The Cambridge Handbook of Child Language

The best survey of the subject available, *The Cambridge Handbook of Child Language* brings together the world's foremost researchers to provide a one-stop resource for the study of language acquisition and development. Grouped into five thematic sections, the handbook is organized by topic, making it easier for students and researchers to use when looking up specific in-depth information. It covers a wider range of subjects than any other handbook on the market, with chapters covering both theories and methods in child language research, and tracing the development of language from prelinguistic infancy to teenager. Drawing on both established and more recent research, the *Handbook* surveys statistical learning; the crosslinguistic study of language acquisition; prelinguistic development, and topics in semantic, pragmatic, and narrative development; bilingualism; sign languages; specific language impairment, language and autism, Down syndrome and Williams syndrome. The field of child language research is multi-disciplinary: the book will be an essential reference for students and researchers working in linguistics, psychology, cognitive science, speech pathology, education and anthropology.

EDITH L. BAVIN is Professor in the School of Psychological Science at La Trobe University, Australia.

CAMBRIDGE HANDBOOKS IN LINGUISTICS

Genuinely broad in scope, each handbook in this series provides a complete state-of-the-field overview of a major sub-discipline within language study and research. Grouped into broad thematic areas, the chapters in each volume encompass the most important issues and topics within each subject, offering a coherent picture of the latest theories and findings. Together, the volumes will build into an integrated overview of the discipline in its entirety.

Published titles

The Cambridge Handbook of Phonology, edited by Paul de Lacy
The Cambridge Handbook of Linguistic Code-switching, edited by Barbara E. Bullock and Almeida Jacqueline Toribio
The Cambridge Handbook of Child Language, edited by Edith L. Bavin

Further titles planned for the series

The Cambridge Handbook of Sociolinguistics, edited by Rajend Mesthrie and Walt Wolfram
The Cambridge Handbook of Endangered Languages, edited by Peter Austin

The Cambridge Handbook of Child Language

Edited by
Edith L. Bavin

CAMBRIDGE UNIVERSITY PRESS
Cambridge, New York, Melbourne, Madrid, Cape Town,
Singapore, São Paulo, Delhi, Tokyo, Mexico City

Cambridge University Press
The Edinburgh Building, Cambridge CB2 8RU, UK

Published in the United States of America by Cambridge University Press, New York

www.cambridge.org
Information on this title: www.cambridge.org/9780521883375

First published 2009
Paperback edition published 2012

Printed in the United Kingdom at the University Press, Cambridge

A catalogue record for this publication is available from the British Library

Library of Congress Cataloguing in Publication data
The Cambridge handbook of child language / Edith L. Bavin, editor.
    p.   cm. – (Cambridge handbooks in linguistics)
Includes bibliographical references and index.
ISBN 978-0-521-88337-5
1. Children – Language – Handbooks, manuals, etc.   2. Language acquisition –
Handbooks, manuals, etc.   3. Language arts (Early childhood) – Handbooks, manuals,
etc.   4. Verbal ability in children – Handbooks, manuals, etc.   I. Bavin, Edith Laura.
II. Title.   III. Series.
P118.C36   2009
401′.93–dc22

                                                        2008045117

ISBN 978-0-521-88337-5 hardback
ISBN 978-1-107-60542-8 paperback

Contents

Figures

Tables

Contributors

Shanley Allen, School of Education, Boston University.

Edith L. Bavin, School of Psychological Sciences, La Trobe University.

Judith Becker Bryant, Department of Psychology, University of Florida.

Heike Behrens, Englisches Seminar, Universität Basel.

Ruth A. Berman, Linguistics Department, Tel Aviv University.

Eve V. Clark, Department of Linguistics, Stanford University.

Stephen Crain, Macquarie Center for Cognitive Science, Macquarie University.

Suzanne Curtin, Departments of Linguistics and Psychology, University of Calgary.

Katherine Demuth, Department of Cognitive and Linguistic Sciences, Brown University.

Rory A. DePaolis, Department of Communication Sciences and Disorders, James Madison University.

Cristina D. Dye, Department of Neuroscience, Georgetown University.

Claire Foley, Department of Slavic and Eastern Languages, Boston College.

Angela D. Friederici, Department of Neuropsychology, Max Planck Institute for Human Cognitive and Brain Sciences, Leipzig.

Susan Goldin-Meadow, Department of Psychology, University of Chicago.

Barbara Höhle, Linguistics Department, University of Potsdam.

Dan Hufnagle, Departments of Psychology and Linguistics, University of Calgary.

Tamar Keren-Portnoy, Language and Linguistic Science, University of York.

Laurence B. Leonard, Department of Speech, Language and Hearing Sciences, Purdue University.

Diane Lillo-Martin, Department of Linguistics, University of Connecticut and Haskins Laboratories.

Catherine Lord, Autism and Communication Disorders Center, University of Michigan.

Barbara C. Lust, Department of Human Development/Cornell Institute for Social and Economic Research, Cornell University.

Rhiannon J. Luyster, Autism and Communication Disorders Center, University of Michigan.

Barbara Zurer Pearson, Academic Liaison, University of Massachusetts, Amherst.

Fiona M. Richardson, School of Psychology, University of London.

Jesse Snedeker, Department of Psychology, Harvard University.

Sabine Stoll, Department of Linguistics, Max Planck Institute for Evolutionary Anthropology, Leipzig.

Erik Thiessen, Psychology Department, Carnegie Mellon University.

Michael S. C. Thomas, School of Psychology, University of London.

Michael Tomasello, Department of Developmental and Comparative Psychology, Max Planck Institute for Evolutionary Anthropology, Leipzig.

J. Bruce Tomblin, Department of Speech Pathology and Audiology, University of Iowa.

Kamil Ud Deen, Department of Linguistics, University of Hawaii.

Virginia Valian, Psychology and Linguistics, Hunter College and The City University of New York (CUNY) Graduate Center.

Marilyn M. Vihman, Language and Linguistic Science, University of York.

Acknowledgements

A book of this nature involves many people and a lot of cooperation. I owe particular thanks to a number of people without whom the volume would not have been completed. The following deserve special thanks and I am extremely grateful to each one.

First, the authors have done a fantastic job covering so many topics in our field. They have been extremely responsive to my comments and suggestions. Andrew Winnard from CUP suggested the handbook and has been supportive of the whole endeavour. Joanna Garbutt from CUP also provided advice and support. Thanks also to the indexer, Sue Lightfoot. It has been a delight working with the copy-editor, Gwynneth Drabble, the production editor, Jodie Barnes and the assistant editor, Sarah Green. Katherine Demuth was extremely helpful in the planning stages, making valuable suggestions about content and possible authors; she has also been a sounding board at other stages in the project. The people who read individual chapters provided constructive feedback to individual authors; this can only have improved the contents. I am grateful to the Institute for Advanced Study at La Trobe University which, through the help of Julia Anderson, generously provided me with office space during 2007. Nadia Petruccelli gave me invaluable assistance in the final few months of putting the chapters and references together. Finally, my partner, Malcolm Macmillan, has always been an inspiration. His wonderful patience and support are truly appreciated. Thanks Mac.

1

Introduction: perspectives on child language

Edith L. Bavin

1.1 Introduction

This handbook aims to provide an overview of current theoretical approaches and research in a range of topics related to child language. The field is multidimensional, as illustrated by the many courses on child language or language acquisition that are taught in departments of Linguistics, Psychology, Cognitive Science, Speech Pathology, Education and Anthropology. This cross-disciplinary nature of the field is reflected in this handbook, which is aimed at upper level undergraduate students up. Graduate students and researchers will find the chapters invaluable. Clinicians also will find some of the chapters of interest. In this introductory chapter I present a general overview of the field and some of the recent developments. In section 1.4 I discuss the organization of this volume and provide an overview of each chapter.

1.2 The study of child language

There are different approaches to the study of child language, and researchers investigate different aspects of the language acquisition process. For example, some will focus on testing particular theoretical claims; others on developmental, cognitive or social factors in the acquisition process; others on the development of a particular feature of language; and others on what we might learn about language development from studying what goes wrong in particular situations. The chapters in this volume illustrate differences in theoretical perspective, language features investigated and methods used. They cover a range of theoretical issues and topics on aspects of the child's developing language system. The topics range from the infant's discrimination of sounds, segmentation of linguistic units and prelinguistic communication to children's phonological, lexical, grammatical, semantic and pragmatic development. Additional topics include bilingualism and atypical language development. Each chapter presents the current state of knowledge in a particular area.

A number of questions underlie the theorizing and research on language acquisition. A crucial question is 'What does the child bring to the task of language acquisition?' (or 'What is the 'initial state?') There is disagreement in the field as to whether linguistic concepts are innate or whether general cognitive abilities are sufficient for the child to acquire a language. The issue, then, is to what extent domain specific or domain general tools are involved in acquiring a language. A related question is: Are there constraints or biases that influence the child's acquisition of language, and if so what is their origin? This question is discussed in relation to the prelinguistic domain: infants' segmentation of the input language, as well as their development of word learning, that is, the mapping of form and meaning. Some of the word learning literature argues for innate biases. However, biases develop with exposure to a language (e.g. see Smith 1999). There are other questions – fundamental to particular aspects of the study of child language – questions related to crosslinguistic and crosscultural similarities in the course of language acquisition, whether there are different trajectories in acquiring one or two languages and how the study of atypical language development informs theories of typical language acquisition. Chapters in the handbook take up these and other issues.

1.3   The past two decades: developments in the field

In the past two decades acquisition research within the nativist (generativist) tradition, pioneered by Noam Chomsky, has focused on the principles and parameters theory. The theory supports the notion of Universal Grammar (see Ch. 2, Ch. 14), assuming universal principles of language and parameters that constrain possible variation across languages. Also in the past two decades, emergentist approaches to language acquisition have developed. MacWhinney (1999: xvii) describes emergentism as a way of 'linking a growing understanding of the brain with new theories of cognition'. Emergentism does not reject nativism; it provides 'accounts in which structures emerge from the interaction of known processes' (p. x). As reflected in this handbook, a large proportion of the current research on child language is based on emergentism.

Shifts in theoretical perspectives have led to new questions and new approaches. For example, the statistical learning approach has investigated how well infants can detect patterns in the linguistic input. There have also been advances in understanding the relationship between cognitive development and language development (e.g. see Bowerman & Levinson 2001). The emergentist coalition model of word learning (Hollich *et al.* 2000) has been proposed, a model in which domain general attentional processes, lexical principles and social pragmatic cues are all involved in the process of word learning, with different cues applying at different stages. The factors that help 'bootstrap' the infant into language have been researched, as has the continuity in development from prelinguistic to linguistic knowledge. Infant segmentation of the input language, their early vocalizations and their gesture use have been investigated in relation to how these early developments are linked to the child's developing linguistic system. Some of the research has targeted the natural course of language development; other research has focused on atypical language development. Verb learning has been a major issue in the past decade (e.g. see Hirsh-Pasek & Golinkoff 2006); the research undertaken has informed much of the theoretical debate. While still limited in terms of the number of languages investigated, crosslinguistic research has provided valuable information about the impact of language-specific factors on the acquisition process, as well as generating discussion about language universals. There have been developments in research on sign languages also. In the context of atypical language development a focus of theorizing has been on the relationship between language and cognition.

Research on language acquisition has benefited from new technologies, including online methods of testing children's developing language knowledge (e.g. see Sekerina *et al.* 2008). The intermodal preferential looking paradigm (Hirsh-Pasek & Golinkoff 1996) has influenced research on infants' and toddlers' knowledge of words and structures. For example, research on verb learning using this paradigm has investigated the age at which children are able to generalize new verbs to different structures. These research findings have informed theoretical claims about young children's knowledge of abstract syntactic categories, and whether the structure in which a verb appears helps in determining something about its meaning, that is, whether there is support for 'syntactic bootstrapping' (e.g. Naigles 1996, Fisher 2002b, and see Ch. 13).

Another technological advance has been the development of eye tracking, used to tap children's online processing of language structures (see Ch. 18). Eye tracking is used to investigate the interpretations being made by the listener at specific points in an utterance, for example an utterance that is potentially ambiguous. It has been used more recently to investigate structural priming – the effect of one structure on subsequent uses of that structure.

The use of neurophysiological measures to examine the brain's response to language-related stimuli has increased. As discussed by Friederici (Ch. 4), while no single method provides a range of information with the necessary fine-grained spatial and temporal resolution required to determine the relationship between particular brain regions and language functions, the use of event related potentials, for example, has added to our understanding of the neural commitment to language, the link between brain maturation and language development. Research using imaging techniques has informed the study of bilingualism and of sign languages.

There have been additions to the number of languages included in the database of the Child Language Data Exchange System (CHILDES). Monolingual data, bilingual data and data from language-impaired children are available for researchers to access, and new tools for analysing the data have been developed. These are readily available to researchers (MacWhinney 2000, http://childes.psy.cmu.edu/).

There has been an increase in the number of studies using parent report measures for documenting developments in infant and toddler communication. For example, the Macarthur–Bates Communicative Development Inventories (Fenson *et al.* 1994, 2007, www.sci.sdsu.edu/cdi/cdiwelcome.htm) are used widely in English-speaking communities to identify variation in the development of prelinguistic communication, vocabulary and features of early grammatical development. The inventories have also been adapted for use with other languages.

Much progress has been made in the study of child language in the past two decades. I have outlined some of the developments; these and others are evident in the chapters of this volume.

1.4   The handbook: an overview

The handbook is divided into five parts. Part I focuses on theoretical and methodological perspectives on language acquisition. It covers the formal linguistic nativist approach and emergentist approaches. Issues of learnability and innatism are discussed in depth. One chapter focuses on statistical learning; another focuses on neurocognition, the link between brain development and the young child's response to linguistic stimuli. There is also a chapter showing the need for crosslinguistic typological research. Each of the chapters included in Part I provides an overview of a different way of approaching the study of child language, giving a rationale for the approach and some of the evidence supporting it. Methodological approaches are influenced by the theoretical perspective taken by researchers. The chapters in parts II, III, IV and V take up issues and approaches introduced in Part I. Many of the chapters include some crosslinguistic data.

The main focus of Part II is prelinguistic development, with two chapters on infants' speech perception and one chapter on the relationship between gesture and language development. Part III covers the structural aspects of language: phonology and grammar, with chapters on the development of phonology and theoretical explanations; factors influencing the acquisition of grammatical categories; verb argument structure; complex sentences; and the morphosyntax interface, with an emphasis on verb agreement. Part IV, covering the age range from toddler to teenager, focuses on semantic and pragmatic development. The chapters in this section discuss lexical meaning, sentence scope, sentence processing, pragmatic development and the development of structures and narrative organization. Part V examines different contexts of language acquisition. Included are chapters on bilingualism and sign languages and four chapters on atypical development. These four chapters cover specific language impairment (SLI), autism spectrum disorder (ASD), Williams syndrome and Down syndrome. The final chapter discusses the issue of how the brain adapts to overcome underlying deficits, and if compensation leads to alternative pathways to language acquisition in order to preserve language functioning.

A brief overview of each chapter is presented in the following sections.

1.4.1 Part I: theoretical and methodological approaches

Valian (Ch. 2) introduces the concepts of nativism and learnability. As she states, discussions about nativism focus on whether the child's mind has content independent of experience. There is disagreement amongst researchers working in the language domain as to the nature of the 'initial state', that is, what the child brings to the task of acquiring a language. The nativist perspective represented in this chapter assumes innate linguistic content, that is, abstract linguistic concepts. The 'final state' (the mature state) is viewed as a formal theory of language. According to this view, acquisition involves the mapping of particular forms from the language of the child's environment to the innate abstract categories. Opponents assume that abstract syntactic categories are learned but, as Valian points out, additional mechanisms would then be required to explain how the abstract categories are built up. The chapter draws on 'poverty of the stimulus' arguments, using the 'case filter' as an example of abstract syntactic categories for which there is no evidence in the input. The special nature of language is illustrated with examples from animal communication, language development in special circumstances and the early language knowledge that children seem to demonstrate.

Representing an opposing theoretical position to that presented in chapter 2, Thiessen (Ch. 3) provides an overview of Statistical Learning. Statistical Learning focuses on the fact that regularities in language occur at the phoneme, syllable, word and phrase level. The major task for the child in acquiring a language is detecting the regularities (patterns) in the input language. Pattern detection is clearly not domain specific; general cognitive abilities, not domain (language) specific, are assumed to be used in identifying the patterns. From the regularities detected, categories can be built by linking items that behave similarly. Research using natural languages as well as artificial stimuli reveals that infants are remarkably adept at detecting regularities, for example transitional probabilities. These can serve as cues to word boundaries. That experience with language affects learning is taken up in chapters 7 and 8.

Friederici's chapter (Ch. 4) on the neurocognition of language development illustrates that language development is closely linked to brain maturation. Neurophysiological measures are used to examine the brain's response to language-related stimuli. Event-related potentials (ERPs), in particular, have been used to document changes in infants' brains. Comparisons can then be made with an adult (mature) model, developed on the basis of ERP components generated by the adult brain in response to different language stimuli and aspects of language processing. ERP research on infant's discrimination of phonetic features, stress patterns and phonotactics is discussed in the chapter, as is research on lexical learning, which suggests that between 12 and 18 months of age there is some 'stabilization' between form and meaning. Friederici cites research with two year olds focusing on lexical and syntactic properties, showing that the 'structure building' processes are already in place but more development is required for the adult-like neural mechanisms which support syntactic processes.

Tomasello (Ch. 5) presents a usage-based approach to language development: 'structure emerges from use'. This is opposed to the theoretical position presented in chapter 2. Tomasello emphasizes the primacy of pragmatics in human communication. For example, even from the age of about one year, shared understandings are evident in infants' communication. It is assumed in this approach that children rely on general cognitive skills in constructing their language. These skills help in identifying the intentions of mature language users as well as the distributional patterns of the language. As patterns become entrenched young children generalize to form abstract linguistic categories specific to their language. Naturalistic and experimental evidence discussed in the chapter supports the approach: that children initially learn on an item-by-item basis and build up abstract categories.

In the final chapter in Part I (Ch. 6), Stoll discusses the need for crosslinguistic typological research. She provides an overview of some of the crosslinguistic research that has been undertaken, which has provided valuable insights into similarities and differences in the course of language acquisition. However, the number and range of languages for which acquisition data is available represents a small percentage of the world's languages. Stoll argues that systematic comparisons of typologically different languages are necessary for identifying universals in acquisition. However, she also indicates some of the inherent problems in conducting research in culturally and linguistically diverse contexts. The existing data, some of which is available on the Child Language Data Exchange System (CHILDES), are not always comparable given different methods are used and different aspects of language researched.

1.4.2   Part II: early development: precursors to linguistic development

Three chapters comprise the early development section. They cover infant speech perception, crosslinguistic perspectives on segmentation and categorization in early language acquisition, and gesture use. Curtin and Hufnagle (Ch. 7) provide a comprehensive overview of research on infant speech perception, and some of the models proposed to explain the reorganisation of infants' perceptual abilities. The models differ in the assumptions made about the role of experience and the nature of innate biases. The research discussed in the chapter supports the Statistical Learning approach. That is, while biases are evident at birth, exposure to a language rapidly shapes infants' perceptual abilities. Categories emerge and are reorganized on the basis of perceptual learning and exposure to the language of the environment. More abstract phonemic representations emerge later.

In discussing infant speech perception in relation to segmenting of words, Höhle (Ch. 8) takes up the interplay between innate processing capacities and language particular properties. She focuses on information that may be used by infants in the early steps to language. Sensitivity to rhythmical information available at birth influences the rapid acquisition of rhythmic features of the language in the child's environment. Infants seem to rely on rhythmic as well as non-rhythmical features in the task of segmenting words from the input language. Höhle cites examples from typologically different languages to illustrate that rhythmical and distributional information at the phoneme, syllable and word level are relevant in the task of segmenting and categorizing.

In the third chapter in this section, Goldin-Meadow (Ch. 9) focuses on the close relationship between gesture and speech. She argues that gesture 'serves as a window on the child's communicative abilities'. The chapter discusses the changing function of gestures in a child's early years and the transition to speech. Gesture use is a precursor of the spoken word and a predictor of developing language. Goldin-Meadow proposes that gesture use may influence the cognitive state of the child; it might encourage language feedback, so helping to promote language learning by influencing the language input received. Included in the chapter is research with different groups: typically developing children, late talkers, deaf 'home-signers', children with Down syndrome, children with unilateral brain damage, and children with specific language impairment (see Tomblin Ch. 23, Leonard Ch. 24).

1.4.3 Part III: phonology, morphology and syntax

The chapters in Part III represent different theoretical views, explanations and data on the acquisition of phonology, morphology, syntax and semantics. Vihman, DePaolis and Keren-Portnoy (Ch. 10) draw on Dynamic Systems Theory (Thelen & Smith 1994) in explaining the continuity between babbling and first words. Lexical and phonological learning, they argue, requires the development of representations that integrate perception and production. Powerful learning mechanisms are proposed to explain development changes, as skills emerge and act as the catalyst for behavioural change. Babbling practice provides the resources for the identification and shaping of early word forms. Detailed examples are provided to illustrate that both distributional and item learning account for the development of a child's phonological system.

In chapter 11 Demuth takes a different perspective in linking phonological and language development, drawing on recent developments in phonological theory to explain developmental patterns across languages. She focuses on research that investigates the interactions between segments and higher level prosodic structures (e.g. prosodic words). Frequency in the input and competing 'markedness' constraints are discussed as two factors that contribute to variability in production, both within and across languages. However, as Demuth points out, it is not yet clear which units need to be considered in determining frequency. The chapter illustrates that the production of grammatical morphemes is constrained by children's developing prosodic representations. As discussed, it is those grammatical morphemes that are prosodically licensed that children are likely to produce.

Behrens (Ch. 12) provides a comprehensive account of factors that influence the acquisition of inflectional morphology and word formation. In contrast to the theoretical approach taken in chapter 15, Behrens adopts an emergentist perspective – children rely on language-specific heuristics to build up grammatical categories – and supports the usage-based approach discussed in chapter 3. She includes Brown's (1973) classic study of the acquisition of English morphology, but also draws on crosslinguistic data to illustrate how children build up morphological paradigms, how morphological development is measured and the different criteria used to determine productivity. Critical evaluation is provided on a number of explanations that have been proposed for the acquisition of grammatical morphology. She discusses recent research on the acquisition of past tense, Slobin's (1985c) operating principles, and the Competition Model.

In chapter 13, Allen discusses different theoretical approaches to explaining how children determine in which structures particular verbs are used by mature language users. She considers the innatist and usage-based positions, presenting arguments for and against semantic bootstrapping and syntactic bootstrapping. Drawing on evidence from children's spontaneous productions, elicited productions and experimental work testing comprehension of different structures, she shows that different conclusions are often drawn. Allen also discusses that much evidence in support of the usage-based approach could represent syntactic priming (Fisher 2002a), and the more recent proposal for 'weak abstract representations'. The chapter covers the acquisition of argument structure alternations, focusing on passive and dative structures, and in identifying the challenges posed for acquisition by ellipsis of arguments in the input language, Allen discusses preferred argument structure.

The topic of chapter 14 is complex structures. Lust, Foley and Dye, taking a Universal Grammar perspective, argue that complex structures provide a 'core domain' for investigating aspects of syntactic and semantic knowledge including hierarchical structure; constituent order; locality domains recursion; and principles of Universal Grammar, such as structure dependence. The authors focus on four types of structures that are traditionally referred to as complex sentences: complementation, coordination, adverbial subordinate clause adjunction and relative clauses. For each of these structures, the chapter presents the challenge they pose for acquisition and data from early spontaneous speech as well as from experimental work. The authors argue that the young child brings knowledge about the linguistic system, for example, knowledge of control structures, branching direction and anaphora. They propose an integration of language-specific and potentially universal syntactic knowledge over the course of development.

Also adopting the Universal Grammar approach, Deen (Ch. 15) discusses the interaction of syntax with morphology, specifically three components of the morphosyntax interface. For readers not familiar with the formalism used in this approach a brief summary is provided. A main focus of the chapter is a detailed comparison of patterns in the development of verb inflection in languages with rich morphology (e.g. Italian) and morphologically poor languages (e.g. English), and in languages that allow null subjects and those that require overt subjects. The chapter examines the theoretical explanations that have been proposed for the omission of verb inflections by children: a deficit in inflectional knowledge, a deficit in converting a syntactic representation into a string of morphological items, or a deficit in the underlying syntactic representation.

1.4.4 Part IV: semantics, pragmatics and discourse

A range of possibilities exist for what a new word could mean, but children seem to target an appropriate preliminary meaning rapidly. Many researchers who work on the acquisition of word meaning have argued that children are guided in the task of word learning by constraints (or biases). These include the 'shape bias' and 'mutual exclusivity'. Such constraints limit the possible form–meaning mappings for the child. There is disagreement, however, about the origin of the constraints, whether they are innate or learned from identifying patterns in the input language. Clark (Ch. 16) adopts a different approach. She argues that children treat language as a cooperative endeavour, making pragmatic assumptions about communication; from these assumptions they 'pick up' information that helps them in developing a lexicon. Clark argues that joint attention, physical co-presence, and conversational co-presence are all factors that assist children in targeting an appropriate form in the input language with which to encode preliminary meanings associated with objects and events in their world.

Adopting a Universal Grammar approach, specifically the principles and parameters theory, Crain (Ch. 17) discusses the emergence of semantic knowledge. He illustrates that semantic scope in human languages is similar to that of classical logic. Different structures containing logical operators, e.g. *not, every, any*, are illustrated from several languages. He compares different entailment relations that apply in English and Japanese in simple negative statements with disjunction. The difference can be captured by a parameter of variation. Initially young English- and Japanese-speaking children make similar interpretations for these structures. This finding can be accounted for by the 'subset principle' within the theoretical framework adopted. Other topics discussed in the chapter include children's knowledge of isomorphism and inverse scope. Much of the research testing this knowledge adopts a truth verification task.

A recent development in the field is the use of eye-gaze paradigms to investigate the development of language comprehension, from word recognition to sentence interpretation. In chapter 18, Snedeker outlines the processes involved in understanding speech and discusses the reasons why it is important to understand the development of children's processing, not just to inform acquisition theory but also to provide insights into the architecture of the adult comprehension system. She discusses some of the research that has been undertaken using the 'visual world paradigm' to investigate lexical (verb bias), prosodic and referential effects on adults' and children's interpretation of potentially ambiguous syntactic structures. She also cites more recent experimental work that combines structural priming and eye-gaze analysis to investigate how children represent argument structure. The priming studies demonstrate that by age three years children employ abstract grammatical representations in online comprehension.

Language acquisition involves more than the mapping of form and meaning. It also involves knowing how to use the forms appropriately in different situations. This is the area of pragmatics. In chapter 19 Becker-Bryant discusses the developmental progression of pragmatic behaviours and the family and peer influences that affect the development of pragmatic competence. While infants demonstrate some rudimentary knowledge of conversational behaviour, the associated skills become more sophisticated over the childhood years. Initiating and sustaining conversations, perspective taking, responding to feedback, requests, are some of the topics included in the chapter, but there is much more. The chapter also covers the adolescent years – when different registers are used for different social functions, e.g. to indicate group identity, and the use of mobile phones and the internet mean conversations are not always face-to-face.

Berman (Ch. 20) focuses on the functions of linguistic forms in children's narratives. Different functions develop and new structures emerge as children master the global level of discourse organisation. Such development depends on children's linguistic and cognitive abilities. Berman discusses 'reference' and 'cohesion' with examples to illustrate some of the different strategies used by children in maintaining reference. She also includes research on 'temporality' and 'connectivity'. While the chapter on complex clauses in Part III of this volume focuses on structure at the sentence level, Berman's chapter examines the 'syntactic architecture' of texts: syntactic packaging combined with thematic and discourse criteria. As Berman points out, while command of the morphosyntax of a language is largely mastered by the age of five years, it takes many years for speakers to recruit the forms 'flexibly and skilfully' in extended discourse.

1.4.5   Part V: varieties of development

Most children in the world are exposed to more than one language. In chapter 21 Pearson proposes that the study of bilingual and multilingual children can inform researchers about the process of language acquisition. The chapter introduces terminology used in classifying individuals with exposure to two or more languages, and with varying levels of competence in the languages. It covers linguistic behaviours associated with bilingualism (e.g. code-switching), and research findings showing some advantages for bilinguals over monolinguals (e.g. in cognitive development), as well as some delays (e.g. vocabulary development). Pearson cites neuro-imaging studies which have investigated how the two languages are represented in the brain. Other topics include the development of phonology, syntax and semantics in early bilinguals compared to second-language learners. A section on the practical implications of bilingualism looks at the types of schooling that promote development in two languages.

In chapter 22, Lillo-Martin provides an overview of research over the past twenty years on the acquisition of sign language, with an emphasis on the acquisition of sign language by deaf children born to deaf parents. The chapter discusses similarities and differences between the acquisition of sign and spoken language, and how the study of sign language can inform researchers about grammar, the nature of language and acquisition in general. About 95 per cent of deaf children have hearing parents and many are not exposed to sign language from birth; this provides a unique context for investigating the nature of language and language acquisition. The chapter includes examples of the types of errors in young children's production of signs, and discusses the development of specific structures, with examples from American Sign Language, Brazilian Sign Language and the Sign Language of the Netherlands.

Specific language impairment (SLI) has been widely discussed in the literature in the past few years. Chapter 23 is the first of two chapters focusing on SLI. The chapter focuses on what is known about the course and aetiology of SLI. Tomblin discusses the criteria commonly used for identifying SLI: a discrepancy between performance on language and non-verbal IQ measures. He also cites research comparing the language of children with SLI and other developmental disorders (see Ch. 25 & Ch. 26), with evidence suggesting that children with SLI 'occupy a similar region'. The persistence of language difficulties of children with SLI is discussed in relation to whether SLI represents deviant or delayed acquisition. The cause of SLI is not known. However, genetic, neurological and environmental factors have been shown to have an influence on SLI; Tomblin cites research in these areas, as well as giving an overview of the academic and social outcomes of children who have persistent language difficulties.

In the second chapter on SLI (Ch. 24), Leonard discusses features of the language of SLI and explanations that have been proposed. While all areas of language can be affected, from phonology to narratives and conversation skills, much of the research in English has focused on morphology, specifically past tense and agreement morphology and the inappropriate use of optimal infinitives in contexts requiring tense and agreement marking. The grammatical morphology affected differs across languages. Verb agreement is not problematic for all languages; when it is, the nature of the difficulties varies. Leonard illustrates this with data from English, German, Swedish, Italian, Spanish and French. Research in the area of SLI represents different theoretical views: formal accounts which assume innate linguistic knowledge, and processing accounts which do not; rather they emphasize memory and processing limitations. Leonard proposes that neither approach provides a full account of the language difficulties evident in SLI.

Chapter 25 gives an overview of the language of children with autism (ASD). Luyster and Lord discuss early developments in communicative behaviour and features of the language of children with ASD. The research cited shows impairment in preverbal communication (e.g. eye contact). There is variability in language development for children with ASD. Some remain nonverbal; for those who develop spoken language the structural features are often intact. The main deficit is in the area of pragmatics, the appropriate use of language in social contexts. The authors discuss the reason for discrepancy in results across different research studies, suggesting they reflect the lack of a generally accepted standardized measure of language in ASD. The chapter touches on genetic factors and cites electrophysiological studies which indicate some atypical associations between language and brain structure and function.

In the final chapter, Richardson and Thomas (Ch. 26) discuss what we know about the development of language in two genetically defined disorders (Williams syndrome and Down syndrome) and how it informs our understanding of normal language development. The authors illustrate that cognitive ability cannot reliably predict language development in all areas. Evidence of such dissociation is relevant in discussions about the modular nature of language, and whether the modular system emerges or is part of the initial state. One view favours 'residual normality'. The neuroconstructivist view is that 'normal performance' could be achieved through atypical means. That is, there may be 'compensation'; different underlying mechanisms may lead to 'normal performance'. As discussed by the authors, fundamental questions about the functional organization of the language system and the extent to which it is constrained by the processing properties of human neurology remain.

Part I

Theoretical and methodological approaches

2

Innateness and learnability

Virginia Valian

2.1 Introduction

This chapter addresses five questions. (1) What is the debate between nativism and empiricism about? (2) If there is innate linguistic content, what are good candidates for it? (3) What are the arguments for and against nativism? (4) What acquisition mechanisms are there? (5) What kind of empirical evidence do we presently have that would allow us to decide whether humans innately have some linguistic knowledge?

2.2 The nativism–empiricism debate

2.2.1 The central question

The central question about nativism is whether the child's mind has content independent of experience. The important word is 'content'. By content I mean knowledge, in the form of concepts and propositions. It is not controversial that humans are more sophisticated learners and users of information than any other species. Researchers may disagree about just how to characterize learning and memory mechanisms, but everyone agrees that all species have built-in methods of acquiring information. The nativism–empiricism debate is about content: does the mind have any content prior to experience? All learning mechanisms operate on content of some sort. It is the nature of the content that divides nativists and empiricists.

The least sophisticated content is primitive categories for classifying sense data, categories like colour and form. Those categories allow us to group together stimuli that share properties (such as redness). Perceptual categories such as lines and angles allow us to recognize a stimulus we

My thanks to Janet Fodor for extensive discussion, and to Mary C. Potter and Gary Marcus for helpful comments on the manuscript.

have encountered before. Empiricists and nativists alike accept rudimentary categories that are based on physical properties. It is when we move beyond perceptual categories to concepts that differences between empiricists and nativists arise. Strict empiricism rules out any innate knowledge in any realm, but it is possible to accept innate concepts in some domains and reject them in others. To take one example, it is possible to be a nativist with respect to non-linguistic concepts but an empiricist with respect to language. A concept in the cognitive domain might be the notion of an agent of an action or the notion of logical (predicate–argument) structure in thinking, concepts that might be useful in the acquisition of language. A concept in the linguistic domain might be the notion of syntactic categories like noun or verb. According to content nativism in linguistics, some abstract linguistic concepts, such as syntactic categories, are necessary in order to explain the child's eventual knowledge. Empiricism denies such innate content.

Is there a middle ground between nativism and empiricism, or a way of avoiding the nativism–empiricism controversy altogether? To say, for example, that humans are 'biased' or 'predisposed' to learn language might seem to be a middle ground. But it is only while they retain their vagueness that biases or predispositions appear to be a middle ground. If, once they are fleshed out, the biases involve the absence of innate syntactic content, then they are empiricist; if they involve innate syntactic content, then they are nativist. Interactionism (Elman *et al.* 1996, Thelen & Smith 1994) is sometimes presented as an alternative to either nativism or empiricism, as is constructivism (e.g. Tomasello 2003 and Ch. 5). In both cases, the organism is seen as actively contributing to whatever knowledge is acquired. But a mind could be active without having prior linguistic content, and it is the postulation of innate content that marks the nativist. Since both interactionism and constructivism either argue against innate syntactic content or assume that it does not exist, those positions are also forms of empiricism.

2.2.2 Preliminaries and terminology

The question of what linguistic concepts are innate can be asked about every aspect of language, from phonology to pragmatics, but this chapter will focus on syntax (and morphosyntax), since that is where debate is concentrated. Although syntactic concepts are no more complex or abstract than semantic concepts, there is nevertheless less debate about semantics, perhaps because it is (incorrectly) seen as part and parcel of cognition.

In the key arguments advanced by nativists and empiricists, conceptions of the 'final state', that is, the mature mental grammar, are closely related to conceptions of the 'initial state', that is, what linguistic concepts are innate. Much of the dispute between nativists and empiricists follows from their different judgments about the correctness of formal linguistic descriptions of language as an approximation of people's mental grammars. With different conceptions of the final state, different conceptions of the initial state are likely. The more abstract and complex the final state, the more likely a rich initial state is. A nativist need not adopt a complex picture of the final state, but adopting a complex picture makes it more likely that one will be a nativist, because input can only provide examples, not abstract structure itself.

In this chapter I use a formal linguistic theory – the framework of principles and parameters theory – as an approximation of the child's final state, because it offers specific proposals about language universals that can be the basis for hypotheses of what is innate. In addition, formal theories cover a broad range of syntactic phenomena and aim for systematicity and coherence. My choice of a formal theory is compatible with also seeing language as a vehicle for a wide range of communicative intentions.

Nativism commits someone neither to a particular grammatical theory nor to a particular philosophy of linguistics. Nativism is compatible with a wide range of theories, such as Head-Driven Phrase Structure Grammar (HPSG, Sag & Wasow 1999), minimalism (Chomsky 1995), and lexical–functional grammar (Bresnan 2001). Nativism is equally compatible with a theory of language as a theory of people's psychological (or biological) states (Chomsky 2006) or as a theory of abstract objects (Katz 1981).

2.2.3   Examples of what is acquired: categories and word order

Two 'simple' aspects of language are acquired early by all speakers: syntactic categories and word order. (Sections 2.6.5 and 2.6.6 provide more detail.) Syntactic categories fall into two main linguistic types: **lexical** and **functional**. The lexical categories are nouns, verbs, adjectives and adverbs, and, in some cases, prepositions. Functional categories include determiners (words like *the* and *my*), inflectional elements (such as tense on a verb and auxiliaries in English), and complementizers (such as the *that* of 'I knew that she was happy'). Functional categories typically contribute less to the meaning of a sentence than lexical categories do. That children separate nouns from pronouns is seen by the absence of errors like 'big he' (Bloom 1990b).

Nativists and most empiricists agree that children's grammars – at some point – include abstract syntactic categories and represent word order in terms of abstract categories. Disagreements concern the origin of categories (and when they are acquired; see Section 2.6.5). Nativists typically start with the hypothesis that at least some syntactic categories, or the features that make up those categories, are innate; empiricists will start with the hypothesis that none are innate, but rather are induced based on exposure to the distribution of those elements across the language.

Does this mean that nativists leave no role for learning? No, learning can still have an important role, for example, in determining what categories particular words belong to. But, crucially, what is learned is not the abstract categories themselves. Instead, learners will acquire a mapping between the innate abstract categories and the particular words in the learner's target language that belong to each category. For empiricists, the hypothesis that no categories are innate means that the only way of acquiring them is by learning. Among the earliest such proposals is one by Braine (1963), proposing that children construct a pivot-open grammar in which certain words or word combinations, like *here's a*, act as pivots which the child can finish with a wide range of words (almost always nouns). More recent proposals include lexically specific formulae (Pine & Lieven 1997, Pine & Martindale 1996), lexically based learning, and usage-based learning (Tomasello 2003 and Ch. 5). After the child has amassed a number of such cases, he or she creates categories for the different words.

The agreement about the child's state, at least by age 5, with respect to syntactic categories and word order makes it possible in principle to examine different learning mechanisms to see what innate content, if any, is required in order for the mechanism to arrive at those categories.

2.3 Candidates for innateness: linguistic universals

The principles-and-parameters framework offers linguistic universals as candidates for innateness. Linguistic universals are principles and properties that (a) are true of every language and (b) define what it is to be a language. It is not enough just to say (a). Properties that are true of all languages may hold because of irrelevant properties of speakers rather than because of properties of language.

The existing sentences in all languages are, for example, of finite length. But the finite length of any given sentence is due to speakers' limited cognitive systems (and limited lifetimes), rather than due to speakers' language. We would not want to say that finite length is a linguistic universal. Speakers acquire a theory of their language that allows for sentences of any length whatsoever, even though people cannot physically produce sentences that would take more than a lifetime to utter.

For two reasons linguistic universals are good candidates for what could be innate syntactic content. First, universals set the defining conditions on what could be a language. Whatever is innate should not be particular to a single language but to language. Second, any child can learn any language. If anything is going to be innate, it is the abstract linguistic features that allow a child to be an omnicompetent language learner.

Linguistic universals are of two types: **absolute** and **relative**. Absolute universals are syntactic principles or structures that appear in every language (Chomsky 1981). One reason to expect all absolute universals to be innate is that, by definition, they hold for every language. They are the best linguistic survival kit a child could have. Another reason for hypothesizing their innateness is that absolute universals are abstract and cannot be directly perceived from exposure to sentences. Later in this chapter I will give the case filter as an example.

What I am calling relative universals are of two types. One type is the building blocks of syntax – **syntactic features and categories**. The entire stock of features and categories may be innate, or only a subset may be innate. Not every language uses every feature and category. Some languages, for example, have a genuine future tense, but English does not. Tensed main verbs in English are either present or past tense. The 'future' in English is carried by the modal *will*, or combined forms like *be going to*; main verbs themselves do not have a future form. French main verbs, in contrast, have present, past and future tenses. Even if all features are innate, they will not all surface in any particular language, just as future tense does not surface in English.

In addition, the members of a given category may differ from one language to another. For example, in English, possessive pronouns behave like articles and cannot be combined with them ('the my ball' is impossible in English). In Italian, however, possessive pronouns behave like adjectives and can be combined with articles. Thus, the innate specification of categories must be abstract. An innate syntactic category will not come with a list of examples, because the exact examples will vary (if only within a narrow set of boundaries). Similarly, no particular word order can be innate. In some languages, like English, function words tend to precede lexical categories within a phrase (*the ball*), but in other languages, function words tend to follow lexical categories. The dominant English word order is subject–verb–object, but in other languages other orders are possible.

The second type of relative universal is **parameters**. Parameters define dimensions of linguistically significant variation, such as whether the subject of a verb must be overt. Another parameter concerns word order: in English the verb comes before its object, but in Japanese the object comes before its verb. Parameters are typically two-valued; each language takes one value or the other for each parameter. Parameters are an important type of linguistic universal, since they map out what syntactic variation is possible. By hypothesis, all parameters are innate, and each is independent of every other. The child's task is to choose, over the course of development, which value of each parameter characterizes his or her language. Parameters are relative universals because, for a given language, only one value can be correct.

A useful heuristic for identifying candidates for innateness is that they be universal in one of these two senses – absolute or relative. Within linguistics, the set of absolute and relative universals is referred to as Universal Grammar. Universal Grammar forms the upper bound of innate syntactic content. But the upper bound is not necessarily also the lower bound. A nativist could take a much more modest position and propose that only some universals are innate, while others can be inferred.

2.4   Logical arguments for innateness

2.4.1   Types of linguistic evidence

The main logical argument given to support the claim of innate syntactic content is the argument from the poverty of the stimulus. This argument states that input contains too little information from children to reach the final state; the input is impoverished. Most examples of poverty of the stimulus arguments are related to two structures: subject–auxiliary inversion in questions in English (see Pullum & Scholz 2002, and responses by, among others, Fodor & Crowther 2002, Legate & Yang 2002) and anaphoric *one* in English (see Hornstein & Lightfoot 1981, Lidz *et al.* 2003b, and responses by Regier & Gahl 2004, Tomasello, 2004). I will not review those examples but, in section 2.3.1, I consider a syntactic phenomenon commonly referred to as the case filter.

Claiming that the input is impoverished is different from claiming that it is noisy or degenerate. The former claim is that input to children lacks information that would allow children to acquire certain syntactic principles or regularities. The latter claim is that input to children includes run-on or incomplete sentences, false starts, and perhaps some outright ungrammaticalities. Speech to children tends to be short, free of hesitations, and generally free of outright errors, though it does contain a reasonable number of fragments and sentences without subjects about 5 per cent of the time. The language acquisition mechanism is obviously built to withstand a certain amount of noise in the input.

The important question is how the mechanism copes with impoverished input. Input, in the form of speech to the child (or speech that the child hears), is called positive evidence. That speech illustrates sentences of the language. It is evidence that certain words and phrases occur. Two other possible types of evidence are negative evidence and indirect negative evidence. Negative evidence is responses from the child's interlocutor either that a certain way that the child has just spoken is ungrammatical or that the child should replace his or her formulation with the one the interlocutor has just produced. If, for example, the child says "I knowed it" and the parent says, "Oh, you knew it", the use of *knew* for *knowed* could constitute negative evidence (sometimes also called implicit correction, negative feedback, a recast, or a reformulation). Similarly, if a child says "That the last one" and the parent says, "That's the last one" the use of *that's* for *that* could constitute negative evidence.

Indirect negative evidence is the absence of a structure that the child would expect to see, given a starting hypothesis. If, for example, an Italian child thought that subjects might be required, their consistent absence in sentences like *Piove* 'It's raining' might be sufficient for the child to revise that hypothesis.

All three sources of evidence are imperfect and require inferences on the child's part. Although adults' errors in talking to children are few, they might temporarily mislead the child. Negative evidence is also imperfect, both because it does not occur every time the child makes a mistake and because the child might not recognize it as a correction. Data from my laboratory, based on twenty-one child–mother pairs, suggest that parents provide 'implicit' corrections for about 25 per cent of children's ungrammatical utterances. More to the point is that the child might not recognize the use of *that's* for *that* as a correction. Indirect negative evidence requires the child both to have a specific hypothesis and to determine whether the absence of confirmatory speech is due to syntactic or nonsyntactic reasons. People never produce triply embedded sentences to children, for example, but they should not take that as evidence that triple embeddings are ungrammatical.

2.4.2 An example of a poverty-of-the-stimulus argument: the case filter

Consider examples 1–5; only 1 is grammatical. (The * indicates ungrammaticality.) What distinguishes the examples is that (2) – (5) all have the incorrect case for one or both pronouns. *Case* refers to the syntactic function that a noun or pronoun plays in a sentence. It is not the same as the semantic role, as is apparent by the contrast in (1) and (1'). The first person is the person doing the greeting in both sentences, but in (1) the pronoun has nominative case (*I*) and in (1') it has objective (or accusative) case (*me*). Similarly, the third person is the one being greeted in both sentences, but in (1) the correct form is *him* and in (1') it is *he*.

(1) I greeted him yesterday; (1') He was greeted yesterday by me.

* (2) Me greeted him yesterday; *(2') Him was greeted yesterday by I.

* (3) My greeted him yesterday; *(3') Him was greeted yesterday by my.

* (4) I greeted he yesterday; * (4') He was greeted yesterday by I.

* (5) I greeted his yesterday; * (5') His was greeted yesterday by me.

Case is a syntactic property that noun phrases (NPs) have as a function of their relation to another category, such as a verb, a preposition, an inflectional element like tense or another noun phrase. English has three cases: nominative, objective (or accusative) and possessive (or genitive; see Carnie 2006, for an introduction to case and other syntactic properties and relations). Although case is only visible on pronouns in English, the case filter claims that it is *invisibly* present on all overt nouns in English. If we replace *I* with *the girl* in (1), *the girl* has nominative case even though the case is not overtly visible. In some languages, such as Hungarian, most cases are visibly present on all overt noun phrases, both pronouns and nouns. And some languages, again like Hungarian, have many cases – upwards of ten.

The case filter is an example of an *absolute* universal within government-and-binding theory. It is the requirement that all overt nouns and pronouns in every language have case; different cases may have distinct morphological forms, as with first person pronouns in English, or may be abstract and have no external form, but only a positional relation to another grammatical element that can assign case to the noun or pronoun in question, as with full lexical noun phrases in English and all nouns and pronouns in Thai. (The word 'filter' is used because structures containing an overt NP that is not cased are filtered out).

Even though case is largely morphologically absent in English, there are examples that show it is grammatically present and, in the example of objective/accusative case, assigned by the verb (or preposition) just to its left. Without the concept of case, the ungrammaticality of certain sequences is otherwise inexplicable. In (6), the verb *consider* assigns objective case to *Jane*.

(6)   Lee considered Jane to be happy

*(7)   Lee considered she to be happy

(8)   Lee considered her to be happy

The ungrammaticality of (7) and grammaticality of (8) show that the position right after the verb, if filled by a noun or pronoun, is one that receives objective case; otherwise *she* would be an acceptable substitution for *Jane*. *She* would be acceptable if the following verb, instead of being an infinitive, were tensed, as in 'Lee considered she would be happy [to receive the package]'. In that case, the tensed verb assigns nominative case to the pronoun.

If an element intervenes between the verb and the following noun, case cannot be assigned and the resulting string of words is ungrammatical. In (9) it is possible to put the adverb *quickly* directly after the main verb *considered*, although it is a bit awkward.

(9)   Lee considered quickly whether to go

*(10)   Lee considered quickly the matter

(11)   Lee quickly considered the matter

(12)   Lee considered the matter quickly

In (10) the sequence is worse than awkward; it is not grammatical. The important difference between (9) and (10) is that in (10) there is no overt object NP whereas in (10) there is (*the matter*). Since, in (10), an adverb intervenes between the verb and the NP to which it would otherwise assign accusative case, the sentence is ungrammatical. If the adverb is moved so that it does not intervene between the verb and its object, as in (11) or (12), the sentences are grammatical. In English, then, if an element intervenes between the verb and its noun, objective case cannot be assigned.

A sequence like (13), which is easily understood, and is very similar in surface form to sentences like (6), (8), and (9), is nevertheless ungrammatical.

The NP *Jane* is uncased: *whether* intervenes between *considered* and *Jane*, preventing the verb from assigning case to the NP.

*(13)   Lee considered whether Jane to go

Neither *she* nor *her* can substitute for *Jane*, also showing that the position is one which cannot receive case. If it could, at least one cased form of the pronoun would be legitimate. (Again, the sentence can be saved by changing the infinitive to a tensed verb, as in 'would go'.) Without the case filter, the ungrammaticality of (13) is inexplicable. (13) violates the case filter, and is thereby ungrammatical.

The concept of the case filter presupposes the concept of grammatical case, the category of NP, and a syntactic mechanism for assigning case. That mechanism in turn involves reference to syntactic categories like verb and preposition. The claim that all NPs in every language must have case is thus embedded in a linguistic system. Only within that system does the claim have meaning. If the case filter is innate, so are the concepts that comprise it.

The case filter is a good example of a poverty of the stimulus argument. Native speakers of English show, by their acceptance or rejection of the sequences in (1) – (13), that a concept like the case filter is part of their mental grammar. But there is no evidence in the input that could lead speakers to put it there. Case does not correspond to concepts that might be more easily inferred from context, such as 'agent of an action' or 'object of an action'. Case is purely syntactic (and, in languages with overt case, morphosyntactic).

There is no way to acquire the case filter from positive evidence. Unlike examples with subject–auxiliary inversion, where there is disagreement about how many possibly informative examples might exist in speech to children, in this context there are no examples. There is also no way to acquire the case filter from negative evidence. Even if children spontaneously produced sequences like (10) and (13) (of which there are no known examples), and received reformulations by their caregivers, nothing in the reformulation could allow the child to infer the case filter or the concepts that make it up. Indirect negative evidence could lead children to wonder why no sequences like (13) are in their input. They might expect to hear combinations of sequences like (6) and (9). But there is no path that could take children from the absence of such combinations to the syntactic components of the case filter.

2.4.3   Arguments against nativism

Arguments against nativism generally take the form of parsimony arguments. If acquisition can be explained without recourse to innate content, then no innate content should be proposed. The fewer entities – mental or otherwise, innate or acquired – the better. Nativism seems to posit more entities than empiricism and thus to be less preferable. But parsimony is a comparative notion that demands (a) two theories for (b) the same body of facts. Parsimony chooses between two specific competing explanations of the same set of phenomena. If one theory accounts for more data than another, the fact that it uses more entities than another theory is not a violation of parsimony. Parsimony never comes into play.

The need for a comparable set of data is one reason that the conception of the final state is so important in language acquisition theories. If very little knowledge of an abstract character is acquired, very few mental concepts – innate or otherwise – will be required to explain that knowledge. If a great deal of abstract knowledge is acquired, many more concepts will be encompassed. The example of the case filter is a case in point. Empiricist theories have not addressed its acquisition. Since nativists and empiricists tend to disagree about the nature of the final state, parsimony is usually an irrelevant principle: the two positions are not explaining the same set of phenomena and thus cannot be evaluated with respect to parsimony.

An alternate approach is to stay closer to the data. Some investigators have analysed corpora from early child speech and concluded that the child does not – during the specific time period when the observations are made – have one or another abstract syntactic category, such as determiners (e.g. Pine & Martindale 1996). Instead, the child has local and limited knowledge about particular words that function as verbs or determiners in the adult system. If syntactic categories like determiners play no role in the young child's performance, they appear otiose. One can achieve a simpler and more parsimonious account of the child's behaviour by omitting the possibility of such innate categories and postulating that they develop later, after the child has abandoned narrow, lexically specific generalizations.

But if the child does eventually acquire knowledge of an abstract category, as almost everyone agrees is the case, he or she must – within this empiricist approach – shift at some point from a set of unrelated small-scale word patterns to an organized category. Such qualitative differences must be accounted for in some fashion, either by invoking additional concepts or additional mechanisms. Something may have been saved by ruling out innate categories, but something will be spent by postulating as yet undetermined mechanisms. The extent to which the initial parsimony yields a net saving is thus unknown.

One important goal of language acquisition theories is an explanation of how the child arrives at his or her final state. It is not enough to describe one or another point in development. If the child shows no clear knowledge of a concept at one time, but does show knowledge of it at a later time, the theory of development must state how that change takes place.

Nativists solve part of the problem of syntactic development by postulating a continuous process in which the child learns how to map innate categories and structures onto input. The initial learning mechanism continues until learning is complete. Thus, the nativist does not postulate unknown learning mechanisms of unknown complexity. Rather, the complexity of the system is known, in principle, at the outset: this innate content, this learning mechanism. The contrast between the two approaches to development demonstrates their incomparability. They are not explaining the same phenomena and thus neither can be rated as more or less parsimonious than the other.

Whether development actually *is* continuous in the nativist's sense is irrelevant to the logic of the continuity argument. What is important is that development *could* be continuous in the way the nativist postulates. The possibility of continuity, coupled with a final state of knowledge of abstract categories, means that we cannot assess theories with respect to parsimony or simplicity until we have competing theories of how knowledge develops to an agreed-upon final state.

2.5   Mechanisms of acquisition and learnability

Any theory of acquisition has to show that the knowledge postulated for the prior state, plus a particular learning mechanism, plus the input, will yield the knowledge postulated at the subsequent state. Learnability theories seek to lay out those elements: what combination of the learner's initial stock of concepts, mechanism of acquisition, and input will yield a particular intermediate or final state (see, for example, Berwick & Niyogi 1996, Fodor 1998a, Gibson & Wexler 1994, Lightfoot 1989, Wexler & Culicover 1980, Yang 2002). When learnability researchers try to model acquisition of an entire language, they discover enormous difficulties even when they provide the model with a great deal of innate content. Such learnability models often propose a form of acquisition called triggering. A trigger is a minimal input – perhaps only a single sentence – which is sufficient to set the correct value of a binary-valued parameter. On such a model, parameter values are not learned. Rather, a parameter is like a switch, set in one position or the other by positive evidence. There are a number of difficulties with the model of triggering, but for our purposes the important point is that triggering is not psychologically plausible. It idealizes acquisition as instantaneous once the appropriate datum arrives (to a mind prepared to receive it). But since children do not appear to make instantaneous decisions, the idealization appears to misstate the actual acquisition process.

One possible model of acquisition is hypothesis-testing (e.g. Valian 1990), which can be constrained or unconstrained. In nativist theories, hypothesis-testing is constrained by absolute and relative universals. The analogy is to theory confirmation in science, although there is no implication that the child consciously tests hypotheses. For parameters, the hypotheses are constrained by the possible values, which incoming data are used to choose between. In the case of syntactic rules, such as subject–auxiliary inversion, the hypotheses will be constrained by innate knowledge of possible syntactic structures – the fact that linguistic rules are structure-dependent.

Thus, the child would never entertain the structure-independent hypothesis that the first auxiliary in a sentence with an embedding ('The girl who is happy is singing') is the one which is inverted yielding the incorrect 'Is the girl happy is singing?' instead of 'Is the girl who is happy singing?' (see Crain & Nakayama 1987 for relevant data). Rather, the child will only entertain the hypothesis that the auxiliary of the matrix clause can be inverted. In the case of syntactic categories, hypotheses will be directed to which specific categories are instantiated in the learner's language. Hypothesis-testing need not be nativist. It can be unconstrained by any innate syntactic content, though it might be constrained by cognition. Nativist hypothesis-testing differs from triggering not in whether linguistic content is assumed to be innate – in both sets of theories, there is innate linguistic content – but in what mechanism is proposed. In hypothesis-testing, learning takes time.

Any form of hypothesis-testing uses one or another form of distributional analysis to evaluate the incoming data. Distributional analysis is essentially a form of pattern analysis in which learners observe what elements of a sequence go where, what elements can substitute for other elements, and what elements tend to occur together. Many different instantiations of such models have been proposed for different aspects of language acquisition (Cartwright & Brent 1997, Freudenthal et al. 2006, Mintz 2003, Redington et al. 1998; see Thiessen Ch. 3 for a discussion of statistical learning). Models differ in what units they presuppose. For example, most models aimed at acquisition of syntactic categories assume that individual words (and sometimes morphemes) are available to the child; the bracketing of speech into words is assumed already to have taken place. Non-nativist theories try to eliminate any syntactic information, such as information about what categories to aim for. Models of isolated pockets of syntax at particular points in the acquisition sequence can achieve at least limited success with relatively little by way of innate content, although even models limited to acquisition of syntactic categories have had only partial success (e.g. good accuracy but low completeness, Mintz 2003, or the reverse). Given the failure of taxonomic linguistics, it seems unlikely that a purely taxonomic approach to language acquisition could be successful. There are no non-nativist theories that have tackled acquisition of the entire grammar.

I am omitting here a range of curve-fitting models like dynamical change models, and connectionist models. In these models learning mechanisms are seen as continuous and what is learned is seen as discontinuous. What a given network learns appears to change qualitatively over the course of development, even as the mechanisms remain constant. In some cases, proponents of such models see knowledge acquisition as a mirage: knowledge does not genuinely take place but only appears to (Thelen & Smith 1994, see Spelke & Newport 1998, for a reinterpretation). For such models, no comparison is possible with models of knowledge acquisition, since they are explaining different things.

In other cases, proponents sometimes propose the models as knowledge acquisition devices, but without any need for innate concepts (Elman *et al.* 1996). In that case, the issues are whether the models presuppose some of the concepts that are supposedly learned and whether they succeed in modelling acquisition. Critiques of these models vary (for a summary of critiques of connectionism and replies, see Bechtel & Abrahamsen 2002, also see Marcus 2003, Valian 1999).

2.6 Empirical evidence concerning nativism

Several characteristics of language acquisition show that language is *special*. (1) Only humans acquire a full language. (2) Language appears to be independent of other cognitive abilities: even profoundly cognitively impaired individuals have close-to-normal syntax; syntactic deficits occur in individuals with no cognitive impairment. (3) Acquisition occurs most easily and fully during early childhood. (4) Some linguistic impairments appear due to certain genetic mutations. (5) Children's early knowledge of syntactic categories and word order, and the precursors of that knowledge, suggest innate content. Let us consider these characteristics of acquisition in turn.

2.6.1 Animals and language

That only humans acquire a full language is clear. Some species have communication systems that encode a limited amount of information, but no species encodes remotely as many concepts as those encoded by the languages humans acquire, and no species' communication system has the form of the languages that humans acquire.

Take the dance of the honeybees, for example, which encodes the distance and direction of a source of food or possible new site for a hive. The dance does not encode the altitude of the site, despite the possible relevance of that information (von Frisch 1967). Nor does the dance differentiate between food or a new hive. In addition, the nature of the encoding is very different from that of languages humans acquire: direction is encoded by the angle of the dance and distance by the number of waggles in the dance. This system is thus a continuous rather than discrete system of the sort used in human language (Janda 1978). There is nothing akin to grammatical categories and nothing akin to a phenomenon like word order. Vervets have alarm calls that appear to differ depending on the identity of the predator, but, again, there is nothing akin to syntactic categories or word order.

Thus, on two grounds, naturally occurring animal communication systems differ from the languages humans acquire. First, they are not effable (Katz 1978): they do not contain the means that would allow communication of more than a tiny number of concepts and there is no evidence that any of the communications are propositional in nature. Second, they bear no syntactic similarity to the languages that humans acquire. Although the lack of language among animals shows that animals differ from humans, it does not entail that humans have innate syntactic concepts and animals lack them. Humans might differ from animals in their computational power alone, or in the extra-syntactic concepts they have.

Studies that attempt to expose animals to language or to teach them language might provide a better comparison. Animals that have been studied include chimpanzees, bonobos, dolphins and grey parrots. The results suggest that animals can use symbols (at least occasionally) in connection with the objects they refer to, can make limited requests using symbols, and can follow limited commands made by humans (see Kako 1999, for discussion and summary). None of these animals, however, shows evidence of syntactic categories.

If no special innate endowment were required to acquire language, then any two species with identical abilities to learn and remember information and with identical repertoires of cognitive concepts should be able to acquire language on the basis of the input provided. If one of the two species is nevertheless unable to learn language, that provides an argument for innate content. The problem, however, is that it is impossible to be certain that we have creatures who are cognitively identical. Bonobos (one of two species of chimpanzee, sometimes called a pygmy chimpanzee) and humans, for example, have highly similar learning abilities and similar cognition; they also share about 98 per cent of their DNA. But the small differences between bonobos and humans might be just those that are relevant to language. Because arguments for innate content based on cross-species differences crucially rely on the assumption of cross-species similarity of the non-linguistic systems and of learning mechanisms, the arguments can only be suggestive.

With those caveats in mind, consider a particular bonobo, Kanzi. Kanzi's experimenters spoke English to him, attempting as much as possible to duplicate conditions in which a human child acquires language (Savage-Rumbaugh *et al.* 1993). The experimenters also accompanied their speech by points to lexigrams on a keyboard for major words, including 'nouns' and 'verbs'. Lexigrams did not include function morphemes, so the system did not fully duplicate the auditory system. Since Kanzi could not produce speech, he had to use a combination of points to objects, gestures and lexigrams, a clear handicap compared to a normal child, a handicap that precluded Kanzi's using function words like *a* and *the*. Kanzi began learning the lexigrams for single words when just a few months old. By the age of 5 years, his sequences were 1.15 items long (only 10 per cent of his utterances were more than one item long; Greenfield & Savage-Rumbaugh 1990). They remained at that length for the next three years. In his short utterance length and failure to develop more complex utterances Kanzi was very different from a human child.

In comprehension tests at age 8, Kanzi appeared to understand a wide range of sentences, such as "Take the snake outdoors," "The surprise is hiding in the dishwasher," "Get Rose with the snake" (Savage-Rumbaugh *et al.* 1993). After hearing such sentences, Kanzi carried out the correct action almost 75 per cent of the time on average. Indeed, he was correct more often than a child aged 1;6 to 2 years who was tested on similar materials and averaged 65 per cent. Impressive though Kanzi's achievements were, he may typically have answered correctly on the basis of his knowledge of the individual items, the most plausible combination of those items, and an order of mention strategy. For example, when told to "Pour the milk in the bowl," Kanzi performed the correct action. In this particular case, other than by eliminating one of the items, it is hard to see how Kanzi could get the command wrong. The correct action is the most plausible combination of the individual words and follows order of mention.

In production, Kanzi failed to develop agent–action word order, instead systematically using action–agent order, despite the input. If input determined what rules a learner would form, then 'smart' animals like bonobos would acquire a regularity as simple, obvious, and robust as the agent–action order. Kanzi seemed to have the concepts of agent and action, he was a good learner generally, and he had an enriched environment. But he did not learn the agent–action order. Kanzi's gaps seem more plausibly explained as due to inadequate mental representation than deficient learning processes. Kanzi does not seem to bring the same syntactic concepts to the task that children do (see also Terrace 1987, for discussions of earlier failures with chimpanzees).

The import of Kanzi's data is to illustrate the argument that the speech data to which children are exposed underdetermines what they will acquire. Bonobos' failure to absorb the regularities in their input demonstrates that no matter how 'transparent' and input-dictated a regularity appears to those of us who acquire it, it is opaque to a learner who cannot represent that regularity in its hypothesis space. We do not know why Kanzi did not represent word order as human children do, even after massive exposure. Although it seems likely that bonobos lack the innate syntactic ideas that humans have, it is also possible that they have different learning mechanisms or different cognition. Kanzi's data, however suggestive, do not *prove* that humans have innate syntactic concepts. His data are primarily useful to us in showing that rich input doesn't by itself yield learning.

Even under conditions of great enrichment, animals do not develop anything like a full language, while humans, even under conditions of great impoverishment, do. For example, deaf children born to hearing parents who do not want their children to learn sign language create a limited gesture system that uses some of the devices, such as word order and inflection, that natural languages use (Goldin-Meadow 2003b, 2005 and Ch. 9).

Another example is the evolving sign language of deaf individuals in Nicaragua. Before 1977, Nicaraguan deaf individuals had no access to other deaf individuals or to schooling. After the revolution, in 1977, 25 deaf individuals were brought together to a school and others joined them in successive years. By 1983 there were 400 individuals of various ages receiving education together (Senghas 2003). The first group developed a common, albeit limited, gestural system. Young individuals who entered the school later, and who were exposed to the limited sign system of the first group, developed the system further, so that it now encoded properties that were not initially present, such as a syntactic means for representing the positions of objects (Senghas 2003, Senghas & Coppola 2001, Senghas *et al.* 2004).

The examples of children with greatly impoverished or no input contrast strikingly with the examples of chimpanzees. The contrast makes it clear that *something* innate distinguishes animals and humans, but it does not entail that that something is innate content.

2.6.2 Dissociation between language and cognition
When we turn to individuals with various forms of cognitive impairments, we find some conditions where syntax is close to normal, as with individuals with Williams syndrome (see Richardson & Thomas Ch. 26). And there are forms of linguistic impairment that leave cognition relatively intact. Such examples again suggest that language is special and at least in part distinct from other cognitive systems. But they do not entail innate syntactic content.

2.6.3 Sensitive period
Language acquisition is most likely to be complete if acquired in childhood, though there are exceptional examples of individuals acquiring native-like fluency in a new language as adults. This argues that language is different from other aspects of cognition which people typically improve at with age, until reaching a plateau. But, again, it does not argue for innate content.

2.6.4 Genetic involvement
A family known as KE has been studied for years because of the language difficulties of some of its members, difficulties which are now known to

be due to a mutation in just one gene, FOX2P, involving one nucleotide change (see Marcus & Fisher 2003, for review and Tomblin Ch. 23). Even though only a single change on a single gene is involved, that gene has multiple effects, perhaps by influencing the actions of other genes (Marcus & Fisher 2003). Tests of syntax comprehension and production are not the only places where individuals with the mutation show deficits. Affected individuals also have difficulties telling apart words and non-words; indeed, that difference alone can distinguish affected and unaffected family members (Watkins *et al.* 2002); affected individuals have some cognitive and motor difficulties as well. Further, the FOX2P gene is found in a number of species and, even in humans, is related to lung and other organ functions as well as cognitive function. Finally, other forms of language delay and impairment show no mutation on FOX2P. As with the considerations we have examined in sections 2.6.1 and 2.6.3, the genetic data strongly suggest that humans are wired to learn language. But the data leave unanswered the question of whether the wiring involves syntactic content or a linguistic ability that does not involve content.

2.6.5   Syntactic categories and their precursors

A nativist view of category acquisition places an abstract specification of categories in the child's grammar as part of the child's initial state. For a nativist, the child's task is then to find out what words fall into each category and how that category behaves in the child's target language; input plays the role of providing specific information. On an empiricist view, the child creates the categories on the basis of regularities in the input and context.

Children appear to have knowledge of categories, including functional categories, very early. Consider, for example, the class of determiners: articles like *a* and *the*, demonstratives like *this* and *that*, possessive pronouns like *my* and quantifiers. Spontaneous speech data demonstrate that children use determiners appropriately as soon as they start putting words together – between the ages of 18 and 28 months (Abu-Akel *et al.* 2004, in a longitudinal investigation of seventeen 18 month olds; Ihns & Leonard 1988, in a longitudinal investigation of a 2 year old; Valian 1986, in a cross-sectional study of six 2 year olds; Valian *et al.* in press, in a cross-sectional study of twenty-one 2 year olds).

Experimental data show that very young children attend to and understand determiners, using them to aid in noun repetition (Gerken *et al.* 1990, with 2 year olds) or to pick out a stuffed animal or block (Gelman & Taylor 1984, with 2 year olds). Eighteen month olds and older infants parse a speech stream better if they hear a genuine determiner than a nonsense form or function word from a different class (such as *and*), and, often, better than if they hear no determiner (Gerken & McIntosh

1993, Kedar *et al.* 2006, Zangl & Fernald 2007). Even though children at 18 months seldom produce determiners, their comprehension is improved when they hear real determiners, indicating that they have a determiner slot which they expect to be filled appropriately. Eleven month olds prefer to look at monosyllabic nouns that are preceded by real, rather than nonce, determiners (Hallé *et al.* in press); 14–16 month olds listen longer to test passages where a nonsense noun is in a verb context rather than a noun context (Höhle *et al.* 2004); 18 month olds look longer to a visual target if it is described by a sentence with a determiner before the noun than if a different short word precedes the noun (Kedar *et al.* 2006). Thus, there is strong evidence that even infants have the category determiner.

Sceptics have questioned whether 2 year olds actually have a category determiner, proposing instead that children have lexically specific formulae (Pine & Lieven 1997, Pine & Martindale 1996), but subsequent work suggests that children are not bound by frames in their use of determiners (Valian *et al.* in press). Children's only error with respect to determiners is their failure to use them in all the contexts where they are required. The reason for those omissions may be prosodic rather than syntactic (Demuth Ch. 11, Gerken 1994): if unstressed syllables do not fit a prosodic template for a language, they will tend to be omitted.

Precursors to a full understanding of determiners are revealed by experiments with very young infants: 8 month olds use *the* to segment speech using nonce nouns, but find the nonsense syllable *kuh* equally useful (Shi *et al.* 2006c). Young infants thus appear initially to have an underspecified representation, accepting a high-frequency vowel whether it appears in *the* or *kuh*. Twelve month olds exposed to a miniature artificial language are able to use the combination of high-frequency markers yoked with either one- or two-syllable words to form categories (Gómez & Lakusta 2004). Even though the items in the language have no meaning, infants form the categories quickly. Since these categories are not natural language categories, the main force of the experiment is to demonstrate that children do not form item-specific representations as their first hypothesis, but more abstract representations.

2.6.6 Word order and its precursors

Word order and categories are intimately entwined. To get word order right, the child either has to have memorized a very large number of sequences or to have coded those sequences in terms of categories. Children do get word order right, both within a phrase (for example, placing determiners in front of adjectives, and placing determiners and adjectives in front of nouns) and within a sentence (correctly ordering the major elements of a sentence, such as the subject, verb and object). As with categories, children's spontaneous speech is ordered appropriately as soon as children put words together.

Sceptics have proposed that 2 year olds do not understand that English word order is subject–verb–object (Akhtar 1999, Akhtar & Tomasello 1997), based on studies with nonce verbs, in which 2 year olds do not correct wrong word orders that experimenters use with nonce verbs. They do, however, produce correct orders with those verbs (Fisher 2002a), and other features of the experiments leave open whether, in some of the experimental situations, 2 year olds drew the correct inferences about the nature of the experimenter's game (Naigles 2002). Even children younger than 2, however, are sensitive to word order. Sixteen month olds, for example, listen longer to sequences displaying correct word order than to those with incorrect word order (Shady 1996).

Precursors to word order sensitivity are apparent in infants ranging from 7 to 12 months of age. Seven month olds exposed to artificial language sequences, quickly acquire order-dependent patterns (Marcus *et al.* 1999), and work with miniature artificial languages demonstrates sensitivity to order among 12 month olds (Gómez & Gerken 1999). Notably, tamarins can acquire some of the same patterns that human infants do, but not all; the ones that tamarins cannot acquire involve recursion (Fitch & Hauser 2004, Hauser *et al.* 2002). Eight month olds are sensitive to whether high frequency items like determiners occur first or last in a phrase: Japanese 8 month olds preferred to hear a highly frequent nonce syllable after low-frequency syllables, while Italian children preferred the reverse pattern (Gervain *et al.* in press). As with category data for infants, the importance of these experiments is their demonstration that children's first hypotheses are abstract, rather than item-based.

2.7   Inference to the best explanation

Observational and experimental data on two year olds' behaviour suggest that, as soon as children can string words together, they are operating with abstract syntactic categories and understand the basic word order pattern of their language. Experiments with even younger children demonstrate that infants under the age of one year form abstract categories and rules rather than lexically specific ones. Taken together, the data provide more specific empirical evidence about innate syntactic content that go beyond the claim that language is special, and the data suggest what the precursors to acquisition are. When taken together with the argument from poverty of the stimulus, the data make a strong case for innateness of syntactic content. The data do not compel that interpretation, but they support the inference of innate content as the best explanation.

Suggestions for further reading

Linguistic Review (2002). 19(1/2), 1–223.

Lust, B. (2006). *Child language: Acquisition and Growth*. Cambridge: Cambridge University Press.

Pinker, S., & Jackendoff, R. (2005). The faculty of language: what's special about it. *Cognition*, 95, 201–236.

Valian, V. (in press). *Input and Innateness: Controversies in Language Acquisition*. Cambridge, MA: MIT Press.

3

Statistical learning

Erik Thiessen

3.1 Introduction

Language is a uniquely human endowment – no other animal communicates using a system as rich or inventive as human language. Statistical learning approaches to language emphasize the richness of human communication: it is the primary source of data from which the child identifies the patterns in their native language. Statistical learning refers to the process of identifying units in the input, such as words or categories, by discovering what features of the input predict other features, and grouping features that are likely to co-occur. It is a domain general ability, meaning that learners can discover these statistical relations in many different types of input, including language, music, vision and other sensory modalities (Fiser & Aslin 2001, Saffran *et al.* 1997). Humans, from infancy to adulthood, and several species of animals show evidence of statistical learning, suggesting that the mechanism that gives rise to statistical learning is both evolutionarily old and present from – or near to – birth (Kirkham *et al.* 2002, Toro & Trobalon 2005). This presents a challenge for theories of language that emphasize learning: if animals and adults are capable of statistical learning, why do infants learn language more successfully than any animal, and most adults (e.g. Johnson & Newport 1989)? To begin to answer this question, it is necessary to understand what statistics learners can detect, how the characteristics of the learning mechanism and the learner affect learning, and how these characteristics change with age.

The definition of statistical learning – the process of using likelihood of occurrence to group elements in the environment – is in some ways similar to the definition of associative learning. Association is clearly an important component of statistical learning, which requires the ability to associate two stimuli that are likely to co-occur. But the two kinds of learning are not identical; there are many examples of associative learning that are not statistical learning, such as fear conditioning and food aversion. Bregman (1934) found that, while infants could be conditioned to fear rats by pairing them with the presentation of a loud noise, it is much more difficult to condition them to fear inanimate objects, such as wooden blocks or swatches of cloth (cf. Cook & Mineka 1990). Even though the statistical relation between loud noises and the inanimate objects is the same as the relation between loud noises and rats, learning proceeds differently. Similarly, consider food aversion: the well-known distaste for a particular food that can be acquired when sensations of nausea follow shortly after eating the food (Bernstein & Borson 1986). This aversion can develop even after several experiences in which the food was not associated with nausea – that is, even though there is, statistically, a low probability of the food leading to unpleasant outcomes.

Saffran *et al.*'s (1996b) experiments on word segmentation in infancy provide a concrete example of statistical learning. In their experiments, infants heard a nonsense language made up of four three-syllable words, such as *golabu, padoti, tupiro* and *bidaku*. Within a word, syllables always predicted each other; after *go, la* occurred 100 per cent of the time. At the end of a word, however, the next syllable is unpredictable, as any of the other three words could subsequently occur. This mimics a property of natural languages: sound sequences are typically more predictable within words than at word boundaries (e.g. Swingley 2005). After listening to the artificial language, infants were able to distinguish between predictable sequences (words like *golabu*) and unpredictable sequences (sequences that crossed word boundaries, like *bupado*). Infants' ability to distinguish between the predictable and unpredictable sequences indicates that they were able to identify which syllables cohered by identifying the statistical relations between syllables.

The defining feature of statistical learning, then, is not that it leads to associations between A and B, but that the formation of these associations is governed by the statistical relationship between A and B. In the remainder of this chapter, we will examine statistical learning in more detail, focusing on three questions. First, to what statistical features of the environment are learners sensitive? Second, how is statistical learning constrained? Finally, how do the characteristics of the learning organism affect the outcome of statistical learning?

3.2   To what statistical features of the environment are learners sensitive?

Statistical learning is guided by the statistical information in the environment. But what statistics do learners detect? The literature on statistical learning contains a wide variety of examples. At a descriptive level, we can group these statistics into two broad categories: conditional statistics and distributional statistics. Conditional statistics specify the likelihood of some event Y, given information about whether some other event X has occurred. These conditional statistics are a subtler metric of the strength of the relation between two events than the simple frequency of their co-occurrence.

Distributional statistics assess the central tendency and variability of members of some population, such as a distribution of colours ranging from a prototypical blue, to blue-green, to a prototypical green. How likely is each colour to occur? Which colour is most common? Those familiar with Bayesian statistics might see some similarity between the categories of conditional and distributional statistics, and the ideas of conditional and prior probabilities. While distributional statistics and conditional statistics have a different flavour at a descriptive level, they may arise from the same mechanisms, a question we will discuss in section 3.2.3.

3.2.1 Conditional statistics

Transitional probability is the most familiar statistic in the statistical learning literature, and it provides an excellent introduction to conditional statistics. The transitional probability between two items, X and Y, can be formalized as the number of times the sequence X-Y occurs, divided by the number of times X occurs. If the sequence X-Y occurs 50 times, and X occurs 100 times, then the transitional probability between X and Y is 0.5. When X occurs, it is followed by Y 50 per cent of the time. Both infants and adults can use transitional probabilities to group items that are highly likely to co-occur (Aslin *et al.* 1998). For example, infants can use transitional probabilities to group syllables, and segment words from fluent speech (Saffran *et al.* 1996a). Indeed, infants are sensitive to transitional probabilities from 2 months of age, if not before (Kirkham *et al.* 2002).

In experimental demonstrations of statistical learning, the sequences with high transitional probabilities are very high indeed (often approaching or equalling 1.0), whereas the sequences with low probabilities contain at least one juncture with a transitional probability at or below 0.33. Adults are able to make distinctions between high- and low-probability sequences when the distinction is less extreme (e.g. Saffran *et al.* 1996b). As yet, it is unclear what minimum difference in transitional probabilities learners need to differentiate between sequences, or if this 'just noticeable difference' changes as a function of the learner's age, or of the type of the stimuli.

While our discussion of transitional probabilities has so far been limited to X and Y pairs in which Y immediately follows X, many of the relations infants and adults learn involve regularities between elements that are not immediately adjacent. This is especially true of languages. While *the* predicts that a noun will follow, the noun can follow several words later (as in *the* big brown *dog*). If learners' statistical sensitivity were limited to detecting relations between adjacent items, it would be a severely limited learning tool. However, several experiments have demonstrated that both infant and adult learners can detect non-adjacent transitional probabilities (Newport & Aslin 2004, Creel *et al.* 2004). That is, in sequences where X and Y are separated by intervening, unpredictable elements – such that listeners might be exposed to XAY, XBY, XCY – participants are able to learn that X predicts a following Y.

Though transitional probabilities are clearly useful and informative, there are many different kinds of conditional statistics available to learners beyond transitional probabilities. One such is co-occurrence probability, the likelihood that two (or more) events occur together. While transitional probabilities assess sequential relationships, co-occurrence statistics measure simultaneous relations. Both infants and adults are sensitive to co-occurrence statistics (Chun & Jiang 1999, Younger & Fearing 1998). Thus, transitional probabilities are but one example of the kinds of conditional statistics to which learners are sensitive. This suggests that statistical learning may be applied in a wide variety of different learning situations.

One of the reasons that conditional probabilities are so useful to learners is that they are a more sensitive measure of the strength of the relation between two (or more) items than simple frequency of co-occurrence. Consider the causal reasoning situation that Schulz and Gopnik (2004) presented to preschool children. In their experiment, two objects, A and B, are possible causes for an event X. Children are twice shown that A and B, together, cause event X to occur. They are then shown once that A, alone, causes the event to occur. B, seen once alone, does not. Critically, children have seen B three times, and more often than not, B preceded event X. But the conditional probability between A and X (100 per cent) is much higher than the conditional probability between B and X. Accordingly, children determined that A was the cause of the event, and B was not a cause.

Several subsequent experiments have confirmed that young children and even infants are successful at using these kinds of conditional probabilities to identify causal relations (e.g. Sobel & Kirkham 2007, Sobel *et al.* 2004). Similarly, several theorists have proposed that conditional probabilities might play a critical role in infants' discovery of referential relations between words and objects (Yu & Smith 2007). If a word occurs in the presence of three objects, A, B, and C, it can be difficult to determine to which of those objects the word refers. If the word is uttered a second time, in the presence of objects B, D and E, the conditional probability between the word and object B is relatively higher than the conditional relation between the word and other objects, which can provide a cue for word learning. The fact that conditional statistics are useful in such disparate situations as causal reasoning and word learning provides some insight into how widely useful conditional statistics might be.

3.2.2 Distributional statistics

While conditional statistics are clearly informative, they are not the only kind of statistical information to which learners attend. An additional group of statistics can be described as *distributional* statistics, as opposed to conditional statistics. Distributional statistics reflect the relative frequency of an event. For example, if X occurs seventy times, and Y occurs thirty times, we might say that the distributional probability of X is 70 per cent. As such, distributional statistics reflect information about the central tendency, and variability, of a group of events. Even very young infants are sensitive to these kinds of distributional statistics (e.g. Dougherty & Haith 2002, Maye *et al.* 2002).

Distributional statistics have long been suggested to be important for various aspects of language learning (e.g. Reber & Lewis 1977). Indeed, distributional statistics may play a role in one of the most striking linguistic developments in the first year of life: infants' adaptation to the phonemic structure of their native language. At birth, infants distinguish between phonemic contrasts not found in their native language. After their first birthday, infants are primarily sensitive to those sounds that are phonemic – indicate a difference in meaning – in their native language (e.g. Werker & Tees 1984). The phonemic categories that a language employs affect the distribution of sounds in the input (Werker *et al.* 2007). Sounds near the prototypical centre of a category occur frequently. Sounds that fall between phonemic categories – and as such are ambiguous – are comparatively rare. Infants are sensitive to this kind of distributional information. When exposed to a bimodal distribution of sounds – a distribution with two modes, and a sparsely populated region between the two prototypical centres – infants are more likely to discriminate between the two prototypes. When exposed to a distribution where one central sound occurs most frequently, infants are less likely to discriminate (Maye *et al.* 2002). This kind of sensitivity to distributional probabilities may explain how infants adapt to the phonemic structure of their native language in the first year of life.

One aspect of distributional statistics is the ability to identify the most common feature or pattern in the input, as in responding differently to unimodal or bimodal distributions. Sensitivity to distributional information can allow learners to, for example, learn a pattern that regularly occurs, but is occasionally violated (e.g. Saffran & Thiessen 2003). But another aspect of distributional statistics is information about variability. Variability can be thought of as a measure of whether the distributional probabilities of a set of two (or more) events are equivalent, or skewed. In a situation where all of the events have roughly equal distributional probabilities, there is high variability: any of the possible events is equally likely to occur, so it is impossible to predict which one will occur. In a situation where one of the events has a markedly higher probability, there is lower variability, as it is likely that the probable event is the one that will occur next.

Adult learners can be exquisitely sensitive to the variability in their environment (e.g. Mueller *et al.* 1974). Infants are also sensitive to variability in the environment, although they may respond to variability differently than adults (Hudson Kam & Newport 2005). Variability has been argued to play a particularly important role in many kinds of learning: variable elements may serve to highlight invariant structural elements in the input (e.g. Gómez 2002). For example, when learning to identify meaning in speech, listeners must learn that some changes in the acoustic signal indicate a difference in meaning (as in *big* vs. *pig*). Other changes in the acoustic signal, such as changes in speaker identity (two different speakers saying *pig*), do not signal a difference in meaning. Acoustic information that is not meaningful may vary more widely than acoustic information that indicates a difference in meaning. Singh (2008) argues that speaker variability focuses infants on the phonemic identity of words.

3.2.3 Are distributional and conditional statistics tracked by the same learning mechanism?

At a descriptive level, conditional statistics and distributional statistics appear to capture different kinds of information. Conditional statistics describe the strength of the relation between two or more items, while distributional statistics describe the central tendencies and variability of a distribution of items. While both entail learning from the statistical structure of the environment, an important question to ask is whether they are really the same kind of learning. That is, do they arise from the activity of the same learning mechanisms? There are a variety of ways one could attempt to resolve this question. As with all questions of mechanism, no single approach will be definitive, so we will discuss two: formal approaches and behavioural approaches.

A formal approach emphasizes identifying the computations that learners perform. And at a formal level, there are indeed similarities between conditional and distributional statistics. Both kinds of statistics require learners to track at least a rough approximation of the frequency of events in the environment. Indeed, conditional probabilities can be thought of as a special case of distributional probabilities. A conditional probability is simply a context-sensitive distributional probability. Distributional probabilities track the likelihood of some event, Y. Conditional probabilities track how likely Y is to occur in a particular context: after X. As one would expect from probabilities with so much in common, several computational architectures are capable of learning from both kinds of statistics (e.g. Christiansen *et al.* 1998, Vallabha *et al.* 2007).

Despite these similarities, much work at the formal level remains necessary for a complete understanding of statistical learning. It is not clear which formal statistics best approximate the statistical regularities to which learners are sensitive. Consider transitional probabilities. Some authors have suggested that *mutual information* may better simulate learners' statistical intuitions (e.g. Redington *et al.* 1998, Swingley 2005). Transitional probability computes relations unidirectionally, moving forward in time – after X has occurred, what is the probability that Y will occur next? Mutual information captures the strength of a relationship in both directions – not only whether X is likely to predict Y, but what is the likelihood that Y has been preceded by X. These relations are not identical; while there is a high probability that the word *dog* is preceded by *the*, there is a much lower probability that *the* leads to *dog*, as many words can follow *the*.

In many situations, transitional probabilities, mutual information and other formal statistical indices of relatedness highlight the same cohesive units in a sequence. However, in some situations they make different predictions, and recent research has begun to examine which kinds of statistics best capture learners' performance (e.g. Aslin *et al.* 1998, Xu & Tenenbaum 2007). While it is unlikely that learners are computing formal statistics, understanding which formal statistics best characterize learning will lead to more precise definition of the underlying learning mechanisms that capitalize on the statistical regularities in the environment. Thus, it is important to remember that when we speak of transitional probabilities, or any other formal statistic, these are only an approximation of the statistics learners are performing, and perhaps not an optimal approximation. This uncertainty makes it difficult to assess, at a formal level, whether sensitivity to conditional and distributional statistics is mediated by the same or different learning mechanisms.

Related to the question of what formal statistic best expresses how learners detect relations between X and Y is an additional formal question: what are X and Y? That is, what are the primitive units over which these computations are performed, and do they differ as a function of the kind of statistic learners detect? For example, consider the synthesized speech Saffran *et al.* (1996b) used to assess whether infants use transitional probability as a cue to word segmentation. This language contains four three-syllable nonsense words: *tupiro, golabu, bidaku, padoti*. In a speech stream like this, there are two especially likely units over which to compute transitional probabilities: syllables and phonemes. Infants may be computing the transitional probabilities between units like *bi* and *da*, or units like /b/ and /i/. In Saffran *et al.*'s original language, transitional probabilities were higher within words than at word boundaries for either kind of unit of computation. Subsequent experiments indicate that infants may rely primarily on computations between phonemic units (Newport *et al.* 2004). Similarly, phonemes seem to be privileged over syllables in the identification of non-adjacent transitional probabilities (Newport & Aslin 2004). However, there is likely no single answer to the question of which units of representation are the primitive units of computation. Different types of stimuli will entail different primitives, and even within the same type of input, learners can use different units as a function of the structure of the input (Saffran *et al.* 2005).

A complementary approach to the question of underlying learning mechanisms focuses on behavioural data. If sensitivity to different kinds of statistical information arises from different learning mechanisms, then there should be a divergence in the age at which sensitivity emerges, or species that show sensitivity to one kind of statistic, but not another. Adults, of course, are sensitive to both conditional and distributional statistics (Saffran *et al.* 1996b). By 8 months, infants are also sensitive to both conditional and distributional statistics (e.g. Maye *et al.* 2002, Saffran *et al.* 1996a). Currently, there is little data to indicate at which age sensitivity to these kinds of statistical information first emerges (though see Kirkham *et al.* 2002). Animal models may also be informative with regard to this question. If sensitivity to distributional and conditional statistics arises from different mechanisms, it would be logically possible to find a species sensitive to one, but not both. Clearly, species other than humans are sensitive to many kinds of statistical relations, (e.g. Kluender *et al.* 1998, Toro & Trobalon 2005), so future research comparing the commonality of sensitivity to these kinds of information across species may yield new insights.

In summary, statistical learning refers to learning that is guided by the statistical structure of the environment. But as we have seen, there are a variety of potential statistical relations to which learners could attend. Even beyond the two broad types of statistical information – conditional and distributional statistics – there are a multitude of potential statistical relations available based on the elements of computation: for example, phonemes, syllables, words and phrases. How can learners possibly sort through this multitude of potential statistics, and discover useful relations? This is the question we address in section 3.3.

3.3   Constraints on statistical learning

One of the perils of statistical learning is what Pinker (1997) has termed a 'combinatorial explosion'. There are, in principle, an infinite number of statistical relations a learner might attempt to track in the input. There are multiple types of statistics, multiple possible units of statistical analysis and multiple distances over which one might attempt to identify regular patterns. But while there are an infinite number of possible statistics a learner might compute, there are only a finite number of exemplars a learner experiences to determine which statistics are fruitful. For learning to succeed, statistical learning must be constrained such that not all statistics are equally likely to be considered.

An additional argument for constraints on statistical learning arises from the study of language. Across the globe, linguistic systems share deep commonalities in the way that they are organized, despite surface dissimilarities (for discussion, see Pinker 1994). If languages are learned via an unconstrained learning mechanism, languages should vary more widely than is actually observed. One way to resolve this apparent quandary is to suggest that linguistic universals arise from children's innately endowed linguistic abilities, including innate knowledge about the structure of language (e.g. Pinker & Bloom 1990). This is the central hypothesis of the Universal Grammar tradition. The key prediction of Universal Grammar is that language learning is constrained in ways that are unique to language. That is, infants learn about language using innate knowledge or mechanisms that are domain-specific; crosslinguistic similarities are a result of these domain-specific constraints on language acquisition.

3.3.1 Constrained statistical learning

An alternative perspective suggests that language is learned, at least in part, via domain general statistical learning mechanisms. However, these mechanisms are constrained, such that not all relations are learned equally well (e.g. Fiser & Aslin 2005, Newport & Aslin 2000, Saffran 2003, Saffran & Thiessen 2003). Importantly, these constraints are not specific to language. Instead, just as statistical learning is a domain general process, operating on many different kinds of input, the constraints on statistical learning are domain general. According to this framework, the similarities across languages are one source of evidence that can identify the constraints on statistical learning. These crosslinguistic similarities arise because learners are not blank slates; they prefer certain kinds of statistical relations. Human languages have been shaped by generations of language learners. Linguistic structures that fit with the constraints on statistical learning – and thus are easier to learn – survive, while structures that do not fit within the constraints on statistical learning are less likely to persist. To the extent that constraints on statistical learning exist, they also simplify the combinatorial explosion problem, as some statistical relations will never be considered. But learning in non-linguistic domains should be similarly constrained.

This proposal immediately raises two related questions: is there evidence to suggest that statistical learning is constrained, and, if so, what are these constraints? Research with infants strongly indicates an affirmative answer to the first question. Constraints on statistical learning exist; infants learn some patterns more easily than others (e.g. Saffran 2002, Saffran & Thiessen 2003). Research with adults, and computational simulations, suggests similar conclusions (e.g. Endress *et al.* 2005, Peperkamp *et al.* 2006). Note, however, that results from adults present an interpretational difficulty. When these results indicate that adults' learning is constrained, especially in ways that would appear adaptive for language, the constraints may have arisen from adults' experience with language.

According to the constrained statistical learning framework, the constraints on learning should be consistent with crosslinguistic structure. Saffran and Thiessen (2003) tested this claim by exploring infants' learning of phonotactic regularities. Phonotactics refers to the patterns of sound combinations a language allows. A phonotactic regularity in English, for example, is that /fs/ can occur at the ends of syllables (as in *giraffes*), but not at the beginning. Crosslinguistically, phonotactic regularities quite often involve generalizations across classes of sounds, such as voiced sounds or fricatives. Phonotactic regularities that govern a mix of sounds from multiple classes (e.g. two fricatives and a stop consonant), with no higher order commonality between them, are less common crosslinguistically (Chomsky & Halle 1968). Saffran and Thiessen found evidence that English-learning infants learn patterns that are more likely to occur crosslinguistically more easily than patterns which are unlikely to occur crosslinguistically.

Findings of this nature can potentially provide explanations for why languages show the types of patterns they do. Patterns that are difficult for infants – the primary language learners in a community – may be less likely to be preserved in language. But critically, according to the constrained statistical learning hypothesis, the difficulty in learning does not arise from knowledge or constraints that are specific to language. Instead, these are constraints on the learning mechanisms themselves, which should apply across a number of domains. As such, one of the primary empirical claims of the constrained statistical learning hypothesis is that the constraints on learning from linguistic stimuli should also constrain learning of non-linguistic stimuli. While this claim has not been exhaustively examined, at least one series of experiments has found similar constraints operating over both linguistic and non-linguistic stimuli (Saffran 2002).

3.3.2   How constraints simplify the learning environment

The constrained statistical learning framework makes an additional claim, which is that the constraints on learning simplify the learning problem. In particular, constraints should make a 'combinatorial explosion' less likely. An example of this kind of constraint is the embeddedness constraint proposed by Fiser and Aslin (2005). Using visual stimuli, they found that participants who had discovered a superordinate structure were insensitive to the statistical relation between subordinate elements of the super-structure. For example, while participants were able to identify that shapes A, B and C predicted each other (they were all members of a three-shape complex with high co-occurrence statistics), they failed to identify that shapes A and B, or B and C, were related. While this is initially counterintuitive, this embeddedness constraint may be highly adaptive; it limits the number of potential computations a learner performs.

Constraints need not absolutely limit learners from performing certain kinds of computations. Some constraints simply bias learners to preferentially seek out one kind of relation, but these constraints can be overridden in the face of appropriate input. This kind of 'soft' constraint can be seen when learners are required to identify transitional probabilities between non-adjacent items. Learners appear to preferentially identify adjacent transitional probabilities; they only discover non-adjacent transitional probabilities under certain conditions (e.g. Creel *et al.* 2004). But the nature of the input can support learners' ability to discover non-adjacent transitional probabilities. When presented with three-item strings of the form 'X-A-Y', for example, the variability of the middle element affects the likelihood of detecting the non-adjacent relation between X and Y. When the A position has low variability (it is filled by only a few possible exemplars), learners are less likely to detect the non-adjacent relationship. But when the A position has high variability, learners are more likely to detect it (Gómez 2002).

Similarly, learners can be prompted to change their preference for the primitive elements over which they attempt to characterize statistical relations. When presented with a series of tones, there are two possible relations infants could compute: the absolute pitch of each tone, or the relative pitch between tones (how much each tone moves up or down in pitch compared to the previous tone). While young infants are sensitive to both, they appear to preferentially rely on absolute pitch, at least when segmenting a tone stream based on transitional probabilities (Saffran & Griepentrog 2001). That is, when both relative and absolute pitch cues are available, infants weight absolute pitch more heavily. However, this preference is not absolute. If the characteristics of the input are such that absolute pitch is less informative than relative pitch, infants will use relative pitch to segment the tone sequence (Saffran *et al.* 2005).

3.4   How the characteristics of the learner influence statistical learning

So far, we have discussed the structure of input, and the nature of learning mechanisms, as the factors that determine learning outcomes. But identical input to identical learning mechanisms can lead to different outcomes as a function of the characteristics of the learner. Once again, an example from food aversion serves to illustrate this point. Rats easily learn an aversion to tastes that precede nausea. By contrast, rats do not easily learn an association between audiovisual cues and nausea (Garcia & Koelling 1966). Many species of birds, however, show a different pattern of learning. Quail learn to avoid visual cues preceding nausea; this may be due to the fact that many birds rely heavily on vision in their search for food (Wilcoxon *et al.* 1971). The characteristics of the organism bias it to identify some relations in the environment, and ignore others. In the remainder of this section, we will examine how the characteristics of human learners influence statistical learning, with a particular focus on information processing, perception and prior experience.

3.4.1 How information processing, perception and prior experience influence statistical learning

Statistical learning is considered to be a form of implicit learning, because learners frequently seem unaware of what, if anything, they have learned (Saffran *et al.* 1997, Stadler 1992). However, even implicit learning can be affected by information processing abilities, such as attentional control (e.g. Stadler 1995), and statistical learning is no exception (Baker *et al.* 2004). Infants identify statistical relations more quickly in stimuli that hold their attention (Thiessen *et al.* 2005). And while statistical learning can proceed in the absence of focused attention, learners appear to be greatly impaired when they are forced to divide their attention between two sources of input in the same modality, such as speech and tones (Toro *et al.* 2005). In addition to attention, working memory has been argued to play an important role in determining the statistics which learners are able to detect (Newport 1988).

The way in which a learner perceives the input also has a significant effect on their ultimate learning. Consider modality as an example. When exposed to audio stimuli, listeners are quite adept at identifying sequential regularities: A occurs, then B, then C (e.g. Saffran *et al.* 1996a). When exposed to visual items, however, learners are less adept at identifying sequential regularities. Instead, learners seem best able to detect relations among items that co-occur simultaneously (Conway & Christiansen 2005, Saffran 2002). Structurally, the relations can be identical across modalities – A can predict B in both vision and audition – but perceptual modality affects how well learners identify them. Perception has other, more subtle effects on statistical learning. One of the earliest examinations of statistical learning (Hayes & Clark 1970) noted that some elements in an auditory stream are more salient than others, and this may influence grouping. Subsequent research has supported this notion. For example, identifying non-adjacent statistical relations is facilitated if there is a perceptual similarity between the non-adjacent elements (Creel *et al.* 2004).

The relation between perception and statistical learning is bidirectional. Just as perception affects statistical learning, statistical learning has an effect on perception (e.g. Maye *et al.* 2002, Werker & Tees 1984). Indeed, statistical learning has been argued to play an important role, not only in the development of speech perception, but also in the development of visual perception (e.g. Fiser & Aslin 2005). It is worth noting, though, that infants are typically much more flexible in allowing input to shape their subsequent perception. Adults, likely due to their greater previous experience, are much more entrenched in their representations than infants (e.g. Iverson *et al.* 2003b).

As the prior discussion indicates, another characteristic of the organism that affects statistical learning is prior experience. What a learner knows affects what they are subsequently able to learn. Consider word learning as an example. Any novel label could, in principle, refer to any item in the current visual scene, or even to absent items (Quine 1964). One way to alleviate this problem is through repeated references to words. The first time an infant hears a word, it may be in the presence of four items, A, B, C and D – and, as such, it may be ambiguous which item the word labels. But if the infant hears the word a second time, in the presence of items B, E, F and G, the likelihood that the word refers to item B is greatly increased. Infants are sensitive to this kind of cumulative statistical information in making word–object pairings (Yu & Smith 2007).

In addition to using statistical information to identify word–object relations, children simplify the word-learning problem because they have several biases or adaptive assumptions (Markman 1991). At least some of these biases may develop as a result of children's sensitivity to statistical information in their environment. One of these assumptions is the shape bias: the assumption that words refer to categories of objects with the same shape. The shape bias appears to develop as a function of children's experience (Landau *et al.* 1988). Consistent with this hypothesis, young children can be trained to show the shape bias by exposure to new labels that refer to objects with similar shape (Smith *et al.* 2002). Samuelson (2002) argues that children develop the shape bias in response to their experience with words in their language – essentially, they detect that the words that they learn refer to objects with similar shapes. Learning regularities like the shape bias, which constrain future hypotheses, occurs across several different domains as a function of the statistical regularities in the input (Kemp *et al.* 2007).

While previous experience constrains subsequent statistical learning (e.g. Curtin *et al.* 2005), these constraints are often adaptive, in that they are shaped by, and well suited to, the characteristics of the input. Indeed, statistical learning, if it were not shaped by previous experience, would be insufficient for many of the learning challenges a child faces. For example, even though transitional probabilities have been widely investigated as cues to word boundaries, transitional probabilities alone are not sufficient to identify word boundaries in fluent, natural speech. Word segmentation is much more successful when learners also incorporate phonotactic, rhythmic and other acoustic cues (e.g. Christiansen *et al.* 1998, Thiessen & Saffran 2003, Yang 2004). Statistical learning can help learners identify the function of these acoustic cues – for example, whether stress signifies the beginning or the end of a word in fluent speech (Thiessen & Saffran 2007) – which then constrain subsequent learning. While this is a highly adaptive strategy, it does come at a cost. Better adaptation to one environment often means being poorly adapted to a different environment (e.g. Best & McRoberts 2003). This idea of adaptation to an environment has important implications for discussing change in learning outcomes as a function of age.

3.4.2 The effect of age-related changes in constraints on language learning

Each of these organism-level constraints on statistical learning – information processing abilities, perception and prior experience – changes as a function of age. This may help to explain one of the great puzzles of language acquisition: why it is that young infants are more successful in acquiring language than adults (Johnson & Newport 1989). This has been referred to as a critical, or sensitive, period, to emphasize the idea that if a learner does not master language before puberty, they are unlikely to ever achieve full linguistic competence. While at least some adult language learners achieve native-like levels of fluency (Birdsong & Molis 2001), a clear consensus in the literature is that adults find it more difficult to acquire language than do infants and young children (e.g. Bialystok & Hakuta 1999).

This presents an apparent paradox for theories of language acquisition that emphasize learning. Adults, like infants, are quite capable of statistical learning – indeed, adults are often tested using stimuli that are more complex than what is typically presented to infants (Fiser & Aslin 2005, Saffran et al. 1997). If statistical learning is critical to language acquisition, and adults can learn from the statistical structure of linguistic input just as well as infants, why do adults have difficulty learning language? One answer to this paradox is to assert that statistical learning plays, at most, a peripheral role in language acquisition. Language acquisition, from this point of view, is accomplished largely by mechanisms that are specific to language, and available only to infants. Adults are unable to learn language as well as infants because they lack access to these language-specific learning mechanisms (e.g. Chomsky 1965).

An alternative approach to resolving this paradox is to argue that the constraints on statistical learning change with development, as a function of the age and prior experience of the learner. One example of this approach is the entrenchment hypothesis: that what adults have learned about their first language conflicts with their second language, and makes language learning as an adult more difficult (e.g. Theakston 2004). Clearly, experience with the first language can interfere with second language processing. However, the entrenchment hypothesis has some difficulty explaining why adults with little to no prior experience with language – such as deaf adults exposed to sign language for the first time – show impaired language development (e.g. Senghas et al. 2004).

A second example of the approach focusing on developmental changes in constraints on learning is Newport's (1990) 'Less is More' hypothesis. According to this hypothesis, infants are better suited to learning language because of their information processing limitations, especially limitations on attention and memory. Adult language learners' errors frequently consist of what Newport (1988) has termed 'frozen forms': utterances in which whole words or phrases are produced, without appropriate awareness of their constituent words or morphemes. This may indicate that adults' ability to perceive and remember complex stimuli is actually too good. Adults' superior information processing abilities (Pelphrey & Reznick 2003) may allow them to store and process entire complex chunks of language, such as phrases. Young children, by contrast, may be able to process and store only component parts of linguistic stimuli. This may be advantageous, if it forces children to analyse language in appropriate components, such as words rather than phrases, or morphemes (like plural -*s* or past tense -*ed*) rather than whole words.

Evidence consistent with Newport's (1988, 1990) Less is More hypothesis includes research suggesting that adults actually acquire some aspects of language more successfully when they are distracted (Cochran *et al.* 1999). Additionally, children are more likely to regularize irregular linguistic productions, whereas adults are more likely to reproduce them faithfully (Hudson Kam & Newport 2005). Some computational modelling suggests that learning language is facilitated when early exposure to the linguistic system is limited to simpler input, which children's processing limitations might accomplish (Elman 1993, but see Rohde & Plaut 1999). Indeed, a variety of experimental data suggests that some of the most substantial changes in linguistic behaviour can occur when learners are unaware of what they are learning (e.g. Kaschak *et al.* 2006, Reber & Lewis 1977). This is often the case with children, but less clearly true of adults. Though much research remains to be done to understand age-related changes in language learning outcomes, the Less is More hypothesis illustrates an important point. Infants and adults exposed to the same input may internalize very different representations over which to perform statistical computations, as a function of their prior experience, information-processing skills and perceptual abilities.

3.5   Conclusion

Statistical learning appears complex – it requires a sophisticated memory system that tracks, at least approximately, frequency, distribution and co-occurrence. With a plethora of statistics available in the environment, one might expect learners to be overwhelmed by the wealth of information, especially infant learners. Fortunately, infants are able to integrate these different statistics as they learn about their native language, rather than being overwhelmed. Consider stress as an example. Stressed syllables are louder, longer and higher pitched than their unstressed counterparts. Older infants and adults exposed to English use stress as a cue to word boundaries (e.g. Jusczyk *et al.* 1999a). This is an adaptive strategy, as most content words in English begin with a stressed syllable (Cutler & Carter 1987). But how do infants discover that stress is a useful cue to word boundaries from their exposure to English?

Thiessen and Saffran (2003) proposed that statistical learning plays an important role in this process, in a variety of different ways. When transitional probabilities and stress cues to word boundaries are placed in conflict, 6-month-old infants follow transitional probabilities, rather than stress cues (Thiessen & Saffran 2003). It may be the case that transitional probabilities are one of the earliest cues that infants use to segment words from fluent speech (cf. Kirkham *et al.* 2002). If so, then the words infants segment from fluent speech via transitional probabilities could provide them with experience with lexical forms, from which they could identify the relation between stress and word position. Learning the association between stress and word position is, in turn, a statistical learning problem – although it entails different statistics than transitional probabilities. From lexical forms, infants can detect a correlation between lexical stress and word onsets. This is a co-occurrence statistic, rather than a transitional probability. Experimental results indicate that infants can indeed learn correlations between stress and word position from exposure to words in which there is a regular correlation between stress and word position (Thiessen & Saffran 2007).

As learning to use lexical stress as a cue to word boundaries indicates, learning can require infants to detect different kinds of statistics. In the case of lexical stress, transitional probabilities help infants identify word boundaries, and co-occurrence statistics highlight where, in the newly discovered words, stress is occurring (Thiessen & Saffran 2007). Learners – whether they are infants, adults, or animals – must flexibly integrate varying kinds of statistical information, both in brief learning episodes and over a lifetime of experience. No single statistic will provide enough information to identify the structure of input as complex as language. The fact that statistical learning has been implicated in infants' learning about many different aspects of language, including phonotactic structure (Chambers *et al.* 2003), prosodic structure (Thiessen & Saffran), word meaning (Yu & Smith 2007), phrase structure (Morgan *et al.* 1989), and the grammatical class of words (Mintz 2002), indicates that there is much more to statistical learning than transitional probabilities.

Suggestions for further reading

Bialystok, E., & Hakuta, K. (1999). Confounded age: Linguistic and cognitive factors in age differences for second language acquisition. In D. Birdsong (Ed.), *Second Language Acquisition and the Critical Period Hypothesis* (pp. 161–181). Mahwah, NJ: Lawrence Erlbaum Associates.

Elman, J. L., Bates, E. A., Johnson, M. H., Karmiloff-Smith, A., Parisi, D., & Plunkett, K. (1996). *Rethinking Innateness*. Boston: MIT Press.

Pinker, S. (1994). *The Language Instinct*. New York: HarperCollins.

Saffran, J. R., Aslin, R. N., & Newport, E. L. (1996a). Statistical learning by 8-month-old infants. *Science*, 274, 1926–1928.

4

Neurocognition of language development

Angela D. Friederici

4.1   Introduction

Children's entrance into language has been described at different levels,
either primarily considering the acoustic–phonological input and the regularities therein (see Thiessen Ch. 3) or stressing the importance of social
aspects (see Tomasello Ch. 5). The empirical evidence upon which these
approaches are based is mostly behavioural in nature. The neurocognitive
approach outlined in the present chapter goes beyond behavioural data
and covers two developmental aspects: first, it contributes to the description of the developing language system based on language-related neural
markers, and second, it adds to the description of the maturation of those
brain systems that support language functions. Both aspects may not be
independent from each other, and thus, information about the maturation
of brain systems may be of value for investigating an adequate description
of language acquisition.

4.1.1   Neurophysiological methods

Multiple brain imaging methods are available, but up to now no single
method provides the full range of information necessary to describe the
function–brain relationships with a fine-grained spatial and temporal
resolution. Functional magnetic resonance imaging (fMRI) and positron
emission tomography (PET) provide good spatial resolution, allowing
conclusions to be drawn about which brain areas are involved in a particular process, but their temporal resolution is limited to about one second.
Moreover, PET is an invasive technique and thus not applicable in non-
clinical studies. The fact that both techniques do not tolerate movement
makes them difficult to use in children. Near infrared spectroscopy
(NIRS, also called optical imaging) is another method that, like fMRI,
registers the hemodynamic response of the brain. Its spatial resolution is

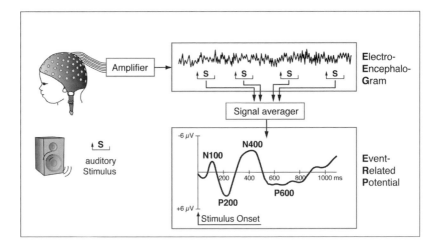

Figure 4.1 The electroencephalogram (EEG) is recorded from scalp electrodes implemented in a cap. The online EEG is averaged over several stimuli (S) of the same type and time locked to the onset of S. The result of this average procedure is the event-related brain potential (ERP). Different ERP components can be identified which are labelled according to the polarity (negativity: N, positivity: P) and their latency (200 for 200 ms). Note that negativity is plotted up.

low, but it is much easier to use in infants and children as the registration system is mounted directly on the child's head.

The methods of electroencephalography (EEG) and magnetencephalography (MEG) both have high temporal resolution of the order of milliseconds, but their spatial resolution is somewhat limited. As EEG registration is the method used most extensively in developmental studies, we will describe this method in more detail.

Neurophysiological measures register the brain's response to inputs directly, not necessarily requiring the infant's attention. Thus, these measures can easily be applied to newborns and very young infants. The most frequently used neurophysiological measure in infants and young children is the measurement of event-related brain potentials (ERPs) as registered with EEG (Fig. 4.1). ERPs reflect the brain's activity in response to a particular stimulus event with high temporal resolution.

Brain responses are averaged and time-locked to the onset of the stimulus. Each time-locked, averaged waveform typically shows several positive or negative peaks at particular latencies after stimulus onset. Each peak, or component, has a characteristic pattern. Each different component's polarity (negative/positive inflection of the waveform relative to baseline) together with latency (in milliseconds) and scalp distribution (e.g. over frontal or other brain regions) allow us to determine the cognitive processes associated with each of them. Changes in the dimensions of ERPs can indicate changes in the cognitive mechanisms they reflect. For example, a longer latency can be interpreted to reflect a slowing down of a particular cognitive process, while a smaller amplitude could indicate a reduction in processing demands or efficiency. A change in the cortical region supporting a particular process, on the other hand, may be reflected in the topography of the ERP.

4.1.2   Neurocognition of language in the adult brain

An adequate description of the developing language system and its neural basis requires respective knowledge about the mature system in the adult. Against the background of an adult model, we will be able to identify the course of development.

In the following paragraphs, therefore, we will briefly sketch the neural basis of language processing in the adult and then review the relevant studies on the neurocognition of language development.

Our knowledge about the neural basis of language processing in the adult has increased considerably over the past two decades due to the advent and systematic use of neuro-imaging techniques. Before that time, our knowledge about the relationship between particular language functions and brain regions was based on studies with brain-damaged patients. The resulting classical neuroanatomical model of language functions localized language to the left hemisphere within two regions: Broca's area, located in the inferior frontal cortex, and Wernicke's area in the superior temporal cortex (see Fig. 4.2). Until the 1970s, Broca's area was thought to be responsible for language production, while Wernicke's area was thought to support speech perception and language comprehension. Systematic studies triggered by developing psycholinguistic theories led to a revised neuroanatomical

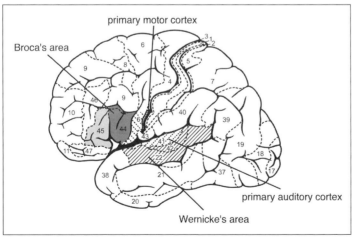

Source: adapted from Brodmann, 1909

Figure 4.2 Schematic view of the left hemisphere. Brain areas are differentiated according to their cytoarchitectonic characteristics and numbered by Brodmann (1909). Broca's area comprises Brodmann Areas (BA) 44 and 45 and Wernicke's area comprises BA 22 and 42.

model of language processing. This model, which deemed Broca's area responsible for syntactic processes and Wernicke's area responsible for semantic processes, has again been revised on the basis of the neurophysiological studies of the last two decades.

The present view identifies different networks consisting of specific brain areas and the connections between them, which support different aspects of language processing such as phonology, syntax and semantics. The analysis of acoustic speech input is performed by primary and secondary auditory cortices in the left and right hemispheres. Phonetic processing involves the left superior temporal sulcus and the dorsal (superior) portion of Brodmann Area (BA 44). The ventral (inferior) portion of BA 44 together with the anterior portion of the superior temporal gyrus (STG) supports initial, local syntactic phrase structure building, whereas the more anterior portion of BA 44, at the transition to BA 45, together with the posterior STG, supports the processing of structural and thematic assignments across phrases. Semantic processes are based in a temporo-frontal network consisting of the left STG and BA 45/47. Prosodic processes are mainly located in the right hemisphere (STG and BA 44) as are discourse processes (STG and BA 45/47) (for a review see Bookheimer 2002, Friederici 2002, Hickok & Poeppel 2007).

With respect to the time course of language processing, a number of specific ERP components have been found to correlate with particular aspects of language processing in adults, namely phonological (prosodic), semantic, thematic and syntactic processes (for review see Friederici 2002, Bornkessel & Schlesewsky 2006). The ERP components generated by the mature brain in response to different aspects of processing can be used as an adult neurocognitive model against which the developmental changes in the ERP pattern are interpretable. We will discuss different adult ERP components in the context of the relevant developmental data.

4.2 Neurocognition of language development

In the following section, we will review those ERP studies that contribute to the question of how the language processing system develops over the first years of life, starting from phonological discrimination and continuing with the build up of lexical and syntactic knowledge.

4.2.1 Discriminating phonological information

The information upon which infants can rely at the very beginning of language learning are the phonological cues in the speech input. In order to extract these cues and regularities from the auditory input, the infant first must be able to discriminate between different phonological parameters at the segmental and suprasegmental levels.

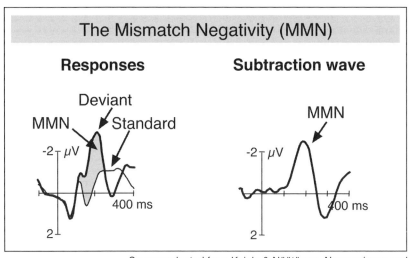

The Mismatch Negativity (MMN)

Responses   Subtraction wave

Source: adapted from Kujala & Näätänen, *Neuroscience and Biobehavioural Reviews*, 2001

Figure 4.3 The mismatch negativity (MMN). Left panel: in a passive auditory oddball paradigm, rarely occurring stimuli (deviant or oddball) are presented among frequently occurring stimuli (standards). Grey shading indicates the difference between the two stimulus conditions. Right panel: the subtraction wave depicts the brain response to deviant stimuli minus the brain response to standard stimuli.

At the segmental level, behavioural studies have shown that infants as young as 1–4 months of age discriminate consonants and vowels (Eimas *et al.* 1971, for a review see Jusczyk 1997). Neurophysiological studies have added to this considerably. One ERP paradigm that has proved to be particularly useful in investigating young infants' abilities to discriminate between phonetic features is the so-called Mismatch Negativity paradigm. In this paradigm a rarely occurring (deviant) stimulus is presented within a sequence of standard stimuli. Deviant and standard stimuli usually differ in one crucial feature. In adults, the discrimination of these two stimulus types is seen as a negative deflection with a peak latency of 100 to 200 ms following change onset (see Fig. 4.3). This negative deflection is labelled Mismatch Negativity (MMN) (for a review see Näätänen *et al.* 2001). Whereas the amplitude of the MMN is mainly modulated by the discrimination abilities of the subjects being investigated and the magnitude of the physical difference between deviant and standard stimuli, MMN latency primarily depends on the deviance onset and is related to the demands of sensory discrimination (for recent reviews, see Näätänen *et al.* 2001, Picton *et al.* 2000).

Negative mismatch responses have already been reported in infants, and even in preterm newborns (e.g. Cheour *et al.* 1997, 2002, Cheour-Luhtanen *et al.* 1995, 1996, Kushnerenko *et al.* 2002, Martynova *et al.* 2003, Morr *et al.* 2002, Weber *et al.* 2004). The negative response in newborns, however, typically does not reveal the sharp negative deflection of the adult MMN.

Instead, a long-lasting negative wave or a rather late negative response occurs (Cheour *et al.* 2002, Cheour-Luhtanen *et al.* 1995, 1996, Martynova *et al.* 2003). In 3-month-old infants, a sharp negative deflection can be observed (Cheour *et al.* 1997, Kushnerenko *et al.* 2002, Morr *et al.* 2002). Several other studies, however, reported a broad positive response in the infants' ERPs that was more prominent for the deviant stimulus (Dehaene-Lambertz 2000, Dehaene-Lambertz & Baillet 1998, Dehaene-Lambertz & Dehaene 1994, Dehaene-Lambertz & Peña 2001, Friederici *et al.* 2002, Leppänen *et al.* 1997). There are several reasons that may contribute to whether we observe a negative or a positive deflection as a mismatch response, including differences in the infants' state of alertness (Friederici *et al.* 2002), methodological differences such as filtering the data (Trainor *et al.* 2003, Weber *et al.* 2004), and the coexistence or overlap of two types of mismatch responses (He *et al.* 2007). In general, the available studies suggest a developmental transition from mismatch triggered positive deflections during early developmental stages towards negative deflections and MMN in later developmental stages. Given the differences in ERP patterns of the MMN response in young infants and adults, the discrimination process could be viewed as being qualitatively different, possibly more acoustically based early in development and phonemically based later on.

Independent of these considerations, the MMN response can be taken to functionally indicate discrimination in the auditory domain. Mismatch negativity responses have been observed for phonetic features in different languages such as Finnish, German and English, for vowel contrasts (Cheour *et al.* 1997, Friederici *et al.* 2002, 2004, Leppänen *et al.* 1999, Pihko *et al.* 1999) and for consonant contrasts (Dehaene-Lambertz & Baillet 1998, Rivera-Gaxiola *et al.* 2005) indicating that infants are able to discriminate different phonemes independent of their target language between 1 and 4 months.

Evidence for language-specific phonemic discrimination, however, only seems to be established between the ages of 6 and 12 months (Cheour *et al.* 1998a, Rivera-Gaxiola *et al.* 2005). These ERP studies indicated that younger infants, aged 6 and 7 months, show discrimination for phonemic contrasts that are both relevant and not-relevant to their target language, whereas older infants, aged 11 and 12 months, only display a discrimination response for phonemic contrasts that are relevant to their target language. These results are in agreement with behavioural data reporting language-specific reactions during the second half of the first year of life (Aslin *et al.* 1981, Werker & Tees 1984).

More recently, language-specific brain responses in an ERP study were shown in infants as young as 4 months old for a phonological contrast marking stress (Friederici *et al.* 2007). In this study, they used bisyllabic items whose first syllable was short and the second long or vice versa. German infants reacted more strongly to items with stress on the second syllable, a stress pattern which is infrequent in their target language, while French

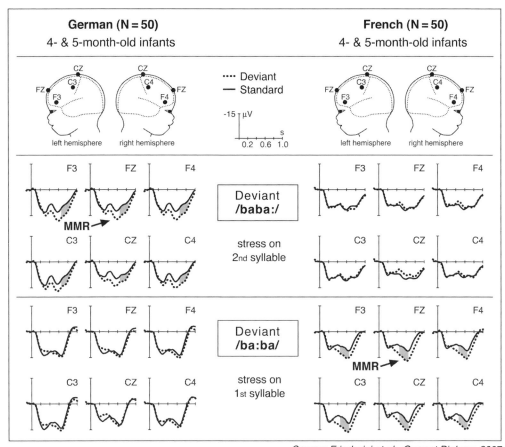

Source: Friederici et al., Current Biology, 2007

Figure 4.4 Averaged ERPs per condition (standard: solid line; deviant: dotted line) for each language group (German: left panel / French: right panel) and item type: for items with stress on the second syllable (top panel) and items with stress on the first syllable (bottom panel). The shaded area indicates the time window chosen for statistic analysis in which the effect was statistically significant. MMR = mismatch response.

infants reacted more strongly to items with stress on the first syllable, a stress pattern infrequent in their target language (see Fig. 4.4). These data thus provide evidence for language-specific brain reactions at the age of 4 months.

In these Mismatch Negativity studies, stimuli usually consist of single syllables or bisyllabic pseudowords. Although they clearly indicate the infants' sensibility to phonetic features early during development, they cannot speak to the issue of how infants are able to segment the incoming speech stream into lexically or syntactically relevant units.

4.2.2 From auditory input to lexical form

To acquire lexical knowledge, infants have to segment words from the auditory stream. Before lexical knowledge is established, segmentation might be aided by knowledge of a given language's potential word forms, such as dominant stress patterns or possible phonotactic structures (e.g. possible beginnings and endings) of words.

4.2.2.1 Stress information

Behavioural studies suggest that stress information is used at around 7.5 (Jusczyk *et al.* 1999a) to 9 months (Houston *et al.* 2000) of age. The ability to segment bisyllabic words with stress on the first syllable from speech input was found at the age of 7.5 months, but word segmentation effects for bisyllabic words with stress on the second syllable are only reported at 10.5 months of age (Jusczyk *et al.* 1999a). Neurophysiological studies, however, suggest that infants are sensitive to stress information as early as 4 months of age and, moreover, that they react specifically to the preferred stress patterns of their target language (Friederici *et al.* 2007). The main effect of conditioning was lateralized to the left hemisphere, suggesting that language dominance may be established early. Functionally, this finding indicates that infants have already established knowledge about the dominant stress patterns of their target language by the age of 4 months.

The ability to use word stress for word recognition during speech perception was shown in a recent ERP study of infants learning Dutch (Kooijman *et al.* 2005). In that study, 10-month-old infants recognized two-syllable words with stress on the first syllable in continuous speech after they had heard the words in isolation. Recognition was reflected in a greater negativity between 350 and 500 ms over the left hemisphere for familiar words compared to unfamiliar words.

4.2.2.2 Phonotactic information

Besides information about syllable stress, phonotactic cues signalling word onset or offset could also be used to segment words from an auditory sequence. Behaviourally, it was shown that 9-month-old infants are able to use this information for word segmentation in minimal contexts, but only when cues were spoken in an infant-directed manner (Friederici & Wessels 1993, Jusczyk & Luce 1994). These behavioural studies are interesting, but they cannot resolve whether this phonotactic knowledge is lexically relevant at that age. Neurophysiological studies, however, can determine lexical relevance. The applicable correlate in the ERP is the so-called N400 component, a negative waveform peaking at around 400 ms. In adults the N400 effect is observed not only for aspects of lexical meaning, but also for aspects of lexical form. The amplitude of the N400 is larger for semantically incongruous words than for congruous words, and also larger for pseudowords than for words (for reviews see Kutas & Van Petten 1994). The N400 can thus be used to investigate lexically relevant knowledge both at phonotactic and semantic levels.

To investigate this issue, a paradigm appropriate for both adults and young children is used in which the participant is shown a picture of an object and at the same time is presented with an auditory stimulus. This stimulus may be a word matching or not matching the object's name, or it may be a pseudoword that is phonotactically legal or illegal. Using this paradigm, developmental changes were observed between the ages of 12 and 19 months (Friedrich & Friederici 2005a, 2005b). At 19 months the ERP effects are similar to those of adults, i.e. an N400 effect was found for incongruous (non-matching) words and phonotactically legal pseudowords, but not for phonotactically illegal pseudowords. At 12 months, however, no N400 effects were observed. These data indicate that at the age of 14 months, but not at 12 months, both real words and phonotactically legal pseudowords are considered as possible word candidates, but phonotactically illegal pseudowords have already been excluded from the native language lexicon (Friedrich & Friederici 2005a).

There appears to be a developmental transition between the age of 9 months, when phonotactic knowledge about word onsets and word offsets is used for word segmentation (Friederici & Wessels 1993), and the age of 19 months, when phonotactic knowledge about phonotactically legal and illegal lexical forms is established (Friedrich & Friederici 2005a, 2005b).

4.2.2.3 Familiarity and recognition of word form

What happens between 9 and 19 months of age? How can we describe the build up of lexical knowledge, which is the mapping between semantic meaning and phonological word form? Given the available data one might assume two stages in the development of lexical knowledge: a familiarity stage and a recognition stage. That is, before the child is able to recognize the phonological word form as referring to a specific meaning, there may be a stage which can be described as 'familiarity' with a phonological form.

There are ERP studies suggesting that children are trying to map sounds onto meaning at about 11 months of age. Such a mapping has been proposed based on a negative deflection observed around 200 ms post stimulus onset at 11 months of age in response to listening to familiar versus unfamiliar words (Thierry *et al.* 2003). There are, however, some concerns about the statistical techniques used in this study, as the analysis was performed to cover every millisecond of recording without applying a correction for multiple comparisons, thus challenging the authors' interpretation.

Using a picture–word priming paradigm, an early fronto-central negativity between 100–400 ms in 12, 14, and 19 month olds was also found for auditory target words that were congruous with a picture compared to incongruous words (Friedrich & Friederici 2005a; Fig. 4.5 displays the ERPs at frontal electrode F7). This early effect was taken to be too early for a semantic N400 effect and was, therefore, interpreted as a phonological–lexical priming effect reflecting the fulfilment of a phonological (word) expectation built up after seeing the picture of an object. At this age, infants seem to have some lexical knowledge, but the word form referring to a given object (meaning) might not yet be sharply defined, allowing

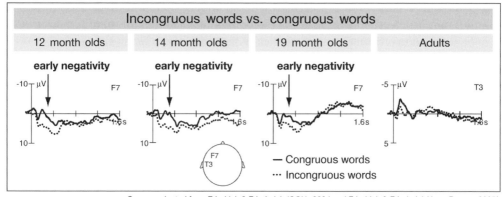

Source: adapted from Friedrich & Friederici, JOCN, 2004 and Friedrich & Friederici, NeuroReport, 2005b

Figure 4.5 The phonological–lexical priming effect, i.e. early negativity, for the comparison of congruous and incongruous words in different age groups. Note the different microvolt scales for the different age groups.

phonetically similar words still to be considered as possible word candidates. This interpretation is supported by the finding that 12 and 14 month olds showed an ERP difference between known words and phonetically illegal words, but not between known words and phonetically legal words (Friedrich & Friederici 2005a). These data support the idea of a transition from a familiarity stage to a recognition stage during the development and build up of lexical knowledge.

4.2.3   From lexical form to word meaning

The studies discussed so far suggest a gradual development and establishment of the lexicon, i.e. the mapping from word form to meaning and its internal organization. For a review of the behavioural evidence concerning word learning, see Werker and Yeung (2005).

In ERP research, the N400 effect has not only been used to investigate phonotactically relevant aspects of the lexicon, but first and foremost, it has been used to evaluate semantic knowledge. It has been interpreted to reflect the process of semantic integration. It is assumed that a perceived word has to be integrated into the semantic memory of the perceiver in order to be 'understood' (Kutas & Federmeier 2000). In the study of semantic processes in infants and young children, the adult N400 has been used as an ERP template against which the ERPs for semantic knowledge and processes during early development are compared.

In an ERP study on the processing of words whose meanings infants either did or did not know, infants between 13 and 17 months old showed a bilateral negativity for unknown words, but 20 month olds showed a negativity only in the left hemisphere (Mills *et al.* 1997). This result was interpreted as a developmental change towards a hemispheric specialization for word processing. In a more recent study, the effects of word

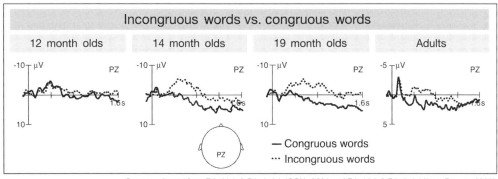

Source: adapted from Friedrich & Friederici, JOCN, *2004* and Friedrich & Friederici, NeuroReport, *2005* b

Figure 4.6 The N400 as an index of lexical–semantic processes, here showing a picture–word incongruity effect. Grand-average ERP at electrode PZ for the different age groups. Note the different microvolt scales for the different age groups.

experience (training) and vocabulary size (word production) were tested (Mills *et al.* 1997). In this word-learning paradigm, 20 month olds acquired novel words either paired with a novel object or alone. After training, the infants' ERPs showed a repetition effect, indicated by a reduced N200–500 amplitude, in response to familiar and novel unpaired words, whereas an increased, bilaterally distributed N200–500 was found for novel paired words. This finding was taken to indicate that the N200–500 is linked to word meaning. However, it is not entirely clear whether the N200–500 reflects semantic processes only or if phonological familiarity also plays a role. The interpretation of this early effect as semantic is challenged by data showing that semantic effects in adults are observed later in reference to the N400 and by the phonological–lexical priming effect reported by Friedrich and Friederici (2005b). It is possible that the early onset of this effect in infants as compared to adults reported by Mills *et al.* (1997) is due to infants' relatively small vocabularies. A small vocabulary results in a low number of phonologically possible alternative word forms, allowing the brain to react early, i.e. after hearing a word's first phonemes.

A clear semantic context N400 effect at the word level has been demonstrated for 14 and 19 month olds (Friedrich & Friederici 2005a, 2005b) (see Fig. 4.6), but not for 12 month olds. The ERP to words in picture context showed a centro-parietal, bilaterally distributed negatively deflected wave between 400–1400 ms, which was more negative for words that did not match the picture context than for those that did (Fig. 4.6 displays the parietal electrode PZ). Compared to adults, this N400-like effect reached significance later and lasted longer. There were also topographic differences of the effect as children showed stronger involvement of frontal electrode sites than adults. The latency differences suggest slower lexical–semantic processing in children than in adults. The more frontal distribution seen in children could either mean that their semantic processing is still more image-based (adults show a frontal distribution when pictures instead of words are processed; West & Holcomb 2002) or that they may have to activate more attentional resources during semantic processing (in adults frontal activation is correlated with increased attention; Courchesne 1990).

The first appearance of the semantic N400 effect in neurophysiological measures at the word level is closely related to the time point at which fast mapping abilities are observed. The ability to learn new words after only a few representations has been demonstrated behaviourally in 13, 14, and 15 month olds, but not in 12 month olds (Schafer & Punkett 1998, Werker *et al.* 1998, Woodward *et al.* 1994). This might suggest a causal relationship between the N400 neural mechanism and word-learning capacity. It has been proposed that the observed transition in word learning may reflect a developmental change from slow associative learning towards fast mapping (Friedrich in press). A possible underlying mechanism might be that slow associative learning is based on a one-to-one mapping from entire word forms to semantic concepts. Fast learning, on the other hand, may be possible once words and semantic concepts are broken into semantic features allowing a novel (feature-based) organization of lexicon and semantic memory, thereby enabling an easy integration of new words into memory. The underlying assumption here is that mapping is achieved at the featural level.

4.2.4   From auditory input to sentential structure

In addition to word knowledge, the child must acquire the syntactic rules according to which words are combined in a sentence. One possible way to extract structural information from auditory input lies in the fact that syntactic phrase boundaries and prosodic phrase boundaries largely overlap. Each prosodic phrase boundary is a syntactic boundary although not every syntactic boundary is marked phonologically. Acoustically prosodic phrase boundaries are marked by three parameters: preboundary length, pitch and pause. It has been argued that prosodic information might aid in the acquisition of syntactic units and the relationships between them (Gleitman & Wanner 1982).

4.2.4.1   Prosodic information

Behavioural studies have shown that 6-month-old infants use converging cues of either pitch and pause or pitch and preboundary length for clause segmentation (Seidl 2007). This indicates that infants at this age weigh different prosodic cues and that, similar to adults, pause is not the only relevant cue.

In adults a particular ERP component has been found to correlate with the processing of prosodic boundaries, i.e. intonational phrase boundaries (IPh). This ERP component is a positive shift occurring at the IPh called the closure positive shift (CPS) (Steinhauer *et al.* 1999). This ERP component was observed not only when the IPh was marked by preboundary length,

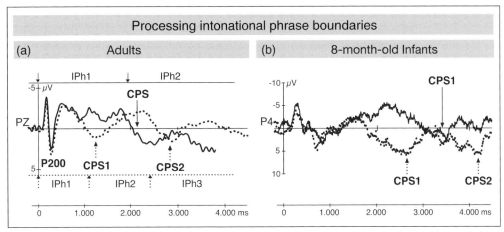

Source: adapted form Friederici, *TICS*, 2005 and Steinhauer *et al.*, *Nat. Neurosci.*, 1999

Figure 4.7 The CPS (closure positive shift) as an index of processing intonational phrase boundaries. (a) Grand-average ERP for adults at electrode PZ. Vertical line indicates sentence onset. IPh1, IPh2 and IPh3 bars indicate the length of the two intonational phrases in sentence type A ([Kevin verspricht Mama zu schlafen] IPh_1 [und ganz lange lieb zu sein] IPh_2 / [Kevin promises Mum to sleep] [and to be a good boy for a while]) represented as solid line, and the three intonational phrases in sentence type B ([Kevin verspricht] IPh_1 [Mama zu küssen] IPh_2 [und ganz lange lieb zu sein] IPh_3 / [Kevin promises] IPh_1 [to kiss Mum] IPh_2 [and to be a good boy for a while] IPh_3) represented as dotted lines. Arrows indicate the CPS. (b) Grand-average ERP for 8-month-old infants at electrode P4 for sentence type A (solid line) and sentence type B (dotted line).

pitch, and pause, but also when the pause cue was deleted (Steinhauer *et al.* 1999). The CPS component is distributed over left and right parietal recording sites for spoken sentences in which segmental and suprasegmental information are present. It is, instead, lateralized to the right hemisphere for hummed sentences in which only segmental information is present (Pannekamp *et al.* 2005). This suggests that suprasegmental information is primarily processed in the right hemisphere, which is supported by brain-imaging studies in adults (Meyer *et al.* 2002, 2004).

In infants, similar right hemispheric dominance in the processing of sentential prosody was found for 3 month olds in an imaging study using near-infrared optical spectroscopy (Homae *et al.* 2006). This finding suggests that the neural mechanism of processing prosodic information is in place quite early during development.

When investigating infants' brain responses specifically to the processing of IPh boundaries, we find that 8-month-old infants (Pannekamp *et al.* 2006, see Fig. 4.7) and even 5-month-old infants (Männel & Friederici submitted) demonstrate the ERP component known to correlate with the processing of IPh boundary information. These data indicate that the neural mechanisms known to support the processing of the acoustic cues of clause boundaries are established before the age of 6 months, allowing the infants to behave accordingly when they reach 6 months of age (Seidl 2007).

4.2.4.2   Structural regularities

To learn the structure of the language into which the infant is born, he or she cannot rely on phonological cues alone but must also consider positional regularities of elements in the speech input. Behavioural studies have shown that by the age of 8 months, infants calculate transitional probabilities within three-syllable strings in a miniature, artificial grammar (Saffran *et al.* 1996a). With a somewhat more complex artificial grammar, learning of transitional probabilities was demonstrated in 12 month olds (Gómez & Gerken 1999). A study with 7 month olds suggested that infants' learning at that age might go beyond statistical learning, possibly involving the extraction and representation of algebraic rules (Marcus *et al.* 1999).

In natural languages crucial grammatical information is not necessarily encoded in adjacent elements, e.g. for subject–verb agreement (he *looks* vs we *look_*). The learning system has to recognize the relationship between the pronoun (*he/we*) and the inflection (*-s/-Ø*) by abstracting from the intervening verb stem. For an artificial grammar, Gómez (2002) has shown that adults and 18-month-old children can learn non-adjacent dependencies in an AXB pattern for 3-syllable strings under some circumstances.

For a natural language, Santelmann and Jusczyk (1998) reported that 18-month-old children learning English can track the relationship between *is* and verb-*ing* (e.g. *is digging* vs. *can digging*). However, work by Tincoff *et al.* (2000) indicated that the relationship between the auxiliary and the progressive (*-ing*) is represented only between specific items (*is-ing*) and is not generalized to *are-ing* or *were-ing* combinations in 18 month olds. Moreover, it was demonstrated that the children's capacity to recognize non-adjacent dependencies relied on their ability to linguistically analyse the material between the two dependent elements. Recognition of dependency relationships was possible for 19-month-old German children only when the intervening material was clearly marked (e.g. as in English, where adverbs are marked by the inflection *-ly*, as in *is energetically digging*), but not in the absence of a clear morphological marker (Höhle *et al.* 2006). Thus, non-adjacent dependencies in natural languages can be acquired under particular circumstances around the age of 18–19 months as demonstrated by behavioural studies.

It would be of special interest to also have ERP data regarding this issue as these may be able to identify the type of processing mechanism underlying the children's behaviour given that specific ERP components related to particular syntactic processes have been reported.

4.2.5   Syntactic processes

In adults, two ERP components are identified to correlate with syntactic processes, each assumed to reflect specific subprocesses. For syntactic violations in a grammatical string, an early left anterior negativity (ELAN, 100–200 ms) has been observed for local phrase structure violations, and a somewhat later left anterior negativity (LAN, 300–400 ms) was found for the violation of non-adjacent elements (e.g. subject–verb agreement). Both of these negativities reflect the automatic detection of a structural violation usually followed by a late positivity (P600) reflecting processes of syntactic reanalysis and repair (for a review see Bornkessel & Schlesewsky 2006, Friederici 2002).

Unfortunately, up to now there are no published studies on the processing of syntactic structure in artificial grammars in very young infants. In an initial step, we conducted an ERP study with 6-month-old German infants coming from monolingual families. They had to learn the relation between an auxiliary and a verb inflection (Italian: *sta*-verb-*are* vs. *puo*-verb-*ando*). Preliminary results suggest that 6-month-old German infants are able to learn these dependencies as violations elicit a centro-parietal positivity resembling the P600. Further studies are certainly necessary in order to be able to describe the underlying mechanisms, but this type of ERP component (P600) suggests that these 6-month-old infants have processed the incorrect sequences as strings that violate a syntactic rule.

For natural languages, the available ERP studies suggest that a late positivity can be observed at the age of 2 years. For local phrase structure violations (e.g. *Der Löwe im brüllt* 'The lion in-the roars') a late positivity (P600) was reported in 24-month-old German children. At this stage, however, no early negativity was present (Oberecker & Friederici 2006. see Fig. 4.8a). An early anterior negativity (child-specific ELAN) in addition to the late positivity (P600) was found in children at the age of 32 months (Oberecker *et al.* 2005. see Fig. 4.8b).

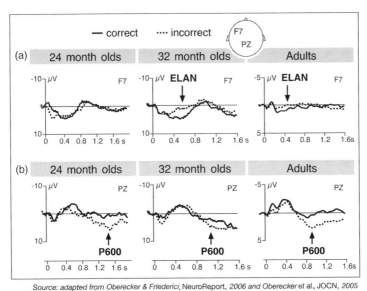

Source: adapted from Oberecker & Friederici, NeuroReport, 2006 and Oberecker et al., JOCN, 2005

Figure 4.8 The ELAN-P600 pattern as an index of syntactic processes. ELAN stands for early left anterior negativity and is displayed in the upper row (a). P600 stands for a late, centro-parietal positivity and is displayed in the lower row (b). Grand-average ERPs at selected electrodes (F7, PZ) across the different age groups. Note the different microvolt scales between children and adults.

Violations of non-adjacent dependencies in English (e.g. *will matching*) did not elicit a significant late positivity even in 30-month-old English children, but only in 36 month olds (Silva-Pereyra *et al.* 2005). This difference may be explained by the fact that the German study (Oberecker & Friederici 2006) tested local dependencies (word category violation), which may be easier to process than the non-local dependencies (modal verb-inflection agreement) tested in the English study. It is not surprising that the ELAN effect, which is taken to reflect highly automatic phrase structure building processes (Friederici 2002) is present only late during development as it may need time to be established. In contrast, the P600, which is taken to reflect processes of syntactic integration, is present at 24 months.

Given that the pattern of the syntactic ERP effects observed by Oberecker and Friederici (2006) is very similar to that of adults, we can conclude that the basic brain mechanisms supporting syntactic processes are similar to adults once the ERP components are present. However, all these ERP components still have a longer latency suggesting that the underlying processes are still not as fast as in adults.

4.3 Summary: Neurocognition of language development

The neurophysiological studies discussed in this review provide information on language development which is complementary and in addition to behavioural studies. They are schematically presented in Figure 4.9.

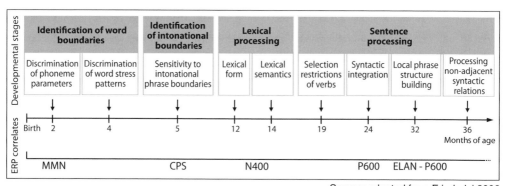

Source: adapted from Friederici 2006

Figure 4.9 A schematic overview of the developmental stages of auditory language perception and the ERP correlates that provide the possibility to investigate phonological, semantic and syntactic processes. The developmental stages can be viewed as interrelated steps during which novel information is extracted and processed on the basis of previously acquired knowledge. Once the basic phonological processes are established, phonemic knowledge is used to identify and represent the first lexical forms and create a larger lexical–semantic knowledge base, which is then used to process meaning in sentential context. The depicted time course of the different developmental stage is an approximation and is based on the ERP studies available in the literature. This also holds for the relation between the developmental age and the ERP components reported in the different studies discussed in the text.

For the phonological discrimination observed early during infancy, the differences in the polarity and scalp distribution of ERP effects suggest that infants rely on processes that are dissimilar from those in adults, possibly reflecting acoustically based rather than phonemically based processes. The similarity of the neurophysiological markers for prosodic processes and a similar right hemispheric basis may be taken to indicate similar brain mechanisms involved in the processing of intonational phrase boundaries in infants and in adults. The ERP studies on lexical learning nicely show the developmental trajectory from familiarity-based to recognition-based processes and suggest a gradual build up and stabilization of the mapping between phonological word form and meaning between the ages of 12 to 19 months. With respect to the build up of structural knowledge and the ability to process non-adjacent dependencies, both necessary for the acquisition of syntactic rules, we clearly need further studies. The data available so far indicate that local structure building processes are present at the age of 2 years and that non-adjacent syntactic relations are computed around the age of 3 years. However, from these data it is also clear that it takes some further development before the neural mechanisms supporting syntactic processes are adult-like.

Suggestions for further reading

Friederici, A. D. (2002). Towards a neural basis of auditory sentence processing. *Trends in Cognitive Sciences*, 6, 78–84.

   (2005). Neurophysiological markers of early language acquisition: From syllables to sentences. *Trends in Cognitive Sciences*, 9, 481–488.

   (2006). The neural basis of language development and its impairment. *Neuron*, 52, 941–952.

Friederici, A. D., & Thierry, G. (eds.). (2008). *Early Language Development: Bridging Brain and Behaviour: Vol. 5. Trends in Language Acquisition Research*. Amsterdam: John Benjamins.

5

The usage-based theory of language acquisition

Michael Tomasello

5.1   Introduction

The usage-based approach to linguistic communication may be summarized in the two aphorisms:

- meaning is use
- structure emerges from use

'Meaning is use' represents an approach to the functional or semantic dimension of linguistic communication. It originated with Wittgenstein (1953) and other pragmatically based philosophers of language, who wanted to combat the idea that meanings are things and instead focus on how people use linguistic conventions to achieve social ends. 'Structure emerges from use' represents an approach to the structural or grammatical dimension of linguistic communication. It is implicit in the work on grammaticalization and language change of many historical linguists, and has been made explicit by Langacker (1987, 2000) and other usage-based linguists, who want to combat the idea of a wholly formal grammar devoid of meaning and instead focus on how meaning-based grammatical constructions emerge from individual acts of language use.

Drawing on the work of many other researchers, Tomasello (2003) proposes a usage-based theory of language acquisition. Paralleling the two aphorisms above, the proposal is that children come to the process of language acquisition, at around one year of age, equipped with two sets of cognitive skills, both evolved for other, more general functions before linguistic communication emerged in the human species:

- intention-reading (functional dimension)
- pattern-finding (grammatical dimension)

'Intention-reading' is what children must do to discern the goals or intentions of mature speakers when they use linguistic conventions to achieve social ends, and thereby to learn these conventions from them culturally. Intention-reading – including skills of joint attention – is the central cognitive construct in the so-called social-pragmatic approach to language acquisition (which is most often used in the study of word learning; Bruner 1983, Nelson 1996, Tomasello 1992, 2000d, 2001). 'Pattern-finding' is what children must do to go productively beyond the individual utterances they hear people using around them to create abstract linguistic schemas or constructions. As a summary term for such things as categorization, analogy and distributional analysis, pattern-finding is the central cognitive construct in the so-called usage-based approach to the acquisition of grammar (Goldberg 1995, 2006, Tomasello 2000a, 2003).

These theoretical positions on the functional and grammatical dimensions of language use and acquisition are minority positions in the field. Essentially, they represent the view that the pragmatics of human communication is primary, both phylogenetically and ontogenetically, and that the nature of conventional languages – and how they are acquired – can only be understood by starting from processes of communication more broadly. In this chapter I provide a synoptic account of the usage-based approach to language acquisition, in both its functional and grammatical dimensions.

5.2   Prelinguistic communication

In the usage-based view one must always begin with communicative function, and it turns out that human infants communicate in some fairly sophisticated ways before they have acquired any linguistic conventions (see Goldin-Meadow Ch. 9). For example, almost all infants communicate by pointing before they have acquired any productive language, and many also use some kind of iconic or conventionalized gestures as well. Interestingly and importantly, other animal species, including our nearest primate relatives, do not communicate with conspecifics in these ways. This suggests that human pointing and other gestures may already embody forms of social cognition and communicative motivation that are unique to the species, and that are necessary as a first step on the way to linguistic conventions both phylogentically and ontogenetically (Tomasello 2008).

The interesting thing about pointing is that there is almost no information *in* the gesture itself; it basically says 'look in that direction and you'll know what I mean'. So where does the meaning come from? One can say it comes from context, but this has a very special significance with respect to human communication; specifically, it means mutually understood context. One person could point for another in exactly the same way to exactly the same clock on the wall, for example, and mean everything from 'what a beautiful clock' to 'our friend is late', depending only on their shared experience and attention prior to the pointing act. From their earliest communicative pointing, infants understand and produce pointing gestures in the context of some such joint attentional frames or common conceptual ground (Tomasello *et al.* 2007). For example, if an 18-month-old girl is engaged in cleaning up toys with an adult, and the adult points to a toy across the room, she will fetch it and clean it up also – assuming that the adult pointing gesture is relevant to their shared activity. But if another person enters the room and points to the exact same toy in the exact same way at a comparable moment, even though the infant herself has been engaged in cleaning up (with the first adult), she does not interpret this pointing gesture as relevant to her own activity egocentrically and so she does not clean up the toy but instead shares attention to it declaratively or gives it to the new adult (Liebel *et al.* in press).

Even young infants do not just communicate about what they understand of the world, but about the shared understandings they have with other potential communicative partners. Infants have the ability to construct such shared understandings – in the form of specific formats, scripts, routines or joint attentional frames in specific interactive contexts – from around the first birthday, and these structure their earliest intentional communication (Bruner 1983, Tomasello 1988). The cognitive aspect of these joint attentional frames comprises precisely those conceptualizations that will later structure young children's complex utterances: agents acting on patients, agents giving things to others, objects being in locations or moving to locations, objects changing states, people in various psychological states and so forth. Importantly, when children communicate in specific instances of such situations or events, they comprehend both their role and the role of the communicative partner. For example, in the diary observations of Carpenter *et al.* (unpublished data) a 14-month-old boy on two different occasions wants his chair pushed up to the dining room table in preparation for mealtime. On one occasion he and his mum are standing next to the table and so he points to the chair; on another occasion he and his mum are standing next to the chair and so he points to the table. This suggests that this child already has some understanding – which he knows he shares with his mum – about preparations for mealtime, where his chair goes at the table, and so forth, that serve as a kind of background topic for the communicative act. He then highlights for his mum, by pointing, the aspect of the situation he wants her to focus on – the one that is new for her – so that she can discern his communicative intention (that the chair be placed under the table in its usual place). On other occasions, with a different joint attentional frame as common ground, it is easy to imagine that this child might point to his chair wanting to be placed in it, or point to the empty space at the table simply to indicate dispassionately that the chair that is normally there is missing (and indeed the Carpenter *et al.* observations include several from prelinguistic children indicating absent referents; see also Lizskowski *et al.* 2007).

In terms of communicative motives, it is well established that infants point for both imperative and declarative motives before language (Bates *et al.* 1979, Carpenter *et al.* 1998). Recent research has even documented that 12-month-old infants point helpfully to inform others of things they are ignorant about. For example, if the mother is searching for something and the child knows where it is, even 12-month-old infants will inform her of this with no desire for the object themselves (Lizskowski *et al.* 2006). The imperative, declarative and informative motives underlying infants' prelinguistic communication are of course exactly the same motives that will structure their early language in the coming months.

Infants' prelinguistic gestural communication, therefore, already includes a species-unique ability to construct with others various kinds of joint attentional common ground to serve as background topic for the attention-directing act of pointing – comprising such things as agents, locations, objects, etc. – as well as species-unique motives for communicating (declarative and informative) that are the exact same motives with which they will use their earliest language. Indeed, many of young children's earliest uses of language are actually accompanied by pointing or other gestures, and these partition the communicative intention in ways that demonstrate the equivalence of gesture and language from a communicative point of view; for example, the child might point to the door while saying "Daddy" to indicate what he might later indicate with "Daddy leave" or some such (Iverson & Goldin-Meadow 2005). In general, prelinguistic communication paves the way for the acquisition of the 'arbitrary' linguistic conventions that infants use, initially, in exactly the same kinds of situations, for exactly the same kinds of communicative motives, as their early gestures.

5.3   Utterances and words

When we turn to children's early linguistic communication, the most basic unit of linguistic experience, and the one with which children begin, is not the word but the utterance. An utterance is the smallest unit in which a person expresses a complete communicative intention – that is, an intention that another person attend to something within the joint attentional frame and so do something as a result – and it thus corresponds to prelinguistic communicative acts such as pointing. Like an act of pointing, an utterance is used to both direct a recipient's attention to something referentially, and also to express a communicative motive (imperative, declarative, informative and others), typically through some form of emotional expression in the face and/or voice. When the child either comprehends or produces an utterance such as 'Birdie!' (to point it out) or 'Hold!' (to request), he or she understands a full communicative act, comprising both reference and motive – even though the form is simply a single adult word expressed with a certain emotion. These so-called holophrases are thus already, in a very simple way, composite structures.

When an adult speaks to him or her, then, what the child is attempting to do most urgently is to comprehend the overall communicative intention behind the utterance; what does the adult intend for me to attend to and to do in the joint attentional situation? At the same time, he or she is also attempting to determine the communicative function of particular constituents within the utterance. This is a kind of 'blame assignment' procedure in which the child attempts to determine the functional role of a constituent in the utterance as a whole. This requires that the child determine, to some degree of specificity, the communicative intention of the whole utterance; one cannot determine a novel sub-function without knowing something about the overall function. Presumably, particular utterance constituents such as words are most easily identified – and emerge as independent units – when the same phonological form appears in different utterances over time with some functional consistency. Thus, if the child hears 'There's the ball', 'Gimme my ball', 'The ball's rolling', 'The ball's bouncing', 'I want a ball', 'Throw the ball', 'That ball's Jeffery's', 'Where's your ball?', etc., the word *ball* comes to exist as a potential utterance constituent for future use when the child needs to indicate one of a certain class of objects as one sub-function of an utterance. One thing that facilitates this process is if the adult stresses the key word, as an indication of its referential newness, and its associated referent is indeed new to the situation (Grassman & Tomasello 2007).

As a non-linguistic example, a young girl may see her father use a stapler and understand that his goal is to staple together two pieces of paper. In some cases, the girl may understand also that the sub-goal/function of placing the papers inside the stapler's jaws is to align them with the stapling mechanism inside the stapler, and that the sub-function of pressing down on the stapler is to eject the staple through the two papers – with both of these sub-functions being in the service of the overall goal of attaching the two sheets of paper. The girl does not need to understand all of this to mimic an adult stapling papers with the same stapler over and over again (analogy: child can say "There-ya-go" over and over again without understanding its internal constituents). But to the extent that the girl does not understand these sub-functions, she will be lost when she encounters some new stapler in which the sub-functions are effected by a different means, for example, one whose stapling mechanism does not require pressing down but rather squeezing. Only to the extent that the girl understands the relevant sub-functions, will she be able to adapt to new situations creatively by, for example, adjusting her behaviour to effect the same outcome with the new stapling mechanism. In the same way, the child may hear an adult say "I stapled your papers" and comprehend not only the utterance and its overall communicative intention, but also, for example, the words *I* and *stapled* and their communicative sub-functions in the utterance (the contributions they are making to the utterance as a whole), along with the phrase *your papers* and its communicative sub-function in the utterance (and the sub-sub-functions of *your* and *papers*). As in the case of the stapler, it is only if the child performs some kind of blame assignment that she will be able to comprehend the constituent linguistic elements in a deep enough way to enable her in the future to use them creatively in novel utterances (Tomasello 2003).

This is the way children learn words. That is, children do not try to learn words directly; they try to comprehend utterances and in doing so they often must comprehend a word in the sense of determining the functional role it is playing in the utterance – and they see commonalities in this functional role across utterances. The lexicon, as it were, is thus only an emergent phenomenon in the sense of Bybee (1998). This is true despite the fact that the process is sometimes obscured in Western middle-class culture because parents and children often establish highly frequent utterance schemas for naming objects (e.g. 'That's a __'. 'It's a __', 'Here's the __', etc.). Children understand quite well the overall function of these utterances as well as the function of the open slot, with the new word in the slot always serving to name the new object in the situation. This gives the impression that what children are doing is mapping a single word onto a single object or action, or concept thereof, as in most theories of word learning (e.g. Bloom 2000, Markman 1989). But if 'mapping' means simply associative learning, this is clearly not how things work. Children are attempting to understand how the adult is using an utterance (and its constituents as sub-elements) to direct their attention. The process is not one of association or mapping but of intention-reading and blame assignment.

We may use children's learning of new words in an experiment as an example. Akhtar and Tomasello (1996) had an adult set up a joint atten-tional game with 24-month-old children in which a novel action was performed always and only with a particular toy character on a particular substrate (e.g. Big Bird on a swing, with other character–action pairings demonstrated as well). She then picked up Big Bird and announced "Let's meek Big Bird", but the swing was nowhere to be found – so the action was not performed. Children thus never saw the new word *meek* paired with the corresponding action. But later, when the adult handed them a new toy and told them to 'Meek it', they searched for (and found) the swing and used it to swing the new character, thus demonstrating their understand-ing of the action intended. The only way they could do this was to under-stand the adult's intentions with respect to the key objects and actions in this jointly understood situation when she originally said "Let's *meek* Big Bird." – and something of the particular intentions behind the use of *meek* – even though she never actually did it. That is to say, the child had to identify the aspect of the adult's overall communicative intention not covered by the known parts of the utterance *let's* and *Big Bird* and connect it to the unknown word *meek*. To learn a new word, children must extract it from a larger utterance and connect it with the relevant aspect of the joint attentional frame they share with the adult.

In many ways this process is even clearer for word types other than nouns and verbs for concrete objects and actions. Thus, many function words can **only** be learned through efforts to isolate their functional contribution in some larger and less predictable set of phrases. For example, Tomasello (1987) reports that his daughter learned the preposition *of* from such expressions as *piece of ice, piece of bread, scared of that*, and *scared of monsters*. It is hard to conceive of any method of acquisition here other than some process of extracting *of* from larger expressions and attempting to discern its function in the overall utterance. Levy and Nelson (1994) make a similar argument about children's earliest uses of causal and temporal terms as *because, so, since, and, but, before* and *if*. And, of course, there can be no question of mapping or association when what is involved is not learning a word per se, but rather learning which referential term of several to choose for a given referent – for example, *the chair* or *that chair in my room* or *it* – in different communicative situations. Learning to make these pragmatic choices in the conventional way – so-called referential choice – requires children to understand why a person chose one means of expression rather than another, that is, her intentions in making the choice (Matthews *et al.* 2006).

5.4   Schemas and constructions

This communication-based, usage-based way of looking at things means we cannot explain children's acquisition of grammatical competence by starting with individual words, learned in isolation, and then gluing them together with abstract meaningless rules, as in the very common 'words and rules' approach (Pinker 1999). Instead, we must begin with children's comprehension and production of whole, meaningful utterances. We then investigate how children *extract* words (with their functions) from utterances and, at the same time, how they find analogical patterns across utterances (based mainly on communicative function) and thereby *abstract* meaningful grammatical constructions.

A linguistic construction is prototypically a unit of language that comprises multiple linguistic elements used together for a relatively coherent communicative function, with sub-functions being performed by the elements as well. Consequently, constructions may vary in their complexity depending on the number of elements involved and their interrelations. For example, the English regular plural construction (N+s) is relatively simple, whereas the passive construction (NP *was* VERB*ed by* NP) is relatively complex. Constructions also vary in their abstractness, from abstract constructions such as the English plural and passive, to various concrete idioms such as *kick the bucket* and *hold one's breath*. Importantly, even the most abstract constructions are still symbolic, as they possess a coherent, if abstract, meaning in relative independence of the lexical items involved (Goldberg 1995). Thus, we know the general profile of the event when we hear 'The dax got mibbed by the gazzer', even though we know none of the individual content words.

Children begin, as noted above, by producing holophrases – one unit utterances with an intonational contour expressing communicative motive. Their earliest multi-unit utterances soon form schemas or constructions, but ones that are highly concrete, not abstract (i.e. based on particular words and phrases, not abstract categories). From the point of view of linguistic form, the utterance-level constructions underlying children's earliest multi-word utterances come in three types: word combinations, pivot schemas, and item-based constructions.

5.4.1   Word combinations

Beginning at around 18 months of age, many children combine two words or holophrases in situations in which they both are relevant – with both words having roughly equivalent status. For example, a child has learned to name a ball and a table and then spies a ball on a table and says, "Ball table". Utterances of this type include both 'successive single-word utterances' (with a pause between them; Bloom 1973) and 'word combinations' or 'expressions' (under a single intonational contour). The defining feature of word combinations or expressions is that they partition the experiential scene into multiple symbolizable units – in a way that holophrases obviously (by definition) do not – and they are totally concrete in the sense that they are comprised only of concrete pieces of language, not categories.

5.4.2   Pivot schemas

Beginning at around this same age, however, many of children's multiword productions show a more systematic pattern. Often there is one word or phrase that seems to structure the utterance in the sense that it determines the speech act function of the utterance as a whole (often with help from an intonational contour), with the other linguistic item(s) simply filling in variable slot(s) – the first type of linguistic abstraction. Thus, in many of these early utterances one event-word is used with a wide variety of object labels (e.g. 'More milk', 'More grapes', 'More juice') yielding a schema such as 'More __'. Following Braine (1963), we may call these pivot schemas or constructions (see also Lieven *et al.* 1997, 2003).

Not only are pivot schemas organized only locally, but even within themselves they do not have syntax; that is, 'Gone juice' does not mean something different from 'Juice gone' (and there is no other marking to indicate syntactic role for elements in pivot schemas). The consistent ordering patterns in many pivot schemas are very likely direct reproductions of the ordering patterns children have heard most often in adult speech, with no communicative significance. This means that although young children are using their early pivot schemas to partition scenes conceptually with different words, they are not using syntactic symbols – such as word order or case marking – to indicate the different roles being played by different participants in that scene.

5.4.3   Item-based constructions

Item-based constructions go beyond pivot schemas in having syntactic marking as an integral part of the construction. For example, children barely two years of age respond appropriately to requests that they 'Make the bunny push the horse' (reversible transitives) that depend crucially and exclusively on a knowledge of canonical English word order (e.g. DeVilliers & DeVilliers 1973b, Hirsh-Pasek & Golinkoff 1996). However, the syntactic marking in these item-based constructions is still verb specific, depending on how a child has heard a particular verb being used. Thus, in experimental studies, when children who are themselves producing many transitive utterances are taught a new verb in any one of many different constructions, they mostly cannot transfer their knowledge of word order from their existing item-based constructions to this new item until after their third birthdays – and this finding holds in comprehension as well (Tomasello 2000d, 2003). These findings would seem to indicate that young children's early syntactic marking – at least with English word order – is only local, learned for different verbs on a one-by-one basis. What little experimental evidence we have from nonce verb studies of case-marking languages (e.g. Berman 1993, Wittek & Tomasello 2005) is in general accord with this developmental pattern.

The main point is that unlike in pivot schemas, in item-based constructions children use syntactic symbols such as morphology, adpositions and word order to syntactically mark the roles participants are playing in these events, including generalized 'slots' that include whole categories of entities as participants. But all of this is done on an item-specific basis; that is, the child does not generalize across scenes to syntactically mark similar participant roles in similar ways without having heard those participants used and marked in adult discourse for each verb specifically. This limited generality is presumably due to the difficulty of categorizing or schematizing entire utterances, including reference to both the event and the participant roles involved, into more abstract constructions – especially given the many different kinds of utterances children hear and must sort through. Early syntactic competence is therefore best characterized as a semi-structured inventory of relatively independent verb-island constructions that pair a scene of experience and an item-based construction, with very few structural relationships among these constructional islands.

5.4.4 Abstract constructions

Between two and three years of age, children begin constructing some more abstract constructions, with fewer particular lexical items necessary. However, despite their abstractness, each of these has a particular function in the sense of the communicative contexts in which it is appropriately used. Examples of some early abstract constructions in English are as follows:

1 Identificationals, attributives, and possessives
   Serve to identify an object or to attribute to it some property. Most common for the identification function: *It's a/the X; That's a/the X; or This's a/the X*. Most common for the attributive function: *It's X; That's X*. Most common for the possessive function: *(It's) X's _; That's X's/my _; This is X's/your _*.

2 Simple transitives and intransitives
   Serve to indicate or request an activity or state of affairs. Transitives (NP + V + NP): prototype is a scene in which there are two participants and one acts on the other (e.g. *Daddy cut the grass*). Intransitives (NP + V): prototype is an activity involving a single participant; either an actor does something (e.g. *Mummy smiled*; unergatives) or something happens to something (e.g. *The vase broke*; unaccusatives).

3 Datives, ditransitives, and benefactives
   Serve to indicate or request the transfer of objects (and other things) between people. Dative (NP + V + NP *to* NP): *He gave it to Mummy*. Ditransitive (NP + V + NP + NP): *Daddy sent her a present* or *Daddy told me a story*. Benefactive (NP + V + NP *for* NP): *She did it for me*.

4 Locatives, resultatives, and causatives
   Serve to indicate or request spatial or causal relations. Early locatives include such things as *Put NP in/on/ the NP, Take NP off my shirt, NP's under the NP*, etc. Resultatives indicate outcomes of actions and include such things as *NP eat NP all up, NP wash it off, NP push it down*, etc. Causatives prototypically involve as a first verb make, let or help, as in *Make NP do it, Help NP do it* or *Let NP do it*.

5 Passives and reflexives
   Serve to indicate things happening to people or things, who are not active agents. Children's early passives (NP + *be/get* + V + *by* NP) are such things as *Spot got hit by a car* or *Mummy got sick* or *It was taken by a bear*. Reflexives are such things as *I hurt myself*.

6 Imperatives and questions
   Many of the above construction types can be used as imperatives to request certain kinds of actions, typically without a subject as in: *Push it here, Smile, Don't do that, etc*. Many of the above construction

types can be used as questions to request certain kinds of information. While mature questions are quite complex, two very common formulae early on are: *What NP doing?* and *Where NP (going)?* Slightly later they start with such things as : *How do ...*, *What are ...*, and *Where is ...* .

The key theoretical point is that when we conceptualize children's early grammatical competence not in terms of abstract computational rules with no semantic content, but rather in terms of constructional patterns conventionally associated with particular semantic content, the acquisition processes needed are not so different from those we need for word learning. The child needs first to see that when the adult produces an utterance that fits a particular linguistic pattern (construction), he or she intends a particular kind of meaning. To see similarities among different utterances, young children need skills of schematization and analogy – skills they also use in other domains of cognitive activity (Gentner & Markman 1997).

5.5   Common objections

More formally oriented theorists object on a number of grounds to this usage-based, item-based approach to child language acquisition. The three most common objections are: (1) it cannot deal with more complex constructions, especially those involving two verbs and syntactic embedding; (2) it does not specify how the generalization/abstraction process is to be constrained, and (3) it does not deal with the so-called 'poverty of the stimulus'.

5.5.1   Complex constructions

Many more formally oriented theorists agree that the kind of account given above works for the very earliest stages of language acquisition – for very simple constructions – but it does not work for more syntactically complex constructions. Recent research has found, however, that complex constructions may not be so different if children's actual productions are looked at carefully (Diessel 2004).

For example, among the more complex constructions in English are sentential complement constructions. The prototype is an utterance like 'I know she hit him' and 'I think I can do it'. Diessel and Tomasello (2001) looked at young English-speaking children's earliest utterances with sentential complements from 2 to 5 years of age. They found that virtually all of them were composed of a simple sentence schema that the child had already mastered combined with one of a delimited set of fixed phrases containing a complement-taking matrix verb (see also Bloom 1992). The matrix verbs were of two types. First were epistemic verbs such as *think* and *know*. As one example, in almost all cases children used *I think* to indicate their own uncertainty about something, and they basically never used the verb *think* in anything but this first person, present tense form; that is, there were virtually no examples of *He thinks ..., She thinks ...*, etc., virtually no examples of *I don't think ..., I can't think ...*, etc. and virtually no examples of *I thought..., I didn't think ...*, etc. And there were almost no uses with a complementizer (virtually no examples of *I think that ...*). It thus appears that for many young children *I think* is a relatively fixed phrase meaning something like *Maybe*. The child then pieces together this fixed phrase (or one of the other similar phrases like *I hope ..., I bet ...*, etc.) with a full proposition, with its function being as a sort of evidential marker (not as a matrix clause that embeds another as in traditional analyses). The second kind of matrix verbs were attention-getting verbs like *Look* and *See*, used in conjunction with full finite clauses. In this case, children used these 'matrix' verbs almost exclusively in imperative form (again almost no negations, no non-present tenses, no complementizers), as in 'See the dog eating a bone,' suggesting again an item-based approach not involving syntactic embedding. (See Brandt *et al.* submitted, for very similar findings in German – even though German subordinate clauses have a different word order from main clauses.)

A second example is relative clauses. Textbook descriptions focus on so-called restrictive relative clauses – e.g. 'The dog that barked all night died this morning' – in which the relative clause serves to identify a noun by using presupposed information (both speaker and listener already know that there was barking all night – that's why it can be used as identifying information). Because relative clauses are a part of a noun phrase argument, they are classically characterized as embedded clauses. Diessel and Tomasello (2000) studied four English-speaking children between ages 1;9 and 5;2 in quantitative detail and made a surprising discovery: virtually all of these children's earliest relative clauses were of the same general form, and this form was not the form typically described in textbooks. Examples would be:

> Here's the toy that spins around
> That's the sugar that goes in there

What is noteworthy here is: (1) the main clause is a presentational construction (predicate nominal or closely related), basically introducing a new topic using a previously mastered fixed presentational phrase such as *Here's the..., That's the ...* ; and (2) the information in the relative clause is not presupposed, as in textbook (restrictive) relative clauses, but rather is new information about the just-introduced referent. Again, the main point is that, when examined closely, even this very complex construction is firmly based in a set of simpler constructions (copular presentationals) that children have mastered as item-based constructions some time before relative clauses are first acquired and produced. Even in German, where again relative clauses have a different word order from simple main clauses, this same basic acquisition pattern is found (Brandt *et al.* 2008)

Finally are questions. A particularly interesting phenomenon is so-called inversion errors. English-speaking children sometimes invert the subject and auxiliary in wh-questions and sometimes not – leading to errors such as 'Why they can't go?' A number of fairly complex and abstract rule-based accounts have been proposed to account for these errors, but in a more detailed analysis Rowland and Pine (2000) discovered the surprising fact that the child they studied from age 2 to 4 consistently inverted or failed to invert particular wh-word–auxiliary combinations on an item-specific basis. He thus consistently said such incorrect things as *Why I can… ? What she will… ? What you can… ?*, but at the same time he also said such correct things as *How did… ? How do… ? What do … ?* In a recent experiment, Ambridge *et al.* (2006) elicited inversion errors from 4-year-old English children and confirmed this pattern. Young children do not seem to have an overall rule for forming questions, or even wh-questions, but rather they have a collection of more item-based schemas that presumably will become a set of more coherent and abstract constructions later in ontogeny.

5.5.2 Constraining constructions

In all theories of language acquisition, there must be some constraints on children's linguistic generalizations and abstractions. Classically, a major problem for formal theories is that as the rules and principles are made more elegant and powerful through theoretical analyses, they become so abstract that they generate too large a set of grammatical utterances – and so constraints (e.g. the subjacency constraint) must be posited to restore empirical accuracy. In usage-based theories children are abstracting as they learn, but they cannot do this indiscriminately; they must make just those generalizations that are conventional in the language they are learning and not others. It is thus clear that any serious theory of syntactic development, whatever its basic assumptions, must address the question of why children make just the generalizations they do and not others.

We may illustrate the basic problem with so-called dative alternation constructions. The situation is that some verbs can felicitously appear in both ditransitive and prepositional dative constructions, but others cannot; for example:

He gave/sent/bequeathed/donated his books to the library.
He gave/sent/bequeathed/*donated the library his books.

Why should the other three verbs be felicitous in both constructions, but *donate* be felicitous only in the prepositional dative? The three verbs have very similar meanings, and so it would seem likely that they should all behave the same. Another example is:

> She said/told something to her mother.
> She *said/told her mother something.

Again, the meanings of the verbs are very close, and so the difference of behaviour seems unprincipled and unpredictable (Bowerman 1988, 1996). Other similar alternations are the causative alternation (*I rolled the ball; The ball rolled*) and the locative alternation (*I sprayed paint on the wall; I sprayed the wall with paint*) – both of which also apply only to limited sets of verbs.

One solution is quite simple. Perhaps children only learn verbs for the constructions in which they have heard them. Based on all of the evidence reviewed above, this is very likely the case at the earliest stages of development. But it is not true later in development, especially in the 3-to-5-year age period. Children at this age overgeneralize with some regularity, as documented most systematically by Bowerman (1982b, 1988, see Pinker 1989, for a summary of evidence): 'Don't giggle me' (at age 3;0) and 'I said her no' (at age 3;1). It is thus not the case that children are totally conservative throughout development, and so this cannot be the whole answer. A second simple but untrue solution is that when children make overgeneralization errors adults correct them, and so children's overgeneralization tendencies are constrained by the linguistic environment. But this is not true in the sense that adults do not explicitly correct child utterances for their grammatical correctness with any frequency (Brown & Hanlon 1970). Adults, at least Western middle-class adults, do respond differently to well-formed and ill-formed child utterances (e.g. Bohannon & Stanowicz 1988, Farrar 1992), but this kind of indirect feedback is generally not considered by most theorists sufficient to constrain children's overgeneralization tendencies, and it is far from consistent.

Given the inadequacy of these simple solutions, three factors have been most widely discussed. First, Pinker (1989) proposed that there are certain very specific and (mostly) semantic constraints that apply to particular English constructions and to the verbs that may or may not be conventionally used in them. For example, a verb can be used felicitously with the English transitive construction if it denotes 'manner of locomotion' (e.g. *walk* and *drive* as in 'I walked the dog at midnight' or 'I drove my car to New York'), but not if it denotes a 'motion in a lexically specified direction' (e.g. *come* and *fall* as in *"He came her to school' or *"She falled him down'). How children learn these verb classes – and they must learn them since they differ across languages – is unknown at this time. Second, it has also been proposed that the more frequently children hear a verb used in a particular construction (the more firmly its usage is entrenched), the less likely they will be to extend that verb to any novel construction with which they have not heard it used (Bates & MacWhinney 1989, Braine & Brooks 1995, Clark 1987, Goldberg 1995). And third, if children hear a verb used in a linguistic construction that serves the same communicative function as some possible generalization, they may infer that the generalization is not conventional – the heard construction pre-empts the generalization. For example, if a child hears 'He made the rabbit disappear', when she might have expected 'He disappeared the rabbit', she may infer that *disappear* does not occur in a simple transitive construction – since the adult seems to be going to some lengths to avoid using it in this way (the periphrastic causative being a more marked construction).

Two experimental studies provide evidence that indeed all three of these constraining processes – entrenchment, pre-emption and knowledge of semantic subclasses of verbs – are at work. First, Brooks *et al.* (1999) modelled the use of a number of fixed-transitivity English verbs for children from 3;5 to 8;0 years – verbs such as *disappear* that are exclusively intransitive and verbs such as *hit* that are exclusively transitive. There were four pairs of verbs, one member of each pair typically learned early by children and typically used often by adults (and so presumably more entrenched) and one member of each pair typically learned later by children and typically used less frequently by adults (less entrenched). The four pairs were: *come–arrive, take–remove, hit–strike, disappear–vanish* (the first member of each pair being more entrenched). The finding was that, in the face of adult questions attempting to induce them to overgeneralize, children of all ages were less likely to overgeneralize the strongly entrenched verbs than the weakly entrenched verbs; that is, they were more likely to produce 'I arrived it' than 'I comed it'.

Second, Brooks and Tomasello (1999a) taught novel verbs to children 2.5, 4.5, and 7.0 years of age. They then attempted to induce children to generalize these novel verbs to new constructions. Some of these verbs conformed to Pinker's (1989) semantic criteria, and some did not. Additionally, in some cases experimenters attempted to pre-empt generalizations by providing children with alternative ways of using the new verb (thus providing them with the possibility of answering 'What's the boy doing?' with 'He's making the ball tam' – which allows the verb to stay intransitive). In brief, the study found that both of these constraining factors worked, but only from age 4.5. Children from 4.5 showed a tendency to generalize or not generalize a verb in line with its membership in one of the key semantic subclasses, and they were less likely to generalize a verb to a novel construction if the adult provided them with a pre-empting alternative construction. But the younger children showed no such tendency.

Overall, entrenchment seems to work early, from 3;0 or before, as particular verb island constructions become either more or less entrenched depending on usage. Pre-emption and semantic subclasses begin to work sometime later, perhaps not until 4 years of age or later, as children learn more about the conventional uses of verbs and about all of the alternative linguistic constructions at their disposal in different communicative circumstances. Thus, just as verb–argument constructions become more abstract only gradually, so also are they constrained only gradually.

5.5.3   Poverty of the stimulus

The fundamental argument for the existence of an innate universal grammar – and against the kind of item-based, usage-based approach advocated here – is the argument from the poverty of the stimulus. Chomsky has made this clear in a number of places, and it has recently been reiterated by Crain and Pietroski (2001). The problem is that the argument is formulated in terms of a formal generative grammar as adult endpoint and a child who has available only behaviouristic learning theory – which enables him or her only to string words together in a Markov chain (with no understanding of phrasal organization or any other structure–function correlations), making blind associations and inductive inferences in the process (with no conceptual understanding of linguistic function at all). But, as Tomasello (2003) argues, there is no poverty of the stimulus if linguistic competence is conceived not as a set of formal, algebraic rules but rather as a structured inventory of meaningful grammatical constructions, with the child possessing sophisticated learning skills involving categorization, analogy and distributional learning. There is certainly no poverty of the stimulus when it comes to the particular constructions children learn. Each of those listed in the preceding section – e.g. transitives, ditransitives, passives, questions, etc. – are heard by young children many dozens or hundreds of times each and every day for several years before they have mastered them on an abstract level (Cameron-Faulkner *et al.* 2003). And, importantly, the acquisition of these constructions is determined in large measure by the frequency (cue availability) and consistency (cue reliability) with which children hear them – along with their complexity (cue cost) of course (Lieven & Tomasello 2008). Indeed, relatively precise predictions about age of acquisition may be made crosslinguistically by quantifying these three input variables (Bates & MacWhinney 1989, Chan *et al.* in press, Dittmar *et al.* 2008).

The poverty of the stimulus problem only arises in very abstract arguments against approaches that recognized no kind of structure dependency within utterances (again, presumably behaviourism). Chomsky (1980) gives the following example of question formation in English.

(1)   a. The man is tall.
       b. Is the man __ tall?

(2)   a. The man who is smoking is tall.
       b. *Is the man who __ smoking is tall?
       c. Is the man who is smoking __ tall?

The idea is that forming simple questions such as 'Is the man tall?' could be done on the basis of either of two hypotheses: move the first-occurring auxiliary to the front or move the auxiliary from the main predicate to the front. To differentiate between these two hypotheses children supposedly need to see examples like (2c) in which the subject NP contains a relative clause with an auxiliary (which did not move to the front). Chomsky (1980: 40) has famously claimed that children almost never hear such sentences. But in an analysis of some written corpora and corpora of child-directed speech, Pullum and Scholz (2002) find many of just the right kind of examples that children need, such things as:

(3) Can those who are leaving early __ sit near the door?

(4) Is the boy who was crying __ still here?

(5) Could those who are coming __ raise their hands?

But actually, if one thinks about it for a bit, children do not really need to encounter such sentences at all (Elman 2001). If children understand NPs with relative clauses – if they understand that the whole phrase is used to make one act of reference – then there would never be any temptation to extract an auxiliary from it; they would simply understand that that unit stays together as one functional unit. It may be said that this is simply another way of stating that children understand structure dependence. True. And that is the point. If we allow children to have some notion of meaning or function, then they understand structure of sentences to the extent needed to form a conventional English yes–no question. Modern usage-based theorists are not behaviourists who believe the child works with unstructured linear strings, but rather they are cognitivists who believe in structure – just not of the purely formal kind.

5.6   Conclusions

The usage-based theory of language acquisition makes the fundamental claim that language structure emerges from language use. This applies at the level of individual words, as their communicative function derives from their use, as well as at the level of grammar, as structure emerges from patterns of use of multi-unit utterances. Historically, the structure of a language emerges through processes of grammaticalization. Ontogenetically, children hear individual utterances and then (re-) construct the abstract constructions of a language. All of this is done with general cognitive processes, and universals of linguistic structure derive from the fact that people everywhere have the same set of general cognitive processes. As noted at the outset, Tomasello (2003) argues that we may segregate these general cognitive processes into the two overall headings of: (1) intention-reading, comprising the species unique social cognitive skills responsible for symbol acquisition and the functional dimensions of language, and (2) pattern-finding, the primate-wide cognitive skills involved in the abstraction process. More specifically, these two kinds of general cognitive abilities interact in specific acquisition tasks to yield four specific sets of processes:

- *Intention-Reading and Cultural Learning*, which account for how children learn conventional form–function pairings, including everything from words to complex constructions;
- *Schematization and Analogy*, which account for how children create abstract syntactic constructions (and syntactic roles such as subject and direct object) out of the concrete utterances they have heard;
- *Entrenchment and Pre-emption*, which account for how children constrain their abstractions to just those that are conventional in their linguistic community; and
- *Functionally Based Distributional Analysis*, which accounts for how children form paradigmatic categories of various kinds of linguistic constituents (e.g. nouns and verbs).

Together these processes account for how children construct a language, that is, a structured inventory of linguistic constructions, from the language they hear being used around them. Further insights into how these processes work in detail are given in Lieven and Tomasello (in press) and Abbot-Smith and Tomasello (2006), mainly in the form of patterns of linguistic input that facilitate these processes – for example, type frequency for analogy, token frequency for entrenchment, statistical patterns leading to paradigmatic categories and all aspects of cue validity – and processes of exemplar-based learning and categorization. Tomasello (2003) also argues that connectionist accounts – at least in their current form in which almost everything is based on distributional analysis with no account of communicative function – are not sufficient to account for language acquisition. Children acquire language first and foremost by understanding how others use language.

Suggestions for further reading

Diessel, H. (2004). *The Acquisition of Complex Sentences*. Cambridge: Cambridge University Press.

Goldberg, A. (2006). *Constructions at Work*. Oxford: Oxford University Press.

Lieven, E., & Tomasello, M. (2008). Children's first language acquisition from a usage-based perspective. In N. Ellis (Ed.), *Handbook of Cognitive Linguistics and Second Language Acquisition* (pp. 168–196). New York and London: Routledge.

Tomasello, M. (2001). Perceiving intentions and learning words in the second year of life. In M. Bowerman & S. Levinson (Eds.), *Language Acquisition and Conceptual Development*. Cambridge: Cambridge University Press.

Tomasello, M. (2003). *Constructing a Language: A Usage-Based Theory of Language Acquisition*. Cambridge, MA: Harvard University Press.

Tomasello, M. (2008). *Origins of Human Communication*. MIT Press.

6

Crosslinguistic approaches to language acquisition

Sabine Stoll

6.1   Introduction

Human language is the only communication system with extensive variation in form and meaning across the groups of its users. Human language
comes in a great many varieties, and the structures we find in grammars of
individual languages and in the way meanings are expressed vary to an
impressive degree. Currently, there are about 6,000–7,000 languages
spoken.[1] For only about half of these we have some kind of basic grammatical description and for only about 10 per cent do we have good and
elaborate analyses. Yet in-depth description of the adult language is a
prerequisite for any acquisition study. Even though in the last forty years
a lot of crosslinguistic language acquisition research has been conducted,
it is still for only about 2 per cent of the world's languages that we have at
least one acquisition study. For even these 2 per cent, however, we may
only have acquisition studies devoted to one individual feature or aspect of
language development.

   Furthermore, this small sample is heavily biased toward Indo-European
languages of Western Europe with the bulk of research still concentrated
on English. This bias manifests itself even in the titles of works on language acquisition. English is the default case: if there is a title about the
acquisition of language or some feature of language without naming the
language, then we can assume the work is on English; if the work bears on
any other language, that language is normally named in the title.

   A problem of this small biased sample is that we take English and a few
other Indo-European languages as the prototype for acquisition. Yet it is well

My warm thanks go to Edith Bavin, Balthasar Bickel, Gabriella Hermon, Elena Lieven and Dan Slobin for helpful
comments.

[1] In addition, there is a large number of sign languages (see Sandler & Lillo-Martin 2006) but I limit myself in
     this chapter to spoken languages.

known that these languages are typologically unusual; English and the Indo-European languages of Northwestern Europe for which we have acquisition data (e.g. French, Italian, German) exhibit a large number of linguistically rare phenomena (cf. Dahl 1990, Haspelmath 2001). A prominent example is the relative construction with relative pronouns (e.g. *whom* in *the woman whom I saw* or *that* in *the mouse that ate the cheese*). This construction raises specific acquisition issues (see Diessel & Tomasello 2000), but it is not attested in many other languages where its function is taken over by structurally different constructions (e.g. Comrie & Kuteva 2005).

Thus a substantial part of our knowledge about language acquisition is built on specific constructions prominent in languages of Europe that have been well described, but we do not have information about how other, more widespread, constructions are acquired. Generalizing from the acquisition of one or a few languages to language in general is comparable to biologists studying one unusual mammal species, such as whales, and making generalizations from that to all other mammals. It is well known that children learn the language of their environment but languages differ and we need to include in our research the range of features that children may have to acquire. Acquisition studies of less well-documented languages and, in general, a more crosslinguistic perspective on acquisition is a top priority in the field.

Crosslinguistic language acquisition research is usually understood in two different ways. First, and most frequently, the term is used for acquisition studies of languages other than English. Studies of this type of research, for instance, investigate how ergative structures are acquired in Quiche Mayan, or how grammatical morphology is acquired in Turkish. Results of such studies are often used to test theories of language acquisition that are developed on the basis of research on English, or that are informed by general speculation about the nature of grammar.

The other type of crosslinguistic research is inherently comparative, and languages for comparison are selected on the basis of typological differences or similarities. I will use the term 'typological language acquisition research' for this type of research. The goal is to systematically explore commonalities and differences in the acquisition of specific linguistic features across different languages. Languages are grouped typologically on the basis of shared features. For example, word order has often been used to define types of languages; English has a predominantly subject–verb–object pattern (SVO), whereas Welsh has a predominantly VSO order and Japanese has a SOV order. A variety of features is used to classify languages into typologies, for example case marking. Some languages are classified as Ergative–Absolutive while others are Nominative–Accusative, identified on the pattern of case marking used. A language with ergative case marking typically treats the subject of an intransitive sentence like the object of a transitive sentence while the subject of a transitive sentence is distinct. However, there is variation within this general pattern (Van Valin 1992). The advantage of the 'typological language acquisition research' approach is that a range of crosslinguistic variation is covered.

There has been an increase in the number of studies comparing acquisition across languages. Despite this, most research – even when on less well-studied languages – still focuses on one language; typological acquisition research is relatively rare. Some typological studies are Pye *et al.* (2007), Slobin (1997b) and Strömqvist *et al.* (1995). The use of different data sets, different methods or different criteria for coding makes it difficult to compare across languages. This complicates post hoc comparisons and meta-analyses and creates a considerable challenge to a full-scale typological approach.

In the remainder of this chapter I discuss some examples of variation across languages and theoretical and methodological challenges posed by language variation. I then review one example of an intra-genealogical acquisition study, a study that compares languages within language families and one example of an inter-genealogical acquisition study that compares languages across families.

6.2 Variation across languages

6.2.1 Some theoretical views
Variation is found at all linguistic levels: phonology, morphology, syntax, semantics and pragmatics. In addition, there is considerable variation in the context in which learning occurs. The main question of typological language acquisition research is whether and if so, how, the actual course of language acquisition is affected by differences across languages, as well as cultures. However, language acquisition research is very much guided by what language is understood to be, and this affects how typological research can be conceived.

In approaches to language acquisition which adopt a nativist perspective (see Valian Ch. 2), linguistic diversity and variation originally played a marginal role. This has changed somewhat in current work that incorporates data from a wider range of languages. Within nativist approaches explanations of how children deal with variation range from performance factors to the assumption of innate mechanisms. In one version of the theory to account for variation across languages, a small set of parameters was proposed to limit the possible syntactic variation. For example, the pro-drop parameter distinguishes languages which allow pronoun subjects to be non-overt, as in Italian, and languages which require pronoun subjects, as in English (Hyams 1989b).

In contrast to approaches which assume innate language structures, the cognitive, constructivist or usage-based theories (e.g. Bybee 1985, Langacker 1987, Tomasello 2000b and Ch. 5) assume that children construct their languages from a small set of item-specific and low-scope constructions. For usage-based approaches, crosslinguistic variation is of key importance because item-specific constructions are necessarily also language-specific, and the variation in linguistic structure is likely to have an impact on how individual constructions are learned (Slobin 1985a).

Dan Slobin has been leading a visionary initiative over the past two decades in expanding our understanding of similarities and differences in the acquisition of languages of different types. His work has focused, in part, on how languages differ in what is grammaticized, and the problem of form–function mapping in the acquisition process, that is, detecting linguistic forms and assigning a meaning/function to each. He launched a large pioneering project that culminated in five volumes, with sketch descriptions of the language acquisition of twenty-eight languages ranging across a wide range of families (e.g. Slobin 1985a, 1985b, 1992, 1997a, 1997b).[2] A number of language acquisition researchers provided selective, mostly uniform, summaries of what we know about the acquisition of these languages. The rationale behind his approach was that different types of languages pose different types of acquisition problems and the crosslinguistic method is a 'method for the discovery of general principles of acquisition' (Slobin 1985a: 5).

Slobin's goal was to use this crosslinguistic data to determine the relative difficulties in acquiring formal devices (Slobin 1973). The assumption that the 'rate and order of development of the semantic notions expressed by languages are fairly constant across children learning different languages' (Slobin 1973: 187) is difficult to evaluate. The complexity measure of forms consisted in comparing time of first use and time of mastery. As Bowerman (1985) pointed out, this is a very difficult measure to apply, since it is far from clear how first use should be coded and whether the establishment of time of acquisition can be assessed from very different types of data collected from a small number of children. In addition, the time of acquisition will depend on the criterion used by the researcher, the data and the method. The data used in Slobin's collections stems from a number of different resources: diaries, experiments and longitudinal studies of children of varying ages, across different time spans and stages of development. That is, the data is heterogeneous. However, the chapters provide valuable insights, and some similarities and differences in the acquisition of different languages emerged.

It has often been assumed that the more complex a feature the more difficult it is to learn (Slobin 1985a). The crucial challenge, however, is to ascertain what complexity consists of. Complexity can be measured along a number of dimensions, and in order to understand development

---

[2] The languages represented include: English, German, Hebrew, Japanese, Kaluli, Polish, Romance languages (with particular emphasis on French), Turkish, ASL, Hungarian, Georgian, West Greenlandic, Quiche Maya, Warlpiri, Mandarin, Sesotho, Scandinavian languages, a comparison of Estonian, Finnish and Hungarian, Finnish, Greek and Korean.

processes, an understanding of the complexity is needed, not just of the form of a structure, but also its function and its interrelation with other structures in the language. Interacting with complexity of form is how consistent and how transparent their functions are. Bates and MacWhinney (1987, 1989) proposed the Competition model to account for some of the different patterns of acquisition found across languages. In this model, mechanisms determining the ways in which cues combine or compete are described and the strength with which a cue is used is directly proportional to the informational value or cue validity. Cue validity is the product of cue availability (proportion of time a cue is present) and cue reliability (proportion of time when the cue is present that it indicates the correct solution) (McDonald 1986, McDonald & MacWhinney 1989). When there are several morphological forms with one function and several functions for one form, cue validity and reliability are affected. For example, if a particular case form is used to mark some nouns but not others, that form is low in validity. The extent to which word order is important in helping children determine who did what to whom has been investigated within the Competition model. Animacy, case marking, agreement or stress may be used in the early stages, depending on the language being acquired (cf. Bates *et al.* 1982, 1984, MacWhinney & Bates 1989). In English, for instance, word order is the dominant cue for young children, but in Hungarian it is animacy and, in Turkish, case marking. That is, young children learning different languages focus on different cues, not necessarily word order, and they are not necessarily the predominant cues which adult speakers of the language rely on.

6.2.2 Conceptualization and linguistic relativity

A large body of research suggests that language is tightly connected with the conceptualization of the world (e.g. Bowerman & Choi 2003, Lucy 1992, Slobin 1996). This research focuses on linguistic relativity which states that the grammar and the lexicon of a language systematically influence how a speaker of this language perceives and conceptualizes the world around. Even concepts like time and space have been shown to be conceptualized differently across languages and cultures. In the spatial domain, Levinson (2003) postulates three major linguistic frames of references that are grammaticalized or lexicalized in the languages of the world: intrinsic ('the man is inside the house'), relative ('the man stands to the right of the house') and absolute ('the man is to the north of the house'). Children will need to learn which of these modes of orientation is relevant in the language of their surroundings. Thus finding out how children learn a language also means finding out how their conceptualization of the world develops.

Korean and English differ both in their conceptualization of space and the linguistic expressions that encode spatial distinctions. In a pathbreaking typological study, Choi and Bowerman (1991) compared the acquisition of Korean and English spatial terms. Where Korean uses verbs to encode spatial concepts, English uses predominantly adpositions. In English a distinction is made between *in* (enclosure of a figure in some container) and *on* (contact of a figure with some object – for support). In contrast Korean distinguishes the kind of fit. For example, *nehhta* 'put loosely in or around' contrasts with *kkita* 'interlock, fit tightly'. Choi *et al.* (1999) found that children from 18–23 months show sensitivity to these language-specific differences. That is, infants are attuned to the way in which their language conceptualizes space. The linguistic input affects concept formation from the earliest stages.

6.2.3 Phonological systems

Children need to learn individual sounds and their phonological contrasts. There are approximately 3,000 categorically distinct sounds used in living languages and there are quite a few more that would in principle be possible – the IPA generates over 50,000 possible symbol combinations (p.c. Ian Maddieson). In their first year, babies build up language-specific phonetic prototypes which help to organize sounds into categories (Kuhl *et al.* 1992, also see Curtin & Hufnagle Ch. 7 and Vihman *et al.* Ch. 10). This also holds for children acquiring tone language such as Yoruba (Niger-Congo, Nigeria) (Harrison 2000). Languages differ in the number of phonemes in their sound system. Rotokas (North Bougainville family, Papua New Guinea) is the language with the smallest known inventory (11 phonemes), whereas !Xóõ (Tuu family, Botswana) is at the other extreme with approximately 153 phonemes. Out of the 122 consonants of !Xóõ there are about 83 clicks which are preferred word-initially over nonclicks (Maddieson 2005, Traill 1985). Clicks are known to be complex to produce and range among the most complex articulatory speech sounds. Children learning such a complex sound system might differ systematically in word-learning strategies from children learning languages with a smaller inventory. Children who still have a small vocabulary may be very selective in their choice of words, that is, either actively avoid words which are difficult to pronounce or substitute consonants systematically (for a summary, see Macken & Ferguson 1983). In fact, clicks are reported to be acquired late in Xhosa (Mowrer & Burger 1991) and closely related Sesotho (Demuth 1992), but the functional load of clicks in these Bantu languages is considerably lower than in the non-Bantu ('Khoisan') languages of Southern Africa. However, the acquisition of 'Khoisan' languages has not yet been documented and so it is not known if clicks are acquired earlier than in Xhosa and Sesotho.

6.2.4 Words

There are different types of words, phonological and grammatical words, and their structure and identification differ from language to language. To illustrate why the study of diversity is crucial but difficult, let us consider an example which shows how our theories are driven by the data we use. Morphology directly influences the kind of words we have in a language (more analytic or synthetic – see Behrens Ch. 12) but this interrelation has not been addressed in studies of word acquisition. A study on the acquisition of verbs in five Mayan languages (Pye *et al.* 2007) showed that even in closely related languages the children's first verb forms differ, depending on the morphology of the particular language (see Section 6.6.1). Words are language-specific constructions and generalizations are difficult to make without taking a wide range of factors into consideration.

It has been taken as common ground that the order of morphemes within a word is fixed and that free permutation of the morphemes is not possible. Any change in order is assumed to create a word with a different meaning. This assumption was confirmed for the languages that have been documented so far. Recent research on words in Chintang (Sino-Tibetan, Eastern Nepal), however, (Bickel *et al.* 2007), shows that prefixes can freely permutate within a word without any change in meaning or other consequences, such as dialect change or pragmatic differences. Thus, speakers freely vary between forms like *u-kha-ma-cop-yokt-e* (3NONSG.A-1NONSG.P-NEG-see-NEG-PST EXCL) and *kha-u-ma-cop-yokt-e, ma-kha-u-cop-yokt-e* 'they didn't see us (EXCL.)'.[3] Free prefix permutation severely reduces the amount of repetition available in the input, but we have at present no idea of how children manage to successfully cope with this feature.

A major finding in word learning has been that children in their early word use tend to prefer nouns over verbs (Gentner 1982). Gentner's observation is based on a number of languages including English, German, Japanese, Kaluli, Mandarin and Turkish. The generalization, however, is based on a survey of early vocabulary studies collected from a variety of independent studies conducted by different researchers. Subsequent studies on other languages (Tzeltal: Brown 1998a, Mandarin Chinese: Tardif 1996, Korean: Choi & Gopnik 1995), and a reanalysis of the English data have shown mixed results; verbs seem to be more represented in the early vocabulary of Korean, for example. It is likely that the use of different data sets or maternal checklists or spontaneous speech samples, yield different results (Clark 2003). An additional factor is the context in which a spontaneous speech sample is collected (Tardif *et al.* 1999). Similarities across English and Mandarin have been found if the context is kept constant.

Estimating the frequency of nouns and verbs presupposes that we can easily distinguish between nouns and verbs in the speech of a child. However, this can be often a challenge both in child language and in some languages in general such as, for example, Riau Indonesian and colloquial Jakarta Indonesian (Gil 2000).

---

[3] 3NONSG.A = third person nonsingular agent, 1NONSG.P = first person nonsingular Patient, NEG=negative, PST = past, EXCL. = exclusive.

6.2.5 Verb morphology

A considerable challenge to acquisition is posed by morphology. Some languages have a lot of morphology such as for instance Mohawk (Iroquoian, United States, Canada); other languages such as English or Mandarin Chinese have very little morphology and Vietnamese has none. In verbs, for instance, languages vary as to how many grammatical categories can be expressed within a single verb form. Based on a world-wide survey, Bickel and Nichols (2005) report a range between 0 (Vietnamese, with no evidence of any inflectional form in the verb), and 13 (Koasati). Grammatical categories expressed in the verb can cover a wide range, from more familiar categories like tense, aspect or negation to less well-known but widespread categories like evidentiality (grammatical marking of evidence for a statement) and mirativity (grammatical marking of new and unexpected information) to less common categories like honorificity or switch-reference. A child learning a language which obligatorily expresses honorificity in verb forms (e.g. Maithili: *daur-l-ak* 'run-PST-3nh', 'he ran' (non honorific), *daur-l-aith* 'run-PST-3h 'he run' (honorific)), has a more complex task of verb learning in the sense of pattern-to-world matching than a child learning a language which does not even express person systematically.

The more verbal categories encoded, the more verb forms a given language exhibits. English expresses three grammatical categories in the verb: person of subject, number of subject and tense, with only two forms to mark them. For example, in *She works* the *-s* encodes the person and number of the subject and tense; in *She worked* the *-ed* expresses tense. In contrast, the Sino-Tibetan language Chintang obligatorily encodes eight categories and speakers of the language need to make choices in all eight (tense, mood, aspect, polarity, person of subject, number of subject, person of object, number of object). A transitive verb in this language has up to 983 distinct forms (Bickel *et al.* 2007). Even though with many verbs, some of these forms are rarely used, they are still part of the grammar of adults, and children will acquire them.

The number of verb forms to acquire adds complexity to the task of acquisition, but the way the forms are encoded also adds complexity. Turkish, for example, is agglutinating: that is, each morpheme encodes one meaning. In contrast, Russian and Polish are inflectional languages, in which forms combine several elements of meaning. Exact repetitions of verbs in agglutinating languages like Turkish (as well as in languages with very little verbal morphology like English) are statistically much more likely than in 'inflectional' languages like Polish, and exact repetitions become even more rare if the number of categories increase as in a polysynthetic 'inflectional' language like Chintang (Tibeto-Burman, Eastern Nepal). Thus, in English constructions like *I saw you, He saw me, We saw them*, the verb form is repeated no matter what person or gender is involved. In Polish there is a different verb form for each person and in addition the gender of the subject is also marked at the verb, e.g. *ja go zobaczyłam* (I him saw.1SG FEM) 'I saw him', *ty nam zobaczyłas* (you us saw.2SG FEM) 'You saw us', but *ty nam zobacyłes* (You us saw.2SG MASC) if the addressee is masculine. Thus the probability for exact repetitions of verb forms is much lower in a language like Polish than in English.

For languages like Chintang the likelihood of exact repetition is even less. For a sentence like 'I saw you', Chintang differentiates the three verb forms *copnehẽ, copnace* and *copnanihẽ*, with different suffixal strings depending on whether the object 'you' is singular, dual or plural, respectively. 'You saw me' involves an altogether different pattern of tense and agreement marking, involving a prefix: *acobehẽ* 'You (singular) saw me', *acobaŋcihẽ* 'You (dual) saw me', *acobaŋnihẽ* 'You (plural) saw me' (Bickel *et al.* 2007).

In summary, verb forms in morphologically rich languages are more variable and the child has to master many more forms and combinations of forms and the appropriate contexts of use.

An area in which similarities in acquisition patterns have been reported is in the acquisition of tense/aspect. Data on tense and aspect are available from a wide variety of historically unrelated languages (see Li & Shirai 2000). There is a strong correlation between tense and grammatical and lexical aspect. Grammatical aspect is a formal category of some languages encoding the temporal structure of an event (e.g. perfective vs. imperfective aspect). Lexical aspect, also called Aktionsarten, is an inherent property of predicates categorizing events into states, activities, telic (goal-directed) events, and other such types. Perfective verb forms, that is, forms portraying events as unstructured wholes (such as the Russian form *dat'* 'give.PFV') and telic Aktionsarten, that is, verbs including a goal or result in their lexical semantics (such as *buy*) typically appear in the past tense form of a verb, whereas imperfective aspect and atelic Aktionsarten typically appear in the present (or nonpast) form (Shirai *et al.* 1998). However, there is variation in the acquisition of tense and aspect across languages. It is unclear whether the variation is due to differences in the language-specific structures that are being acquired, or because researchers use different criteria for identifying acquisition or different types of data on which to base their conclusions. For example, some data have been collected through observation while other data have been elicited in experimental settings. Another likely source of variation is the discourse context of aspect usage, which has been shown to cause substantial variation in a study on the acquisition of Russian aspect (Stoll 2001, 2005).

6.3   Variation in context

Children learn their language from their environment, and there is much descriptive work on the input that children receive. There is not only variation in the structures that children have to learn, but also in their cultural and linguistic contexts (Lieven 1994, Ochs & Schieffelin 1984). Studying the linguistic environment of children can help answer two important questions. First, are there any commonalities of qualitative changes made by the caretakers when talking to the child, in other words do all cultures somehow facilitate their speech when talking to children (not necessarily in the same way)? Second, does the input influence development; that is, do we find correlations between certain features in the input and the language development of the child?

As discussed by Ochs and Schieffelin (1984), some cultures are more child-centred while others are more situation-centred. The difference relates to the values and beliefs of the society. In a child-centred society, as is typical with urban industrialized Western groups, a child is assumed to be a communicative partner from birth and caregivers will talk to a young baby as if the baby can understand, and will even answer for the baby; in addition, a baby's vocalization will be interpreted as a word. In contrast, in situation-centred societies, a young baby is not assumed to be a communicative partner and so child-directed speech does not play the same role. In fact, children may not be addressed directly until they start to produce intelligible words (e.g. Quiche Mayan: Ratner & Pye 1984, Kaluli: Schieffelin 1985). Other features also vary, such as prompting a child to use appropriate language or even speaking for the child. However, it is difficult to compare directly across cultures because we may not have captured all the contexts in which adults talk to children (de León 1998). Thus we do not know the extent to which children learn language structures from the language addressed to them and from language they overhear,

Research on the dyadic interaction between mothers and their children in Western, literate, urban contexts (that is, child-centred) has identified a series of features characterizing child-directed speech: shorter and simpler utterances, higher pitch (Fernald & Kuhl 1987, Fernald et al. 1989), exaggerated intonation, few errors (Snow & Ferguson 1977). None of these adaptations, which should facilitate acquisition, applies universally. Higher pitch, for example, was long assumed to be a good candidate for a universal of child-directed speech. It has even been found in tone languages such as Mandarin Chinese (Grieser & Kuhl 1988, Papousek et al. 1991). However, there are societies in which higher pitch seems absent from child-directed speech because it is reserved for other registers, as Ratner and Pye (1984) suggest for Quiche Maya (though for an alternative interpretation, see Fernald et al. 1989). A study by Fernald et al. (1989), comparing prosodic modifications in mother's and father's speech to preverbal children in languages with considerably diverse prosodic structures (French, Italian, German, Japanese and both British and American English) suggests that even though there are common patterns found in the input there are language-specific variations. Repetition has also been reported for the speech addressed to young children in, for example,

Tzeltal (Brown 1998b), English (Cameron-Faulkner *et al.* 2003) and also in a recent comparative study of Russian, English and German (Stoll *et al.* in press).

6.4 Methods for investigating language acquisition

A main problem for typological research is the comparison across studies. If, for instance, we want to compare the acquisition of aspect in French, Russian and English using the results of already available studies we would encounter a number of difficulties. Researchers may have collected different types of data and with different research methods, number of participants and age range of the children. There is a wide range of methods used in language acquisition research: experimental paradigms, structured elicitations using a uniform stimulus kit, picture identification and observations in naturalistic or laboratory contexts. Experiments are used to test what children can do both in production and comprehension in a specific context, but they raise methodological and practical issues for typological research. Experiments for investigating typological similarities and differences in acquisition patterns need to be equivalent across language groups, but this can be difficult for a number of reasons. For example, one experimental paradigm for research on very young children's comprehension is the intermodal preferential looking paradigm (IPL) (Golinkoff *et al.* 1987). In this paradigm, children are simultaneously presented with two pictures and an auditory match for one of the pictures. It is assumed that if children understand the input they will look longer at the matching picture, although there are problems in interpreting what it is the children have actually understood. However, even though the design is relatively simple, the technical and practical prerequisites can be a challenge if one wants to conduct such an experiment in the field. For such an experiment an electricity supply is needed but is not always available. In addition, there needs to be a location where the experiment can be conducted without interruption from others. This means that IPL testing is more or less restrained to the specific cultural context of technically advanced societies.

Any kind of data collection needs to be conducted in collaboration with a native speaker of the language and for experimental or comparative research it needs to be conducted in a uniform context for all participants. In various cultures there can be difficulties in finding assistants who can deal with the experimental situation appropriately. Further, the instructions of the experiment need to be equivalent across languages. Any differences can bias the results considerably. Keeping the instructions constant is not a trivial task, for example, one language may have obligatory articles while another does not which results in differences in the stimuli.

Another problem is in developing stimuli that can be compared across languages. The use of picture prompts (or videos) for instance presupposes that children of the culture are familiar with pictures or videos, but this may not be the case. The choice of stimuli can also introduce a bias. Familiarity with the stimuli can bear significantly on the results. Consider the acquisition of ergativity; if we want to compare its acquisition in Quiche Mayan children (Mexico), Warlpiri (Australia) and Inuktitut (Canada), we might have difficulties in finding stimuli that are equally common and appropriate in the three societies and ecosystems. Another example is if we want to test children's understanding of transitivity comparing Russian with English and other languages we need to be aware that case marking of objects in Russian is different for masculine animate nouns than for masculine inanimate nouns; neuter nouns and feminine nouns have yet another ending. The researcher must decide which gender groups to use. If all gender/animate combinations are included, the number of items to test will be large and the task may be too long for young children. However, to restrict the stimuli to one case would render the data not representative.

Thus it can be a challenge to control the conditions without biasing the results. It is less difficult to conduct an experiment across closely related languages and cultures than in unrelated languages or very different cultures. This does not mean that typological/crosscultural research is impossible but it is important to be aware of introducing potential biases that are unrelated to the research questions.

We expect that a situation is understood more or less in a similar enough way. However an important point to keep in mind is that there are cultural differences. As Greenfield (1997) has argued, in order to use a test developed for one culture in another, the cultures must share values, knowledge and communication. For example, there needs to be agreement on the merit of particular responses to particular questions. In addition, we cannot assume a universal function of questions; testing a child on something for which we know the answer may not be appropriate. Also, knowledge may be held jointly in some cultures so it will not be culturally appropriate to test an individual; a group session would be more appropriate.

Further, the context for an experiment is always quite specific and does not necessarily translate to other linguistic contexts (Stoll 2005, Tardif *et al.* 1999) or performance in general (Richards 1994). Depending on the exact design, the stimuli and the procedure, very different results can be obtained as shown for instance by various results on the acquisition of the transitive construction in English (Abbot-Smith & Tomasello 2006).

The goal of longitudinal naturalistic acquisition studies is to gain a representative sample of the language of a child or a group of children and the linguistic context over a specific developmental period. These data constitute an important resource. The main advantage is that we obtain spontaneous speech samples. However, one of the problems is that the resources required are extensive. In addition, the time commitment is huge; data need to be transcribed, translated with glosses for morphemes and also coded so that patterns of development can be analysed. This requires the help of research assistants who are native speakers of the language.

There are several questions that need to be decided in developing such a project: How many children to record? With whom to record them? In which situations? At what time of the day? At what intervals? With or without observer? Are there siblings and will they be in the recording? Answers to these questions have a direct influence on the sample of speech obtained (Hoff-Ginsberg 1991). Three issues are of particular relevance. First, small samples make generalizations to the population problematic, especially since there is variability in how children develop (Bates *et al.* 1988, Lieven 1997, Lieven, Pine & Barnes 1992). With only a small sample, there is no way of knowing what the normal range of development is. Second, the density of sampling can influence the results. Since the frequency of occurrence of linguistic structures varies, the frequency of sampling influences the probability of how often a linguistic feature will be encountered. Thus, if we are interested in a rarely occurring linguistic feature, we might severely underestimate the age of emergence just because our sample is not dense enough (Tomasello & Stahl 2004). Third, the situation in which the sampling occurs influences the data obtained (Hoff Ginsberg 1991). Bornstein and colleagues (Bornstein *et al.* 2000, 2002) found that the recording situation strongly affects children's output. Children acquiring English were more likely to produce longer utterances if they are recorded at a time that the mother judged would provide an optimal sample of speech than when, for example, the child plays by herself with the mother nearby. In order to make generalizations, we need to have an overall picture of the typical day of a child and choose contexts which best allow for comparisons across cultures. Fourth, the interpretation of the child data requires that we know how the output of the child correlates with the input of the caretakers (Stoll & Gries in press). In addition we need methods to compare the data of children learning different languages meaningfully and these methods still need to be developed. This is an important task of future research.

6.5   Child Language Data Exchange System

An important source of data from a variety of languages was developed in the early 1980s by Brian MacWhinney and Catherine Snow; this is the Child Language Data Exchange System project (CHILDES). CHILDES provides a series of tools to transcribe and analyse data to facilitate empirical language acquisition research. It hosts corpora on about thirty languages. English is the best represented language with several corpora that are morphologically glossed. Three other languages, Irish (Guilfoyle), Sesotho (Demuth) and Indonesian (Gil), are represented by corpora that are translated and morphologically glossed for both child and interactors (Indonesian and Sesotho) and for the child only (Irish). In addition, CHILDES contains corpora of five languages, which are glossed but not translated, and there are corpora of three languages, which are translated but not glossed. All other corpora of the remaining languages are transcripts only.

The lack of glossing and translation limits the way the data can be used for analysis since quantitative analysis is limited to orthographically identifiable structures. For typological work, glossing and translations are required. Given the amount of resources needed to build up a transcribed, translated and glossed longitudinal corpus, it is clear why not all the corpora in CHILDES have been glossed and translated yet. However, the data available help in making crosslinguistic and typological comparisons possible. The data is free for researchers to access as are the tools available for analysis.

6.6   Typological studies of language acquisition

Slobin (1997d) called the two major ways of engaging in typological language acquisition studies based on the sampling of languages intra-typological and cross-typological. To avoid confusion with the term 'cross-linguistic studies', I will use the standard terms used in typology, namely intra-genealogical studies for studies which compare languages within language families and inter-genealogical for studies which investigate the acquisition of a feature across language families. I focus only on studies here that were designed as typological studies thus excluding studies that evaluate very different data sets.

6.6.1   Intra-genealogical studies

Since the grammars of closely related languages usually do not differ as strongly as grammars of unrelated languages we can hold several variables constant, which potentially otherwise might influence our results. Intra-genealogical studies (e.g. Smoczynska 1985, Strömqvist *et al.* 1995) also constitute an important basis for inter-genealogical studies.

To illustrate how intra-genealogical studies operate I present the findings of a recent study of early verb forms in five Mayan languages (Pye *et al.* 2007). The key feature in this study is that the same method of analysing longitudinal data is used in all five languages. The study starts from the observation that children learning Quiche, Q'anjob'al and Yukatek produce many more combinations of verb root plus suffixes than children learning Tzeltal and Tzotzil, who produce a high proportion of bare verb roots. Even though the morphology of the languages is similar, there are differences in the position of some affixes, such as the position of an affix that marks verb transitivity and mood, and there are other differences in the structure of the inflectional paradigms. These fine-grained differences make the comparisons of early verb forms in these languages a natural experiment. The data for comparison are early verb forms occurring in natural speech, and a

sample of child-directed speech. A range of factors in the input were correlated with the use of bare verb forms in the children's data. The factors
include: the frequency of verbs occurring without prefixes, verbs in
sentence-initial position, the number of imperatives used, and what are
called 'right-edge factors', that is, the frequency of occurrence of verb
forms without suffixes at the right edge of a sentence. The main significant
factor turns out to be the frequency with which adults produce verb forms at
the right edge of words and sentences. Contexts vary significantly in the five
languages in which the verb root can occur without an overt suffix. In Tzeltal
and Tzotzil verb roots can appear simultaneously at the right edge of the verb
stem and the right edge of the sentence. In the other three languages the verb
root only occurs at the right edge of the verb stem but not at the end of the
sentence because these have status suffixes that need to appear at the right
sentence edge. The study shows that if the researchers had restricted their
analysis to Tzeltal and Tzotzil, they would have concluded that children are
drawn to the 'semantic kernels' of verbs. However, the results from Quiche,
Yukatek and Q'anjob'al show that the input influences why Tzeltal and
Tzotzil children favour the extraction of verb roots (Pye *et al.* 2007). This
study exemplifies how intra-genealogical studies can reach a high level of
precision in testing variables in closely related languages.

6.6.2 Inter-genealogical studies

In inter-genealogical studies, features are investigated independent of
language families. Studies of this type range from small-scale studies
including two languages to larger studies with a number of languages.
Such typological studies provide in-depth insights into how children
acquiring different languages compare in the acquisition of a specific
feature (e.g. Allen *et al.* 2006, Bowerman *et al.* 1995, Imai & Gentner 1997,
Johnston & Slobin 1979). A key characteristic here is the justification for
the choice of languages. The choice of languages depends on the variables
a researcher is interested in.

A discussion of Slobin's typological study of motion verbs (Slobin 1997d),
which is part of a larger typological study on narratives (Berman & Slobin
1994), illustrates this kind of research. The study was influenced by Talmy's
(1985) typology of the way languages code path and manner of movement.
On the one hand, there are what he calls 'verb-framed' languages, which
encode paths by the verb, and leave out the manner of the motion completely or express it in a complement (typically a gerund), e.g. Spanish *salió
(corriendo)* 'he exited (running)'. The other type of motion verbs are what
Talmy calls 'satellite-framed' languages, where the verb root expresses
manner of motion and particles (adpositions, adverbs) are used to express
the path; e.g. *She ran out of the house.* In Slobin's study the languages were
chosen depending on the way they express motion. The use of motion
verbs was then investigated in a narrative experiment with a picture book

without words as a stimulus (*Frog, Where are you*?, Mayer 1969). The experiment was conducted with English, German, Spanish, Turkish and Hebrew-speaking children. In comparing the narratives of children learning verb-framed and satellite-framed languages, distinct styles emerged. English children, for instance, devoted more narrative attention to the dynamics of movement along a path because of the availability of verbs of motion that trace out detailed paths in relation to ground elements. This is shown in the number of different verb types used in the two languages. English children used many more verb types expressing motion than did Spanish children. Spanish speakers, by contrast, gave relatively more attention to static scene setting (Slobin 1997d). This dichotomy was later extended to a third group of languages, where manner and path were balanced across different parts of speech (Thai, Warlpiri and several other languages of different families, see Strömqvist & Verhoeven 2004). The inclusion of a wider range of languages helped develop theories about linguistic categories and also about the acquisition of these categories.

6.7   Conclusions

The past few decades have seen considerable progress in the study of language acquisition across a wide range of languages, including some endangered languages such as Tzeltal, Tzotzil, Yukatec and Inuktitut. This research is a pressing task because more than half of the approximately 7,000 languages (and thus linguistic diversity) are severely endangered. Language acquisition research of little-known languages requires extensive collaboration with field linguists and social anthropologists. This makes typological language acquisition resource intensive. However, it is only by conducting such research that our understanding of the diversity of human language and the effect of this diversity on language acquisition can be fully understood.

Suggestions for further reading

Berman, R. A., & Slobin, D. I. (1994). *Relating Events in Narrative: A Crosslinguistic Developmental Study*. Hillsdale, NJ: Lawrence Erlbaum Associates.

Bowerman, M., & Brown, P. (Eds.). (2007). *Crosslinguistic Perspectives on Argument Structure: Implications for Learnability*. Mahwah, NJ: Lawrence Erlbaum Associates.

Pye, C., Pfeiler, B., de León, L., Brown, P., & Mateo, P. (2007), Roots or Edges? Explaining variation in children's early verb forms in five Mayan languages. In B. Pfeiler (Ed.), *Learning Indigenous Languages: Child Language Acquisition in Mesoamerica* (pp. 15–47). Berlin: Mouton de Gruyter.

Slobin, D. I. (Ed.). (1985–1995). *The Crosslinguistic Study of Language Acquisition*. (Vols. 1–5). Mahwah, NJ: Lawrence Erlbaum Associates.

Part II

Early developments

7

Speech perception

Suzanne Curtin
Dan Hufnagle

7.1   Introduction

Prior to the onset of productive language, infants demonstrate a range of speech perception abilities. Their ability to perceive numerous speech sounds, segment speech, learn frequent patterns and hone in on the appropriate linguistic units for the ambient language is impressive. Speech perception research has revealed that these abilities not only provide the basis for learning native-language sound categories, but also the basis for learning syllable structure and segmenting and storing words. Early preferences for speech over other environmental sounds and for infant-directed speech over adult-directed speech help guide infants' attention to the relevant information in the speech input. These prelinguistic speech perception abilities demonstrated in infancy result in a strong foundation for later language development. In this chapter we will focus on early infant speech perception abilities and discuss how speech perception shapes early word learning and the linguistic categories that emerge from the growing lexicon.

The chapter begins with an overview of infants' perceptual abilities at birth. We then provide a review of language-general speech perception capabilities demonstrated by infants over the first few months of life. This is followed by a discussion of the ways in which infant speech perception abilities change as a result of experience with the target language. We then review findings exploring how infants use different properties of language input to find and identify words in the speech stream. By the time infants are 12 months of age they have learned a great deal about sound categories and what constitutes a word. We provide a review of how learning about sounds and words influences early word–object associations. We complete the chapter by discussing various theoretical approaches that have been proposed to account for speech perception development and early word learning.

7.2   Perceptual abilities at birth

Prior to birth, infants' speech perception is shaped by experience. Neonates exhibit changes in sucking behaviour depending on whether the infants hear stories that were read by their mothers during the last few weeks of pregnancy or whether they hear novel stories (DeCasper & Spence 1986). Newborns also prefer their mother's voice to the voices of other females (DeCasper & Fifer 1980). They prefer to listen to infant-directed speech (Cooper & Aslin 1990), which has higher pitch, longer vowels, wider pitch variation and increased rhythmicity compared to adult-directed speech (Fernald 1985, Werker & McLeod 1989).

A useful and potentially necessary starting point for infants is the ability to separate speech sounds from non-speech sounds, and it has been proposed that there is an initial bias for listening to speech over other types of sounds (Jusczyk 1997). Indeed, newborns listen longer to speech than to non-speech sounds that are matched in complexity and spectral frequency (Vouloumanos & Werker 2007). These early preferences and biases allow the infant to direct attention to certain properties of the speech signal thereby facilitating language acquisition.

Exposure to speech at these very early stages activates specialized areas of the brain (Dehaene-Lambertz & Peña 2001). Optical imaging studies with neonates reveal greater activity in the left hemisphere than the right when presented with normal forward speech but not when backward speech is presented (Peña *et al.* 2003). Studies using functional magnetic resonance imaging (fMRI) reveal distinct patterns of activation to the two types of speech (Dehaene-Lambertz *et al.* 2002). The results of these studies suggest that some of the basic psychoacoustic and cognitive capabilities that are essential for speech perception are available to the infant at or just before birth. However, these capabilities are not necessarily unique to humans. Non-human primates demonstrate similar abilities, suggesting reliance on general processes of the primate auditory system (Ramus *et al.* 2000, Tincoff *et al.* 2005).

Young infants demonstrate the ability to discriminate different speech sounds. Discrimination of stop consonants has been demonstrated in newborns by heart-rate deceleration (Lecanuet *et al* 1995). Newborns can discriminate some vowel categories, as indicated by event-related potential research (Cheour-Luhtanen *et al.* 1995). Within a few months, they are able to discriminate vowels that are not phonemically distinguished in the native language (Swoboda *et al.* 1976, Trehub 1976) and discriminate some vowels that are acoustically quite similar (Marean *et al.* 1992). Asymmetries in vowel perception have been observed in discrimination tasks. Newborns use the most extreme 'point' vowels in the vowel space (e.g. /i/ and /u/) as reference anchors. This results in reduced discrimination for vowels that are close to the point vowels in phonetic space (e.g. /I/ and /U/) when the point vowel is presented first and used for comparison. The non-point vowel is subsumed into the point vowel category. This does not happen, however, when the non-point vowel is the standard (Polka & Bohn 2003).

Categorical perception of consonants has been shown in young infants using high-amplitude sucking procedures (Bertoncini *et al.* 1987) and by event-related potentials recorded from the scalp in 3 month olds (Dehaene-Lambertz & Gliga 2004). Seminal work examining categorical perception found that infants discriminate consonant tokens if they are pulled from either side of the adult voice onset time (VOT) category boundary (e.g. /ba/ from /pa/), but do not discriminate two tokens from within one side of the category boundary (Aslin *et al.* 1981, Eimas *et al.* 1971). However, research with 3–4 month olds has shown graded, within-category perception of VOT under different testing conditions (Miller & Eimas 1996). Specifically, when infants are familiarized with the prototypical exemplar and then tested on a non-prototypical member of a category, discrimination is difficult. However, when familiarized with the non-prototype and then presented with the prototype, discrimination of VOT is observed. This ability to discriminate within-category tokens persists to 8 months (McMurray & Aslin 2005). These findings suggest that although categorical perception may be the most easily revealed, within-category sensitivity is also possible.

Infants demonstrate discrimination of consonants in the ambient language as well as contrasts that occur in other languages (see Saffran *et al.* 2006 for a review). Kikuyu-learning infants of 4 months of age can discriminate the voicing contrast (ba vs. pa) found in English, but not in Kikuyu (Streeter 1976). Guatemalan infants at 4.5 to 6 months old are also able to discriminate the English voicing contrast but, surprisingly, not the voicing contrast found in their native Spanish language (Lasky *et al.* 1975), which employs a different voicing distinction than English (Lisker & Abramson 1967). One explanation for this finding is that the English voicing contrast is aligned with a language-general voicing boundary (Jusczyk 1997). Infants learning a language such as Spanish where the voicing distinction does not align with this general boundary must reset or shift their perceptual categories (Aslin & Pisoni 1980). Experience with the target language will provide appropriate information about the relevant speech sound contrasts for the language.

Many of the studies exploring discrimination of consonants and vowels present the contrast in single syllable units (e.g. /ba/). Infants can, however, perceive some phonetic contrasts in multisyllabic strings in initial position (**b**ada vs. **g**ada) as well as in medial position (da**b**a vs. da**g**a) (Jusczyk & Thompson 1978). Within these longer sequences, infants are also sensitive to a number of prosodic cues, such as vowel duration (Eilers *et al.* 1984) and pitch peaks (Bull *et al.* 1984). Infants demonstrate great sensitivity to prosodic information, especially rhythmicity. Newborns discriminate languages from different rhythmical classes (Mehler & Christophe 1995,

Mehler *et al.* 1988, Nazzi *et al.* 1998). By 2–4 months infants are able to discriminate languages from within a single rhythmical class (e.g. English and Dutch), and soon after begin to discriminate between two dialects from within the same language (e.g. American and British English; for a review, see Nazzi & Ramus 2003). The ability to discriminate languages based on rhythmic class helps to lay the foundation for speech segmentation by highlighting units for segmentation.

7.3   Learning language-specific sound categories

Infants are able to perceive a number of speech contrasts from birth, but these contrasts may not correspond with the speech sound contrasts that are used by the individual languages that the infants are learning. Before 6 months of age, infants discriminate a range of consonant and vowel contrasts present in their native language as well as contrasts found in other languages. Listening experience over the first year of life leads to improved discrimination for more difficult phonetic distinctions in the native language (Kuhl *et al.* 2006, Polka *et al.* 2001). Experience with the ambient language also leads to a decline in the ability to discriminate non-native contrasts.

Unlike young infants, adults fail to discriminate similar sounds that are not part of their native language inventory (Pisoni & Lively 1995). Pioneering work by Werker and Tees (1984) documented the rapid decline of this ability at the end of the first year of life. They compared Hindi- and English-speaking adults' and 6 to 12 month olds' discrimination of the Hindi retroflex-dental /da/–/Da/ place distinction and the voiceless aspirated-breathy voiced /tʰa/–/dʰa/ distinction. Predictably, Hindi-speaking adults discriminated minimal pairs better than English-speaking adults. However, 6- to 8-month-old English learners also discriminated the Hindi contrasts. On the other hand, 10 to 12 month olds performed like English-speaking adults and failed to discriminate (Werker 1989, Werker & Tees 1984). Listening experience in one's native language triggers this decline in the ability to perceive non-native distinctions. This pattern of decline has been replicated in a number of distinctions using the Conditioned Head Turn procedure (Anderson *et al.* 2003, Pegg & Werker 1997, Werker & Lalonde 1988), the Visual Habituation discrimination task (Best *et al.* 1995), and event-related potential research (Cheour *et al.* 1998b, Kuhl & Coffey-Corrina 2001, Rivera-Gaxiola *et al.* 2003).

This reorganization of perceptual abilities, where native-language contrasts are preserved and non-native contrasts are lost, occurs earlier for vowels than consonants. As with consonant perception, infants are able to discriminate across a range of vowel categories within the first few months of life. However, by 6 months of age infants already appear to be less sensitive to non-native vowel contrasts. For example, Kuhl and colleagues (1992) observed a language-specific perceptual bias when testing within-vowel-category discrimination with English and Swedish 6-month-old infants, in which non-prototypical (i.e. non-native) vowels were perceived as part of the native language category. Polka and Werker (1994) found that English-learning 4-month-old infants could discriminate non-English vowel contrasts found in German, whereas 6 to 8 month olds showed more sensitivity to English than German contrasts, and 10- to 12-month-old infants were unable to discriminate the German contrasts. In a follow-up study, Polka and Bohn (1996) found that although infants at all of the ages tested (4–12 months) could discriminate all vowel contrasts presented (native and non-native), an asymmetry was observed by 6 months of age with native prototypical vowels affecting the perception of non-prototypical vowels. The reason for the earlier reorganization of the perceptual space of vowels might be because vowels carry much of the basic prosodic information that infants are attracted to in early infancy (Fernald 1992, Mehler *et al.* 1988).

The functional reorganization from language-general to language-specific speech perception (Werker 1995) is clearly evident in infants who are raised in a monolingual environment. Infants in bilingual environments demonstrate a unique developmental trajectory when tuning to the categories of their native languages. Catalan, Spanish and Catalan–Spanish bilingual infants were tested on their discrimination of the vowel distinction /e/–/E/ (as in /dethi/ and /dEthi/) that is used in Catalan but not in Spanish (Bosch & Sebastián-Gallés 2003). All three groups discriminated the /e/–/E/ contrast at 4 months of age. The Spanish monolingual infants stopped discriminating it at 8 months, but the Catalan monolingual group continued discrimination. The bilinguals failed at discrimination at 8 months, but demonstrated success at discrimination once again at 12 months of age, resulting in a U-shaped developmental pattern for discrimination. This finding with bilinguals suggests that listening experience alone does not result in maintenance of a distinction. Further support comes from a study with French- and English-learning infants (Burns *et al.* 2003). Infants were tested on their ability to discriminate both the French phonemic voice–voiceless contrast (/ba/–/pa/) and the English phonemic voice–voiceless contrast (/ba/–/pa/, but phonetically [pa]-[pʰa]). By 10–12 months of age the French infants were better at discriminating the French distinction than the English one. Similarly, the English infants at this age were better at discriminating the English than the French contrast. However, like the Spanish–Catalan 8 month olds, the bilingual English–French infants failed to show evidence of discriminating either contrast at 10–12 months. Further tests with 17–20-month-old bilingual infants revealed two distinct patterns of discrimination: half of the older bilingual infants successfully discriminated both the French and the English contrasts, and half the infants only discriminated one or the other. These results suggest that many bilingual infants are dominant in one of their languages from infancy.

The age at which perception becomes language-specific is not the same for all speech sound contrasts. When this happens for a specific contrast depends on a number of variables. The salience of a particular contrast likely plays a role. Support for this comes from the fact that vowel perception becomes language-specific a few months earlier than consonant perception (Kuhl *et al.* 1992, Polka & Werker 1994). Moreover, acoustically quite distinct contrasts that lie completely outside the phonological space of the native language (e.g. click contrasts) may continue to be discriminated even without listening experience (Best *et al.* 1988). Frequency also plays an important role. Infants stop discriminating two non-native phones that are variants of a single highly frequent native phone at a younger age than they do variants of a less frequent native phone (Anderson *et al.* 2003). While these factors contribute to when language-specific perception for a specific contrast may arise, how this reorganization might be accomplished remains unclear.

Stochastic processes and similarity metrics have been proposed to explain perceptual reorganization. An artificial language learning study by Maye *et al.* (2002) tested whether or not statistical learning may play a role in phonetic category reorganization. Two groups of infants were familiarized to different distributions of eight tokens of /da/ spanning a continuum from [da] to the unaspirated, voiceless [ta]. All infants heard all eight tokens, but one group heard a distribution of stimuli that corresponded to a single phonetic category, and the other group heard a distribution of stimuli that corresponded to two categories. Infants in the two-category group were better able to discriminate the endpoint stimuli (e.g. the most extreme /da/ and /ta/ stimuli) than were infants in the one-category group even though those tokens were equally frequent across groups (see also Maye & Weiss 2003).

Distributional learning has also been shown to facilitate discrimination of a difficult phonetic contrast when that contrast defines categories that serve a functional role in the native language, such as differentiating between words. Maye *et al.* (2008) demonstrated that exposure to a bimodal distribution in 8-month-old infants' input can lead to increased discrimination of prevoiced /g/ versus short-lag /k/ (unaspirated voiceless) consonants. This exposure also helps with the discrimination of an unfamiliar contrast sharing the same phonetic feature as the contrast presented during familiarization (e.g. /d/–/t/). These findings reveal that infants are sensitive to the frequency distribution of speech sounds in the input and that infants demonstrate sensitivity during the age range in which developmental changes in speech perception are observed. Therefore attention to the statistical distribution of speech sounds in the input is one of the factors driving speech perception reorganization over the first year of life.

7.4   Learning language-specific syllable sequences

During the first year of life, infants not only begin to figure out the specific sound categories of their language, but also the phonotactics. Phonotactics are the language-specific co-occurrences of speech sounds in different syllable positions (*i.e.* 'pt' does not occur word initially in English but can occur at the end of a word, such as *kept*). Cues to phonotactic regularities tend to be probabilistic rather than categorical. For instance, the sequence 'ft' tends to occur more often within a word ('after') than across word boundaries ('off to', 'tough to') (Mattys & Jusczyk 2001a). Similar to findings in phonetic perception (Maye *et al.* 2002), artificial language learning studies have shown that infants use distributional statistics to learn about the phonotactics of the ambient language (Chambers *et al.* 2003, Saffran & Thiessen 2003).

Between 6 and 9 months, infants develop knowledge of phonotactic regularities in their language (Jusczyk *et al.* 1993b). For example, an English-learning infant will listen longer to a word beginning with the legal 'str' sequence than the unacceptable 'rst' sequence and show the opposite pattern for word endings. At 9–10 months infants in a monolingual learning environment show a preference for listening to lists of words that correspond to native language phonotactics (Jusczyk *et al.* 1993b). Bilingual learning infants show a preference by this age for the phonotactic patterns of the dominant language in their input (Bosch & Sebastián-Gallés 2001). Jusczyk *et al.* (1994) found that infant preferences could most parsimoniously be explained by input frequency. When presented with nonsense words with two equally legal phonotactic sequences, infants of 10 months consistently show a preference for the stimuli with the more commonly occurring sequences. Chambers *et al.* (2003) familiarized 16.5 month olds with CVC syllables which had restrictions on which consonants could occur in initial position and which ones could occur in final position (e.g. /bæp/ but not /pæb/). Infants in this study listened longer to novel sequences in the test phase that did not conform to the phonotactic regularities observed in the familiarization phase. Infants demonstrate sensitivity to native language phonotactics, but it is possible to teach infants novel phonotactic patterns.

Recent studies have begun to explore the role of word position in infants' preference for native-language phonotactics. Jusczyk *et al.* (1999c) demonstrated that 9-month-old infants prefer lists of non-words that share common word-initial consonants to lists of non-words with varying word-initial consonants, but they have no preference for lists of non-words that share common word-final consonants. Similarly, Zamuner (2006) found that Dutch 10-month-old infants discriminate voicing and place of articulation contrasts in word-initial position, but fail to discriminate these contrasts in word-final position. Only by 16 months are infants able to discriminate place of articulation contrasts in word-final position, but these infants still fail to discriminate the voicing contrast. Moreover, 9- and 11-month-old Dutch-learning infants show no preference for legal versus illegal voicing phonotactics when this contrast occurs word-finally (Zamuner 2006). These results suggest that early on infants are only sensitive to contrasts and sequences of segments in salient positions. Further support for this comes from Karzon (1985) who demonstrated that 1- to 4-month-old infants are better able to discriminate the middle syllable in *marana* vs. *malana* if it is emphasized with infant-directed prosody. Together, these studies illustrate that infants' speech perception is poorer when contrasts occur in non-initial positions.

Kajikawa and colleagues (2006) explored sensitivity to word-level phonotactic patterns in English and Japanese monolingual infants at the ages of 6, 12 and 18 months. All of the test words in their study were phonotactically legal in English (*neek*, *neeks* and *neekusu*), but only *neekusu* is legal in Japanese. They found that English-learning infants could discriminate between *neek* and *neeks* at 18 months of age, but the Japanese infants could not. At 6 and 12 months, neither the English nor the Japanese infants could discriminate these forms. All infants at all ages could discriminate *neeks* and *neekusu*. However, at 18 months Japanese infants diverged slightly in their discrimination of *neekusu* and *neeks* from the English infants, beginning to treat them similarly, suggesting sensitivity to the legal sound sequences in their native language.

7.5   Finding words

Spoken words do not occur in isolation; rather they form a continuous stream. One of the tasks that infants face is segmenting this continuous stream into smaller units. Research examining speech segmentation has found that infants begin this process between 6 and 8 months of age. Infants use familiar word forms to aid segmentation. If a highly frequent form such as *mummy* precedes an unfamiliar word, then segmentation of the unknown form is facilitated (Bortfeld *et al.* 2005). Support for the role of familiar forms comes from preference studies in which the infant is first familiarized to CVC words (cup) and then presented with passages containing those words at test and also passages containing minimally different foils (tup) (Jusczyk & Aslin 1995). Infants of 7.5 months demonstrated a listening preference for the familiar passages, suggesting they extracted these words from the speech stream.

Familiar words are not enough for infants to excel at segmentation. The number of word forms that any individual infant is familiar with by the time he or she begins segmenting is highly variable. Moreover, even infants who are familiar with a large number of word forms do not know enough of these forms to segment many more words when infants begin segmentation in earnest. For this reason, it is important to examine other information in speech that may help with word segmentation. Several potential cues to word boundaries have been identified, such as prosodic, rhythmic and segmental information, transitional probabilities, phonotactics and stress (see Saffran *et al.* 2006 for a review). All of these cues are part of the distributional properties of the speech input. Eight-month-old infants are able to segment the speech into 'words' using the statistical information available about the co-occurrence of syllables (transitional probabilities) (Saffran *et al.* 1996b). Syllables themselves carry other information, such as phonotactic and prominence information (word stress). Probabilistic information in the form of phonotactics is used for segmentation by 9 months of age. When infants of this age are presented with sequences of consonants that are typically found within a word versus consonant sequences that typically occur across a word boundary, they listened longer to sequences containing the clusters typically occurring within a word (Mattys *et al.* 1999). This suggests that infants have knowledge of which consonant clusters tend to occur with words and those that occur at boundaries.

Infants are sensitive to the alternation of strong and weak syllables at a very young age (Gerken 2004, Mehler & Christophe 1995, Mehler *et al.* 1988, Nazzi *et al.* 1998). English-learning 7.5-month-old infants use strong syllables to determine the presence of certain words in fluent speech (Newsome & Jusczyk 1995). When infants were exposed to strong syllables of two-syllable words, for example 'king' for 'KINGdom' (stressed syllable in all caps), and then passages containing the entire word, the infants did not listen longer to passages that contained the entire word than to passages that contained no familiar targets. Moreover, when infants were exposed first to the passages with the entire word, they did not listen longer to the strong syllable in isolation. Thus, infants were doing more than just matching strong syllables, indicating that they were matching the entire word.

In an artificial language learning task, Curtin *et al.* (2005) exposed 9- and 7-month-old infants to an unparsed speech stream that stressed every third syllable. During test, infants preferred (i.e. listened longer to) sequences that corresponded to an initially stressed sequence from the familiarization phase. This was the case even though all of the test sequences had equally stressed syllables. They further found that when 7-month-old infants segment stress-initial sequences from the speech stream they have a listening preference for items that are identical in their segments and their stress patterns (DObita, DObita) over ones that were segmentally the same but had stress shifted to an adjacent syllable (DObita, doBIta). Taken together, these studies support the claim that stress is a salient cue that can be used by infants to parse the continuous speech stream (Jusczyk *et al.* 1999a).

The items used in the experiments of Curtin and colleagues (2005) and Jusczyk and colleagues (1999a) corresponded to a trochaic pattern (strong–weak stress), and it may be the case that infants were segmenting speech based on the trochaic pattern that is found in their native language. This type of language-specific preference for a particular rhythmic pattern may guide segmentation (Jusczyk *et al.* 1999a, Polka *et al.* 2002). Infants are sensitive to changes in stress patterns between 1 and 4 months of age

(Jusczyk & Thompson 1978), and sometime between 6 and 9 months of age they begin to orient to the predominant stress pattern of the language they are learning (Echols *et al.* 1997, Jusczyk *et al.* 1993b). Infants exposed to a predominately iambic language (wS), such as Canadian French, segment only wS words (Polka *et al.* 2002). When English infants are presented with wS forms, such as 'guiTAR', they misparse iambic wS patterns. Here, they segment 'TAR' as an initial syllable. If 'TAR' is consistently followed by an unstressed word (e.g. *is*), infants treat 'TAR#is' as a single unit (Jusczyk *et al.* 1999a). However, if two strong syllable words are adjacent, as in 'COLD ICE' or 'PACK ASH', then infants do not misparse these sequences as a single unit, and by 11 months, English-learning infants no longer mis-segment wS words (Mattys & Jusczyk 2001a).

The specific dialect of a language that infants are exposed to may also influence segmentation. While 8-month-old infants exposed to Canadian French demonstrate segmentation of wS items (Polka *et al.* 2002), infants of this age who are exposed to European French do not demonstrate segmentation of words (Nazzi *et al.* 2006). Even by 12 months they fail to segment bisyllabic units, but demonstrate evidence of segmenting individual syllables. It is not until 16 months that European French infants are segmenting whole units (Nazzi *et al.*). It is possible that the cues for iambic patterns have different degrees of salience in different dialects. It is also possible that different testing procedures across these studies yield divergent results. Further crosslinguistic and cross-dialectical studies are required to elucidate these findings.

The infant has a number of potential cues available to help segment the speech stream. Not all cues will provide the same information about where a potential word boundary may exist, nor will all cues necessarily be of equal salience. If all these cues are available, the question arises as to which cues might be used more often and when different cues might facilitate segmentation. To address this, Johnson and Jusczyk (2001) pitted coarticulation (information about the effect of an adjacent sound on the production of a speech sound) and stress against transitional probabilities to determine if either one could override the statistical information. They found that both coarticulatory and stress information override transitional probabilities when infants are 8 months of age. However, when transitional probabilities and stress provide conflicting cues to boundaries, infants around 6 months of age pay more attention to transitional probabilities than to stress information (Thiessen & Saffran 2003). Likely the interplay between different cues to segmentation, such as stress and statistical information, changes over the course of development.

7.6   Early word recognition

Infants can recognize the sound patterns of their names as young as 4.5 months (Mandel *et al.* 1995), and by 6 months, they can recognize their names in ongoing speech (Mandel *et al.* 1995, Mandel-Emer 1997). By 11 months of age, French and English infants can recognize frequent familiar words without any training (Hallé & Boysson-Bardies 1994, Vihman *et al.* 2004), but 9 month olds do not. Similar results have been obtained with ERP studies. Infants as young as 11 months demonstrate recognition for familiar word forms, even though they do not necessarily understand these words (Thierry *et al.* 2003). Infants' ability to remember words, whether or not they are tied to meaning, is impressive. Newborns can remember a simple word form for over 24 hours (Swain *et al.* 1993). Jusczyk and Hohne (1997) demonstrated that by 9 months, infants are able to retain the sound patterns of frequently presented words for up to two weeks.

In order to recognize words there needs to be similarity between the word currently being processed and the stored form. However, the degree of required similarity appears to change depending on the age of the child. Recognition at 7 months seems to require segmental information to be an exact match. If there is a change in the initial consonant of the exposure words (*cup* to *tup*), then infants fail to recognize the word (Jusczyk & Aslin 1995, see also Stager & Werker 1997). This is also the case for speaker voice. At 7.5 months there is reduced recognition of a word if it is produced by a speaker with a very different voice (male to female) from the original production (Houston & Jusczyk 2000). Reduced recognition holds even if the voices are both female but with very different voice characteristics, suggesting it is not only gender differences but also the overall degree of differences that influence recognition (Houston & Jusczyk 2003). Lower level cues also affect word recognition. Seven-month-old infants recognize words they have segmented only if they agree in coarticulation information (information concerning the effect of an adjacent sound on the production of a speech sound) (Curtin *et al.* 2001). Word recognition is optimal when all aspects, such as speaker affect, speech rate and pitch, match the form the infant heard during exposure (Singh *et al.* 2004).

Younger infants require information to match between the target word form and the stored one. However, as infants develop, they seem to pay less attention to segmental information. At 9 months infants pay attention to prosodic cues over segmental cues (Mattys *et al.* 1999). At 11 months, if the onset consonant in an unstressed syllable changes (e.g. *canárd* to *ganárd* 'duck') infants treat both words as familiar (Hallé & Boysson-Bardies 1996). This is not the case if the phonetic detail occurs in a stressed syllable. Here, infants tend to treat the mispronounced word as unfamiliar (Vihman *et al.* 2004). Shifting the stress to another syllable in segmentally equivalent forms diminishes word recognition for 7-month-old infants (Curtin *et al.* 2005), but it does not affect word recognition at 11 months (Vihman *et al.* 2004). In tasks measuring memory for familiar words, infants older than 11 months begin to place more importance on segmental phonetic information than on suprasegmental and indexical (e.g. speaker voice, affect) cues. Infants will now recognize a word even when affect, gender and other such cues are varied (Singh *et al.* 2004). By the end of the first year, infants are learning what information is important for word recognition. The linguistic knowledge gained during this time provides the foundation for building a lexicon. Learning the relationship between sound patterns and meaning is not an easy task, but with stored word forms, the infant can begin the process of mapping words to meaning (Jusczyk 1997).

At the initial stages of word learning, detailed information about the word form is stored. Evidence for this stems from word recognition tasks using familiar objects and familiar words. Data using a two-choice visual fixation paradigm indicates that infants of 14 to 23 months, when presented with a display of two known objects, will shift their gaze and look longer towards a target object (e.g. a baby) when they hear its correct pronunciation as opposed to a close, but incorrect, pronunciation (e.g. *vaby*; Swingley & Aslin 2000, 2002). While overall word familiarity influences recognition, the effect is also observed for recently acquired words (Bailey & Plunkett 2002). It has been argued that neighbourhood density may play a role as well because it is difficult to learn a new word (e. g. *gall*) that is similar to a well-known word (*ball*), even at 20 months (Swingley & Aslin 2000). This is further supported by eye-tracking studies that have found that 24 month olds respond more quickly when distinguishing words that differ in all segments (*dog* vs. *tree*) than to ones with much overlap in their segments (*dog* vs. *doll*) suggesting infants are attending to word-initial information (Swingley *et al.* 1999). Moreover, infants at 18–20 months look just as quickly and reliably to the appropriate object when presented with partial words as they do when presented with the entire word (e.g. *baby* [bey] and [beybi]; Fernald *et al.* 2001).

7.7   Early word–object associative learning

When infants first begin to map words onto concepts, they need to hold in memory information about the sound pattern of the word and link that sound pattern to the concept. Research examining infants' discrimination and categorization of speech sounds has demonstrated that reorganization and fine-tuning of phonetic categories takes place over the first 12 months of life (see Saffran *et al.* 2006 for a review). Is the phonetic knowledge accrued over this time available to guide early word learning? To address this question, Werker and colleagues (1998) outlined an associative word-learning task known as the Switch task to test whether infants use phonetic detail to direct word learning. In this task, infants are presented with two word–object pairings. For half the trials they see Object A paired with spoken Word A, and on the other half of the trials infants see Object B paired with Word B. Infants are habituated to these pairings, and once their looking time declines by a preset amount the test phase begins. Infants are presented with two types of test trials. 'Same' trials are made up of the appropriate pairing between a familiar word and familiar object (e.g. Word A and Object A). 'Switch' trials contain a familiar word and a familiar object, but with a mismatch in the pairing (e.g. Object A with Word B). If the infant has learned to associate the words with their appropriate objects, they should be surprised when there is a mismatch in the pairing. As a result, they should look longer during the Switch than the Same trial. If they have only learned the words and objects, but have not associated them with one another, then there should be no difference in looking times for either type of test trial. Infants of 14 months, but not younger, can learn words and the appropriate association with their objects in this procedure as long as the objects are moving (Werker *et al.* 1998), and if the newly learned words are phonetically dissimilar (e.g. [lɪf] and [nim]) (Stager & Werker 1997).

It is not until infants are 17 months of age that they can succeed at this task if the words are phonetically similar as in, [bɪ]/[dɪ], even though younger infants can discriminate these syllables in a simple discrimination task (Stager & Werker 1997). To account for these findings, Stager and Werker proposed a 'resource limitation' explanation. They suggested that infants 14 months of age fail in this task because they are not yet accomplished word learners. In other words, the computational demands required for linking words and object hinder their ability to attend to and access the phonetic detail that distinguishes between words.

This finding has been demonstrated across a number of studies using a range of contrasts (Pater *et al.* 2004). One manipulation presented the [b]–[d] contrast in an appropriate word form such as [bɪn] vs. [dɪn]. Still, infants of 14 months failed in this condition. Even if the acoustic salience of the contrast is increased infants continue to fail at this task. Indeed, infants of 14 months also fail on the potentially less confusable voicing distinction [bɪn]–[pʰɪn] and on a voicing + place distinction, [pʰɪn]–[dɪn] (Pater *et al.* 2004). In a task in which infants physically manipulated and grouped objects with the same labels together, infants of 20 months failed to learn words that differ minimally in only their word-medial vowel, even when acoustically quite distinct vowels were used (Nazzi 2005). In contrast, findings by Curtin and colleagues (submitted) suggest that 15-month-old infants are able to learn novel words that differ only in one vowel sound in a Switch task. They argue that richer acoustic properties of vowels facilitate infants' performance with these similar-sounding words, but that not all contrasts will be equally discriminable. Infants only succeeded in utilizing the vowel pair that was distinguished by the first formant and failed with vowel pairs that were distinguished by the second formant. These results demonstrate that infants initially use some acoustic cues before others and do so before they use consonant features.

Support for the resource limitation explanation comes from findings where infants of 14 months with particularly large vocabularies successfully notice a switch (Werker *et al.* 2002a, Werker & Fennell 2004). Their success is presumably due to the fact that they are more accomplished word learners. The resource limitation hypothesis has been further elaborated in a series of studies that demonstrated that if the cognitive demands required of the task are lessened by presenting infants with minimally different known words (e.g. 'ball' [bal] vs. 'doll' [dal], which are minimal pairs in many North American dialects), then 14 month olds succeed (Fennell & Werker 2003). Additionally, when the load is reduced by increasing object familiarity by simply allowing the infant to interact with an object over a period of weeks without it being given a label, infants of 14 months are able to learn minimally different words (Fennell 2004). In tasks where the labels of known objects are mispronounced, researchers have found that infants as young as 14 months detect subtle phonetic differences (Bailey & Plunkett 2002, Fennell & Werker 2003, Swingley & Aslin 2002). Furthermore, when learning two new words, infants of 14 months are able to notice mismatches in word–object pairings if the demands of the task are lessened by providing infants with pictures of both referents simultaneously (Ballem & Plunkett 2005).

In a series of studies, Thiessen (2007) explored whether contexts in which children have heard the relevant, phonetically similar contrasts is a factor in their ability to succeed in this word-learning task. More specifically, Thiessen tested a distributional account, which predicts that children will use phonetic contrasts when they experience the two phones in very distinct contexts. For example, since [da] and [tʰa] are very similar contexts, they form a dense neighbourhood. However, if infants encounter these forms in lexical contexts that contain greater phonetic variability, perhaps the phonetically similar words that are differentiated by the /d/–/t/ contrast would be less likely to interfere. To test this hypothesis, Thiessen (2007) familiarized 15 to 16 month olds with three word–object pairings: the novel word *daw* paired with a novel object, *dawbow* paired with another novel object, and *tawgoo* also paired with a novel object. In the Same trial, infants saw the appropriate pairing of *daw* with its object. In the Switch trial, the *daw* object was paired with *taw*. If distributional information in the form of lexical context plays a role in allowing children to use phonetic contrasts, then they should reliably notice a switch, and indeed, 15 to 16 month olds are successful. While more exposure is not enough to reduce resource demands (Thiessen 2007), prior exposure, such as hearing sequences in a word segmentation task, which require the infant to pull word-like units from the continuous speech stream, can help infants learn word–object associations at 17 months (Graf Estes *et al.* 2007a).

The results of these studies suggest that there are a number of factors involved in early word learning. The specific contrast being tested, whether a consonant or a vowel, will influence the outcome. Task differences suggest that infants store the information about sound sequences that make up the word, but access to that information depends on whether the infant is performing a recognition task or a retrieval task and also depends on whether or not the infant is familiar with one or more of the words. Additionally, more experienced word learners successfully notice minimally differing word pairs. Thus, while the overall picture is complex, infants are clearly able to store information about the sound sequences that make up words and match these sequences to meaning. While there may be instances where they do not detect fine phonetic details, infants are successfully learning about meaningful words.

7.8   Theoretical approaches

Aslin and Pisoni (1980) outlined four possible models for the development of speech perception. The universal model argues that infants are born with sensitivities to native and non-native phonetic contrasts, and experience functions to only maintain the existing built-in sensitivities. Without experience, sensitivities to non-native contrasts will be lost. Similarly, the attunement model argues that while biases exist at birth, experience functions to shape them more precisely and ultimately to converge on the adult categories. The ability to discriminate contrasts is driven by experience according to the perceptual learning model. The overall rate of development is dependent on frequency of contrasts in the language input, the acoustic discriminability of contrasts, and the infant's attention. Finally, the maturational theory argues that development occurs following a predetermined schedule. In this case, whether or not a child can discriminate a contrast is completely independent of experience. No model by itself can account for all of the findings related to developmental speech perception, nor can one alone account for other speech developments occurring over the first two years of life.

Other models of developmental speech perception have been proposed to explain general and language-specific perception of speech sounds. Two specific models are the Perceptual Assimilation Model (PAM, Best 1994, Best & McRoberts 2003) and the Native Language Magnet model (NLM, Kuhl 1993). PAM provides a 'direct realist' account of native and non-native speech perception (Best 1994). Young infants perceive speech categorically by recovering information about the distal object from the acoustic signal – specifically information about the vocal tract configuration as represented in gestural phonology (Browman & Goldstein 1986). Non-native speech segments will be perceived according to how they might be assimilated to native categories (see Best & McRoberts 2003, for an extension of PAM). Non-native sounds will be discriminated if they are assimilated into two different native language speech categories, but if the non-native sounds are assimilated to a single native language category, they will not be discriminable.

Acoustic cues, rather than vocal tract gestures, are the source of information available to the listener according to the NLM (Kuhl 1993). NLM categories emerge in multidimensional space, and initially, this type of category structure results in asymmetries in discrimination. Frequently heard instances emerge as new prototypes of categories, which then redefine or even merge initial categories (Kuhl 1993, 2004). Studies with infants demonstrate that these best instances of a phonetic category act as perceptual magnets and pull nearby tokens into their perceptual space. Thus perceptual asymmetries are evident as poorer performance if a prototype of the category is used as a standard in a discrimination task.

Both of these models focus exclusively on the development of sound categories and do not focus on the role of speech perception in word learning. A unified account of how language experience affects perception of native-language sound categories and word recognition in infancy was proposed by Jusczyk (1997). According to WRAPSA (word recognition and phonetic structure acquisition), as the acoustic signal enters the auditory system a set of 'auditory analysers' provides a description of the signal. Over the course of acquisition, the output of the auditory analyser is weighted to give prominence to features that are required for contrasting different words. Once the signal is weighted, pattern extraction takes place. At this time, the signal is segmented into units that temporally group together prominent features into syllabic units. WRAPSA assumes that infants first have access to prosodic information, then syllabic, and only later on in development do they have access to phonetic information. In order to recognize words, representations act as probes. If a close match is obtained between a probe and an existing representation of a known word, then the word is recognized and its meaning (if represented) is accessed. If no match can be found, the probe will either be reprocessed or stored as a new entry with or without meaning.

PRIMIR (Processing Rich Information from Multidimensional Interactive Representations) is a new theoretical framework (Werker & Curtin 2005). PRIMIR utilizes the fact that there is rich information available in the speech input, and claims that infants can pick up this information and organize it along a number of multidimensional interactive planes. Access to information depends on the joint activity of three dynamic filters: initial biases (such as preferences for speech over non-speech), developmental level of the child and requirements of the task the infant is facing. These filters work together to direct attention to one plane (or more).

PRIMIR assumes that the same general statistical learning mechanisms are operating over different levels of analysis simultaneously. Thus, prosodic analysis, segmentation of the speech stream, extraction of syllables, forming phonetic categories and storing word forms happen simultaneously, with each level further influencing the category formation and the information pickup at all other levels. Categories of all types will emerge based first on natural clusters that become reweighted and reorganized as a function of listening experience and perceptual learning. This results in language-specific phonetic and indexical categories and a preference for frequent phonotactic sequences and stress patterns. All this information is used to segment words from the speech stream and recognize word forms. Word forms are sequences that have been identified as possible lexical candidates that eventually or simultaneously become linked to meaning. Within the PRIMIR framework, they are stored as exemplars.

The earliest representations are richly detailed and encode phonetic and indexical information. Over time, with the establishment of a sufficient vocabulary containing multiple phonological contrasts in multiple positions, more abstract phonemic representations emerge. Phonemes may emerge in staggered fashion and will likely be positionally bound at first. Some abstract representations may not be solidified until the child learns to read (Werker & Curtin 2005).

7.9 Challenges

From birth through the first year, infants modify general speech perception abilities to conform to the categories and structures that are relevant to their native language. The field is awash with empirical findings from recent decades, providing great insight into the development of speech perception. Yet it is still just the beginning. Rich information exists in the speech stream, and its statistical patterns allow learners to induce linguistically relevant structure. Some of the information that infants can use is now known, but it is unclear whether this information is necessary or sufficient to account for language development. We still do not know the extent of the information that is available to infants. Another challenge is understanding the interaction of maturation and other developmental events on the kinds of information that infants acquire and use in the development of speech perception.

Suggestions for further reading

Aslin, R. N., & Pisoni, D. B. (1980). Some developmental processes in speech perception. In G. H. Yeni-Komshian, J. F. Kavanagh & C. A. Ferguson (Eds.) *Child Phonology: Vol. 2, Perception* (pp. 67–96). New York: Academic Press.

Jusczyk, P. W. (1997). *The Discovery of Spoken Language*. Cambridge, MA: MIT Press.

Saffran, J. R., Werker, J. F., & Werner, L. (2006). The infant's auditory world: Hearing, speech, and the beginnings of language. In D. Kuhn & R. Siegler (Eds.), *Handbook of Child Psychology: Vol. 2. Cognition, Perception, and Language* (6th edn., pp. 58–108). New York: John Wiley.

Werker, J. F. & Curtin, S. (2005). PRIMIR: A developmental framework of infant speech processing. *Language Learning and Development*, 1(2), 197–234.

Werker, J. F. & Tees, R. C. (1984). Cross-language speech perception: Evidence for perceptual reorganization during the first year of life. *Infant Behavior and Development*, 7, 49–63.

8

Crosslinguistic perspectives on segmentation and categorization in early language acquisition

Barbara Höhle

8.1   Introduction

The previous chapter has shown how infants' speech perception is shaped by the developing phonological system and how this process discharges into the establishment of lexical representations and the processing of content words. The present chapter will follow the issue of interactions of innate processing capacities and the specific requirements of the language to be learned with a specific focus on crosslinguistic research including the initial steps infants take to enter the specific morphosyntactic system of the target language.

One of the fascinating questions of language acquisition research concerns the nature of the interplay of innate prerequisites the child brings to solve this task and the impact of the different conditions of experience provided by the child's exposure to one or more language(s) and their specific structural features. Language acquisition is a developmental area in which the target of the learning process is the subject of multiple variations. Even though the crosslinguistic variation can be described within a restricted set of dimensions or parameters that constrain the grammatical options a language can take (Chomsky 1981), we have to assume that the learning mechanisms involved are characterized by at

I thank Jürgen Weissenborn for his long-lasting cooperation in our common research on the early acquisition of function words and for his comments on an earlier version of this contribution. The research cited in this paper was supported by several grants by the German Science Foundation (DFG HO 1960/5–1/2; HO 1960/6–2; HO1960/8–1). Last but not least, I thank my colleagues from the Special Research Cluster Information Structure (SFB 632). The possibility for the cooperative work in this framework sharpened my view on crosslinguistic variation and the necessity of its incorporation into acquisition research.

least some flexibility to cover this variation. The crosslinguistic enterprise of language acquisition research initiated by Slobin and his coworkers (Slobin 1985a, 1985b, 1992, 1997a, 1997b) has demonstrated that to a certain degree different kinds of languages pose different kinds of acquisition tasks to the child. As a consequence we see that specific structural features of the language to be learned have an impact on the acquisition process from very early on. Nevertheless, it is far from being clear how and when the child – equipped with some kinds of universal mechanisms to acquire a language – adapts to these specific problems that every language poses to the acquisition process.

The flexibility of the learning mechanism and the variation in the type of information that these mechanisms rely on will be the focus of this chapter. Looking at two tasks that the child has to master and seems to master within the early phases of language acquisition – namely the segmentation of the speech input into linguistically relevant units and the assignment of these units to syntactic categories – we will see that learners seem to use various different cues to solve these problems. An overview on existing data on language processing and language learning capacities in children within the first two years of life will show that there is no unique trajectory of language acquisition across languages but that this trajectory is shaped by specific features of the target language from early on.

Many of the questions that we are looking at in this chapter have already been asked in Peters' contribution to Slobin's *Crosslinguistic Study of Language Acquisition* (1997b). Peters argues that the acquisition pattern of the morphosyntactic system of a language is heavily dependent on prosodic as well as on features of the morphological system of the language. The interaction of these features can make the morphosyntactic system easier or harder for the child to track thus accounting for the differences in the developmental speed observed across different languages (cf. the contributions in Slobin 1985a, 1985b, 1992, 1997a, 1997b). According to this view grammatical morphemes are relatively easy to acquire when they are frequent, have a fixed position relative to an open-class stem, a clear function, an easily recognizable form, and thus are, on the basis of these properties, easy to segment. These parameters define classes of languages corresponding to typological groupings that should allow predictions about how similar or dissimilar acquisition patterns in different languages are. Thus, it has been shown that the acquisition of Turkish case markings proceeds very fast and is accomplished already by age two (Aksu-Koc & Slobin 1985) while the acquisition of case markings is still in progress in German learners at age four (Clahsen 1984, Mills 1985) even though the Turkish case system has a higher number of cases than the German system. Probably the differences in the form of case marking between German and Turkish are relevant for this developmental asynchrony. While Turkish is an agglutinating language with a highly transparent form–function relation given by clearly segmentable affixes that typically mark only one morphosyntactic category, German has an inflectional system with the typical fusion of several morphosyntactic categories into one affix. This example demonstrates that the manner of encoding grammatical features in the language and thereby in the input to the child is crucial for how easily the child finds the information necessary to acquire the specific grammatical features of the target language in his or her input.

In the following sections we will ask how typological differences of this kind interact with the mechanisms that young children use for their earliest steps into language acquisition. We will focus on two domains that have been researched quite intensively and at least across some languages during the last years, namely the acquisition of segmentation routines for words and the syntactic categorization of these linguistic elements.

8.2   Some methodological remarks

Since we are looking at an early phase of language acquisition comprising mainly the first eighteen months of life we will present mostly experimental data from studies using one of the methods that have been established for the study of early language acquisition and processing (for an overview see Jusczyk 1997). Most of the studies that will be discussed have used the headturn preference paradigm. Some others – especially those that have studied newborns – were run with the high amplitude sucking paradigm. Nevertheless, even using the same experimental paradigm there is still a lot of variation in methodological details of the studies. The outcome of experiments with infants can be heavily influenced on slight experimental variations including the number of trials used, the duration of the familiarization phase if included, the number of different stimuli, etc. Studies using the headturn preference paradigm have found familiarity effects (i.e. longer listening times to familiar stimuli) as well as novelty effects (i.e. longer listening times to unfamiliar stimuli) in experiments with very similar setups (Thiessen & Saffran 2003). This might be the result of an interaction involving the complexity of the stimuli presented and the developmentally changing capacities of the child to process them that has not yet been understood in its full complexity (cf. Burnham & Dodd 1999, Houston-Price & Nakai 2004). Nevertheless, according to the model by Hunter and Ames (1988) phases of familiarity preference and novelty preference might be present even within one single experiment making the duration of testing to a variable heavily influencing whether we find a familiarity preference, a novelty preference or even a null effect when listening times are averaged over all trials of an experimental session. Thus, comparing the performance of children across languages using these experimental techniques is an enterprise that implies a high degree of methodological comparability of the experiments with respect to the kind of stimuli, the age of the children that typically only is distributed over a very narrow range and the number of trials used. Our review will show that research fulfilling these requirements is just going to be started in the areas under consideration.

8.3   Crosslinguistic issues in word segmentation

8.3.1   Rhythmical typology and rhythmical sensitivity

So far, the typological approach has been followed most consequently by research on the emergence of word segmentation capacities in children learning stress-timed and syllable-timed languages. Traditionally, stress-timed languages (e.g. most of the Germanic languages) are considered to base their rhythm on the recurrence pattern of stressed syllables while syllable-timed languages (e.g. most of the Romance languages) base their rhythm on the syllable per se (Pike 1945). Abercombrie (1967) made a more general claim assuming that rhythmical structure is based on the iso-chrony of the rhythmical units leading to the expectation of a constant timing of the stressed syllables in stress-timed languages and of constant timing of all syllables in syllable-timed languages. As phonetic analyses of the crucial temporal intervals in languages of these two classes did not yield much evidence for the isochrony hypothesis (Dauer 1983, Roach 1982) other phonologists have proposed that the auditory impression of a specific rhythmical structure is a by-product of other phonological prop-erties like the complexity of syllable structure and the reduction of unstressed syllables (Dauer 1983, Nespor 1990). In fact, Ramus and col-leagues (Ramus *et al.* 1999) showed that clustering of languages by their proportion of vocalic intervals and the variability of consonantal intervals leads to groupings that are in accordance with the traditional classification of stress-timed, syllable-timed and mora-timed languages (i.e. languages like Japanese or Tamil where the rhythm of which is supposed to depend on the mora – a subsyllabic unit determining the syllable weight (Otake *et al.* 1993)). The clusters found reflect the difference between languages with respect to the typical syllable structure. Stress-timed languages have complex and variable syllable structures ranging from simple CV syllables to syllables with complex consonant clusters in onset and coda. In con-trast, syllable- and mora-timed languages show less variable syllable pat-terns with a dominance of simple CV syllables leading to a high proportion of vowels and high homogeneity of the syllable structures observed. Adult listeners are able to perceive differences between languages based on exactly these cues (Ramus *et al.* 2003).

But what about children? Infants' ability to discriminate between differ-ent languages seems to reflect exactly the boundaries set by these rhyth-mical groupings. Nazzi and colleagues (Nazzi *et al.* 1998) have tested systematically the ability of newborns to discriminate languages of the respective types. They found that French newborns discriminate between languages of different rhythmic groups (e.g. English from Japanese or English from Italian) but not between languages of the same rhythmic group (e.g. English from Dutch or Italian from Spanish). This shows that infants are equipped with the perceptual mechanisms sensitive to the phonetic features that constitute the rhythmical structure of language. Using different types of synthesized Dutch and Japanese speech strings, Ramus (2002) demonstrated that the discrimination capacities of newborns are in fact dependent on the rhythmic properties of the speech input and not on more general intonation patterns.

This sensitivity to rhythmical information seems to be the basis for a fast acquisition of at least some rhythmic or prosodic features specific to the target language. At the age of 5 months English-learning infants already show a high sensitivity for the rhythmical features of their native language. Even though they are still not able to discriminate foreign languages belonging to the same rhythmical class (e.g. German vs. Dutch) they can discriminate their native language, i.e. English, from other languages belonging to the same rhythmical class (e.g. Dutch) (Nazzi *et al.* 2000). The observation of a very early acquisition of prosodic features of the target language is supported by data showing that German infants as young as six months prefer to listen to trochaic as compared to iambic syllabics while French infants of the same age do not show an analogous behaviour (Höhle *et al.* submitted). Asymmetrical brain responses to trochaic and iambic bisyllables by German and French 4 month olds probably already reflect the sensitivity to the rhythmical pattern typical for the target language (Friederici *et al.* 2007).

On the background of these findings it is surprising that Jusczyk *et al.* (1993a) did not find a preference for the trochaic pattern (that is, with strong–weak stress) in English-learning infants before the age of 9 months. The currently existing data do not allow us to decide whether this reflects a real delay for English learners due to some crucial differences between the languages looked at or whether methodological differences between the studies in the different languages are responsible for the diverging results for learners of the rhythmically similar languages German and English. While the study with German and French learners only used simple CVCV sequences that showed only prosodic but no segmental variation, the study with English learners used a whole set of different English trochaic and iambic words (that is, words with strong–weak stress).

8.3.2 Using rhythm to segment speech

Adapting the metrical segmentation strategy initially proposed for speech processing in adults (Cutler *et al.* 1986) to language acquisition, many researchers proposed that the rhythmic sensitivity of infants plays a crucial role in determining a segmentation strategy for the detection of word boundaries in the native language (Curtin *et al.* 2005, Echols *et al.* 1997,

Houston *et al.* 2000, Jusczyk *et al.* 1999a, Morgan & Saffran 1995, Nazzi & Ramus 2003, Nazzi *et al.* 2006). In stress-timed languages there is a coincidence of the boundaries of metrical feet and of word boundaries. The initial boundary of a metrical foot – defined by a strong syllable – is a reliable cue for an initial word boundary for a reasonable number of content words in these languages. In fact, counts for English have shown that about 90 per cent of the content word tokens in a corpus of spoken language have an initial strong syllable (Cutler & Carter 1987). For German, the proportions are similar: about 96 per cent of the bisyllabic words have a stressed syllable as their initial syllable. Children learning English and German, as well as children learning Dutch (which is a stress-timed language very similar to English and German with respect to word stress), from early on use a segmentation strategy that is adapted to this correlation of stress and word boundaries (Höhle 2002, Houston *et al.* 2000, Jusczyk *et al.* 1999a). Learners of these languages between eight and nine months old have been shown to be successful in segmenting words with initial strong stress out of continuous speech but not words with an initial weak syllable. This suggests that they use a metrical segmentation strategy that takes strong syllables as being word-initial and attaches following weak syllables to the strong one. This is exactly what the hypothesis of a rhythmically triggered segmentation strategy would predict.

For a full evaluation of the hypothesis that early segmentation is determined by rhythmic properties, data from languages not belonging to the stress-timed class are necessary. So far, only French has been investigated under this question. Nazzi and colleagues (Nazzi *et al.* 2006) provide evidence that twelve-month-old French learners segment their speech input into syllables but are not able to correctly segment bisyllabic words. Only at the age of sixteen months were French learners able to detect new bisyllabic words in continuous speech. These results suggest a delay of French learners in segmenting multisyllabic words from continuous speech compared to learners of the stress-timed languages as reported above. If French has a high proportion of monosyllabic words, starting out with a syllabic segmentation strategy might be appropriate in this language, providing the child with an initial lexicon of a sufficient size to establish additional segmentation routines based on other kinds of information. But even monosyllabic French words are sometimes hard to segment on the basis of a syllabic segmentation routine due to the fact that word initial resyllabification processes (liaison) are regularly observed in French words starting with a vowel. For instance, the definite singular article forms (*la*, *le*) lose their vowel and the remaining consonant is attached to the word beginning (*le ami* > *l'ami*). This raises the question which other cues may help learners to find word boundaries (see Curtin & Hufnagle Ch. 7). In general, phonotactic regularities (Friederici & Wessels 1993, Jusczyk *et al.* 1993b, Mattys & Jusczyk 2001b) as well as allophonic cues (Johnson & Jusczyk 2001, Jusczyk *et al.* 1999b) and transitional probabilities (Thiessen & Saffran 2003, Saffran *et al.* 1996a) between sylla-bles provide useful information for word segmentation that infants can process. But the efficiency of these cues in a given language depends heavily on its specific phonological features, i.e. in languages with only simple syllable structures phonotactics might be less informative than in languages allowing complex consonant clusters. So far the role of these other cues has not been studied for French learners.

The situation for French provides a more complicated picture when data from learners of Canadian French are taken under consideration. Polka and Sundara (2003) report segmentation of bisyllabic words as early as 8 months of age using the same experimental method as Nazzi *et al.* (2006). It is still unclear which differences between Canadian French and European French are relevant for the diverging findings. Nevertheless, the discrepancies observed challenge the hypothesis that the assignment of a language to a rhythmical group is the single factor that predicts which kind of segmentation routine infants learning the language initially use. More research on different languages, especially on languages not belong-ing to the stress-timed language category, is clearly needed.

8.3.3   Further phonological cues to word boundaries

Assuming that children use all kinds of cues that their speech input provides, one may ask what other kind of information supports the child to solve the segmentation task. Our group has looked at early segmenta-tion processes in Turkish infants. Turkish is interesting to look at due to several features (cf. Kabak & Vogel 2001). First of all, Turkish is a language belonging to the syllable-timed group. Second, Turkish – in contrast to French – has lexical stress with main stress on the final syllable in most words. Third, Turkish has vowel harmony with the restriction that all vowels within one word have to belong to one and the same of two differ-ent harmony classes based on the front–back distinction with front vowels forming one class and back vowels forming the other class. If two syllables with vowels not belonging to the same harmony class appear in adjacent syllables there is a very high probability of a word boundary between the syllables.

In a series of experiments we tested Turkish infants' sensitivity for vowel harmony. Already at the age of six months Turkish infants preferred to listen to bisyllabic non-words that obey the Turkish harmony restric-tions compared to bisyllabic sequences, the vowels of which did not stem from one class. German six month olds tested with the same material did not show any listening preferences for the harmonic or the non-harmonic sequences. This suggests that the preference observed for the Turkish infants is not due to general acoustic preferences for sequences of vowels with similar articulatory features. In contrast, the Turkish infants' prefer-ence for vowel harmonic sequences seems to be the result of their exposure to a language that systematically uses vowel harmony in their lexical inventory. Being sensitive to this feature, six-month-old Turkish infants may be ready to use it for word segmentation.

This was tested in a second experiment with nine-month-old Turkish learners. In this experiment the influence of vowel harmony as a cue to word boundaries was tested by presenting strings in which a word boundary was or was not marked by a following non-harmonic syllable. The results of this study indicate that the Turkish infants' segmentation of continuous speech is supported by harmony information. This shows that infants use different types of cues provided by their ambient language to find a solution for the segmentation problem. In addition, infants seem to acquire knowledge about typical word forms in their language in a very fast manner within the first months of life. This can either be rhythmical patterns as shown for the German learners as well as non-rhythmical information as co-occurrence patterns of specific segments as is the case for vowel harmony in Turkish.

This observation still leaves us with some sort of hen-and-egg problem (cf. Thiessen & Saffran 2003). If six month olds know the features of typical word forms in their language they must have solved the segmentation problem – at least partly – before the age of six months. Language-specific features like a trochaic dominance or the existence of vowel harmony in the lexical inventory must be a result of having recognized that these features exist in the ambient language, which is only possible on the basis of already segmented words. As a consequence Thiessen and Saffran suggest that children start out the segmentation process with distributional analyses of transitional probabilities between segments – a process that is not dependent on prior knowledge of at least some features of the target. By these mechanisms first word forms are identified that serve as input for the analysis of phonological features being typical for word forms in the respective language. Evidence for their account is provided by findings that seven-month-old English learners weight transitional probabilities as a more reliable cue for a boundary than prosodic cues while the reverse pattern showed up for nine month olds. The fact that a trochaic bias is not present in six month olds but is in nine month olds (Jusczyk *et al.* 1993a) is in accordance with this developmental trajectory as well as the observation that segmentation of bisyllabic words is present before the age of nine months (Jusczyk *et al.* 1999a) and the fact that unstressed closed-class elements can already be segmented by seven month olds (Höhle & Weissenborn 2003).

But if the delay of English learners is not only due to the method used in the study it would suggest that English learners are slower in recognizing the typical features of word forms in their language than, for instance, German or Turkish learners. If this is the case we have to ask which features of German and Turkish that are not present in English might aid the process of finding words in the former languages. Rhythmically,

German and English form one class leaving Turkish aside. But, morphologically, German and Turkish have a lot of common properties even though the two languages traditionally belong to different typological classes with respect to their morphological system – Turkish as an agglutinating and German as an inflecting language. Nevertheless, what both languages have in common and what puts them apart from English is their rich system of affixes appearing at the edges of words, with a high frequency making them excellent candidates for markers of word boundaries. Given infants' sensitivity for recurrent patterns these elements should be salient for the infants from very early on. Evidence for this assumption will be presented in the following sections.

8.3.4 Function morphemes and their role for segmenting the speech stream

8.3.4.1 Bound grammatical morphemes

In our outline of a morphological typology of different languages we saw that Turkish belongs to the synthetic agglutinating languages with many affixes that can be attached to one stem forming a morphologically very complex word. In addition, due to the word-final stress that always moves to the last affix of the word these affixes have a high degree of perceptual saliency. These features may support the acquisition of the morphosyntactic system that Turkish learners have mastered already by the age of two years (Akcu-Koz & Slobin 1985).

In contrast the form–function relation in inflectional languages like German is more opaque. But, due to formal syncretisms, the number of different affixes is highly restricted in German with only around twelve different inflectional endings that can stand for over some dozens of different combinations of morphosyntactic categories. This leads to a very high frequency of occurrence for the single forms of the inflectional affixes in German. Again, following the assumption that infants are highly sensitive to frequently occurring segments, they should have a firm representation of these segments from early on. In addition, while unstressed syllables belonging to a word stem are not generally reduced to schwa, German inflectional endings only involve schwa as a vocalic part. This makes the usefulness of German inflectional endings as markers for word boundaries even higher.

The question now is whether – given their probably low degree of perceptual salience caused by not being stressed and the reduced vowel – infants can process them. Recent research has provided some evidence for this. Blenn *et al.* (2003) as well as Pelzer and Höhle (2006) have shown that German ten month olds respond to the affixes of noun phrases occurring within continuous speech. They presented the infants with sentences involving noun phrases with concordant morphology, i.e. every member of the phrase had the same dative plural affix (e.g. *diesen jungen Katzen* 'these young cats') and the same sentences involving non-concordant dative singular phrases (e.g. *dieser jungen Katze* 'this young cat'). It is important to note that both types of phrases are grammatical in German. The infants showed a listening preference for the sentences involving the concordant (but grammatical) phrases compared to the sentences involving the non-concordant phrases. First of all, this result shows that children as young as ten months process unstressed affixes as they constituted the only difference in the form of the two sentence types, all other word forms being identical across the sentences. In a second experiment, the authors presented English children of about the same age with the same German material using the same procedure. English children did not respond differently to the concordant and non-concordant affixes. This suggests that the reaction of the German children was already based on some experience they have with the crucial affixes from their prior exposure to German, and was not only a response to the dense reoccurrence of some sound patterns within a restricted domain. In the former case no differences between the German and the English infants should have appeared. As Pelzer and Höhle (2006) suggest, this sensitivity might help the German infants to segment whole phrases marked concordantly out of continuous speech. To test this, they presented ten-month-old German learners in a further experiment with passages containing sentences with either concordant or non-concordant noun phrases. Then the infants were tested with isolated noun phrases, the familiar ones from the passages and some new concordant and non-concordant ones. The infants showed a listening preference for the concordant noun phrases as compared to the non-concordant ones only for the noun phrases that had already appeared in the passages. Again, this result suggests that infants do not simply respond to the recurrences of identical endings within a phrase as this should have led to a general preference for the concordant phrases. Instead, the result suggests that due to the recurring affixes concordant phrases are easier to segment from the passages and easier to memorize, leading to better recognition of the concordant than the non-concordant phrases in the test phase. As the unfamiliar phrases had not been presented before in continuous speech, neither segmentation nor memorization tapped their processing during the test phase.

In German, the appearance of concordant phrases is restricted to single instances of noun phrases depending on the gender of the noun, the grammatical case and phonological features of the noun itself. Thus, concordant phrases in German are rather the exception than the rule, making the finding that the German children respond to this feature even more intriguing. A question for further research would be how children learning a language that makes more heavy use of this feature (e.g. Spanish, Italian) respond to it. So far, our results suggest that very young children are able to process affixes and might build up some sort of representation for them early in their language acquisition process. The recognition of these items in the speech input may facilitate its further analysis. This does not imply that the children already have a representation of the morphosyntactic functions of the affixes but that they have the capacity to establish a form representation of these items that allows for an identification of these elements across utterances.

In languages that make less use of inflectional endings, free-standing grammatical morphemes may have a similar function as structural anchor points in the sense of Valian and Coulson (1988). Function words such as *the* in English share some of the properties described for the affixes above, typically having a high frequency of occurrence and often appearing at the edges of syntactic units like phrases or clauses. Similarly, we can ask for evidence that children are sensitive to these elements from early on.

8.3.4.2 Free grammatical morphemes

One of the first experiments that provided evidence that infants can detect function words within continuous speech comes from Höhle and Weissenborn (2003) looking at German infants. Using an experimental design that had been conceived by Jusczyk and Aslin (1995) to study the detection of lexical words in continuous speech, seven to eight month olds and six month olds were familiarized with different function words and other unstressed closed-class elements including determiners as well as prepositions. After the familiarization they were presented with text passages either including one of the familiarized items or not. Only the seven to eight month olds but not the six month olds showed significant longer listening times to passages including a familiarized function word than to passages not including a familiarized item. According to these results, the older infants had detected the crucial elements in continuous speech despite the fact that they had the typical features of unstressed closed-class elements in continuous speech, for instance showing only half of the duration of the corresponding words presented in isolation. This suggests that – at least for German learners – there might be less perceptual disadvantages for unstressed functional items than previously thought.

These findings for German learners are supported by findings from even younger French learners. Shi *et al.* (2006b) did a similar experiment in which six month olds were familiarized with one determiner (either *la* 'definite article, singular feminine' or *des* 'indefinite article, plural') and then tested with noun phrases including the familiarized determiner or not. Infants showed a familiarity effect for the phrases including the familiarized determiner. A further experiment using two phonetically highly similar functors (*la* 'the' and *ta* 'your') failed to show an enhanced attention to the phrase containing the familiarized determiner. This suggests that the representations the six month olds build up for the word forms during the familiarization phase are not fully phonetically specified. We cannot decide whether the fact that French learners have reacted to the function words at a younger age than the German children tested by Höhle and Weissenborn (2003) is due to methodological differences in the experiments or whether it reflects systematic differences in the speed of the acquisition processes in the two languages. A crucial difference between the two studies is the complexity of the stimuli presented during the test phase. While Shi and colleagues tested with isolated noun phrases that included the critical determiner always in initial position, Höhle and Weissenborn used whole sentences. Thus, the crucial elements were embedded in longer strings having material before and after them. This may have rendered their detection harder than in the material used by Shi and colleagues.

Further results meanwhile suggest that young children are not only able to detect these elements in continuous speech but also build up form representations for them from early on. Höhle and Weissenborn (2000) found that German learners' ability to recognize determiners as familiar items starts around the age of eleven months. They familiarized eleven month olds with bisyllabic sequences, either representing a noun phrase including the definite article plus a monosyllabic noun (e.g. *der Kahn* 'the boat') or a bisyllabic word, the first syllable of which did not constitute a word form by itself and the second syllable of which was segmentally identical to the noun of the noun phrases (e.g. *Vulkan* 'volcano'). The noun phrase as well as the bisyllabic words represented an iambic metrical pattern. In the test phase, passages were presented in which only the strong syllable of the familiarization items appeared in new contexts. Only the children who had been familiarized with the noun phrases responded with longer listening times to the passages including this syllable, but not the children familiarized with the bisyllabic words. This suggests that the children had segmented the noun phrases during the familiarization but had represented the bisyllabic words as one unit. Since the only difference between the familiarization strings was constituted by the form of the first syllable we assume that the children – based on an already existing form representation of the determiner – had segmented this item out of the string and were left with a second monosyllabic item. Nine month olds did not yet show this effect.

Findings pointing in a similar direction are reported by Shi *et al.* (2006c) for English learners. They showed that eleven to thirteen month olds but not eight month olds preferred to listen to sequences consisting of combinations of a real determiner or pronoun and a nonsense word (e.g. *the breek*, *his tink*) than to sequences in which the functor had been replaced by a nonsense syllable (e.g. *ris tink*). Effects for even younger English learners were obtained by Shi *et al.* (2006a). They familiarized eight and eleven month olds with nonsense words (e.g. *breek*) preceded by a high (*the*) or a lower (*her*) frequency function word or by nonsense syllables that were phonetically very similar to the real function words (*kuh, ler*). In the test phase of the experiment only the nonsense words were presented for testing their recognition. The eleven month olds showed longer listening times to the nonsense word that had been familiarized together with the high frequency existing determiner (*the*) as compared to the nonsense functor.

For the low-frequency function word no effect was observed. The pattern of the eight month olds was different. They showed longer listening times to those nonsense words that had either been familiarized with *the* or with *kuh* than to those familiarized with the functor with the lower frequency or its phonetic foil. This suggests that both age groups recognize the high frequency functor as a familiar string in the input and therefore seem to segment the string before the nonsense word, which facilitates the recognition of the item in the test phase. While the phonological representation of the high frequency function word *the* seems to be already quite specific for the eleven month olds, it is still underspecified for the eight month olds leading to the same results for the real and the nonce function word.

Similar results for French learners were obtained by Shi and Lepage (in press). They familiarized eight month olds with sequences of either the French indefinite plural determiner *des* or the 1st person singular possessive pronoun in the plural form *mes* or a nonsense syllable *kes* together with an infrequent French noun. In the test phase infants were only presented with the isolated nouns. Shi and Lepage found that the infants listened longer to those nouns that had been familiarized together with one of the existing function words during familiarization than to the nouns that had been presented with a preceding nonsense syllable. To test for frequency effects of the functors used, Shi and Lepage ran a second experiment in which the personal pronoun *mes* was replaced by the less frequent form for the 2nd person plural *vos*. This form did not yield the same effect that had been observed for the more frequent form *mes* in the first experiment. This frequency effect supports the assumption that already existing first lexical representations of frequent functors help the child to segment their speech input by providing information about word boundaries of items being adjacent to these functors.

Even though the experiments with the German, French and English learners are very similar with respect to the methods used, their results are not the same. Höhle and Weissenborn (2000) found a comparable effect only for German infants of about eleven months but not for nine month olds. The items used in the German study were two forms of the definite article, i.e. the singular masculine form *der* and the singular neuter form *das*. The missing effect for the German nine month olds may be due to the more complex article paradigm in German as compared to French, and to the more systematic use of articles in French as in German. German has three different gender forms and the article forms are different for the four cases leading to a paradigm involving twelve positions (ignoring number) that are filled by six different forms. French, on the other hand, has only two different genders and no case marking leading to only two word forms in the respective word classes (again ignoring the plural). The situation for English is even more simple with only one single form of the definite article *the* even including the plural. Even though the German system has a lot of syncretisms the higher form inventory must lead to a lower frequency of the single forms of the paradigm.

Summarizing, the results for German, French and English uniformly show that children learning these languages process and establish a form representation of functional elements from early on. The crucial factor for this early acquisition seems to be the high frequency of the corresponding forms as frequency can account for the asynchronous acquisition found across different function words within languages as well as for differences found across languages. Due to their high frequency, functional elements may well be accessible to infants' processing and learning mechanisms that have been proven to be highly proficient in computing frequency distributions of sound patterns (Jusczyk *et al.* 1994, Mattys & Jusczyk 2001b, Maye *et al.* 2002, Onishi *et al.* 2002, Saffran *et al.* 1996a). The cross-linguistic comparison suggests that the acoustic salience of the realization of functional elements in the speech stream does not make good predictions about their acquisition. With respect to acoustics, English determiners should be the less salient ones in the languages considered as they are generally realized as unstressed syllables with schwa vowels. In German, determiners are unstressed as well, but the degree of vowel reduction is generally lower than in English. In French there are some function words with only schwa vowels (e.g. *le, te, se*) while the majority have full vowels (e.g. *la, mon, les*). If perceptual saliency defined by these parameters determines the rate of acquisition we would expect the English infants to be the last in acquiring function words – an expectation that is contradicted by the data. This raises the question whether stress is as crucial for infants' speech processing as typically assumed (e.g. Bates & Goodman 1999, Gleitman & Wanner 1982). So far, there is no empirical evidence supporting the claim that infants have special problems in processing unstressed material (E. K. Johnson 2005, Jusczyk & Thompson 1978). Adults' disadvantages in the processing of unstressed words might thus be the result of changing attentional parameters (Cutler & Foss 1977, Cutler & Swinney 1987).

Building up a first form representation of these elements of course does not imply that children already have established knowledge about the morphosyntactic functions of grammatical morphemes. The data presented above show that children have established some form of representations of frequently occurring sound patterns on which they map corresponding parts of the incoming signal. This mapping process may support an initial structuring of the signal (Valian & Coulson 1988).

8.4   Crosslinguistic issues in the syntactic categorization of words

8.4.1   Categorizing words

The question about how different syntactic categories are established during language acquisition is a matter of intense debate. Within nativist accounts it is assumed that the knowledge on the existence of different syntactic categories is part of Universal Grammar and that the child's acquisition task consists in identifying instances of these categories in the language they are learning (e.g. Pinker 1984). According to Pinker's semantic bootstrapping hypothesis children are equipped with universal linking rules between semantic properties and form class. By the use of these linking rules children would assign a word referring to an object to the class of nouns and a word referring to an action to the class of verbs. This aids children to bootstrap into a first lexicon involving syntactic category information about the items included. This syntactic classification of the first lexical items allows the child to perform an analysis of the distributional patterns the words typically occur in. These distributional patterns substitute the use of meaning–class relations as a more reliable cue to syntactic category membership of new words.

Accounts not sharing the assumption of an initial linguistic endowment assume that syntactic categories emerge during the acquisition process by mapping syntactic categories onto conceptual ones (Gentner 1982) or by identifying similar features of initially syntactically non-categorized items (Tomasello 2000c). In other proposals input cues like phonological properties of the word forms themselves or distributional information is considered as the basis for the construction of syntactic categories (Maratsos & Chalkley 1980).

8.4.2 Phonetic and phonological cues to word category

The discussion about a possible impact of phonetic or phonological information on word categorization goes back to Gleitman and colleagues' (Gleitman & Wanner 1982, Gleitman *et al.* 1988) proposal that the correlation of stress and syntactic category, at least for the closed–open-class distinction, might be useful for the learner to discover the morphosyntactic distinctions typically associated with these two categories.

Only recently, phonological correlations between open- and closed-class items corresponding roughly to lexical and grammatical morphemes and their potential role in language acquisition have been the subject of empirical studies. Based on the observation that function words are typically more minimal in their phonological form, Shi and colleagues (Shi *et al.* 1998) have investigated different features relevant for phonological complexity vs. minimality in English, Mandarin Chinese and Turkish infant-directed speech. They found that in all three languages under investigation the average lexical item had significantly more syllables, more complex syllables, higher vowel durations and a higher relative amplitude than the average functional item. Besides these features holding for all three languages there were single cues only observed in single languages depending on the specific phonological systems of the respective language, e.g. in Turkish lexical items were harmonic to the preceding syllable in more cases than functional items, in Mandarin Chinese more marked tones occurred in lexical than in functional items, in English a higher amount of vowel reduction was observed in functional as compared to lexical items. Even though comparing the means yielded significant differences between the two classes there was a high amount of overlap with respect to every single feature under study so that none of the cues on its own had the power to allow a reliable assignment of a given item to one of the two classes. But simulations with self-organizing neural networks showed that using these cues simultaneously led to a reliable assignment of items to the two grammatical classes.

The data provided so far suggest that the input contains acoustic and phonological cues that a learner might use for a rudimentary classification into lexical and functional items. The question now is whether the learner has the capacities to make use of these cues. Data by Shi *et al.* (1999) suggest that this is the case. They found that English-learning infants make a categorical distinction between English lexical and English function words that were representing the typical features observed for the two word classes.

There are indications that word forms may contain phonological cues that allow a more fine-graded categorization within these broad classes, i.e. the categorization of nouns and verbs (Durieux & Gillis 2001, Kelly 1996). But so far there is no empirical evidence that children of the age considered here use these cues to categorize nouns and verbs.

8.4.3 Distributional cues to word category

Most recent research has looked at distributional information as a cue to syntactic categorization of words. From a linguistic point of view distributional information should be the most reliable cue for the syntactic categorization of word forms as syntactic categories are established by words sharing the same distributional properties. Based on the observation that children are sensitive to functional morphemes, the assumption that functional morphemes provide important structural information that children use to categorize content words is not far away. Functional morphemes can be seen as providing the structural frame of a sentence with empty slots for the insertion of content words. The idea of structural frames is supported by Soderstrom and colleagues (Soderstrom *et al.* 2007) who found that sixteen-month-old English learners notice the misplacement of an inflectional ending but not the misplacement of a non-inflected content word within a given sentence. This is in line with findings by Shafer *et al.* (1998). They presented ten- and eleven-month-old English learners with normal passages and with passages in which some of the function words had been replaced by nonsense syllables. Using the ERP technique they found differences in the eleven month olds' brain responses for the normal and the modified passages suggesting that these infants have some sensitivity to the distribution of elements with typical function word shape in speech. These findings support the assumption that infants begin building a syntactic structure based on function morphemes and their relationships. If this is the case these morphosyntactic structures provide crucial information on the syntactic categories of the content elements appearing within these structures.

The first evidence for this scenario was presented by Brown (1957), who found that three to five year olds' interpretation of a new word is dependent on its morphosyntactic environment, e.g. by relating *a sib* to a presented object and *sibbing* to a presented action – a finding that has been verified by a number of more recent studies with toddlers (Eyer *et al.* 2002, Gelman & Markman 1985, Taylor & Gelman 1988) and with even younger children (Bernal *et al.* 2007, Katz *et al.* 1974, Waxman & Booth, 2001, 2003).

A study with German learners suggests that the morphosyntactic environment not only helps the child to find a referent for a new word but that the new word is assigned to a syntactic category with specific distributional features. Höhle *et al.* (2004) presented fifteen month olds with noun phrases consisting of the German indefinite article and a new non-existent word form (*ein pronk* 'a pronk'). After familiarizing infants with these noun phrases the new word was presented within another syntactic environment either constituting another frame for the noun use of the word (e.g. *dieser pronk* 'this pronk') or constituting a frame for the verb use of the same new word (e.g. *sie pronk* [1] 'she pronk'). The children showed a listening preference for the use of the new word in the verb context, suggesting a novelty effect for the ungrammatical structure. These results suggest that German learners use the appearance of a determiner before an unknown word to assign the new word to a syntactic category that we would call nouns. The fact that they accept the use of the new word in environments that are lexically different from but syntactically identical to the environment in which the word had occurred before shows that children as young as fifteen months have some generalized knowledge about the syntactic features of at least some syntactic classes and do not generally exploit syntactic knowledge in an item-by-item fashion (Tomasello 2000c). Mintz (2006) provided evidence that even younger children of 12 months use distributional information to categorize new words.

In contrast to the bigrams used by Höhle *et al.* (2004), Mintz tested the reliability of so-called frequent frames for assigning new words to a syntactic category. Frequent frames are constituted by non-adjacent

---

[1] Note that the use of the new word as verb form does not necessarily request the adding of an inflectional ending in German. Furthermore, a replication of the experiment using a new non-existent word form that could also be an inflected verb form (e.g. *melt*) yielded the same results. It is important for the interpretation of the results that a group of infants familiarized with a pronoun context (*er pronk* – 'he pronk') and presented with the same sentences during testing did not show the same effect.

word pairs with a variably filled one-word slot between them that occur with a high frequency in the child's input (Mintz 2003) like e.g. *to … it*. The elements constituting the frequent frames are not necessarily function words. Mintz argues that the frequency of co-occurrence of the words constituting the frame by itself makes it likely that the existence of the frame reflects a systematic aspect of the language and is not a product of chance. This in turn suggests that the words occurring within this frame share systematic properties like the syntactic category. From the analyses of several corpora of child-directed speech, Mintz (2003) could show that child-directed speech contains frequent frames of the above type and that in fact the different words occurring in these frames had a high degree of overlap with respect to their syntactic category. Interestingly, most of the frequent frames observed in these corpora were frames for verbs.

Children can only make use of these frames if they are able to learn and process non-adjacent dependencies. This capacity has been shown for children in their second year of life across different languages (Gómez 2002, Höhle *et al.* 2006, Santelmann & Jusczyk 1998). Mintz (2006) tested whether English-learning children would be able to use the information given by frequent frames for a syntactic categorization of the words occurring within the frames. Similarly to Höhle *et al.* (2004) infants were familiarized with new words within a context providing either a syntactic frame for a noun or for a verb and then were tested with the same words in either a different frame for the familiarized category or in a different frame indicating another syntactic category for the enclosed word. As the German learners in the Höhle *et al.* (2004) study, twelve-month-old English learners showed a novelty effect for the presentation of the new words in a frame indicating another syntactic category than the familiarized one. These results show that already at the end of the first year children can use distributional information for determining the syntactic category of new words.

The question arises whether the concept of frequent frames can be applied to other languages having a more complex morphological system than English. As described by Mintz (2006), frequent frames are defined by pairs of word forms. Converting this concept to a language like German raises the question as to whether a language with a richer inflectional system contains a reliable number of frequent frames. Due to the gender and case marking system in German the single form *it* can be replaced by at least five different forms of the personal pronoun. This means that one single frame in English, *to … it*, will be distributed to five different ones in German, leading to a lower frequency of the frame in German as compared to English. These crosslinguistic differences suggest a typological differentiation in the definition of frequent frames that not only takes word forms as possible constituents of a frame but also bound grammatical affixes. For instance, German verb forms are marked systematically by inflectional endings which are – at least partially – unique for this word class. This leads to the hypothesis that in inflecting and agglutinating languages affixes are used as category markers by infants from early on, a hypothesis that – to my knowledge – has not been tested yet.

8.5 Some conclusions

Our overview on early segmentation and categorization abilities in young children shows that basically there might be two kinds of information that are especially relevant for the early steps of young children into language acquisition, namely rhythmic information and distributional information on different kinds of linguistic levels including the phoneme, the syllable and the word level.

Several studies have raised the question of whether there is a dominance relation between rhythmical and segmental statistical cues of one type of cue being weighted over the other by young children (Johnson & Jusczyk 2001, Mattys *et al.* 1999, Thiessen & Saffran 2003). The present results for English children suggest an initially stronger reliance on transitional probabilities between segments that turns into a dominance of prosodic cues around the age of nine months. Nevertheless, the dominance of prosodic cues might only have a short life span, given the fact that by the end of their first year of life English learners are able to correctly identify iambic words which would not be possible based on a metrical segmentation strategy alone. Thus, additional cues like, e.g. phonotactic and allophonic cues, as well as the growing influence of top-down processes by the mapping of already established lexical form representations to sequences of the incoming signal make the processing system more flexible and more efficient (Höhle *et al.* 2006, Kedar *et al.* 2006, Zangl & Fernald 2007).

A still open, important question is whether the available evidence concerning patterns of the hierarchy and interaction of different cues for the initial segmentation and categorization of the speech input as well as the changes these patterns may undergo that is still based on only a handful of languages will turn out to be universal or not. That is, given the fact that actually only a minimal proportion of the about 6,000 different languages across the world (Haspelmath *et al.* 2005) have been studied with respect to the critical structural properties and their impact on acquisition until now, an answer to this question will require both research on a much broader variety of languages – specifically focusing on typologically very different groups like tone languages or polysynthetic languages – and corresponding comparative acquisition research. Initial steps in this direction have been taken (Mattock & Burnham 2006) but strengthening and broadening crosslinguistic approaches to early language acquisition is still a major challenge for the future.

Suggestions for further reading

Jusczyk, P. W. (1997). *The Discovery of Spoken Language*. Cambridge, MA: MIT Press.

Nazzi, T., & Ramus, F. (2003) Perception and acquisition of linguistic rhythm by infants. *Speech Communication*, 41, 233–243.

Peters, A. (1997) Language typology, prosody, and the acquisition of grammatical morphemes. In D. I. Slobin, (Ed.) *The Crosslinguistic Study of Language Acquisition: Vol. 5, Expanding the Contexts*. Mahwah, NJ: Lawrence Erlbaum Associates.

9

From gesture to word

Susan Goldin-Meadow

9.1   Gesture's role in learning language

When people talk, they gesture and those gestures often convey ideas not found in the talk. Even more striking, the information conveyed in gesture and not in speech typically reflects knowledge that speakers don't know they have about a task, and is the first sign that they are ready to learn that task (Goldin-Meadow 2003a). In this chapter, the task to be learned is language, and my goal is to explore the role that gesture plays in the learning process.

Because gestures are produced along with speech and thus in the service of communication, they take on the intentionality of speech (although they rarely come under conscious control). But gestures are not part of a codified system – their forms and meanings are constructed in an ad hoc fashion in the context of the speech they accompany. It is precisely because gestures are produced as part of an intentional communicative act and are constructed at the moment of speaking that they are of interest to us. They are communicative acts that are free to take on forms that speech cannot assume or, for a child at the earliest stages of language learning, forms that the child cannot yet articulate in speech. And, as we will see, children use gesture before they are able to speak.

9.2   Gesture can serve as a stepping stone to first words

At a time in their development when children are limited in what they can say, gesture offers an additional avenue of expression, one that can extend the range of ideas a child is able to express. And young children take advantage of this offer (Bates 1976, Bates *et al.* 1979). Strikingly, even deaf children acquiring sign language produce gestures (Capirci *et al.* 1998).

Children typically begin to gesture between 8 and 12 months. They first use deictics, pointing or hold-up gestures whose meaning is given entirely by the context and not by their form. For example, a child of 8 months may hold up an object to draw an adult's attention to it and then, several months later, point at the object. Children do not use their early pointing gestures merely to direct attention to an object or themselves; they use them to influence the mental states of others (Tomasello *et al.* 2007). As such, pointing gestures constitute the child's first foray into establishing common ground with another person in order to affect how that person acts, feels or thinks.

Pointing gestures typically precede spoken words by several months and give children an easy way to refer to objects before they have words for those objects. But note that an adult has to follow a pointing gesture's trajectory to its target in order to figure out which object the child means to indicate. In this sense, pointing gestures resemble context-sensitive pronouns such as *this* or *that* more than they resemble nouns. Despite their reliance on the here-and-now, however, pointing gestures constitute an important early step in symbolic development and pave the way for learning spoken language. In fact, a large proportion of the nouns that eventually appear in a child's vocabulary can be predicted from looking at that child's earlier pointing gestures (Iverson & Goldin-Meadow 2005).

In addition to deictic gestures, children produce conventional gestures common in their cultures, for example, nods and side-to-side headshakes (Guidetti 2005), and also iconic gestures, although the number tends to be quite small and variable across children (Acredolo & Goodwyn 1988). For example, a child might open and close her mouth to represent a fish, or flap her hands to represent a bird (Iverson *et al.* 1994). Children do not produce beat gestures (which pattern with the rhythm of language) or metaphoric gestures (which capture abstract meanings, for example, moving the hand forward to indicate the future) until later in development, around the time that they begin to tell narratives (McNeill 1992).

Unlike a pointing gesture, the form of an iconic gesture captures aspects of its intended referent – its meaning is consequently less dependent on context. These gestures therefore have the potential to function just like words and, according to Goodwyn and Acredolo (1998), they do just that. Children use their iconic gestures to label a wide range of objects (trees, rabbits, rain). They use them to describe how an object looks (big), how it feels (hot), and even whether it is there (all gone). They use them to request objects (bottle) and actions (out). However, there are differences across children, not only in how often they use iconic gestures, but also in whether they use these gestures when they cannot yet use words. Goodwyn and Acredolo (1993) compared the ages at which children first used words and iconic gestures symbolically. They found that the onset of words occurred at the same time as the onset of gestures for only thirteen of their twenty-two children. The other nine began producing gestural symbols at least one month before they began producing verbal symbols – some began as much as three months before. Importantly, none of the children produced verbal symbols before they produced gestural symbols. In other words, none of the children found words easier than gestures, but some did find gestures easier than words.

Children vary widely in how quickly their vocabularies grow. Can looking at early gesture use in children and parents help us predict this variability? Rowe *et al.* (2008) videotaped fifty-three children in their homes during their daily activities every four months between 14 and 34 months. At 42 months, children were given a standardized vocabulary test, the Peabody Picture Vocabulary Test. Interestingly, the rate at which children used gesture at 14 months predicted the size of their vocabularies at 42 months, even after taking into account the number of words the children and their parents produced at 14 months. Early gesture can predict the trajectory of child vocabulary development.

Not surprisingly, children stop using iconic gestures as words as they develop. They use fewer gestural symbols once they begin to combine words with other words, whether they are learning English (Acredolo & Goodwyn 1988) or Italian (Iverson *et al.* 1994). Thus, there seems to be a shift in attitude toward gesture over development. This shift has been experimentally verified by Namy and Waxman (1998) who tried to teach 18- and 26-month-old English-learning children novel words and novel gestures. Children at both ages learned the words, but only the *younger* children learned the gestures. The older children had already figured out that words, not gestures, carry the communicative burden in their worlds.

Children thus exploit the manual modality at the very earliest stages of language learning. Perhaps they do so because the manual modality presents fewer burdens. It certainly seems easier to produce a pointing gesture to indicate a drum than to articulate the word *drum*. It may even be easier to generate a drum-beating motion than to say *drum* – children may need more motor control to make their mouths produce words than to make their hands produce gestures. Whatever the reason, gesture does seem to provide an early route to first words, at least for some children.

9.3 Gesture becomes integrated with speech during the one-word period

Even though they treat gestures like words in some respects, children very rarely combine their gestures with other gestures and, if they do, the phase tends to be short-lived (Goldin-Meadow & Morford 1985). But children do frequently combine their gestures with words, and they produce these word-plus-gesture combinations well before they combine words with words. Children's earliest gesture–speech combinations contain gestures that convey information redundant with the information conveyed in speech; for example, pointing at an object while naming it (Greenfield & Smith 1976). The onset of these gesture–speech combinations marks the beginning of gesture–speech integration in the young child's communications.

The proportion of a child's communications that contains gesture seems to remain relatively constant throughout the single-word period. What changes over this time period is the relationship gesture holds to speech. At the beginning of the one-word period, three properties characterize children's gestures: (1) Gesture is frequently produced alone, that is, without any vocalizations at all, either meaningless sounds or meaningful words. (2) On the rare occasions when gesture is produced with a vocalization, it is combined only with meaningless sounds and not with words; this omission is striking given that the child is able to produce meaningful words without gesture during this period. (3) The few gesture-plus-meaningless sound combinations that the child produces are not timed in an adult fashion; that is, the sound does not occur on the stroke or the peak of the gesture (cf. Kendon 1980).

Some time during the one-word period, two notable changes take place in the relationship between gesture and speech (Butcher & Goldin-Meadow 2000). First, gesture-alone communications decrease and, in their place, the child begins to produce gesture-plus-meaningful-word combinations for the first time. Gesture and speech thus begin to have a *coherent semantic* relationship with one another. Second, gesture becomes synchronized with speech, not only with the meaningful words that comprise the novel combinations but also, importantly, with the old combinations that contain meaningless sounds (in other words, temporal synchronization applies to both meaningful and meaningless units and is therefore a separate phenomenon from semantic coherence). Thus, gesture and speech begin to have a *synchronous temporal* relationship with one another. These two properties – semantic coherence and temporal synchrony – characterize the integrated gesture–speech system found in adults (McNeill 1992) and appear to have their origins during the one-word period.

This moment of integration is the culmination of the increasingly tight relation that has been evolving between hand and mouth (Iverson & Thelen 1999). Infants produce rhythmic manual behaviours prior to the onset of babbling. These manual behaviours entrain vocal activity so that the child's vocalizations begin to adopt the hand's rhythmical organization, thus assuming a pattern characteristic of reduplicated babble (Ejiri & Masataka 2001). These rhythmic vocalizations become more frequent with manual behaviours (e.g. arm swinging, hand banging) and less frequent with non-manual behaviours (e.g. leg kicking, torso bouncing). Thus, by 9 to 12 months, the time when children produce their first words and gestures, the link between hand and mouth is strong, specific, and stable, and ready to be used for communication (Iverson & Fagan 2004).

9.4   Gesture paves the way to two-word combinations and beyond

The onset of gesture–speech integration sets the stage for a new type of gesture–speech combination – combinations in which gesture conveys information that is different from the information conveyed in speech. For example, a child can gesture at an object while describing the action to be done on that object in speech (pointing to an apple and saying "give"), or gesture at an object while describing the owner of that object in speech (pointing at a toy and saying "mine", Greenfield & Smith 1976). This type of gesture–speech combination allows a child to express two elements of a proposition (one in gesture and one in speech) at a time when the child is not yet able to express those elements within a single spoken utterance. Children begin to produce combinations in which gesture conveys different information from speech (point at box + "open") at the same time as, or later than – but *not* before – combinations in which gesture and speech convey the same information (point at box + "box", Goldin-Meadow & Butcher 2003). Thus, combinations in which gesture and speech convey different information are not produced until *after* gesture and speech become synchronized, and thus appear to be a product of an integrated gesture–speech system (rather than a product of two systems functioning independently of one another).

In turn, combinations in which gesture and speech convey different information predict the onset of two-word combinations. Goldin-Meadow and Butcher (2003) found in six English-learning children that the correlation between the age of onset of this type of gesture–speech combination and the age of onset of two-word combinations was high and reliable. The children who were first to produce combinations in which gesture and speech conveyed different information were also first to produce two-word combinations. Importantly, the correlation between gesture–speech combinations and two-word speech was specific to combinations in which gesture and speech conveyed *different* information – the correlation between the age of onset of combinations in which gesture and speech conveyed the *same* information and the age of onset of two-word combinations was low and unreliable. It is the *relation* that gesture holds to speech that matters, not merely gesture's presence.

These findings were replicated on ten additional children learning English (Iverson & Goldin-Meadow 2005) and three learning Italian (Iverson *et al.* 2008). Despite the fact that the Italian children were immersed in a gesture-rich culture and had larger gestural repertoires than the American children (although, interestingly, they also had smaller spoken vocabularies), they still used gesture–speech combinations to convey sentence-like ideas several months before they expressed these ideas in two-word combinations.

Gesture thus serves as a signal that a child will soon be ready to begin producing two-word sentences. What happens next? Gesture could continue to expand a child's communicative repertoire, combining with words to convey increasingly complex ideas. Alternatively, after serving as an opening wedge into two-word sentences, gesture could cease its role as a forerunner of linguistic change. Ozcaliskan and Goldin-Meadow (2005a) observed forty children at 14, 18 and 22 months to address this question, and found that the types of gesture–speech combinations children produced changed over time and presaged changes in their speech (e.g. GIVE gesture + "I paint" was produced several months before the child produced comparable two-predicate combinations entirely in speech, "Give and I paint"). Ozcaliskan and Goldin-Meadow (2008) continued to observe these same forty children until 34 months to determine whether gesture remains at the cutting edge of change as children flesh out their skeletal linguistic constructions with additional arguments (e.g. GIVE + point at brush + "I paint"). They found that once a linguistic construction was established in a child's repertoire, the child no longer used gesture as a stepping-stone to elaborate the construction. Gesture thus appears to be a forerunner of ground-breaking linguistic change, but not change that merely fleshes out a construction.

In sum, once gesture and speech become integrated into a single system (as indexed by the onset of semantically coherent and temporally synchronized gesture–speech combinations), the stage is set for the child to use the two modalities to convey two distinct pieces of a single proposition within the same communicative act. Moreover, the ability to use gesture and speech to convey different semantic elements of a proposition is a harbinger of the child's next step – producing two elements within a single spoken utterance, that is, producing a simple sentence.

9.5   Once language is mastered, gesture is a harbinger of things to come in other cognitive domains

Over time, children become proficient users of their spoken language and no longer need gesture to expand their linguistic devices. But gesture does not drop out of their communicative repertoires. Instead it continues to be at the cutting edge of children's knowledge but in domains other than language. Older children frequently use hand gestures as they speak (Jancovic *et al.* 1975), gesturing, for example, when asked to narrate a story (e.g. McNeill 1992), give directions (e.g. Iverson 1999) or explain their reasoning on a series of problems (e.g. Church & Goldin-Meadow 1986). And children continue to convey information in gesture that is different from the information they convey in speech (Goldin-Meadow 2003a). More importantly, children who produce gestures that convey information not found in speech on a task appear to be in a transitional state with respect to that task – they are more likely to profit from instruction and make progress on the task than children whose gestures overlap with their speech (Church & Goldin-Meadow 1986, Perry *et al.* 1988, Pine *et al.* 2004). Thus, once language is mastered, gesture begins to mark children as being ready to learn other cognitive tasks.

Gesture continues to accompany speech throughout childhood (and adulthood), forming a complementary system across the two modalities. At all ages, gesture provides another medium through which ideas can be conveyed, a medium that is analog in nature. It is, in addition, a medium that is not codified and therefore not constrained by rules and standards of form, as is speech.

9.6 Children are also gesture comprehenders

Children not only produce gestures – they also receive them. There is good evidence that children can understand the gestures that others produce by 12 months. For example, children look at a target to which an adult is pointing at 12 to 15 months (Butterworth & Grover 1988, Leung & Rheingold 1981, Murphy & Messer 1977). But do young children integrate the information they get from the pointing gesture with the message they are getting from speech?

Allen and Shatz (1983) asked 18 month olds a series of questions with and without gesture, for example, "What says meow?" uttered while holding up a toy cat or cow. The children were more likely to provide some sort of response when the question was accompanied by gesture. However, they were no more likely to give the *right* response, even when the gesture provided the correct hint (i.e. holding up the cat vs. the cow). From these observations, we might guess that, for children of this age, gesture serves merely as an attention-getter, not as a source of information.

Macnamara (1977) presented children of roughly the same age with two gestures – the pointing gesture or the hold-out gesture (extending an object out to a child, as though offering it) – and varied the speech that went with each gesture. In this study, the children did respond to the gesture, although nonverbally – they looked at the objects that were pointed at, and reached for the objects that were held out. Moreover, when there was a conflict between the information conveyed in gesture and speech, children went with gesture. If the pointed-at object was not the object named in the speech, the child looked at the object indicated by the gesture.

From these studies, we know that very young children notice gestures when they are produced along with speech and can even respond appropriately to it. However, we do not know whether very young children can take information conveyed in gesture and integrate it with information conveyed in speech. To find out, we need to present children with information that has the possibility of being integrated. Morford and Goldin-Meadow (1992) did just that in a study of children in the one-word stage. The children were given 'sentences' composed of a word and a gesture, for example, "push" said while pointing at a ball, or "clock" said while producing a GIVE gesture (flat hand, palm facing up, held at chest level). If children can integrate information across gesture and speech, they ought to respond to the first sentence by pushing the ball, and to the second by giving the clock. If not, they might throw the ball or push some other object in response to the first sentence, and shake the clock or give a different object in response to the second sentence. The children responded by pushing the ball and giving the clock – that is, their responses indicated that they were indeed able to integrate information across gesture and speech. Moreover, they responded more accurately to the "push" + point at ball sentence than to the same information presented entirely in speech – "push ball". For these one-word children, gesture + word combinations were *easier* to interpret than word+word combinations conveying the same information.

One more point deserves mention – gesture + word combinations were more than the sum of their parts. Morford and Goldin-Meadow (1992) summed the mean number of times children pushed the ball when presented with the word "push" alone (0.7 out of 12 possible) with the mean number of times children pushed the ball when presented with the point at ball gesture on its own (1.0 out of 12). That sum was significantly smaller than the mean number of times children pushed the ball when presented with the "push" + point at ball combination (4.9 out of 12). In other words, the children needed to experience *both* parts of a gesture + word combination in order to produce the correct response. Gesture and speech together evoked a different response than either gesture alone or speech alone.

Kelly (2001) found the same effect in slightly older children responding to more sophisticated messages. The situation was as natural as possible. A child was brought into a room and the door was left ajar. In the speech only condition, the adult said, "It's going to get loud in here" and did nothing else. In the gesture only condition, the adult said nothing and pointed at the open door. In the gesture + speech condition, the adult said, "It's going to get loud in here" while pointing at the door. The adult wanted the child to get up and close the door, but he didn't indicate his wishes directly in either gesture or speech. The child had to make a pragmatic inference in order to respond to the adult's intended message.

Even 3 year olds were able to make this inference, and were more likely to do so when presented with gesture + speech than with either part alone. Kelly summed the proportion of times 3 year olds responded correctly (i.e. they closed the door) when presented with speech alone (0.12) and when presented with gesture alone (0.22). That sum (0.34) was significantly smaller than the proportion of times the children responded correctly when presented with gesture + speech (0.73). Interestingly, 4 year olds did not show this emergent effect. Unlike younger children who needed both gesture and speech in order to infer the adult's intended meaning, 4 year olds could make pragmatic inferences from either speech or gesture on its own. Thus, for 3 year olds (but not 4 year olds), gesture and speech must work together to co-determine meaning in sentences of this type. Gesture on its own is ambiguous in this context, and needs speech (or a knowing listener) to constrain its meaning. However, *speech* on its own is ambiguous in the same way, and needs gesture to constrain its meaning. It appears to be a two-way street.

9.7 The gestural input children receive

Very little is known about the gestures that children receive as input during development. Bekken (1989) observed mothers interacting with their 18-month-old daughters in an everyday play situation and examined the gestures that those mothers produced when talking to their children. She found that mothers gestured less frequently overall when talking to a child compared to an adult, but produced proportionally more simple pointing gestures. Shatz (1982) similarly found that, when talking to young language-learning children, adults produce a small number of relatively simple gestures (pointing gestures rather than metaphoric and beat gestures).

More recently, Iverson *et al.* (1999) observed Italian mothers interacting with their 16- to 20-month-old children, and found that the mothers gestured less than their children did. However, when mothers did gesture, their gestures co-occurred with speech, were conceptually simple (pointing or conventional gestures), referred to the immediate context, and were used to reinforce the message conveyed in speech. In other words, mothers' gestures took on a simplified form reminiscent of the simplified 'Motherese' they used in speech. In addition, mothers varied widely in their overall production of gesture and speech, some talking and gesturing quite a bit and others less so. And those differences were relatively stable over time despite changes in the children's use of gesture and speech (see also Ozcaliskan *et al.* 2005b).

Moreover, the gestures parents produce seem to have an effect on their children's gestures. Namy *et al.* (2000) found that the number of gestures parents produced during a book-reading task with their 15-month-old children was highly correlated with the number of gestures the children themselves produced. Indeed, the majority of gestures acquired by infants appear to be derived from gestural or motor routines that parents engage in with them, either deliberately (e.g. the itsy-bitsy spider song which is accompanied by a finger gesture depicting a spider crawling motion) or unwittingly (e.g. sniffing a flower) (Acredolo & Goodwyn 1988, Goodwyn & Acredolo 1993). There are, in addition, crosscultural differences in gesture rates, reflected in both parents and children. For example, Goldin-Meadow and Saltzman (2000) found that Chinese mothers gestured significantly more when talking to their orally trained deaf children (and to their hearing children) than did American mothers. In turn, the Chinese deaf children produced more gestures than the American deaf children (Wang et al. 1993).

The gestures adults produce not only have an effect on child gesture, they also affect child speech. Children are more likely to learn a novel word in an experimental situation if it is presented with gesture than without it (Ellis Weismer & Hesketh 1993). And when parents are asked to teach their children in the one-word stage gestures for objects and actions, children not only learn the gestures but their verbal vocabularies increase as well (Goodwyn et al. 2000). Rowe et al. (2008) examined the impact of parental gesture on child language in a naturalistic setting and although they did not find a direct effect of parental gesture on child vocabulary growth, they did find an indirect effect: The more a parent gestured when her child was 14 months, the more her child gestured at 14 months and the larger the child's spoken vocabulary 2.5 years later.

The gestures parents produce seem to have an impact on how often children gesture and may even influence the ease with which children learn new words. However, parental gesture cannot be essential for either development. Children who are blind from birth not only are capable language learners (Andersen et al. 1984, Landau & Gleitman 1985), but they also gesture when they talk even though they have never seen anyone gesture. Indeed, on certain tasks, congenitally blind children produce gestures at the same rate and in the same distribution as sighted children (Iverson & Goldin-Meadow 1998). Children do not have to see gesture in order to use it.

9.8 Gesture in children who are having difficulty learning language

Some children cannot easily learn the spoken language that surrounds them and end up being language-delayed. Do such children turn to gesture?

Thal et al. (1991) observed a group of children in the one-word stage who were in the lowest 10 per cent for their age group in terms of size of productive vocabulary. They characterized the children's verbal and gestural skills at the initial observation session when the children ranged in age from 18 to 29 months, and then observed each child again a year later. They found that some of the children were no longer delayed at the one-year follow-up – they had caught up to their peers. The interesting point about these so-called 'late bloomers' is that they had actually shown signs of promise a year earlier – and they showed this promise in gesture. The late bloomers had performed significantly better on a series of gesture tests taken during the initial observation session than did the children who, a year later, were still delayed. Indeed, the late bloomers' gesture performance was no different from normally developing peers. Thus, children whose language development was delayed but whose gestural development was not had a better prognosis than children who were delayed in both language and gesture. At the least, gesture seems to reflect skills that can help children recover from language delay – it may even serve as one of those skills.

If gesture and speech are part of the same system, children who show delays in language learning ought to show delays in gesture as well, and they do. Ozcaliskan *et al.* (2008) observed eleven children with early uni-lateral brain injuries between 18 and 30 months, and compared them to forty typically developing children observed over the same time period. The children with brain injury produced gesture–speech combinations conveying sentence-like ideas several months before they conveyed the same ideas entirely in speech, just as the typically developing children did. However, the children with brain injury were delayed by several months in both types of combinations. Along the same lines, Iverson *et al.* (2003a) observed five children with Down syndrome (mean age 48 months) and matched them on language level, essentially vocabulary size, with five typically developing children (mean age 18 months). The typically devel-oping children were already producing the types of gesture–speech combi-nations that herald the onset of two-word speech. The children with Down syndrome were not, suggesting that, despite their age, they were not yet ready to produce two-word utterances.

What happens to children whose language continues to be delayed at later stages of development? Some children fail to acquire age appropriate language skills yet they seem to have no other identifiable problems (i.e. no emotional, neurological, visual, hearing or intellectual impairments). Children who meet these criteria are diagnosed as having specific language impairment (SLI; see Leonard Ch. 24, Tomblin Ch. 23). Evans *et al.* (2001) studied a group of SLI children ranging in age from 7 to 9.5 years. They asked each child to participate in a series of Piagetian conservation tasks, and compared their performance to a group of normally developing children who were matched to the SLI children on number of correct judgments on the tasks. The task-matched normally developing children turned out to be somewhat younger (7 to 8) than the children with SLI (7 to 9.5).

The question that Evans and her colleagues asked was whether the children with SLI would turn to gesture to alleviate the difficulties they had with spoken language. They found that the children with SLI did not use gesture more often than the task-matched children without SLI. However, the children with SLI were far more likely than the task-matched children to express information in their explanations that could *only* be found in gesture. When Evans and colleagues coded gesture and speech together, they found that the children with SLI produced significantly more conserving explanations than the task-matched children without SLI. It may not be surprising that the children with SLI knew more about conservation than their task-matched peers – they were older. However, all of the 'extra' knowledge that the SLI children had was in gesture. The children seemed to be using gesture as a way around their difficulties with speech.

Throughout development, speakers seem to be able to use gesture to detour around whatever road-blocks prevent them from expressing their ideas in words. These detours may not always be obvious to the ordinary listener, to the researcher, or even to the clinician. They may reside, not in how much a speaker gestures, but in the type of information the speaker conveys in those gestures. It is important to note that the gestures SLI children produce do not form a substitute system replacing speech. The children's gestures are no different from the gestures that any speaker produces along with talk. Children with SLI exploit the gesture–speech system that all speakers employ and use it to work around their language difficulties.

9.9   Gesture in children who do not have a model for language

We turn next to a situation in which children are unable to acquire spoken language. It is not, however, because they cannot acquire language – it is because they cannot hear. It is extremely difficult for deaf children with profound hearing losses to acquire spoken language. If these children are exposed to sign language, they learn that language as naturally and effortlessly as hearing children learn spoken language (Lillo-Martin 1999 and Ch. 22, Newport & Meier 1985). But most deaf children are not born to deaf parents who could provide them with input from a sign language from birth. Rather, 90 per cent of deaf children are born to hearing parents. These parents typically do not know sign language and would prefer that their deaf children learn the spoken language that they and their relatives speak. As a result, a number of profoundly deaf children of hearing parents are sent to oral schools for the deaf – schools that focus on developing a deaf child's oral potential, using visual and kinesthetic cues and eschewing sign language to do so. Unfortunately, most profoundly deaf children do not achieve the kind of proficiency in spoken language that hearing children do. Even with intensive instruction, deaf children's acquisition of speech is markedly delayed when compared either to the acquisition of speech by hearing children of hearing parents, or to the acquisition of sign by deaf children of deaf parents. By age 5 or 6, and despite intensive early training programmes, the average profoundly deaf child has only a very reduced oral linguistic capacity (Mayberry 1992).

Do deaf children who are unable to learn spoken language and are not yet exposed to sign language turn to gesture to communicate? If so, do the children use gestures in the same way that the hearing speakers who surround them do (i.e. as though they were accompanying speech), or do they refashion their gestures into a linguistic system reminiscent of the sign languages of deaf communities?

Deaf children who are orally trained do use gesture to communicate and these gestures even have a name – 'homesigns'. It may not be all that surprising that deaf children exploit the manual modality for the purposes of communication – it is, after all, the only modality accessible to them, and they see gesture all of the time when their hearing parents talk to them. What is surprising, however, is that the deaf children's gestures take on both the *functions* and the *forms* found in natural languages (Goldin-Meadow 2003b), and thus look quite different from the gestures that young hearing children produce.

In terms of language functions, the homesigners use gesture to request objects and actions from others and make comments on the actions and attributes of objects and people in the room. But they also use gesture to refer to objects and events that are not perceptible to either the speaker or the listener. For example, one deaf child produced the following string of gesture sentences to indicate that the family was going to move a chair downstairs in preparation for setting up a cardboard Christmas chimney: He pointed at the chair and then gestured 'move-away'. He pointed at the chair again and pointed downstairs where the chair was going to be moved. He gestured 'chimney', 'move-away' (produced in the direction of the chair) and 'move-here' (produced in the direction of the cardboard chimney). Homesigners also use gesture to tell stories, to make generic statements, to talk to themselves, and to comment on their own and others' gestures.

In terms of language forms, homesigners often combine their gestures into strings (unlike hearing children who rarely do so) and those gesture strings have many of the properties of sentences. For example, home-signers' gesture combinations are structured, with underlying predicate frames that influence how likely it is that a gesture will be produced for a particular argument, and with surface level devices that indicate 'who does what to whom'. In addition, the gestures are themselves composed of parts (akin to morphemes) and are marked differently when serving noun-like vs. verb-like roles.

Thus, homesigners use gesture systems that contain many of the basic properties found in all natural languages. It is important to note, however, that their gesture systems are not full-blown languages, and for good reason. The children are developing their gesture systems on their own without a community of communication partners. Indeed, when home-sign children are brought together into a community (as they were in Nicaragua after the first school for the deaf was opened in the late

1970s), their sign systems begin to cohere into a recognized and shared language. That language becomes increasingly complex, particularly after a new generation of deaf children learns the system as a native language (Kegl *et al.* 1999). The manual modality can take on linguistic properties, even in the hands of a young child not yet exposed to a conventional language model. But it seems to grow into a full-blown language only with the support of a community that can transmit the system to the next generation.

The homesigners had not been exposed to a conventional sign language and thus could not have fashioned their gesture systems after such a model. They were, however, exposed to the gestures that their hearing parents used when they talked. These parents were committed to teaching their children English and therefore talked to them as often as they could, and when they talked, they gestured. The parents' gestures might have displayed the language-like properties found in their children's gestures. It turns out, however, that they did not (Goldin-Meadow 2003b) – the parents' gestures looked just like any hearing speaker's gestures.

Why didn't the hearing parents display language-like properties in their gestures? In fact, the children's hearing parents did not really have the option of displaying language-like properties in their gestures simply because the parents produced all of their gestures with talk. Their gestures formed a single system with the speech they accompanied and had to fit, both temporally and semantically, with that speech – they were thus not 'free' to take on language-like properties. In contrast, the deaf children had no such constraints on their gestures. They had essentially no productive speech and always produced gesture on its own, without talk. Moreover, because gesture was the only means of communication open to these children, it had to take on the full burden of communication. The result was language-like structure. The homesigners may (or may not) have used their hearing parents' gestures as a starting point. However, it is very clear that the children went well beyond that point. They transformed the speech-accompanying gestures they saw into a system that looks very much like language.

9.10 Gesture is versatile: it can be language or it can play a role in helping children learn language

Gesture is versatile. It can serve as a substitute for language in the hands of a child who is not exposed to a model for language. Gesture thus offers us what may be the clearest window onto the skills that children themselves bring to language learning. These are the skills that interact with the language model to which a child is exposed in the typical process of language learning.

But gesture is important even when children are exposed to a language model. Gesture provides the first sign that children are ready to learn their first words and sentences. It thus reflects changes that are about to appear in a child's developing language. There is, moreover, the possibility that gesture plays a role in bringing those changes about in at least two ways (Goldin-Meadow & Wagner 2005).

First, gesture offers a mechanism by which children can point out their thoughts to listeners who might then calibrate their speech to those thoughts, thereby facilitating the learning process. Indeed, there is evidence that mothers 'translate' their children's gestures into words, providing timely models for how one- and two-word ideas can be expressed in the child's language (Goldin-Meadow *et al.* 2007). As a second example in older children and another task, children on the verge of learning a maths task gesture differently from children who are not ready to learn that task, and teachers take advantage of this signal, altering the instruction they give a child as a function of the gestures the child produces on the task (Goldin-Meadow & Singer 2003). Learners can thus signal through their gestures that they are in a particular cognitive state, and listeners use that signal to adjust their responses accordingly, providing input that the learner might not have got had he or she not gestured.

Second, gesture can play a role in learning by influencing the learners themselves. For example, encouraging school-aged children to produce gestures conveying a correct problem-solving strategy increases the likelihood that those children will solve the problem correctly (Broaders *et al.* 2007, Cook *et al.* 2008). Thus, the act of gesturing seems itself to play a role in learning in general, leaving open the possibility that gesturing also plays a role in language learning. For example, the act of referring to an object in gesture could facilitate learning the word for that object in toddlers at the early stages of language learning. Future work is needed to explore whether gesture promotes language learning not only by influencing the linguistic input the learner receives, but also by influencing the learner's own cognitive state.

In sum, gesture can serve as a window onto the child's communicative abilities, one that often provides a view of the child that is distinct from the view provided by speech. Moreover, gesture can expand children's communicative resources when they are at the one-word stage, and predict with some precision when those children will begin producing two-word sentences. To the extent that early gesture predicts later language learning, we can begin to use its absence as an early marker of language learning that may go awry. But gesture has the potential to go beyond reflecting early language learning abilities to play a role in causing changes in those abilities. If so, gesture may turn out not only to be an early diagnostic for difficulties in later language learning, but also to be a technique by which language learning can be improved.

Suggestions for further reading

Capirci, O., Montanari, S., & Volterra, V. (1998). Gestures, signs, and words in early language development. In J. M. Iverson & S. Goldin-Meadow (Eds.), *The Nature and Functions of Gesture in Children's Communications* (pp. 45–60). San Francisco: Jossey-Bass.

Goldin-Meadow, S. (2003a). *Hearing Gesture: How Our Hands Help Us Think.* Cambridge, MA: Harvard University Press.

   (2003b). *The Resilience of Language: What Gesture Creation in Deaf Children can Tell us about how All Children Learn Language.* New York: Psychology Press.

Iverson, J. M. & Goldin-Meadow, S. (2005). Gesture paves the way for language development. *Psychological Science*, 16, 368–371.

McNeill, D. (1992). *Hand in Mind.* Chicago: University of Chicago Press.

Tomasello, M., Carpenter, M., & Liszkowski, U. (2007). A new look at infant pointing. *Child Development*, 78, 705–722.

Part III

Phonology, morphology and syntax

10

A dynamic systems approach to babbling and words

Marilyn M. Vihman
Rory A. DePaolis
Tamar Keren-Portnoy

10.1   Introduction

What is the developmental function of babbling in relation to language, if any? How is it related to the child's first words, and can this relationship shed any light on the highly controversial issue of the origins of grammar in acquisition? Studies of both infant speech perception and early vocal production have produced a wealth of findings over the past thirty-five years, but theoretical progress has been slow, with deductive ideas drawn from linguistic theory often masking the coherent evidence provided by observational and experimental studies.

Dynamic systems theory (Thelen & Smith 1994), with its emphasis on the role of variability in developmental advance, on the independent emergence of related skills as a self-organizing catalyst for behavioural change and on the deep interconnectedness between perception and action and learning, offers a promising perspective on early speech development. While reviewing the empirical findings of studies of production and of links between perception and production this chapter will also consider the relationship of those findings to dynamic systems theory.

10.1.1   The challenge: construction of a first system

A central concern of the study of child language is to account for the developmental source of linguistic knowledge. In one influential approach to this problem innately given Universal Grammar (or UG) is assumed to provide the knowledge of linguistic structure that serves as the starting point for language acquisition, leading to the basic question: *What exactly needs to be learned?* (Peperkamp 2003). This must then be followed by the question of the nature of the triggering process needed to establish the specifics of a given language: *How does the child recognize the critical data that will make it possible to set the appropriate parameters, or to rerank constraints in the appropriate way?* (see for example, Fikkert 1994, Lleó & Prinz 1997). For approaches that deny the existence of UG, such as the constructivist approach (see Menn 2006, Tomasello Ch. 5), the questions are the converse: *With what knowledge, if any, does the child begin?*, followed by the complementary question: *How can the child gain knowledge of linguistic structure or system?*

The role of phonology in the development of linguistic knowledge is often given short shrift by researchers interested in word learning (e.g. Bloom 2000, Hollich *et al.* 2000), while production is similarly disregarded by researchers focusing on perceptual advances. Yet before a child can begin to develop linguistic meaning or make referential use of words he or she must be able to represent and access word forms or phrases, which can then come to be associated with recurrent situations, objects or events. Furthermore, it seems shortsighted to assume that perceptual advances alone can suffice to account for language learning. A long tradition of both diary and planned observational studies has found wide individual differences in the rate and pathway of emergence of word production and phonological knowledge across children developing normally, even within the same ambient language group (see Vihman 1996); experimental group studies of word recognition and learning shed little light on this critical aspect of phonological development since it is individuals that learn words, not groups. It is evident that both lexical and phonological learning depend on the development of representations that integrate perception and production; this remains a central issue which has so far attracted insufficient attention.

In this chapter we will adopt the second position identified above, which looks for broad biological foundations to language but posits no specific linguistic knowledge as part of that foundation. Following Braine (1994) we will argue that it is a powerful learning mechanism – coupled with the speech motor system – rather than innate knowledge of linguistic principles that can be identified as the source of the remarkable human capacity for language. Pierrehumbert (2003: 118) proposed that the phonological system is 'initiated bottom-up from surface statistics over the speech stream, but refined using type statistics over the lexicon'. She does not elaborate on the source of the lexical knowledge that supports the second cycle of statistical learning, however. We argue below that the missing link is production experience, which brings the specific adult lexicon to which the child is exposed into focus and into partial or incipient mastery, leading, as Pierrehumbert says, to a new cycle of statistical learning based on types, not tokens. We will seek to show how that learning is first fuelled by the maturational emergence within the first year of vocal production of adult-like syllables. We will demonstrate the role played by babbling practice in supporting attention to and memory for first words, and we will argue that those early words in turn provide a database for distributional learning, the proximal source of emergent phonological systematicity.

10.1.2 Dynamic systems theory (DST) and the origins of grammar

In general, developmental ideas have been scarce in the literature on phonological acquisition, which has tended to draw instead on formal models of adult language and to apply them in a deductive way to child language patterns. Yet when we turn to such a deeply developmental theory as that of Thelen and Smith (1994), we find that their ideas have a remarkable degree of correspondence with the empirical findings which have accumulated over the past thirty-odd years of intensive study of infant speech perception and production, despite the fact that those findings are outside the domain of Thelen and Smith's own research (although Thelen 1991 relates dynamic systems ideas to the development of vocal production).

A key dynamic systems idea is that we must examine *process* in order to understand the origins of structure, which also means accepting *variability* as the very stuff of development. 'In detail … development is messy … What looks like a cohesive, orchestrated process from afar takes on the flavor of a more exploratory, opportunistic, syncretic, and function-driven process in its instantiation' (Thelen & Smith 1994: xvi). In what follows we will first provide a brief account of the process by which babbling is transformed into the first word production.

Nonlinearity is found again and again in empirically grounded accounts of language acquisition as well as in other areas of development. The notion of a predictable succession of categorically distinct 'stages' is generally revealed, on closer analysis, to be a false lead. 'The boundaries of *progressive stages* are … blurred by seeming regressions in performance and losses of previously well-established behaviors' (Thelen & Smith 1994: xvii; our italics). In what follows we will illustrate the nonlinearity of early phonological development, in which the first largely accurate word forms give way to a long period of template-based production, which is less accurate but also more systematic, reflecting the first steps in the construction of a phonological grammar.

According to Thelen and Smith (1994: 247), in a discussion of the emergence of successful reaching for objects in the first year:

From the messy details of real time – from the variability and context sensitivity of each act – global order can emerge … Knowledge … is not a thing, but a continuous process; not a structure, but an action, embedded in, and derived from, a *history of actions*. (our italics)

In what follows we will attempt to account for the emergence of flexible word-production patterns – different for each child, in accordance with the differences in individual histories of exposure, of 'intake', of early vocal production preferences and of first word use.

10.2   The starting point: biological precursors

Interest in early speech patterns has grown considerably since Jakobson (1941/68) made the claim that babble is wholly unrelated to early word forms, which he took to signal the onset of *linguistic* production. These ideas were shown to be untenable over thirty years ago (Oller *et al.* 1976, Vihman *et al.* 1985); babbling is now generally accepted as providing the raw material for early words. The continuity between babble and first words should not, however, be taken as evidence that the onset of canonical babbling (Oller 1980) is primarily a language-driven activity. There is strong evidence that babble is just one of many rhythmic motor skills that come online in the first year of life, providing the infant with the tools with which to gain knowledge of the world (Iverson *et al.* 2007, Thelen 1981). In Piaget's terms (1952), babble is a kind of 'secondary circular reaction', a perceptuomotor link that helps to lay the foundations for intelligent behaviour.

Campos *et al.* (2000) document the cascading effect of cognitive advances springing from the ability to initiate locomotion. Considered in a social context, the onset of babble can be expected to have a similar cascading effect. Currently there is a growing consensus that babble is best viewed as a multimodal activity, involving both proprioceptive and auditory experience. This provides powerful support for perceptuomotor learning, an excellent illustration of the way that simple linear progression in a basic motor system makes possible the learning of complex cognitive structures (cf., e.g. Rochat 1998, Westermann & Miranda 2004).

The babbling patterns of infants are highly individual and yet subject to very simple biological constraints. The earliest stable supraglottal consonants produced (excluding glides, which are difficult to distinguish from vowels) are stops and nasals (Locke 1983, McCune & Vihman 2001), both of which can be articulated by simple raising and lowering of the jaw. Davis and MacNeilage (1995) have formulated this process in terms of the frame/content theory of early speech organization. In their account, early speech is dominated by successive cycles of mandibular oscillation (the 'frames'), in which the starting tongue position determines both consonant and vowel. Thus, alveolar stops co-occur with front vowels (e.g. [di]), velar stops with back vowels (e.g. [ko]), and bilabial stops with central vowels (e.g. [ba]).[1] As babbling becomes more variegated, combining different consonants within a single vocalization, the infant gains control over the 'content' within each syllable, leading to a wider range of consonant/vowel combinations. The co-occurrence of consonants and vowels in early speech has been found to hold in numerous languages (but see Chen & Kent 2005).

---

[1] For an introduction to phonetics we refer readers to Ladefoged (2006).

The gaining of voluntary motoric control over a specific consonant is the next step toward incorporating these articulatory gestures into early words. McCune and Vihman (2001) tracked these simple early speech patterns – termed vocal motor schemes (VMSs) – in twenty infants. They characterize a VMS as 'a generalized action plan that generates consistent phonetic forms … a formalized pattern of motor activity that does not require heavy cognitive resources to enact' (McCune & Vihman 2001: 152). They operationalized the onset of a VMS as the production of ten or more occurrences of a given consonant in each of three out of four successive 30-minute observational sessions. The VMS thus incorporates an element of both consistency and stability over time. Attainment of a VMS means that the infant is able to consistently access a speech-like motoric pattern with the expenditure of only very limited cognitive resources – freeing those resources to support the novel attentional and memory tasks of associating an arbitrary sound pattern with a meaning.

10.3 The role of babbling: the accuracy of first words, 'preselection' and the 'articulatory filter'

Contrasting their findings with the 'course of phonological development as it has been previously reported' Ferguson and Farwell (1975: 429) noted a number of 'surprising tendencies' in the course of their analysis of the first words of three children acquiring English. The surprises included (a) the relative 'accuracy' of many early child words, with later regression to more primitive forms, (b) the great variability of the early word forms, and finally (c) the 'seeming great selectivity of the child in deciding which words he will try to produce' (Ferguson & Farwell 1975: 429).

The finding of early accuracy has been supported in many subsequent studies (cf. Appendix B in Vihman 1996, which includes the first recorded words of twenty-seven children each acquiring one of seven different languages). To illustrate this, Table 10.1 presents the first four words of a Dutch child, Thomas (based on Elbers & Ton 1985).

Like most early words, the Dutch target words are one or two syllables in length and include mainly early learned consonants (labial and coronal stops, the glide /j/, and /s/, less common in early words but still one of the core consonants in babbling as well as words: See Locke 1983). Somewhat unusually, however, two of the words include two different places of articulation, with a change of both place and manner in *pus*.[2] The child forms are remarkably close to the adult models, if we allow for cluster reduction and a substitution of [x] for /s/ in most forms of /pus(jə)/. Thomas'

---

[2] Elbers and Ton note that eight of Thomas' first twenty words involved more than one place of articulation; only one violates the sequence front–back seen in *part* and *pus*. This is typical of early melodic patterns: See Jaeger 1997, Vihman and Croft 2007.

Table 10.1. First word forms: relative 'accuracy'

Thomas (Dutch, 15–16 months)		
adult form	*gloss*	*child form*
/auto:/, /o:to:/	'car'	[at], [atə], [aut], [auto:], [o:t], [o:to:]
/hap/, /hapjə/, /hapi/	'a (little) bite'	[ap], [apə], [hap], [hapə], [hab], [habə]
/pa:rt/, /pa:rtjə/	'horse, horsie'	[pa:t], [pa:tə], [ba:t], [ba:tə]
/pus/, /pusjə/	'cat, kitty'	[pusj], [pəx], [bəx], [pux], [bux]

first four words fit the characterization of (more or less) 'accurate'; they are also seemingly 'preselected' for their relatively simple and accessible target forms. Interestingly, Elbers and Ton note that the babbling patterns [at(ə)], [pa:t(ə)] and [bəx], recorded during 'playpen monologues' when the child was alone, 'are already present in babbling *before* their corresponding words are reported to be produced' (1985: 557).

What then is the mechanism underlying the evident 'preselection' of forms to attempt? How can the child know what *not* to attempt? Vihman (1993) proposed that an 'articulatory filter' might be mediating the input, rendering salient those patterns with which the child was already familiar from his or her own babbling production. In this model, the emergence of adult-like syllables, in the middle of the first year, provides the child with a valuable resource (a kind of 'bootstrap', or easily accessible facilitator) for focusing in on selected portions of the fast-moving input speech stream. The tool would be deployed involuntarily: once one or more consonants have been well practised – some weeks or months after canonical babbling begins – the child's attention is likely to be captured by sound patterns that constitute a 'good enough' match to his or her own babbled productions, just as adult attention is sometimes captured by overhearing a highly familiar proper name, for example, embedded in a conversation not consciously attended (Wood & Cowan 1995). By 'good enough' we mean here roughly the same thing as was intended above by 'accurate'. Such an implicit experience of a match of own vocal pattern to input speech would eventually lead to the child's use of such patterns in relevant frequently repeated or routine situations; the consequence would be a small number of known lexical items, the first identifiable words, typically produced only in limited contexts (Vihman & McCune 1994; see Figure 10.1).

A recent experimental study confirmed the existence of something like an 'articulatory filter' by testing the effect of well-practised consonants (VMS) on the child's attention to non-words embedded in short sentences (DePaolis 2006). DePaolis recorded the infants every one or two weeks from 9 to 10 months on and tested them as soon as they had mastered at least one supraglottal consonant to VMS criterion. In order to administer the perception test as soon as the child showed a reliable production

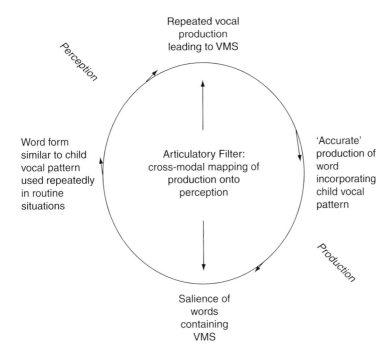

Figure 10.1 The matching of self- and other-produced vocal patterns to own production, supported by a familiar situational and/or verbal context, helps the infant to 'choose' relatively accurate first words.

preference, VMS was defined operationally either as in McCune and Vihman (2001, see section 10.2), or, alternatively, as fifty or more occurrences in the course of one to three sessions.[3] Testing involved presentation of three types of brief contrasting passages of five sentences, each passage consisting of nine uses of non-words featuring (a) the child's VMS (e.g. for /p/b/, *bapeb*), (b) another child's VMS (e.g. for a child producing /t/d/ to less than VMS criterion, *deeted*), or (c) the fricatives /f/v/, which are seldom if ever used to VMS criterion in this period (e.g. *vufev*). The passages consisted of simple sentences with one or two content-word slots filled with the relevant non-word type.

Testing the children within a week of the recording session in which the first VMS was identified proved critical, as the testing revealed a bipolar response to the non-word passages: Of the eighteen children tested, half had only a single VMS; of those nine children, six showed greater attention to the passages featuring their own VMS, while of the nine with multiple VMSs, all but one showed the reverse pattern, greater attention to the 'other-child' VMS passage. Thus, the extent of a child's prior use of a

---

[3] Voicing differences were disregarded in tallying infant consonant production, both because infants do not control voicing in word production at this age (Macken 1980) and because voicing is difficult to transcribe reliably.

particular consonant had, as predicted, an effect on his or her perceptual attention to that consonant – but the effect shifted from attention to what is familiar to attention to what is novel with the mastery of a second consonant.

Interestingly, production practice has been shown to affect semantic processing as well. In an event-related potential study in which infants heard familiar words that were presented together with (but slightly following) pictures that did or did not match the words, Friedrich (2007) found an 'N400 effect' at 14 months but not at 12 months (see also Friederici Ch. 4).[4] Strikingly, 12 month olds as a group did show an early differential response to the matching vs. the mismatching picture–word pairs (interpreted as a priming effect of the pictures in the case of matching words only), indicating that (most of) the words were recognized when presented in the matching condition. In the mismatch condition conflicting information from picture vs. word was the likely cause of the infants' failure to recognize the words; as a consequence, there was no associated meaning search and no N400 effect. In contrast, a subgroup of 12 month olds with high early word production (five to twenty-nine words) did show the N400 effect, with significantly stronger responses in the children reported to be saying the most words – indicating that these precocious infants were accessing the familiar words and responding with an effort at semantic integration even when the words were out of context in relation to the images they were looking at.

10.4   Word templates: the beginnings of phonological organization

10.4.1   Holistic early word representations: production vs. perception

Early production studies gave rise to the claim that the first phonological representations are whole-word based (Ferguson & Farwell 1975) and 'holistic' or 'schematic' (Waterson 1971). The claim is now controversial, since recent experimental studies, addressing either word recognition or word learning, have seemed to suggest that early (perceptual) representations are, on the contrary, 'finely detailed', giving rise to the 'phonetic specificity' hypothesis (based on eye-tracking: Swingley 2003, Swingley & Aslin 2000, 2002; preferential looking: Bailey & Plunkett 2002; or the 'switch paradigm': Fennel & Werker 2003, Werker et al. 2002b). These studies test children's ability to detect differences between novel or familiar words that are minimally distinct phonetically, which involves little or no involvement of prior knowledge, whereas the production studies

---

[4] In adults, a larger negative deflection (N400) in response to unexpected than expected words in a given context is taken to reflect the effort of semantic integration.

necessarily involve accessing representations in long-term memory, often in the absence of any immediate verbal or situational priming.

The nature of infant 'phonological representation' is as yet poorly understood. Different results are obtained, depending on accentual pattern (English vs. French: Vihman *et al.* 2004) and task demands – specifically, word recognition, word learning and word production. The task differences are important: in the case of word recognition, both the word form and the contextual situation or the image of a referent object may be expected to prime memory for the word and its associations, making the memory load negligible (as in the Swingley and Plunkett studies).

In the case of word learning significant attentional resources must be allocated to the problem of retaining the arbitrary sound–meaning link, as Werker and her colleagues have argued (cf. also Storkel 2001, who made the same point on the basis of a word-learning experiment with 3 year olds). This should make the task of learning new words particularly difficult for children who lack a stock of well-practised production patterns or routines to support memory for the new word form. One indication of this is the finding, reported by Werker *et al.* (2002b), that after habituation training to associate /bɪ/ to one novel object and /dɪ/ to another, the only 14 month olds who responded with surprise to the 'switch trial', in which the new 'word form' is associated with the wrong object, were those with a reported production vocabulary of over twenty-five words (whereas the 17 month olds were 'successful' as a group in showing word learning in this sense). The fact that a larger production vocabulary has been found to be associated with advanced performance as regards both semantic processing of familiar words and novel word learning is a strong indication that production experience supports the accessing and use of familiar word representations (cf. also Mills *et al.* 1997).

The contradiction between the apparently 'detailed' representations suggested by perception experiments and the holistic representations imputed to children on the basis of production studies can be reconciled, then, if we bear in mind that word production requires cognitive resources above and beyond what is required for word recognition or even new word learning – in particular, memory and planning as well as motoric skill. As children begin to make use of larger numbers of word types they must rely on temporarily activated representations for production, often showing regression in accuracy in the word forms they produce. These later representations, although dependent on perceptual experience of a sound pattern, give us good reason to accept Waterson's (1971) judgment that they are holistic 'schemas' or, in our terms, templates, in which the child's previous production practice strongly influences his or her memory for word forms. We will support this contention with examples, below, and will address the question of the source of the holistic representations in our discussion of learning mechanisms.

10.4.2 Whole word phonology: variability

Several arguments for whole word representation as the basis for production are summarized in Vihman and Croft (2007: 689); we review them here, beginning with illustration and discussion of the first, 'variability'. The three remaining arguments – holistic match of child to adult form, similarity among child forms, and response to challenges – will be discussed in the next section.

1. *Variability*: A sound may be produced differently in different early words, and individual words may be more or less variable (Ferguson & Farwell 1975). This suggests that although the child has gained knowledge of particular words ('item learning'), he or she has not yet developed abstract categories of sounds.

Ferguson and Farwell (1975) famously reported twelve widely varying pronunciations of the word *pen* produced in the course of a single session at about 15 months by K, one of the two American children they observed, with alternate production of labial or alveolar, oral or nasal onset, or neither, and with a range of oral or nasal low to mid vowels, as shown in (1):

(1) [mã° (im.), ᴧ̃ (im.), dɛ^dn, hɪn, ^mbõ, pʰɪn, tʰn̩ (x3), bɑʰ, dʰaʊ˜n, buã]⁵

The child K seems to have a holistic auditory image of the word but no clear vocal match for it within her existing repertoire, even with the support of an immediately preceding adult production;⁶ the exploratory variation, which seems primarily to target the articulatorily unfamiliar final nasal, clearly reflects the perceptual influence of the final nasal on the word as a whole.

A similar example of a 'hard word', attempted six times by an English child, Jude (also aged 15 months, but already producing twenty-five words in a half-hour session, which corresponds to a cumulative lexicon of over fifty words: Vihman & Miller 1988), is *circle*, variously produced, in full or partial whisper, as:

(2) [tʂɬu, tʂtʰə (x2), tʰ tʰ, tṇtɬjṳ (im.), kʰtɬṳ (im.)]

Here we see evidence of child attention to the sibilant and its co-occurrence with a stop and a lateral, although the place of the stop appears to be uncertain as does the sequencing of the various segments, again despite the presence of an immediate adult model in two cases. It is evidently not the individual sounds themselves that Jude cannot accurately reproduce,

⁵ im. 'imitated'. Note that K had produced no more than eight or nine words in a session spontaneously at this point.
⁶ In the full listing of child variants for each word that Ferguson and Farwell included in a later reprint of this paper (1977) we find that K, in the three preceding weekly recording sessions, had produced onset oral and nasal labial stops but only two codas, a weak [ᵏ] in [mã̃ᵏbu] *monkey* (im.) and [x] in [bʷux] *book*. A nasal vowel occurred once, for the first time, in the previous session: [æ̃] *on*, and also in two other words in the current session: [mã̃] *me/mine* and [hɪʌ̃], [ᵐkjũ] *thank you*.

since each of them is produced in at least one attempt at the word. Similarly, there is no reason to believe that he cannot perceive the adult segments. Instead, his difficulty appears to derive from the planning and production of the word pattern as a whole, in sequence, with its rapidly changing series of consonantal gestures.

The children's 'underlying representations' cannot easily be inferred from these production efforts. They are better described as dynamic or fleeting than as set or stable (or reliably accessible), with apparent influence on the momentary remembered form of the word not only from the percept of the target word itself but also from coexisting ('whole word') production patterns in the child's repertoire – patterns which must be accessed for vocal expression.

10.4.3   Templates in the word production of three late talkers.

Three further arguments for whole word phonology were cited in Vihman and Croft (2007).

2. *Holistic match of child to adult form*: Comparison of early child words to their adult models on a segment-by-segment basis is often difficult, as Waterson (1971) showed in the case of her son 'P'. Instead, the child appeared to be targeting a 'whole gestalt'.
3. *Similarity among child forms*: The interrelation between the child's own words may be more evident than the relation to the adult models (Macken 1979).
4. *Response to challenges*: The 'gestalts' or 'templates' which are taken to underlie the common patterning of a child's words can be seen as responses to one or more challenges posed by the segmental sequence or structure of the word form as a whole. The primary challenge, in most cases, is the difficulty of producing different consonants, vowels or both within a single syllable of a word (e.g. *pen*) or across syllables (*circle*).

The relationship of child to adult form and the sources of child difficulty have already been illustrated by the two sets of variable forms presented above for K and Jude, one just beginning to produce words, the other (Jude) having a considerably larger lexicon. Appreciation of the patterning seen in a child's word forms requires that one consider the full set of word forms produced in a given session, however, or over a delimited period of time (e.g. Priestly 1977).

In order to further illustrate these principles and to show their interrelationship we draw here on patterns observed at the 'twenty-five-word point' (25wp: the first half-hour recording session with twenty-five or more words) of each of three British children who were late to begin talking. Similar patterns, templates or 'canonical forms' (Menn 1983) from younger children have been reported in numerous studies, beginning with Waterson (1971) and Menn (1971). For recent crosslinguistic data illustrating template use see Vihman and Kunnari (2006), based on longitudinal observations, and Vihman and Croft (2007), based on diary studies.

Two of the children whose data we present here (Elise and Tony) were identified at 30 months as '(expressive) late talkers' on the basis of having a score within 3 months of chronological age on the Reynell-III Receptive Scale and a score of 6 months or more below chronological age on the Reynell-III Expressive Scale.[7] These children thus differ from the younger children whose data have been presented in illustration of the development of templates in earlier studies by virtue of their larger (age-appropriate) receptive lexicon. It is all the more striking that their limited phonetic resources should result in patterns that resemble those of the younger children. At the same time, their wider ranging lexical targets mean that the 'adaptations' observed are sometimes even more radical than those reported for younger children. The process of induction of templatic patterns that we describe under learning mechanisms, below, can be understood to be the same.

1. Jack (26 months.)[8]

    In this session Jack, who was engaged primarily in 'book reading' with his mother, actually produced fifty-two different word types altogether, excluding word combinations, onomatopoeia and doubt-fully identifiable forms. All of the words were produced spontaneously at least once. Two word patterns dominate Jack's production: CVVN, or monosyllables including a diphthong and nasal coda, and CVGlV, or disyllables with a medial glide.

    a. CVVN: Some of these forms are relatively accurate (designated as 'select' in Table 10.2). In each of these 'selected' words the rhyme matches the target, although initial clusters are reduced and the

Table 10.2. Later word forms: the emergence of a CVVN pattern

Jack <CVVN>			
Select		Adapt	
clown	[daʊn]	boat	[beɪn]
crane	[heɪːn]	ladybird	[laːbwaʊm]
green	[giːn]	moon	[buːən]
paint	[beɪn] (x2)	spoon	[m̩buːm]
plane	[deɪːin]	worm	[beʊm]
train	[dəɪn]		

---

[7] When first seen, at 25 months, Jack was not yet producing combinations despite having a reported vocabulary of over 100 words on the Oxford CDI (Hamilton *et al.* 2001). At 2;6 he scored within the normal range for both expression and comprehension on the Reynell, however, and so he cannot be considered a true 'late talker'.

[8] We discuss the children's word patterns here in order of child age at the 25wp.

Table 10.3. Later word forms: the emergence of a disyllabic CVGlV pattern

JACK <CVGlV>	
ADAPT	
banana(s)	[bɛːː | aʊ]⁹
bubbles	[bɔːwuːə]
guitar	[giːaː]
Harriett	[heɹjɛː]
pizza	[mbia, biə]
strawberries	[dauːwi]
toast	[dəuːːa]

onset consonant sometimes changes in unexpected or atypical ways (*crane, plane*). In other cases ('adapt') the words show 'adaptation' to the emergent template. For example, two words show consonant harmony (*ladybird, spoon*) and two (*boat, ladybird*) show a change of stop to nasal coda. In two further cases Jack draws out or creates a diphthong: *moon, worm*.

There are three additional CVVC forms with a non-nasal coda. *Plate* [beɪtʰ] seems regular and 'accurate' but does not participate in the pattern; its co-occurrence in the same session with [beɪn] for *boat* shows the unevenness of template use. The remaining two forms have coda [k]: *bike* [maɪʔkʰ] (with its anomalous onset) and *grape(s)* [geɪk], with consonant harmony.

   b. CVGlV: In the case of this template there are no 'accurate' or 'selected' productions, although the pattern applies most closely to adult open monosyllables with a long vowel:[10] *bee* [biːa], *no* [nəuːːə], *ski* [ɲiːa], *two* [duːə]. Note that most of these forms also occurred in the same session as monosyllables, CVV₀: *no* [nəuː], *ski* [gi] (x2) and *two* [duː]. The most striking adaptations, however, involve longer words produced with this pattern (Table 10.3). These forms seem to reflect Jack's ease in producing diphthongs, which he can also extend into a second syllable.

2. Elise (33 months.)

Drawing on Elise's 25wp, with 23 imitated and 25 spontaneous words (omitting onomatopoeia), we find a single strong pattern, in which [s] or [ts] are added or substituted for final consonants or clusters.

   a. Monosyllables: In the case of monosyllables Elise sometimes seems to be targeting a plural form (*bees, eyes*), but there is reason to doubt that the final *-s* ever has morphological value (cf. *pink, red*:

---

⁹ The vertical line represents a brief pause or break between the two syllables.

¹⁰ All forms are presented here as transcribed; a glide is necessarily present in the disyllabic forms, even where not indicated, as a transition to the final vowel.

Table 10.4. Later word forms: the emergence of a monosyllabic fricative coda pattern

Elise monosyllables <CV(V)s/ts>			
Select		Adapt	
birds	[baːdsː, bɛː[p]s]	*bees*	[weɪːɕ]
cat(s)	[[t]ɛtsːː]	*bike(s)*	[baɪs]
eyes	[aɪs]	*books* (im.)	[bɪdʔsː]
horse (im.)	[^{h}aɪːts]	*cake* (im.)	[k^{h}iːːʃts]
		cloud (im.)	[waɪːːsːː]
		dog(s)	[dəʔtsː]
		pig	[bɪds] (x4)
		pink (im.)	[bits]
		red (im.)	[weʔðs]
		sheep (im.)	[wɪtsː]
		shoes	[ʒəts]
		socks	[dədsː]
		trees	[wiːːs̪ːː]

im. = imitation

Table 10.5. Later word forms: the emergence of a disyllabic fricative coda pattern

Elise <V_oCVCVs/x/ts>	
Adapt	
ladybird	[əbɛbɛːts]
pirate	[wɛwets]
fairy (im.)	[hɛːwix]
microphone	[həʔdudɛs]
lady	[ɛdiːʃ]
rabbit	[haʔpiːsːː, baʔbiːtsː]
T-shirt	[əʔtɛtʃ]
telescope	[tetətɛːs]

Table 10.4). In addition, Elise produces two monosyllables with coda /n/, *arms* [æːːn] (imitated) and *mouse* [mãn, mãn^{t}, mãn$^{\theta}$] (this may reflect a confusion of *mouse* and *man*, based on a picture involving both a mouse and a pirate).

b. Disyllables. These forms sometimes include the fricative or affricate coda in the first syllable: *cross bones* [dəsbaːn], *icecream* [wisbɹiːː] and even *chicken* [dɪdsən] (with possible metathesis of the sibilant release of the onset affricate), all imitated. More often the coda is in word-final position, for both vowel- and consonant-final word targets (see Table 10.5).

Elise's remaining disyllabic forms with codas have either /m/ (*balloon* [ǝlǝuːm] or /t/ (*boat* [bǝʔatʰ], *pepper pig* [haʔbɛbɪtʰ], both imitated). Interestingly, although Elise sometimes inserts a final [s] where none is warranted, she never omits a coda altogether when the target has one.

3. Tony (35 months.)

    Tony, the latest of the three children to reach the 25wp (when he produced 33 different words spontaneously), has a dominant word pattern <V_oCVV_o>, the largest subset of which shows the more specific pattern <V_owVV_o>. In both cases Tony tends to add a filler [(h)V] before the word if there is none in the target.

    a. Stop or nasal: In the case of words *not* produced with medial [w], labial and velar stops and nasals occur initially or medially (Table 10.6); in the case of two target words with /f/ onset Tony produces anomalous substitutions (*fly, four*) – in both cases using an output pattern that serves elsewhere for a 'selected' word (*bye, go*). There is also one disyllabic target adapted for production with reduplication of the velar-onset first syllable ('*copter* [gɒʔgɒʔ] (x2)), which is again similar to a frequent output syllable (cf. *(a) car, all gone* as well as *go*).

    b. Medial <w>. This more specific pattern is produced as a match to target ('selected') in five words or phrases, while in ten additional words Tony imposes the pattern, sometimes at the expense of quite radical changes to the target word form (e.g. *carry, soil*: Table 10.7). In addition, two words are adapted to this template but include a (harmonizing) labial coda: *bum* [awʌm], *Tom* [ǝwɑːːm]. Tony produces codas in only three other words, all monosyllabic targets; all harmonize coda with onset: *beep* [biːpʰ], *dig* [hɛgɪg] and *stuck* [gɒkʰ, ɒʔgʊkʰ]. It is striking that Tony uses no coronal consonants at all.

Table 10.6. Later word forms: the emergence of a <VCV> pattern

TONY <V_oCVV_o>			
SELECT		ADAPT	
(a) ball	[ɒːbɔː] (x4)	*please*	[heɪ biː]
(a) bike	[æʔbaː]	*train*	[ɒgeɪːːː]
bye	[baɪ]	*fly*	[ǝbaɪ]
(a) car	[hægaː, aːgaː] (x2)	*four*	[ǝgɔːː]
all gone	[ɔːgɒ]		
go	[gǝuːː]		
(oh) no	[ŋǝuːː (x3), ɔːǝŋǝu]		
more	[mɔː] (x3)		

Table 10.7. Later word forms: the emergence of a <VwV> pattern

TONY <V_owVV_o>			
SELECT		ADAPT	
all wet	[aː wɛʔ]	*aeroplane*	[aʊwɛ]
away	[aweɪ]	*carry*	[əwiə]
hurray	[həweɪ]	*flowers*	[aːwe]
wee	[wiːː] (x2)	*fly*	[ɒʔwaɪːː]
whoa	[wəuː]	*over*	[əuːwɛ]
		soil	[hawaʊ, əwaʊː]
		that way	[ɒ.weɪ]
		up there	[ʌʔbwɛː, aːbwɛː]
		wheelbarrow	[aʔwɛː, awɛː]
		wire	[əːwaːː, ɛwa]

Alongside his strong labial bias, expressed in his 'choice' or discovery of <w> as a template consonant, he also produces many words with [g] and substitutes a velar nasal in the word *no*.

The patterns we see in the words produced by these three late talkers reflect, as do the patterns of younger children, their reliance on a small core consonant inventory, one which primarily consists of stops, nasals and glides. Beyond that, we see in the many 'adapted' forms, or forms which fail to match the target (even in cases where the child clearly has the necessary articulatory or phonetic resources to make a more accurate match, e.g. Jack's *boat, toast*), evidence that the children are inducing generalized patterns from their own output. That is, once the child has learned a certain number of adult-based words, usually at the fairly slow pace characteristic of 'item learning', word learning becomes easier (as evidenced by a rapid increase in new word production). This greater facility can be ascribed to the emergence of one or more well-practised 'motor plans' or templates that serve to support attention and memory to the form–meaning link. We see this as the beginning of phonological systematicity – in other words, as an emergent phonological grammar, in which the child goes beyond individual word forms to develop patterns representing possible word shapes which are based on the intersect between his or her own output forms and common input patterns.

10.5   Learning mechanisms

Studies of artificial grammar learning in adults (e.g. Reber 1967) already suggested the importance of statistical or 'distributional' learning over forty years ago, but it is only in the past decade that experimental findings have made it clear that children, like adults, automatically tally distributional regularities in the environment (Saffran *et al.* 1996a; also see Thiessen Ch. 3). This learning capacity is not restricted to speech (i.e. is not 'domain specific'), however, but has been shown to apply automatically to any regularly recurring sequence in the infants' environment (Kirkham *et al.* 2002). If we relate these findings to the host of experimental studies of prelinguistic responses to speech reported in the 1990s (Jusczyk 1997), we can conclude that over the course of the first year infants gradually gain a sense of input language patterning as regards sequences at any level of linguistic organization – segments, syllables, accentual patterns, words, phrases, clauses. Based on adult studies (e.g. Saffran *et al.* 1997), it is clear that this learning occurs in the absence of any specific intent to learn or even of (conscious or focused) attention to linguistic patterning as such.

However, word *production* requires that the child register arbitrary form–meaning relationships; the word forms repeatedly used in a given situation must persist in the child's memory, together with their context of use (or meaning), in order to lead to recognizable word use. This need not imply conscious attention or a specific intention to learn. Rather, the routine recurrence in a given situation of a sound pattern familiar from the child's own vocal practice can be taken to prime the child to produce that pattern in the often experienced situation (see Fig. 10.1). Each such use – which necessarily involves motoric effort (Elbers & Wijnen 1992) – can be expected to strengthen the memory trace, making future deployment of the same pattern more likely (Edelman 1987) and supporting memory for both form and meaning. Such early word production, supported by the experience of a perceptual match, can be taken to be the source of the relatively 'accurate' first words, as indicated above. This is 'item learning'; each word must be remembered individually as a whole, form and meaning together. It is thus quite different from the rapid, automatic registering of recurrent regularities ('distributional learning').

Current thinking in neuroscience supports the idea of a dual memory system. It is widely accepted that the hippocampus is required to consolidate detailed, multimodal episodic memories, which are the basis of learning from unique experiences, such as the item learning just described (McClelland *et al.* 1995, Squire & Kandel 1999). Furthermore, the registering and recall of arbitrary form–meaning pairs also generally depends on processing in the frontal lobes (known to be involved in the selection of percepts for focused attention). In contrast, the registration of regularities – the essence of distributional learning – occurs even in the face of hippocampal damage, permitting amnesic patients to abstract structure from a set of related items, for example (Knowlton & Squire 1993).

There is thus ample evidence to support a distinction between two types of learning – one probabilistic, statistical, sensitive to distributional properties such as frequency of occurrence and sequential patterning, the other responding to chance conjunctions of unrelated elements (notably, for our purposes, the arbitrary association of form and meaning), essential for the construction of a lexicon. What is most important is the idea that once motor production begins to highlight words in the input, leading to item learning, the 'input' to the child's distributional learning mechanism will necessarily begin to include the child's own word forms. This is a critical change: now the internal structure of the first words – the 'selected' target words, as (1) filtered through the child's primitive speech production mechanism and (2) analysed through distributional learning – will automatically be induced, providing the child with implicit phono-logical patterns that can be 'projected' onto the input speech stream, 'capturing' possible words to say which will gradually become more ambi-tious, less close to the vocal patterns actually available to the child. The new words need only share a minimal resemblance to the induced pat-terns and will be altered in individual ways, resulting in templates such as those described here.

The whole process is data-driven from the bottom up and self-organized through the powerful learning mechanisms highlighted above. Furthermore, at the same time that the infant is producing new word forms that conform to an internally developing templatic system, he or she is also gradually moving closer to the adult system through ongoing implicit comparison of child to adult word forms. As suggested by Pierrehumbert (2003), who supposed that the process happens only much later than the period of the first words, once the child has a much larger lexicon, 'type statistics' can be induced from his or her internal word representations, creating more or less well-defined templates and greatly facilitating and accelerating the process of further lexical learning.

10.6   Conclusion. From babble to words: a developmental account

In order to better understand the processes that might account for the origins of phonological system we have presented some of the evidence to support the essential continuity between babbling and first words. We also claimed that babbling is only one of many manifestations of the child's general motoric development, with its rhythmic base and its cascading socio-cognitive consequences. And we argued that a child's babbling prac-tice provides the essential resources for the identification and shaping of early word forms. We provided experimental evidence to back up the claim that the apparent preselection of adult targets reflects implicit multimodal matching of the child's own vocal production patterns to frequent input speech sequences. In dynamic systems terms, maturational advances in vocal production – primarily the emergence of rhythmic canonical babbling syllables in the middle of the first year – provide fuel for a phase-shift to first word production. But the presence of speech-like syllables in repertoire is not in itself sufficient to catalyze this shift. Instead, the normal environment of a growing child – the presence of talking caretakers, the infant's sense of reward elicited by the production of vocal forms that echo some of that talk, the proprioceptive feedback obtained from the articulation of the syllables which provide that reward – makes available numerous supporting experiences to tune those syllables in the direction of the ambient language and eventually to register, in the child's mind, matching input sequences along with their situational context or meaning (see also McCune 1992).

The route from babbling to words that we described is 'universal' but also highly individual, since the starting points (the particular first syllables or consonants to be mastered) differ as do the pathways followed. We noted that particularly challenging word forms may give rise to an exceptional degree of variability (for evidence of an increase in the variability of a child's word forms in the weeks immediately *preceding* the first manifestation of a stable templatic pattern see Vihman & Velleman 1989, Vihman *et al.* 1994). We also considered both first words (Table 10.1) and later words (three late talkers). In all cases we saw individual phonetic constraints deriving from variable motor skills and practice and we saw that those constraints translated into particular pathways leading to phonological structure. Non-linearity was reflected, if indirectly, in the late-talker word patterns, in which the 'adapted' word forms were sometimes quite remote from their targets yet close to many other forms produced by the child. As outlined by Thelen and Smith, knowledge here again reflects the history of actions of each child, although we did not here trace individual babbling patterns through the accurate first words to the generalized patterns of the later words. We did see that the children construct knowledge each in their own way, based on their own specific perceptuomotor experiences. Finally, we argued that there is no need to posit innate knowledge structures (UG) in order to explain the emergence of language. The learning mechanisms we invoke, unique in humans due to the combinatory power of distributional and item learning, seem to us to be sufficient to account for the formation of a phonological system.

Suggestions for further reading

Ferguson, C. A. & Farwell, C. B. (1975). Words and sounds in early language acquisition. *Language*, 51, 419–439. Reprinted with Appendix in W. S.-Y. Wang (Ed.). (1977). *The Lexicon in Phonological Change* (pp. 7–68). The Hague: Mouton.

Pierrehumbert, J. (2003). Phonetic diversity, statistical learning, and acquisition of phonology. *Language and Speech*, 46, 115–154.

Thelen, E. & Smith, L. B. (1994). *A Dynamic Systems Approach to the Development of Cognition and Action*. Cambridge, MA: MIT Press.

Vihman, M. M. (1996). *Phonological Development*. Oxford: Basil Blackwell.

Vihman, M. M. & Croft, W. (2007). Phonological development: Toward a 'radical' templatic phonology. *Linguistics*, 45, 683–725.

11

The prosody of syllables, words and morphemes

Katherine Demuth

11.1 Introduction

Much of the early work on the acquisition of phonology focused on the transition from babbling to first words (see Vihman 1996 for review, and Ch. 10). Over the past fifteen years research has increasingly begun to examine children's later phonological development at higher levels of prosodic structure (e.g. the syllable, the prosodic word and the phonological phrase). This new focus has been stimulated in part by new approaches to phonological theory (e.g. Optimality Theory: Prince & Smolensky 2004), as well as other developments in understanding prosodic structure more generally. This has provided the tools needed for investigating children's early language productions as the outcome of a series of competing constraints rather than rules, where simple (unmarked) structures are predicted to appear earlier than those that are more complex. At the same time, there has been an increase in the availability of longitudinal, phonetically transcribed corpora of child speech between the ages of 1–3, in languages such as Dutch, Japanese, European Portuguese, English and French. Some of these data also provide information about the language input (child-directed speech) children hear. Researchers have subsequently been able to use both frequency and markedness considerations in making within-language and crosslinguistic predictions about the course of phonological development. This chapter first reviews some of the structures that are important to the study of prosodic development. It then highlights some of the recent findings regarding prosodic development, identifying areas for further research.

11.2 Prosodic structures

To investigate the structure of children's early syllables, words and morphemes it is useful to consider the prosodic hierarchy in (1) (Nespor & Vogel 1986, Selkirk 1984, 1996). In particular, prosodic words (PWs) (also called phonological words) are composed of feet (metrical units) and syllables. These PWs may also be embedded in higher level phonological phrases (PPs), phonological utterances and intonational phrases.

(1) The prosodic hierarchy

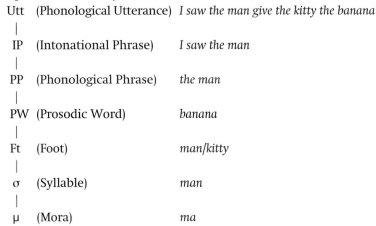

Utt (Phonological Utterance) *I saw the man give the kitty the banana*

|

IP (Intonational Phrase)   *I saw the man*

|

PP (Phonological Phrase)   *the man*

|

PW (Prosodic Word)   *banana*

|

Ft (Foot)   *man/kitty*

|

σ   (Syllable)   *man*

|

μ   (Mora)   *ma*

Syllables in turn are composed of an onset consonant and a rhyme, as in (2). The rhyme consists of an obligatory nucleus, and an optional coda. These subsyllabic units are called moras. Thus, monomoraic syllables contain only a nucleus, whereas bimoraic syllables may contain either a vowel plus coda consonant (*dog*), a diphthong (*play*), or a long/tense vowel (*see*).

(2) Basic syllable structure

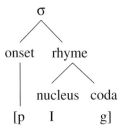

σ

onset   rhyme

nucleus coda

[p   I   g]

Some languages also permit complex (branching) onsets and codas. These are realized as consonant clusters. The consonant clusters permitted vary depending on the language. However, most consonant clusters obey the sonority sequencing principle (SSP), where sonority is greatest in the nucleus, and decreases toward the edges of the syllable (Clements 1990, Selkirk 1984). This is captured by the sonority hierarchy in (3), where each sound can be categorized in terms of one of seven manners of articulation (Ladefoged 1993). More sonorant segments tend to fill the nucleus of the syllable, and less sonorous segments tend to fill onset and coda positions. In the case of consonant clusters, sonority typically falls from the nucleus outward. For example, in the word *blend* /blɛnd/, /ɛ/ is a vowel, /b/ and /d/ are stops; /l/ and /n/ are a liquid and nasal, which are both less sonorant than a stop, but more sonorous than a vowel.

(3) The sonority hierarchy
     stops > affricates > fricatives > nasals > liquids > glides > vowels
     least sonorant   ⟶   most sonorant

   Languages differ in the types of syllable structures, foot structures, and PW structures permitted. Children must therefore learn what types of prosodic structures their target language allows. Moras play an important role in languages such as English and Dutch, where stress assignment is sensitive to the syllable weight (how many moras it contains), and where stress generally falls on heavy syllables (i.e. those containing two moras of structure). Foot structure also differs from language to language. Languages such as English and Dutch permit one-syllable bimoraic feet such as in *dog*, whereas Bantu languages like Sesotho have only monomoraic syllables, and therefore disyllabic feet, as in *nama* 'meat'. Languages also differ in the directionality of feet, many exhibiting Strong-(weak) trochaic feet (English, Dutch), but some exhibiting binary or longer (w)(w)S iambic feet (e.g. K'iche', French). Binary feet can be disyllabic (4a) or monosyllabic (bimoraic) (4b). They therefore constitute well-formed minimal words (McCarthy & Prince 1994). Some languages also permit words containing only a light (monomoraic) syllable, or a subminimal word (4c). Subminimal words are generally considered to be marked and unusual since they are PWs that do not contain a foot. However, words of this type are permitted in Romance languages and Japanese.

(4) Prosodic words composed of a foot (a, b), and a subminimal word (c).

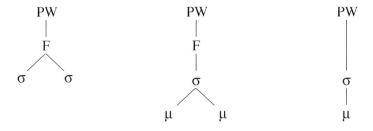

(a) disyllabic foot (*kitty*)   (b) bimoraic foot (*dog*)   (c) monomoraic
                                                                  subminimal word

   The frequency of different PW shapes varies from language to language. Although both English and Spanish permit four-syllable PWs containing two feet (5a), as well as a foot plus an initial unfooted syllable (5b), both are much more frequent in Spanish. In contrast, English and Dutch contain many monosyllabic and disyllabic PWs like those in (4a) and (4b).

(5)   Prosodic words composed of more than one foot

(a) two feet (*e.g. alligator*)   (b) one foot plus an initial unfooted syllable (*e.g. banana*)

With these structural preliminaries, we can now consider how children learn these various prosodic structures. We first review early findings in the field, and then discuss more recent research.

11.3   Prosodic development: early observations

Although much of the early research on the acquisition of phonology focused on segments, some European researchers began to focus on the word as an important unit in children's early phonological organization. Drawing on insights from Firth (1948), Waterson (1971, 1987) proposed that children's early phonologies could best be characterized by holistic, non-segmental prosodic units. These findings were followed by proposals by Allen and Hawkins (1978, 1980) that English-speaking children's early words tended to take the rhythmic form of disyllabic trochaic (Strong–weak) feet (e.g. *kitty*). They observed that children's early words are often augmented (*cup > cupy*) or truncated (e.g. *banana > nana*) in form, both processes resulting in a trochaic foot. They further proposed that such early word shapes might be universal, representing the default, or unmarked form of early words.

Following research on the prosody–syntax interface (Selkirk 1984), Matthei (1989) investigated across-word processes in children's early speech. Consistent with Allen and Hawkins (1978, 1980), he found that some lexical items were augmented to a disyllabic trochaic foot when produced in isolation (6a–b). However, when the two are combined into a larger phonological phrase, both were phonologically reduced (6c), again yielding a disyllabic trochaic foot.

(6)   Child   Adult Target
  (a) [ˈbebi]   /ˈbebi/   'baby'   (1;5)
  (b) [ˈbʊkɔ]   /ˈbʊk/   'book'
  (c) [ˈbebʊ]   /ˈbebiz ˈbʌk/   'baby's book'

Around the same time, Macken (1978, 1979) found that some children exhibited templatic patterns in their early words. That is, some children went through a period of development where their early words exhibited certain distributions of consonants, such as only labial consonants word-initially, and only coronal consonants word-medially. Thus, words such as Spanish *Fernando* were realized as [mano], and *libro* 'book' as [pito]. Such findings lead to proposals that children had both a perception and a production representation (Kiparsky & Menn 1977, Menn 1983, Menn & Matthei 1992) (though others disagree: Smolensky 1996). The early research from several of the above researchers began to lay the ground-work for thinking of children's early phonologies in terms of output constraints.

By the 1980s, acquisition researchers had experienced the limitations of rule-based, segmental accounts of children's early productions (e.g. Smith 1973), and had begun to explore other approaches to understanding the nature of early phonological systems. Demuth (1993) used an autosegmental approach to the acquisition of Bantu tonal systems. She showed that 2-year-old Sesotho-speaking children had no problem learning lexical tones, but only acquired grammatical tone melodies (tone sandhi) around the age of 3. Other researchers used similar non-linear approaches to understanding the aspects of phonological development in both first- and second-language acquisition (e.g. Archibald 1995, Yavas 1994). The field was therefore ripe for exploring new approaches to phonological acquisition.

11.4   The emergence of unmarked prosodic structures

Early on, Jakobson (1941) had proposed that children begin language acquisition by initially producing a maximally different set of 'unmarked' consonants (i.e. those that are easy to produce, and widely found amongst the world's languages). Although this proposal has never been verified at the segmental level, phonologically simple structures, such as stop consonants (e.g. /p/, /t/, /k/) and simple CV syllable structures (such as /ba/), do tend to be acquired early.

Several researchers began to expand this idea to account for the early appearance of other structures in children's early phonologies. For example, Fee (1995) and Demuth and Fee (1995) suggested that both weak initial-syllable truncation (*banana* > *nana*) and reduplication/vowel epenthesis (e.g. *dog* > *dada*) could be understood in terms of markedness. Drawing on developments in prosodic phonology (Nespor & Vogel 1986, Selkirk

1984, 1996), they proposed that children's early productions exhibit prohibitions against more 'marked' prosodic structures such as syllable-final coda consonants (e.g. *dog*) and initial weak (unstressed) syllables (*banana*). Observing that the same types of constraints could also account for early word-shapes in Dutch, they proposed that perhaps children learning all languages would exhibit a similar stage of early development, where prosodic words were both minimally and maximally a binary foot, or 'minimal word'.

Similarly, Gnanadesikan (2004) proposed that the 'emergence of the unmarked' could help account for the fact that children tended to preserve the least sonorant consonant in cases of consonant cluster reduction at the beginnings of words (e.g. *tree > tee*, *stop > top*). Pater (1997) then integrated these proposals, showing that children's early word truncations could be understood in terms of markedness constraints at both the level of the syllable and prosodic word. Thus, *banana* is often truncated to *bana*, preserving the least sonorant (least marked) consonant in the syllable/word onset. Note that such truncations also indicate that children have perceived at least the onset of the weak, unstressed syllable, even though they have not fully produced it.

11.5   The acquisition of syllable structures

The importance of syllables as units of phonological analysis was a relatively neglected area of research until the work of Clements and Keyser (1983). Further research pointed to the importance of the sonority hierarchy and the sonority sequencing principle for understanding some of the crosslinguistic restrictions on syllable structures (see (2), (3), and (4) above). These developments set the stage for examining how and when different types of syllable structures are acquired, both within and across languages. Thus, although there are certainly individual differences in the timing of acquisition within a given language, there are also robust crosslinguistic differences.

11.5.1   Coda consonant acquisition

Many children's earliest syllable structures consist of simple CV structures, with coda consonants omitted. Over time, children develop the ability to produce coda consonants, and other, more marked, complex syllable structures. Interestingly, coda consonants tend to appear earlier in languages where codas and coda clusters are common. Lleó (2003) reports that some German-speaking children begin to use coda consonants while still babbling. In contrast, she finds that Spanish-speaking children's first use of coda consonants is much more delayed, with many coda consonants still being omitted after the age of 2. Demuth and McCullough (in press-a) find that French-speaking children exhibit an intermediate scenario, producing most coda consonants around 1;8 years. These cross-linguistic differences in the timing of coda consonant acquisition can be explained by the interaction of at least two factors: the overall frequency of coda consonants in the ambient language, and the prosodic position in which they occur within the word. For example, using an elicited production task with novel words, Kirk and Demuth (2006) found that English-speaking children were much more likely to produce coda consonants in stressed or word-final syllables, as compared with unstressed and/or word-medial syllables. They suggest that this is due to the fact that both stressed and final syllables, in English and many other languages, tend to be longer in duration than medial or unstressed syllables. This may provide young language learners with more time to articulate more complexity within the syllable. It is perhaps not surprising, then, that coda consonants are acquired later in Spanish, since many of these occur in unstressed and/or word-medial position. Thus, some of the within-speaker variability in the production of coda consonants may be a function of the prosodic contexts in which these appear. This may also help explain some of the crosslinguistic differences in when coda consonants are acquired. Thus, both frequency and prosodic context play a role in the determining when coda consonants may emerge.

These findings do not address the types of consonants that are first acquired in the coda. On markedness grounds it might be expected that more sonorous consonants would be acquired in the coda first. However, in a corpus study of English child-directed speech, Stites *et al.* (2004) found that alveolar stops are the most frequent coda consonants in English. In a longitudinal study of child speech they also found that most English-speaking children's first coda consonants are alveolar stops rather than the less frequent, phonologically less-marked sonorant coda consonants. Kehoe and Stoel-Gammon (2001), in a larger cross-sectional study, confirmed this finding, showing that /t/ was the first coda consonant acquired by most children, followed quickly by /d/. Thus, although frequency and markedness typically pattern together, children may show a preference for frequency over markedness effects in their early productions, all else being equal. This raises questions about the notion of markedness as a whole, and its relationship to frequency for learners of a particular language. It also raises the question of which linguistic units learners are using for calculating 'frequency'. For example, Zamuner *et al.* (2004) show that coda consonant production is a function of neighbourhood density. That is, it is the frequency of the rhyme + coda, rather than simply the coda consonant itself, that is the best predictor of accuracy in coda consonant production, at least for English. On the other hand, /ʁ/ is one of the most frequent consonants in French, yet several studies have found that at least some French-speaking children have persistent problems with the production of /ʁ/ (e.g. Demuth & McCullough in press-a, dos Santos 2007,

Rose 2000). This may be due to articulatory problems with this uvular fricative, or due to its variable realization in the input children hear.

11.5.2   Consonant cluster acquisition

Research on the structure of the syllable has provided a framework for examining the acquisition of consonant clusters as well. Some of the early research focused on consonant cluster reduction in children with phonological delay, where various explanations were given for why clusters are simplified the way they are (e.g. Chin & Dinnsen 1992, Gierut 1999) (see Bernhardt & Stemberger 1998 for review). Following Pater (1997), some researchers proposed that children typically preserve the least marked onset, i.e. the least sonorant segment of the cluster (e.g. Barlow 1997, Ohala 1996, 1999). Thus, in a word like *stop*, the obstruent /t/ would be preserved, but in a word like *sleep*, the /s/ would be preserved. Others noted the limitations of the sonority account (e.g. Barlow 1997, 2001). Goad and Rose (2004) proposed that children preserve the consonant that is the head of the syllable (e.g. *plate > pate; slate > late)*. However, Pater and Barlow (2003) show that some children simplify *sneeze* to *neeze*, but *sleep* to *seep*. Jongstra (2003) therefore proposed that when the sonority distance is close, the segment contiguous with the nucleus will be preserved (*sneeze > neeze*), whereas when the sonority distance is sufficiently far, the least sonorous segment will be preserved (*sleep > seep*). However, a recent study of cluster simplification calls all the above into question, noting that features from both consonants often remain in cluster reduction (e.g. *spin > fin*) (Kirk 2008). Most of these studies have been carried out in Germanic languages; it is possible that research on other languages might shed light on these issues.

The studies mentioned above all examine word- and syllable-onset clusters. Only a few studies have investigated the acquisition of word- and syllable-final clusters. One might predict these to be later acquired since codas are more marked than onsets. However, Lleó and Prinz (1996) found that final clusters were acquired several months earlier than word-initial clusters in a longitudinal study of German-speaking 1–2 year olds. Levelt *et al.* (2000) also found that the majority of the children in the Dutch CLPF corpus acquired word-final before word-initial consonant clusters, though both patterns occur, probably due to equal frequency in children-directed speech. Kirk and Demuth (2005) found that English-speaking 2 year olds were more accurate at producing word-final as opposed to word-initial consonant clusters. In English, coda clusters are more frequent than onset clusters. Interestingly, the English-speaking children in their study also exhibited better production of final nasal + *s* and stop + *s* clusters than final nasal + stop and *s* + stop clusters. Furthermore, children often metathesized the *s* + stop clusters (*wasp > waps*), suggesting that frequency or articulatory factors may be involved. Note also that the most accurately produced clusters are those that typically occur with morphologically complex forms, suggesting that morphology may provide a further perceptual or production advantage for these coda clusters.

To explore these issues further, Demuth and Kehoe (2006) examined the acquisition of consonant clusters in French. They found that 2 year olds were more accurate at producing onset rather than word-final clusters in picture identification tasks, a finding confirmed in a subsequent longitudinal study (Demuth & McCullough in press-a). Some researchers have proposed that some word-final consonants in French (and other languages) prosodify as onsets to empty-headed syllables (e.g. *partir* 'to leave' /paʁ.ti.ʁØ/) (Charette 1991). It is possible that this structure is more marked, and therefore later acquired, though Goad and Brannen (2003) claim that such structures are universal at early stages of acquisition. Rose (2000) noted, however, that one child from his longitudinal study of two children learning Canadian French had acquired /ʁ/ in word-final position, but had /ʁ/ as a coda word-internally. He therefore proposed that this child had a coda representation for /ʁ/ in all positions. However, others have also noted that the acoustic and articulatory characteristics of French /ʁ/ are extremely variable, both within and between speakers (see Demuth & McCullough in press-a). Little is known about the acquisition of segments that are variably realized in the input, or where the syllabic representation is ambiguous (see discussion in Kehoe *et al.* 2008, Rose 2000).

11.6 The acquisition of prosodic word structure

Initial research on the acquisition of PW structure (Demuth 1995a, Pater 1997) suggested that children had an early awareness of word-minimality effects, and that this could be captured in terms of constraint interactions. Using acoustic evidence, Ota (1999) also showed that Japanese-learners exhibit compensatory lengthening of the vowel when a coda is omitted, thereby preserving moraic (and minimimal word) structure. But Japanese is a mora-timed language. What about word-minimality effects in a syllable-timed language like French, where CV subminimal words are also permitted? Demuth and Johnson (2003) examined this issue in longitudinal data from one French-speaking child. They found that her earliest words (1;3–1;5) were all target or reduplicated CVCV forms. As in other languages, her early grammar showed a highly ranked constraint against word-final (coda) consonants, resulting in either reduplicated CVCV repairs, or truncated CV outputs. Interestingly, she also reduced some disyllabic CVCV words to monosyllabic CV form. Further analysis showed that segmental constraints against fricatives, velar stops and clusters were more highly ranked than faithfulness to syllable preservation and/or word minimality (see dos Santos 2007, for similar observations from another child who does have velar consonants). Demuth and Johnson (2003) show that CV subminimal words account for 20 per cent of all words French-speaking children hear. They suggest that learners are sensitive to the high-frequency phonological structures of the target language, and quickly begin to adjust their grammars (constraint ranking) to accommodate such forms. Note that such a perspective on the development of early grammars minimizes the role of universal markedness. Rather, higher frequency phonological forms become the 'unmarked' structures on a language-specific basis.

This issue has been subsequently pursued in several other studies. For example, Goad and Buckley (2006) proposed that one Canadian French-speaking child did show early word-minimality effects through compensatory vowel lengthening (CVC > CV:), though no acoustic analysis was provided. However, analysis of two French children showed no systematic lengthening of the vowel when the word-final consonant was missing (Tremblay & Demuth 2007). The number of subjects examined in all these studies is small, suggesting that further study with more children at the early stages of acquisition (1–2 years) is required to resolve this issue. Returning to English, Demuth *et al.* (2006) examined word-minimality in four children between the ages of 1–3. Although some children showed apparent compensatory vowel lengthening, this occurred on both monosyllabic and disyllabic words, and on both long/tense as well as short/lax vowels. If learners were using compensatory lengthening to preserve word-minimality, one would expect it to be restricted to monosyllabic words with short/lax vowels, where a second mora of structure is required to preserve a bimoraic foot, or minimal word. Further acoustic analysis of three children's compensatory processes found that two of the children exhibited compensatory lengthening for missing codas with all vowels, whereas only one (older) child showed compensatory lengthening only for target words with a short/lax vowel (Song & Demuth in press). This suggests that English-speaking children may initially compensate for omitted coda segments, and only later (around the age of two) come to realize that English has word-minimality constraints. The English findings contrast with those of Ota (1999) for Japanese. However, since coda consonants are always moraic in Japanese, it is possible that compensatory lengthening is due to segmental factors here as well. Alternatively, perhaps children become more aware of moraic structure and its consequences for PW structure earlier in a mora-timed language. This is obviously an area for further crosslinguistic research.

Roark and Demuth (2000) proposed that the frequency of syllable and prosodic word shapes in the input children hear may help determine the PW structures children use in their early utterances. In a corpus study of child-directed speech they showed that most words in English are monosyllabic, whereas Spanish has many more trisyllabic and quadrasyllabic words. They suggested that these word-shape characteristics may account for English-speaking children's tendency to truncate words like *banana* until around 2;6 years (Pater 1997). In contrast Spanish-speaking children permit larger PWs much earlier (see also Lleó 2006). Further support for a frequency-based account comes from studies of European Portuguese (Vigário *et al.* 2006). However, Prieto (2006) suggests that the relative frequency of foot shape, rather than PW shape, helps explain why Catalan learners (but not Spanish learners) exhibit a stage of development where they truncate disyllabic S(w) PWs. Finally, Ota (2006) suggests that lexical frequency effects best account for the few cases of truncation found in child Japanese. Thus, frequency effects at different levels of prosodic structure may help determine the relative ranking of constraints in the grammars of children learning different languages, resulting in different truncation patterns in early PW development.

Critically, these patterns of truncation appear to be due to phonological, not perceptual or articulatory constraints. For example, Carter and Gerken (2004) found that children left a prosodic 'trace' of the missing syllable (realized as a silent duration) when they omitted the initial unstressed syllable of a three-syllable word. This suggests that, in some cases, children have 'planned' for the syllable, even though no segmental content is realized. Such 'covert contrasts' in children's early speech are often missed in traditional phonetic transcription. This raises questions about the extent to which other 'omissions' in child speech may be realized at some level of analysis, suggesting the need for a developmental model of speech planning/production.

11.7   The acquisition prosodic morphology

Drawing on insights from the prosodic hierarchy, researchers began to examine children's acquisition of grammatical morphemes. Since many grammatical morphemes are variably produced for a certain period in development, syntacticians have often claimed that children's morpho-syntactic representations take time to be fully acquired. However, researchers have also begun to find that some of the variability in children's production of grammatical morphemes is not random, but predictably constrained by aspects of children's developing prosodic representations. That is, there may be phonological (as well as syntactic and semantic) restrictions on children's use of grammatical morphemes. For example, researchers of Bantu languages such as Sesotho reported that children tend to produce noun class prefixes with monosyllabic stems before consistently producing them with disyllabic stems (Connelly 1984). Demuth (1994) suggested that children first produce noun class prefixes that can constituted part of a disyllabic foot (*mo-tho* 'person'), tending to omit those that are unfooted (*mo-sadi* > [sadi] 'woman'). Demuth and Ellis (in press) have recently shown that this tendency holds until the age of 2;3.

Selkirk (1996) shows that different languages prosodify grammatical function items at different levels of structure (7). She also suggests that unfooted grammatical morphemes that were prosodified at the level of the phonological phrases (PPs) (7b) violate constraints on well-formed prosodic structure, where each level of the prosodic hierarchy is immediately dominated by the next higher level (e.g. syllable > foot > PW, etc.). Thus, grammatical morphemes that are prosodified as free clitics (7b) (e.g. French) require the child to produce a marked type of structure. This is also the case with the affixal clitics in (7d) (e.g. Spanish). In contrast, grammatical morphemes that can be prosodified as an internal clitic as part of a foot (7c) should be the easiest and earliest acquired. We hypothesize that this is the form that the earliest noun class prefixes assume in Sesotho. Finally, those grammatical morphemes that themselves constitute a PW (7a) (as in German) will require the child to produce yet another 'word'.

(7)   The prosodic structure of grammatical function items

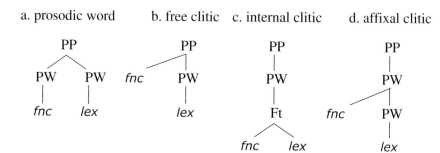

a. prosodic word   b. free clitic   c. internal clitic   d. affixal clitic

Gerken and colleagues (Gerken 1994, Gerken & McIntosh 1993) have also found that English learners were more likely to produce grammatical morphemes such as pronouns and determiners when these could be prosodified as part of a foot (e.g. Tom [hit the]$_{Ft}$ pig vs. Tom [wanted]$_{Ft}$ the pig). Gerken (1996) then showed that this could also be captured in terms of Selkirk's (1996) markedness constraints. Thus, children's variable omission of grammatical function items could be understood in terms of prosodic constraints, where those that could be prosodified as part of a foot were more likely to be produced at a certain stage of acquisition.

Lleó (1996) had long noted that Spanish-speaking children (unlike German-speaking children) exhibit the use of (proto)determiners from the beginning of their speech. This was explained in terms of the high frequency of Spanish three-syllable words, which required a monomorphemic structure like that in (7d). This then provides Spanish-speaking children with the prosodic structure needed for the early use of determiners (Demuth 2001, Lleó 2001, Lleó & Demuth 1999). Further support for this Prosodic Licensing Hypothesis came from the fact that three-syllable words that are truncated to two syllables are nonetheless accompanied by a (proto)determiner (e.g. *la muñeca* 'the doll' > [a'meka], Demuth 2001). This suggests that Spanish-speaking children can use the prosodic structure in (7d) at this point in development, and can fill the initial prosodic slot with either lexical or functional material.

Research on other languages similarly shows that young children are more likely to produce grammatical morphemes that are prosodically licensed than those that are not. For example, Demuth and Tremblay (2008) showed that French-speaking children consistently use determiners with monosyllabic words around 1;10 years, whereas consistent use with disyllabic and trisyllabic words lags by two and four months, respectively. This suggests that the early determiners are prosodified as part of the foot, and that determiner use with two- and three-syllable words appears only once these can be prosodified at the level of the PP (7b). Similarly, Demuth and McCullough (in press-b) found that English-speaking children had significantly higher use of articles when these could be prosodified as part of a foot with the preceding word. In contrast, children tended to omit articles that remained unfooted (those prosodified at the level of the PP) (e.g. *Tom [hit the]$_{FT}$ ball* vs. *Tom [wanted]$_{FT}$ (the) ball*). This pattern persisted for 4–5 months, disappearing as the children approached 2–2;6 years. Note that this is about the same time that children begin to more reliably produce the initial unstressed syllables of lexical items like *banana* (cf. Pater 1997).

The prosodic licensing of grammatical morphemes appears to occur at the level of the syllable as well, where some children exhibit syllable structure (phonotactic) restrictions on the acquisition of English third person -s (e.g. Stemberger & Bernhardt 1997). That is, children are much more likely to produce this grammatical morpheme when it occurs as a simple coda consonant than when it forms part of a consonant cluster (e.g. *sees* vs. *hits*) (Song *et al.* in submission). This suggests that there is still much to be discovered about the phonology–syntax interface in children's developing grammars, where constraints on prosodic representations may account for much of the variable production of grammatical morphemes.

These findings suggest that children's acquisition of grammatical morphemes is closely tied to the development of prosodic representations. Given that many grammatical morphemes are unstressed prosodic clitics, their acquisition is dependent on the development of higher level prosodic structures. The Prosodic Licensing Hypothesis therefore provides a framework for exploring the development of higher level prosodic representations, and how this changes over time. It also provides a principled means for making predictions about the course of grammatical morpheme development within and across languages. As shown in the case of Spanish determiner acquisition, however, these developments are also closely tied to the prosodic properties of the lexicon.

11.8   The future of phonological acquisition

11.8.1   Theoretical developments

The field of phonological acquisition has been significantly influenced by the developments in phonological theory, including the prosodic issues outlined above. Many other developments in phonological theory have implications for our understanding of children's phonological systems as well, and this will continue to develop in years to come. The recent development of constraint-based approaches to the study of phonological systems (e.g. Prince & Smolensky 2004) provides a framework for investigating interactions between different types of constraints in the developing system, and for viewing phonological acquisition as a constraint-satisfaction problem. This provides a much-needed vocabulary for understanding what constraints change over time.

11.8.2   Frequency versus prosodic factors

There is still the problem of understanding the mechanisms underlying phonological change. Researchers have long known that lexical frequency plays an important role in psycholinguistic processing (e.g. MacDonald *et al.* 1994), and infant speech perception studies show that infants are also sensitive to the frequency of the segments and prosodic structures they hear (e.g. Anderson *et al.* 2003). It has also long been known that 3–5 year olds' representation of familiar, high-frequency words is more robust in both perception and production than that of novel and low-frequency words (Edwards *et al.* 2004). And, as noted above, researchers have found frequency effects on children's production of syllable and prosodic word structures.

One of the challenges to the study of frequency effects is what to count. Demuth (2001) suggests that language learners may be keeping track of the statistics of structures at all levels of the prosodic hierarchy, as well as the segmental interactions therein. For example, much of the research on lexical acquisition finds that children's accuracy in the production of lexical items is closely related to neighbourhood density (Edwards *et al.* 2004, Storkel 2004). Thus, some of the variability found in the acquisition of syllable structures, as well as words and morphemes, may be explained by the frequency with which these occur in the lexicon. However, as mentioned above, there are also limits to the frequency accounts. Across different prosodic contexts, other contextual and/or gestural planning phenomena may better account for some of the variable production found. For example, the position within the word or within the phonological utterance (Hsieh *et al.* 1999), as well as the presence or absence of stress, may also play an important role in determining the nature of children's early syllable, word and morpheme productions. Such issues are not currently incorporated into models of early acquisition. Controlling for such prosodic factors may provide a clearer understanding of children's phonological competence and the factors that contribute to variability in production.

11.8.3   Articulatory and acoustic factors

Given the complexities of language production, there may also be acoustic and/or articulatory evidence that children are actually approximating certain contrasts and that these are not heard by the listener/transcriber. There has been renewed recent interest in investigating such 'covert contrasts' (e.g. Scobbie *et al.* 2000), providing acoustic evidence for children's developing phonological representations For example, Stoel-Gammon and Buder (2002) show that most English-speaking children control extrinsic vowel lengthening before voiced/voiceless consonants by the age of 2 (see also several of the studies mentioned above). Little is known about the prosodic organization of children's early productions, and how this interacts with both prosodic constraints and planning/production. Further study of children's developing articulatory abilities, and their acoustic correlates, may help to address these issues.

11.8.4   Sources of data

Another challenge to the field has been the lack of longitudinal phonetically transcribed data from multiple children between the ages of 1 and 2. This type of data is particularly important since children are actively acquiring the phonology of their language during this time – a point at which it is often difficult to conduct elicited production experiments. Several new longitudinal corpora are now becoming available on CHILDES (MacWhinney 2000). Many of these include interactions with parents, providing important information about the input children hear. Some corpora contain acoustic files and/or phonetic transcription, allowing for the acoustic/phonetic analysis of both child and adult speech. Phonological and phonetic analysis tools (e.g. PHON tools – see CHILDES (Rose *et al.* 2006) and Praat tools (Boersma & Weenink 2005)) are now also available to facilitate phonological and acoustic analysis.

11.9   Conclusion

The field of phonological acquisition has grown significantly since the 1990s, beginning to more systematically explore interactions between the acquisition of segments and higher level prosodic structures. This has been possible due to several developments in phonological theory, as well as the increasing availability of early, phonologically transcribed longitudinal language acquisition data. Both have allowed researchers to more thoroughly explore the nature of the constraints on children's early phonologies, and how these change over time. This in turn has allowed the field to begin to make testable predictions about the factors that influence the process of phonological development. These advances can now begin to provide a clearer picture of how phonological systems are acquired in normally developing individuals, with implications for better understanding the nature of language delay.

Suggestions for further reading

Archibald, J. (Ed.). (1995). *The Acquisition of Non-linear Phonology.* Hillsdale, NJ: Lawrence Erlbaum Associates.

Bernhardt, B., H., & Stemberger, J. P. (1998). *Handbook of Phonological Development from the Perspective of Constraint-Based Nonlinear Phonology.* San Diego: Academic Press.

Bernhardt, B., H., Gilbert, J., & Ingram, D. (1996). *Proceedings of the UBC International Conference on Phonological Acquisition.* Somerville, MA: Cascadilla Press.

Demuth, K. (2006). Crosslinguistic perspectives on the development of prosodic words. *Language and Speech,* 49(2), 129–135.

Goad, H., & Rose, Y. (2003). Segmental-prosodic interaction in phonological development: A comparative investigation. *Canadian Journal of Linguistics,* 48(3/4), 139–452.

Kager, R., Pater, J., & Zonneveld, W. (2004). *Constraints in Phonological Acquisition.* Cambridge: Cambridge University Press.

12

Grammatical categories

Heike Behrens

12.1   Introduction

This chapter addresses the acquisition of inflectional morphology and word formation with a focus on the processes of generalization that have been identified in intensive crosslinguistic research. Section 12.1 provides definitions of the terms *grammatical* and *categories*, and presents evidence for the language-specific nature of these morphological paradigms. Regarding the acquisition of morphological categories, criteria for the assessment of children's development are discussed (Section 12.2), and it is shown how children generalize over inflectional morphology (Section 12.3) and word-formation processes (Section 12.4). Here, I will focus on the different factors that contribute to the identification of morphological regularities and their interaction with other aspects of language. Finally, it will be shown how different theories try to capture the interaction of these linguistic aspects (Section 12.5).

In linguistic terminology, morphology deals with the grammar of words (Booij 2005), whereas syntax is concerned with the relationship between words. This distinction is not an absolute one as some languages encode morphologically what others encode by specific syntactic constructions or lexically through circumscription, e.g. English forms the passive by a syntactic operation (*Peter hugs his dog* → *The dog is hugged by Peter*), Latin or Sesotho do so by inflection.

In the hierarchy of grammatical relations, words have properties regarding the syntactic functions they can represent (part-of speech category or word class), as well as their internal makeup (stem, inflectional and derivational affixes or stem changes) and the word formation they can take part in (compounding, derivation and conversion). Typological research shows that languages differ widely regarding the categories they encode morphologically, and the way in which they do so. Thus, the term 'grammatical category' requires clarification on the notion of what is *grammatical* as well as how to conceive of a *category*.

12.1.1 What is grammatical?

The term 'grammatical' refers to the syntactic and morphological properties of a language. Morphology and syntax are related to phonology, on
the one hand, and semantics and pragmatics, on the other. Phonological
and prosodic properties of the stem may determine the declension class a
word falls in or the allomorphs. For example, the English plural morpheme has three different realizations (-s, -z, or -əz) depending on the
noun stem (cf. *cats, pigs* and *horses)*. Likewise, grammatical categories can
encode semantic distinctions like tense and aspect, or pragmatic ones like
honorifics (different forms to encode degrees of politeness).

Slobin (1997c: 277) defines a *grammatical morpheme* as follows:

Prototypical grammatical morphemes are affixed to content words, are
general in meaning, phonologically reduced, and not etymologically transparent. Familiar examples are elements like plural markers on nouns and
tense/aspect inflections on verbs. Another obvious type of grammatical
morpheme is represented by 'little words' like prepositions and auxiliaries, which consist of small sets of items occurring in syntactically fixed
positions.

From a typological perspective, languages differ widely in their division
of labour between syntax and semantics, and in the number of categories
they distinguish morphologically. Fixed-word-order languages like Chinese
have no grammatical morphology and few function words, whereas richly
inflecting languages like Latin or Inuit languages can have highly complex
categories. On the function side, there seem to be some universal tendencies
of what is encoded by grammatical morphology, but they are by no means
deterministic (Section 12.1.3).

12.1.2 What is a category?

There are two main views of how to think of categories: a formal one and a
prototypical or emergent one (see Smith 2005, Taylor 2003). In classical
philosophy, categories were conceived as binary with clear boundaries:
one is a member or one is not. Such binary approaches form the basis for
the binary nature of inflectional categories (see Ud Deen Ch. 15) and the
part-of-speech classification in Generative Grammar. Chomsky (1970)
hypothesized that words can be classified by the features [±N] and [±V].
Supposedly, [±N] and [±V] are features of Universal Grammar, and their
combination yields four lexical categories: Verb [−N +V], Noun [+N −V],
Adjective [+N +V], Preposition [−N −V], which are taken to be universal
syntactic primitives (Chomsky 1970; for review on the history of this
classification see Eschenlohr 1997). If grammatical categories followed
such a binary organization, all words and word forms should be classifi-
able in an unambiguous fashion, and the task for the learner is to identify
these categories. However, the features [±V] and [±N] have no defining

properties other than 'nouniness' and 'verbiness'. It is not clear on what basis the child would come up with the correct classification if labels like nouns and verbs were to refer to innate categories, rather than language-specific heuristics (Sasse 1993: 647).

A different approach to categorization emphasizes the fuzziness of category boundaries and emphasizes that categories tend to show proto-type effects in a number of domains (Taylor 2003). Prototypical members of a category are accessed faster in the mental lexicon, tend to be more frequent and the like. This suggests that category members are not equal, as assumed in the classical tradition. However, the prototype version cannot explain why we can build categories on the fly, i.e. see similarities or analogies between different entities or events. For this reason, several cognitive psychologists emphasize that categories are emergent and flexible (Smith 2005). Moreover, humans are very good at establishing relational analogies (Gentner 2003) between items that have no or only very little surface similarity (*x* is to *y* as *a* is to *b*). These powerful generalization skills explain why the human mind is a very efficient and flexible categorizer, in fact much more adaptable than if it was equipped with a set of prespecified categories (Gentner 2003).

12.1.3 Are there grammaticizable notions?

Grammatical categories cannot be defined on formal grounds, but their linguistic function or meaning could be specified, for example because certain semantic distinctions are part of the human genetic prespecification. Spelke and colleagues distinguish four innate core knowledge systems that facilitate later learning based on experience. These four systems

represent inanimate objects and their mechanical interactions, agents and their goal-directed actions, sets and their numerical relationships of ordering, addition and subtraction, and places in the spatial layout and their geometric relationships   (Spelke & Kinzler 2007: 89).

Similar concepts were developed in Cognitive Linguistics (see Slobin 1997c: 266). Typological comparisons revealed that only few notions are encoded by closed-class items (in particular notions like tense, aspect, causativity, voice, mood and person), whereas other notions do not seem to be encoded grammatically at all, although they are part of our everyday experience: Languages do not tend to encode colour grammatically or the state-of-mind of the speaker, i.e. whether he was interested or bored (Talmy 1985; see also the summary in Slobin 1997c). In addition, grammaticalization processes in different languages seem to go in similar directions. These findings suggest that these processes and representations are common to all humans and thus not the product of the individual mind. If that were the case, two different acquisition models would be needed: one for identifying the – potentially unlimited – semantic richness of open-class lexical items, as well as a look-up mechanism for the semantically constrained set of closed-class grammatical categories (Slobin 1997c: 267). Subsequent typological research on differences between languages as well as courses of acquisition in different languages has shown, however, that form and meaning are not neatly carved up in entirely predictable packages of closed-class items with a constrained set of meaning, and lexical items with variable meaning. But if such predictability is not there, if open- and closed-class meaning form a cline rather than two distinct sets, children would not be helped by specific innate knowledge about grammaticizable notions (Slobin 1997c: 309). Instead, cognitive factors like language processing and concept formation, as well as social aspects of communication, will interact with the specific affordances of the form–function relations found in language types and in individual languages.

12.1.4 Crosslinguistic differences and 'typological bootstrapping'

Form–function correspondences vary systematically between language types, and also within languages of the same type. Language types can be distinguished according to the nature of inflectional paradigms as in the classic distinction between isolating languages like Chinese with no or very little grammatical markers. Inflection can be agglutinative like in Turkish, where affixes for different grammatical categories are added to the stem. Typically, each grammatical category is represented by a different morpheme such that there is a one-to-one mapping of form and grammatical function. But inflection can also be fusional or synthetic. In fusional languages, inflectional morphemes typically encode several functions (e.g. case plus number or tense plus agreement in German), in (poly) synthetic or incorporating languages affixes not only consist of grammatical markers, but also other words or their pronominalized forms can be incorporated into a single word (e.g. Inuit languages, see Allen Ch. 13).

The number of grammatical categories possible or obligatory in a language as well as the nature of the morphology (additive or fusional/ synthetic) will affect what the language-learning child will have to pay attention to. Systematic crosslinguistic comparisons started with Slobin's (1973) study on cognitive prerequisites of language, where he operationalized the differences between languages in order to find out what makes language learning easy or hard. He found, for example, that children learning Turkish, a very regular agglutinative language, acquired certain grammatical notions much earlier than children learning Serbo-Croatian, a language with highly complex inflectional morphology.

In order to understand more about these generalization processes, two questions have to be addressed: how can we measure children's morphological development, and how can we assess the productivity of their linguistic representations?

12.2 Measures of development

12.2.1 Compositional or holistic forms?

Acquiring morphology can be an additive and a deconstructivist process. In the additive scenario, the child starts out with an uninflected stem and learns to add morphological markers, including building up the inflectional paradigm for each grammatical category. Such order of acquisition is typical for languages like English with relatively little morphology, and where the stem of a word corresponds to the citation form (*to laugh*). The child then adds agreement, aspect and tense morphology, for example (*laugh-s, laugh-ing, laugh-ed*). Morpheme-order studies (Section 12.3.1) examine the typical order of acquisition and provide hypotheses for such order.

In the deconstructivist scenario, children start out with complex morphological forms and analyse their internal constituency only later. They have stored the form holistically, just like a second-language learner who may know a greeting formula in the new language without being aware of its structure. This is typical for richly inflected languages where children never or only rarely encounter stems in isolation. But it is also found in other languages, when children pick up forms in an unanalysed fashion. Consider the closest relatives of English: German and Dutch. Here, the infinitive (the citation form of the verb) has an inflectional suffix (*mach-en* or *mak-en* 'to make'). Strictly speaking the form is compositional which raises the question of how to conceive of such forms if there is no evidence that the child is aware of its internal structure: To assume at face value that the child has access to the compositional structure of a complex morphological form would be an overestimation. Thus, criteria for productivity are needed (Section 12.2.2).

The assessment of productivity also affects a more general measure of linguistic complexity, the mean length of utterance (MLU; Brown 1973). For the early stages of language development, the MLU turned out to be a more reliable measure of children's language development than age alone. MLU works best in language where acquisition is predominantly an additive process. Brown (1973) computed MLU in morphemes, but this turned out to be disadvantageous for languages with a richer inflectional repertoire because the complex nature of words inflates the MLU, although the inflectional markers may not be productive. Thus, MLU is now more commonly measured in words, which renders a problem for polysynthetic languages.

12.2.2 Criteria for productivity

The major methodological issue in child language study is the assessment of productivity. In the context of child-language research, productivity refers to the internal analysis of a form, not the productivity of the morphemes as such, i.e. whether they are synchronically used to inflect new words that enter the language. That is, acquisition researchers need to find out whether children are aware of the internal structure of a string of their language, and whether the child has developed generalizations and is able to apply them to new contexts.

The most straightforward criterion for acquisition seems to be the *adult-like provision* of the morpheme(s) under investigation. Brown (1973) set a criterion of 90 per cent provision in obligatory contexts. The problem here is to define *obligatory context*: The linguistic and the non-linguistic context has to be taken into account in order to decide whether, for example, the use of a particular tense marker or the definite or indefinite article is required (Brown 1973: 255–256 & 259–270, Cazden 1968). The 90 per cent criterion of provision in obligatory contexts measures the endstate of development. At the onset of development, the criterion of contrast or alternation marks the beginning of paradigm building (Section 12.3.3). Here, the child has to use at least two different inflectional forms of the same word stem as the first sign of creativity. Alternatively, one could look for the occurrence of a morpheme with different words, e.g. the plural morpheme on different nouns. The criterion of contrast is not a strict one. Some researchers prefer a criterion of at least three different forms in order to reduce the chance that the child has simply memorized two or three inflected plural forms without having noticed their morphological constituency. There are a number of reasons why these criteria are widely used. The main reason is the indeterminacy of the notion of 'onset of productivity'. While having a contrast of three or four or five forms seems better than having a contrast of just two forms, there is no absolute dividing line between acquired/non-acquired. Thus, setting a number is just an operational criterion to fix the minimum number of exemplars. A second reason is that a low number is often used because of the nature of the data set. In many cases, it is just not possible to find more than two or three relevant examples within a single transcript, either because the inflectional category is rather rare (e.g. the passive) or because the inflectional category shows a lot of allomorphy such that the individual allomorphs have low token frequency.

More clear-cut examples for productivity are children's *overgeneralization errors*, most notably in the form of overgeneralization, when a wrong allomorph is applied, e.g. a regular form for the irregular one (e.g. *go-ed* instead of *went*). Since it is unlikely that the child hears *goed* in the input, she or he must have made up the form. Such effects can be reproduced experimentally by testing children on nonce words, for example in the famous *wug*-tests by Berko (1958). She presented children with unfamiliar nouns and verbs and elicited plural, past tense or progressive forms. The use of nonce words ensures that children cannot rely on their memory because they have not heard that word before. To pass such tests, children have to learn the nonce word first, i.e., the task demand is higher than when inflecting a familiar word. Thus, nonce word tests estimate the upper end of productivity rather than the onset.

In their study on early passives in Inuktitut, Allen and Crago (1996: 139–143) list several other criteria that are less frequently used to assess productivity. *Innovative forms* by conversion of a word to a different word class reveal productivity, for example, as in 'It balls' in response to the question 'What does the ball do?'. *Self-corrections* can also serve as an indicator that the child is aware of morphological forms.

In languages with several affixes, errors in the *ordering of the morphemes* can also serve as a diagnostic. This would be the case if children, for example, would be aware of the scope effect of the different positions of the passive morpheme in an agglutinating language like Inuktitut (Allen & Crago 1996: 141).

Yet other criteria for acquisition could be set by comparing the *frequency of the child's use with adult use*, the degree to which the child exploits the *semantic and pragmatic domain* of that marker, or the *semantic and pragmatic appropriateness* of the child's use of a morpheme (Brown 1973: 255).

12.3 The acquisition of inflectional morphology

12.3.1 Morpheme order studies

The order of the acquisition of grammatical morphemes has been one of the foremost issues in acquisition research. Within each language, morpheme-order studies define the typical pathway of acquisition and can therefore serve for diagnostic purposes of children's development. From a crosslinguistic perspective, differences in the order of acquisition of 'similar' morphemes can provide information on cognitive, phonological, semantic and distributional factors that influence children's segmentation and classification processes.

In Brown's seminal study on the development of language in three American children (Adam, Eve and Sarah, cf. the Brown corpus in the CHILDES database; MacWhinney 2000), the emergence of morphology marks Stage II in their development (Brown 1973). Before this, individual words are combined without a clear encoding of the semantic or grammatical relationship that holds between them, thus evoking the impression of 'telegraphic speech'. The reason for the later emergence of grammatical functors is that in order to acquire them, the child has to sort out numerous semantic and formal variables. Regarding formal variables, Brown (1973, 249–250) distinguishes factors that affect perceptual salience (e.g. the amount of phonetic substance, stress, serial position, high and stable frequency) and factors of grammatical complexity (e.g. phonological properties of the stem and stem changes, class membership of the stem, number of allomorphs; see also Peters 1985: 1055 for segmentation heuristics).

Semantically, grammatical functors can encode numerous relations like possession, case, number, gender, tense, aspect, modality, voice and so forth). The results of the analysis of longitudinal samples of spontaneous speech from Adam, Eve and Sarah was that there is a high correlation in the rank order of fourteen grammatical morphemes that reached the 90 per cent criterion of provision in obligatory contexts (Brown 1973). In stage II (MLU 2.25) the present progressive, the plural and the prepositions *in* and *on* were acquired. In stages III and IV (MLU 2.75 and 3.50) the past irregular (e.g. *ran*), third person irregular (e.g. *has*), uncontractible copula (e.g. *is* in 'She is happy') and articles became productive, followed by third person and past regular, the uncontractible auxiliary (e.g. *is* in 'It is running') and the contractible auxiliaries (as in 'It's running') and copula (as in 'She's happy') in Stage V (MLU 4.00). These results were confirmed in other studies for English, for example in a cross-sectional study by Jill de Villiers and Peter de Villiers (1973a). Like in Brown's study, MLU was a better predictor of development than age. A comparison of different studies using different methodologies (including imitation and nonce word tasks) generally supports the rank order of acquisition for English morphology found in Brown's study and its stringent and systematic criteria for scoring productivity (Brown 1973: 273–290).

But what accounts for the systematicity found in the acquisition of English morphemes? First, these are data from the same language, American English, thus it can be assumed that children are faced with the same input properties such that the same processing factors (perceptual salience and grammatical complexity) determine the ease of acquisition. If this was the case, differences between languages are predicted because different languages posit different acquisition spaces (Section 12.1.4). Alternatively, the morphemes could unfold along a semantic–pragmatic scale in the sense that it is more relevant for children to encode ongoing events or plurals than rather abstract auxiliaries. If semantic factors play the most important role, crosslinguistic similarities will be expected (Section 12.5).

12.3.2   Generalization and schema formation

But before investigating different theories to account for the acquisition of morphology, let us first focus on the onset of morphological paradigm building, i.e. the trajectory between first, most likely lexically specific or item-based morphological markers and the earliest generalizations. In a usage-based perspective, generalization over experience leads to schema formation (Langacker 2000). Thus, generalization is a bottom-up process. On the one hand, repeated encounter of particular strings in a language leads to entrenchment, i.e. the memory traces for that string become more robust. With an increasing amount of stored linguistic experience, the child will start to register commonalities between certain forms and the functions they encode. For example, the child may notice that some forms that denote events or activities receive an *-ing* suffix when referring to ongoing events or activities, but an *-ed* when referring to the past. The child can now relate the forms of a stem to one another, but can also relate all those forms marked by *-ed* or *-ing*, thus forming grammatical categories. Acquisition then is a process from low-level schemas where the related strings still share a lot of surface similarity, to more abstract schemas. Bybee (1995) attributes development to the different roles of type and token frequency: while high-token frequency leads to strong entrenchment, high-type frequency leads to generalization. This also explains why high-frequency irregular forms (like the English irregular verbs) remain in the language although their inflectional pattern is no longer productive, and why they may be acquired early despite of their irregular status (see the results from morpheme-order studies above).

From the perspective of a child engaged in communicative acts, the child is confronted with whole utterances, not individual words or morphemes. Tomasello (2003: 174) sees the emergence of grammatical categories as a process of identifying their function in larger communicative units:

(1) On the level of an *expression*, children have to identify communicative intentions in the input (e.g. *I wanna see it*), and they have to be able to reproduce these expressions.

(2) Children form a *pivot schema* by forming a schema on the one hand, and a slot-filler category on the other (e.g. *throw ball, throw can, throw pillow*).

(3) Next, children form item-based constructions as second-order symbols (e.g. *Mary hugs John, John hugs Mary*).

(4) Then, children form abstract constructions like syntactic roles based on analogy (*A hugs B, X kisses Y*).

(5) They form paradigmatic categories (e.g. part-of-speech categories or inflectional paradigms) based on categorization by distributional analysis.

12.3.3 Paradigm building

Evidence for the item-based nature of acquisition mainly comes from distributional analyses where it is shown that children do not acquire the full paradigm at once. Moreover, the limited nature of the formal paradigm may be related to semantic associations. In their analysis of British children's use of the various inflectional forms of the verb *go*, Theakston *et al.* (2002) showed that the children assigned different functions to the forms (e.g. *going* for intentionality, *gone* for disappearance) and did not seem to be aware that these forms belonged to the same inflectional paradigm. Likewise, Behrens (2003) found that children learning German, Dutch and

English seem to acquire the different functions of the highly polysemous and polyfunctional verb *go* (or *gehen* and *gaan*, respectively) in different orders, in accordance with the frequency with which the different functions are used in the input language.

An international research team coordinated by Wolfgang Dressler is studying the processes in acquiring pre- and proto-morphology in more detail. They have focused not only on distributional patterns and the relation between children's language and the input they receive, but also on more general, possibly universal patterns in crosslinguistic acquisition; they have explained this by bottom-up processes (e.g. Bittner *et al.* 2003).

In the pre-morphological phase identified in this research, the child might exhibit individual form–function correspondences, for example by not only using linguistic symbols in a rote-learned, but adult-like fashion, but also by encoding certain aspects by idiosyncratic meanings. For example, a child might not yet distinguish the nominal or predicative use of particular words morphosyntactically, but could mark the predicative function through extragrammatical means (Bittner *et al.* 2003), such as truncating word forms to establish a morphological contrast, using filler syllables, or producing onomatopoeic reduplications (e.g. *run run*) (e.g. in German, a common baby-talk word for 'bed' is *heia*, and 'to sleep' is *heia machen* 'make heia' or reduplicated *heia heia machen*). In a comparison of the acquisition of verb morphology in various languages (including Germanic and Romance languages as well as Finnish, Lithuanian, Greek, Turkish, Croatian and Yucatec Mayan) the first stage of generalization (so-called proto-morphology) showed the greatest individual variation: children start to generalize based on the analogies they perceive, and individual patterns can show in lexical spurts of the verb category as opposed to more continuous acquisition of verbs and their morphology. The verb spurt tended to be more pronounced than in languages with little verb morphology rather than those with richer morphology, but individual differences were attested in all languages under investigation. Subsequently, children acquired a number of inflectional contrasts for individual verbs, and started to generalize the inflectional properties to other verbs. Again, the concrete manifestations of these generalizations may be child-specific, more general patterns seemed to emerge when children had acquired a critical mass of exemplars that allowed them to draw generalizations over a larger number of exemplars (Bittner *et al.* 2003).

Three major conclusions can be drawn from such studies: first, the order of emergence of (verb) morphology is not a direct frequency match of the adult language (see also Wijnen *et al.* 2001). Second, generalization can be source- as well as product-oriented. In a source-oriented construction of complex morphological forms, the child adds morphemes to the stem. For example, the child may have identified a particular suffix as the past tense marker in English and so adds it to all stems treated as verbs. In a product-oriented generalization, the child would adjust forms to the schema of the inflected forms in the adult language. For example, in German a string consisting of the article *die* followed by a bisyllabic noun ending on *-(e)n* has a very high likelihood of encoding a plural. Children might try to match their own plural forms to the schema 'bisyllabic noun ending on *-(e)n*'. This product or schema orientation explains certain truncation of nouns that cannot be accounted for by a simple addition of inflectional morphemes (Behrens 2002, Bittner 2000, Köpcke 1998). For example, the German words *Apfel* 'apple' and *Vogel* 'bird' form the plural by vowel raising of the stem, without adding a suffix (*Äpfel, Vögel*). This is a 'bad' German plural from the schema perspective, because the *ending* is ambiguous between singular and plural forms. Children try to produce better plural forms by adding suffixes (*Apfel-n, Vogel-n*) but also by truncating the stem (*Apf-en, Vog-en*). Thus, Gestalt and schema-oriented approaches contribute to the identification of the basis on which children generalize as children have to relate the source (stem) to the product (inflected form) of morphological processes.

Third, morphological development does not follow a strictly U-shaped learning trajectory, discussed often in relation to English past tense acquisition, in which children start out with rote-learned and target-like forms (e.g. *ran*), then segment the rote-learned forms and start to overgeneralize the most regular pattern(s) to irregular stems (e.g. *runned*), and finally 'relearn' the irregular forms (See Marcus *et al.* 1992). Such a development predicts errors especially in the second phase. Instead, errors occur throughout development and may change in nature over time.

Behrens (2002) investigated the error rates and error patterns in a German child's learning of the plural in German. Throughout the first 6 months of morphological development, some subsets of nouns were not susceptible to errors. For example, nouns ending with schwa always take the *-n* plural, and the child never made an error on this class. Other, less predictable plural classes showed much higher error rates, irrespective of type frequency of that plural class – probably because the child at this early age did not have enough linguistic experience to generalize based on type frequency, and because some of the more uncommon allomorphs apply to nouns with high-token frequency. Crucially, the error patterns changed with development: initially, the child overgeneralized, in particular the *-n* ending; a little later, he made frequent errors with nouns that do not take a plural suffix, because these nouns violate the iconicity principle – that plurals should be marked (Köpcke 1998). These results show the need for fine-grained analyses, or experimental work, to find out about children's generalization patterns.

The time course of acquisition is important; error patterns may change within just a few weeks or even days. Such change is indicative of learning processes as conceived of in dynamic systems theory (DST; cf. van Dijk 2004, van Geert 1994). As discussed above, morphology requires the integration of multiple interrelated components of language. In DST is it assumed that changes in one aspect of a complex system affect other components. Only a system that is not developing is stable. Learning phases, then, are characterized by higher variability because previously established units become destabilized. Variation, often in the form of apparent regress, is thus an indicator of development (van Geert 1994).

To sum up, research on the emergence of morphological paradigms shows that children start out with rather small generalizations, and build up the inflectional paradigms in a piecemeal fashion. There seems to be agreement in the literature that the concrete nature of inflectional paradigms has to be learned in a language-specific fashion (see Ud Deen Ch. 15, Section 15.5.1), and that complexity of a morphological paradigm affects its acquisition. To assess complexity and the factors that contribute to the ease or difficulty in the acquisition of morphology is the subject of a number of processing models of morphology (see Section 12.5).

12.4   The acquisition of derivational morphology and compounding

Derivational morphology and word formation processes are studied far less extensively than inflectional morphology. The focus of the studies is on compounding where two lexical stems are combined to form a new word (*nose beard* for *moustache*; Becker 1994) and on the formation of agentive nouns (*kiss* → *kisser*). Also, some more specific semantic domains have been studied in some detail, for example prefixes for undoing actions like *un-* in English (Clark 1993: 219–238) or ways to encode causative events (Bowerman 1974).

In principle, the rules for word formation can be acquired by the same generalization mechanisms that help children to acquire inflectional morphology. When children try to fill lexical gaps, they may rely on the derivational and compounding patterns they have identified in their target language. For example, children can change the part-of-speech category of a word, either through conversion (word-class change without overt morphological marking as in English) or by applying the appropriate affixes to a noun root as in Slavic languages (see Clark 1993: 198–218). As with inflectional morphology, overgeneralization and lexical innovations based on regular word formation strategies are attested. The generalization processes rely on the regularity in the adult language, as well as on the semantic abstractness of the resulting lexemes (Becker 1994b, Clark 1993). Word formation errors and overgeneralizations are attested as early as errors and overgeneralizations in inflectional morphology.

12.5 Theories

There is a range of explanatory theories that either claim universal constraints on the acquisition of morphology, or that emphasize the properties
specific to the language or language type, that affect the processability and
therefore account for the relative ease or difficulty of acquisition. Unlike in
syntax acquisition, there are only a few proposals regarding concrete innate
representations of morphology. In the principles and parameters and the
minimalist version of Generative Grammar, a systematic relationship
between the inflectional properties of verbs and verb movement is assumed
(See Blom 2007 for an overview of different versions of the theory; Ud Deen
Ch. 15 for a recent generativist account; Dimroth *et al.* 2003 for a semantics-
based theory).

But in the second half of the twentieth century, there were prominent
proposals that assumed that children may rely on the prespecification
from general cognition or semantics. Jean Piaget proposed a stage model
of development and assumed that language development depends on the
prior development of the relevant concepts in general cognition (See
Johnston 1985). Slobin (1985c) initially assumed that children's grammatical acquisition would be driven by their functional need because, he
hypothesized, all children would be involved in similar kinds of activities,
facing similar communicative requirements. What unites the so-called Basic
Child Grammar that he proposed are the functions encoded. Children
would have to search for the appropriate means to encode them in their
target languages. These assumptions are now widely refuted (Slobin 1997c),
there seems to be agreement that children acquire form and function in
synchrony (Section 12.5.4).

Regarding the acquisition of morphological categories, the major contemporary theories can be described as processing models. The Dual
Mechanism model (Section 12.5.2) conceives of the human processor as
being divided between a module that handles regular inflection, and a
memory storage for the holistic storage of analytical forms. In contrast,
single mechanism models assume that there is no principled division
between regular and irregular morphology, but that children learn all
morphology by generalization over the input patterns they take in
(Sections 12.5.1 and 12.5.2).

12.5.1 Dual route versus single route processing

A second domain is concerned with whether inflectional morphology is
processed in two different ways. It has been proposed that the human
processor is designed to process regular morphology by compositional and
rule-governed processes such that the inflectional morpheme is added
to the stem (Clahsen 1999a, Marcus 2000, Marcus *et al.* 1992, Pinker

1999, Pinker & Prince 1991). Irregular forms have to be memorized, i.e. they are stored holistically in the mental lexicon. In language processing, the speaker would first search through the stored inventory of irregular forms, and if the item is not found there, compose the regular form by rule. Failure of look-up results in overgeneralization errors. For example, a speaker wanting to encode the past tense form of *go* fails to retrieve *went* and consequently produces *go-ed* by rule.

Single-route models do not make a categorical distinction between regular and irregular morphology, but assume that all degrees of regularity can be learned on the basis of generalizing over the input children hear (Elman *et al.* 1996; see also the discussion in Clahsen 1999a). In the course of the past two decades, processing models have been refined and can now be tested using a variety of data types and methods (longitudinal, cross-sectional, experimental, computational).

12.5.2   Operating principles

What accounts for the ease of acquisition? Slobin (1973, 1985c) formulated forty so-called operating principles that children were assumed to make use of when processing their target language (see Slobin 1985c: 1251–1256). These operating principles are assumed to guide children in their initial segmentation of speech (Peters 1985), and provide strategies and procedures for attending to and storing the input they receive, and for deriving linguistic patterns from it by organizing segmented elements into units and mapping them to their function (Slobin 1985c). For example, inflectional morphology often surfaces as suffixes, and thus children would pay attention to the end of a unit and store it separately from the unit (Slobin 1985c: 1251). Operating principles would need to be flexible enough to allow the acquisition of typologically different languages and thus account for the variable mappings between different levels of representation attested in different languages. For example, children should strengthen particular solutions that have proven successful to similar problems. Strengthening explains why gender is acquired early in Hebrew, where it is a pervasive category that is relevant for a wide range of agreement phenomena and plural formation, whereas it is acquired late in Romance languages, where it only plays a marginal role (Slobin 1985c).

But the concept of operating principles, although psychologically plausible, was criticized at the time. This was because the operating principles were designed to deal with the divergent processing problems different languages pose, and offered a large repertoire of strategies and learning procedures. There were a number of problems raised. First, they lacked predictive power as there was no theory of when to apply which operating principle (Bowerman 1985, Hakuta 1988). Second, the underlying assumption was that children's language development would follow the same cognitive development irrespective of the language being acquired.

The first problem was addressed in the Competition Model developed by Elizabeth Bates and Brian MacWhinney (Bates & MacWhinney 1987, see also the extended version in MacWhinney 2004b, 2005), the second problem led to a rethinking of the relationship between thought and language in theories of linguistic relativity (Bowerman 1985, 1994, Bowerman & Choi 2003, Slobin 1997c, 1997d).

12.5.3 Competition model

From a processing perspective, each language and dialect has its own affordances regarding cues it offers for learning its structure. Bates and MacWhinney (1987) conceptualized these cues as being in competition with one another such that the ease or difficulty of acquisition can be predicted by the validity of a cue (a function of its availability and reliability) in relation to the cost of processing it. Morphological markers that show a one-to-one mapping of form and function have the highest cue validity (e.g. the very regular agglutinative affixes found in Turkish); cues that have several functions have lower validity. Cue cost computes the difficulty of processing: affixes, for example, are easier to process than subtle phonetic changes of the stem. Frequent elements are easier to detect and to store than low frequent ones.

The competition model allows prediction of the order of acquisition in different languages. Regarding syntactic transitivity, for example, word order is a very reliable cue in English, but less reliable in German, where subjects and direct objects can be reordered. In German, case marking on the definite article of masculine nouns is the most reliable cue, but not always available (because not all nouns are masculines, and not all masculines are accompanied by the definite article).

A study on German revealed that young children rely on word order, and only older children are able to process case cues (Lindner 2003; see also Kempe & MacWhinney 1998). Thus, the competition model allows us to compute the effect of the relation between different cues on acquisition. Similar ideas are currently explored in probabilistic theories of language (e.g. Bod *et al.* 2003). Probabilistic models have been applied to the acquisition of part-of-speech categories through observing co-occurrence statistics (Redington *et al.* 1998) or through multiple-cue integration, i.e. prosodic, phonological and distributional cues (Christiansen & Monaghan 2006).

12.5.4 Linguistic relativity

Several researchers assumed that children across the world will start out to learn languages based on the same functions and similar if not same semantics, because (a) they would perceive visual stimuli in the same way, e.g. spatial configurations, (b) they are involved in similar events and activities, e.g. scenes where an agent manipulates an object), (c) their general cognitive development would proceed in similar fashion. For example, it should be cognitively easier to refer to past events that resulted in an observable change-of-state than to encode abstract temporal relations like *before* and *after*. This is because they may involve a different deictic *origo* than the here-and-now, and the order of events may be different from the order specified in the utterance (e.g. Before John went to Paris he spent five days in London).

However, research in typologically different languages and their acquisition has shown that not only do languages differ in how they divide up 'semantic space', but language itself plays an important role in directing children's linguistic and non-linguistic categorization (Bowerman 1985, 1994, Slobin 1997d, Stoll Ch. 6). Children need to pay attention to those categories that are (obligatorily) encoded in their language: Turkish children, for example, need to keep track of whether an event they report on has been observed directly or not, since Turkish encodes evidential modality (Aksu-Koç 1998).

12.6   Summary and outlook

This chapter has focused on generalization processes as well as theories and methods to account for the developmental processes observed. Analysis of children's spontaneous speech or systematically elicited data has informed us about the time course and nature of generalization, as well as on individual differences in children's learning trajectories. Crosslinguistic comparisons have led to deeper insights into the factors that influence acquisition. The five volumes edited by Slobin (1985–1995) present detailed descriptions of the acquisition of morphosyntax in a wide range of typologically different languages, while the chapters in Berman and Slobin (1994) systematically compare data from narratives, as do chapters in Strömqvist and Verhoeven (2004).

Through experimental work it has been possible to operationalize the variables found in the language and in learner's development (e.g. Thomas & Gathercole, 2007, on the interaction of grammatical gender and phonological mutation in Welsh), and computational models of development help to identify the processes necessary for integrating interacting linguistic variables. However, while these models are very successful in dealing with the form side of language, they are currently less well suited to integrate semantic and pragmatic factors, simply because these are hard to implement.

Morphological categories pose a language-specific acquisition problem that involves the integration of multiple cues and domains (phonology, prosody, semantics, pragmatics, syntax). Generalization seems to proceed in a usage-based and piecemeal fashion. While there is a substantial body of research showing how and in what order children build the paradigm of a particular inflectional category, there is less insight into the gradedness of the child's representation regarding the function of these miniparadigms.

Suggestions for further reading

Berman, R. A., & Slobin, D. I. (Eds.). (1994). *Relating Events in Narrative: A Crosslinguistic Developmental Study*. Hillsdale, NJ: Lawrence Erlbaum Associates.

Bowerman, M., & Levinson, S. (Eds.). (2001). *Language Acquisition and Conceptual Development*. Cambridge: Cambridge University Press.

Li, P., & Shirai, Y. (2000). *The Acquisition of Lexical and Grammatical Aspect*. New York: Mouton de Gruyter.

Slobin, D. I. (Ed.). (1985–1995). *The Crosslinguistic Study of Language Acquisition*. (Vols. 1–5). Mahwah, NJ: Lawrence Erlbaum Associates.

Strömqvist, S., & Verhoeven, L. (Eds.). (2004). *Relating Events in Narrative: Vol. 2. Typological and Contextual Perspectives*. Mahwah, NJ: Lawrence Erlbaum Associates.

13

Verb argument structure

Shanley Allen

13.1   Introduction

In syntax, an argument is defined as 'a noun phrase bearing a specific grammatical or semantic relation to a verb and whose overt or implied presence is required for well-formedness in structures containing that verb' (Trask 1993: 20). Arguments can be identified in two ways: in terms of syntactic roles with respect to the verb such as Subject and Object, and in terms of semantic roles in relation to the verb such as Agent (entity that instigates an action) and Patient (entity that undergoes an action). Argument structure is the specification of the number and types of arguments required for a verb in that structure to be well-formed. For instance, an intransitive structure requires one Subject argument (e.g. *John laughed*) while a transitive structure requires both a Subject and an Object (e.g. *John built the cabinet*). Stereotypically the Subject is an Agent and the Object is a Patient, as is the case in the two examples just cited. However, one does not need to look far to find exceptions to this. For example, the Subjects in *The cabinet broke* and *Mary liked the cabinet* are not Agents since they do not perform any action (*cabinet* is a Patient, *Mary* is an Experiencer). In addition to the intransitive and the transitive, many more complex argument structures occur and have been studied extensively (see Levin 1993 for a review of over eighty argument structures used in English). Some common structures include the passive (e.g. *The cabinet was built by John*), the ditransitive (the prepositional dative, e.g. *John gave the cabinet to Mary*, or the double object dative, e.g. *John gave Mary the cabinet*), and the causative (the lexical causative, e.g. *John broke the cabinet*, or the periphrastic causative, e.g. *John made the cabinet break*).

All verbs in a language must be used in at least one argument structure, but most verbs may appear in two or more structures as indicated in the examples just cited. Thus, many researchers have argued that the lexical entry for each

Thanks to James Anglin and Edith Bavin for helpful discussions and comments on earlier drafts of this chapter.

verb in the mental lexicon must specify which argument structures a verb permits in the form of subcategorization frames (e.g. Baker 1979, Oehrle 1976). Others have argued that subcategorization frames are unnecessary because so much of a verb's argument structure can be derived from its meaning (e.g. Levin 1993, Pinker 1989). For example, most verbs of change of state (e.g. *break, bend, melt, drop*) can appear in both intransitive and lexical causative structures (e.g. *The cabinet broke, John broke the cabinet*). Other well-defined subtypes of verbs such as verbs of appearance and occurrence (e.g. *appear, arise, happen, recur*) can be used in the intransitive structure but not the lexical causative structure (e.g. *The rabbit appeared, *The magician appeared the rabbit*). Thus, if one can appropriately identify the relevant meaning of a given verb, one can determine the argument structure of that verb. Still other researchers have argued that not verb meanings but rather construction meanings are the essential starting point for under-standing argument structure (e.g. Fillmore *et al.* 1988, Goldberg 1995). For instance, it is clear from the sentence structure alone that *John mooped the ball to Mary* describes an event of transfer and that *John mooped the ball onto the table* describes an event of caused motion; knowing the meaning of the verb is not necessary to understanding much of the meaning of the sentences.

The main task that children face in learning argument structure is determining which verbs can appear in which argument structures. Consider an English-speaking child who wants to tell a friend about her experiences observing an otter in the zoo. How does she learn that she can describe this event by saying *I saw an otter* but not *I looked an otter*? Although both verbs have similar meanings, *see* is transitive and *look* is intransitive. If that otter then precipitously descends from the land into the water, the English-speaking child can describe that event by saying either *The otter dropped into the water* or *The otter fell into the water*. But how does she learn that *The zookeeper dropped the otter into the water* is perfectly grammatical while *The zookeeper fell the otter into the water* is not permitted? Although both verbs can be used in the intransitive structure with Patient Subjects, only *drop* can be used in the lexical causative structure. And if the zookeeper subsequently brings the otter over to show it to the child, how does she know to describe this event as *The zookeeper carried the otter to me* and not *The zookeeper carried me the otter* – in other words, that *carry* can be used in the prepositional dative but not the double object dative? Indeed, children often overgeneralize argument structures belying their struggle in figu-ring out the appropriate patterns (e.g. *Don't giggle me* to mean 'Don't make me giggle', Bowerman 1982a). Given the complexity of the system, learn-ing argument structure is clearly no small task.

This chapter reviews a representative sample of the extensive literature on the acquisition of argument structure. Section 13.2 outlines three theoretical debates that have driven the research on argument structure acquisition: is early knowledge related to argument structure innate or lexically driven? Given innate building blocks, do children break into argument structure using verb meaning or sentence structure? How strong are argument structure representations at the outset and how do they develop over time? Section 13.3 illustrates the relevance of particular argument structures to these theoretical debates in a brief review of the work on the acquisition of passives and datives. Finally, section 13.4 discusses how children can learn argument structure when arguments are often omitted in caregiver speech, and how children's use of different forms for arguments (e.g. noun phrase, pronoun, omitted) relates to their understanding of information flow in the discourse.

13.2   Theoretical approaches

13.2.1   Bootstrapping using innate knowledge

Consistent with the generative linguistic approach to language development, one prominent theory of the acquisition of argument structure is that children are innately endowed with key knowledge that helps them break into the system. This includes (1) apparently universal *syntactic categories* such as noun and verb, (2) basic understanding of the potential *syntactic relations* between the two such as Subject and Object, (3) basic knowledge of the *semantic roles* or functions of arguments such as Agent and Patient, and (4) expectations about the likely links between syntactic roles and semantic functions (i.e. *linking rules*), such as that the Agent of an action is also likely to be the Subject of a verb (Gleitman *et al.* 2005, Pinker 1984, 1989). Children are assumed to use this innate knowledge to 'bootstrap' themselves into a fully abstract and adult-like system of argument structure. However, there are two conflicting approaches about the direction in which this bootstrapping occurs to solve the linking problem: from semantics to syntax (semantic bootstrapping – Pinker 1989) or from syntax to semantics (syntactic bootstrapping – Gleitman 1990).

13.2.1.1   Semantic bootstrapping

Under the semantic bootstrapping account, children focus first on the semantics of the event denoted by a verb, homing in on the meaning of that verb (Pinker 1984, 1989). For example, they notice through observation that a running event typically involves an Agent who does the running, and that a pushing event typically involves an Agent who does the pushing and a Patient that gets pushed. When children later hear an utterance like *John runs* or *Bill is pushing the car*, they use their innately specified linking rules to infer that the Agent is the Subject and the Patient is the Object. With repeated similar experiences, children map this information about Subjects and Objects to facts about word order, noun and verb morphology and other indicators of syntactic roles. Pinker and his colleagues conducted several spontaneous speech and elicited production studies indicating that appropriate and overgeneralized utterances involving various argument structure alternations are largely constrained by semantic classes (Gropen *et al.* 1989, Pinker 1989, Pinker *et al.* 1987). For example, they found that children's dative overgeneralizations do not extend to verb classes that do not allow it and, in studies using novel verbs, children prefer to generalize the passive structure to novel verbs of action rather than novel verbs of experience, mirroring the verb class distribution of passives with real verbs. Some supportive evidence for children's early sensitivity to verb classes comes from a non-linguistic task showing that infants have expectations as to the participants associated with particular events. Gordon (2003) showed infants videos of either a 'giving' event in which two people approach each other and exchange a stuffed bear, or a 'hugging' event in which two people approach each other and hug but the bear does not change hands. After habituation to the event, infants are then shown the same video but without the bear. Infants' eye movements indicate that they search for the missing bear in the 'giving' condition but not in the 'hugging' condition.

The semantic bootstrapping approach has been challenged on several fronts. First, the links between syntactic and semantic categories have been shown to vary too much across languages for universal linking rules to be plausible (Bowerman & Brown 2007, Slobin 1997c). Second, later spontaneous speech analysis revealed that many Subjects in the first utterances of English-speaking children were not Agents, thus violating the proposed default linking rules (e.g. *I like it*, *Pete hurt by car*; Bowerman 1990, Lieven *et al.* 1997). Third, a detailed analysis of causative overgeneralization errors indicates that they are common in verb classes that strongly prohibit the lexical causative such as verbs which are not dynamic (e.g. … *the cold stayed them awake*, 2;11) or for which the caused event is not brought about directly (e.g. *I want to watch you this book*, 4;3), and that such overgeneralizations persist until age 12 which is much later than Pinker's theory would predict (Bowerman & Croft 2007). Fourth, Goldberg and her colleagues (Casenhiser & Goldberg 2005, Goldberg 1995, 1999, 2006, Goldberg *et al.* 2004, 2005) provide evidence that innate linking rules are not needed for semantic bootstrapping; rather, children can use the verb that is the most frequently used in a given construction to '[facilitate] the association of the meaning of the verb in the construction with the construction itself, allowing learners to get a "fix" on the construction's meaning' (Goldberg *et al.* 2004: 310). For example, their analysis of spontaneous interactions between twenty-seven children aged 2;4 and their caregivers showed that *put* was the most frequently used verb in the caused motion construction (e.g. *John put the book on the table*) appearing in about a third of child and caregiver uses, and that *put* was not used in any other construction than caused motion so was an excellent predictor of that construction. Subsequent experiments with adults and children aged 5–7 provide evidence that participants can learn an argument structure construction on the basis of limited input data, and that highly frequent use of one verb in that construction in the input facilitates learning. All of these challenges show that semantic bootstrapping as proposed by Pinker (1989) does not work.

13.2.1.2 Syntactic bootstrapping

Another set of challenges to semantic bootstrapping comes from those who claim that semantics is not dependable as a cue to argument structure (Gleitman 1990, Gleitman *et al.* 2005). First, children under radically different exposure conditions (e.g. blind vs. sighted, with vs. without exposure to natural language) acquire much the same representations for verbs (Goldin-Meadow 2003b, Landau & Gleitman 1985). Second, many verbs are identical to each other except in one respect which is difficult to distinguish just from observation of the event (e.g. *chase* vs. *flee*), and some verbs do not refer to observable states or events (e.g. *think, know*; Gleitman 1990). Third, even for more 'concrete' verbs it is not a straightforward task to pick out the event in a real world scene denoted by a particular verb (Gillette *et al.* 1999, Snedeker & Gleitman 2004).

These researchers instead propose syntactic bootstrapping – that children attend first to the number of arguments a verb has and the syntactic arrangement in which they appear and then use that information as a 'syntactic zoom lens' (Fisher *et al.* 1994) to bootstrap themselves into the meaning of the verb. If a child hears a sentence like *The rabbit ziffs the ball to the elephant*, she or he is likely to hypothesize that *ziff* is a verb of transfer such as *give* or *throw*; a verb of placement (*put*) or perception (*see*) would not fit the syntactic frame. The efficacy of this process has been confirmed by many comprehension studies using the preferential looking paradigm (see Naigles & Swensen 2007 for a review). For example, Naigles (1990) showed two groups of 24 month olds a video in which a rabbit repeatedly pushed a duck into a squatting position while both rabbit and duck circled their arms. One group heard the accompanying phrase *The rabbit is gorping the duck* (transitive) while the other heard *The rabbit and the duck are gorping* (intransitive). Then both groups saw the two events separated – pushing to squat on one screen and arm-circling on another – while hearing *Where's gorping now? Find gorping!* The group exposed to the transitive utterance selected the pushing event while the group exposed to the intransitive utterance selected the arm-circling event. Since both groups saw the same initial video, there would be no reason to expect such a differentiation in interpretation of the verb *gorp* under the semantic bootstrapping account. Similar results have been found for slightly older children (Bavin & Growcutt 1999, Hirsh-Pasek & Golinkoff 1996) including that children can interpret non-causal verb meanings (Naigles & Kako 1993), can use multiple syntactic frames to learn verb meaning (Naigles 1996), can interpret verb meaning even when information about arguments is minimal (i.e. both arguments specified with pronoun *she* – Fisher 1996, 2002b), and can use syntactic frames to distinguish the meanings of perspective verbs (*chase, flee*) and mental state verbs (*think, believe*) (Fisher *et al.* 1994, Papafragou *et al.*

2007). Naigles and colleagues show that children as young as age 2 can adjust their interpretation of a known verb to fit a new syntactic frame (e.g. acting out a bringing event upon hearing *Noah goes the elephant to the ark*), illustrating that they derive meaning as least as much from the syntactic frame as from the verb (Naigles *et al.* 1992, 1993). Syntactic bootstrapping also holds in languages other than English. Children use the number of arguments in sentences to extend causative meanings to familiar verbs presented in transitive frames and non-causative meanings to familiar verbs presented in intransitive frames in languages as varied as Mandarin Chinese, Kannada and French (Lee & Naigles 2008, Lidz *et al.* 2003a, Naigles & Lehrer 2002).

Work cited in the previous paragraph indicates that children's argument structure representations are sensitive to the number of nouns in a sentence. More recent work has investigated whether children are also sensitive to the semantic roles of those arguments and thus to the linking rules between semantics and syntax that are central to argument structure. In a preferential looking study by Gertner *et al.* (2006), 21 and 25 month olds were simultaneously shown two video clips with arguments in opposite roles (e.g. bunny gorping duck, duck gorping bunny). They looked longer at the screen for which the semantic role in the video event matched the syntactic role in the accompanying speech, for both Subject–Agent (e.g. *The bunny is gorping the duck!*) and Object–Patient (e.g. *He is gorping the duck!*), indicating their sensitivity to linking rules. Similar results using a different paradigm were found for slightly older children by Fernandes *et al.* (2006).

13.2.2   Usage-based learning

The strong form of the two bootstrapping accounts just described assumes that children break into argument structure aided by innate linguistic knowledge. An alternative view, the usage-based learning approach, is that children use only general cognitive mechanisms to learn argument structure on the basis of generalizations from the input (Tomasello 2000a, 2003, and see Ch. 5). This approach has its foundations in studies of spontaneous speech. Tomasello's (1992) detailed analysis of one child's speech before age 2 showed that each verb seemed to be an 'island' with its own argument structure (e.g. *eater* for the verb *eat* and *runner* for the verb *run*), a pattern later confirmed in data from several other children (Lieven *et al.* 1997, McClure *et al.* 2006). Tomasello hypothesized that these first verb-specific argument structures are gradually generalized by the child to more abstract categories such as Agent, Subject and intransitive verb, eventually leading to verb-general representations of argument structure only after age 3;0. Children's overgeneralization errors are also rare before age 3;0, suggesting that they have not yet formed initial generalizations (Bowerman 1982a, Pinker 1989). Finally, the strong effect of input frequency on the emergence of productivity of argument structures in children is consistent with a usage-based view (Allen & Crago 1996, Demuth & Kline 2006, Gordon & Chafetz 1990).

More powerful evidence for the usage-based approach comes from three types of elicited production studies: novel verb generalization, weird word order, and training. In a typical *novel verb generalization* study (Tomasello & Brooks 1998), children at 2;0 and 2;6 were taught one verb modelled as intransitive (e.g. *The ball is dacking*) and another as transitive (e.g. *Jim is tamming the car*). The experimenter then asked the child 'What's AGENT doing?' attempting to elicit transitive structures. Although children typically produced a new transitive sentence for the verb modelled as transitive (e.g. *He's tamming the car*), very few produced a transitive sentence for the verb modelled as intransitive (e.g. *He's dacking the ball*). Several similar studies in English, Hebrew and Spanish eliciting transitive structures from novel verbs modelled in either neutral, intransitive or passive frames consistently show similar results, implying that children younger than 3;0 do not yet have an abstract representation of these structures (see Tomasello 2000a and references therein). The same finding holds for elicited production studies using the dative alternation as discussed in section 13.3.2 (Conwell & Demuth 2007, Gropen *et al.* 1989).

In the *weird word order* paradigm, children hear an experimenter describing events using novel and familiar verbs in a weird word order (e.g. *Ernie Bert pushing* to describe Ernie pushing Bert) or with incorrect linking relations (e.g. *The frog is pushing the lion* to describe an action in which the lion is Agent and the frog is Patient) and are then asked to describe similar events in their own words. Children younger than 3;6 typically 'correct' the word order from Subject–Object–Verb to Subject–Verb–Object for frequent familiar verbs; for novel verbs and infrequent familiar verbs they either use the weird order or avoid using the verb altogether (Abbot-Smith *et al.* 2001, Akhtar 1999, Matthews *et al.* 2005). Both English- and German-speaking children aged 2;4 'correct' the semantics–syntax linking for familiar verbs; German-speaking children also do so for novel verbs but English-speaking children mostly avoid using them (Abbot-Smith *et al.* in press).

The third type of elicited production study involves *training* children in use of either intransitive–transitive (e.g. *This tiger is bouncing* / *This tortoise is bouncing this tiger*) or passive–transitive alternations (e.g. *The tiger's gonna get bounced* / *The tortoise is gonna bounce the tiger*) for a set of familiar verbs, then presenting them with a novel verb in either intransitive or passive and encouraging them to use it in the transitive. Trained children aged 2;6 generalized the transitive structure with novel verbs more than twice as often as a group of control children who did not receive training indicating that developing a representation of the transitive structure is influenced by input frequency (Abbot-Smith *et al.* 2004, Childers & Tomasello 2001). Overall, the results of both spontaneous speech and elicited production studies suggest that 2-year-old children restrict their use of a verb to the syntactic frame in which it is learned and do not easily generalize to other frames as would be predicted if they had innate knowledge of categories such as Agent and Subject (Tomasello 2000a).

13.2.3   Weak abstract representation

Fisher (2002a) critiques the strong version of the usage-based approach while acknowledging its valuable contributions to understanding the role of lexical learning in acquisition. She argues that many of the findings interpreted by usage-based theorists as lack of abstraction could rather be interpreted as evidence of syntactic priming (Bock 1986) – children persist in using the learned syntactic frames because they have just heard them – or as evidence of appropriate conservatism – children know that not all English intransitive verbs can be used transitively (e.g. *sleep*, *giggle*). More importantly, she points out that a non-trivial number of 2 year olds in studies claimed to support a strong usage-based theory in fact generalized novel verbs to new sentence frames (Abbot-Smith *et al.* 2001, Brooks & Tomasello 1999b) or changed ungrammatical to grammatical word orders (Akhtar 1999). Finally, she notes that virtually all of the evidence for the usage-based approach derives from production studies which arguably require active behavioural decision making and thus relatively strong syntactic representations. In contrast, comprehension studies using the preferential looking paradigm, which places fewer performance demands on children and thus is more sensitive to weak syntactic representations, have provided evidence for abstract representations of argument structures as young as 2;0 (see section 13.2.1.2). Supported by these three types of evidence, Fisher suggests that 2-year-old children do in fact have abstract representations of the syntactic frames in question although they are weaker than those of older children and adults. In their reply to Fisher's critique, Tomasello and Abbot-Smith (2002: 210) concede that young children may 'have a weak transitive schema – one that enables certain kinds of linguistic operations but not others – whereas older children have a stronger and more robust schema based on a wider range of stored linguistic experience'.

Growing out of this interaction between Fisher (2002a) and Tomasello and Abbot-Smith (2002), the research on argument structure acquisition has now largely turned towards exploring the nature of weak argument structure representations and how they strengthen over time in interaction with lexical learning. Most of the literature published after 2003 from both the syntactic bootstrapping and usage-based approaches is framed within this discussion. For example, a study of spontaneous speech in 2 year olds stresses the 'limited scope formulae ... which serve as building blocks for more abstract structures' in addition to the many verb-specific patterns found (McClure *et al.* 2006: 693), and the weird linking study mentioned earlier takes care to point out that 80 per cent of the ten

English-speaking children who used a transitive structure with a novel verb corrected the linking (indicating a verb-general representation of the transitive structure) in addition to noting that the other twenty children avoided the novel verb (Abbot-Smith *et al.* in press).

In addition, several researchers have begun to explore this question using priming – a paradigm particularly sensitive to revealing representation strength. In a typical *production priming* study, an experimenter models one argument structure in picture descriptions with several verbs and then asks the child to describe a new picture with a different verb. The child's use of the primed argument structure is taken to indicate that he or she has a verb-general representation for the structure that can extend to a new verb. Savage *et al.* (2003) showed that 6-year-old English-speaking children could easily generalize the passive structure to new verbs after being primed with five passive utterances, but 3 and 4 year olds could only generalize if all the primes were identical except for the verb (e.g. *It got pushed by it* and *It got caught by it* rather than *The brick got pushed by the digger* and *The ball got caught by the net*) and thus had high lexical overlap with the potential target utterance. A follow-up study with 4 year olds revealed that the effect of priming was stronger when varied verbs were used in the priming phase than when a single verb was used, and the effect of varied primes persisted for up to a month suggesting that learning occurred during the study (Savage *et al.* 2006). Huttenlocher *et al.* (2004) found productive generalization of both transitive/passive and dative structures with 5 year olds using methods similar to Savage *et al.* (2003). Finally, Shimpi *et al.* (2007) found weak but productive generalization of both transitives/passives and datives with 4 year olds when ten passive examples were modelled in the priming phase (i.e. double the amount used by Savage *et al.* 2003), and with 3 year olds when children's responses were interspersed with the primes rather than the primes and responses occurring in separate blocks. The production priming results taken together indicate that 3 year olds have weak representations of the passive and dative structures that can be accessed under favourable experimental conditions, and that this representation gradually gets more robust through the age of 5 or 6. A recent study has tested *comprehension priming* using eye-tracking with children aged 3 and 4 (Thothathiri & Snedeker 2008). Children heard several sentences asking them to manipulate objects in a display in front of them. Two prime utterances used either the prepositional dative or the double object dative (e.g. *Give the lion the ball* or *Give the ball to the lion*). Then a test utterance was presented using either the primed or non-primed dative structure, but that was ambiguous between the two until after the onset of the first post-verbal noun (e.g. *Give the bird the dogbone* or *Give the birdhouse to the sheep*). Children's eye gaze was analysed to determine whether they expected the test utterance to have the same structure as primed. Four year olds showed a stronger comprehension priming effect than 3 year olds, consistent with the interpretation that young children have a weak syntactic representation of the two dative structures that strengthens with development.

13.3   Trajectory and patterns in the acquisition of argument structure alternations

Looking at argument structure acquisition from the point of view of theory often focuses on abstract questions for which data are secondary. In this next section, we focus on argument structure acquisition from the point of view of the structures themselves – specifically passive and dative – in order to get a sense of the trajectory and patterns of development within one structure.

13.3.1   Passives

Typical passives are shown in the (b) sentences in (1) and (2), with their active transitive counterparts in the (a) sentences.

(1)   a. The cat chased the dog.
      b. The dog was chased by the cat.

(2)   a. Marion climbed the big tree.
      b. The big tree was climbed by Marion.

In the active transitive sentences the Agent appears in Subject position while the Patient appears in Object position. In passive sentences the linking between syntactic roles and semantic roles changes: the Patient appears in Subject position while the Agent optionally appears in an adjunct phrase introduced by the preposition *by* in English. This entails that the standard word order also differs for the two structures: Agent–Verb–Patient for active transitives and Patient–Verb–Agent for passives. The passive is permitted crosslinguistically for virtually all transitive action verbs like those in (1) and (2) with Agent Subjects and Patient Objects. However, only a subset of non-action verb classes for which the Subject and Object are linked to other semantic roles permit the passive, and those classes differ across languages (Pinker *et al.* 1987). For instance, psychological verbs permit passivization in English (e.g. *The paintings were admired by the tourists*) but verbs of pure possession do not (e.g. *A new game was had by the brothers*). From the discourse perspective, the passive focuses attention on the Patient of the transitive action and defocuses the Agent.

The passive has been the most frequently studied argument structure in the acquisition literature. It is an ideal test of whether children's apparent comprehension and production of argument structures derive from a true understanding of the argument structure of a particular verb, or reflects knowledge of the real-world context or the most frequent or default pattern that occurs with that verb in the input. In addition, the differential distribution of the passive across semantic classes of verbs predicts that children will quickly learn and easily overgeneralize passives using verbs with Agent Subjects and Patient Objects, but will learn the passive of other classes of verbs more slowly (Pinker *et al.* 1987).

Four main findings concerning passives have been central to the literature on argument structure acquisition. First, passives do not typically appear in English spontaneous speech until around age 4, and children's early comprehension and production of passives is strongly influenced by their reliance on the word order and linking patterns of the much more frequent active structure and by their knowledge of real-world context (see O'Grady 1997 and references therein). Both comprehension and production errors involve reversing the roles of the arguments – treating the Patient Subject as if it were the Agent and the Agent in the adjunct *by* phrase as if it were the Patient. Children also comprehend and produce passives earlier when the Agent and Patient are non-reversible as in (2) (i.e. one cannot say *Marion was climbed by the tree*) than when they are reversible as in (1), reflecting the influence of real-world plausibility of events. Indeed, English-speaking children may not fully understand the argument structure of passives until age 6 or later even though they produce passive structures earlier than that.

A second finding is that children are sensitive to semantic classes of verbs in learning the passive. Two semantic classes are typically distinguished: action verbs and non-action verbs. In two separate studies involving children aged 3–11, Sudhalter and Braine (1985) tested children's ability to identify the Agent (for action passives) or Experiencer (for non-action passives). Children aged 3–6 performed almost twice as well on passives containing action verbs (54–58 per cent) as compared to non-action verbs (26–29 per cent). Even for 11 year olds there was a clear difference between the two types of verbs (85 per cent for action; 70 to 77 per cent for different types of non-action). Similar results have been found in other studies using both real verbs (e.g. Gordon & Chafetz 1990, Maratsos *et al.* 1985) and novel verbs (Pinker *et al.* 1987).

Third, the timing of passive acquisition is affected by the frequency of use of passives in the input. English-speaking children's production and comprehension of the passive increases when frequency of passive input is increased as part of experimental conditions (Baker & Nelson 1984, Brooks & Tomasello 1999b, Pinker *et al.* 1987, Vasilyeva *et al.* 2006). Input frequency may also explain the difference in time of acquisition between action and non-action passives since action passives are much more frequent in child-directed speech (Gordon & Chafetz 1990). In addition, the passive is learned earlier in languages in which it appears more frequently in the input. Passives are acquired and productively used as early as between 2;0 and 2;8 in Sesotho, K'iche' Mayan, Zulu and Inuktitut, languages in which passives occur as much as forty times more frequently in the input than in English (Allen & Crago 1996, Demuth 1989, Demuth & Kline 2006, Pye & Quixtan Poz 1988).

Finally, three types of evidence support the finding that children develop abstract representations for the passive structure in English some-time after age 3, although earlier for other languages such as Inuktitut (Allen & Crago 1996). First, children overgeneralize the passive structure with verbs (or nouns used as verbs) that do not normally passivize and thus could not have been heard in the input. However, passive overgeneralizations are not frequent, are virtually non-existent before 2;6, and typically do not start appearing until well after age 3 in English (Pinker *et al.* 1987). Examples shown here are from English (3a), German (3b) and Inuktitut (3c) (Allen & Crago 1996, Pinker *et al.* 1987).

(3) a. Until I'm four I don't have to be gone (= taken to the dentist). (3;6).
     b. Der Löffel ist besuppt.
        'The spoon is souped.' (3;6)
     c. Siaqri-tau-vuq.
        slide-PASSIVE-INDICATIVE.3SINGULAR.SUBJECT
        'It was slidden.' (3;3, child's foot slid on a slippery surface)

Second, several elicited production studies show limited evidence of gene-ralizability of the passive (see section 13.2.2). Brooks and Tomasello (1999b) taught children (mean ages 2;11 and 3;5) two novel verbs in either the active transitive or passive structure, using utterances such as *Big Bird meeked the car* or *The car got meeked by Big Bird* (for an action in which Big Bird pulled a car in a clear glass jar up through a clear glass tube affixed to a ramp). Children in both transitive and passive conditions were then asked questions focused on the Agent (e.g. *What happened to Big Bird?*) and the Patient (e.g. *What happened to the car?*) to see if they could use the new verb in the modelled structure and generalize it to the other structure. Children taught the transitive structure virtually always responded with the tran-sitive, even for the Patient-focused questions which adults would answer with the passive. In contrast, children taught the passive structure often used transitives in their responses (20 per cent at 2;11, 55 per cent at 3;5). In addition, about 40 per cent of children in a follow-up study who were taught one verb in the transitive and the other in the passive produced at least one passive structure with the transitive-modelled verb. These results suggest that children age 3;5 and younger have some verb-general repre-sentation of the active structure, but a weaker representation of the passive which is revealed under less stringent experimental conditions. The final type of evidence, priming studies, is discussed in section 13.2.3.

13.3.2 Dative alternation

Verbs which permit the dative alternation may appear in either the pre-positional dative construction (4a) or the double object construction (4b).

(4) a. John gave the book to Mary.
     b. John gave Mary the book.

Most verbs of transfer which take Patient and Recipient Objects allow the alternation such as *give, bequeath, take, send, slide, throw, sell, build, prepare* and *tell*. However, the double object construction is not permitted with Latinate verbs (e.g. *John donated the library the book*), in situations where the Recipient cannot reasonably be construed as a possessor of the Patient (e.g. *John sent China the book*), or with a variety of semantic classes of verbs including verbs of saying (e.g. *John confessed Mary the secret*), verbs of manner of speaking (e.g. *John barked Mary an order*), and verbs of selection (e.g. *John selected Mary a necklace*). The alternation is also restricted by the form in which the arguments are realized: the double object dative is atypical when the Patient is a pronoun (e.g. *?John gave Mary it*), and much more common than the prepositional dative when the Recipient is a pronoun (e.g. *John gave her the book*). From a discourse perspective, the prepositional dative highlights the transfer event while the double object construction highlights the endstate of transfer (usually possession of the Patient by the Recipient).

    Children comprehend and spontaneously produce both forms of the dative alternation from a relatively early age. The first spontaneous forms appear in children's speech in English when their utterances have a mean length of two words; this corresponds to ages between 1;6 and 3;4 depending on the child (Campbell & Tomasello 2001, Gropen *et al.* 1989, Snyder & Stromswold 1997, Viau 2006). Several different verbs appear in children's earliest dative constructions although *give* is one of the first verbs produced and the most frequently used. In spontaneous speech transcripts of seven children aged 1;3–5;1, Campbell and Tomasello (2001) found that the majority of children used some dative alternation verbs in both possible constructions (*give, get, make, show, bring, read*), some in only the double object construction (*tell, feed, hand, pay*), and some in only the prepositional dative construction (*fix, leave, open, take*); this differentiation occurs in adult speech as well (Thothathiri & Snedeker, 2008). Campbell and Tomasello also found that most verbs which appeared in one or other of the dative constructions had first appeared in the child's data in a simple transitive construction where the child was the implied recipient (*Read story, Give that*) or where the child specified the recipient in later conversation (*Make a cake, I may give some*).

    The above-mentioned studies all find that the first use of the double object construction typically precedes or occurs at the same time as the first use of the prepositional dative; Viau (2006) shows an average temporal gap of 3.3 months between the two in his transcript study of twenty-two children. This difference may be influenced by input frequency since the double object construction occurs more often in speech to English-speaking children, even though both dative constructions are used frequently in the input with multiple verbs (Campbell & Tomasello 2001, Snyder & Stromswold 1997). It may also be influenced by semantic differences between the two constructions such as the emphasis on motion of the Patient (prepositional dative) vs. eventual possession of the Patient (double object construction) proposed by Gropen *et al.* (1989). Viau (2006) provides evidence that linguistic elements containing the semantic primitive HAVE, assumed to underlie possession in the double object construction, are acquired earlier than those containing the semantic primitive GO which is assumed to underlie the motion component of the prepositional data.

Evidence pertinent to the development of verb-general representations of the dative alternation comes from the same three sources as for the passive: overgeneralizations in spontaneous speech, elicited production studies and priming studies. The latter is discussed in section 13.2.3. Gropen *et al.* (1989) summarize literature showing that children rarely overgeneralize the dative alternation, that dative overgeneralizations begin appearing younger than passive overgeneralizations and continue for several years, and that they appear only after children have begun using the dative forms correctly. Their own study of transcripts from five children shows that overgeneralizations account for about 5 per cent of the double object constructions produced, and occur only once in every 4,000 or so utterances. Some examples compiled by Gropen *et al.* are shown in (5).

(5) a. I'll brush him his hair. (2;3)
     b. How come you're putting me that kind of juice? (2;4)
     c. I said her no. (3;1)

White (1987) showed that children age 3–5 can interpret and act out overgeneralized double object constructions, while Mazurkewich and White (1984) found that 9 year olds judged as grammatical almost half of the erroneous overgeneralized double object constructions on a grammaticality judgment test. These results suggest that children have some abstract representation of the dative structures from relatively early in acquisition but take a long time to work out the limits of the pattern.

Gropen *et al.* (1989) also conducted an elicited production study to test the strength of children's verb-general representations of the dative alternation. They taught four novel verbs each denoting a novel event (e.g. sliding a ball through a tunnel to a mouse at the other end), two with the double object dative and two with the prepositional dative. After each verb was taught, they asked the child to describe the event with questions eliciting both the double object construction (e.g. *Can you tell me what I'm doing with the mouse?*) and the prepositional dative (e.g. *Can you tell me what I'm doing with the ball?*). The children in their study, aged 6–8 years, easily generalized the novel verb to the non-modelled structure. In a similar study with 3 year olds in which the children were simply asked to describe the novel event to their caregiver, Conwell and Demuth (2007) found that virtually all child descriptions used the modelled construction.

However, children in a follow-up study who heard one action described with the double object dative and the other with the prepositional dative used the non-modelled construction in 31 per cent of their own descriptions. This suggests that children have an understanding of the dative alternation that they can use productively in at least some circumstances, consistent with the 'weak representation' hypothesis (see section 13.2.3).

Demuth and colleagues (Demuth *et al.* 2005, Demuth *et al.* 2003) studied the extent of 3- to 12-year-old children's verb-general representations in a Sesotho construction closely related to the dative – the double object applicative containing benefactives as shown in (6) – which is used productively by Sesotho-speaking children as early as age 2;1 (Demuth 1998).

(6) a. Mosadi   o-rek-el-a   ngwana   dijo.
         woman   AGREEMENT-buy-APPLICATIVE-MOOD   child   food
         'The woman is buying food for the child.'
                                                       (Demuth *et al.* 2005: 424)

   b. Banana   ba-a-mo-pheh-el-a.
       girls   AGREEMENT-PRESENT-OBJECT(BENEFACTIVE)-cook-
                 APPLICATIVE-MOOD
       'The girls are cooking (the meat) for her.'
                                                       (Demuth *et al.* 2005: 425)

Sesotho has no prepositional alternative for benefactives, and thus use of the double object construction is not subject to semantic restrictions related to verb classes as in English. However, the order of Patient and Benefactive arguments following the verb is constrained semantically such that the argument highest on the animacy hierarchy (human > animal > inanimate) must appear closest to the verb as in (6a); the order is not fixed if both arguments have the same level of animacy. Children as young as four years showed sensitivity to the ordering of arguments in a forced choice grammaticality judgment task (3 year olds showed sensitivity in some but not all conditions), although children's judgments also became more adult-like with age. Double object constructions with both objects expressed are not common in Sesotho caregiver speech – only two examples in 98 hours – since the arguments are commonly expressed as morphemes on the verb or omitted as shown in (6b) (Demuth *et al.* 2000). Therefore, these results show that children can abstract verb-general representations from the input at relatively young ages even for low frequency structures.

13.4 Argument realization

Much of the literature on argument structure acquisition assumes that arguments are always present in caregiver speech to provide the full input necessary to child learners, and that children always produce all the arguments that a verb requires. However, this is not the case in so-called *pro-drop* languages such as Spanish where arguments may be realized by agreement markers on the verb (7a), and in so-called discourse-oriented languages such as Mandarin Chinese where arguments may be omitted when retrievable from the discourse context (7b).

(7) a. Habl-o   con mi abuel-a   cada dia.
         speak-1SINGULAR.SUBJECT with my grandparent-FEMININE every day
         '(I) speak with my grandmother every day.'

     b. Bei1.
         carry
         '(The child) carried (the puppy to Grandma).'

                                                              (Lee & Naigles 2005: 530)

The omission of arguments thus poses two challenges: how do children receive sufficient data from the input to learn argument structure, and how do they display their knowledge of argument structure?

13.4.1   Argument omission in caregiver speech

As just noted, arguments are frequently omitted in caregiver speech in many languages. Rispoli (1995) found that only 1 per cent of transitive sentences in his Japanese caregiver data had two overt case-marked arguments while 90 per cent had one or no arguments whose syntactic role was usually not identified. Narasimhan, Budwig and Murty (2005) found similar results for caregiver Hindi: only 7 per cent of transitive sentences contained two arguments while 44 per cent contained no arguments. In caregiver Inuktitut, Skarabela (2006) found that fewer than 15 per cent of arguments were realized overtly (data are not separated by verb type) although most of the omitted arguments were indexed by person/number agreement markers on the verb which indicate syntactic role. How do children learning these languages receive the data they need to determine the argument structure of verbs in their language?

  Bowerman and Brown (2007) discuss three ways in which children could receive this information from the input. First, even though any given utterance may contain only one or none of the required arguments for a verb, across several utterances it is likely that all the arguments will appear. They cite an example from Clancy (1996) in which a Korean caregiver refers to an event involving sticking plastic shapes to a board variously as 'shall auntie stick?' (Agent), 'stick this' (Patient), and 'stick there' (Location) – using all three arguments of the verb *pwuthita* 'stick' but across three separate utterances. Thus a child who is able to keep track of all of the instances of one verb will eventually have the requisite evidence to determine a verb's argument structure. At a more general and comprehensive level, Lee and Naigles (2005) show probabilistic associations between number of arguments and verbs of different semantic classes for Mandarin Chinese, another language with frequent argument omission. In a study of 7,884 tokens of the 60 most frequent verb types in data from caregiver speech to ten different children aged around 1;10, they found that object NPs followed transitive verbs (e.g. *mai3* 'buy') significantly more frequently than intransitive verbs (e.g. *ku1* 'cry'), full clauses followed internal/communication verbs (e.g. *siao1* 'say') significantly more frequently than motion verbs (e.g. *pao3* 'run'), and locative phrases followed motion verbs significantly more frequently than internal/communication verbs. These and other results from their study are very similar to findings for a comparable database of caregiver English (Naigles & Hoff-Ginsberg 1995, 1998) even though Mandarin has rampant argument ellipsis and English does not.

A second source of evidence is the other linguistic tendencies that co-occur with verbs of certain argument structures. Rispoli's (1987, 1995) study of Japanese caregiver speech revealed that transitive and intransitive verbs are differentially associated with such properties as the animacy of the Patient and the speech act of the utterance in which the verb occurs. Wittek (2007) shows for German that the use of the adverbial *wieder* 'again' is a reliable cue to one argument structure pattern in that language. Although German requires arguments in most cases, such a cue could also work well in a language with argument ellipsis.

A third possibility is that children can glean information even from omitted arguments because of their knowledge of the discourse effects on argument realization. Adults realize arguments in various forms depending on the accessibility of the referent to the interlocutor (see Ariel 1990 and references therein). A referent newly introduced into discourse is deemed inaccessible and realized as a full noun phrase whereas a referent just mentioned in the previous utterance is already accessible to the interlocutor and thus typically appears as a pronoun or is omitted. Children as young as 2 years are also sensitive to accessibility features in realizing arguments in their own speech (e.g. Allen 2000, Clancy 1997, Guerriero *et al.* 2006, Matthews *et al.* 2006, Narasimhan *et al.* 2005, Serratrice 2005; see Allen *et al.* 2008 for a review). In one typical spontaneous speech study, Allen (2000b) investigated children's sensitivity to eight accessibility features in over 3,000 arguments from four children aged 2;0–3;6 speaking Inuktitut, a language characterized by rampant argument omission. She found that children were significantly more likely to realize arguments overtly when they were newly introduced to discourse (vs. given), absent from the physical context (vs. present), contrasted with other referents (vs. not contrasted), and ambiguous as to the referent in context (vs. unambiguous). A follow-up study found that children were more likely to realize an argument the less accessible it was: fully accessible arguments were realized overtly in only 18 per cent of cases while arguments inaccessible for all features (i.e. newly introduced, contrasted, ambiguous) were realized overtly in 86 per cent of cases (Allen 2007b). In a typical experimental study, Matthews *et al.* (2006) assessed the effects of joint attention on argument realization in one hundred English-speaking children aged two, three and four years. Participants viewed ten short video clips (e.g. clown jumping, fairy eating an apple). For one block of five clips, the experimenter was watching the screen with the child (i.e. accessible because of joint attention); for the other, the experimenter was not able to view the screen (i.e. not accessible because of lack of joint attention). After viewing each clip, participants were asked to recount the clip to the experimenter with the request "What happened? What did you see?" The three and four year olds, but not the two year olds, chose different linguistic forms (noun vs. pronoun) to realize the referents depending on whether the interlocutor shared attention to the video or not. Although the studies just described do not directly assess whether children are able to use the input to learn argument structure in argument omission languages, they show that children manipulate argument form according to accessibility in their own speech and thus may well recognize the implicit presence of an argument in the input in situations where an argument would normally be required but is omitted for reasons of accessibility.

13.4.2   Preferred argument structure in child speech

The distribution of children's lexical vs. omitted (or pronominalized) arguments in spontaneous speech can also reveal their knowledge of argument structure. As discussed in the previous section, an argument which is not accessible in the discourse is likely to be realized as a lexical noun phrase, while an argument which is accessible is likely to be pronominalized or omitted depending on the typology of the language. Du Bois's (1987) study of adult narratives in Sakapulteko Maya as well as much further work in languages of varying typologies reveals that choices about argument realization also have relevance to argument structure (Du Bois *et al.* 2003). In particular, there is a strong correlation between the syntactic role in which an argument is realized, the accessibility of that argument and the morphological form in which it appears – a pattern which Du Bois has named Preferred Argument Structure. Utterances are typically restricted to a maximum of one lexical and one new argument per clause (typically the same argument), and new and lexical arguments are typically not expressed as the Subject of a transitive verb but rather as an Object or as the Subject of an intransitive verb. Speakers thus reveal their knowledge of argument structure through their differential expression of new vs. given referents and lexical vs. non-lexical arguments in different syntactic roles.

Several spontaneous speech studies have shown that young children also follow the patterns of Preferred Argument Structure. In a study of four Inuktitut-speaking children aged 2;0–3;6, Allen and Schröder (2003) found that only 0.2 per cent of children's transitive clauses contained more than one lexical or new argument, and only 1 per cent of Subjects of transitive verbs were realized as lexical forms or arguments new to the discourse. Clancy (2003) found the same pattern for speakers of Korean aged 1;8–2;10: only 5 and 2 per cent of transitive clauses contained more than one lexical or new argument respectively, and only 13 and 3 per cent of Subjects of transitive verbs contained lexical forms and new arguments respectively. Similar results hold for children aged 1;9 and 3;0 learning Japanese and English (Guerriero *et al.* 2001), children aged 2;10–4;3 learning Hindi (Narasimhan *et al.* 2005), and children aged 2;0–2;5 learning Tzeltal Mayan (Brown 1998c). These results are striking given the divergent typologies of the languages with respect to whether they allow argument omission and whether they mark syntactic role, and show that children across languages are highly sensitive not only to individual links between referent accessibility and argument realization but also to the broader argument structure patterns this entails. (See Clancy 2003 for arguments that the nature of children's early activities is the underlying source of their early sensitivity to Preferred Argument Structure.)

13.5 Conclusion

As noted in the introduction to this chapter, the research on the acquisition of argument structure has been driven by determining what mechanism children use to break into the system. Theories range from generalization from the input on the basis of initial item-by-item learning on the one hand, to guidance from innate linguistic knowledge on the other. It is clear by now that some elements of both these positions are true – children's early knowledge of argument structure is not adult-like regardless of whatever innate knowledge they may have, yet children have much more sensitive early knowledge than was previously believed. Current research focuses on deepening our understanding of the nature of the knowledge that children bring to the task of learning argument structure, and investigating how various factors such as input frequency and processing ability interact with the argument structure system to mediate development towards adult-like knowledge.

Suggestions for further reading

Allen, S. E. M., Skarabela, B., & Hughes, M. (2008). Using corpora to examine discourse effects in syntax. In H. Behrens (Ed.), *Corpora in Language Acquisition Research* (pp. 99–137). Amsterdam: Benjamins.
Bowerman, M., & Brown, P. (Eds.) (2007). *Crosslinguistic Perspectives on Argument Structure: Implications for Learnability*. Mahwah, NJ: Lawrence Erlbaum Associates.

Gleitman, L. (1990). The structural sources of verb meanings. *Language Acquisition*, 1, 3–55.

Naigles, L., & Swensen, L. (2007). Syntactic supports for word learning. In E. Hoff & M. Shatz (Eds.), *Blackwell Handbook of Language Development* (pp. 212–231). Malden, MA: Blackwell.

Pinker, S. (1989). *Learnability and Cognition: The Acquisition of Argument Structure*. Cambridge, MA: MIT Press.

Tomasello, M. (2000a). Do young children have adult syntactic competence? *Cognition*, 74, 209–253.

14

The first language acquisition of complex sentences

Barbara C. Lust
Claire Foley
Cristina D. Dye

14.1 Introduction

14.1.1 'Complex' vs. 'simple'

The term 'complex sentence' generally describes all sentences which are not 'simple' sentences. It traditionally covers all cases where more than a single clause is involved, as in sentential coordination (e.g. *Mary dances and Anne sings*), adverbial subordinate clause adjunction (e.g. *Anne dances when Mary sings*), and cases where some form of sentence-internal clausal embedding is involved as in sentence complementation (e.g. *[Mary claims [that Anne wrote a book]]*) or relativization (e.g. *[Mary reads the book [that Anne wrote]]*) (brackets display the multi-clausal factor). This descriptive characterization is not fully valid however. Sentences with non-clausal coordination (e.g. *Mary and Anne wrote a book*) or various forms of nominal and verbal embedding or adjunction (e.g. *the enemy's destruction of the city*) fall between 'simple' and 'complex' categories. In fact any 'simple' sentence which involves an operation, such as question formation, implicitly involves a relation between distinct clausal variations.

In this chapter we will review highlights of recent research on sentence types commonly described as 'complex' in keeping with the traditional background. However we will do so in a manner which suggests that there is no firm line between 'complex' and 'simple' sentences.

14.1.2 Complex sentences as a core

Complex sentences in many ways provide a core domain for investigation of the acquisition and development of syntactic and semantic knowledge.

We are grateful to Edith Bavin and James W. Gair for their careful reading and many helpful suggestions. All errors are our own.

Their study can lead us in the investigation of the most basic aspects of syntactic and semantic knowledge, such as those summarized in (i)–(v).

(i)   *Hierarchical structure*: The elements of a sentence appear not merely in a temporal or linear order but also form a hierarchy of constituents
       Example: Within the sentence *Mary sings [when Anne dances]* the bracketed clause forms a subordinate constituent

(ii)   *Order*: Not only words but also constituents may be related in different orders
       Example: Some clausal constituents may appear initially or finally, as in *Mary sings [when Anne dances]* and *[When Anne dances] Mary sings*

(iii) *Locality domains*: Hierarchical structure and order inform the range for some grammatical operations, e.g. anaphora (where the reference or meaning of a linguistic element depends on an antecedent)
       Example: *Mary believes [that Anne admires herself]* permits coreference between *herself* and *Anne*, but not between *herself* and *Mary*.

(iv)   *Recursion*: Human language includes the capacity to generate an infinite set of sentences by having an operation apply to its own output
       Example: *Mary believes [that Anne claims [that Paul thinks [that Chris says …*

(v)   Linguistic principles such as *Structure dependence*: Operations in human language depend not merely on linear order but on structure (Chomsky 1988, Lust 2006: 55)
       Example: Question formation involves operations that refer not simply to the order in which words appear but to their structural role, as in: *Is [the man [who is tall]] in the room?*

Complex sentences in essence make overt what may be only implicit in simple sentences. For example, they often reveal overt complementizers, which may introduce sentential complements (e.g. *Mary claims [**that** Anne wrote a book]*), and which are generally silent in simple sentences. They provide domains for reduction of redundancy, therefore leading to null sites or ellipsis (e.g. *Mary sings and Mary dances → Mary sings and Ø dances*) and implicate all the principles involved in these (e.g. principles of anaphora, which determine the interpretation of the null sites). They provide barriers for certain long distance operations.

Complex sentences provide a domain where various fundamental questions regarding the nature of a 'Language Faculty' can be more critically investigated. For example simple word associations, which may be involved in simple sentences (as in the 'verb island' constraint of Tomasello 1992 for example, and Ch. 5), cannot account for long-distance operations and need not be confounded to the same degree that they are in simple sentences. Lexical and functional category development can be dissociated through investigation of complex sentence domains. Whereas linguistic principles such as structure dependence can be probed in simple sentences, they are more easily revealed in complex sentence structures.

While there is much research on the young child's first words and first simple sentences stemming from classic early work (e.g. Brown 1973), there has been relatively little work which has probed early formation of complex sentences (with a few exceptions, e.g. Bowerman 1979, Diessel 2004). The time may have come for a more comprehensive integration of research on complex sentence formation with a view towards assessing the underlying linguistic knowledge it reveals.

14.1.3　The purpose and structure of this chapter

Here we cull basic discoveries on the acquisition of complex sentences. In our brief review we examine what the child knows about the linguistic system that underlies complex sentence formation and related operations (e.g. i–v above) and how this knowledge is revealed throughout the course of development. To this end we focus on selected research that has probed the theory of Universal Grammar (UG) in language acquisition. This theory seeks to define 'both a set of universal *principles* which capture what underlies language structure across languages, and a finite set of *parameters* to account for possible crosslinguistic variation' and at the same time to explicate a Language Faculty which may account for the human capacity for language (Lust 2006: 55; see Chomsky 1981, 1988). Research on language acquisition in this framework investigates the degree to which knowledge of linguistic principles constrains language acquisition and affects its development. It emphasizes discovering the knowledge of the grammatical system underlying particular constructions, especially the capacity for recursion, hierarchical structure and structure dependence.

A contrasting perspective on language acquisition views complex sentences as built from simpler constructions, which are concrete instances of language use, i.e. individual pairings of form and function (e.g. Goldberg 1995). Under this approach language acquisition is a process of gradually building larger constructions from the experience of smaller ones. This general approach has been applied to the study of the acquisition of several types of complex sentences (see Diessel 2004 and references therein). This chapter cites exemplary research from this paradigm in the relevant sections below.

The present chapter is organized as follows: section 14.2 reviews the acquisition of complementation, section 14.3 the acquisition of coordination, section 14.4 the acquisition of adverbial subordinate clause adjunction and section 14.5 the acquisition of relative clauses. In section 14.6 we briefly consider results of this overview with regard to leading questions regarding the study of language acquisition in the field today.[1]

---

[1]　Due to length limitations this chapter does not address additional issues related to complex sentences such as the acquisition of wh-questions and long-distance binding (e.g. de Villiers 1995). For these the reader is referred to Lust *et al.* (1994), Crain and Thornton (1998, Ch. 22), Guasti (2002, Ch. 6).

14.2   Complement clauses

14.2.1   The acquisition challenge

We may define 'complement clauses' as clauses embedded in one of the argument slots of the verb in the main clause. Complement clauses, as in (1)–(2), involve structural embedding wherein one clause is embedded within another. In addition they integrate structural phenomena such as the complementizer as head of a clause, the finiteness of the embedded clause, pro forms like pronouns or null sites, anaphora (e.g. principles of 'control', which semantically identify the null subject of a non-finite complement termed 'PRO' in certain generative theories), as well as specific lexicon involved in main verbs. There is considerable variation across and within languages in complement clauses especially regarding the degree of syntactic and semantic integration between the complement and the matrix clause. Specific dimensions of variation include whether the complement clause is finite or non-finite, whether the complementizer is overt or covert and whether it is +/– wh, as illustrated in (1)–(3).

(1)   finite, overt C, +wh
      Mary asked whether they would leave.

(2)   finite, covert C, –wh
      Mary said they would leave.

(3)   non-finite, overt C, +wh
      Mary asked where to go.

Complements also vary with regard to the nature of their subject, i.e. overt as in (1)–(3) above or null as in (4)–(7) below. Complements with null subjects may vary with regard to the nature of the null subject and its relation with matrix clause arguments, that is, whether subjects or objects control them:

(4)   Subject control:
      Mary$_i$ tries [PRO$_i$ to leave].
      Mary$_i$ promised Joe [PRO$_i$ to leave].

(5)   Object control:
      Mary told Joe$_i$ [PRO$_i$ to leave].

Languages vary in the form and function of complement clauses as in the French examples (6) and (7), where the indirect object is marked by a preposition.

(6)   Marie a promis à Jean de partir
      'Mary promised (TO) John to leave.'

(7)   Marie a dit à Jean de partir
      'Mary told (TO) John to leave.'

The child learning a given language needs to discover which type(s) of complement clauses occur in the target language and how these may vary within the language.

14.2.2 Complement structures in early spontaneous speech

Production of complement clauses has been reported even before MLU 2 in spontaneous speech (Bloom *et al.* 1980, 1989, Limber 1973), e.g. (8)–(10). These utterances may or may not reveal overt complementizers.

(8) no Kathryn want play with self

                  (K11, 22.3, MLU 1.92, Bloom 1970: 161)

(9) Tu crois lé pieure là?
 = *Tu crois qu'elle pleure là?*
 you think COMP: she cry there
 'Do you think she is crying there?'

                  (French, 1;11, Dye 2005:17)

(10) Chcem pić dżem w słoiku
 I-want to-drink jam in jar
 'I want to drink (the) jam in (the) jar'

                  (Polish, Jaś, 2;0, Smoczyńska 1985: 643)

Bloom *et al.* (1989) documented very early clausal complements to English epistemic and perception verbs in children's spontaneous speech. Diessel and Tomasello (2001) analysed finite complement clauses in the spontaneous speech of children acquiring English, arguing that these clauses occur with only a few different verbs in early utterances. Diessel and Tomasello argue that the main clause verb serves only as a kind of epistemic or attention-getting frame for the clause, and thus that these utterances reflect only one proposition. This view, which suggests that early complement clauses do not reflect true grammatical embedding, contrasts with findings from a body of research uncovering grammatical constraints in early complements. We turn next to these findings.

14.2.3 Complement clause and control

Most of the acquisition research on complement clauses has focused on what has been termed 'control structures' (e.g. (4) (5)) and children's interpretation of the null subject of the complement. Early work uncovered a general preference for object as antecedent. Chomsky (1969) tested children (5–9 years) on the comprehension of structures like (11) and (12):

(11) Bozo <u>tells</u> Donald PRO to hop up and down

(12) Bozo <u>promises</u> Donald PRO to hop up and down

She reported that many children tend to interpret the matrix clause object as the controller of the embedded clause subject in both structures, incorrectly interpreting (12) to mean 'Bozo promises Donald that Donald would hop up and down'. This empirical finding was subsequently replicated (e.g. Cohen Sherman & Lust 1986, Eisenberg & Cairns 1994, Hsu *et al.* 1985, 1993). Similar findings have been reported for French and Spanish (Clark 1985 and references therein). Chomsky (1969) proposed that this behaviour could be explained by a minimum distance principle (MDP) (Rosenbaum 1967). The MDP has often been interpreted to mean that children choose the matrix object because it is the 'nearest', where 'nearness' refers to linear distance in the word string, reflecting a performance strategy.

Theoretically, if children could rely on a performance strategy such as the surface MDP they could bypass adult grammar. For example, Hsu, Cairns and Fiengo (1985) tested sixty-four children aged 3;2 to 8;3 on complement and adjunct control structures through an act-out task and proposed several distinct 'stages' or 'grammar types': (i) object oriented (ii) mixed subject–object (iii) approaching adult and (iv) adult. As these authors point out their proposal raises the question of how or why the child might move from one stage to the next.

Maratsos (1974) predicted that if the MDP were a simple performance strategy then children would misinterpret null subjects in passive, object-control sentences such as (13), because here PRO is nearest to the 'by'-phrase not to the syntactic subject.

(13)   Mary$_i$ was told by Joe [PRO$_i$ to leave].

The results of an act-out task with forty 4 and 5 year olds did not support this prediction; children correctly interpreted (13) (see also Goodluck 1978, Tavakolian 1978).

In addition, Cohen Sherman (1983) and Cohen Sherman and Lust (1986, 1993) provided evidence against the stage theory. They tested developmental groups of children on both comprehension and production on both non-finite subject and object control structures (14a,b) and finite (non-control) structures (14 c,d) with and without pragmatic lead (i.e. a preceding sentence introducing one of the arguments of the main clause).

(14)   (This is a story about Tom/Billy)
        a. Tom$_i$ [promises Billy$_j$ [PRO$_i$ to eat the ice cream cone]].
        b. Tom$_i$ [tells Billy$_j$ [PRO$_j$ to eat the ice cream cone]].
        c. Tom$_i$ [promises Billy$_j$ [that he$_{ijk}$ will drink the milk]].
        d. Tom$_i$ [tells Billy$_j$ [that he$_{ijk}$ will drink the milk]].

Seventy-two children (3 to 8 years) were tested in a production (elicited imitation) and a comprehension (act-out) task. Results replicated previous findings regarding preference for matrix object as controller. However, they additionally revealed a correlation between PRO and infinitival complements on the one hand and between lexical pronouns and finite complements on the other hand, suggesting that children know about the finite/non-finite distinction in embedding types and about the distribution of null or lexical subjects in each. Children did not allow pragmatic context (in the form of pragmatic lead) to influence interpretation of the subject in infinitival clauses (14a,b) but did so in the interpretation of the subject of finite complements (14c,d) suggesting that children know that control of null subjects in non-finite complement structures is obligatory. The results of Eisenberg and Cairns (1994) support the early availability of grammatical knowledge of control.

Young children acquiring Mandarin Chinese (ages 2;6 – 5;0, mean age 3;9, N = 95) have also been shown to distinguish control from non-control structures (Chien & Lust 1983, 1985). They distinguished grammatical subjects from topics in these control structures, reducing redundancy in an imitation task in sentences like (17) to produce (18) but resisting this in sentences like (15). A reduction of topic as in (16) is ill-formed since it appears to yield a topic-controlled gap in an obligatorily subject-controlled position.

(15) Xiǎohuá, jiějie   xǐhuān Xiǎohuá dài   màozi.
      Xiǎohuá, older sister like   Xiǎohuá wear hat
      'Xiǎohuá, (her) older sister likes Xiǎohuá (to) wear (a) hat'

(16) * Xiǎohuá$_i$, jiějie xǐhuān Ø$_i$ dài màozi.

(17) Xiǎohuá, bàba   xǐhuān baoa   kàn   diànshi.
      Xiǎohuá, father like   father watch TV
      'Xiǎohuá, (her) father likes (her) father to watch TV'

(18) Xiǎohuá, bàba$_i$ xǐhuān$_j$ Ø$_i$ kàn diànshi.

Cohen Sherman and Lust concluded that a principle of minimal distance that is structure dependent selects the object as the 'unmarked' option in control structure like (14a,b). Pinker (1984) suggests that the child's preference for object interpretation is a default hypothesis reflecting what crosslinguistically is the unmarked option; verbs like 'promise', which are rare across languages, would require additional learning.

14.2.4 Distinguishing complement from coordinate clauses

Children acquiring Mandarin also differentiate complement from coordinate structures (Chien & Lust 1983, 1985). They distinguish the anaphora in 'control' constructions like (15) from that in coordinate sentences. Young children's ability to distinguish complement and coordinate structures has also been shown in English (Cohen Sherman & Lust 1993). Complement sentences as in (14) were compared with sentences involving coordination (19).

(19) a. [The turtle$_i$ tickles the skunk$_j$] and [Ø$_{i,*j}$ bumps the car].
      b. [The turtle$_i$ tickles the skunk$_j$] and [he$_{i,*j}$ bumps the car].

In an act-out task children chose different antecedents for the two sentence types, favouring the object in complement structures, but the subject in coordinate structures.

14.2.5 Summary of findings on complementation

There is evidence for early productivity of complement clauses in child language and evidence that children know about the distribution and interpretation of empty category subjects (e.g. PRO) in these clauses as well as about a principle of minimality involved in assigning reference to the embedded subject. This principle appears to reflect structure dependence. At the same time children's errors in antecedent choice reveal that they are acquiring language-specific lexical knowledge such as the distinction between subject and object control verbs such as *promise* and *tell*.

14.3 Coordination

14.3.1 The acquisition challenge

Coordination provides perhaps the most basic recursive device of natural language grammars, illustrated in the Dr Seuss (1965) example in (20) and a paradigm case of complex sentence formation. (For an in-depth discussion of the complexities of coordination and its acquisition see Lust *et al.* in press.)

(20)   When tweetle beetles fight, it's called a tweetle beetle battle, **and** when they battle in a puddle, it's a tweetle beetle puddle battle. **And** when tweetle beetles battle with paddles in a puddle, they call it a tweetle beetle puddle paddle battle. **AND** ....

   Although seemingly simple, coordination involves many of the most fundamental syntactic aspects of language knowledge, including structural configuration. Various constituents can be coordinated and must obey certain structural constraints, ruling in sentential coordination (21a) and phrasal coordination (21b), but ruling out (22), where a noun phrase and a verb phrase are conjoined.

(21)   a. Ben's band bangs and Bim's band booms
       b. [[Bim] and [Ben]] lead bands with brooms

(22)   *[[Ben] and [bang booms]] make tweetle beetles happy

Various forms of anaphora productively apply in coordination. Antecedents may either precede or follow the proform or gap, ((23)–(28)) illustrating this variation. Coreferential elements are underlined.

(23)   Tweetle beetles battle and *[they]/[Ø] use paddles.*

(24)   Tweetle beetles Ø and Pudgy Wuggies carry paddles.

(25) Tweetle beetles carry [Ø] and [Ø] use paddles.

(26) Tweetle beetles make [Ø] and Pudgy Wuggies carry [paddles].

(27) Tweetle beetles battle in puddles and Pudgy Wuggies do [Ø] too.

(28) Tweetle beetles battle Pudgies and so do Wuggies [Ø].

Constraints apply to these operations, as in (29) or (30).

(29) * Tweetle beetles carry paddles and use [Ø].

(30) *Tweetle beetles battle in puddles and Pudgy Wuggies [Ø].

Coordination is also a domain for syntactic constraints on various operations. For example, there are constraints against wh-questions reaching
into the coordinate clause as in (31), and also constraints requiring 'across
the board' operations, as in (32) where the 'what' question must apply in
both clauses:

(31) *What do Tweetle beetles carry paddles and [Ø].

(32) *What do Tweetle beetles like [Ø] and Pudgy Wuggies hate paddles.

In the acquisition of coordination, then, the child must assemble knowledge about constituent structure, anaphora, and a wide array of essential
linguistic operations. This knowledge must provide the infinite but constrained productivity involved in these recursive structures. Coordination
also involves semantic and pragmatic factors such as those related to
temporal order, or causality. Specific coordinating connectives may integrate such features in their morphology (e.g. 'but' integrating a negation
feature, or 'because' integrating causality). Children must integrate their
developing cognitive, syntactic, semantic and pragmatic knowledge; in
doing so they will, for example, overcome an 'order of mention strategy'
(e.g. Beilin & Lust 1975, Clark 1973).

Coordination varies across languages in how it is realized including
whether coordinate connectives are overt (e.g. they are not in Mandarin
(33) or (34)), whether and how they vary morphologically across coordination types and the degree to which coordinate and adverbial clause structures are distinguished syntactically and/or semantically.

(33) suanlah-tang
      sour-hot soup
      'hot and sour soup'
                                                    (Chao 1968/1976: 483)

(34) wo   mai   piao   jin – qu
      I   buy   ticket enter-go
      'I bought a ticket and went in/I bought a ticket to go in'
                                                    (Li and Thompson 1981:595)

The child must then not only acquire a constrained, productive grammar of coordination, but map that to a language-specific lexicon and grammar.

14.3.2 Coordination in early spontaneous speech

Sentential coordinations as in (35)–(36) appear to be developmentally primitive; they are in place when phrasal or reduced coordinations appear, e.g. (37).[2]

(35) There water and there water (group MLU 2.36, Lust & Mervis 1980)

(36) Mae de matta no sorede Yū-chan ga   nete-ta   keredo
     front at waited FP and   Yū   NOM sleeping-was however
     'Ø waited at the front and Yū was sleeping though'
                                        (33 months, Lust *et al.* 1980)

(37) Tora to   raion kowai n   da   yo
     tiger and lion frightening is   GEN COP FP[EMPH]
     '(The) tiger and (the) lion are frightening!'
                                        (34 months, Lust *et al.* 1980)

Examples from left-branching languages such as Japanese show early productivity of the left-branching embedding representation of coordination, as in (38) from Japanese child speech and (39) from a comparable study of Sinhala (Gair *et al.* 1998).

(38) Kore ni   notte   yochien   iku no
     this in   ride-GER Ø kindergarten go   FP
     'Ride on this and go to kindergarten'
                                        (36 months, Lust *et al.* 1980)

(39) mamə [gedərə gihilla] kææmə kææwa
     I   home go-LA food   eat-PAST
     'I went home and ate'[3]
                                        (2.11, Gair *et al.* 1998)

14.3.3 Early coordination is not a 'simple' developmental primitive

A review of experimental research on the acquisition of coordination relative to adjunction has *not* supported the claim that early coordination involves simple linearization or juxtaposition (Lust 1994). For example, in a study of coordination with VP-ellipsis structures like (40), children as young as 3;0 were found to compute multiple interpretations of the 'does

---

[2] See Lust (1981) and deVilliers *et al.* (1977). Note that 36 and 37 are examples from Japanese.
[3] LA is a conjunctive participle; it can sometimes have the semantic meaning of 'when'.

too' clause, including those in (40a–d), while ruling out ungrammatical interpretations like (40e) and others.

(40)   Oscar bites his apple and Bert does too
       a. O_i bites O_i's apple and B_j bites B_j's apple iijj
       b. O_i bites O_i's apple and B_j bits O_i's apple iiji
       c. O_i bites B_j's apple and B_j bites B_j's apple ijjj
       d. O_i bites E_k's apple and B_j bites E_k's apple ikjk
       e. *O_i bites O_i's apple and B_j bites E_k's apple iijk

Within the domain of coordination, children thus demonstrate competence for ellipsis, knowledge of ambiguity, variable binding and structure-dependence (see Foley *et al.* 2003). Here coordination does not appear to be a 'simple' early structural type.

14.3.4 Distinguishing coordination from complement and adverbial clauses

Several studies across languages have provided evidence that young children distinguish coordinate from adjoined or embedded clauses, both syntactically and semantically. As noted in section 14.2.4, children distinguish complement and coordinate structures in English and Chinese. Additional evidence comes from a study investigating pro-drop in subordinate clauses where children acquiring English (2;2 to 4;5) imitated structures like (41)–(42) (Núñez del Prado *et al.*1993).

(41)   Mickey sings and Mickey/he whistles.

(42)   Pluto coughs when Pluto/he wakes up.

In their imitations children reduced the second subject (noun or pronoun) to a null subject significantly more in coordinate structures (15.3 per cent of all items) than in subordinate structures (2.4 per cent of all items). When they imitated adverbial structures like (42), they reduced the noun to a pronoun or retained the pronoun.

14.3.5 Crosslinguistic variation

Left-branching languages (such as Chinese) differ systematically from right-branching languages (such as English), as reflected in children's early forms of coordination. For example, in elicited imitation, English-speaking children (ages 1.11–3.1, mean age 2.6) found the [V [O+O]] structure (43) most accessible (Lust 1977) but Chinese-speaking children (ages 2.0–4.5, mean age 3.3) found the [[V+V] O] (44) significantly more accessible (Lust & Chien 1984).

(43)   [Eat [the crackers and the cake]]

(44)   [[XI-yi-xi   ye   ca-yi-ca]   wawa]
       [[wash   and   dry]   the doll]

These results provide evidence that children consult the branching direction (or head direction) of the grammar of the language they are acquiring and that this parameter of variation affects early, even simple, sentence formation. Research on Japanese coordination (Lust & Wakayama 1979, 1981) supports this view. The effects of right- and left-branching language differences on simple sentences are also seen in studies of subject pro-drop in simple sentences (Mazuka *et al.* 1986, 1995, cf. Bloom 1990a) (See also Weissenborn 1992).

14.3.6   Conclusions on the acquisition of coordination

Children distinguish coordinate and adjoined or embedded clauses, both syntactically and semantically, early in acquisition. Directionality in the specific language being acquired influences coordination (both in anaphora direction and in the direction of phrasal coordination). Sentential coordinations appear to be developmentally primitive; they are in place when phrasal or reduced coordinations appear. Children integrate pragmatic and cognitive knowledge over the course of development in coordination. The course of acquisition continuously integrates general linguistic principles and language-specific knowledge.

14.4   Adverbial subordinate clauses

14.4.1.   The acquisition challenge

Sentences with adverbial subordinate clauses adjoin one clause to another:

(45)   Jane uses a computer [when she works]

Although it appears closely related to a coordinate clause, the adverbial clause domain provides different possibilities for syntactic and semantic operations. For example, subject pro-drop is not allowed in the adverbial subordinate clause domain in English (46), although it is in coordinate clauses (47).

(46)   Jane uses a computer [when she/*Ø works]

(47)   Jane uses a computer and Ø works

Diessel (2004: 152–156) summarizes several syntactic, semantic and pragmatic factors which distinguish coordinate and adverbial subordinate clause structures.

   Adverbial clauses may vary in finiteness and in the type of syntactic domain they provide, distinguishing (46) and (48) in terms of whether a lexical pronoun or a null subject is allowed and distinguishing the type of anaphora they involve (e.g. bound or free).

(48)   Jane uses a computer [when *she/ Ø working]

Table 14.1. Types of knowledge that must be integrated in adverbial clauses

Universal features of language	Language-specific features
• Hierarchical structure	• Directionality
• Adjunction	• Lexical forms for anaphoric elements
• Clausal architecture	• Lexical and semantic knowledge of connectives
• Constraints on anaphora	

Depending on the language, adverbial clauses may also vary in direction-ality appearing either in postposed/right-branching position as in (46) above or in preposed/left-branching position, as in (49) below:

(49) [When she/ *Ø works], Jane uses a computer.

   It has been hypothesized that the unmarked direction of adverbial sub-ordinate clause adjunction in a language reflects the 'principal branching direction' of a language as either right or left, and that this determines systematic differences between right- and left-branching languages. This directionality interacts with the reference of pronominal elements. In (46) and (49), coreference is possible between the subjects of the two clauses but it is not in (50), reflecting a violation of one of the principles of anaphora (Principle C) (See Crain & McKee 1985, Lust *et al.* 1992 for dis-cussion of acquisition of this area).

(50) *She$_i$ uses a computer when Jane$_i$ works.

Table 14.1 summarizes the universal and language-specific features of language knowledge that a child must integrate in the domain of adverbial clauses.

14.4.2   Adverbial clauses in early spontaneous speech

Children acquiring English tend to produce temporal clauses very early, as in the examples in (51) and (52) from a 2 year old. These clauses may be introduced by an overt element, as in (52) or not, as in (51). They may appear before the main clause, as in (51), or after, as in (52).

(51) Child (sitting in his car seat): I get out!
      Mother: Not yet!
      Child: Get home, get out.
      Mother: Yes. Then you'll get out.
                                       (2;1,23, Clark 2003: 259)

(52) The toast make a noise when you put butter on.
                                       (2; 4,26, Clark 2003: 259)

14.4.3 Adverbial clauses and principles of anaphora

Configuration, directionality and finiteness of the adverbial clause domain interact with the determination of reference for anaphoric elements in adverbial clauses. Lust *et al.* (1986) probed knowledge of these interactions in a study of structures like (53)–(56) in English.[4]

(53) Pronoun, forward: Billy dropped the penny [when he saw the cat]

(54) Null, forward: Johnny washed the table [when Ø drinking juice]

(55) Pronoun, backward: [When he coloured the books] Tommy drank milk

(56) Null, backward: [When Ø dressing the baby] Daddy dropped the book

Using both imitation and act-out tasks, Lust *et al.* found that children acquiring English distinguished between the null and overt proforms in these structures according to the finiteness of the subordinate clause (e.g. in an imitation task they frequently converted the null subjects in non-finite sentences to pronoun subjects with tensed predicates.)

Within a given language, both the directionality and the interpretation of the anaphora appear to vary according to the configuration of the clause. For example, in Hindi in clauses introduced by the adverbial *jab* 'when', children were found to generalize directionality over null and overt anaphora, linking a forward antecedent-proform to right-branching structures, and a backward antecedent-proform to left-branching structures (Lust *et al.* 1995). In Sinhala and Japanese, children differentiated two types of adverbial clauses in terms of their finiteness, their configuration (position at which the adverbial clause was joined) and the anaphora involved (e.g. Gair *et al.* 1998, Lust *et al.* 1985, Oshima & Lust 1997). These results reveal that knowledge of the structure of adverbial clauses is integrated with knowledge of different forms of anaphora and with knowledge of directionality of adjunction within and across languages; this knowledge is evident from an early age.[5]

14.4.4 Conclusions on adverbial clauses

Study of the acquisition of adverbial clauses demonstrates that children integrate knowledge of hierarchical structure (e.g. attachment of an adverbial clause at different hierarchical points in a sentence), recursion (e.g. through capacity for adjunction) and the lexicon (e.g. various proforms either lexical or null), with language-specific directionality, with constraints on anaphora and with the meaning of the connectives that introduce adverbial clauses.[6]

---

[4] Also see Goodluck (1981).   [5] Also see Mazuka (1996, 1998).

[6] See, for example, Winskel (2004) and references therein for discussion of the acquisition of temporal clauses in terms of their semantic content.

14.5   Relative clauses

14.5.1   The acquisition challenge

Relative clause structures like those in (57) reflect the linguistic property of recursion.

(57)   This is [[[*the train* [that hit *the bus* [that bumped *the car* [that …

Other relative clauses are illustrated in examples (58)–(61) (from Tavakolian 1981). In each of these examples, the relative clause is bracketed and the head of the clause italicized. The examples vary depending on whether the main clause subject or object is modified (58, 59) vs. (60, 61) and whether the gap within the relative clause appears in subject (58, 60) or object position (59, 61).

(58)   SS (main clause subject is modified; gap in subject position)
        The *sheep* [that jumps over the rabbit] stands on the lion.

(59)   SO (main clause subject is modified; gap in object position)
        The *lion* [that the horse kisses] knocks down the duck.

(60)   OO (main clause object is modified; gap in object position)
        The horse hits the *sheep* [that the duck kisses]

(61)   OS (main clause object is modified; gap in subject position)
        The duck stands on the *lion* [that bumps into the pig]

Languages differ in a number of grammatical features associated with relative clauses. For example, in Mandarin the head of the relative clause may be lexically specified (62) or null (63) (from Mandarin, Packard 1987). (The *e* indicates the gap; Packard glosses the modification marker *de* with the abbreviation MOD.)

(62)   wo   kan e_i de shu_i
        I   read e_i MOD $book_i$
        'books which I read'

(63)   wo   kan e_i de $Ø_i$
        I   read e_i MOD $Ø_i$
        'the one(s) which I read'

Korean permits internally headed relative clauses, as in example (64) from K.-Y. Lee (1991). (See Andrews 1985 for examples of syntactic features associated with relative clauses in other languages.)

(64)   chayk pilyekanke   nayil   kackookessumnita
        book borrow-go-PAST-COMP tomorrow bring-COMP-come-FUT-DECL
        '(I) will bring back the book I borrowed tomorrow.'

In dimensions of relative clause syntax such as the overt realization of the elements appearing as head at clause boundaries and in gap position, languages vary in what they permit.

14.5.2   Relative clauses in early spontaneous speech

Reports of early production of relative clauses in English natural speech include structures like the examples in (65)–(66) (also see Hamburger 1980, Tomasello Ch. 5).

(65)   Look I got!
         = Look what I've got (showing a cookie he had been given)
                                                      (1;11,22, Clark 2003: 251)

(66)   Herb work ə big building have ə elevator'n it
         = Herb works in a building that has an elevator
                                                      (2;0,9, Clark 2003: 251)

These proto-relatives may be characterized by the presence of a clause or a clause-like segment in a typical noun phrase position (65) or juxtaposed to a noun phrase (66).

14.5.3   Lexically headed relative clauses

Much of the early work on the acquisition of relative clauses focused on children's interpretations of relative clauses that differed in whether they modified a main clause subject or object, and in whether they included a gap in subject or object position within the relative clause, as in (58)–(61) above. For example, in a study of English lexically headed relative clauses with twenty-four children aged 3 to 5 years, Tavakolian (1981) reported that the children interpreted relative clauses modifying a main clause object as if they modified the subject, corresponding to a coordinate structure, as in (67). A total of 63 per cent of the interpretations of OS structures were of this nature.

(67) Stimulus: The sheep jumps over the *rabbit* [that stands on the lion].
      Interpretation: sheep jumps over rabbit, sheep stands on lion

   Using an act-out task to test children's understanding of relative clauses, Goodluck and Tavakolian (1982) found that the animacy of an embedded object influenced whether children could successfully act out a sentence containing a relative clause. If the object was animate, as in (68), it was harder than if the object was inanimate, as in (69).

(68) The dog kicks the horse that knocks over the sheep.

(69) The dog kicks the horse that knocks over the table.

Hamburger and Crain (1982) reported that when the context supplied two exemplars of the head noun (e.g. two horses for (68)), thus satisfying a felicity condition, children aged 3 to 5 years produced fewer errors with OS sentences. (For related research see Crain & Thornton 1998, Kidd & Bavin 2002 and references therein.)

Some production studies have also probed the distinction between subject and object relative clauses. Demuth (1995b) investigated production of relative clauses in the spontaneous speech of three children acquiring Sesotho (one sampled at ages 2;6 and 3;0, one at 2;6 and 3;2 and one at 4;0–4;1). By the age of about 3, the younger children use as many subject relative clauses as the child at four years of age. In contrast, the number of object relatives increases from almost none at 3 years of age to 40 per cent of relative clauses at age 4. Demuth also reports that in the early data children frequently use the relative suffix on the embedded verb in Sesotho (glossed RL below), but that the clause-boundary relative marker (glossed REL) is either missing or is included only in cases where it also represents agreement. The example in (70) illustrates a child's omission of REL and inclusion of RL (both markers are obligatory in the adult language).

(70)   Mane   enkile   teng
         = *mane moo*   *ke-e-nk-ile-ng*   teng
         LOC REL   1SG-9PN-take-PERF-RL   there
         'Over there where I took it'

(Sesotho, 2;6, Demuth 1995b)[7]

Demuth concludes that a developmental trend from subject to object relative clauses exists in Sesotho, and that children initially distinguish relative clauses from other clauses (as indicated by the verbal suffix), but have not yet determined the syntactic status of the REL marker.

The overt realization of the elements appearing at clause boundaries has also been investigated in the acquisition of French. Labelle (1990) conducted an elicited production study with 108 children (3–6 years old) acquiring French. The study elicited relative clauses by asking children to choose one of two pictures to put a sticker on. The pictures depicted a character or object involved in two different activities; the most natural way to distinguish them would be to use a relative clause (e.g. for an object relative clause *The ball that he is catching* or *The ball that he is throwing*). In this study children produced the complementizers that introduce subject and object relative clauses (*qui* and *que*) far more frequently than the overt operators that introduce oblique relative clauses (e.g. the locative relative clause marker *dans laquelle* 'in which'). See also Guasti and Shlonsky (1995) and Foley (1996).

---

[7] 9PN = gender/number class 9 pronominal.

14.5.4   Findings for free or headless relatives

The term 'headless' refers to the absence of a nominal head, as in example (71). A series of studies has compared the development of lexically headed relative clauses like those discussed in section 14.5.3, and 'free' or 'headless' relative clauses. In a study of ninety-six children between the ages of 3;6 and 7;7 Flynn and Lust (1981) tested headless relative clauses, as in (71), and lexically headed relative clauses, as in (72)–(73). Examples (72) and (73) differ in whether or not there is semantic content in the head (*balloon* versus *thing*).

(71)   Fozzie Bear hugs [what Kermit the Frog kisses]

(72)   Ernie touches [the balloon [which Big Bird throws]]

(73)   Cookie Monster eats [the thing [which Ernie kicks]]

Using an elicited imitation task they found that children performed significantly better on the free relatives than on the lexically headed; there were no significant differences for structures involving head nouns with semantic content and those without. These findings indicate that, consistent with early spontaneous speech data, headless relatives may be developmentally primitive. The authors argue that free relatives provide an especially direct route to nominalization of the clause, and to subsequent embedding under an NP within the main clause.

A primacy for headless relatives appears to also characterize the acquisition of Mandarin Chinese. Packard (1987) analysed the spontaneous speech of twenty-seven Taiwanese children in two age groups (2;0–2;5 and 2;6–2;11), counting examples of nominal modifiers with the *de* marker, including forms with and without overt heads. In Packard's full set of 6,209 utterances, referring expressions with *de* modification appeared in both age groups, but the percentage of such utterances with a lexical head increased from 18.7 per cent of referring expressions in the younger group to 47.3 per cent in the older group.

In Korean, K.-Y. Lee (1991) analysed the spontaneous speech of 36 children (ages 1;4 to 3;9; see also Lee *et al.* 1991). She reports findings pointing to the earlier productivity of relative clauses without a lexical nominal head than with a lexical head. Lee found that children produced relative clauses like (74) ,which are introduced by the clause marker/complementizer *kes*.

(74)   Mok-ey   ke-nun-*ke*   ya?
       Neck-LOC   wear-PRES-COMP   INT?
       'Is it the one (you) wear on the neck?' (referring to her mother's necklace)
                                                            (Korean, 1;11, K.-Y. Lee 1991)

Kes operates as a complementizer in adult Korean but generally does not appear in adult relative clauses of this form.[8] Children nevertheless insert *kes*, a finding compatible with Murasugi's (2000) report that children

---

[8] *Kes* introduces sentential complements and also appears at the boundary of internally headed relative clause structures (K.-Y. Lee 1991).

acquiring Japanese insert the particle *no* in relative clauses where it is not grammatical in adult Japanese:

(75) buta san-ga   tataiteru   no   taiko
     piggy-NOM   is-hitting   *no*   drum
     'the drum that the piggy is playing'
                         (Japanese, 2;11, Murasugi 2000: 235)[9]

Murasugi argues that *no*, which is a genitive marker, can instantiate the head of CP. In both Japanese and Korean, children appear able to generalize an element appearing in complementizer position in the adult grammar to introduce relative clauses. In Quechua also, children spontaneously produce more headless relatives than other forms (Courtney 2006). Taken together, these findings suggest a developmental path that leads from the free relative to the lexically headed form. It may be the case that when the free relative more directly corresponds to the lexically headed form it assists the acquisition of lexically headed forms. (Foley 1996). Children appear to be integrating knowledge of adjunction with other grammatical components needed for embedding within a nominal phrase.

   This picture of development as a process of integrating grammatical components is supported by findings from the acquisition of Tulu. In an elicited imitation experiment Somashekar (1999) compared the development of several relative clause types in monolingual children aged 2;5 to 6;6. These types included the verbal adjective, where the embedded verb inflects for tense but not agreement; in another type, the correlative, the embedded verb inflects for both tense and agreement, as in (76).

(76) [yeer$_i$ kuuli   dekk-ye-naa]   aaye$_i$ eDDennaaye.
     who$_i$ teeth   washed-3MASC.SG.-Q   he$_i$ good:3MASC.SG
     'He who brushed (his) teeth is good.'

Children often converted correlatives (and other relative clauses) to verbal adjectives. Importantly, when they did so they also frequently made the required change on the inflection of the embedded verb, including the tense marker but omitting agreement, as required by the syntax of Tulu. Such frequent conversions in Somashekar's data suggest that children begin early to integrate the syntax of clausal structure with the syntax of embedded verb inflection.

14.5.5   Semantics in relative clauses

Additional recent work on relative clauses has examined various cognitive semantic aspects of relativization (e.g. Ozeki & Shirai 2005 for Japanese and Korean). Fragman *et al.* (2007) report children's early awareness of the restrictive/non-restrictive distinction in English.

---

[9] Murasugi's gloss assumes *buta san* (noun and honorific) is a single lexical item.

14.5.6 Conclusions on relative clauses

Research findings suggest that while lexically headed relatives develop over time, free or headless relatives appear foundational to the development of lexically headed forms. While some studies propose a developmental course in which complex relative sentences expand from simple sentences (e.g. Diessel & Tomasello 2005), the patterns of development reviewed here cannot be so described.[10] For example, at very early stages Tulu-speaking children reveal a capacity to relate clausal structure and verbal morphosyntax. Korean-speaking children add a clausal head *kes* and Japanese-speaking children add *no* to early relatives, even when not occurring in the adult language in these structures. These results are consistent with children's continuous access to a capacity for complex sentence structure and recursion, and with the need to acquire and integrate language-specific knowledge, such as branching direction, verbal inflection and lexical forms (e.g. of elements introducing and potentially heading relative clauses).

14.6   Conclusion

In this chapter we have suggested that just as there is no clear grammatical distinction between simple and complex sentences, so there is no fundamental distinction in acquisition between simple and complex sentences. The data do not support a view that complex sentences develop from simple sentences in an additive fashion. For example, sentences with relativization and/or complementation do not simply expand from simple sentences, and early coordinated and adverbial sentences do not reflect flat juxtaposition of component parts. A second example is the apparent absence of a stage at which children's early grammars allow coordination but not adjunction (Lust 1994).[11] In several studies young children were found to distinguish coordinate from non-coordinate structures, apparently consulting the clausal and hierarchical structure of their language in order to do so. It does not appear that at a first 'stage' children have competence only for simple sentences and at a subsequent 'stage' they gain competence for complex sentences.

Instead, there is evidence for complex sentence grammar from the beginning of productive combinatorial speech. Children's language shows an early sensitivity to parametric crosslinguistic variation in grammatical factors related to complex sentence formation, such as directionality of adjunction and to finite/non-finite distinctions in clausal adjunctions. This has led some to speculate as to how these early sensitivities might arise even before the child speaks a first word (Mazuka 1996).

---

[10] See also Crain *et al.* (1990) for a contrasting view of development.

[11] See Tavakolian (1978), Lebeaux (1990), Cohen Sherman and Lust (1993) and Cairns *et al.* (1993).

While there clearly is an effect on complex sentence formation from the development of simple sentence grammar, at the same time there is evidence that the grammar of complex sentences also affects children's simple sentence formation early in development.

We have also discovered evidence of developmental phenomena. For example, sentential coordinations appear developmentally primitive relative to other types of coordination. Relative clauses without lexical heads appear developmentally primitive to those with heads. Yet the form of development we observe here is not a simple addition of one concrete construction to another. For example, the developmentally primary sentential coordinations or relative clauses without nominal lexical heads are both complex structures, superficially at least as complex as the coordination and relative clause types they provide foundations for.

In general, our review coheres with Bloom's (1970: 138) observation that in early language acquisition, 'increase in structure or complexity [i]s not a matter of simply increasing length of utterance by adding structure to structure or adding elements within a structure'. Development appears to involve integration of language-specific structure, the lexicon, and cognitive and semantic features, with potentially universal syntactic knowledge in the course of mapping to a specific language grammar.

Suggestions for further reading

Bloom, L., Rispoli, M., Gartner, B., & Hafitz, J. (1989). Acquisition of complementation. *Journal of Child Language*, 16, 101–120.

Diessel, H. (2004). *The Acquisition of Complex Sentences*. New York: Cambridge University Press.

Limber, J. (1973). The genesis of complex sentences. In T. Moore (Ed.), *Cognitive Development and the Acquisition of Language*. New York: Academic Press.

Menyuk, P. (1969). *Sentences Children Use*. Cambridge MA: MIT Press.

Roeper, T. (2007). *The Prism of Grammar*. A Bradford Book. Cambridge MA: MIT Press.

15

The morphosyntax interface

Kamil Ud Deen

15.1 Introduction

This chapter investigates the acquisition of morphology in child language, and considers various possible explanations for the empirical facts. The discussion revolves around the *morphosyntax interface*, a term used to refer to the confluence of two areas of language, morphology and syntax, and the processes involved in linking these two. A morpheme is the smallest unit of meaning in language, and the study of morphemes is referred to as morphology. Morphemes include regular words (e.g. *girl, eat, beautiful, etc.*), but also smaller units of language such as prefixes (e.g. *un-, re-*), suffixes (e.g. *-s, -ed, -ing*), etc. The way in which these morphemes are ordered depends on a variety of different factors, including properties of the sound system, properties of the morphemes themselves, as well as properties of the grammatical system. This latter system is referred to as syntax – the abstract set of principles that govern the ordering and interpretation of morphemes in a sentence. The morphosyntax interface, therefore, is the locus of interaction of these two areas of language.

Many linguistic phenomena arise out of this interface of morphology and syntax, including the familiar passive construction, questions and inflection. The focus of this chapter is inflectional morphology – a classic example of a linguistic phenomenon that is both syntactic and morphological in nature (see Behrens Ch. 12). Inflection is a variation in the form of a word that is conditioned by a particular grammatical context. For example, the verb *eat* occurs in a variety of different forms, including *eats, eating, ate*. The choice of which of these forms a speaker uses is determined by the context in which the word occurs – *eats* occurs in a habitual or historical present context; *eating* occurs after an auxiliary verb in the present progressive context, etc. These different forms represent different inflectional forms of the verb. Languages vary as to which kinds of inflection they exhibit, but typical examples of inflection are agreement on the verb for person (e.g. a verb in

English often has -s attached to the end when the subject of the sentence is third person, singular), number (e.g. the noun in English has -s attached when indicating that the referent is plural), case (e.g. nominative, accusative, genitive pronouns in English), tense, modality, aspect, etc.

The morphosyntax interface is an important area of research in the study of child language because children exhibit (i) interesting patterns in the acquisition of inflectional morphology, and (ii) significant cross-linguistic similarities in the nature of those patterns. In particular, this chapter asks the question of whether the patterns in the acquisition of morphology have as their source (i) a lack of knowledge of inflectional morphology, (ii) a lack of syntactic knowledge, or (iii) problems with the conversion of a syntactic representation into a string of morphemes.

The chapter begins with a discussion of the architecture of the morpho-syntax interface (Section 15.2). This section begins with an overview of the theoretical framework in which the ensuing discussion is couched (for read-ers who are not familiar with the theory), and is followed by a description of how the morphosyntax interface is organized. Section 15.3 then describes the major findings in the acquisition of inflectional morphology, stating five important generalizations. Section 15.4 describes the Root Infinitive phe-nomenon. These two sections establish the empirical facts which then serve as the background for section 15.5, in which we discuss several recent theories, categorized into those that propose a deficit in (i) inflectional knowledge, (ii) the process of converting a syntactic representation into a morphological string, and (iii) the underlying syntactic representation.

15.2   The morphosyntax interface

15.2.1   The generative approach to language

This chapter assumes a model of language that was first proposed by Noam Chomsky (1957). The details of this model have changed over the last fifty years, but the basic approach remains unchanged. Simplifying the model somewhat, the idea is that all sentences in a language are generated by a computational system that is comprised of a finite set of principles oper-ating on a set of lexical items. These lexical items are manipulated by the finite set of principles within a highly constrained hierarchical structure, which takes the form of a binary branching tree. The hierarchical structure associated with the sentence 'The girl chased the mouse' is shown in (1).

(1)

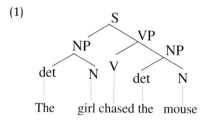

The words in the sentence are arranged in pre-specified positions in the terminal nodes of the syntactic tree in (1), which are labelled according to the function that they perform. Terminal nodes are the locations on the tree which do not branch any further. So the determiner *the* (sometimes also referred to as an article) occurs within a node labelled *det*, the noun *girl* occurs within a node labelled N, the verb *chased* occurs within a node labelled V, etc. These various nodes are grouped into *phrases*, which take as their label the major element within that phrase. So *the girl* constitutes a phrase which takes the label Noun Phrase (the noun being the major element within that phrase). The rest of the words are categorized in a similar fashion.

The top node on the tree in (1) is labelled S because it represents the entire Sentence. In the 1980s, this label was changed from S to Inflectional Phrase (IP), in recognition of the fact that in a wide variety of languages the highest positions of the tree are typically reserved for inflectional kinds of elements. This top node branches downwards in a binary fashion, with the next two nodes down labelled NP and VP. This division represents a basic division in any sentence: that of subject and predicate. The NP stands for the subject noun phrase, and the VP stands for the verbal predicate. Finally, the grammatical object (*the mouse*) occurs deeper within the VP, within another NP.[1]

This formalism has several important characteristics. First, all nodes that are labelled alike are assumed to function alike. For example, NPs should be interchangeable, and in fact this is largely true (e.g. 'The mouse chased the girl', where the object NP has been switched with the subject NP, is a grammatical sentence). Second, the overall structure has a 'nested' characteristic. That is, each binary branching node is nested within another binary branching node, except for the very top node. This creates a series of hierarchically embedded structures that are basically of the same type. Note that the VP consists of not only the verb, but also the NP that corresponds to the grammatical object. This captures the intuition that the predicate is more than just the verb, but is affected by the properties of the object. Thus this nested structure allows for groupings of words into linguistically meaningful units. We will return to this characteristic in our discussion of syntactic accounts of child language in section 15.5.3. And finally, this model has a finite set of principles, which together with the stipulated structure have the capacity to generate an infinite set of sentences. This *generative capacity* is appealing because it provides a mechanism to explain how children are able to acquire the ability to understand and produce an infinite set of sentences without having to learn each and every one of them.

---

[1] The structure described here is obviously Anglo-centric. While the structures for other languages differ from that outlined here, the basic tenets of this framework remain constant (e.g. binary branching, phrasing).

15.2.2 The interface

It is generally accepted that in producing a grammatical sentence, the particular morphemes we produce, both their form and relative order, are a reflection of this underlying syntactic representation of the sentence. The idea is that a speaker creates a syntactic representation of a sentence, translates that into a series of lexical and morphological items (often referred to as 'linearization'), and then actually physically pronounces them. The listener, who does not have access to the underlying intended syntactic representation, perceives the lexical and morphological items, takes note of their form and order, and decodes them into a syntactic representation. The morphosyntax interface (MI) refers to this interaction of syntax with morphology. Minimally, the MI includes the following three components:

I.   syntax
II. conversion algorithm
III. morphology

Each of these areas are studied extensively in adult language, especially I and III. The conversion algorithm II receives somewhat less attention, although it is assumed in virtually every theory of syntax and/or morphology. The precise mechanisms of the conversion from syntax to morphology (and vice versa in comprehension) are not very well understood, but there are several formal descriptions of how morphology links up with syntax.

Within the generativist approach to language acquisition one well-known formalization is Baker's (1988) Mirror Principle, which holds that the overt order of a string of morphemes is either a direct reflection of the underlying architecture of a syntactic tree, or its exact mirror image. Thus if one observes a string of morphemes as in (2a), one can assume (by the Mirror Principle) that the underlying structure of that sentence is as in (2b), or its exact mirror image (2c).

(2) a.   Observed order of morphemes: A – B – C

The underlying assumption to this approach is that the conversion algorithm is a simple reader of the terminal nodes of the tree. So in the case of (2b), the tree is read from left to right, top to bottom, while in (2c), the tree is read from right to left, bottom to top. This produces a linearized string of abstract categories, each of which is then matched to appropriate items in the lexicon. An example from English is 'I chase mice', which would be represented as the structure in (2b), where *I* would be A, *chase* would be B and *mice* would be C. On this approach, the properly functioning MI involves the output of a syntactic component, the correct conversion algorithm, and appropriate access to a full lexicon. If any one of these components is deficient in any manner (as may be the case with children), then the process may produce non-adult-like utterances.[2]

Now, if a child produces an utterance that is morphologically unadult-like (e.g. a typical young child utterance missing 3rd person singular *-s* in English, such as 'Mummy eat cookies today'), it is not immediately clear where the source of that error lies: it could conceivably be any one of the three components to the morphosyntax interface in (I–III), or indeed some other domain entirely.[3] Hyams (1989a) refers to this as the Domain Problem: when the child produces an error, it is not immediately clear which domain of language is responsible for that error. As such, over the last several years, various theories have been put forward to explain essentially the same set of facts, each appealing to a different domain. We shall discuss several of these theories below, but first we must establish what those basic empirical facts are.

15.3   Some properties of the acquisition of morphology

Over the last few decades, several important generalizations have emerged from the study of morphology in child language. While there are exceptional cases, the generalizations presented here are good rules-of-thumb that might guide a researcher's first analysis of child data. Following these five generalizations, we discuss the phenomenon known as Root Infinitives (also known as Optional Infinitives).

15.3.1   Five generalizations
15.3.1.1   Generalization 1. Inflection acquired before age 5
Typically developing children are remarkably good at acquiring inflection. Over the last few decades, children acquiring a wide range of languages have been found to exhibit high degrees of control (about 80 per cent

---

[2] This kind of direct linking between syntax and morphology is widely assumed in the literature. For example, Pollock's (1989) split-INFL hypothesis was based upon the observation that negation occurs in a different relative order with finite verbs versus non-finite verbs. This was used as evidence that the syntactic position to which finite verbs move in the syntax is different from that of non-finite verbs. The details of this proposal are beyond the scope of this chapter, but the reader is referred to Pollock's original paper, as well as Haegeman (1991) and Carnie (2006) for an overview.

[3] An obvious candidate is phonology. There have been several influential proposals that seek to explain the omission of inflectional elements (including grammatical subjects) as phonological processes, e.g. Gerken (1991), Gerken and McIntosh (1993) and Demuth (2007). I do not discuss these here because they do not directly relate to the morphosyntax interface.

correct in obligatory contexts) over inflectional morphology by about age 5 or earlier. This is a remarkable feat when one considers that children are rarely (if ever) explicitly taught the form, meaning or context of inflectional morphemes. Nevertheless, children come to know the inflectional systems of their language at a very early age.

In fact, if a child uses target inflectional morphemes in less than 50 per cent of obligatory contexts at an age when the inflectional morphology would typically be acquired, this is often taken by speech pathologists as an initial indication that the child has a language disorder. For example, Rice and Wexler (1996b), using data from thirty-seven American children aged 4;4 to 5;8 diagnosed with specific language impairment (SLI) (see Tomblin Ch. 23 and Leonard Ch. 24,) and forty age-matched normal children, find that the unimpaired children used third person singular -s, past tense -ed, and the auxiliaries be and do in over 80 per cent of obligatory contexts, while the SLI children produced all four of these morphemes in less than 50 per cent of obligatory contexts.

15.3.1.2   Generalization 2. Early acquisition in inflectionally rich languages

A somewhat counterintuitive finding is that children acquiring languages that have a rich inventory of inflectional morphemes seem to acquire that system significantly earlier than children acquiring languages relatively meagre in inflection, such as English. For example, Guasti (1993/94) investigated the speech of three children (aged 1;8–2;7) acquiring Italian, and reported that the children began producing agreement before the age of 2, and the rate of error never rose above 3 per cent. Furthermore, omission of inflection was very rare, although avoidance of certain forms (e.g. plural) was attested. Guasti concluded that the agreement system is in place from very early on, perhaps even as young as 2 years of age. Similarly, Deen (2004) reports that children acquiring Swahili (a Bantu language spoken in Eastern Africa with a very rich set of inflectional morphemes) converge on the correct agreement system before age 3, producing less than 2 per cent errors and omitting agreement less than 20 per cent of the time. Results such as these have been found in a wide variety of languages, including Spanish (Grinstead 2000), Catalan (Grinstead 2000), Sesotho (Demuth 1992) and German (Poeppel & Wexler 1993), and stand in contrast to the acquisition of inflections in morphologically poorer languages such as English, in which children often do not acquire the agreement system of their language until approximately age 4 years (Brown 1973, see Phillips 1995 for a review).

15.3.1.3   Generalization 3. Regular inflectional systems are easier

Inflectional systems that are regular and that contain very few exceptions are acquired earlier and with fewer errors than those that have exceptions. One way to measure whether children have acquired the inflectional system of a language is whether they commit errors in production (errors of *commission*). Committing errors in production is a special kind of error (the other kind being an error of *omission*, see Generalization 5). Examples of such errors are the use of a first person agreement marker in a third person context, or the use of singular morphology in a plural context (or vice versa). It has generally been found that children acquiring languages with systematic and regular inflectional systems produce far fewer errors of this sort than children acquiring languages with irregular or unpredictable inflectional systems.

A good example of this is the difference between Italian and Brazilian Portuguese (BP). Italian has a very regular system of verb agreement, shown in (3a) below. As discussed above, Italian children acquire agreement very early and with few errors. However, BP has a rather unusual inflectional paradigm, shown in (3b).

(3) a. Italian   b. Brazilian Portuguese
    1st sg   (io) scriv – o   1st sg   Eu es'crev – o
    2nd sg   (tu) scriv – i   2nd sg   Você es'crev – e
    3rd sg   (lui/lei) scriv – e   3rd sg   Ele es'crev – e
    1st pl   (noi) scriv – iamo   1st pl   A gente es'crev – e
    2nd pl   (voi) scriv – ete   1st pl   Nós escre'v – emos
    3rd pl   (Loro) scriv – ono   2nd pl   Vocês es'crev – em
                                     3rd pl   Eles es'crev – em

In Italian, each person/number has a distinct morpheme associated with it, and no single morpheme refers to more than one person/number. This is a regular, unmarked agreement system. Compare this to the BP system, which is significantly different. Notice that the only morpheme in BP that uniquely corresponds to a single person/number the way all six do in Italian is first person singular. The remaining morphemes are either conflations of multiple person/number references, or are complicated in some other way. The morpheme *-e* is used with second person singular, third person singular and first person plural subjects. So *-e* seems to occur in all three persons, and in both the singular and plural. Furthermore, *-em* occurs when the subject is either second or third person, plural. And finally, there are two (seemingly non-distinct) forms for first person plural: *-e* and *–emos*. Thus the BP agreement system is significantly less regular and predictable than that of Italian.

Rubino and Pine (1998) investigated the acquisition of inflection in one child acquiring BP. They found that while errors in the singular are relatively low (2.1 per cent), errors in agreement with plural subjects occurred at a rate of 28 per cent. The researchers argue that this high rate of error shows that children do not acquire inflection as easily and as rapidly as is usually thought, and that children acquire agreement on verbs in a piecemeal fashion. However, the plural is exactly where most of the irregularity of the BP agreement system occurs, and so it is not surprising that agreement errors would arise in the plural. When faced with a system that has unexpected irregularities, the child simply tries to regularize the system, resulting in error. Such errors are very common in other domains of child language involving exceptional morphology. Consider overgeneralization in English verb morphology: children often go through a stage during which they sometimes produce past tense verbs such as *goed*, *runned* and *eated* (see Behrens Ch. 12, Section 12.2.2). In this case, children have acquired the past tense rule of English (add -*ed* to the verb stem) and have not learned that this generalization only applies to certain verbs. Children must learn these cases one by one through positive exposure to each example. Similarly, in BP the child has learned the regular pattern but has not learned the irregular portions of the agreement paradigm. We shall return to BP in our discussion in section 15.3.1.5.

15.3.1.4 Generalization 4. Grammatical subjects often omitted

Languages can be classified into those that allow null subjects (e.g. Italian, Spanish, Japanese, Swahili) and those that require an overt subject (e.g. English, French) with finite verbs.

(4)   English   Italian
  a. Overt subject: I ate the cake   Io ho mangiato la torta
  b. Null subject: * ate the cake   Ho mangiato la torta

A feature of child English is that grammatical subjects are omitted at very high rates. Valian (1991) reports that five English-speaking children (mean age: 2;0) produced null subjects in approximately 31 per cent of non-imitative, non-imperative utterances. In a group of older children (mean age: 2;5), that proportion dropped to 11 per cent. Thus as the children matured and they began to acquire the inflectional system of their language, a higher percentage of subjects occurred. How are subjects related to inflection? Grammatical subjects are related to inflection and the MI in a very real sense: the grammatical case required by subjects is referred to either as nominative case or ergative case (depending on the kind of language in question). Considering nominative case, within generative frameworks of language, it is widely assumed to be assigned by some inflectional category such as tense or agreement (which one depends on the language and particular theory). But because subjects require case assignment, they are very closely related to this inflectional category. That grammatical subjects and inflectional morphology develop in child language together in real time is therefore not a coincidence. Subjects *are* inflectional in nature.

15.3.1.5 Generalization 5. Errors of omission predominate, errors of commission are rare

When children do make errors, they overwhelmingly make errors of omission, as shown in (5). Such errors include the omission of inflectional elements (e.g. 5d–f), but also the omission of the 'carrier' of inflection, (e.g. the copula verb in 5b and the auxiliary verb in 5c), as well as other elements that are thought to be related to inflection, such as determiners (5a). Examples (5a,c) are from Radford (1990), (5b) from Becker (2000), (5d) from Brown (1973), (5e) from Demuth (1992), and (5f) from Deen (2005).

(5) Errors of omission – very common
    a.   Paula play ball   Determiner Omission
         target: Paula plays with <u>the</u> ball
    b.   I in the kitchen   Copula Omission
    c.   baby talking   Auxiliary Omission
    d.   He bite me   Agreement Omission
    e.   Ø – qet – il – e   Agreement Omission, Sesotho
         target: ke – qet – il – e
                  1sg–finish–PAST–IND[4]
                  'I finished'
    f.   alafu a – Ø – rud – i   Tense Omission, Swahili
         target: alafu a – li – rud – i
                  then 3sg–PAST–return–IND
                  'Then he returned.'

Such errors are widely reported in the literature for a number of languages, including German (Poeppel & Wexler 1993), Inuktitut (Swift & Allen 2002), Japanese (Clancy 1985), Kaluli (Schieffelin 1985), Quechua (Courtney 1998), Polish (Smoczyńska 1985), Sesotho (Demuth 1992), Siswati (Kunene 1979), Swahili (Deen 2002, 2005), Turkish (Aksu-Koc & Slobin 1985) and Zulu (Suzman 1991). Not only are errors of omission attested in a wide range of languages, within each language omission often occurs at high rates. For example, Sano and Hyams (1994) report that in the speech of three children acquiring English (data available on CHILDES, MacWhinney 2000), at certain stages over 70 per cent of third person singular verbs were missing the obligatory *-s*. They investigated the speech of Eve (age 1;6–1;10), Adam (2;3–3;0) and Nina (2;4–2;5), and found the rate of omission of *-s* in third person singular contexts was 78, 81 and 75 per cent, respectively.

Deen (2005) reports similar results in the acquisition of Swahili. The Swahili verb is inflected minimally for subject agreement (SA), tense (T) and mood, as shown in (6), and children at early stages omit subject agreement and tense at high rates (see Table 15.1).

(6) Swahili minimal verbal complex: SA –T – V – Mood
    Example: ni – li –   anguk- a
               1sg –PAST– fall –   IND
               'I fell.'

---

[4] IND = indicative mood.

Table 15.1. Rate of omission of agreement and tense in Swahili

Child	Age	Agreement omission (%)	Tense omission (%)
Haw	2;2–2;6	72.1	70.3
Mus	2;0–2;3	54.5	40.0

Table 15.2. Rate of agreement errors in a range of languages

Child	Language	Age	Utterances	Percentage error	Source
Simone	German	1;7–2;8	1,732	1.0	Clahsen & Penke (1992)
Martina	Italian	1;8–2;7	478	1.6	Guasti (1993/1994)
Diana	Italian	1;10–2;6	610	1.5	Guasti (1993/1994)
Guglielmo	Italian	2;2–2;7	201	3.3	Guasti (1993/1994)
Claudia	Italian	1;4–2;4	1,410	3.0	Pizzuto & Caselli (1992)
Francesco	Italian	1;5–2;10	1,264	2.0	Pizzuto & Caselli (1992)
Marco	Italian	1;5–3;0	415	4.0	Pizzuto & Caselli (1992)
Gisela	Catalan	1;10–2;6	81	1.2	Torrens (1995)
Guillem	Catalan	1;9–2;6	129	2.3	Torrens (1995)

So the omission of inflectional morphology is crosslinguistically common and occurs at high rates. Errors of commission (also known as errors of substitution), while not unheard of, are much less common. An example of an error of substitution is an agreement error such as 'I eats dinner', in which third person agreement incorrectly occurs in a first person context. In an analysis of the speech of ten English-speaking children (age range 1;6–4;1), Harris and Wexler (1996) identified 1,724 verbs that occurred in the first person singular context, of which only 3 occurred with the incorrect third person singular -s suffix – a remarkably low error rate of 0.17 per cent. Similarly, Deen (2004) investigated the speech of two children (age 2;10–3;0 and 1;8–2;1) acquiring Swahili, and found that the rate of errors of agreement were extremely low. The older child produced a total of 3 agreement errors out of 224 verbal utterances (an error rate of 1.3 per cent), and the younger child produced 1 error out of 197 verbal utterances (an error rate of 0.5 per cent). Table 15.2 (adapted from Sano & Hyams 1994) shows the rate of errors in agreement in a number of children acquiring various languages.

In calculating error rates, it is important to ensure that a fine-grained analysis is performed so that the contexts in which errors are more prevalent can be identified. Consider the hypothetical data set in Table 15.3, in which the rate of error has been calculated for each file. The overall error rate for this corpus is 1.05 per cent (31/2, 945). Such a low error rate confirms Generalization 5, and fits well with the rest of the data presented in Table 15.2. However, this error rate masks an apparent spike in errors in file 2, where the error rate is more than 5 per cent.

Table 15.3. Hypothetical data set showing variation in error rates across files

File	Utterances	Errors	Percentage	File	Utterances	Errors	Percentage
1	370	1	0.27	4	260	1	0.38
2	425	24	5.65	5	525	1	0.19
3	565	4	0.71	6	800	0	0

Furthermore, it is possible that upon closer examination of file 2, one might discover that a large number of errors occur only in certain contexts or with certain morphology or with certain lexical items – facts that would be lost if a file-by-file analysis were not performed. In fact, this is what is found by Rubino and Pine (1998) in their study of the Brazilian Portuguese child discussed in section 15.3.1.3. They found that while the overall rate of error in subject–verb agreement was in line with other languages (44/1,464 = 3.01 per cent), the rate of error was significantly higher in the plural (14/50 = 28 per cent) than in the singular (30/1,414 = 2 per cent). Because there are many more examples of singular verbs than plural verbs, when the data are aggregated across all contexts, it gives the impression of a very low error rate.

However, the unusually high error rate reported for BP is not due to the low frequency of plurals in BP, as Rubino and Pine suggest. As Deen (2004) points out, their argument predicts that because plurals are generally rarer in child speech and child-directed speech than singular verbs, children crosslinguistically should do worse on plural agreement. But in the speech of two Swahili children studied by Deen, the rate of error in the singular was very low (0.5–1.47 per cent), and there were *no errors* in the plural. Deen argues that the elevated rate of errors in BP is essentially because of the irregular nature of the agreement paradigm (see (3b)). Thus the elevated rate of errors that Rubino and Pine report is due essentially to Generalization 3 and not to an exception to Generalization 5.

15.4 Root Infinitives

A Root Infinitive (RI) is a verb that is marked with overt non-finite morphology and that occurs in a root (main) clause. Examples of RIs from a variety of languages are provided in (7).

(7) a. Thorsten das   hab-en   German
       Thorsten that have-INF
       'Thorsten has that.'
    b. Papa   schoen wass-en   Dutch
       daddy shoes wash-INF
       'Daddy washes (the) shoes.'

c. Ferm-er   yeux   French
   close-INF   eyes
   '(I have) closed (my) eyes.'

The verbs here are not just missing inflection, but are overtly marked as infinitives. In adult language, this is generally ungrammatical (although non-finite verbs do occur in certain root clauses). For example, the appropriate form of the verb in (7a) in adult German would be the finite *hat*, not *haben*. This could be taken as a potential exception to Generalization 5 above – that is, use of the infinitive in finite connects could be construed as an error of commission. However, as we will see, this is not the case.

One of the most striking facts about RIs is that the occurrence of the morphological infinitive is not a morphological error. Rather, by positioning the infinitival verb in a position reserved for non-finite verbs, children exhibit knowledge that the form they are using is indeed a non-finite form. Take German as an example. In adult German main clauses, finite (inflected) verbs occur in the second position (8a), while infinitives occur at the end of the sentence (8b). The boxes indicate the different forms of the verb used in different contexts.

(8)   a.   Ich   sehe   viele   Leute   Finite German Verb
           I   see.1sg   many   people   Verb in second position (V2)
           'I see many people.'

      b.   Ich   möchte [viele   Leute   seh-en]   Non-finite German Verb
           I   want   [many   people   see-INF]   Verb in final position
           'I want to see many people.'

Following most generative approaches, in German finite main clauses the verb must move leftward from its final position to the second position in the clause structure. The first movement is to I(nflection) Phrase (referred to as S in (1)), and then a second movement to a position referred to as C(omplementizer). The first position in the clause structure is usually filled by the subject of the sentence, although any other element (e.g. the grammatical object, negation, an adverb) may also be in first position. This is referred to as the V(erb)-2 phenomenon. In non-finite sentences, however, the verb does not move leftward to C, and so it remains in sentence-final position, as in (8b). The details of how and why this happens are not relevant for our purposes, only that finite verbs occur in the second position of the sentence, while non-finite verbs occur in the final position of the sentence. Thus finiteness predicts the position of the verb in German.

In an analysis of RIs in child German, Poeppel and Wexler (1993) found that, with few exceptions, inflected verbs occurred in the (correct) second position (197/208) while uninflected verbs (RIs) occurred in the (correct) sentence-final position (37/45). That is, the use of infinitival morphology is

Table 15.4. Use of RIs and non-RIs

Use of RI by children	Non-use of RI by children
Danish (Hamann & Plunkett 1998)	Catalan (Grinstead 2000)
Dutch (Weverink 1989)	Inuktitut (Swift & Allen 2002)
Faroese (Jonas 1995)	Italian (Guasti 1993/94)
Flemish (Krämer 1993)	Japanese (Sano 1995)
French (Pierce 1989)	Quechua (Courtney 1998)
German (Poeppel & Wexler 1993)	Sesotho (Demuth 1992)
Swedish (Platzack 1992)	Spanish (Grinstead 2000)
	Swahili (Deen 2002, 2005)
	Zulu (Suzman 1991)

not an error in the sense that the child simply lacks knowledge of the inflectional system. Rather, the fact that children produce verbs in positions that conform to the underlying syntactic requirements shows that children possess an understanding of the syntactic requirements of German.[5] This kind of form–position contingency has been found in other languages, including Dutch (Wijnen 1997) and French (Pierce 1989).[6]

Table 15.4 lists some of the languages in which children have been reported to produce RIs, and languages in which children rarely produce RIs.

Why children produce infinitives in some languages and not others is still unclear: to date there is no satisfactory explanation. One obvious solution is that the default verb form (if there is one) varies across languages, but this solution runs into problems once a wide range of languages is considered.[7]

15.5 The source of the omission and RIs

So far we have seen that children crosslinguistically acquire inflection by age 5 (earlier in morphologically rich languages). Initially children may omit inflections and in some languages produce root infinitives. Both these phenomena have the potential to inform us about the acquisition of the MI since they both involve morphological elements that are closely

---

[5] There are several additional arguments to support the conclusion that RIs are reflective of knowledge of the syntactic requirements of the adult language. For example, RIs in child language tend to occur with null subjects, while finite verbs tend to occur with overt subjects. This is because the absence of case features on a non-finite verb results in the failure to license an overt subject. See Deen (2005) for summary of the languages in which this empirical result has been reported. Additionally, RIs tend to occur in modal contexts (e.g. Wijnen, 1997) – a property common to adult infinitives too.

[6] In French, the form–position contingency relates to the position of the verb with respect to negation. Inflected verbs in adult French occur to the left of negation (see 2a–b). Children exhibit the same form–position contingency here too: when RIs occur, they occur to the right of negation *pas*, but when the verb is inflected, it consistently occurs to the left of negation.

[7] One additional question is whether children acquiring English actually use RIs. Several researchers have argued that the bare verb used by young English-speaking children is the English equivalent of the RI (e.g. Wexler 1994), and has the same underlying cause as the RI in other languages.

tied to the underlying syntax. What could the source of these errors be? There are at least three possibilities, listed in (9).

(9)   a. Deficits in morphological knowledge
      b. Deficits in syntax–morphology conversion
      c. Deficits in syntactic knowledge.

The first (9a) refers simply to a lack of knowledge of the morphological properties of a language. A child that has not learned, for example, the full agreement paradigm in the target language may not know which morpheme to produce in a certain context, and thus may omit morphology. We will refer to this process as morphological learning – learning the properties of the various inflectional paradigms in the target language.

The second (9b) is a problem with converting the syntactic representation into a morphological string. Assuming that morphological learning has taken place, it is possible that the very algorithm for producing the appropriate string of morphemes is somehow impeded, resulting in the absence of the target morpheme. There are two ways that this could occur: (i) the algorithm itself is incorrect, or (ii) processing resources to execute the conversion are insufficient, resulting in omission of inflection.

The third (9c) is a child syntactic component that is somehow different from that of the adult. If the underlying syntactic representation that feeds into the conversion algorithm is somehow non-adult-like, then the output will be similarly deviant from the adult norm. There are many classes of theories within this category, including what I refer to as Structural Divergence theories and Underspecification theories.

15.5.1   Morphological learning

The first possible source for the omission of inflection in child language is that the child has simply not learned the full morphological paradigm yet, and so is not in a position to produce the appropriate morpheme. There are several reasons why such an explanation may be attractive. First, we know that the morphological form of inflection must be learned by children on the basis of exposure. That is, no theory of child language posits language-specific morphemes (e.g. -ed) as innately specified. Second, we know that the acquisition of inflection is difficult for second-language learners, and the intuition is that this is because of the difficulty in learning morphological paradigms (think of all the memorizing involved in learning the verb conjugations in a language like French).

While such an explanation may account for some of the errors children produce, it faces serious problems. First, and perhaps most serious, if the child has not learned the morphological paradigm of inflection, then we would expect a higher rate of errors of commission. For example, if the child only knows first and third person morphology in the Italian verbal paradigm, then we might expect the child to use a high rate of first or third person morphology in second person contexts. However, as we saw earlier, the rate of errors of commission is uniformly low across all three persons. Second, if morphological learning is the underlying problem, we expect children learning morphologically rich languages (like Italian and Swahili) to acquire their morphology later than children learning languages that are morphologically meagre – the more there is to learn, the longer it should take to learn. But this is clearly not the case, as we saw in Generalization 2. And finally, a lack of morphological learning cannot account for the RI facts – despite infinitival morphology in root clauses, children nevertheless adhere to the syntactic properties of infinitives, and when verbs are fully inflected, they consistently occur in the correct position. This shows that children have knowledge of the properties of the various inflectional forms. In sum, while the absence of morphological knowledge may account for some of the acquisition facts, few researchers take this approach seriously.

15.5.2 Morphosyntax conversion

A second possibility is that the delay in the acquisition of inflectional morphology occurs because of a lack in ability to faithfully render the syntactic representation into a string of morphological items. How might this happen? Recall that this is by far the least studied aspect of the MI and so relatively little is known about how it actually operates. To date, there have been no proposals of a breakdown in the conversion algorithm itself. There are several logical reasons for this. First, *why* is it that a child has a different conversion algorithm? Other than the fact that inflection is delayed, there are no logical or empirical reasons to suggest that this process is any different from the adult. Second, how could a child learn that a particular conversion algorithm is incorrect? What kinds of evidence would inform the child that the conversion algorithm (and no other aspect of the MI) requires revision? There is nothing known about how this mechanism works, and so little can be said about how and why a child could fix a problem in the conversion algorithm.

The process of conversion is undoubtedly a resource-demanding process, involving at least the following four steps: (i) reading of the output of the syntactic component, (ii) matching of terminal syntactic nodes to items in the lexicon, (iii) retrieval of those items from the lexicon and (iv) assembly into a string of morphemes. The resources required to quickly and accurately execute this conversion in real time during speech is undoubtedly substantial. And so it is possible that the processing demands are so rigorous that an immature processor (such as that of a 3-year-old child) is simply not powerful enough to cope (see Behrens Ch. 12, Section 12.5, for additional perspectives on the processing approach to morphology).

There have been several proposals in the literature that suggest reduced processing power as the source of a variety of child errors (e.g. L. Bloom 1970, P. Bloom 1990a, O'Grady 2005, Valian 1991). Perhaps the most well-known proposal is that of Paul Bloom (1990a), who argued that the omission of overt grammatical subjects in child English (and presumably other languages) is due to reduced processing capacity. Bloom argued that the immature processor is not able to cope with the production of a full sentence, and so the least communicatively important portions of a sentence – grammatical subjects – are omitted by children. Subjects are considered less important for communicative purposes because often the subject is old information, and so may be omitted without any real loss in meaning.

Bloom's specific proposal is that the longer a sentence, the greater the pressure exerted on the processor – the more items to process in a single utterance the more resource-demanding that particular utterance is. He therefore predicts that when an utterance contains more words, the child is more likely to omit a subject. Bloom calculated the average length of utterances containing overt subjects and those without subjects, and found a correlation. For example, in the speech of one child, he found the mean length of VP with past tense verbs when the sentences include a subject was 2.432 words (n = 44), and when the subject was null 2.833 (n = 36, a statistically significant difference). He concludes that this correlation arises because of limits on processing capacity, and that as the child matures, this processing bottleneck opens up, reducing the rate of omission of subjects.

Bloom's proposal is innovative in that it presents an articulated theory of how processing limitations result in morphosyntactic effects in child language.[8] Can such an approach account for the delay in acquisition of inflectional morphology and/or the RI phenomenon? On first blush, this approach holds promise. It fits well with Generalization 1 (children acquire inflectional morphology before age 5 years), since at young ages, the child's immature processor is not capable of coping with the pressures of producing inflectional morphology in real time. But by age 5, the child's processor is powerful enough such that no omission is necessary. Second, this approach is consistent with Generalization 5. The production of any morphology, even incorrect morphology, requires processing resources. So, logically, limitations on processing capacity should lead to limits on the amount of inflection produced, not to the incorrect use of inflection (that is, errors in commission).

However, limits on processing resources should apply to all children. Thus children crosslinguistically would be expected to exhibit equal difficulty with the acquisition of morphology, in contrast to Generalization 2 (morphologically rich languages are acquired earlier than morphologically poor languages). Furthermore, the correlation between sentence length and the presence/absence of inflection in languages other than English does not hold. For example, Deen (2005) investigated whether the omission of subject agreement and the omission of tense in child Swahili

---

[8] While this particular approach is now generally considered somewhat simplistic (see Hyams & Wexler 1993 for specific criticisms), it serves to illustrate the logic of this approach.

is correlated to utterance length, and found no statistically significant correlation for either. Thus Bloom's explanation applies selectively to grammatical subjects in English, which is inconsistent with the idea that the delay in inflection stems from a general property of development in the child's processing capacity. In general, approaches that propose problems with processing capacity tend to predict much larger deficits in inflection than are actually observed. We turn now to theories that suggest deficiencies in the syntactic component of the MI result in the delay in the acquisition of inflectional morphology, as well as the occurrence of RIs.

15.5.3 Syntax

15.5.3.1 Structural divergence

Considering Baker's Mirror Principle, on the face of it, the significant rate of omission of inflection might suggest that children's underlying syntactic competence is severely deficient. Models that posit gross discontinuities in the syntactic component of the child grammar and the adult grammar have been largely refuted on empirical and theoretical grounds, but it is instructive to review the arguments.

We saw earlier that English children produce bare verbs at high rates. To account for this phenomenon, Radford (1986) argues that children go through a stage in which they do not have any syntactic structure above the VP, as in (10). This area of the syntactic tree (above the VP) is often referred to as *functional* structure. He argues that the use of such bare structures is not unique to child language, since adults sometimes produce them. For example, in sentences such as 'I consider [John smart]', the second clause *John smart* (referred to as a small clause) is analysed as having no functional structure, and consists of essentially the same structure as in (10). Radford points to various similarities between adult small clauses and child speech in that both (i) show an absence of verbal agreement, (ii) show an absence of copula verbs, (iii) allow non-nominative subjects, e.g. 'I consider him /*he smart'. Radford argues that children go through this small-clause stage at an early age, and then leave this stage as the child's grammar matures. All children are predicted to go through a small clause stage, since this stage occurs because of an immature linguistic system. Thus Radford's Small Clause Hypothesis (SCH) is an example of a proposal in which the child syntactic component is argued to be substantially different from the adult syntactic component.

(10)   Child syntactic structure

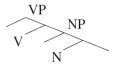

(11)   Adult syntactic structure

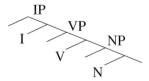

The SCH, in its time, was influential: it accounted for a wide set of facts in an elegant manner. However, there are problems, one of which is that child speech is rarely devoid of *all* inflectional material. As pointed out earlier, young children produce bare verbs at a rate as high as 80 per cent. But that means 20 per cent of child utterances include the appropriate inflectional morphology. It would be difficult to explain this if there was no functional structure available, as the SCH holds. A second problem is that children acquiring morphologically rich languages do not appear to go through anything like the small clause stage that Radford hypothesized. Italian children, for example, almost never produce bare verbs – in fact, they produce large amounts of inflectional morphology at early ages, as described earlier. Thus the theory that inflectional categories are completely absent in child language at early stages is not supported by the empirical data.

15.5.3.2   Truncation

Partly in response to the problems with the small clause hypothesis, Rizzi (1994) put forward a theory that accounts for the optionality of inflection in child language and that has a mechanism to deal with observed crosslinguistic variation. Rizzi argues that for every adult sentence, the top node of the syntactic tree is specified as a Complementizer Phrase (CP for short). The CP is typically the position that introduces words such as *that* and *for* in complex sentences such as 'I think that John is happy.' Such words are referred to as complementizers, and hence the label CP. The CP position is also associated with wh-questions. Notice that question words such as *who, what, which*, etc. (the so-called wh-question words) typically occur at the beginning of a sentence. However, they are often interpreted in some other position. Consider the sentence 'What did John eat?' The question word *what* is interpreted as the object of the verb *eat*. This suggests that at some level, this word originates in that object position. However, because it is pronounced at the front of the sentence, it must move from that object position to a position that is structurally higher. This movement is shown in (12).[9]

---

[9] The [e] in (12b) signifies the now-empty position from which the wh-word moved. Notice that the auxiliary verb *did* is necessary in question formation of this type, and it in fact undergoes movement as well: from the base form of 'John did eat what' to 'What did John [e] eat [e]'. The auxiliary verb is unlabelled in this tree for reasons of clarity, but see Haegeman (1991) for a clear description of how wh-question formation works within this framework.

(12)

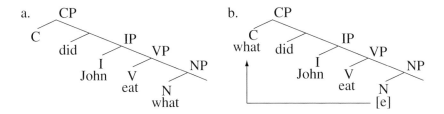

Rizzi argued that for every sentence that an adult produces, the top node of the structure is always a CP (whether a question or not, whether a complementizer occurs or not).[10] He refers to this as an axiom of language, and something that is obligatory for all adult speakers. Children, on the other hand, have not set this axiom yet, and so they may specify any node as the top node of the tree. This means that the child utterance need only project up to, say, the VP, and nothing above that is ever projected. Thus a sentence in which the top node is a VP is in fact a grammatical sentence for children. Rizzi refers to this as the Truncation Hypothesis because everything above the node that is specified as the top node is truncated (i.e. never projected). Crucial to the Truncation Hypothesis is that any node may be specified as the top node of the tree. In some utterances, it may be a CP (just like an adult), but in other utterances it may be a VP, or any other node. However, once a particular node is specified as the top node of the tree, everything below that node must be fully projected. For example, it is not possible for the child to specify CP as the top node of the tree, and then omit the IP from projection. So the tree in (13a) is permissible, but the tree in (13b) is not, because it has an intervening projection missing.

(13)

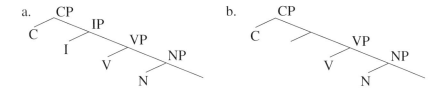

The benefits of this system are numerous (see Guasti 2002 for a thorough and more technical overview of Truncation and its merits). First, because the specification of the top node of the tree is variable, the child may sometimes specify the top node as either CP, IP, VP or NP (that is, the object of the verb). If the top node is specified as VP or NP, inflection will be omitted by the child. Thus the Truncation Hypothesis has a mechanism to

---

[10] The reasons need not concern us, but the argument is essentially one of parsimony: a system that varies from utterance to utterance in terms of what the top node is, is inherently more difficult to learn and less parsimonious.

account for the optionality of inflection. Second, Truncation is compatible with many of the generalizations listed in section 15.3.1. Because the mechanism that correctly specifies the top node as CP matures before age 5, omission of inflection should cease well before age 5 years (Generalization 1). Furthermore, grammatical subjects occur within the IP projection, and thus are vulnerable to Truncation (Generalization 4). Moreover, because Truncation results in the omission of IP, errors of omission are expected. However, when the top node of the tree is specified either as IP or CP, then inflection should occur correctly. Thus errors of substitution are expected to be rare, and the accuracy of inflection such as agreement is expected to be very high (Generalization 5).

Truncation is a neat and elegant hypothesis that enjoys good support in the field. However, there is a significant body of evidence that does not comport with the hypothesis. For example, Deen (2005) shows that while Truncation does predict some of the acquisition facts in child Swahili, there are clause types which clearly defy the system proposed by Rizzi. In particular, the logic of the Truncation Hypothesis is that the projection of the tree occurs up to (and including) the phrase that is specified as the top node of the tree – no intermediate phrase may be omitted. In Swahili, this hypothesis may be tested very precisely because, unlike most European languages, Swahili exhibits multiple inflectional affixes that correspond exactly to the underlying syntactic structure. Consider (6), repeated as (14) below. The structure of the example is provided in (15).[11] Note that the hierarchical order of the syntactic projections corresponds to the linear order of the inflectional morphemes, in accordance with Baker's Mirror Principle.

(14)   Swahili minimal verbal complex: SA – T – V – Mood
        Example: ni –   li –   anguk–   a
                 1sg –   past –   fall –   IND
                 'I fell.'

(15)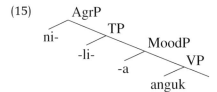

The Truncation Hypothesis makes the following predictions with respect to the Swahili clause. If the root is specified as VP, children should produce verbs that occur without any inflection whatsoever (e.g. *anguk* from the example in (14)). If the root is specified as MoodP, children should produce verbs with mood, but no additional inflection (e.g. *anguka*). If the root is

---

[11] AgrP = Agreement Phrase, and corresponds to Subject Agreement; TP = Tense Phrase. The order verb–mood occurs because the verb moves leftward (much as in German) out of the VP and adjoins to Mood. See Ngonyani (1996) for evidence of this verb movement.

specified as TP, children should omit subject agreement, and nothing else (e.g. *lianguka*). And if the root is specified as AgrP, children should produce adult-like utterances with nothing omitted (e.g. *nilianguka*). Deen finds that children as young as 2 do indeed produce most of these clause types, but never the first one (root = VP): Swahili children never omit Mood. This is unpredicted under Truncation. More importantly, however, Swahili children produce large rates of utterances in which the tense morpheme is missing, but all other inflection remains intact. This is schematized in (16):

(16)   SA – Ø – V – Mood
        Example: ni –   anguk –   a
                1sg – fall –   IND
                'I fell.'

Such tenseless clauses are utterly unattested in adult speech, and are judged as categorically ungrammatical by native Swahili speakers (and thus are very unlikely to be a product of what the children hear). Such utterances (which at early stages make up approximately 20 per cent of children's verbal utterances) are problematic for the Truncation Hypothesis since an intermediate projection (TP) appears to be omitted, while a higher projection (AgrP) occurs. While these facts are problematic for Truncation, they need not necessarily be seen as contradicting Truncation. Rather, a more sensible conclusion might be that while Truncation holds in child language, it is not the only process that leads to omission: perhaps processes independent of truncation (e.g. phonological processes) result in the omission of TP.

15.6   Conclusion

In this chapter we reviewed some of the major findings of the acquisition of inflection over the last decades from a formal grammar perspective. We discussed five broad generalizations that hold across a wide range of languages. The focus was on two of these generalizations: children in a wide range of languages omit inflection at high rates, and children in some languages produce Root Infinitives – root clause non-finite verbs. We discussed three possible sources for these two facts: morphological learning, processing factors and syntax. Within each approach, we considered various recent theories, concluding that while each theory fares well in some respect, no single theory is perfect.

So what does this mean for the study of child language and, more broadly, for linguistic theory? First, the empirical findings point very clearly to significant competence on the part of the child. While child language differs in significant ways from the target language, these differences in no way suggest anything like a global absence of knowledge in any aspect of language. Rather, a more informed view of child language is that it is by-and-large consistent with the adult language, and that any discrepancies arise out of relatively restricted divergence from the adult grammar.

Second, no single theory is sufficient to account for the entire gamut of child data. A realistic view of child language is one that considers different theories, and finds a way to integrate them into a single, encompassing model (e.g. MacWhinney 2004a), However, to move forward in understanding the nature of the human child and the mechanisms that go into acquiring language, we need more sophisticated understanding of (i) each component of the MI and (ii) the acquisition of each area of the MI. This will require crosslinguistic data. Crosslinguistic data have become more available over the last few decades (in part because of the CHILDES project, MacWhinney 2000), but the number of languages on which we have data sets and meaningful interpretations of those data is not sufficient. That being said, data by itself is only useful if meaningful analyses can be conducted on it.

If we are able to disentangle the Domain Problem in the acquisition of inflection, it will inform us not only of the source of the delay in inflectional morphology, but also of how the three components of the MI fit together. Thus child language and the study of the MI hold the potential for great discovery within developmental psycholinguistics, as well as theoretical linguistics and cognitive science more broadly.

Suggestions for further reading

Fletcher, P., & Garman, M. (1997). *Language Acquisition: Studies in First Language Development*. Cambridge: Cambridge University Press.

Goodluck, H. (1991). *Language Acquisition: A Linguistic Introduction*. Cambridge: Blackwell.

Guasti, M.-T. (2002). *Language Acquisition: The Growth of Grammar*. Boston, MA: MIT Press.

O'Grady, W. (1997). *Syntactic Development*. Chicago: University of Chicago Press.

Part IV

Semantics, pragmatics and discourse

16

Lexical meaning

Eve V. Clark

16.1 Introduction

Children produce their first words around age one. They add more, at first rather slowly, but rapidly become adept at pronouncing longer sequences of sounds. They then start adding to their repertoire more quickly, and also begin to combine single words into longer utterances. In comprehension, they appear to go much faster and accumulate a rather larger vocabulary earlier than in production. This asymmetry, of course, continues to hold for adults too.

How do children go about adding words to their vocabulary and learning the meanings they carry? Children appear able to pick up new words quite readily, sometimes from a single exposure. Between the ages of one and two, most children learn to produce between 200 and 600 words, and understand considerably more. Between the ages of two and six years, their vocabulary grows to as much as 14,000 words. (This amounts to about nine new words a day.) And by early adulthood, vocabularies range from 50,000 to 100,000 words (Clark 2009). But children do not learn words in isolation. They learn individual words within the flow of conversation between adults and children.

Adults are a major source for children's early word acquisition because young children infer the possible meanings of unfamiliar words from how other speakers use them. So they learn in the course of conversation as they observe adult usage in context. In doing this, children appear to follow much the same procedures as adults in trying to communicate their own intentions while interpreting those of others. Like adults, they make certain assumptions about communication and conversation – that speakers choose the words and expressions they do for a reason, and if they choose one word rather than another, it is because they mean something else. That is, even very young children appear to assume there are intentions guiding the adult's choices of words, just as there are intentions guiding a person's actions (e.g. P. Bloom 1997, 2000, Woodward & Guajardo 2002).

In doing this, children implicitly follow Grice's cooperative principle from well before they are able to fully observe all its constituent maxims. Their earliest utterances are often impossible to interpret out of context. Errors of omission make their utterances inconsistent with the maxim of quantity (Say as much as you need), while errors of commission are inconsistent with the maxim of manner (Be clear) (Grice 1989). But as children learn more about the meaning of each word and each construction, their utterances become more interpretable to others, and conform more closely to the cooperative principle in conversational exchanges.

The acquisition of a lexicon, the vocabulary of a language, is an enormous project. Words are essential tools as speakers communicate about the world around them. In learning the words of a language and how to use them, children attend first to what the adults around them say and do. Adults in turn offer them the conventional terms to use on each occasion, and so provide the expertise required in the transmission of a language from one generation to the next.

16.2   Two approaches to the acquisition of lexical meaning

How do children limit the possibilities when assigning a meaning to a new term? One approach has been to assume that children start out with certain built-in constraints that place limits on the initial hypothesis-space for possible meanings that might be assigned to specific words when these are first encountered. For example, children could assume that words pick out whole objects (*a cat, a fork, a bottle*) rather than parts or properties (*a paw, a tail, a handle, a cork*); they could assume that each category-type can be designated by only one word rather than by several alternative terms (*the dog* vs. *the dog, the poodle, the vandal, the guard*); and that words pick out only simple category types (*cat, swing, oak*), not complexes of category types (*circus, play, competition*). This view might be characterized in terms of the following constraints (see Markman 1989):

a.   Whole Object constraint: assume that any unfamiliar word picks out a whole object
b.   Mutual Exclusivity constraint: assume that only one term can be applied to each object-type
c.   Taxonomic constraint: assume that each term picks out a single category-type.

Constraints like these would limit the possibilities when children assign preliminary meanings to new words, but they also pose a problem because they must eventually be overridden and ultimately discarded. This is because they are incompatible with how the vocabulary of a language is structured on the one hand, and because they are not reflected in how adults talk to children on the other. Notice that all languages have terms for picking out objects, but they also have terms for actions (*break, run*), properties and states (*green, soft, elated*), and relations (*in, beside*). Moreover, objects and events can be viewed by speakers from different perspectives, with each perspective signalled by the speaker's choice of words. For example, a speaker might talk about the family dog as *the dog, our boxer, that pest, the drooler* or *the postal alarm*. These expressions differ in meaning, yet all of them can refer to the same entity (Clark 1997). Adults use terms for objects *and* for actions, properties, and relations when they talk to young children, and they make use of different perspectives on objects and events, just as they do when talking to adults.

If children rely on built-in constraints early on to assign meanings to unfamiliar words, how do they learn the meanings of words for actions, properties and relations? That is, how do they get rid of the constraints that would block learning in these cases? Notice, too, that their early vocabularies do not contain only nouns, although those predominate for children learning some languages. But children also pick up some terms for actions and properties early on. And how do young children deal with the fact that adults often use more than one term to refer to the same object? If they simply drop earlier constraints to accommodate this, when and under what circumstances do they do this? These questions remain unanswered.

An alternative approach has been to assume that children adopt much the same pragmatic assumptions about communication as adults. That is, from the start they rely on something like the cooperative principle and its attendant maxims (Grice 1989). Central to the working of this principle are factors basic to all communicative exchanges: joint attention, physical co-presence and conversational co-presence (H. H. Clark 1996). When adults talk to each other, they tend to take these for granted. Joint attention is fundamental in language acquisition (Tomasello 1995, Ch. 5 this volume) because children have to learn how to connect the words being spoken with the events being spoken of. They need to learn what the mappings are from words-to-world and world-to-words in order to assign meanings to the words they are hearing. So with young children, adults often make sure they have established joint attention with a child-addressee before they try to convey something to that child (e.g. Estigarribia & Clark 2007). If children are not attending, there is no way to get them to act or supply information. In adult–child exchanges, joint attention is typically accompanied by physical co-presence since, not surprisingly, exchanges with young children nearly always concern the here-and-now – whatever entity, action or relation the conversational participants are attending to. And this physical co-presence is accompanied by conversational co-presence: the adult and child talk together about whatever is happening at their locus of joint attention.

In addition, like adults, very young children observe both conventionality and contrast in language and so use specific words for certain meanings from the start, even when their meanings do not fully coincide with the adult's. The established lexicon of a language is conventional. That is, for particular meanings, there is a term (or construction) that everyone in the community would expect to be used. If the speaker does not use that expression then, people infer, he or she must mean something else. Contrast, the fact that differences in form (in word or construction choice) mark differences in meaning, works together with conventionality. These two principles stem from the assumption that language is designed for communication, and that children, from early on, treat language as a cooperative endeavour. Just as for adults, these principles guide early word use and word interpretation (Clark 1993). This leads children to attend to the conventions and so identify the appropriate terms for use.

How do these pragmatic factors help children acquire the meanings of new terms? Conventionality should lead children to seek the appropriate terms to express particular meanings. In fact, children signal their recognition of the conventionality of language in two ways: first, they aim for adult targets in their own early word uses and repair their own mispronunciations (in as far as they can), and second, they ask for words for the world around them from as early as 1;6 or 2;0. Children also maintain contrasts in their own word uses, opting for the conventional term where they know one, and otherwise, once past the stage of over-extensions, relying on general-purpose deictics or on words coined for the occasion (Clark 1993). Again, children give evidence for all this from before age two.

16.3   Uptake

When children take up a new word, they pick up first on how that word was used on that occasion: this is often called 'fast mapping' (see Heibeck & Markman 1987). They then elaborate this initial information as they learn more about the conventional meaning of each word, connecting words to their neighbours and relations in the same semantic domain, as well as to their word-class and to patterns of use in specific syntactic constructions. Children's earliest meanings typically overlap to a considerable extent with the target adult meanings – largely because their fast mapping stems from observations of actual uses (e.g. Huttenlocher & Smiley 1987). But their resources are limited at first, so they may over-extend many of their early words, stretching their uses beyond adult boundaries. For example, children's first term for an animal, *dog*, say, is often over-extended to pick out cats, sheep, squirrels, and other smallish four-legged mammals as well, and their first term for fruit, *apple* or *orange*, may be over-extended to a range of other small round objects such as balls, grapes, door-knobs, round soaps, spherical candles and so on. At the same time, children who make such over-extensions in production do not make them in comprehension (Thomson & Chapman 1977). Their reliance on over-extensions, then, reflects a communicative strategy where they stretch available resources to refer to things they lack words for. This view is supported by the fact that over-extensions vanish as children acquire the appropriate words for different areas of the original over-extension. Around the same time, typically between 2;0 and 2;6, children also start asking innumerable *What's that?* questions, as they actively solicit words for categories they do not yet have terms for.

16.3.1   Scenarios for uptake

Children are constantly being exposed to unfamiliar words, and need to take account of them in context. What they do with unfamiliar words may not be observable, even though they are in fact doing fast mapping in context. Imagine a child, Anna, holding a drink container and waiting for the adult to fill it with milk. (She already knows the word *cup*, but not *mug*.) The adult then says to her, "Can you give me your mug?" At this point, Anna has only one thing to give, so she can set up in memory what she has inferred about the meaning of the new term *mug* for the next time she hears it:

(1)   Child: New word = MUG
            Category: drink container
            Subtype: kind of CUP
            (Property ??)

This scenario can be compared to a more complex one, where the child, here Ben, has to revise some of his immediate inferences about the use of an unfamiliar word. He is holding two plastic animals, a dog and a cat. And he knows the words *dog* and *cat*. But the adult says to him, "Can you hand me the spaniel?" Ben realizes he needs to hand over one of the animals he's holding, but he does not know which one so he guesses and hands over the cat. And the adult responds with, "No, no, the spaniel." From this Ben now infers that *spaniel* must designate some kind of dog, so he offers the dog instead. So his initial fast mapping for *spaniel* might be represented as (2a), and his revision as (2b):

(2)   a. Child: New word = SPANIEL
              Category: animal (dog-and-cat)
              Subtype: cat ?

      b. Child: New word = SPANIEL
              Category: animal
              Subtype: dog

Both scenarios require that children make pragmatic inferences about a possible meaning in the context where they have heard an unfamiliar word. They can then act upon those inferences as they decide, for example, how to respond to a request (Clark 2007). Inferences like these provide the starting point in establishing conventional meanings for new terms. So their fast mapping of an unfamiliar term begins with assigning a word-form to a referent in context, with a preliminary meaning that could be glossed as 'form X picks out that type of entity/property/action/relation'. Storing some information in memory is critical for children so they can recognize the same word the next time, and eventually try to make use of that word themselves.

Adults also make some direct offers of words, and these offer critical insights into the general process of uptake by children as they begin to build up a meaning for the new word, establishing both reference and sense, from the patterns of adult use in context, along with any other information offered by adult speakers.

16.4   Direct offers of new words

When adults make offers of words that they judge to be new for a young child, they typically rely on specific syntactic frames in making the offer (Clark & Wong 2002). Typical frames include those listed in (3), where the forms in (3c–e) are question/answer sequences where the adult supplies both the question and the answer:

(3)   a. This/that is a———.
      b. Those are called ———.
      c. What is this/that? A ———.
      d. What're these called? They're ———.
      e. What is X doing? He's ———.

The most readily identifiable frames are those for introducing nouns. These nearly always contain a deictic like *this* or *that* to introduce the new noun, as in (3a, b). Occasionally, adults use a question/answer sequence for this (3c, d), but more often rely on such sequences to introduce a new verb, as in (3e).

Consistently used frames are one way to highlight a new term since what is new in an utterance is generally placed in final position. This position carries sentential stress in English, so both position and stress make the new word prominent. Adults also use other highlighting techniques with new words: they use them as single words some of the time, and they tend to use a new word several times in the subsequent exchange (Clark in press).

How do children respond to direct offers of new words? In an analysis of 701 direct offers, I found that children tend to repeat new words in their next turn immediately after hearing them from the adult. They repeat them 54 per cent of the time in the next turn, just as the child does in (4):

(4) D (1;8.2, having his shoes put on;
     points to some ants on the floor):   Ant. Ant.
     Father (indicating a small beetle nearby):   And that's a bug.
     D: **Bug**.
                                                   (Clark, unpublished data)

Repeats like these show that children are attending to the new word and, in repeating it, they thereby ratify the adult's offer. Moreover, their rate of repetition for new words (at 54 per cent) is over double their rate of repeating whatever information is new in the preceding speaker's utterance (at 22 per cent) (Clark 2007). That is, speakers regularly take up what was new in the preceding speaker's turn and treat it as given in their own following turn. This shift of status for information from new to given is common in conversation in general, but the amount of actual repetition is modified by speakers' reliance on other devices to re-refer to an element that is now being treated as given: for instance, adults use pronouns (*he, they*), demonstratives (*that*, in reference to an object, action, or event), and the pro-verb *do* in place of full lexical verbs. With new words, though, repeats signal clearly that children are attending to those words per se.

When children do not repeat the new word, they may acknowledge it with *mmh, yeah, uh-huh*, or *yes* (9 per cent of the time). Or they may simply continue with a semantically consistent response. While this would count as an acknowledgement in an adult–adult exchange, it's harder to assess whether such responses from children in fact indicate attention to and uptake of a new word.

Adults do not stop there. They typically go beyond the offer of the word itself, as in (4), and provide children with additional information about the referent of that word. This information may allow the child to distinguish the referent from near-neighbours, identify distinctive features of various kinds, and so offer more hooks for the child's later use of the word in other appropriate contexts. Take the parent–child exchange in (5):

(5) M(1;10, picking up a toy walrus
     and putting her finger on a tusk):   Big nose.
     Father: No. Those are TUSKS.
     M: **Tusks**.
     Father: They're like big teeth.
                                          (Clark, unpublished data)

After the child M repeats the new word *tusks*, her father adds a comparison to teeth to distinguish tusks still further from the child's initial proposal. In adding information about the referent on such occasions, adults license extended inferences in context about the meaning of the new word just offered. Consider the exchange in (6) and the information the adult offers after providing a new word:

(6) Mo (looking at a
     picture of some owls in a   What are these?
     book with the child):   Those are birdies.
     Ch (1;7.19):   **birdies**.
     Mo: And the name of these kinds of birdies
                                  they call owls. (mother points at the
                                  picture) And they say "hoo-hoo".
     Ch: **hoo**.

                                         (CHILDES: NewEng 20)[1]

After the child's repeat of *birdies*, the mother first ratifies the child's use and then adds the term for the particular sub-kind of bird involved, *owls*. Then she picks up on a distinctive characteristic of owls, namely the sound they make, *hoo-hoo*. So this child can infer both that an *owl* is a kind of bird, and that it is identifiable from the particular sound it makes. In short, adults consistently license further inferences about the meaning of the new word by adding information pertinent to the referent and hence the use of the target word (Clark 2002).

In offering further information, adults may appeal to the child's memory of shared experiences, as in (7):

(7) Parent to child (2;8.11, with a   They're–, they're– he's climbing up a
     picture of someone walking   hill. It's a STEEP hill because it goes …
     up a hill, presenting the   high! It goes high. It goes really high
     adjective *steep*):   really fast. So it's STEEP. Can you say
                                       STEEP? STEEP.[2]
     Child: **Steep!**
     Parent: Steep. Do you like steep hills? Do you
                                       remember – Do you know we walked
                                       up some steep hills this morning on
                                       our walk – when we were looking for
                                       rocks?

                                              (Clark in press)

And they appeal to the child's current knowledge about near-neighbours of the target referent of a new word, as in (8):

(8) Parent to child (3;3.7,   And this one? This one, it
     with a picture of some birds;   looks a bit like a sea-gull. Do
     first talks about bird-types   you remember seeing sea-
     already known to the child, including gulls at the beach?

---

[1] Examples from the CHILDES archive are identified by corpus name and file number.
[2] Capitals signal emphatic stress.

blue-jays and chickadees, then
leads up to the new word, *tern*):

Child:	Mm –hm.
Parent:	This one, looks a bit like a sea-gull, it's called a TERN.

(Clark in press)

Adults often offer quite extensive information about the category type by talking about class membership, parts, properties (including characteristic sounds), motion and function. They also link new words to information about habitat and history, as well as mentioning any personal connections to the referent.

Some typical new-word offers, accompanied by such information, are given in (9)–(13) for some inclusion relations, a property, a part, a function and a comparison with a near neighbour, respectively;

(9) Mother (to Christina, 1;7.7): That's another cat. But that's a
                                              different kind of cat.
                                              It's a cub. It's a baby lion.

(CHILDES: NewEng 20)

(10) Naomi (2;7.16): What is it?
      Father: Those are cobblestones.
                       That's a street made out of stones.

(CHILDES: Sachs 68)

(11) Sarah (2;3.19, points to picture of bare foot of boy sitting in chair)
      Mother: That's his foot.
      Sarah: **Foot**.
      Mother: There's his toes. Where's his toes?
      Sarah: Toes dere.

(CHILDES: Brown/Sarah 3)

(12) Adam (3;2.0): I fold [?hold] my sword.
      Mother: Hmm?
      Adam: I fold my sword.
      Mother: You're folding your sword?
                      That's a knife for cutting chicken.

(CHILDES: Brown/Adam 24)

(13) Child (2;11, looking at a book with mother)
      Mother: Do you know what that one is?
      Child: Ummm.
      Mother: I don't know if you know what that one is.
      Child: That's a snake.
      Mother: It looks like a snake, doesn't it? It's called an eel. It's like a
                    snake only it lives in the water. And there's another one.

(Gelman *et al.* 1998)

In effect, adults offer a range of information that will help children keep one referent-type distinct from another, and allow them to begin setting up a meaning for the target word, based on any inferences they have been able to make from the information offered.

16.5   Putting meanings together

Children start to combine words they can already produce sometime between age 1;2 and 2;0, to produce two-word utterances like *more read, ball there, mummy sock*, or *no cup*. But these combined meanings can be hard to interpret out of context. As L. Bloom (1971) pointed out, an utterance like *mummy sock* may be intended to convey very different meanings, depending on whether the child is identifying the agent who is putting on the child's sock, or identifying the possessor of the sock. As children add inflections on nouns and verbs, as well as other grammatical morphemes, the meanings of their early word combinations become clearer. And they too can start to make use of function words like *the* and *can* as well as of noun and verb inflections. These all offer preliminary information about the kind of thing an unfamiliar word designates on that occasion, namely some kind of object vs. some kind of action. They also become aware that prepositions often mark relations, and adjectives denote properties (e.g. Fisher 2002b, Fisher *et al.* 2006, Hall 2000).

Children can make some use of part-of-speech information from as young as 1;5 when they are able to distinguish proper names from count nouns (e.g. *He's Dax* vs. *He's a dax*), and by 2;6-3;0, they can distinguish count nouns from mass nouns (e.g. *That's ruk* vs. *That's a ruk*). At this age, they can distinguish adjectives from proper names: they extend an unfamiliar adjective (*He's very daxy*) to anything else with the same property but restrict the proper name (*Daxy*) to the original referent. But can they use what they already know about a familiar word to make inferences about an unfamiliar one that co-occurs with it?

What happens when young two year olds are asked to pick out the referent of an unfamiliar noun used with a familiar verb? In one study, children aged 2;0 and 2;6 were first tested on familiar combinations (e.g. *feed + horse, read + book*, or *drink + coffee*) to make sure they knew what the verbs meant. They then heard those verbs combined with unfamiliar nouns and chose probable referents for those nouns from sets of four pictures. They had to identify the referent of the object-noun in sentences containing a familiar verb combined with an unfamiliar noun as direct object, as in 'The mummy feeds the ferret'. The children made appropriate choices at levels well above chance. And a day later, they reliably remembered which picture they had chosen as the referent for each unfamiliar noun. Children the same age were also tested on familiar verbs (e.g. 'Show me something to feed', followed by a set of four pictures) to see whether they had already identified the relevant properties for the object-type (not mentioned) that typically went with each verb. They did even better in this task than in the previous one when they had to take the unfamiliar noun into account as well (Goodman *et al.* 1998).

Studies like this back up the observational research on how adults talk about objects and events, and the effects such talk has on children's acquisition of the relevant patterns in a language. Consider the way adult speakers of English and Korean talk about spatial relations. In English, speakers use the verb *put* in combination with prepositional phrases headed by *in*, for all kinds of containment, as in (14):

(14) a. Put the apples in the bowl.
       b. Put the cassette away in its case.

In Korean, speakers use two different verbs for 'put in', one for loose-fit relations like the one described in (14a), and another for tight fit, in (14b) (Choi & Bowerman 1991). This distinction that adults make in Korean, but not in English, shapes children's acquisition of how to talk about containment from the start, and leads young Korean and English children to categorize spatial arrays differently because of how their language encodes the relevant spatial relations (Choi *et al.* 1999).

Adults, of course, display to children in their everyday speech the relations that hold between verbs and their direct objects, as well as many other patterns of collocation, some involving large classes of co-occurring terms, others restricted to smaller sets or to single idioms. But the range of verbs than can occur with a specific noun, as well as the set of nouns that can occur with a particular verb, offer children important information about how to construct linguistic categories as well as how to construct utterances appropriate for talking about many kinds of objects and events. They learn, for example, that a verb like *open* in English usually involves the removal of some kind of impediment to access: *open the door, open the briefcase, open the jam jar*, etc. but not **open the light, *open the tap*, or **open the apple*, whereas in French, the meaning of *ouvrir* 'to open' appears to mean something more like 'allow access to', and therefore applies to lights (providing light), taps (allowing water to run) and radios (making the sound audible), as well as to doors, windows and briefcases, for instance, although not to such entities as apples and shoes (see also Bowerman 2005).

In summary, children can identify the probable referents of new nouns by drawing (in part) on what they already know about relevant verb meanings. And they can do this as young as age 2;0. This is consistent with other experimental studies of word learning where, after a few exposures to an unfamiliar (nonsense) word in context, children can identify new instances of possible referents from an array of candidate objects (e.g. Clark & Grossman 1998). In actual conversation, of course, children are continually exposed to a much larger range of nouns for the kinds of things that can be fed or drunk or read, and they hear a range of interconnected uses linking familiar and unfamiliar terms all the time (e.g. Bowerman 2005, Callanan 1985, Weizman & Snow 2001).

16.6   Semantic domains

As children learn more words, these can be organized into semantic domains. One domain might comprise all their words for animals and for their young (*dog* and *puppy*, *cat* and *kitten*, *horse* and *foal*) for example, along with some superordinate terms like *animal* and, eventually, *mammal*. They hear associated words for actions specific to each kind of animal, for specific sounds (*bark*, *neigh*, *bray*, *roar*, etc.), and specific kinds of motion (*trot*, *gallop*, *slither*, etc.). They also hear other terms drawn from domains like food, habitat and general development (e.g. Callanan 1985, Clark & Wong 2002). Many of these terms occur in adult follow-ups to explicit offers of new words, where adults talk about distinguishing properties (*fur*, *feathers*, *stripes*), sounds (*roar*, *squeak*, *growl*), typical locations (*zoo*, *farm*, *field*) and activities (*hunt*, *creep*, *fly*). Adults also list other similar kinds in order to 'place' the new word offered in the relevant semantic domain, as in *There's a lion, a leopard, a tiger and a CHEETAH*, and they link basic-level terms to a subordinate or superordinate term, as in *That dog is a spaniel* or *A seal is an animal*. They often offer near-neighbours that contrast with the term under discussion. For example, in talking about size, whether a toy truck will fit under a bridge, say, parents may use not only *big* and *small*, but also *wide* (said of the road or the vehicle), and *high* and *low* (in relation to a bridge) (e.g. Ebeling & Gelman 1994, Rogers 1978).

Some domains take years to acquire, and the meanings children assign to each term may shift as they add words that cut up the conceptual space more finely and learn more about how to use each one (e.g. Ameel *et al.* 2008, Andersen 1975). Many domains themselves become interconnected by all the terms they share in common. Dimensional adjectives like *tall* or *long*, for instance, apply to artifacts and to natural categories of all kinds. Many verbs apply to entities drawn from multiple domains. And so on. In many domains, though, even after several years, children may know little beyond some basic contrasts in meaning. For instance, they may know, by age six, that the words *oak* and *elm* both designate trees, but not be able to identify any instances. That is, they have acquired part of the lexical meaning but they have not yet established the reference for either word. This state of affairs is not unusual: it holds for most adults in some domains as well.

16.7   Words to fill lexical gaps

Children coin new words from an early age. These supplement the established words that they have picked up so far. Young two year olds use nouns as verbs for actions where they do not yet know any established word (e.g. *It bows* [how a violin works], *I broomed her* 'hit her with a [toy] broom', *Can I fire the candle?* 'light the candle', *Don't hair me* 'brush my hair', *Daddy's rugging* 'vacuuming', *You have to scale it first* 'weigh'). They construct noun–noun compounds to talk about sub-kinds (e.g. *plate-egg* vs. *cup egg* for 'fried' vs. 'boiled' eggs; *house-smoke* vs. *car-smoke* for 'smoke from a chimney' vs. 'exhaust', *tea-sieve* vs. *water-sieve* for a small strainer vs. a large one). And by 3;0 they also use some derivational affixes like agentive and instrumental *-er* (e.g. *I'm a good cooker!* 'cook', *You're the sworder and I'm the gunner, The rainer* 'person who drives away the rain', *That's a climber* 'ladder', *I'm gonna turn off the driver* 'ignition key', *The pounder* 'hammer') (Clark 1993).

Languages offer a variety of means for the coining of words. The main devices are compounding and derivation, and different languages favour each of these to differing degrees. Germanic languages, for instance, tend to use a lot of compounding for both nouns and verbs, as well as derivation, while Romance languages favour derivation, especially with suffixes, and make much less use of compounding. Within a language, some options are productive for the expression of specific meanings. For example, English *-er*, added to a verb root, is more productive for the construction of new agent nouns than either *-ist* or *-ian*. Yet *-ist* is locally productive in scientific domains and in music as an agentive suffix (Clark 1993).

In children's coinages, the choices of word-forms for new words depend on several factors. One is transparency of meaning: they construct new words from familiar forms that they already know. This accounts, in English, for early uses of nouns transformed into verbs where children lack a verb for the action they want to talk about, and for noun–noun compounds used to designate objects they want to talk about. Both these word-form types are also relatively simple to construct (they do not require any morphological changes to the roots involved). Simplicity of form is another factor children favour, especially when their knowledge about the structure of words is still limited. With denominal verbs, there are no changes to be made in going from the source noun to the new verb. Much the same holds for noun–noun compounds, where the main modification is the imposition of a primary–tertiary stress pattern on the new compound. One can see these two factors at work in child coinages like *magic-man* (for *magician*) and *volcano-y* (for *volcanic*). *Magic-man* is transparent (*magic* + *man*) and simple, as is *volcano-y* (*volcano* + adjectival *-y*). Notice that in *magician*, the relation to *magic* is obscured by the change from final *k* to *sh* before the *-ian* suffix. In *volcanic*, the change from *volcano* lies in the second vowel that changes value with the addition of the *-ic* suffix. These aspects of word formation tend to be mastered only after children have learnt to read.

The other factor that children appear sensitive to is the productivity of the form–meaning relation used in constructing an innovative word-form. Productive word-formation patterns in each language are those favoured by adult speakers for specific meanings such as agentive nouns, locative nouns, instrumental verbs and so on. So the frequency with which children hear particular word-forms that they can analyse also plays a role. Children pick up on the more productive options in a language first, and only later learn the less productive options available (Clark 1993).

Innovative words are subject to the same pragmatic principles as the rest of the lexicon: new words constructed by the speaker cannot carry the same meaning as an existing word because conventional terms pre-empt any innovations that would carry exactly the same meaning. In effect, coinages must contrast in meaning with existing words. Many coinages from children fail to observe this constraint: they fill the meaning slot for which there is an existing word (but the children do not yet know that word). The novel verb *to scale* temporarily fills the slot for the conventional verb *weigh*. The novel compound *car-smoke* fills the slot for the conventional noun *exhaust*, and the derived form *climber* fills the slot for the conventional noun *ladder*. These innovative forms do not contrast in meaning with the existing conventional forms. They are therefore forms that children will have to give up once they learn the conventional forms. However, it can take time for them to discover that their own coinage in fact has exactly the same meaning as the form used by adult speakers. Finally, innovative words fill lexical gaps for both adult and child. And as children learn more words, they become less likely to coin words that are in fact pre-empted by terms that are already there.

16.8   Meaning beyond the word

Speakers often implicate a meaning that they do not express directly. Rather, they let the addressee infer what they mean from what they say. Consider the exchange in (15):

(15)   A. Have you read *The Kite-Runner*?
       B. I've read Chapter 1.

From this response, Speaker A infers that B has not yet read the whole book, and so cannot simply answer with "yes". But B has started the book so "no" is not a possible answer either. Like adults, children can make inferences from context about the speaker's intended meaning, as in (16):

(16)   Father tapping the edge of D's bowl with a spoon at breakfast –
       D (1;11.28):   *Herb hitting bowl.*
       Father: Why was I hitting your bowl? Why was I hitting your bowl?
       D: *∂ eat ∂ cornflakes.* (D picked up his spoon and finally took a mouthful)

(Clark, unpublished data)

While children readily make such inferences in context, can they make them when the inference depends on the wording for some scale applied to the event? Scales can involve quantifiers like *some* and *all*, where the use of the term *some* in conversation typically implicates *not all*. Or a scale may be based on general (encyclopedic) knowledge about parts vs. wholes, where an action affecting only a part would implicate that the action did not apply to the whole. Or the scale might be an ad hoc one, established in context. For instance, if a task involved three separate subevents, and only one of these was completed, this would imply that the task as a whole remained unfinished.

Can children make the necessary inferences to interpret such scales and derive the relevant scalar implicatures? In fact, children do well from age four on when they are presented with scenarios like those in (17) or (18), and asked to judge whether the puppet involved deserves a reward for completing the task or not:

(17) Quantifier scale: The lion is told he has to eat four oranges and if he
                          does, he'll get a reward; he retires inside a doll's
                          house to eat in peace. When he comes out, the
                          adult asks him: Did you eat the oranges?
      Lion: *I ate some.*

(18) Encyclopedic scale: The dog has to paint the house, and if he does,
                           he gets a reward. He goes off to paint, and
                           when he returns, the adult asks: Did you paint
                           the house?
      Dog: *I painted the roof.*

The responses in these scenarios imply that the lion and the dog respectively failed to complete their tasks and so should not receive a reward. Four year olds make this judgment readily, and withhold the reward. But the same children give the reward in cases where the task is completed, as in (19):

(19) The bear has to fix a broken chair. He goes off to fix it then returns,
      and when he returns, the adult asks: Did you fix the chair?
      Bear: *I fixed it but it was hard.*

Overall, children made appropriate judgments for all three types of scale examined – quantifier (as in (17)), encyclopedic (as in (18)), and ad hoc (Papafragou & Tantalou 2004).

Children's ability to infer intentions emerges early (P. Bloom 1997), but they take longer to learn to identify the implicatures that can accompany uses of specific lexical items in specific contexts, just as they take several years to learn how determiners like *the* and *a* indicate the given vs. new status of a noun phrase (compare *He saw the dog* vs. *He saw a dog*). Learning lexical items is one thing: children pick up words readily in context and make use of the information available in assigning them preliminary meanings. But learning just how each word can be used often takes much longer.

16.9 Conclusion

When children learn word meanings, they take advantage of any information available in context, and make use of joint attention along with physical co-presence to identify the intended referents on each occasion. By correlating joint attention and physical co-presence with the words being used by the adult, children can start on the mapping required as they assign meanings to words. Their earliest meanings result from fast mapping, and may be more limited in scope than the adult's meaning for the same term or expression. Establishing meanings that are closer to the adult's conventional meanings takes time, and may proceed rather slowly as children accumulate observations of adult usage as well as additional information about each referent-type and how it differs from its neighbours.

Words are critical elements in many larger expressions: when they appear in idioms, children may have to interpret them differently from when they occur outside those particular contexts of use. Compare *bucket* in *She filled the bucket with milk* and *He kicked the bucket last week*. Children typically learn non-idiomatic uses of words before they learn idiomatic ones. At the same time, children begin to learn all sorts of collocations among words from the moment they start to combine words into larger (syntactic) units. And, in some cases, they may limit their early combinations to a particular collocation, using a specific noun only with the definite article, and not with an indefinite or a deictic, say, or using a specific verb only with one particular noun as direct object. Here too, as children learn more details about the meanings of the words involved, they begin to use a wider range of combinations to express the meanings they intend, and in doing so, extend the scope of each syntactic construction they are producing (Clark & Kelly 2006, Tomasello 2003).

Lexical meanings are an essential tool for speakers in communicating with others, but words are accompanied in conversation by gaze, by gesture and by affect as well. It is the combination of all these factors that children must master in order to convey their intentions to others. To achieve that, they need to attend not only to the initial context of use when they are first exposed to an unfamiliar word, but also to the myriad uses they observe subsequently. They need to take in the contexts of use plus any added information adults provide about referent-types, whether these are objects, actions, properties or relations. And they need to relate what they learn about each word to any other words that belong in the same semantic domain, that collocate with that word, or that make some more specialized use of it in an idiom or in some figurative extension.

Suggestions for further reading

Bloom, P. (2000). *How Children Learn the Meanings of Words*. Cambridge, MA: MIT Press.

Bowerman, M., & Levinson, S. C. (Eds.). (2001). *Language Acquisition and Conceptual Development*. Cambridge: Cambridge University Press.

Clark, E. V. (2009). *The Lexicon in Acquisition* (2nd edn). Cambridge: Cambridge University Press.

(2003). *First Language Acquisition*. Cambridge: Cambridge University Press.

Gentner, D., & Goldin-Meadow, S. (Eds.) (2003). *Language in Mind*. Cambridge, MA: MIT Press.

Markman, E. M. (1989). *Categorization and Naming in Children: Problems of Induction*. Cambridge, MA: MIT/Bradford Books.

Tomasello, M. (2003). *Constructing a Language*. Cambridge, MA: Harvard University Press.

17

Sentence scope

Stephen Crain

17.1   Introduction

At Logan Airport in Boston, a sign reads: 'All airplanes do not carry pets'. Clearly, this sign is intended to convey the message 'Not all airplanes carry pets' and not the message 'No airplanes carry pets'. Once on board, passengers view a video reviewing the safety features of the aircraft. The video concludes with these instructions: 'If you do not understand any of the safety features of this aircraft, please ask a flight attendant for assistance.' Clearly, the intended message here is 'If there is any safety feature that you do not understand', not 'If you fail to understand every safety feature.' As these examples illustrate, sentences that contain more than one logical operator (e.g. *not, every, any*) are open to interpretation. The alternative interpretations are due to the scope of the operators. The notion of scope is much the same in human languages and in logic. In the sentence 'Every airplane does not carry pets' there are two possible scope relations involving the operators *every* and *not*. On one reading the universal quantifier *every* takes scope over *not*. A paraphrase of this reading is: No airplanes carry pets. On a second reading *not* takes wider scope than *every*. A paraphrase is: Not all airplanes carry pets. The same scope ambiguities arise in logic.

   This chapter reviews some of the literature on children's mastery of scope relations among linguistic expressions in human languages. Two main issues are addressed. One is the extent to which children and adults carve up scope relations along the same lines as standard logic. We will consider a broad range of cases. The second issue is whether or not children and adults assign the same readings to sentences with more than one operator, and if not, why not. These are vexing issues, and far from settled, but the findings from the literature on child language reveal a great deal about the emergence of semantic competence in human languages. Before we turn to child language, it will be useful to briefly review the relevant aspects of scope in classical logic.

17.2   Disjunction and negation in human languages

17.2.1   Semantic scope

Suppose you and your friends Gen and Ted often go to lunch together. Ted usually orders either sushi or pasta. Today, however, Ted doesn't order sushi and he doesn't order pasta. Later you overhear Gen tell someone "Ted didn't order sushi or pasta." Would you agree? Adult speakers of English would agree. Textbooks of logic would also agree. In classical logic, the formula in which disjunction is in the scope of negation is $\neg(A \vee B)$. The truth conditions associated with this formula exclude the possibility of A, and they exclude the possibility of B. And in English, the statement 'Ted didn't order sushi or pasta' excludes the possibility that Ted ordered sushi and the possibility that Ted ordered pasta. So, it looks like English disjunction generates a conjunctive entailment when it appears in the scope of local negation, as in one of De Morgan's laws: $\neg(\mathbf{A} \vee \mathbf{B}) \Rightarrow (\neg\mathbf{A} \wedge \neg\mathbf{B})$.

The conjunctive entailment of disjunction only holds if disjunction is interpreted as inclusive-*or*, as in classical logic. To see this, consider the truth-conditions of disjunction (inclusive-*or*). A statement of the form $(\mathbf{A} \vee \mathbf{B})$ is true in three cases: (i) if A is true but not B, (ii) if B is true but not A, and (iii) if both A and B are true. A statement of the form $(A \vee B)$ is false, therefore, only if both A and B are false. This means that the negation of $(A \vee B)$, namely $\neg(A \vee B)$, is true just in case both A and B are false. It follows that $\neg(A \vee B)$ logically entails $(\neg A \wedge \neg B)$.[1]

In human languages, then, we can determine whether or not disjunction corresponds to inclusive-*or*, as in classical logic, by asking whether negative statements with disjunction give rise to conjunctive entailments. We already witnessed one relevant example from English, "Ted didn't order sushi or pasta." This sentence generates a conjunctive entailment, i.e. 'Ted didn't order sushi and Ted didn't order pasta.' This is *prima facie* evidence that disjunction is interpreted as inclusive-*or* in English. The story is more complex in other languages, as we will see, but we will also see that there is considerable overlap between logical and human languages, including child language.

---

[1] The truth tables in (i) can be used to affirm this logical equivalence.

(i)

A	B	A ∨ B	¬(A ∨ B)	¬A	¬B	¬A ∧ ¬B
0	0	0	1	1	1	1
0	1	1	0	1	0	0
1	0	1	0	0	1	0
1	1	1	0	0	0	0

17.2.2 Syntactic domains

To generate a conjunctive entailment, disjunction must be in the scope of negation. In logic, scope is determined by bracketing. In human languages, syntactic structure generally determines semantic scope. That is, the scope of two logical operators is often determined by examining the structural position of these operators in the constituent structure of the sentence. The key to the structural relationship in human languages is known as c-command. One operator A has scope over another operator B if and only if A c-commands B.[2] For example, in (1a) the negation operator (*not*) c-commands disjunction (*or*). Consequently, the sentence (1a) yields a conjunctive entailment. That is, (1a) entails that if the news didn't surprise Karl or Jeb, then it didn't surprise Karl and it didn't surprise Jeb. By, contrast, the negation operator does not c-command disjunction in (1b), so a conjunctive entailment is not generated. Rather, (1b) is true in three circumstances: (i) if Karl was surprised, but not Jeb, (ii) if Jeb was surprised, but not Karl or (iii) if both Karl and Jeb were surprised.

(1)   a.   The news that Bush won did **not** surprise Karl **or** Jeb
       b.   The news that Bush did **not** win surprised Karl **or** Jeb

17.2.3 Inverse scope

Sometimes syntactic position does not guarantee semantic scope in human languages. For example, (2) is the Japanese translation of the English sentence 'Ted didn't order sushi or pasta.' Adult speakers of Japanese do not judge (2) to generate the same conjunctive entailment as it does in English, namely that Ted did not order sushi and did not order pasta. Rather, adults judge (2) to mean that 'Ted didn't order sushi' *or* 'Ted didn't order pasta.' In logic, the corresponding form is ($\neg$A $\vee$ $\neg$B), which does not entail ($\neg$**A** $\wedge$ $\neg$**B**).

(2)   Ted ga   sushi   ka   pasuta o   tanomanakatta.
      Ted NOM   sushi   or   pasta   ACC   order-NEG-PAST
      'It's sushi or pasta that Ted did not order, but I don't know which one
      he did not order'

Although the Japanese disjunction operator *ka* in (2) is c-commanded by negation in the surface syntax, *ka* is interpreted as if it has scope over negation. Pursuing a suggestion made in Szabolcsi (2002), Goro (2004) proposed that languages vary in the way they interpret disjunction in simple negative sentences. This crosslinguistic variation is due to a parameter. According to the parameter, there are two classes of languages. In one class, which includes Japanese, disjunction is a 'positive polarity item'. In the other class, which includes English, disjunction is not a positive

---

[2] An expression A c-commands another expression B if there is a path that extends upwards to the first branching node above A, and then proceeds downwards to B.

polarity item. By definition, a positive polarity item must take scope over negation. English *some* meets this definition of a positive polarity item, as (3) illustrates. If *some* were interpreted within the scope of negation, the sentence would mean 'Ted didn't eat *any* kangaroo'. Instead, it means there is some kangaroo that Ted didn't eat.

(3) Ted did**n't** eat **some** kangaroo.
     Meaning: There is some kangaroo that Ted didn't eat

Let us indicate the parameter value on which disjunction takes scope over negation as (OR > NEG), and the other value as (NEG > OR). The Japanese setting of the parameter is (OR > NEG). On this setting, disjunction has scope over negation. So disjunction does not yield a conjunctive entailment in simple negative sentences like (2). By contrast, the English setting of the parameter is (NEG > OR), with negation taking scope over disjunction. So, 'Ted didn't order sushi or pasta' generates a conjunctive entailment, as in one of De Morgan's laws: $\neg(\mathbf{A} \lor \mathbf{B}) \Rightarrow (\neg\mathbf{A} \land \neg\mathbf{B})$. At first glance, it looks as though Japanese fails to adhere to De Morgan's laws in simple negative sentences, but since disjunction takes scope over negation in simple negative sentences in Japanese, De Morgan's laws are simply not operative in these sentences.

Positive polarity items (e.g. English *some*, Japanese *ka*) are interpreted as having scope over negation just in case the positive polarity item and negation are in the same clause. However, if negation appears in a higher clause than the one containing the positive polarity item, then negation takes scope over the polarity item, if negation c-commands disjunction. Example (4) illustrates this for English *some*.

(4) You'll **never** convince me that Ted ate **some** kangaroo.
     Meaning: You'll never convince me that Ted ate any kangaroo.

17.2.4 Logic and language reunited

If the Japanese disjunction operator *ka* is a positive polarity item, then Japanese is expected to adhere to De Morgan's laws in sentences in which negation appears in a higher clause than the clause that contains *ka*. This prediction is confirmed, as the examples in (5) illustrate. Disjunction generates a conjunctive entailment in both structures, so the Japanese sentences and the corresponding English sentences have the same meanings.

(5) a. Gen ga   Ted ga   sushi ka pasuta o   tanonda   to   iwanakatta.
        Gen NOM Ted NOM sushi or pasta ACC order-PAST that say-NEG-PAST
        'Gen didn't say Ted ordered sushi or pasta'
        Meaning: Gen didn't say Ted ordered sushi, and she didn't say Ted ordered pasta

b. Gen ga   Ted ga   sushi ka pasuta o   tanomu no   o   minakatta
    Gen NOM Ted NOM sushi or pasta   ACC order-Prt Nmlzr ACC see-NEG-PAST
    (Prt: Present, Nmlzr: Nominalizer)
    'Gen didn't see Ted order sushi or pasta'
    Meaning: Gen didn't see Ted order sushi, and she didn't see Ted order pasta.

Examples like those in (5) indicate that Japanese adheres to De Morgan's laws after all. When negation appears in a higher clause than the clause that contains disjunction, a conjunctive entailment is generated in both Japanese and in English, despite differences in word order. Notice that the disjunction operator, *ka*, precedes negation in Japanese, whereas *or* follows negation in English. This is because Japanese is a verb-final language and negation is attached to the verb. Nevertheless, the Japanese example yields the same truth conditions as its counterpart in English (and all other languages, as far as we know). This shows that the interpretation of disjunction does not depend on linear order. What matters is constituent structure and the structural relations among expressions (e.g. c-command).

17.3   Disjunction and negation in child language

17.3.1   De Morgan's laws in child English
There have been several experimental studies of English-speaking children's interpretation of disjunction in the scope of negation. These studies have revealed that 3- to 5-year-old English-speaking children are aware of the adult interpretation of sentences with disjunction and negation. A representative example is an experiment by Crain *et al.* (2002) using the Truth Value Judgment task. Two experimenters were needed to conduct the study. One acted out the stories using the toy props, and the other manipulated a (wizard) puppet. While the story was being acted out, the puppet watched alongside the child. During each trial, the story was interrupted so that the puppet could make a prediction about what he thought would happen. Then the story resumed, and its final outcome provided the experimental context against which the subject evaluated the puppet's earlier prediction. The puppet repeated his prediction at the end of each story, and then the child subject was asked whether the puppet has 'said the right thing or the wrong thing'. If the child indicated that the puppet had been wrong, they were asked to explain 'what really happened'.

On a typical trial, sentence (6) was uttered by the wizard puppet as a prediction about how events would unfold in a story. It subsequently turned out that the girl who stayed up late received a jewel, but not a dime.

(6)   The girl who stayed up late will **not** get a dime **or** a jewel.

The English-speaking children correctly rejected sentences like (6) in experimental contexts such as this. Children's stated reason for rejecting (6) was that
the girl who stayed up late had received a jewel. This invites the inference that,
in children's grammars, (6) generates a conjunctive entailment – that the girl
will not receive a dime *and* she will not receive a jewel. This shows that English-
speaking children adhere to De Morgan's laws in simple negative sentences.

It is worth noting that the same children accepted sentences like (7) in
the same context. As in (6), negation precedes the disjunction operator in
(7). However, negation does not have scope over the disjunction operator
in (7), so the sentence does not generate a conjunctive entailment. Instead,
(7) implies that the girl will either get a dime or a jewel. We will call this a
'disjunctive' interpretation.

(7)   The girl who did**n't** go to bed will get a dime **or** a jewel.

Children's different responses to (6) and (7) demonstrate their knowledge
that constituent structure, and not linear order, governs semantic scope.

17.3.2   De Morgan's laws in child Japanese

So far, we have seen that English-speaking children adhere to De Morgan's
laws in simple negative sentences; disjunction licenses a conjunctive
entailment in such sentences, both for children and adults. By contrast,
for adult speakers of Japanese, a conjunctive entailment is generated only
if negation resides in a higher clause than the clause that contains disjunction (see the examples in (5)). When disjunction *ka* appears under local
negation in simple negative sentences like (8), adult speakers interpret *ka*
as a positive polarity item, so it takes scope over negation. Therefore, (8)
does not generate a conjunctive entailment for adult speakers of Japanese.

(8)   Butasan-wa ninjin **ka**   pi'iman-wo   tabe-**nakat**-ta
      pig-TOP   pepper or   carrot-ACC   eat-NEG-PAST
      Literally: 'The pig didn't eat the pepper or the carrot'
      Meaning: The pig didn't eat the pepper *or* the pig didn't eat the carrot.

What about child speakers of Japanese? Based on considerations of
language learnability, Goro (2004) made an intriguing prediction – that
Japanese-speaking children would initially generate a conjunctive entailment in simple negative disjunctive sentences, in contrast to adult speakers of Japanese. This prediction was based on the observation that the two
settings of the positive polarity parameter stand in a subset/superset relation. On the Japanese setting of the parameter, disjunction takes scope
over negation (OR > NEG). Therefore, (8) is true in three different sets
of circumstances: (i) when the pig didn't eat the carrot, but did eat the
pepper, (ii) when the pig didn't eat the pepper, but ate the carrot, and

(iii) when the pig didn't eat either one. On the English setting of the parameter, the English counterpart to (8) is true just in case (iii), when the pig didn't eat either the carrot or the pepper. So, on the English setting of the parameter (NEG > OR), simple negative statements with disjunction are true in a subset of the circumstances corresponding to such statements on the Japanese setting of the parameter (OR > NEG).

Suppose children learning English start off assuming the Japanese setting of the parameter (OR > NEG). If so, these children would judge the sentence 'Ted didn't order sushi or pasta' to be true if (i) Ted didn't order sushi, but ordered pasta, or if (ii) Ted didn't order pasta, but ordered sushi, or if (iii) Ted ordered neither. As a matter of fact, the sentence is true only in the last of these circumstances. So, English-speaking children who have 'misset' the parameter would have to expunge those truth conditions that are not consistent with the correct parameter value (NEG > OR). The problem of 'unlearning' turns out to be particularly vexing, as it would require special input from adults, such as corrective feedback. As far as we know, such input is not available to children in sufficient abundance to guarantee that all children achieve the correct parameter setting (see e.g. Pinker 1990).

A way out of this dilemma is for children to initially choose the parameter setting that makes sentences true in the most restricted set of circumstances. Then, if the initial setting is incorrect for the local language, there will be ample positive evidence pointing out the need to switch the setting to the one that generates a wider range of truth conditions. This solution to the learnability problem is called the semantic subset principle (Crain *et al.* 1994). The principle dictates that, whenever parameter values are in a subset/superset relation, children initially select the subset value.

In the present case, the semantic subset principle anticipates that children's initial setting will be the subset reading (NEG > OR), even in languages like Japanese, where adult judgments reflect the alternative setting (OR > NEG). If so, Japanese-speaking children would be expected to initially interpret (8) in the same way the corresponding sentences are interpreted in English. Based on this line of reasoning, Goro (2004) predicted that Japanese-speaking children would generate a conjunctive entailment for disjunction in the scope of negation, even in simple negative sentences. The prediction was confirmed in an experimental investigation of 4- and 5-year-old Japanese-speaking children by Goro and Akiba (2004). They found that the Japanese-speaking children consistently licensed a conjunctive entailment in response to statements like (8).

17.4   Disjunction in the scope of the universal quantifier

17.4.1   The two arguments of the universal quantifier

It will be useful to introduce an additional distinction. Structurally, the universal quantifier *every* combines with the subject noun phrase to form a grammatical unit, e.g. *every student* or *every student in this room*. The subject noun phrase that *every* combines with is called its 'Restrictor'. Once *every* combines with its Restrictor, the entire quantificational expression combines with the predicate phrase (e.g. *swims, speaks French or Spanish*). The predicate phrase is called the Nuclear Scope of the universal quantifier. So, *every student swims* would be represented as: Every R[student] NS[swims].

Suppose you and your friends Gen and Ted board an international flight. During the flight, Gen and Ted order pasta for their meals, but you order sushi. Later, every passenger who ordered pasta, including Gen and Ted, become ill. But, fortunately, you feel fine. Now, suppose you overhear Gen tell someone: "Everyone who ordered pasta or sushi became ill." Would you contradict Gen, saying "No, I ordered sushi, and I feel fine." That's what English-speakers would do. Moreover, if the sentence 'Everyone who ordered pasta or sushi became ill' is translated into Japanese, Russian, or Chinese, the sentences in these languages also carry the same conjunctive entailment – that everyone who ordered sushi became ill <u>and</u> everyone who ordered pasta became ill (contrary to fact). This shows us that disjunction licenses a conjunctive entailment in the Restrictor of the universal quantifier *every*:

(9) Everyone who ordered sushi or pasta became ill.
Everyone R[who ordered sushi or pasta] NS[became ill]
Meaning: everyone who ordered sushi became ill
and
everyone who ordered pasta became ill

In (10) the phrases (*ordered sushi or pasta* and *became ill*) are reversed. This allows us to see how disjunction is interpreted in the Nuclear Scope of the universal quantifier. As indicated in (10a), when disjunction resides in the Nuclear Scope, it receives a disjunctive interpretation (cf. example (7)). The critical point is that disjunction does not license a conjunctive entailment in the Nuclear Scope of the universal quantifier, as indicated by the '*' in (10b).

(10) Everyone who became ill ordered sushi or pasta.
Everyone R[who became ill] NS[ordered sushi or pasta]
a. for every x (x = person), if x became ill, then x ordered sushi or x ordered pasta
b. * → everyone who became ill ordered sushi **and** everyone who became ill ordered pasta

The asymmetry in the interpretation of disjunction in the Restrictor versus the Nuclear Scope of the universal quantifier is summarized in (11).

(11) a. Every R[... or ...] NS[...............]
= Conjunctive Entailment

b. Every R[..............] NS[.... or ....]
= Disjunctive Interpretation

17.4.2 Disjunction and universal quantification in child language

Several studies have investigated the truth conditions children associate with disjunction in the Restrictor and in the Nuclear Scope of the universal quantifier. One, by Gualmini *et al.* (2003), asked 3- to 5-year-old English-speaking children to judge sentences including (12) and (13), produced by a puppet.

(12)   Every woman bought eggs or bananas.

(13)   Every woman who bought eggs or bananas got a basket.

Sentence (12) was presented to children in a story where some of the women bought eggs, but none of them bought bananas. The child participants consistently accepted (12) in this condition, showing that they assigned a 'disjunctive' interpretation when disjunction is in the Nuclear Scope of *every*. In another experimental condition, the same children were presented with sentence (13) in a context in which the women who bought eggs received a basket, but not the women who bought bananas. The child participants consistently rejected the test sentences in this condition. This finding is taken as evidence that children generated a conjunctive entailment of disjunction in the Restrictor of *every*. This asymmetry in children's responses demonstrates children's knowledge of the asymmetry in the two arguments of the universal quantifier – the Restrictor and the Nuclear Scope.

17.4.3 More on the scope of universal quantification
17.4.3.1 Isomorphism and inverse scope

Consider sentence (14), and the two (informal) meaning representations (14a, b):

(14)   Every boy is riding an elephant.
      a. For every boy x, there is a y (y = elephant), x is riding y
      b. There is a y (y = elephant), for every x (x = boy), x is riding y

In (14a), the universal quantifier *every* takes scope over the existential quantifier *there is*, so the meaning is: For every boy, there is a possibly different elephant that the boy is riding. The order of the operators is reversed in (14b) resulting in the meaning: There is an elephant such that every boy is riding that elephant. Since the quantificational expression *every boy* takes scope over (i.e. c-commands) *an elephant* in the constituent structure for (14a), this is called the 'isomorphic' interpretation. The alternative reading, in (14b), is called the 'inverse scope' interpretation. On both readings, however, the universal quantifier *every* ranges over the denotation of the subject noun, *boy*, and the existential quantifier ranges over the denotation of the object noun, *elephant*.

The isomorphic interpretation and the inverse scope interpretation tend to crop up whenever there are two operators. For example, in sentences with the universal quantifier and negation, as in (15), the sentence gives rise to an isomorphic reading and an inverse scope reading. On the isomorphic reading of 'Every horse did not jump over the fence', the subject noun phrase, *every horse* has scope over negation, (15a); the sentence is true only if none of the horses jumped over the fence. On the inverse scope reading, negation has scope over *every horse*, (15b), so the sentence denies the claim that every horse jumped over the fence. So, on the inverse scope interpretation, 'Every horse did not jump over the fence' is true if at least one horse didn't jump over the fence.

(15)   Every horse did not jump over the fence.
   a. For every x (x = horse), ¬[x jumped over the fence]
   b. ¬ For every x (x = horse), [x jumped over the fence]

17.4.4   Isomorphism in child language

In some languages, certain types of sentences with two operators are judged to have only the isomorphic reading. For example, adult speakers of Mandarin Chinese judge sentences like (16) to license the isomorphic interpretation (16a), but not the inverse scope interpretation, (16b). Similarly, the isomorphic interpretation dominates for (17), with the universal quantifier *every horse* taking scope over the indefinite noun phrase *a fence*.

(16)   A horse jumped over every fence.
   a. there is an x (x = horse), for every y (y = fence), x jumped over y
   b. *for every y (y = fence), there is an x (x = horse), x jumped over y

(17)   Every horse jumped over a fence.
   a. for every x (x = horse), there is a y (y = horse), x jumped over y
   b. *there is a y (y = fence), for every x (x = horses), x jumped over y

In groundbreaking research, T. Lee (1991, 1997) tested children acquiring Chinese on a range of sentence structures with two operators. Although children's responses differed from adults in certain respects, the main finding was that, by age 7, children responded like adults in assigning the isomorphic interpretations of sentences like (16) and (17).

Surprisingly, experimental studies of English-speaking children suggested that they, too, have an inherent preference for the isomorphic interpretation of sentences with two operators. One source of evidence was a study of children's productions by O'Leary and Crain (1994). These researchers designed the target sentences to evoke specific negative sentences from children. For example, in one story, it turned out that one dinosaur didn't find anything to eat, but all the others did. When the puppet produced his version of what happened in the story, he got it wrong, as illustrated in (18). In response, children often used the indefinite NP *something* in the scope of negation:

(18) Puppet: Every dinosaur found something to eat.
       Child: No, this dinosaur didn't find something to eat.
       Meaning: this dinosaur didn't find *anything* to eat.

For adults, the sentence 'This one didn't find something to eat' is odd because *something* is a positive polarity item, and hence must take scope over negation. So the sentence means 'there is something that the one dinosaur didn't find to eat' but that wasn't what happened in the story. Clearly, children were using *something* to mean *anything*. This suggests that children intended the isomorphic interpretation in their reply to the puppet in (18). Children were not simply repeating the expression used by the puppet, because they consistently replaced *anything* by *something* in another experimental condition (e.g. Puppet: "Only one of the dinosaurs found **anything** to eat." Child: "No, every dinosaur found **something** to eat.")

Other studies also appear to support the conjecture that children initially adopt the isomorphic interpretation. For example, Musolino (1998) found that children rejected (19) if one of the horses did not jump over the fence. It would seem that they interpreted (19) to convey the meaning -none of the horses jumped over the fence- (the isomorphic interpretation), rather than the meaning -not all of them did- (the inverse scope interpretation).

(19)   Every horse didn't jump over the fence.

17.4.5   Inverse scope in child language

In several recent studies, however, it has been demonstrated that children are able to compute the inverse scope interpretations of sentences with two (or more) operators. The critical experimental factors that are prerequisite to children's understanding of the alternative interpretations of scope ambiguities were investigated by Gualmini (2004). By attending to the felicity conditions on the use of negative sentences, Gualmini was able to evoke both isomorphic and inverse scope interpretations from children across a range of structures, including ones like (20) (also see Crain *et al.* 1996). A central idea in constructing felicitous contexts was anticipated by Bertrand Russell, who pointed out that 'perception only gives rise to a negative judgment when the correlative positive judgment has already been made or considered' (1948: 138). This is called the 'condition of plausible denial'.

By satisfying the condition of plausible denial, Gualmini (2004) demonstrated children's knowledge of an asymmetry in the scope relations of *not* and *some* in the Restrictor versus the Nuclear Scope of the universal quantifier in sentences like (20) versus (21). In (20) the positive polarity item *some* has scope over *not*, resulting in the inverse scope reading. In (21), the universal quantifier cancels the polarity sensitivity of *some*, so *not* and *some* retain their surface scope positions in the meaning representation.

Figure 17.1 The extra-object condition

Therefore, (21) licenses an isomorphic interpretation. Children's behavioural responses to (20) and (21) indicate knowledge of this asymmetry in scope relations.

(20)   Every smurf didn't jump over some hurdle.
       Every R[smurf] NS[did **not** jump over **some** hurdle]
       = Inverse scope Interpretation

(21)   Every smurf who didn't jump over some hurdle cried.
       Every R[smurf who did **not** jump over **some** hurdle] NS[cried]
       = Isomorphic Interpretation

17.4.6   Children's difficulties in assigning scope

Research has uncovered systematic non-adult responses to sentences containing the universal quantifier by preschool and even school-age children, beginning with work by Inhelder and Piaget (1964). Consider the picture in Figure 17.1. Is (22) an accurate description of the picture?

(22)   Every boy is riding an elephant.

If you are like most adults, you judge (22) to be a correct description of the picture. From a logical point of view, the sentence is true because every member of the set denoted by the subject noun, *boy*, has the property expressed by the predicate phrase, *is riding an elephant*. Once you verify that every member of the set of boys is riding an elephant, you judge the sentence to be true. The 'extra' elephant, the one not being ridden by a boy, may have puzzled you, but it does not make the sentence false, because the range of the universal quantifier *every* does not extend to the denotation of the object noun, *elephant*. The adult analysis is represented in (23).

(23)   For every x (x = boy), there is a y (y = elephant), x is riding y

In contrast to adults, preschool and even school-age children sometimes reject (22) as an accurate description of the picture in figure 17.1. When children are asked to explain these negative responses (Experimenter: "Why not?"), children are likely to point to the 'extra' elephant. We will describe three accounts of children's non-adult behaviour in response to sentences like (22).

17.4.6.1   The event quantification account

On one analysis, children produce non-adult responses to (22) because they demand symmetry (i.e. a one-to-one relation) between the boys and elephants. Consequently, children's non-adult performance has been called 'the symmetrical response'. The truth conditions associated with the symmetrical response can be represented using two universal quantifiers, each ranging over a different noun, *boy* versus *elephant*, as in (24). Notice that one universal quantifier ranges over the subject noun, *boy*, and a second universal quantifier ranges over the object noun, *elephant*. On the adult interpretation, with only a single universal quantifier, the truth conditions are limited to those represented in (24a), and do not extend to those in (24b).

(24)   Every boy is riding an elephant.
    a. For every x (x = boy), there is a y (y = elephant), x is riding y
        AND
    b. For every y (y = elephant), there is an x (x = boy), x is riding y
        'For every boy, there is an elephant that the boy is riding, and for every elephant, there is a boy riding that elephant.'

Obviously the sentence 'Every boy is riding an elephant' does not contain two universal quantifiers, so the truth conditions in (24) must be derived from a semantic analysis that contains only a single *every*. One account of children's symmetrical response, by Philip (1995), is called the 'Event Quantification account'.

   According to this account, children analyse sentences like 'Every boy is riding an elephant' using an 'event' variable ('e'), rather than variables that range over individuals (e.g. 'x' and 'y'). On the Event Quantification account, children's symmetrical response eventuates because the universal quantifier *every* ranges over events in which either boys or elephants participate. So, both the subject noun, *boy*, and the object noun, *elephant*, appear in the Restrictor of *every*. The denotations of these nouns form a disjunction, events in which boys participate ('PART') and ones in which elephants participate. The analysis is (informally) represented in (25).

(25) EVERY e R[PART(boy, e) v PART(elephant, e)] NS[e = boy-riding-elephant]

Recall that when the universal qualifier, *every*, has scope over disjunction in the Restrictor, disjunction licenses a conjunctive entailment (see 11a).

(26) EVERY R[… or …] NS[……………] Conjunctive Entailment

Therefore, the representation in (25) yields both (27a) and (27b), from which the truth conditions associated with children's symmetrical responses immediately follow. To see this, compare (27) with (24).

(27) a. EVERY e R[PART(boy, e)] NS [e = boy-riding-elephant]
      AND
      b. EVERY e R[PART(elephant, e)] NS [e = boy-riding-elephant]

Despite its success in explaining children's symmetrical responses, the Event Quantification account fails to explain many of the findings reported in the literature. For example, children acquiring Mandarin Chinese do not manifest symmetrical responses to sentences like 'All the men are carrying water-buckets' in contexts with extra water buckets, not being carried by any of the men (Lee 1997). Moreover, by age 7 children acquiring Mandarin consistently assign an existential wide-scope interpretation to instructions like (28), which they interpret as an instruction to lay a single towel on every child (Lee 1991). On the Event Quantification account, there should be a one-to-one correspondence between towels and children.

(28) (Child's Name) gai yitiao   maojin zai meige   xiaohai shenshang
                      lay one-CL towel   at   every-CL child   body-on
      '(Child's Name) lays a towel on every child'

The Event Quantification account also fails to explain the findings of studies in which the same linguistic expression is interpreted differently by children depending on its hierarchical position in constituent structure. For example, we reported evidence that children know that disjunction licenses a conjunctive entailment in the Restrictor of the universal quantifier, but not in the Nuclear Scope. The standard partitioning of sentences places the subject noun phrase in the Restrictor and the predicate phrase in the Nuclear Scope (see Section 17.4.1) On the Event Quantification account, however, the Restrictor contains both the subject phrase and also components of the predicate phrase. By altering the contents of the Restrictor in this way, the event quantification account fails to explain children's sensitivity to differences in the meaning that depends on preserving the distinction between subject and predicate in constituent structure.

17.4.6.2 The salience account

A second account of children's non-adult interpretation of sentences like 'Every boy is riding an elephant' is offered by Drozd and van Loosbroek

(1999) (cf. Geurts 2003). Children differ from adults in response to such sentences, according to Drozd and van Loosbroek, depending on which of the sets of objects mentioned in the sentence, boys or elephants, is more 'discourse active', i.e. more salient in the context. Let us call this the 'Salience account'. On this account, when the set of boys is discourse active, the sentence is given the adult analysis by children, as in (29). However, when the set of elephants is more salient, the sentence 'Every boy is riding an elephant' is analysed by children as in (30). Children respond "No" when they adopt the analysis in (30), due to the 'extra' elephant. In short, the Salience account introduces two occurrences of the universal quantifier, one ranging over the subject noun, *boys*, and one ranging over the object noun, *elephants*.

(29)   Every boy is riding an elephant.
For every x (x = boy), there is a y (y = elephant), x is riding y
'For every boy, there is an elephant which that boy is riding'

(30)   Every boy is riding an elephant.
For every y (y = elephant), there is a x (x = boy), x is riding y
'For every elephant, there is a boy riding that elephant'

On the adult analysis in (29), children say "Yes" in the extra-object condition, even where there is an 'extra' object, an elephant not being ridden by a boy. When the set of elephants is discourse active, therefore, children are expected to say "Yes" if every elephant is being ridden by a boy, even if there are 'extra' boys, ones not riding elephants. This prediction of the Salience account was investigated in a study by Meroni *et al.* (2006). On one trial, children were shown a picture in which there were four tigers, three of them holding balloons. The test sentence on this trial was (31).

(31)   Every tiger is holding a balloon.

The study was designed to see if children would accept (31) if the balloons were discourse active. To make the balloons highly salient, the experimenter made a special point of the fact that there was a beautiful butterfly on each balloon. Nevertheless, the 3- to 5-year-old children who participated in the experiment consistently rejected the target sentences. In short, children did not behave as predicted by the Salience account.

17.4.6.3   The condition of plausible denial
Children who give non-adult responses to sentences with the universal quantifier, sometimes give adult-like responses in the same experimental contexts. Therefore, both the Event Quantification account and the Salience account propose that children's grammars permit two analyses of sentences with the universal quantifier, a non-adult interpretation and an adult-like interpretation. This raises a learnability problem, because the input from adult speakers of the local language will always be consistent

with one of children's interpretations, namely the adult interpretation. It is difficult to see how, on either account, children could purge their grammars of the non-adult interpretation.

In addition to this theoretical difficulty, children's non-adult responses fail to emerge in certain experimental tasks, such as the Truth Value Judgment task (Crain *et al.* 1996). Crain *et al.* use this observation to argue that children's successful performance in the Truth Value Judgment task is due to the satisfaction of the condition of plausible denial (see section 17.5.3). Essentially, the proposal is that a sentence is felicitous if it answers a question that was under consideration in the discourse context. It is pragmatically felicitous to use the sentence 'Every boy rode an elephant' if the question at issue is 'Did every boy ride an elephant?' This felicity condition was satisfied in Truth Value Judgment tasks by having some boy(s) consider riding a donkey but, in the end, deciding to ride an elephant, just like the other boys. In such experimental contexts, children consistently perform like adults in responding to sentences with a universal quantifier, regardless of the salience of the denotation of the object noun.

17.5   Disjunction in the scope of focus expressions

17.5.1   Disjunction and focus expressions in adult language

The final topic is the acquisition of focus operators. We will discuss English *only* and its counterpart in Japanese, *dake*. Suppose you, your friends Gen and Ted, and several others go out to lunch. Today, Ted orders sushi, rather than pasta. You order beans, and everyone else orders beans or rice. Later, you overhear Gen tell someone "Only Ted ordered sushi or pasta." Would you agree with your friend? That's what English-speaking adults would do. Moreover, if the sentence 'Only Ted ordered sushi or pasta' is translated into Japanese, Russian or Chinese, the sentences in these languages have the same meaning. The sentences convey two messages: (a) that Ted ordered either sushi or pasta, and (b) that everyone else didn't order sushi or pasta. This second meaning component, moreover, licenses a conjunctive entailment – everyone else did not order sushi <u>and</u> everyone else did not order pasta. The same conjunctive entailment is licensed in other languages. These observations are summarized in (32).

(32)   Only Ted ordered sushi or pasta.
    a. Ted ordered sushi or pasta. = Disjunctive Interpretation
    b. Everyone else (being contrasted with Ted) didn't order sushi or pasta. = Conjunctive Entailment

Meaning: Everyone else didn't order sushi and everyone else didn't order pasta.

Following Horn (1996), the meaning of a sentence with the focus operator *only*, such as (32), can be decomposed into two conjoined propositions.

The first proposition pertains to the focus element, *Ted*. This meaning component is called the *presupposition*. Roughly, the presupposition is the original sentence without the focus operator, as shown in (32a). The second meaning component is an entailment generated by the focus operator. This meaning component is called the *assertion*. The assertion pertains to a set of individuals being contrasted with the element in focus (here, Ted), as illustrated in (32b). The assertion entails that the property being attributed to the individual in focus is not a property of anyone in the contrast set.

If the English sentence is translated into Japanese, or any other language as far as we know, the resulting sentence has the same meaning. Consider the Japanese counterpart to (32), namely (33).

(33)   Ted dake ga   sushi ka pasuta o   tanonda
       Ted only NOM sushi or pasta   ACC   order-PAST
       Presupposition: Ted ordered sushi and pasta.
                                    = Disjunctive Interpretation
       Assertion: Everyone else didn't order sushi or pasta.
                                    = Conjunctive Entailment

Recall that the disjunction operator, *ka*, takes scope over negation in Japanese, in simple negative sentences in which disjunction and negation are both contained in the same clause. Notice that the assertion of example (33) is the simple negative sentence 'Everyone else didn't order sushi or pasta.' The assertion is given in Japanese in (34).

(34)   Hoka no   daremo   ga   sushi ka pasuta o   tanomanakatta
       else   GEN everybody NOM sushi or pasta   ACC order-NEG-PAST
       'Everyone else didn't order sushi or pasta'
       Meaning: It's either sushi or pasta that everyone else didn't order

There is a paradox here. The English sentence 'Only Ted ordered sushi or pasta' and its Japanese counterpart both make the same assertion, namely that everyone being contrasted with Ted did not order sushi, and everyone did not order pasta. Yet, if the assertion 'Everyone else didn't order sushi or pasta' is produced in Japanese, it does not carry a conjunctive entailment. Japanese-speaking children will be hard-pressed to 'learn' the meaning of the assertion in sentences with the focus operator *dake*, since this meaning cannot be expressed in a simple negative sentence with *ka*.

This suggests that the status of *ka* as a positive polarity item, with scope over negation, is a 'surface' phenomenon. If *ka* is introduced as part of an entailment that is generated by a sentence with the focus operator *dake*, as in (34), then *ka* retains its position within the scope of negation. And the interpretation of *ka* in the assertion is consistent with De Morgan's laws. That is, 'Everyone else didn't order sushi or pasta' entails that everyone else didn't order sushi and everyone else didn't order pasta. This further reinforces the conclusion that disjunction in human languages is inclusive-*or*, as in classical logic.

17.5.2   Disjunction and focus expressions in child language

Recent experimental research has sought to determine whether or not children know the two meaning components of sentences with a focus expression: English *only*, Japanese *dake*. As noted earlier, 4- to 5-year-old children appear to know that *or* licenses conjunctive entailments in certain contexts, e.g. under negation, and in the Restrictor of the universal quantifier *every*. So, children's interpretation of *or* was used to assess their knowledge of the semantics of *only* (Goro *et al.* 2005). The research strategy in these experiments was to investigate children's interpretation of disjunction *or/ka* in the presupposition of sentences with the focus operator *only/dake* in one experiment, and the meaning of the assertion in a second experiment. One of the test sentences was (35).

(35)   English: Only Bunny Rabbit will eat a carrot or a green pepper.
　　　 Japanese: Usagichan-dake-ga ninjin ka piiman-wo   taberu-yo.
　　　　　　　　 rabbit-*only*-NOM   carrot *or* green pepper-ACC eat-dec

Under the decomposition analysis, the meaning of the sentences in (35) can both be partitioned into two meaning components, as in (36).

(36)   a. *Presupposition*: Bunny Rabbit will eat a carrot *or/ka* a green pepper
　　　 b. *Assertion*: Everyone other than Bunny Rabbit will not eat a carrot *or/ka* a green pepper

Within the *presupposition* component, the disjunction operator *or* yields *disjunctive* truth conditions: Bunny Rabbit will eat a carrot or will eat a green pepper. Suppose that children assign the correct interpretation to *or/ka* in the *presupposition*. If so, children should assign these disjunctive truth conditions, and not the conjunctive entailment of disjunction, so they should accept sentence (36) in the situation where Bunny Rabbit ate a carrot but not a green pepper. This is Experiment I.

In the assertion, *or/ka* licenses a conjunctive entailment – everyone else will not eat a carrot and they will not eat a green pepper. Consequently, if children assign the correct interpretation to *or/ka* in the assertion, they should reject (36) in the situation in which Cookie Monster ate a green pepper (while, again, Bunny Rabbit ate a carrot but not a green pepper). This is Experiment II. To summarize, if children understand both the presupposition and the assertion of 'Only Bunny Rabbit will eat a carrot or a green pepper', then they should accept it in Experiment I, but reject it in Experiment II.

Virtually identical experiments were conducted with English-speaking and Japanese-speaking children, to compare their linguistic behaviour. The experiment employed the Truth Value Judgment task. The main finding was that both English-speaking children and Japanese-speaking children consistently accepted the test sentences in Experiment I, and consistently rejected the test sentences in Experiment II. The two groups of children showed no significantly different behaviour in interpreting disjunction within sentences containing a focus operator, *only* versus *dake*.

The high rejection rate in Experiment II shows that children assigned conjunctive entailments to disjunction in the assertion component of sentences with the focus expression *only/dake*. Children's consistent rejections in Experiment II suggests that they are computing the covert meaning component that is associated with focus operators. Both English-speaking children and Japanese-speaking children were able to compute the derived logical truth conditions of disjunction in the scope of a focus operator. This computation requires children to compute contrast sets, an ability that has been questioned in the literature (cf. Paterson *et al.* 2003). The fact that Japanese-speaking children comprehend the meaning of the assertion, despite the difficulties associated with 'learning' this meaning from experience (especially in Japanese), invites the conclusion that disjunction is innately specified as inclusive-*or*.

17.6 Conclusion

In classical logic, disjunction generates a conjunctive entailment when it appears in the scope of negation, as in one of De Morgan's laws: $\neg(A \lor B) \Rightarrow (\neg A \land \neg B)$. The conjunctive entailment of disjunction is licensed only if disjunction is interpreted as inclusive-*or*, as in classical logic. In human languages, then, we can determine whether the interpretation of disjunction accords with classical logic by asking whether disjunction gives rise to a conjunctive entailment when it appears in the scope of negation. Indeed, a conjunctive entailment is licensed in English in simple negative sentences, as in the example 'Ted didn't order sushi or pasta'. This sentence entails that Ted didn't order sushi and Ted didn't order pasta. In some other languages, however, disjunction does not generate a conjunctive entailment in simple negative sentences. These languages include Japanese and Chinese. But, in contrast to adults, young children learning Japanese and Chinese take disjunction to license a conjunctive entailment in simple negative sentences. Clearly, children acquiring Japanese and Chinese are not simply matching the adult input. Apparently, children appeal to a primitive (innate) concept of disjunction, namely inclusive-*or*.

Despite variation across languages, as far as we know, all languages generate a conjunctive entailment in certain constructions. For example, a conjunctive entailment is generated when negation resides in a higher clause than the clause that contains disjunction. Two other putative linguistic universals have been advanced, also involving disjunction. One is that disjunction licenses a conjunctive entailment in the scope of (the Restrictor of) the universal quantifier. The second universal is that disjunction licenses a conjunctive entailment in the scope of (the assertion) of certain focus expressions, such as English *only*. The findings of experimental investigations reveal that even preschool children know these and other subtle facts about the interpretation of disjunction in the scope of other linguistic expressions. Taken together, the findings from crosslinguistic research and from studies of child language are evidence of the considerable overlap between the meanings of the logical vocabulary of classical logic and the corresponding expressions in human languages, including child language.

Suggestions for further reading

Chierchia, G., & McConnell-Ginet, S. (2000). *Meaning and Grammar: An Introduction to Semantics.* Cambridge, MA: MIT Press.

Crain, S., & Thornton, R. (1998). *Investigations in Universal Grammar: A Guide to Experiments in the Acquisition of Syntax and Semantics.* Cambridge, MA: MIT Press.

Guasti, M. T. (2002). *Language Acquisition: The Growth of Grammar.* Cambridge, MA: MIT Press.

18

Sentence processing

Jesse Snedeker

18.1 Introduction

Human language comprehension is so effortless that it often appears instantaneous. Someone speaks, and we understand them without any awareness of how. It is only when we step back and examine the structure of language that it becomes clear just how complex this ability is. To understand speech, we must: transform the acoustic input into a phonological representation, identify each word that is spoken, integrate these words into a structured syntactic and semantic representation and then use that representation to determine what the speaker intended to convey.

Figure 18.1 illustrates these processes and how they might be connected. The solid arrows represent a pared-down theory of how information flows through the system during comprehension. Most theorists posit additional connections between the different levels of processing but they disagree about whether these interactions are immediate or delayed.

The field of sentence processing examines the combinatorial processes that follow word identification – syntactic analysis, semantic interpretation and pragmatic processing. Until recently there was little research that examined children's sentence processing. This was largely attributable to a lack of appropriate paradigms. Research on adult language comprehension had relied on reading paradigms, dual-task studies and metalinguistic judgments of words or utterances. While these methods provided substantial insight into the mature processing system, the findings for young children were often difficult to interpret. In recent years a number of new techniques have been developed which allow us to study how children comprehend spoken language with more natural tasks.

There are several reasons for studying children's sentence processing. First, it is a critical but poorly understood aspect of child development. By four or five years of age, children have mastered the basics of their native language and amassed an impressive vocabulary. But we know little about

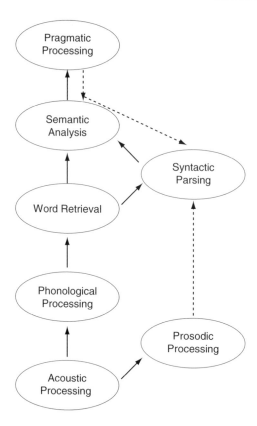

Figure 18.1 A sketch of the processes involved in comprehending spoken language. The solid arrows represent the bottom-up connections that are a part of all theories. The dotted arrows represent the pathways explored in section 18.4.

how they employ this knowledge as they are listening. Are young children able to understand sentences as rapidly as adults? Or is it wiser to slow down when we speak to them? Do they arrive at essentially the same interpretation as adults? Or is our communication with children jeopardized by systematic differences in how we resolve linguistic ambiguity? Mapping the development of language processing could also shed light on some developmental disorders. For example, many children with Asperger's syndrome and Attention Deficit Disorder have problems following spoken instructions, despite average or even superior performance on standardized tests of lexical and grammatical abilities. Sensitive measures of online comprehension could allow us to explore whether these problems stem from deficits in language processing, in contrast with deficits in pragmatic abilities, attention or motivation.

Studying children's language processing may also provide insight into the architecture of the adult language comprehension system. There is general consensus that adults are able to rapidly integrate many sources of information to arrive at a syntactic and semantic analysis of an utterance. But there is considerable controversy about precisely how this is done. Some theorists believe that adult language processing is massively interactive (that every process in Fig. 18.1 connects with and directly influences every other process). Others believe that the flow of information through the system is more constrained (or modular). For example, some theorists propose that during initial comprehension, information from one level flows solely to the level immediately above it. In these modular theories, there is typically a second stage of processing in which a wider range of information sources is used to refine and revise the initial analysis. With experience these revision processes may become so rapid and automatic that it becomes difficult to find evidence of the initial modular stage. Tracing the development of language comprehension in developmental time could help resolve this debate. In the absence of a blueprint, we may be able to discover the underlying structure of sentence processing by watching the building go up.

Finally, studies of children's sentence processing inform the study of language acquisition. As we will see in section 18.5, processing studies can provide data on the nature of children's linguistic representations which bear directly on theories of acquisition. In addition, sentence processing constrains language acquisition. Children acquire language in part on the basis of the utterances they hear. What they learn from an utterance will depend on how they represent it, which in turn will depend on the comprehension process itself (Fodor 1998b).

In this chapter I will briefly describe what we know about adult sentence processing and introduce some of the methods that are used in children's sentences processing. Then I will review two lines of work: one on ambiguity resolution and one on syntactic priming. I will conclude with a discussion of recent directions in the field.

18.2   Methodological issues

Speech gallops along at about 2.5 words per second. To keep pace language comprehension must be both rapid and incremental. In other words, we begin analysing each word as we hear it, rather than waiting until the word or the sentence is complete. For this reason the study of language comprehension requires tools with fine temporal resolution: tools that give us insight into the moment-to-moment changes in cognitive processes rather than merely showing us the final product. These methods are called online comprehension tasks, to distinguish them from the offline tasks used to study children's grammatical knowledge.

For many years research on adult language comprehension primarily examined the comprehension of written language. Text was preferred to speech both because it was much easier to present and because the presentation of each word or phrase could be yoked to the participant's response, providing fine-grained information about processing time. Many paradigms combined reading or listening with a secondary task,

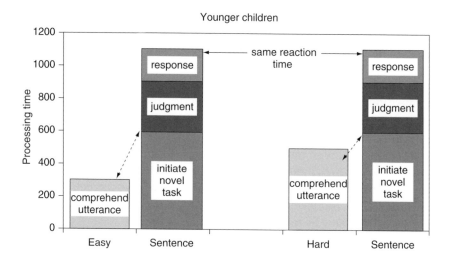

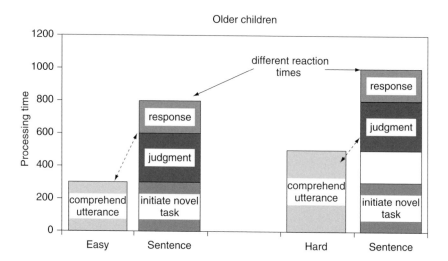

Figure 18.2 Hypothetical example of a reaction-time task in two groups of children. To respond, children must both initiate the novel task and comprehend the sentence. If task initiation is slow (as in the younger children) then differences in linguistic processing will not affect reaction times.

like judging whether the sentence was grammatical or whether a string of letters formed a word. These secondary tasks were used to make inferences about the processing load at different points in an utterance and the kinds of interpretations that were being entertained.

Because these paradigms provided a rich and detailed picture of adult language comprehension, several creative experimenters adapted them for use with children (for reviews see Clahsen 2008, McKee 1996). The results of such studies can be difficult to interpret, primarily because these tasks require abilities – such as reading, executive functions and metalinguistic reasoning – which continue to develop throughout childhood (see e.g. Gombert 1992, Welsh *et al.* 1991). Often in reaction or reading time tasks young children appear to be insensitive to information sources or constraints that guide sentence processing in adults and older children (Kidd 2003, Traxler 2002). But typically the younger children have much longer reading or reaction times in all conditions, suggesting that they find the task more difficult than do older children. Under these circumstances, response times may not be a sensitive measure of language processing. As the response time increases the noise in the data increases as well, making it more difficult to detect effects of a given size. As figure 18.2 illustrates, the presence of a secondary task – like a judgment or button press – further complicates the picture. If young children are slower at initiating the secondary task, that delay can mask any differences in difficulty of the linguistic task. Cognitive psychologists would say that the effect is absorbed into the slack, and thus is not apparent in the reaction time (see Sternberg 1998).

These difficulties led researchers to conclude that children's language processing is best studied with spoken language and no overt task. The challenge, of course, is to figure out how we can get data on online processing under these conditions. Over the past decade two solutions have emerged. First, we can examine the neural correlates of sentence processing using neuro-imaging techniques. The most popular imaging technique for studying children's sentence processing is the measurement of event-related potentials (or ERPs, see Ch. 4). ERPs provide less information about the location of a neural process than methods like fMRI, but they have the temporal resolution necessary for studying language processes, are safe for use with children, and are inexpensive compared to other imaging techniques. Our interpretation of ERP data in children is largely based on what we know about particular ERP effects in adults. One limitation of the technique is that most research designs examine neural responses to anomalous utterances, and thus provide limited information about the evolving interpretation of well-formed utterances.

Recently many researchers have been studying children's online language processing by examining what they look at as they are listening to an utterance (Fernald *et al.* 1998, Nation *et al.* 2003, Song & Fisher 2005, Swingley & Aslin 2002, Swingley & Fernald 2002, Trueswell *et al.* 1999). These methods stem from the intermodal preferential looking paradigm which was developed to study intermodal perception (Spelke 1979) and offline language comprehension (Golinkoff *et al.* 1987), and from the visual world paradigm that was developed by Michael Tanenhaus and his colleagues to study online spoken language comprehension in adults (Tanenhaus *et al.* 1995).

In eye-gaze studies exploring online language processing, children hear a word or a sentence that refers to the visual scene that accompanies it. The visual scene can be a video, a still picture, or a set of objects placed on a tabletop. As the child is listening to the sentence, her gaze direction is recorded. Later the child's eye-movements are analysed with respect to the accompanying utterance, allowing researchers to make inferences about the child's evolving interpretation of the utterance. Eye gaze can be measured in several ways. Some researchers use automated eye-trackers which record an image of the eye and use computer algorithms to infer the direction of gaze. Other researchers simply use a camera which is pointed at the child's face and then code the video by hand. The two methods produce quite similar results (Snedeker & Trueswell 2004).

Why might eye movements be a useful measure of language processing? Because visual acuity is much greater in the fovea (the centre of the retina), we tend to move our eyes to fixate objects that we are attending to. These eye movements are quick, frequent and largely unconscious. Language in turn is a remarkably effective way of altering someone's attentional state. If I say "telephone" you are likely to find yourself thinking of telephones. If there is a telephone nearby that I might be referring to, your eyes will tend to rest on this telephone shortly after the word begins. Eye-gaze paradigms have several advantages for studying children's comprehension. The tasks are simple to administer and typically enjoyable for children. We can examine the comprehension of naturalistic spoken utterances which do not contain anomalies. The measure of interest is based on a spontaneous behaviour which requires no training on the part of the participant. Finally, because the eyes can move several times a second, eye-gaze paradigms provide fine-grained temporal information.

In adults these methods are sensitive to language processing at multiple levels and have been successfully used to explore such diverse issues as: the time course of lexical activation (Allopenna et al. 1998, Magnuson et al. 2003); the integration of syntactic and semantic constraints during sentence processing (Boland 2005, Kamide et al. 2003); and the role of contextual cues in resolving referential and syntactic ambiguities (Chambers et al. 2004). Much of the developmental work has focused on word recognition, demonstrating that one and two-year-old children rapidly and incrementally map phonological input onto lexical entries (Fernald et al. 2006, 1998, Swingley & Aslin 2002, Swingley & Fernald 2002). However several researchers have also examined higher-level processes such as pronoun interpretation (Arnold et al. 2000, Sekerina et al. 2004, Song & Fisher 2005), incremental semantic analysis (Sedivy et al. 2000) and syntactic ambiguity resolution (Snedeker & Trueswell, 2004, Trueswell et al. 1999). While this field is still in its infancy, it has already provided some insights into the origins and development of the language comprehension system and the grammatical representations that underlie it.

18.3   The adult comprehension system

Half a century of systematic exploration has led to a rich (albeit incomplete) understanding of how adult listeners interpret spoken language. While there is still considerable controversy in this field, there is broad agreement on three basic issues (see Altmann 2001, Elman *et al.* 2005, Treiman *et al.* 2003 for reviews). First, language comprehension involves a series of processes which are ordered with respect to one another (see figure 18.1). Phonological processing must begin before words can be recognized. Lexical processes provide semantic and syntactic information which is integrated into structural representations which in turn encode the relations between words. Structured semantic representations are enriched and disambiguated by pragmatic inferences that are guided by information about communication and the context of language use.

Second, each of these processes is incremental. This means that processing at higher levels begins before processing at the lower levels is completed. Many theorists use the metaphor of spreading activation (or cascading water) to capture this relation. As soon as activation (information) begins to accumulate at one level of analysis, it is propagated on to the next level, initiating the higher level process while the lower one is still in progress. Thus word recognition is underway by the time the first phoneme has been heard, syntactic and semantic processing begin as soon as candidate word forms become active (often leading to expectations about words that have yet to be heard), and pragmatic inferences can be made before a clause is completed.

Third, processing at a given level can be influenced by information from other levels, both higher and lower, in the linguistic system. For example, word identification is rapidly influenced by top-down information about the syntactic and semantic context in which that word appears, as well as bottom-up information about the phonological and prosodic form of the word.

To explore this in more detail, let's focus on the syntactic level. In adults syntactic parsing has primarily been investigated by examining the way readers initially interpret, and misinterpret, syntactically ambiguous phrases. For example, consider the sentence fragment (1):

(1)   Mothera destroyed the building with ...

At this point in the utterance the prepositional phrase (PP) beginning with *with* is ambiguous because it could be linked to the verb *destroyed* (VP-attachment), indicating an instrument (e.g. *with her awesome powers*); or it could be linked to the definite noun phrase *the building* (NP-attachment) indicating a modifier (e.g. *with many balconies*). In adults, several different kinds of information rapidly influence the interpretation of ambiguous phrases.

First, knowledge about the particular words in the sentence constrains online interpretation of ambiguous phrases (Taraban & McClelland 1988, Trueswell *et al.* 1993). For instance, the sentence in (1) favours the instrument analysis but if we change the verb from *destroyed* to *liked* the preference flips and the modifier analysis, or NP-attachment, is favoured. This kind of information is often called 'lexical bias' or 'verb bias'. The observed change in preferences could reflect knowledge about the kinds of structures in which each verb is likely to appear (information accessed during word retrieval and then passed on to the syntactic parser), it could reflect semantic knowledge about the arguments of the verb (accessed during word retrieval and passed on to semantic analysis), or it could reflect a more global analysis of the plausibility of different events (pragmatic processing), which influences the relations posited during semantic analysis, which in turn constrains syntactic parsing. All three pathways are shown in Figure 18.1.[1]

Second, adults can use intonation or prosody to resolve attachment ambiguities. If we hear a pause before the preposition (*destroyed the building … with the tower*), we are more likely to assume that the prepositional phrase is attached to the verb phrase and interpret it as an instrument. In contrast, a pause or intonational break before the direct object (*destroyed … the building with the tower*) favours NP-attachment (Pynte & Prieur 1996, Schafer 1997). In Figure 18.1, the pathway by which prosody might influence syntax is shown by the dashed line coming up from prosodic processing to syntactic parsing.

Finally, the situation in which the utterance is used can influence our interpretation (Crain & Steedman 1985). For example, if only one building is under consideration, VP-attachment is likely to be preferred, but if multiple buildings are available then we are more likely to initially interpret the ambiguous phrase as a modifier specifying the building in question (Altmann & Steedman 1988). This type of information is often called referential context. In a reading task the referential context depends upon the information provided in the passage (and the reader's knowledge of the world). In some studies of spoken language comprehension the referential context is limited to the set of objects that the participant can act on. In figure 18.1 the pathway by which referential context might influence parsing is shown by the dashed line coming down from pragmatic processing to semantic analysis and then to syntactic parsing.

The bulk of the evidence suggests that adults rapidly integrate these different information sources to arrive at the analysis that best meets the constraints they have encountered (for a review see Altmann 1998). But disputes continue about the details of this process: do some sources of information establish the candidate analyses while other sources of information weigh in at a later stage (Boland & Cutler 1996, Pynte & Prieur 1996)?

18.4   Syntactic ambiguity resolution in children

The introduction of eye-gaze paradigms enables us to ask parallel questions about the development of online parsing. Trueswell and colleagues (1999) first explored this in a study examining whether children, like adults, can use referential constraints to guide online parsing. Children were given spoken instructions to move objects about on a table while their eye movements were recorded. The critical trials contained a temporary

---

[1] If verb bias effects are actually based on plausibility, then the pathway by which they influence syntactic analysis is the same as the pathway by which referential context has its effect (shown with a dashed line from pragmatics to semantics to syntax).

PP-attachment ambiguity, see (2) below. The verb (*put*) was one that typically appears with a PP argument encoding the destination of the action, thus supporting an initial analysis of the phrase *on the napkin* as VP-attached.

(2) Put the frog on the napkin in the box.

In contexts with just one frog, adults initially looked over to the incorrect destination (the empty napkin) suggesting that they were misanalysing the first prepositional phrase (*on the napkin*) as a VP-attached destination (Tanenhaus *et al.* 1995). But when two frogs were provided (one of which was on a napkin) the participants were able to immediately use the referential context to avoid this garden path, resulting in eye movements similar to unambiguous controls (e.g. *Put the apple that's on the napkin …*).

In contrast five year olds were unaffected by the referential context. In both one-referent and two-referent contexts, children frequently looked at the incorrect destination, suggesting that they pursued the VP-attachment analysis regardless of the number of frogs. In fact, the children's actions suggested that they never revised this misanalysis. On over half of the trials, their actions involved the incorrect destination. For example, for the utterance in (2) many children put the frog onto the napkin and then placed it in the box. By age eight, most children acted like adults in this task, using referential context to guide their parsing decisions about ambiguous phrases.

There are two plausible explanations for this overwhelming preference for the VP-attachment. First, children's parsing preferences could be driven by their statistical knowledge of the verb *put*, which requires the presence of a PP-argument (the destination). Second, children could have a general structural preference for VP-attachment. Such a preference would be predicted by theories of acquisition and parsing that favour simple syntactic structures (i.e. a Minimal Attachment strategy, Frazier & Fodor 1978, Goodluck & Tavakolian 1982) or that ban complex syntactic operations entirely in early stages of development (e.g. Frank 1998). On such a theory, parsing revisions that are based on lexical or referential sources might simply get faster over the course of development (Goodluck & Tavakolian 1982), until the erroneous analyses become undetectable to experimenters measuring adult comprehension (Frazier & Clifton 1996).

Snedeker and Trueswell (2004) explored these two possibilities by manipulating both the bias of the verb and the referential context in which the utterance was used. In this study, children and adults heard globally ambiguous prepositional phrase attachments, as in (3). These sentences were presented in contexts that provided distinct referents for the prepositional object under the two analyses. For example in (3c) both a large fan and a pig holding a fan were provided (see figure 18.3).

(3) a. Modifier Biased: Choose the cow with the fork
    b. Unbiased: Feel the frog with the feather
    c. Instrument Biased: Tickle the pig with the fan

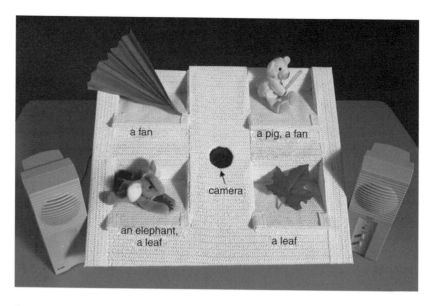

Figure 18. 3 Example of a display for the verb bias and prosody experiments (Snedeker & Trueswell 2004, Snedeker & Yuan 2008). The critical utterance was: *Tickle the pig with the fan.*

Both adults and five-year-old children were strongly swayed by the type of verb that was used in the instructions. When the verb was one that frequently appeared with an instrument phrase (3c), participants began looking at the potential instrument (e.g. a large fan) shortly after the onset of the prepositional object. When the verb was strongly biased to a modifier analysis (3a), participants focused in on the animal holding the object instead. In addition, verb biases strongly shaped the ultimate interpretation that the adults and children assigned to the prepositional phrase: instrument biased verbs resulted in actions involving the target instrument while modifier biased verbs resulted in actions on the target animal. Adults also incorporated referential constraints into their analyses, children showed little sensitivity to the referential manipulation. Although there was a weak effect of referential context on children's eye movements, their ultimate interpretation of the prepositional phrase was based exclusively on verb bias.

Recently Snedeker and Yuan (2008) built upon these findings by using the same sentences and paradigm to explore young children's and adults' use of prosody in online parsing. While prior studies of adult comprehension had found rapid effects of prosody on ambiguity resolution (Kjelgaard & Speer 1999, Snedeker & Trueswell 2003, Steinhauer *et al.* 1999), there was little information available about how adults combined prosodic and lexical cues and no evidence that young children made use of prosody to resolve syntactic ambiguity (Choi & Mazuka 2003). Two prosodic variants of each sentence were created. The modifier prosody had an intonational phrase (IP) break after the verb (*You can tap … the frog with the flower*) while the instrument prosody had an IP break after the noun (*You can tap the frog … with the flower*). The prosody of the sentence was fully crossed with the verb bias manipulation described above, resulting in six different conditions.

When large numbers of participants are tested, paradigms like these can provide detailed information about the time course of language processing. In this study we were able to look at how eye movements changed in 100 ms intervals starting at the beginning of the critical word (e.g. *fork* in 3a). We found that both the children and the adults made rapid use of prosody to interpret the ambiguous phrase. By 200 ms after the critical word began, adults who heard instrument prosody were already looking at the instrument more than those who heard modifier prosody. In children these effects were smaller and emerged a bit later (500 ms after the onset of the critical word). The effects of verb bias were also robust and rapid, indicating that lexical information plays a central role even when strong prosodic cues are present. In children the effect of verb bias appeared as soon as the critical word began (at 0 ms). Since eye movements take approximately 200 ms to programme and execute, this indicates that the children were using information about the verb to guide syntactic analysis immediately after encountering the preposition.

Taken together this set of studies suggests that children's online parsing is rapidly influenced by lexical and prosodic cues but is relatively impervious to referential cues. Snedeker and Yuan suggest that this pattern could reflect either (1) a developmental difficulty in employing top-down cues during comprehension; or (2) the failure of the parsing system to acquire a constraint which is only a weak predictor of syntactic structure (see Trueswell & Gleitman 2004 for discussion).

18.5   Syntactic priming

While most researchers have used online methods to explore the processes that are involved in language comprehension, these methods can also give us insight into the nature of children's linguistic representations. In our recent work on priming, Malathi Thothathiri and I have used an eye-movement paradigm to explore how children represent argument structure.[2]

Languages have systematic correspondences between syntactic relations, such as subject and object, and semantic categories, such as agent and patient or theme. These correspondences allow us to interpret who did what to whom, even when the verb in the sentence is novel. For example, in (4) we all know who the culprit is – even if we never encountered this particular verb and harbour no prejudices against motorists.

---

[2] Allen discusses argument structure in Ch. 13.

(4)   The driver doored the cyclist

Tomasello and colleagues have suggested that young preschoolers use templates based on the behaviour of individual verbs to guide comprehension and production (Tomasello 1992 and see Ch. 5). For example, a young child might have a template for the verb *hit* that captures the knowledge illustrated in (5) and another template for *pinch*, illustrated in (6)

(5)   ___x hit ___y, where X = hitter, Y = hittee

(6)   ___A pinch ___B, where A = pincher, B = pinchee

With these templates children would be able to interpret and produce new utterances with the same verb (such as *The taxi hit the delivery van*). But since the item-based templates do not include abstract syntactic and semantic relations, they would provide no guidance for interpreting utterances with novel verbs like that in (4). Thus, to evaluate children's linguistic representations, researchers typically examine children's comprehension and production of sentences with novel verbs. Almost two decades' worth of research has yielded mixed results and contrasting interpretations. Many novel-verb production studies show limited generalization in young children (Tomasello 2000c) but these results are contradicted by novel-verb comprehension studies that demonstrate robust generalization in children as young as 21 months of age (Gertner *et al.* 2006).

But both types of findings are open to alternate interpretations. Subtle aspects of verb meaning can constrain the use of verbs in sentence structures. For example, *Give me a cookie* is grammatical while *Pull me a cookie* is not (see Pinker 1989). Thus, children may fail at a novel-verb generalization task simply because they have failed to grasp the exact meaning of a new verb (Fisher, 2002a). Conversely, success at a novel-verb task could reflect the use of problem-solving strategies that are unique to novel stimuli, rather than the use of abstract representations (see Ninio 2005, Thothathiri & Snedeker 2008).

Most of the concerns about novel-verb studies stem from their placing children in situations where they are faced with unfamiliar linguistic input. Structural priming is a method by which we can circumvent these issues to explore how utterances with known verbs influence one another. This technique has long been used to investigate the representations that underlie language production in adults (Bock 1986). For example, adult participants are more likely to produce a passive sentence (e.g. *The man was struck by lightning*) after reading a passive sentence (e.g. *The president was confused by the question*) than after reading an active sentence (e.g. *The question confused the president*). Since the two constructions express the same semantic relations, priming can be attributed to syntactic representations or mappings between syntax and semantics. Furthermore, since priming occurs despite the fact that the primes and targets use different nouns and verbs, we can infer that adults have abstract representations that capture the similarities between these sentences.

Production priming has only recently been used to study the nature of children's linguistic abstractions. Some researchers have found evidence for abstract structural priming in three- and four-year-old children (Huttenlocher *et al.* 2004, Song & Fisher 2004). Others have not (Gamez *et al.* 2005, Savage *et al.* 2003).

Recently we developed a novel paradigm that combines structural priming and eye-gaze analyses to investigate priming during online comprehension. Since production tasks are often more difficult for children than comprehension tasks (Hirsh-Pasek & Golinkoff 1996), this may provide a more sensitive measure of children's linguistic knowledge. Because eye-gaze paradigms provide information about how an interpretation changes during processing, this method allows us to explore the locus of the priming effect and rule out alternate explanations that have been proposed for production priming (e.g. priming of the preposition *to*). Critically, this technique allows us to explore the representations that children use when understanding sentences with verbs that they already know. If children have item-specific representations (as assumed under the verb island hypothesis, see Ch. 5) then we would expect priming within verbs but not between verbs. In contrast if children have abstract syntactic or semantic categories, then we would expect to see between-verb priming.

The critical sentences in these studies used dative verbs. Dative verbs, such as *give*, *bring* or *send*, typically appear with three arguments: an agent, a recipient and a theme. In English there are two ways in which these arguments can be expressed, as shown in (7). In the prepositional object construction (7a) the theme appears as the direct object while the recipient is expressed by the prepositional phrase marked by *to*. In the double object construction (7b) the recipient is the direct object while the theme is expressed as a second noun phrase.

(7)   a. Tim gave a half-eaten pomegranate to Chris.
      b. Tim gave Chris a half-eaten pomegranate.

Datives are well-suited for developmental studies of priming. The two dative constructions have the same basic meaning and differ only in how the semantic roles get mapped onto syntactic elements. Thus, priming using datives offers a reasonably clear case of structural priming independent of semantics. In addition, both dative constructions are acquired quite early; children appear to comprehend and produce both forms by age three (Campbell & Tomasello 2001, Gropen, *et al.* 1989).

Children were given sets of trials which consisted of filler sentences, followed by two prime sentences, and then a target sentence. The primes were either direct object or prepositional object datives and the final target sentence was also a direct object or prepositional object dative. Our goal was to determine whether direct object and prepositional object datives would prime the interpretation of subsequent utterances that used a different verb and had no common content words. For example, would hearing *Send the frog the gift* facilitate comprehension of *Show the horse the book*?

To link this priming to eye movements we made use of a well-studied phenomenon in word recognition, the cohort effect (Marslen-Wilson & Welsh 1978). As a spoken word unfolds, listeners activate the lexical items that share phonemes with the portion of the word that they have heard. In the visual world paradigm, this process results in fixations to the referents of words that share phonemes with the target word (Allopenna *et al.* 1998). These effects are particularly strong at the beginning of a word, when all of the phonological information is consistent with multiple words (the members of this cohort). In our studies we used priming as a top-down constraint which might modulate the activation of different members of a phonological cohort.

The target trials were either double object (8a) or prepositional datives (8b).

(8) a. Bring the monkey the hat.
     b. Bring the money to the bear.

The set of toys that accompanied the utterance contained two items that were phonological matches to the initial part of the direct object noun. One was animate and hence a potential recipient (e.g. a monkey) while the other was inanimate and hence a more likely theme (e.g. some money). Thus the overlap in word onsets (e.g. *mon* …) created a lexical ambiguity which was tightly linked to a short-lived ambiguity in the argument structure of the verb. We expected that priming of the direct object dative would lead the participants to interpret the first noun as a recipient, resulting in more looks to the animate match, while priming of the prepositional object dative structure would lead them to interpret it as a theme, resulting in more looks to the inanimate match.

To validate our paradigm, we began by examining priming between utterances which shared the same verb (within-verb priming). Since both item-based grammars and abstract grammars posit shared structure between utterances with the same verb, within-verb priming would be consistent with either theory. We found that young four year olds showed robust within-verb priming during the ambiguous region. Young three year olds were slower in interpreting the target sentences, but when we expanded the analysis window to include the whole sentence, we found a reliable priming effect. Children who had heard double object primes were more likely to look at the potential recipient (the monkey) than children who had heard the prepositional object primes.

To examine the nature of the structures that children use, we conducted parallel experiments in which the prime and target utterances had no

(a) Abstract structural representations

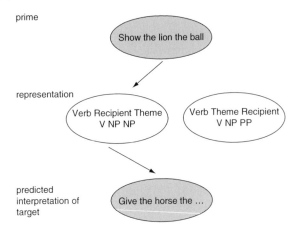

(b) Item-based frames

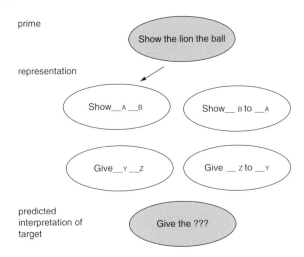

Figure 18.4 Predictions for the between-verb conditions in the priming experiment (Thothathiri & Snedeker 2008).

content words in common (between-verb priming). Under these circumstances the abstract grammars predict priming, while item-based grammars do not (see figure 18.4).

We found that both young four year olds and young three year olds showed between-verb priming. In the three year olds the effect of between-verb priming was almost as large as the effect of within-verb priming, indicating that there was no benefit gained when the two utterances shared a verb. This would suggest that abstract representations play a dominant role in online comprehension in this age group.

18.6   Current issues in children's sentence processing

In this chapter I have described a few studies which illustrate how eye-movement paradigms have been used to study children's sentence processing. The studies on ambiguity resolution demonstrate that four-year-old children, like adults, draw on information from multiple levels of linguistic representation to construct syntactic analyses. While children may fail to make use of some information (like referential context), they rapidly use both lexical and prosodic information to guide their interpretation of an ambiguous phrase. The priming studies demonstrate that children as young as three have abstract grammatical representations which they employ during online comprehension.

However both sets of studies leave many questions unanswered. What is the nature of these abstract representations? And do they shape comprehension in even younger children? Why do four and five year olds fail to revise syntactic misanalyses (Trueswell *et al.* 1999)? Do they fail to notice the error or are they incapable of fixing it? Do younger children also use lexical and prosodic information during parsing?

In the past decade, there has been considerable progress in the study of children's online language processing. In addition to the phenomena we describe here, other researchers have addressed word recognition (Fernald *et al.* 2008), morphological processing (Clahsen 2008), reference resolution (Sekerina *et al.* 2004, Song & Fisher 2005) and the calculation of pragmatic inferences (Huang & Snedeker, 2006), among other topics. Crosslinguistic work is gaining momentum (Choi & Mazuka, 2003; Clahsen 2008; Sekerina & Brooks 2007). New techniques are being developed. There is good reason to believe that the next ten years will bring us even closer to understanding how language comprehension develops.

Suggestions for further reading

Clahsen, H. (2008). Behavioral methods for investigating morphological and syntactic processing in children. In I. Sekerina, E. Fernández & H. Clahsen, (Eds.), *Developmental Psycholinguistics: Online Methods in Children's Language Processing.* (pp. 1–27). Amsterdam: Benjamins.

Fernald, A., Zangl, R., Portillo, A. L., & Marchman, V. A. (2008). Looking while listening: Using eye movements to monitor spoken language comprehension by infants and young children. In I. Sekerina, E. Fernández & H. Clahsen, (Eds.), *Developmental Psycholinguistics: Online Methods in Children's Language Processing.* (pp. 97–135). Amsterdam: Benjamins.

Snedeker, J., & Thothathiri, M. (2008). What lurks beneath: Syntactic priming during language comprehension in preschoolers (and adults). In I. Sekerina, E. Fernández & H. Clahsen (Eds.), *Developmental*

Psycholinguistics: OnLine Methods in Children's Language Processing (pp. 137–167), Amsterdam: Benjamins.

Trueswell, J., & Gleitman, L. R. (2004). Children's eye movements during listening: Evidence for a constraint-based theory of parsing and word learning. In J. M. Henderson & F. Ferreira, (Eds.). *The Interface of Vision, Language, and Action* (pp. 319–346). New York: Psychology Press.

19

Pragmatic development

Judith Becker Bryant

19.1 Introduction

When children are learning language, they must learn more than just phonology, semantics and syntax. Being a skilled language user means knowing how to use one's language appropriately and strategically in social situations. Children need to learn pragmatic skills, also referred to as communicative competence (Hymes 1967). They must learn how to make language work in interactions with their peers, families, teachers and others.

Many skills are involved in pragmatic competence because we use language for so many purposes. Children need to learn to ask questions, make requests, give orders, express agreement or disagreement, apologize, refuse, joke, praise and tell stories. They must learn routines such as *trick or treat* and *happy birthday* and polite terms such as *please* and *thank you, hello* and *goodbye, excuse me* and ways to address others. They must learn to initiate, maintain and conclude conversations; know when to speak or be quiet and how to take turns; to provide and respond effectively to feedback; and to stay on topic. They must know and use the appropriate volume and tone of voice. They need to learn how the meanings of terms such as *I* and *you* and *here* and *there* vary in meaning according to who is speaking and who is listening. They must learn what styles of speech to use; when to use jargon; and when and whether to talk about certain subjects. In some cultures, children must also learn complex forms that include informal and polite pronouns (e.g. *du* 'you' and *Sie* 'You (polite)' in German) or layered systems of terms and expressions (e.g. to convey degrees of respect and social distance in Japanese). With all of these skills, children must learn to be sensitive to their audience and to the situations in which they are communicating.

Audience and situation (i.e. communicative context) involve many levels. There is the immediate context that includes prior conversation, task and setting, relationship between speaker and listener, and listener characteristics. There are also broader contexts such as the culture or cultures in which children develop and communicate. To be competent and effective, all of these contexts must be taken into account.

In the following section I introduce two major theories that have influenced research on pragmatics. Then I discuss the development of pragmatic skills, difficulties in acquiring pragmatic competence, the role of family and others in helping shape pragmatic development and suggestions for future research.

19.2   Theories relevant to the study of pragmatic development

Two major theories that underlie work in pragmatics are speech act theory (Austin 1975) and Piaget's cognitive developmental theory.

19.2.1   Speech act theory

Philosopher John Austin (1975) argued that some sentences do not just describe or report information. Rather, when uttered in the appropriate circumstances by the appropriate individuals, they help speakers accomplish things in the world. For example, when the designated person says, "I now pronounce you man and wife" while conducting a marriage ceremony, that person is actually marrying a man and woman. Austin called such sentences *performatives* or speech acts. Speech acts include, for example, bets, requests, warnings, verdicts, promises and apologies.

Austin also suggested that speech acts have three components:

- the locutionary act, or the act of saying a sentence that makes sense and refers to something,
- the illocutionary act, or the speaker's purpose in saying that sentence,
- the perlocutionary act, or the effect of that sentence on a listener.

For example, a lady dining in a restaurant might say, 'I'm hungry' (a locutionary act). By this, she might intend to make a request for the waiter to take her order (an illocutionary act). The waiter might understand the diner to be making a simple statement of fact (the perlocutionary act). Alternatively, after eating a heavy meal another diner might say, 'I'm hungry', intending to be ironic, and the waiter might bring the dessert menu, concluding that this speaker is still hungry and is making an assertion or request. One needs context to determine what the function of a given sentence form might be.

Note that speech act theory does not deal specifically with children or language acquisition. Rather, it has provided researchers with ideas about which aspects of children's communication to study (i.e. which specific speech acts), the types of at least implicit knowledge children should acquire about communication, and the other competencies (e.g. the ability to draw inferences) that may underlie pragmatic competence.

19.2.2 Cognitive developmental theory

Also influential in the study of the development of pragmatic competence is Jean Piaget's cognitive developmental theory. Piaget introduced the notion of egocentrism. An example of egocentric behaviour is when a child waves at the telephone rather than saying *hello* to Grandma or talks about *the book* his teacher reads at school without explaining which book it was. In Piaget's view, egocentrism is the inability to take another person's point of view, the inability to recognize that others have different knowledge, feelings, thoughts and perceptions or to know what the different knowledge, feelings, thoughts and perceptions might be. In his 1926 book *The Language and Thought of the Child* (1974), Piaget argued that young children think and act more egocentrically than adults. An example of egocentric speech is when a child twice asks someone, "What did you say?" but never listens for an answer (Piaget 1974: 41). Non-egocentric sentences included information adapted to the listener's point of view as well as requests and threats. Piaget found that egocentric speech comprised nearly half of the spontaneous language of children aged four to seven years. He also found in experimental work that children called story characters *she* or *it* without explaining to whom they were referring, left out important information, and did not present events in the correct order, as if they assumed that their listeners already understood what they were talking about. From these data, Piaget concluded that young children are egocentric and unable to take their listeners' perspectives, that 'the effort to understand other people and to communicate one's thought objectively does not appear in children before the age of about 7 or $7\frac{1}{2}$' (Piaget 1974: 139).

Both speech act theory and Piaget's cognitive developmental theory stress the relevance of context for using and understanding language. For the speech act theorists, context meant the participants as well as the task or setting and prior conversation. For Piaget, context meant the immediate physical context as well as characteristics of the listener (e.g. listener knowledge). Subsequent researchers have investigated children in many contexts to see which contextual factors affect the children's language in order to assess specific claims and aspects of these theories.

19.3 The growth of pragmatic skills

It is precisely because pragmatic behaviours are so contextually sensitive that it is difficult to describe clear developmental progressions for each of them. Children usually perform differently in laboratory experiments than in everyday interaction and converse differently with strangers than with those who are more familiar, making it hard to define and assess the level of competence. This section therefore focuses on several domains which provide relatively clear information about development. The developments described are norms; there are of course many individual differences.

19.3.1   Infant speech acts

Infants demonstrate increasing evidence of communicative intent and acquire minimal pragmatic skills over the course of their first year (Clark 2003, Goldin-Meadow Ch. 9). Even before they begin to produce words, they are able to use gesture, intonation and phonemes to communicate requests for objects or actions, their desire to direct others' attention, as well as their refusal of objects or actions. The range of communicative functions infants can express increases dramatically along with their vocabulary (Bates 1976). Common pragmatic expressions such as *please, thank you, uh-oh, hello* and *bye* are typically acquired well before two years (Fenson *et al.* 1994).

One skill necessary for conversation, turn taking, has its roots in the first year. In many cultures, infants enjoy familiar caregiver–infant routines such as give-and-take games and peek-a-boo. Through these caregiver-driven routines, infants learn that particular responses follow specific caregiver behaviours (Reddy 1999).

19.3.2   Conversational skills
19.3.2.1   Taking turns

Although even young infants can alternate turns while communicating with adults, preschoolers rarely overlap turns. However, preschoolers lack the precise timing of turns that older children and adults exhibit. They tend to rely on obvious cues that a speaker has finished, rather than anticipating upcoming conversational boundaries, which often results in long pauses between turns (Garvey 1984). Turn-taking is particularly difficult for children when there are more than two speakers (Ervin-Tripp 1979).

Phrases such as the sentence-initial *and* and fillers such as *y'know* help older children hold the floor and keep their turns more effectively (Garvey 1984, Pan & Snow 1999). The timing of their turns is more precise, and there are fewer long pauses in their conversations. They also acquire the ability to interrupt by offering excuses. Skilled interrupting develops at least through adolescence.

19.3.2.2   Initiating and sustaining coherent conversation

With age, children get better at initiating and sustaining coherent conversations. Toddlers and young preschoolers may use simple strategies like repetition and recasts of their partners' utterances to keep the conversation going (Pan & Snow 1999). Older children can elaborate by adding new but relevant information to the previous speaker's turn (Garvey 1990, Ninio & Snow 1996). They can discuss their day's activities, have prolonged debates about the relative merits of different television shows and enjoy long conversations during pretend play.

Some types of conversations are particularly challenging, however. Conversations over the telephone pose problems for preschoolers even though they have many experiences using telephones (Warren & Tate 1992). Similarly, telephone systems that use interactive speech technology are challenging even for older children because of the vocabulary and conversational conventions they employ (Arunachalam *et al.* 2001).

One way to maintain a face-to-face conversation is to use cohesive devices. These provide ways to link talk to earlier parts of a conversation. Comprehension depends on making the link. For example, five-year-old Ben asks, "Where's Dad?" and his older brother Sam replies, "He's here." The pronoun (or anaphor) *he* helps connect parts of the conversation without the need to repeat a prior phrase ('Dad is here'). Children use anaphora more frequently with age but do not appear to understand it fully until the middle school years. Another linking device is ellipsis, in which a speaker omits part of what was said before. For example, Ben wonders, "Did the dog eat my toy?" When Sam says, "Yes, he did," the missing information ('eat your toy') can be found by referring to a more complete form earlier in the conversation.

Connectives such as *then, so,* and *because* become more frequent and diverse over the preschool years (Garvey 1984, McTear 1988) and beyond (see Berman Ch. 20). More complex forms such as *for example, though,* and *perhaps* that mark relationships among utterances are seldom produced until later adolescence (Hoyle & Adger 1998). This developmental progression applies to English; development of connectives depends in part on the complexity of forms used in a particular language.

19.3.2.3   Giving and responding to feedback

Longer, coherent conversations are also made possible by an increasing ability to convey understanding (or the lack thereof) and to repair conversations when they break down. Two year olds can repeat or verify their utterances when explicitly asked to do so in a familiar and natural situation. Preschoolers may sometimes issue and respond to queries requesting more specific responses. Bilingual preschoolers can switch languages to repair conversational breakdowns (Comeau *et al.* 2007). However, preschoolers are inconsistent and often inept at indicating that they do not understand when others' communication is unclear and at repairing their own speech, especially when their listener's feedback is not explicit or when the situation is unfamiliar or unnatural (Garvey 1984, Lloyd *et al.* 1998). These younger children are also poor at acknowledging that they do comprehend.

School-age children are better able to achieve mutual understanding in conversations. Once they are six, most children are able to mark corrections with phrases such as *I mean*, and they insert *uh-huh*, *right*, *I see* and head nods at appropriate moments to indicate continuing attention and satisfactory comprehension (Garvey 1984, Lloyd 1992). This type of response is referred to as back-channel feedback. During the middle school years and adolescence, children provide more feedback to listeners, with constructive interruptions such as "I know what you mean" promoting conversation. They can also respond appropriately even to subtle feedback such as listeners' quizzical expressions. However, such pragmatic competence continues to develop throughout the life span (Berman 2004a, Hoyle & Adger 1998, Ninio & Snow 1999, Pan & Snow 1999).

19.3.3 Non-egocentric language

In some of the earliest efforts to assess young children's pragmatic behaviour, researchers asked whether preschoolers communicate egocentrically. Using research procedures modelled after Piaget's, these researchers demonstrated that young children are able to take the perspective of the listener in certain circumstances. These studies investigated referential communication, the ability to describe an item from a set of similar items so that a listener can identify it (Lloyd 1992). An everyday example of referential communication is a child describing a particular book he wants his mother to retrieve from a shelf full of books.

O'Neill (1996) had two year olds ask a parent for help retrieving a toy. Children were more likely to name the toy or its location or to point to it when parents did not know its location than when they did. In other words, the children took the parents' knowledge into account when communicating. In contrast, preschoolers made unclear references (e.g. 'this one') and used gestures in trying to communicate with a 'talking' computer (Montanari *et al.* 2004). Preschoolers generally perform better in familiar situations than in experimental situations (Ninio & Snow 1999) and with familiar items (e.g. sets of animals) than unusual items (e.g. abstract shapes) (Yule 1997).

The research does not clearly answer the question of whether preschoolers are egocentric in their attempts to communicate. Their language depends on context. When preschoolers are familiar with a fairly simple, interesting task, their language does not appear to be completely egocentric. This conclusion is not inconsistent with Piaget's theory since Piaget observed that preschoolers sometimes use egocentric language and sometimes use more social language. That is, they may behave egocentrically in certain situations and are more likely to behave egocentrically than older children and adults, especially when the cognitive, linguistic and social demands on them are great.

19.3.4 Requests

Requests are interesting parts of pragmatic competence for at least two reasons. First, requests exemplify the distinctions Austin made among the three components of speech acts: locutionary, illocutionary and perlocutionary acts. Listeners must understand that very indirect, vague locutionary acts (e.g. *lunch time*) and very direct, explicit locutionary acts (e.g. *Get ready for lunch*) may have the same illocutionary purpose and perlocutionary effect. Adults are assumed to infer the meaning of indirect requests by considering both their form and the context of their use. Researchers are interested in whether young children also have this understanding and therefore investigate children's comprehension of indirect requests.

Second, effective speakers take context into account by varying the requests they use in different situations. Speakers have many forms of requests at their disposal, not only in terms of their direct and indirect structure, but in terms of whether they contain semantic aggravators (words or phrases that intensify the request; e.g. *or else, right now*) or semantic mitigators (words or phrases that soften the request; e.g. *please* or giving reasons). Researchers are thus interested in how children produce requests and whether they recognize the relationship between the forms and functions of requests (see Becker 1982, 1984).

19.3.4.1 Comprehension of indirect requests

Both observational and experimental studies indicate that preschoolers respond to indirect requests as requests for action. Two year olds respond as appropriately to requests their mothers phrase as questions as to those phrased directly (Shatz 1978), and three and four year olds respond with appropriate actions when, for instance, telephone callers ask, "Is your Daddy there?" and when someone hints, "It's noisy in here" (Ervin-Tripp 1977).

Other evidence that preschoolers treat indirect requests as requests for action is found in the way children normally refuse such requests. Garvey (1975) observed thirty-six preschool dyads. When children did not want to comply with indirect requests, they often justified and explained in terms of their inability to perform the requested act (e.g. "I can't"), lack of willingness (e.g. "I don't want to"), lack of obligation to comply (e.g. "I don't have to"), or their inappropriateness as the person being asked to comply (e.g. "No, you"). Their comments reveal not only that they viewed indirect requests as requests, but that they understood the conditions under which they could legitimately make requests and the conditions under which they should respond. Experiments also show that preschoolers understand the intent of indirect requests (Ervin-Tripp *et al.* 1987, Leonard *et al.* 1978).

It may be that indirect requests like hints are not very opaque or difficult for young children to understand. Because some indirect requests are so common in everyday speech, they may not require logical reasoning or the conscious consideration of form and context (Gordon & Ervin-Tripp 1984). Preschoolers may routinely hear requests such as "Lunch time" (meaning

'Clean up and wash your hands'), so that their intent has become obvious and the response automatic.

19.3.4.2 Production of Requests

Many contextual factors affect the forms of requests adults use in different situations. They include the roles of the two people conversing, whether the setting is personal or transactional, whether the requested action can normally be expected of the listener, and the relative status or power of the two people. Most of the research on children has focused on status.

In general, like adults, young children tend to address direct requests with semantic aggravators to listeners of lower status and indirect requests with semantic mitigators to listeners of higher status. For example, preschoolers are more likely to use an imperative (e.g. "Gimme an X") with a peer and a more indirect request (e.g. "May I have an X?" "Do you have an X?") with an adult (Ervin-Tripp 1977, Gordon & Ervin-Tripp 1984, Shatz & Gelman 1973). During role play, they have dominant puppets enact more direct requests than submissive puppets do (Andersen 2000). They even make more subtle differentiations, using requests that are more indirect with more dominant, bigger peers than with less powerful peers (Wood & Gardner 1980).

19.3.5 Pragmatic development during adolescence

As children move into adolescence, their expanding social worlds both enable and pressure them to display more sophisticated pragmatic skills. Experience with a greater variety of teachers and peers, exposure to more language forms gained from reading and schooling (Berman 2007), and participation in extracurricular activities such as sports teams and work motivate adolescents to take others' perspectives and use language strategically. Furthermore, pragmatic behaviour reflects normal advances in identity development and increasing autonomy from parents. The social contexts in which adolescents display pragmatic behaviour also expand to include such technologies as cellular (mobile) phones and the internet.

During adolescence, language assumes an especially significant role in marking identity. Appropriate use of current slang expressions and gestures unique to the peer group is critical. These behaviours mark solidarity with members of the groups to which teens belong and assert teens' separateness from other groups and from younger children and adults (Cooper & Anderson-Inman 1998, Greenwood 1998, Heath 1998). Knowing the current labels for the groups themselves and knowing ways of teasing and arguing gain importance in the teen years. Shifting among various registers and language varieties enables adolescents to align themselves with particular age, social class, racial and ethnic groups (Blum-Kulka 2004). Even gossip and verbal relational aggression function to forge teen alliances and manage social boundaries, discover peer norms and explore identity (Parker & Gottman 1989).

The technology available to adolescents affords new opportunities for social interaction. Pragmatic skill is required to shift adeptly among different styles of communicating depending on with whom one is communicating and whether one is speaking on the phone, text messaging or using the internet to communicate through instant messaging, chat rooms, email, social networking sites or blogs. Different terminology is appropriate to different modalities, and the anonymous modalities allow teens to construct identities by means of email addresses, screen names and selective sharing of information (Calvert 2002). Especially for younger adolescents with limited ability to meet peers outside of school, technology provides a mechanism for dyadic communication that promotes friendship as well as for simultaneous communication with many others that promotes group identity formation (Boneva *et al.* 2006).

Communication using technology is also structured differently from face-to-face communication. It offers greater privacy and control but may present more challenges for maintaining conversational coherence (Greenfield & Subrahmanyam 2003). Adolescents can keep multiple channels of communication open and (to some degree) monitor and participate in all of them simultaneously (Greenfield *et al.* 2006). Another difference is that, with chat rooms, related utterances are often separated by several turns of other conversations. Cellular (mobile) phones and the internet enable teens to defer conversations, communicate from almost anywhere at any time and save messages (Ling & Yttri 2006).

19.4   The difficulty of acquiring pragmatic competence

In contrast with morphological and syntactic rules, there are usually not strict rules for pragmatic competence (Abbeduto & Short-Myerson 2002, Becker 1990). Rather, in specific contexts, using or omitting a particular pragmatic behaviour is seen as relatively appropriate or inappropriate. For example, children do not always have to say *please* in order to be polite and appropriate. There are other ways to make polite requests, such as saying "May I watch TV?" The lack of strict prescriptive and proscriptive rules probably makes it difficult for children to learn whether and when to exhibit different behaviours.

Another factor that makes acquisition of pragmatic competence difficult is that many polite forms have no clear referents. That is, it is not obvious what a form such as *please* means. Furthermore, some forms such as *thank you* that seem to have a meaning (in this case, being thankful) are often supposed to be used in situations when their meaning is contradicted (such as when it is appropriate to thank someone who gives you a toy you already have) (Gleason *et al.* 1984). Therefore the learning process is probably different from that for other words.

Third, the conventions for competent communication in one setting (e.g. home) are often different from those in other settings (e.g. school). To the extent that these conventions are different, children may have trouble learning and adjusting to institutional settings and may also be judged negatively (see Section 19.6).

19.5 Influences on the acquisition of pragmatic competence

Acquiring pragmatic competence is difficult, but children have some help. There are a number of ways families and schools contribute to the acquisition process. Furthermore, children's cognitions, knowledge and efforts to learn about communication also facilitate their pragmatic development.

19.5.1 Socialization

In general, it can be said that caregivers 'socialize' language. They use language to help their children become competent members of their societies and cultures, competence reflected in part in the children's language usage (Ely & Gleason 1995, Schieffelin & Ochs 1996). Virtually from birth, infants begin to receive information about some of the pragmatic behaviours that will help them meet their social needs. Much of the structure of conversations may be learned in early interactions between infants and caregivers. Actions and talk (e.g. the use of *hello*, *please*, and *thank you*) are highly organized and predictable during social games or routines such as peekaboo and in give-and-take with objects. Such games provide children clear and consistent information about a small number of socially significant phrases. In these interactions, infants also learn about taking turns, the responsibilities of both participants to keep the interaction going, how to focus on a theme or topic, and how to make the interaction cohere. Caregivers find ways to pull their infants into the interaction, to help infants respond and participate, much as if they were having a conversation (Ninio & Snow 1996).

Once children exhibit some basic pragmatic competence, begin to participate more actively in interactions, and can anticipate sequences of behaviour in the routines, caregivers adapt their interactions (Becker 1990). A number of interesting studies have been conducted on how they do this during the preschool years.

Gleason and her colleagues (e.g. Snow *et al.* 1990) and others (e.g. Herot 2002) have observed that parents often prompt their children to produce appropriate pragmatic behaviours. In order to replicate and extend these findings, Becker (1994) conducted a one-year longitudinal study of five families. Parents audiotaped everyday interactions between themselves and their preschoolers in their homes, mostly at dinner time. Multiparty dinner table conversations appear to promote conversational and narrative skills as well as language socialization more generally (Blum-Kulka 1997, Ely *et al.* 2001). The results of the study showed, first, that parents commented about a wide variety of pragmatic behaviours. They provided input about what children were expected to say (e.g. *please*, *goodbye* and address terms), how children were expected to speak (using the appropriate volume, tone of voice and clarity), when children should speak, and how to stay on topic.

Parents also used a variety of strategies in their comments about and reactions to their preschoolers' pragmatic behaviours:

- prompt
  - direct comment on omission (e.g. "Say 'excuse me' when you cough")
  - indirect comment on omission (e.g. "What's the magic word?")
  - direct comment on error (e.g. "Don't talk with your mouth full")
  - indirect comment on error (e.g. "What did you say?")
  - anticipatory suggestion (e.g. "Don't forget to say 'night-night' to Daddy")
- model
  - provide the appropriate behaviour before the child has the opportunity to produce it (e.g. "Excuse me" as the child coughs)
  - comment on younger sibling's behaviour (e.g. Mother: "What do you say?" Infant: "Thank you." Mother: "You're welcome. Very good!")
  - demonstrate prompts and behaviours as instruction (e.g. Father: "Go get my milk." Mother: "Well, what do you say?" Father: "Please.")
- verbally reinforce following preschoolers' appropriate usage (e.g. "I like the way you say [X]")
- pose a hypothetical situation for didactic purposes (e.g. "What would you say if that ape came up to you and said 'hi'?")
- evaluate retroactively (e.g. "She said her prayers [earlier at lunch] all by herself! Word for word, too. I'm really happy about that.")
- address child's comment (e.g. Child: "It's a bad word, 'ugly'. " Mother: "It's not a bad word, you just use it wrong.")
- evaluate another (e.g. "Right, Jane?")

One of the provocative aspects of these findings is that most of the parents' input was indirect. Specifically, parents' indirect comments on errors and omissions comprised an average of 61 per cent of the total input (49–91 per cent across the families). Indirectness seems a risky way to teach pragmatic competence, because children might not understand what they are supposed to do. The finding that so much parental input is indirect is counterintuitive, because parents believe that displaying competence is important and a reflection of their own socialization competence (Becker & Hall 1989, Bryant 1999). One would think that parents would be explicit in order to maximize the chances of their children performing correctly. Although these are not experimental findings and therefore causal conclusions cannot be drawn, it is likely that indirectness challenges children more cognitively and provides more information about pragmatic conventions than does direct, explicit input (Becker 1988). In fact, mothers of preschoolers believe that indirect responses place cognitive burdens on children by helping them 'to think rather than just parrot' and 'figure it out on [their] own' (Bryant 1999: 134).

The research reported above focuses primarily on middle-class, American families because that is the population on which most of the research has been done. It is important to note that societies and cultures vary greatly with respect to characteristics of caregiver–child interactions, the pragmatic behaviours they value, and the means by which they socialize pragmatic behaviours (Genesee et al. 2004, Schieffelin & Ochs 1986). However, the children ultimately acquire pragmatic competence that is appropriate to their culture.

19.5.2   Fathers and siblings

A number of researchers have suggested that different family members contribute to the acquisition of pragmatic competence in different and potentially important ways. That is, family members who know the child less intimately (e.g. fathers who are secondary caregivers) or who lack the capacity and motivation to tune in to the child's needs (e.g. older siblings) may pressure the child to communicate clearly and appropriately more than would family members who know the child most intimately (e.g. mothers who are primary caregivers) (Barton & Tomasello 1994, Gleason 1975, Mannle & Tomasello 1987, Rondal 1980). Fathers and siblings, in this view, challenge children to adapt and broaden their communicative skills and thus prepare them to talk with strangers and about unfamiliar topics. Thus, fathers and siblings may serve as 'bridges' to the outside world, "leading the child to change her or his language in order to be understood" (Gleason 1975: 293).

There is some evidence to support the bridge hypothesis. Relative to mothers, fathers of infants have been observed to have more breakdowns in communication, spend less time focused on the same object or action, be less successful at tuning in to their children's current focus of attention, make more off-topic replies, and request clarification more often (Mannle & Tomasello 1987, Tomasello et al. 1990). Fathers of preschoolers have also been found to use more imperatives with their children than do mothers (Gleason 1975, Malone & Guy 1982). A meta-analysis demonstrated that, across studies, mothers are more supportive (e.g. they praise, acknowledge) in their speech than fathers (Leaper et al. 1998).

Older siblings are even less tuned in and conversationally responsive than fathers. In general, siblings are more directive, less responsive and less adept than their mothers at using techniques for maintaining conversations with younger siblings and at taking into account the infants' conversational immaturity (Hoff-Ginsberg & Krueger 1991, Mannle *et al.* 1991, Tomasello & Mannle 1985).

Siblings can influence pragmatic competence in additional ways. Some researchers argue that children are motivated to participate in conversations between their mothers and older siblings. Therefore, they learn how to enter conversations effectively (Barton & Tomasello 1991) as well as to maintain a topic and take turns in such complex, triadic conversations (Barton & Tomasello 1994, Hoff-Ginsberg & Krueger 1991). Younger siblings also have the opportunity to observe conversations between their mothers and older siblings and are thereby exposed to a variety of communicative styles.

If siblings influence the acquisition of pragmatic competence, one would expect first-born children to differ from later-born children in their communicative skills. Hoff-Ginsberg (1998) investigated this possibility with one-and-a-half to two-and-a-half year olds. Although, as previous research has shown, the first-born children exhibited more advanced lexical and grammatical development, the later born children had more advanced conversational skills in interactions with their mothers.

There are several limitations in the literature reported above. First, causal conclusions cannot be drawn because the research is descriptive and correlational. Neither experimental studies nor interventions have been implemented to test the influences of families on the acquisition of pragmatic competence. Second, there are many variations across families with similar configurations (Mannle & Tomasello 1987). Not all mothers behave the same way, nor do all fathers or all siblings. For example, Davidson and Snow (1996) failed to find that middle-class, highly educated fathers of nursery school children used more challenging language than mothers. One must also exercise caution in generalizing results of studies of relatively few families. Third, context influences parental behaviour to a greater extent than parental gender does (Lewis 1997). The setting, the task, and other situational characteristics strongly affect how family members interact with children.

19.5.3 Peers

Children are also exposed to multiparty conversations with peers, often in the context of daycare or school. Multiparty conversations allow children to hear more talk, hear greater varieties of talk, and observe and assume different conversational roles than in dyadic conversation (Blum-Kulka & Snow 2002). Such conversations require children to deal with participants' limited background knowledge and to be assertive and clever in finding ways to participate. Peers probably affect pragmatic competence in a variety of ways. They may be similar to siblings as relatively uncooperative conversational partners, and thus contribute to the pressure preschoolers feel to communicate more clearly and effectively (Mannle & Tomasello 1987). Interactions with peers are frequent, sustained and emotionally engaging, and so provide a developmental context that promotes narrative and other pragmatic skills (Nicolopoulou & Richner 2004). Peers also participate in forms of communication that are different from those of adults speaking to children (Blum-Kulka & Snow 2004, Ely & Gleason 1995), but, like adults, may correct peers' pragmatic behaviour (Nakamura 2001). Their special kinds of humour and disagreements, the topics about which they talk, and their explicit socialization about language provide communicative experiences that no doubt complement those experienced with adults.

19.6   The importance of pragmatic skill

Pragmatic skills are important to children's lives. Pragmatic competence predicts later academic skills, is necessary for understanding and functioning in the classroom, and is associated with greater liking by peers and adults.

First, some aspects of preschoolers' pragmatic behaviour are predictive of (and may in fact prepare children for) later literacy (Reeder *et al.* 1996) and mathematical achievement. For example, narrative skills may provide a bridge to print literacy because they can promote the enjoyment of stories and help children learn about the structure and linguistic conventions of stories (Griffin *et al.* 2004, Snow 1994, Snow *et al.* 2007). Skill at structuring narratives and elaborating plots is associated with subsequent reading and writing abilities. Reeder and his colleagues have found a relationship between pragmatic awareness and early writing ability (Reeder & Shapiro 1997). They argue that having the metalinguistic skills to attribute intentions and motives to speakers (to comprehend implicit meanings) may help children develop the ability to understand written language that provides no clues from social interactions (Reeder & Shapiro 1996). Similarly, Snow and Blum-Kulka (2002) suggest that the ability to take multiple perspectives in multiparty conversations aids in text comprehension. There is also some evidence that preschoolers' narrative performance predicts their mathematical ability two years later (O'Neill *et al.* 2004).

Second, children who are pragmatically skilled function better in school (Greenwood *et al.* 2002, Snow & Blum-Kulka 2002) and other evaluative contexts. Children must learn when and how to speak and respond to teachers and peers, how to address teachers, to display their knowledge and obtain information appropriately, to comprehend indirect language (such as knowing that when teachers say "Use your words" they usually intend that children solve conflicts verbally rather than physically), and to modify their behaviour appropriately in different school settings (e.g. playground, cafeteria, classroom). Throughout the life span, pragmatic competence (or the lack thereof) affects teachers' judgments of children's abilities and motivations (Becker *et al.* 1991, Rice 1993) as well as children's opportunities for learning through interactions with peers and teachers (Rice 1993, Silliman & Wilkinson 1991).

The relevance of pragmatic behaviour in schools is particularly salient when the conventions of the classroom are different than those of the home. Cultures vary in how and when children may converse with adults, ask questions, display knowledge, make eye contact, wait for others' responses and use volume. However, teachers evaluate children using the communicative patterns of the culture with which they are most familiar, commonly the majority culture (e.g. Genesee *et al.* 2004, Philips 1993). When the pragmatic practices of home and school are more compatible, children are more comfortable and display their pragmatic competencies more effectively.

Finally, pragmatic competence is important because children who are pragmatically competent are better liked than those who are less skilled. Many researchers have shown that children who are skilled at gaining entry to ongoing social interactions and who are verbally responsive are more popular than children who are less skilled (Dodge *et al.* 1983, Samter 2003). It is advantageous to be able to employ such verbal strategies as greeting, suggesting, asking to join in and making substantive contributions to the interaction (Craig & Washington 1993). Furthermore, Hazen and her colleagues (Black & Hazen 1990, Kemple *et al.* 1992) have shown that three-and-a-half to five-and-a-half year olds who are well liked by their peers (as contrasted with those who are disliked) are better able to initiate and maintain cohesive conversations. These children clearly direct their communication to specific peers, respond appropriately when others try to communicate with them, and can attend to two playmates rather than just focusing on one of them. Other researchers have obtained similar findings for younger (Black & Logan 1995, Gertner *et al.* 1994) as well as older children (Brinton & Fujiki 1995, Place & Becker 1991).

It has been found that in adolescence, those who convey allegiance to the group by using more inclusive pronouns and asking questions are viewed as better peer leaders than those teens who simply talk more. Cassell *et al.* (2006) drew this conclusion from an innovative study of approximately 300 teens participating in an online international junior summit. They analysed messages posted prior to the election of delegates. Not surprisingly, teens and young adults skilled in negotiation and persuasion are more successful professionally (Nippold 1998).

The causal relationship between pragmatic competence and popularity is complex (Black & Logan 1995). Kemple *et al.* (1992) argued that some pragmatic skills (such as the ability to make relevant comments and respond positively and contingently to peers) contribute to young children's initial popularity. Then, further differences in communication skills emerge after children's reputations as being popular or unpopular are established. Unpopular children may avoid communicating with peers in order to avoid rejection. Their poor pragmatic skills serve to maintain their lower status and may preclude their involvement in positive interactions that would help them learn better skills and develop better self-concepts.

19.7   Challenges for conducting research on pragmatic development

In conclusion, future research would benefit from reflection about a number of issues that pose challenges to research in this domain.

1. Serious consideration should be given to the characteristics of context that matter for pragmatic behaviour. Despite the centrality of this construct for pragmatics (and, indeed, all of social science), it has received surprisingly little examination.
2. Even more than with other aspects of behaviour, there is a tension between the use of naturalistic and experimental methods. Both obviously provide complementary types of information, and researchers must keep in mind the potential influence of task on language. For various reasons, many pragmatics researchers are biased towards observational methods.
3. Related to this bias is a tendency to use small samples that yield a great deal of detailed information. Small samples, of course, are potentially unrepresentative.
4. Transcripts may not provide the contextual and paralinguistic details necessary to code pragmatic behaviour accurately. Examples of this problem come from longitudinal data collected by DeHart (1999).
   - "Gee, that's a great idea!" may be a compliment or sarcastic remark.
   - "I really like cows" may be an assertion or an indirect request.
   - "I know!" in response to a partner's comment "And here's a roof for the gas station" may be an expression of sudden insight or a derisive remark about complete obviousness.

   In all three examples, transcripts suggested different coding than videos did.

Suggestions for futher reading

Blum-Kulka, S., & Snow, C. (Eds.). (2002). *Talking to Adults: The Contribution of Multiparty Discourse to Language Acquisition*. Mahwah, NJ: Lawrence Erlbaum Associates.

Kraut, R., Brynn, M., & Kiesler, S. (Eds.). (2006). *Computers, Phones, and the Internet*. New York: Oxford University Press.

Ninio, A., & Snow, C. (1996). *Pragmatic Development*. Boulder, CO: Westview Press.

Piaget, J. (1926/1974). (M. Gabain, trans.) *The Language and Thought of the Child*. New York: New American Library.

20

Language development in narrative contexts

Ruth A. Berman

20.1 Introduction

This chapter considers children's language beyond the boundaries of single utterances in naturalistic speech or of isolated sentences in structured elicitations. Narrative discourse is particularly appropriate for this purpose, since it emerges early in child language in the context of highly scaffolded conversational interchanges (Miller & Sperry 1988, Ninio 1988). Yet children's narratives manifest autonomous text construction only at late preschool age; it takes until around age 9 to 10 years before they demonstrate well-formed global-level organization of narrative structure (Hickmann 1995, Peterson & McCabe 1983); and rhetorical expressiveness consolidates only in adolescence and adulthood (Berman & Nir-Sagiv 2007, Berman & Slobin 1994). Narratives thus provide an advantageous site for tracing the long developmental route from emergence to mastery in language acquisition (Berman 2004b). Second, narratives are a universal type of discourse, familiar to children raised in oral as well as literate cultures (Bavin 2004, de León in press). They thus embody a special relation between the presumably universal mode of thought defined by Bruner's (1986) 'landscape of action' and the impact of typological factors on language-particular modes of expression (Slobin 1982, 2004).

Third, while canonic narratives – at least in western cultures – are all organized around a shared 'action structure' with an initial setting, episodes, resolution and coda (Labov 1972, van Dijk 1980), they cover numerous sub-genres, both fictive (romance, mystery, etc.) and veridical (autobiography, history, etc.). This varied range is reflected in cross-sectional research on children's elicited narratives, including: personal-experience accounts of children aged 3 to 10 years (Peterson & McCabe 1983) and from middle childhood to adolescence (Berman & Nir-Sagiv 2007, Ravid & Berman 2006); stories based on short picture series (Hickmann 2003, Karmiloff-Smith 1979, Nelson 1986); and the 'frog story' picture storybook (Berman & Slobin 1994, Strömqvist & Verhoeven 2004). Narrative discourse has thus come to supplement interactive conversational contexts as a favoured site for language acquisition research with a usage-based approach to child language, where linguistic forms – grammatical morphemes, lexical expressions, syntactic constructions – are examined in relation to the functions they perform in extended discourse.[1]

20.2 Narrative-embedded use of linguistic forms

A key theme of this chapter derives from Slobin's (1973) insight that, with age, new forms are recruited to meet old functions while, concurrently, new functions are realized by familiar linguistic means. This is illustrated in (1) through (3) below by three linguistic categories in the 'frog story' narrative sample (Berman & Slobin 1994): prepositions (*in, on, after*), the English suffix *-ing* and the connective *and*.

(1) Developmental phases in use of prepositions:
1. Spatial [with Concrete Noun]: *in the jar, on the floor, run after the bees*
2. Temporal [with Time/Event Noun]: *in the morning, on that day, after breakfast*
3. Temporal/Causal [with Gerundive]: *in running, on waking, after finding it*
4. Manner/Cause [with Abstract Noun]: *in fun, on his flight, after the discovery*

Several related patterns emerged in this domain. First, with age, children use a wider variety of prepositions to express locative and other relations between predicates and their associated noun phrases, reflecting the general developmental trend to greater lexical specificity (for example, *in, inside, into, within*). Second, they assign more, and more abstract, meanings to familiar terms, so that each of the prepositions in (1) acquires more complex semantic functions. Third, they use these lexical items in different morphosyntactic environments, with gerunds and derived nominals. Functionally, such constructions play a role in narrative **connectivity** – through nonfinite subordination with gerundives – and narrative **evaluation** – through complex adverbials of manner (*in fun, with care*), cause (*on his flight* = *as a result of his fleeing*), and temporality (*after the discovery* = *after he discovered*). Moreover, these quite basic, early acquired prepositions, when used in less frequent, more sophisticated contexts like (1.3) and (1.4), serve for stylistic elevation through higher register, more literate forms of expression.

---

[1] This chapter focuses on the relation between linguistic forms and narrative functions, adopting what Nicolopoulou (1997) calls a 'formalist' psycholinguistic analysis rather than the interpretive, socio-cultural approaches that she advocates, and see, too, Bamberg (in press), Blum-Kulka (2005).

Consider, next, the suffix *-ing*. One of the first bound morphemes acquired by English-speaking children, its use changes markedly with age, as shown in (2).

(2) Changing form/function relations of the English suffixal *-ing*:
  1. Bare main verb:
      And that he – floating off, uh – sitting down [3;3]
      And here, he trying to get the bees [3;11]
  2. Complement of verbs of perception or aspectual verbs:
      I see him snoring [4;9]
      He kept on calling frog [5;10]
  3. Noun Modification – truncated relative clauses:
      The dog was shaking the tree with the beehive hanging from it [9;10]
      The dog is curious about some bees flying overhead [Adult]
  4. Sentence Modification – non-finite adverbial clauses:
      The deer carried him to the edge of a cliff, with his dog chasing after [9;1]
      The three were just sitting around doing nothing [Adult-d]

As with prepositions in (1), development occurs concurrently in syntactic context, semantic content and narrative function. Early, ungrammatical use of bare *-ing* forms without a tensed auxiliary *be*, as in (2.1) reflects young children's tendency to view (present) progressive as the unmarked, basic form of picture-based storytelling. Subsequently, these non-tensed forms are used grammatically, to construct an early type of complement structure (2.2). Later still, they serve for non-finite clause-linkage to create a tightly cohesive type of 'syntactic packaging' (2.3 – and see also Section 20.3.3). At the most advanced phase, non-finite adverbial clauses provide background information to the events described in the preceding clause, so that a linear sequence like *The deer carried him to the edge of the cliff, and/ while/as his dog chased after* may be replaced by a more tightly fused construction in the non-finite subordinate clause *with his dog chasing after* in (2.4).

As a third example, consider the basic coordinating conjunction *and*, examined in children's narrative usage in English (Peterson & McCabe 1988), French (Jisa 1985), and Hebrew (Berman 1996). It, too, serves different, and more varied functions with age, as delineated in (3).

(3) Phases in emerging use of the coordinating conjunction 'and':
  | Phase position / Function | Intention signalled |
  I Utterance-Initial /   'I have more to say:'
      Announcing – in the same conversational turn
  II Clause-Initial /   'Something else / more happened'
      Chaining – in chronological sequence
  III Text-Embedded /   'The events or states are related'
      Chunking – within a given discourse topic

As depicted in (3), use of the coordinating conjunction *and* progresses from the behavioural unit of utterance, to the syntactic unit of clause and on to the discourse unit of text-segment. This reflects a shift from initial associative, communicatively motivated declaration that the speaker is still engaged in talk, to temporal chaining of clauses in sequence and thence to mature syntactic packaging. In monologic narrative contexts, use of *and* reveals a U-shaped developmental curve: three and four year olds use it relatively little as a syntactic connector between temporally related texts (Phase II above); subsequently it may be over used, as a favoured means of chaining clauses – often with a more specific sequential term (e.g. *and then, after that*); and eventually, in more mature narrative texts, *and* is used only occasionally for clause-linkage. For proficient narrators, it is superfluous for marking sequentiality, which they recognize as the default case for narrative temporality, so not needing to be overtly marked.

These examples illustrate a key feature of language development that I have argued elsewhere for various domains in Hebrew (Berman 1986, 2004a). Linguistic forms often emerge early on, typically in the preschool years, but their development manifests a lengthy route via acquisition to mastery.

20.3   Expression of discourse functions in different narrative domains

This section takes narrative functions rather than linguistic forms as the point of departure for analysis: reference to participants in a story – by means of nominal constructions like lexical NPs and pronouns (Section 20.3.1; narrative temporality – through the verbal categories of Tense, Aspect, Mood (Section 20.3.2); and discourse connectivity – by devices for clause linkage (Section 20.3.3).

20.3.1 Reference
The term 'reference' serves here in the narrow sense of relating to entities mentioned in a piece of discourse. Linguistically, reference can be realized by lexical noun phrases – proper nouns, common nouns and complex noun phrases with adjectives, prepositional phrases and/or relative clauses – and also by personal, reflexive and indefinite pronouns, by argument ellipsis, repetition or lexical substitution. Hickmann (2003: 5) provides powerful arguments from this domain for why 'the basic unit of analysis must go beyond the sentence' since 'context dependence is a fundamental property of language'. Narratives are well suited to studying acquisition of referring expressions. For one thing, stories necessarily involve protagonists and report on events that occur to characters (people, animals, robots). In order for interlocutors to know who or what is being talked about as the narrative unfolds, these characters need to be suitably

introduced as new participants in the story, re-referred to by maintaining reference to them, or marked by shifting reference to other participants. In extended discourse, referring expressions constitute 'cohesive ties' (Halliday & Hasan 1976) that serve to link utterances together in a text.

In acquiring reference, children need to integrate local and global processes of text construction, to achieve both linguistic cohesion between utterances and discourse coherence across the text (Hickmann 2004). This involves knowledge of such apparently disparate linguistic domains as determiners and pronouns, null subjects, and dislocations (Berman 1990, Karmiloff-Smith 1981), which then need to be re-represented in integrating bottom-up and top-down processes of text construction (Karmiloff-Smith 1983). Narrative reference thus demands a combination of linguistic and cognitive abilities, including: the distinction between deixis and anaphora and between given and new information (Hickmann 2003, Hickmann *et al.* 1995), awareness of shared information between narrator and interlocutor (Kail & Hickmann 1992, Kail & Sanchez y Lopez 1997), and hence, too, command of a 'theory of the listener' (Berman & Slobin 1994).

Three year olds make use of a range of means for making reference in different languages, including articles and determiners, lexical noun phrases, different kinds of pronouns and person marking on verbs, and zero anaphora (e.g. Bamberg 1986, Karmiloff-Smith 1980, McGann & Schwartz 1988). These devices may be used correctly at the local level of individual utterances or isolated sentences, yet it takes many years to acquire command of reference at a more global discourse level, where account needs to be taken of the text as a single entity or unified whole. In elicited narratives, young preschoolers tend to use pronouns deictically rather than as anaphoric means of achieving textual cohesion, reflecting the fact that they treat narratives as essentially interactive and are as yet unable to take adequate account of interlocutor knowledge. For example, in picture-series descriptions, children may maintain reference by paralinguistic means such as pointing to the characters in the different pictures, they may use deictic picture-oriented terms like *this, that, here*, or else resort to definite and indefinite expressions in a way that appears fairly random (Karmiloff-Smith 1981, Katzenberger 1994, Reilly 1992).

These features of early narrative reference are illustrated by the text of an English-speaking child aged 3;8, based on the 'frog story' booklet (Berman & Slobin 1994: 59), with animate referring expressions underlined.

(4) *It's **a bee**. There's a dog. And there's a frog, and slippers, and another slipper, and there's boots. He's wake up! They put her head in the pot.* Going down. *The dog barked, and here they calling frog. There's bees. And the hole in the tree. Ack!! A owl. And he's running through there and he fell off. Look, oh, he's up there! He's awake. He fell off – in the pool. And there's no head. Then there's a frog. See, he caughted a frog.*

Compare this with (5), the introduction to the same story told by a 10 year old, who uses indefinite noun phrases to introduce the three characters and definite or pronominal reference for recurrent mentions, distinguishing between the boy and the frog by *he* versus *it* (Berman & Slobin 1994: 69).

(5)   There's *a boy* who has *a pet frog* and *a pet dog*, and one night after *he* goes to bed, *the frog* sneaks out. And *he* wakes up and *it's* gone. So *he* and *his dog* look all over the place for *it*. So then *they* go outside and start calling for *it*.

It might be easier for young children to make it clear who they are talking about in their personal-experience accounts, where the narrator is the chief protagonist, so allowing deictic reference and shifts to only one or two other participants. Yet toddlers have difficulty making unambiguous use of referring expressions even in their conversation-embedded narratives, as illustrated by the interchanges in (6) between a mother and her 26-month-old daughter (from Hudson 1993) and in (7) between an investigator and a rather older child (from Peterson & Dodsworth 1991) – with referring expressions again underlined.

(6)   M: Did *you* go swimming in the lake?
      C: Yeah! *I* was running and swimming with *Daddy*.
      M.   With *Daddy*?
      C.   *I* can't swim. But when *I'm* with *Daddy*, *he* kept putting *me* in. *I* can't swim with *him* either.
      M.   **You** can't swim with *who*?
      C.   And *Laura* was there.
      M.   *Laura* was there?
      C.   Yes, and *the two of us* were stepping in the pool.

The interchange in (6) shows that reference specification is difficult for very young children even in highly scaffolded contexts, where considerable shared knowledge with a primary caretaker can be assumed. This difficulty is exacerbated in narratives elicited by an outside investigator, as in (7).

(7)   I.   Can *you* tell me about the barbecue that *you* had?[2]
      C.   We had a barbecue right over here, and *I* told **him** to don't put it … and *I* told *Dan* what *he* was doing. And …
      I.   *You* told *Dan* what **he** was doing?
      C.   Yeah. And when *I* was doing it, *I* turned, pushed *him*, what *I* do, pushed way up high.
      I.   *You* pushed *him* way up high?
      C.   Yes, but *he* turned to go.
      I.   But *he* what?
      C.   **He** turned to go on *me*. *He* didn't come to *my house*.

---

[2]   Different cues might be available to children acquiring morphologically richer languages. For example, in Hebrew, second person pronouns are differentiated for gender (masculine *ata*, feminine *at*) and number (plural *atem*).

As the authors clearly state, 'an almost total lack of identifying referents for her pronouns makes this an incomprehensible narrative' (Peterson & Dodsworth 1991: 412). Such difficulties are compounded when narratives are elicited by methods requiring more autonomous, monologic text construction, as in (4) and (5).

Most psycholinguistically motivated research on narrative reference is based on picture-series elicitations, including the pioneering studies undertaken from rather different perspectives by Karmiloff-Smith (1979, 1981) and Maya Hickmann (1980, 1982), as well as in the work of Nelson and her associates (Nelson 1986).[3] Other studies on reference have used the 'frog story' picture booklet to examine how children compared with adults refer to the protagonists in the same story (for example, Bamberg 1987, in German, Bavin 2000, in Warlpiri, Berman 1990, in Hebrew, Wigglesworth 1990, in English).

Findings of this rich research base have yielded *conflicting interpretations*. For example, Karmiloff-Smith (1981) found that from around six years of age, children rely on 'a thematic subject strategy' as a top-down process for linking utterances across the text: they use the same pronoun all along to refer to a single major protagonist. In contrast, Bamberg's (1986, 1987) analyses indicate that even three year olds can use this strategy, in line with other studies that claim to show very early command of referential forms (e.g. Bennet-Kastor 1983). The bulk of research in this domain, however, suggests that reference to entities (in a story) is a late-developing ability. Thus, using different elicitation materials, the studies of Karmiloff-Smith (1981, 1987), of Hickmann and her associates (e.g. Hickmann 1987, 1995, Hickmann & Liang 1990, Kail & Hickmann 1992), Wigglesworth's 'frog story' (1990) analysis, as well as those of the present author and her associates (e.g. Berman & Katzenberger 1998, Katzenberger 1994) indicate that it takes children until 9 or 10 years of age, or even beyond, to master the system – in the sense of being able to introduce, maintain, and shift reference to characters both appropriately and unambiguously.

Hickmann (1995: 206) concludes from her review of 'diverging findings' for development of anaphoric referential strategies that these highlight 'the importance of adequate control in studies of children's discourse organization'. Thus, Kail and Hickmann (1992) found that 'a direct comparison of narratives produced in the presence versus the absence of mutual knowledge shows that only 9-year-old children differentiate the two situations systematically, while younger children use deixis in both'. Along different lines, Shapiro and Hudson's (1991) comparison of preschool and first-grade children's performance on two types of picture-series stories – one 'event based' with merely sequential structure and the other

---

[3] Specially designed picture series have also been used in doctoral dissertations examining children's developing reference in different languages, including in Cantonese (To Kit Sum 2006) and Hebrew (Katzenberger 1994).

a 'problem-based' story – showed that in the event-based version, children used simpler pronominal reference strategies compared with the more sophisticated linguistic devices they applied in constructing a problem-based story. These studies support Hickmann's (2003: 175–183) conclusion that 'pervasive methodological problems' underlie the study of child language in general and of acquisition of referring expressions in particular.

A rather different, though not inconsistent, explanation for these divergent findings emerges from the question of what is meant by 'knowing' and being able to use such knowledge. A domain-general developmental progression that addresses this question is articulated in Karmiloff-Smith's (1992) model of representational redescription (RR) via reiterated developmental phases – from an initial phase focused on external data, via an internally driven phase, and on to an integrative reconciliation between internal representations and external data – with knowledge at each phase represented and re-represented at four different levels. Against this background, I have argued that the process of linguistic development involves a protracted route from early emergence via acquisition on to mastery in different linguistic domains (Berman 2004a) and in different narrative settings (Berman 1995). Discourse-embedded command of referring expressions involves a complex process of re-organization of linguistic knowledge, rather than a one-step transition from, say, deixis to anaphora, or a simple shift from bottom-up to top-down processing or between local and global command of narrative reference.

The protracted path of reference acquisition and the fact that it is mastered relatively late cannot be explained in terms of complexity of linguistic structure alone. Rather, as noted in section 20.3.1, reference is a **cognitively demanding** domain, requiring such late-developing abilities as: memory retention across stretches of extended discourse; clear grasp of the distinction between new and given information; understanding of mutual knowledge; and the ability to provide sufficient, non-redundant information about who is being referred to at each point in the unfolding story. Coordinating all these facets of information processing along with encoding them by appropriate means of linguistic expression is a formidable task for children, even at school age.

Besides, there is **no one correct way** of referring to participants in a narrative. Wigglesworth's (1997) analysis of Australian English 'frog story' texts produced by 4 to 10 year olds compared with adults shows that participants across age-groups select a range of strategies for referring to characters in their narratives, although proportions differed with age. For example, while the youngest children alone consistently preferred a thematic-subject strategy in referring to the boy as main protagonist, this strategy was favoured by nearly half the 10 year olds, but by only one adult. Starting from age 8, 'an anaphoric strategy', using full nouns to switch reference and pronouns to maintain reference, was adopted by around half the children, and by nearly all of the adults in the group. Similarly,

Katzenberger's (1994), study of picture-series narratives in Hebrew (showing two participants of the same sex and age) found that adults invariably introduce the characters when they first occur in the text by overt, explicit lexical means, and subsequently deploy one of several 'maintain-reference' strategies to refer to them when they recur (Berman & Katzenberger 1998). The adults and some 10 year olds favoured three such means: (1) a 'labelling strategy', introducing characters by a proper name (e.g. *Aliza, Mrs. Cohen*), by role (e.g. *customer, saleswoman*), or appearance *(the redhead, the one in blue)* subsequently repeating these labels or using third person pronouns or subject ellipsis; (2) a 'thematic-subject strategy' selected one of the characters as topic across the text, introduced lexically, subsequently referred to by a personal pronoun or null subject; or (3) a 'parallel presentation strategy' that introduces the two characters together at the beginning by distinct lexical means, and then differentiates them by various means, such as by different activities. Whatever the strategy, all the adults and 10-year-old children referred to the characters in a way that made it possible to identify who was being referred to at each point across their narratives. In contrast, the preschoolers were able to maintain reference to their characters around only one quarter of the time, and they differed from older narrators both in the extent to which character reference was clearly maintained across the text, but also in the strategies they adopted for this purpose. Importantly, use of referring expressions was one of the few variables in Katzenberger's (1994) study that differentiated between 10-year-old schoolchildren compared with adults, supporting other claims for relatively late development of narrative referentiality.

Reference-making strategies need, moreover, to be interpreted in light of **target language typology** – as demonstrated by the Hickmann *et al.* (1996) study of criteria for identifying noun phrases in English, French and German compared with Mandarin Chinese, where pronouns are unmarked for such categories as gender, case or animacy. Other languages have surface morphological cues that serve to disambiguate reference, including person marking on verbs in Italian and Spanish or extensive gender agreement on Hebrew verbs and adjectives (Berman 1990, Katzenberger 1994). These inflections are acquired early, and children can rely on them in identifying a given referent in both interpreting and producing narratives. A related factor is extent of same-subject elision in a given language. Berman and Slobin (1994) found that English-speaking narrators aged 3 to 9 years as well as adults relied heavily on pronominal subjects, Hebrew speakers used null subjects for maintaining reference in one third to half the clauses they produced, and the Spanish narrators hardly ever used pronoun subjects at all. The fact that narrative topic maintenance showed such language-particular trends across age groups confirms Slobin's (1996, 2001) insight that the language used by children is from a young age closer to that of adult speakers of the language than to that of their peers from typologically different backgrounds.

20.3.2 Narrative temporality

As a discourse genre organized around dynamic events that proceed through time, narratives afford a communicative context well suited to studying acquisition of linguistic temporality. Young children's abilities in this connection are considered largely in relation to reference to past time (Eisenberg 1985, Fivush *et al.* 1987, Sachs 1983). Early talk about past events is interpreted as a major cognitive milestone, indicating a removal from the here and now and the ability to refer to displaced objects and events even before children have mastered the relevant linguistic means (past tense, perfective aspect). Ninio (1988) notes that children from around age 20 months refer to completion of events (using diverse grammatical and lexical forms, such as Hebrew *nigmar* 'is-finished = all gone, done', *zehu* 'that's it, no more'). From around 26 months of age, children begin to encode the 'reportative' function of speech to convey information about what happened, the basis for stringing together narrative sequences in 'referential' clauses (Labov 1972). For example, a Hebrew-speaking child aged 2;5 talking about what happened at nursery school, informs her mother: *Rani (na)fal, bel pésa* [cf. adult *Eran nafal ve kibel péca*) 'Eran fell and got (a) wound' = got hurt).

   Linguistically, a critical facet of early narrative development is thus use of past-tense marking. This emerges first, in typologically different languages, with high-frequency change-of-state intransitive verbs (the 'unaccusatives' of generative grammar) often with irregular morphology, like English *fell, broke, spilt* and in perfective aspect in languages like Italian or Spanish – to express a 'resultative perspective' focused on change-of-state events in early child grammar (Slobin 1985c). Later use of past tense morphology applies across verb classes, including dynamic activity verbs, both intransitive (e.g. *went, ran, jumped*) and causative (*hit, dropped, pushed*), and elaborated, in languages with grammatical aspect, by use of imperfective aspect and/or past progressive to mark background states or ongoing events.

   Following Labov and Waltezky's (1967: 20) pathbreaking analysis of narratives as 'one method of recapitulating past experience by matching a verbal sequence of clauses to the sequence of events which actually occurred', researchers have identified the temporal sequencing of linguistic strings as crucial for narrative acquisition. As noted in section 20.2, even young preschool children are able to string together events that took place in the past, while older children come to rely on a consistent **dominant tense** form for anchoring the events recounted. Thus, in the frog-story sample, three to four year olds tended to switch between present and past in describing the events depicted in the pictured storybook, whereas older children, increasingly from age 5 years up, demonstrated a narrative storytelling mode by adhering to largely past-tense forms in such different languages as English, Hebrew, and Spanish (Berman & Slobin 1994).

With age, narratives manifest an increasingly **more variegated temporal texture**, reflected in increasing alternation of forms, moving away from monotonic temporal sequential anchoring of events, and tense-aspect shifting for global discourse purposes (Bazzanella & Calleri 1991, Berman & Nir-Sagiv 2004, Kupersmitt 2006). Extended reliance on aspectual distinctions is revealed by use of past progressive forms in the English 'frog story' sample of five and nine year olds; increased use of past perfect forms in personal experience narratives of adolescents and adults compared with younger children in English and Spanish; and greater reliance on non-finite subordinate clauses in English, Hebrew and Spanish – in both the 'frog story' samples and in personal-experience narratives of older children (Berman 1998, Berman & Nir-Sagiv 2007, Kupersmitt 2006).

Another important development is the ability to go beyond chronological sequentiality in recounting events: by reference to co-occurrent situations expressing temporal relations of **simultaneity** and/or to prior or forthcoming events as the story unfolds expressing retrospection and prospection, respectively). The crosslinguistic analysis of Aksu-Koç and von Stutterheim (1994) on the 'frog story' narratives reveals that, with age, simultaneous events are marked by more specific lexical means (e.g. English *while* or Hebrew *be-od še-* rather than the default temporal conjunction *when, kše-* as subordinators, and a larger range of converbs in Turkish), together with past progressive forms where possible. Reference to temporal **retrospection** occurs in the 'frog story' as a means of relating the 'initiating event' – a boy's pet frog escapes from the jar where it has been kept – and the final resolution, where the boy's search ends in finding a(nother) frog. Different means are used to express the relation, from juvenile *he saw a frog* to *he found his froggie* and on to more explicit formulations like *his lost pet, the frog that ran ~ had run away, the frog he (had) lost*. These expressive alternatives reveal a connection between nominal reference and narrative temporality and demonstrate the repertoire of superficially unrelated linguistic forms that speakers can choose to express syntactic, semantic and narrative functions of temporality. Age-related levels of 'narrativity' range from the semantics of possession (*his = the boy's*) to the discourse function of restrictive attribution (by relative clauses) and/or the temporal function of retrospection (by past perfect aspect). They also point to the role of typology and rhetorical preferences in different target language, for example, whether the language marks pluperfect aspect for expressing prior-to-past versus past events, like Spanish and English (more so in British than American English) or whether (as in German and Hebrew, say) speakers rely on relative clauses alone, without overt aspectual marking of the relation of anteriority.

A third facet of increasingly variegated linguistic temporality is demonstrated by *tense-aspect shifting* for expressing foreground–background distinctions. In Spanish, children from a young age distinguish background situations by use of imperfective forms in contrast to the perfective backbone of narrative events – in personal-experience accounts (Kupersmitt 2006), in retelling of a fable (Sandbank 2004), as well as in the picture-book 'frog story' (Sebastián & Slobin 1994). In Hebrew, a language that does not afford such options, older narrators rely increasingly on present-tense participial forms (the so-called *benoni* 'intermediate' construction) to achieve this discourse function (Berman & Neeman 1994). Sandbank (2004) compared the reconstruction of the same fable by native speakers of Spanish, which has a rich system of grammatical aspectual distinctions, and Hebrew, which lacks inflectional marking of aspect (Berman & Dromi 1984, Berman & Nir-Sagiv 2004). She found that in the introductory setting to the fable, Spanish 6 year olds referred predominantly to activities encoded in the past imperfective (e.g. *Caminaban dos mulas llevando su carga* 'Walked + Impfv two mules carrying their load') whereas in Hebrew, children relied more on reference to states, mainly with the general existential verb *haya* 'be' (e.g. *Hayu pa'am shtey pradot* '(there) were once two mules'). These findings demonstrate the impact of target language typology on the expressive options available to and selected by speaker–writers of a given language. And they illustrate Slobin's (2004) idea of a 'distributed semantics', where diverse linguistic devices conspire together in expressing a given narrative function, such as, say, temporal retrospection or background settings versus foreground events.

20.3.3   Connectivity

The term 'connectivity' refers to discourse-embedded clause-linkage, defined in functional linguistics as 'nexus' (Foley & Van Valin 1984), 'clause-combining' (Haiman & Thompson 1988), 'clause complexes' (Matthiessen 2002), or 'complex sentences' (Bybee & Noonan 2001). Here we consider children's acquisition of two related facets of this domain: lexical markers of inter-clausal relations (Section 20.3.3.1) and the syntactic architecture of groups of clauses linked together syntactically, thematically or discursively (Section 20.3.3.2).

20.3.3.1   Lexical marking of connectivity

As noted in section 20.2, the coordinating conjunction 'and' is the earliest and most ubiquitous marker of connectivity in children's narratives. The excerpts in (8) illustrate 3 year olds' use of 'and' in describing the same scene in different languages (from Slobin 1988).

(8)   English, aged 3;1: *A owl. Flew out of here. And he's running away.*
           German, aged 3;3: *Da kommt ein Vogel. Und da rennt er.*
                   'There comes a bird. And there he runs'.
               Spanish, aged 3;3: *Salio un pajaro immenso. Y un ninito se cayo de cabeza asi.*
                   'A big bird came out. And a little boy fell on his head like this'.

Hebrew, aged 3;6:   *Hine yanshuf.*   *Ve hine hayeled nafal.*
                      'Here's an owl.   And here the boy fell (down)'.

As specified in section 20.3, these immature uses of 'and' are utterance-initial, and hence fail to meet the syntactic function of clause-linkage or to express a conventional temporal or causal semantic relation. Pak *et al.* (1996: 302) argue that initially, for young preschoolers, connectives such as *because, so, then*, occur largely in 'limited, socially defined contexts' and serve interactional rather than ideational functions. Along similar lines, French and Nelson (1985) show that preschoolers use connectives like *and, if*, and *but* more, and more appropriately, when talking about situations that are familiar to them.

Two converging developments occur in acquiring markers of connectivity in narrative contexts. First, the function of particular items becomes semantically more specific with age, while concurrently, older children use a wider range of different connectives along with basic terms like *and, and then, so* (Peterson & McCabe 1991). Dependence on 'and' decreases as other connectives take over (Jisa 1987, Laubitz 1987, Scott 1984), while early marking of temporal relationships gives way to causally chained sequences of events (Kernan 1977, McCutchen & Perfetti 1982).

These trends are confirmed by comparing Hebrew-speaking children's use of connectivity markers in elicited picture-book narratives and personal experience accounts of a fight or quarrel (Berman 1995, 1996). In both contexts, older children use relatively more lexical markers of sequentiality (sentence-modifiers meaning 'then', 'after that', or 'afterwards') than the 3 year olds, increasingly for chaining clauses in sequence. Even in the more complex 'frog story' accounts, such expressions, alone or preceded by the marker meaning 'and', account for fully **one quarter** of the 'free' or independent clauses (single-clause sentences or the main clause of multi-clause constructions) in the 5- and 9-year-old texts but far fewer among the 3 year olds. Increased reliance on overt markers of temporal sequencing is illustrated by texts produced by a preschool 5 year old compared with 9-year-old texts of the two types – translated from the Hebrew originals in (9) and (10).

(9)   a.   Excerpt from Hebrew 'frog story' translated into English [boy aged 5;3]:
           There was a boy that er … that he caught a frog!!
           And afterwards he slept,
           And suddenly did not see it
           And then he said to the dog …
           And – and – he also went outside with his dog to search.
           And afterwards he took it
           And – he said (something) like this
           And they called for it, for the frog!

And afterwards he went down, told him [= the dog] to go down,
Then he caught him [= the dog]
And he [= the boy] thought he [= the dog] (had) chased it away.
He told him [= the dog] to go outside.
And afterwards they walked and walked until they came to a place where
they wanted to see if it [= the frog] was there.

b. Hebrew 'fight' story translated into English [girl, aged 5;3]:
   Yesterday at nursery school I quarrelled with my friend Roni,
   My friend took the doll (away) from me by force
   And afterwards (she) threw it (away).
   And then (she) laughed and said that I deserved it.
   Afterwards I got upset, and cried.
   And afterwards I told (about) her to the teacher.

The texts in (9) are typical of stories told by 5 year olds: Nearly every clause has a sequential introducer, with or without the conjunction *and* to mark event-chaining, indicating that the next step in the story is about to be described. In contrast, 3 year olds use few terms marking sequentiality, since for them 'and' signifies that they are about to describe the next picture (in the 'frog story'), or that another utterance is to follow (in the 'fight' sample). And it is also very different from narrative connectivity marking of 9 year olds, as marked by the underlined elements in (10).

(10) a. Excerpt from Hebrew 'frog story' translated [boy aged 9;5]:
         Once there was a boy, and he had a dog.
         The boy looked inside the jar
         And inside the jar was a frog.
         Afterwards the dog … er afterwards the boy went to sleep and the dog
         climbed on top of him to sleep together,
         And meanwhile the frog went out of the jar.
         Next morning the boy got up, and the dog … also.
         When they looked at the jar, they didn't see the frog.
         And then they started looking for it all over the place, and inside the jar
         ***that** was there.*
         Afterwards the boy went outside, and the dog also.
         When they looked at the jar, they didn't see the frog.
         And so they started looking for it all over the place, inside shoes and
         inside the jar where it was [= had been].
         Afterwards the boy went outside, and the dog also.

      b. Hebrew 9 year old 'fight' story translated into English [boy, aged 9;2]:
         Every night I fight with my brother
         because *he says that only he should take the dog downstairs.*

> *One night he pushed me*
> *And afterwards* [zero] *ran away quickly to his room,*
> *And after that I went downstairs with the dog.*
> [The family lives in an apartment building of several floors]

The 9-year-old texts in (10) make less use of 'and', relying on connectives like those meaning 'because', 'but', 'in order to' or 'until', 'meanwhile' to mark other logical as well as temporal relations between events in the unfolding narrative.

Analysis of personal-experience narratives produced both orally and in writing by grade-school children, middle school, and high school students shows that development in use of connectivity markers – as of other facets of discourse-embedded language use – continues well beyond middle childhood (Berman & Nir-Sagiv 2004). Around adolescence, sequential markers serve to frame entire segments of the narrative, by expressions such as *at first, later on, eventually*. These reflect more global, top-down narrative organization, in place of earlier chaining of one event after another (Berman & Nir-Sagiv 2007). Such growth in variety and flexibility of lexical devices is accompanied by increased variation in syntactic clause-linking constructions as discussed in the following section.

20.3.3.2 Syntactic packaging

Children's acquisition of complex syntax beyond the sentence level has been relatively little studied in narrative contexts. Most such research is on school-age children and pedagogically or clinically motivated, using the so-called 'T(erminable) Unit' – defined as a single finite verb with its associated subordinate and coordinate clauses – to measure the number and type of clauses within one such sentence-like element of (mainly written) discourse (Hunt 1965, Loban 1976, Scott 1988, Scott & Windsor 2000). More functionally motivated criteria of narrative clause-combining were first specified for the 'frog story' narratives in terms of 'syntactic packaging' by Berman and Slobin (1994: 538–554). They found, for example, that 3 and 4 year olds produce mainly isolated clauses in their narratives, while across languages, older narrators typically package clauses together significantly more, rising from around 15 to 40 per cent of total clauses from 3 to 9 years of age in English and Hebrew, while in Spanish, even 3 year olds combine clauses in a single syntactic package around one fifth of the time. These trends interface with changes in the **type** of constructions used for clause combining as a function of both age and target language typology.

Two such means are non-finite adverbial subordination (e.g. *while running away from the owl*) and subject elision (e.g. *The boy climbed the tree and looked in the hole*). Both demonstrate more tightly cohesive syntactic packaging, interacting with the structural options and rhetorical preferences of speaker-writers of different languages (Slobin 1996, 2001, 2004). Developmental progression in types of adverbial embedding in 'frog story' narratives is schematically depicted in (11) for three languages, where > stands for 'earlier than', while parenthesized constructions were not found even in the adult 'frog story' corpus (Berman 1998).

(11)   Developmental progression in types of adverbial subordination:
       English: Finite subordinates > Non-finite participles (*-ing* > *-ed*) >
          (Latinate nominalization e.g. *arrival, search*)
       Hebrew: Finite subordinates > Semi-finite Participle *benoni* forms >
          Derived nominalization > (Non-finite gerundives)
       Spanish: Finite subordinates > Non-finite gerunds > Non-finite
          infinitives

This developmental progression is supported by findings for personal experience narratives produced in writing as well as speech by school-age children and adolescents in these three languages. Berman and Nir-Sagiv's (in press) analysis extends the Berman and Slobin (1994) notion of syntactic packaging by combining syntactic with thematic and discursive criteria of **clause packaging** to characterize the 'syntactic architecture' of texts in different discourse genres (Berman & Nir-Sagiv 2007). We found, first, that **density** of narrative clause linkage increased from 9 year olds to 12 year olds, and most significantly among 16 year olds and adults in all three languages: That is, more clauses were packaged together in a single cohesive unit as a function of age. For example, younger, school-age children's texts often consist of isolated or unconnected clauses, whereas adolescents' (written) narratives average well over two clauses per package.

   The number of clauses packaged together was also affected by target language typology: Spanish revealed the greatest density in this respect (averaging over 4 clauses per package across age-groups) compared with English (slightly over 3 on average) and Hebrew (2.7 per package). Moreover, as suggested by findings from the 'frog story' sample for the developmental progression shown in (11), speaker–writers of different languages showed clear rhetorical preferences in **type of clause packaging**: Spanish used centre-embedded 'nested' type relative and adverbial clauses significantly more; Hebrew speaker-writers preferred paratactic stringing of clauses, typically with same-subject elision; and English participants relied more on complementation and non-finite participial subordination for creating inter-clause connectivity. These trends were evidenced from the youngest age group (9 year olds), demonstrating that children observe the expressive options favoured by adult speaker-writers of their language. Thus, English-speaking 9 year olds used more non-finite subordination than their Hebrew peers, yet they, too, showed clear developmental progression, from less than 5 per cent in the youngest group, up to nearly 10 per cent of the clauses produced by 12 year olds, jumping to nearly 20 per cent among adolescents and adults (nearly 17 and 20 per cent of all clauses respectively). Taken together, these findings point to clause-combining connectivity as a late development, far beyond the time when formal, single-sentence analyses typically stipulate 4 to 5 year olds as having 'acquired' complex syntax.

Same-subject elision, an important means of reference maintenance (Section 20.3.1), also plays a role in narrative connectivity that differs across languages and age groups. Spanish has rich person marking and favours subjectless clauses very widely, and Spanish-acquiring children from early on observe the grammatical requirement of same-subject elision in coordinate and subordinate clauses, as their 'default' option for narrative connectivity (Sebastián & Slobin 1994). Hebrew null subjects are somewhat more restricted and in narrative contexts, Hebrew-speaking 3 and 4 year olds tend not to rely on subject ellipsis, but to overuse repeated subject pronouns (for example, translated from the Hebrew 'frog story' corpus, *This dog **he** also climbs* [3;10], *And the boy **he** went up a tree* [4;9]), while children aged 5 to 9 years old use same-subject elision increasingly for clause linkage in coordination, rather less in subordination, and more mature narrators (a few 9 and 12 year olds and several adults) may use subject elision across entire chunks of texts as their favoured rhetorical option for narrative connectivity (Berman 1988, 1990). In English, same-subject ellipsis occurs rather less in tensed coordinate clauses and not at all in complements or adverbial subordinate clauses, so that, as noted in the preceding subsection, English narrators tend to rely more on pronominal coordination than their Spanish- or Hebrew-speaking peers. For English speaker-writers, null-subject subordination is an option mainly in non-finite clauses, as a late-developing, but favoured means of achieving narrative connectivity (Berman & Nir-Sagiv in press).

20.4   Overall developmental trends

The overview of form–function relations in developing narrative text construction provided in section 20.3 in the domains of reference, temporality and connectivity demonstrates the complex interaction between target language typology – to which children are sensitive from a very young age – and the long developmental route to mastery of different linguistic devices (like non-finite subordination or same-subject elision) at the service of narrative discourse functions (like reference or connectivity). More integrative analysis also points to an age-related interaction between these different linguistic systems, on the one hand, and between command of linguistic forms at the local level of isolated or adjacent clauses and overall, global-level mastery of narrative text organization, on the other. Thus a linguistic device such as same-subject elision serves for both referential clarity and discourse connectivity, while non-finite subordination plays a role both in varying temporal texture and also as a tightly cohesive means of packaging clauses together.

This interweaving of different linguistic forms and narrative functions is illustrated in (12a–d) by Hebrew-language descriptions of the first three pictures in the 'frog story' picture-book. Referring expressions (to animate entities) are underlined, items marked overtly for **temporality** are in bold, connectives are double-underlined, and <subordinate> clauses enclosed in angled brackets. In the glosses, items in parentheses are morphemes that have no surface form in (normative) Hebrew, and square brackets indicate explanatory comments.

(12)   a. Girl, aged 3;5:

ze kelev, ve-magafayim ve-kise. ve-ze yeled. kan, ze kelev **metapes** al ha-yeled. axshav … ve-hu **maxzik** et ha-shaxor ha-ze.

'This/it (is a) dog, and-boots and-(a)-chair. And this (is a) boy. Here, this (is a) dog **climbs** on the-boy. Now … and-he **holds** that black (thing).'

b. Boy, aged 5;2

ha-yeled **yashav** ve-gam ha-kelev. hem **ra'u** ke'ara ve-betoxo cfardea ve-az hayeled **halax lishon** ve-ha-cfardea **yac'a**.

'The-boy **sat** [=was-sitting] and the-dog also. They **saw** + Plur (a) dish and-inside-it (a) frog + Fem and-then the-boy **went to-sleep**, and-the-frog **exited**.'

c. 4th Grade Boy, aged 8;3:

haya le-yeled exad cfardea ,<ve-še-hayeled **yashan**> ha-cfardea **yac'a** ve-hi **barxa** ve-ba-boker <še-ha-yeled **kam**> az hu ra'a <še-hatsintsenet reka.>

'(There) **was** to a boy [= A boy had] (a) frog + Fem, and <that [=when] the-boy **slept**>, the-frog **exited** and she [=it] **escaped** and-in-the-morning <when-the-boy **woke**> then [=so] he **saw** <that the-jar (was) empty.'

d. 6th grade boy aged 11;4:[4]

hayo haya yeled , še- **gidel** cfardea babayit, ve kelev gam . hu **ahav legadel** ota becincenet. Balayla Ø **halax lishon** ve hacfardea **yac'a** mihacincenet. K-še-ba-boker **kam**, Ø ra'a še-ha-cincenet reyka. Ø **hitla-besh** maher. ve Ø **hitxil likro** la mihaxalon .

'Once (upon a time there) **was** (a) boy <that **kept** (a) frog+Fem at-home, and (a) dog, also>. He **liked to keep** her [=it] in (a) jar. At night Ø **went to sleep** and the-frog **exited** from-the-jar. <When in-the-morning Ø **woke**>, Ø **saw** that the-jar (was) empty. Ø **dressed** quickly and Ø **began to-call** her from-the-window.'

The examples in (12) reveal quite typical, age-related developments in all three domains, illustrating the interconnection between the linguistic

---

[4] The symbol Ø represents same-subject elision.

means of expressing different narrative functions. In **reference**, the 3 year old's orientation is largely deictic, while the 5 year old uses pronominal reference, disambiguated in Hebrew by number (plural *they*) and gender (*boy, dog* are masculine nouns, *frog* is feminine). In **temporality**, the 3 year old uses only present tense (with no surface verb in copular constructions in Hebrew), indicating that she is still in 'picture-description' rather than storytelling mode, while from age 5 years, the past tense anchors the narrative, alternating in the school-age texts with present-tense complements that mark simultaneity with past-tense matrix verbs. In **connectivity**, the 8 year old uses subordination for clause-linkage, while the 6th-grader relies extensively on same-subject elision in referring to the boy as topic.

The Hebrew examples also demonstrate the close connection between early command of **local** linguistic means at the level of isolated or adjacent clauses and the later developing mastery of **global** text structure. These different levels of language use are illustrated for three developmental phases by short picture-series based texts in (13) – adapted from Karmiloff-Smith (1983).

(13)   Narrative Action-Structure and Referential Strategies
   a. *Here the rabbit's riding a bike and ... the two cats are playing tennis and ... the dog's kicked a goal and the rabbit's drawing a line 'cos the turtle's won the race and the fox is playing his trumpet and ... the dog's singing with his guitar.*

The text in (13a), representing Karmiloff-Smith's Phase I early narrative development, relies on a Definite nominal strategy for reference, there is no marking of Sequentiality in temporal terms, and there is no overall Action Structure as evidence of an internalized narrative schema. The Phase II text in (13b) relies on a Thematic Subject Strategy to refer to the rabbit as key protagonist, it overtly marks temporal Sequentiality, but it, too, lacks overall narrative organization.

   b. *There is a rabbit riding a bicycle and he ... sees two cats and he ... draws a line for the turtle and he ... sees a dog with a ball and then he sees a fox playing music and then he ... hears some more music.*

In contrast, the Phase III text in (13c) uses a nominal strategy for introducing new referents, who are subsequently referred to by pronouns, with the rabbit as main protagonist referred to by *he* and the other characters by *it* and it alternates skilfully progressive and simple aspect verbs in the present, with past tense used in the concluding 'wrap-up' clause to signify anteriority. Critically, these linguistic forms serve in the framework of a fully developed global action structure based on the script of a (bicycle) race as a top-down organizing principle for narrative construction.

c. *Well, there's a rabbit going for a ride on a bicycle and he passes by two cats who're playing tennis, and then another rabbit … his friend, is drawing a line. It's the finishing line for the bicycle race. And then he rides by a dog playing football, and then there's a fox cheering him with a trumpet, and then they all have a party because he won the race.*

Along with the integration of increasingly varied and more appropriate linguistic devices at the service of different narrative functions, development of discourse-embedded language use also requires concurrent attention to both local linguistic expression and overall text organization.

Table 20.1. Developmental phases in narrative functions of linguistic forms

	Developmental phase		
Linguistic category	I Prenarrative	II Structural	III Rhetorical
Tense-shifting:	Mixed present and past tense; erratic shifting, triggered by local cues	One dominant anchor-tense; grammatical shifting, local sequence of tense constraints	Past ~ present narrative mode, discourse-based shifting and grounding distinctions
Sequentiality markers:	Occasional, utterance-initial	Overused, scattered across texts	Few, selective, marking episodes
Null subjects:	Occasional, some ungrammatical in lone clauses	Grammatical, in adjacent clauses for local connectivity	Across stretches of text, for topic maintenance

Table 20.1 (from Berman 1995) sums up the interplay between acquisition of the principles of narrative organization – from isolated utterances to chaining adjacent clauses and on to overall command of global text structure – and use of linguistic means – in tense–aspect alternations, lexical marking of sequentiality and reliance on null subjects.

In sum, the findings surveyed in this chapter, and summarized in part in Table 20.1, reflect quite general trends in developing form–function relations beyond the isolated utterance or sentence. Grammatical command of morphosyntax at the level of the simple clause is established early on, typically by age 3 years; and complex syntax is largely mastered by age 5. But it takes a long time, well into school age, until speakers are able to recruit these forms flexibly and skilfully in extended discourse, so as to plan and control the flow of information in constructing hierarchically organized (narrative) texts.

Suggestions for further reading

Berman, R. A., & Slobin, D. I. (1994). *Relating Events in Narrative: A Crosslinguistic Developmental Study.* Hillsdale, NJ: Lawrence Erlbaum Associates.

Hickmann, M. (2003). *Children's Discourse: Person, Time, and Space across Languages*. Cambridge: Cambridge University Press.

Peterson, C., & McCabe, A. (1983). *Developmental Psycholinguistics: Three Ways of Looking at a Child's Narrative*. New York: Plenum.

Strömqvist, S., & Verhoeven, L. (Eds.). (2004). *Relating Events in Narrative: Typological and Contextual Perspectives*. Mahwah, NJ: Lawrence Erlbaum Associates.

Part V

Varieties of Development

21

Children with two languages

Barbara Zurer Pearson

21.1   Introduction

The study of bi- (or multi-) lingual children has the potential to inform – or challenge – our ideas about the fundamental process of language learning, its timing and limits, and about the role of the environment in conjunction with factors internal to the child or the languages themselves.

Until recently, childhood bilingualism was considered a special case of language acquisition, rather than the majority phenomenon it is (Crystal 2004). According to a topic search by Bialystok (2007), the number of articles on bilingualism in the corpus selected more than tripled between 1997 and 2005, from an average of 100 articles in 1997 to over 350 in 2005. One- and two-case studies are popular and instructive, but we are also witnessing the study of groups of children and the establishment of large government-funded projects like the Collaborative Research Centre for Multilingualism in Hamburg and the recently instituted Centre for Research on Bilingualism in Theory and Practice at the University of Wales, Bangor. In such centres, much of the programmatic research is devoted to issues in bilingual acquisition.

Crystal (2004) proposes that the innate mechanisms that help children acquire their first language also help them acquire second or subsequent languages in early childhood. In his view, the Language Acquisition Device, or LAD, (Chomsky 1965) is really a 'MAD', or Multilingual Acquisition Device, so innate factors are as crucial for bilingual language acquisition as for monolingual acquisition. On the other hand, bilingual-learning children's more obvious dependence on relatively specific amounts of input from the environment has theoretical implications for the nature of the LAD (or MAD) and also more practically, for the kind of support parents and other interlocutors provide for language learners, what Bruner (1983) called the LASS, the Language Acquisition Support System.

In this chapter I first give a broad descriptive overview of childhood bilingualism and its many manifestations, especially behaviours unique to bilinguals. Then I compare early versus late acquisition of the second language and bilingual versus monolingual acquisition. Finally, I point to practical research on bilingual children in education and communication disorders.

21.2   Terms for talking about bilinguals

The term 'bilingual' takes on slightly different meanings depending on whether it is used to describe an individual, a community or a behaviour. A person is 'bilingual' if he or she can use two languages in communication. Similarly, a community is bilingual if some functions of community life take place in one language and other functions in another. A language practice is bilingual if it mixes elements of two languages either receptively or expressively, or both.

21.2.1   Classifications of bilinguals by skills

The consensus is that individuals who use more than one language fall on a spectrum. At one end is the simultaneous interpreter at the UN who speaks both languages as well as a native and is fully literate in both. At the other end are newborns who hear two languages spoken to them, but who cannot speak or understand even one language, much less two. In between these poles are all degrees of proficiency and use. Preschoolers who are just being introduced to a new language at school that is different from the one they speak at home are often called bilingual because, like the newborn, they have bilingual input and will probably speak two languages at some point in the near future. They will be considered true, **active** bilinguals when they have productive use of two grammars and can produce and understand novel sentences in both the first and second language, even if skills in the languages are not **balanced**. Often a bilingual has only one language that is at the same level as a monolingual's single language. Typically one language is **dominant** and the other is **non-dominant**, or weaker. Which language is dominant at any one point can change over time with new experience and new needs for one or the other language. Also, children younger than age 9 or 10 are vulnerable to loss, or attrition, of a language if they do not use it consistently.

21.2.2   Classification by learning context

Bilinguals differ according to how their two language communities relate to each other. If the learners' dominant language is the community (or majority) language, they would be called **elite** or **elective** bilinguals – for example, French speakers in France who decide to learn Chinese. To be bilingual is a choice since the primary language will already serve their basic needs in the community. The opposite is a **heritage** or **folk** or **immigrant** bilingual, for example Chinese speakers who move to France and must learn French for their daily life and livelihood.

Another defining characteristic is the place where the languages are learned and used. A **home language** may serve for primarily conversational purposes, what Cummins (1979) calls Basic Interpersonal Communication Skills (or BICS). More formal, academic language, typically learned at school or in formal settings, he called Cognitive-Academic Language Proficiency (or CALP). CALP engages all four modalities of language use: understanding, speaking, reading and writing, whereas BICS are more likely oral language only. Those who can read and write as well as understand and speak both languages are bilingual and bi-literate. Those who can only understand and possibly read but do not speak or write the second language are **passive** bilinguals.

21.2.3 Classification by timing

One common classification of bilinguals is based on when the languages were learned relative to one another. Child bilinguals can begin both languages at birth simultaneously or learn one first and then after that one is established, learn the next one sequentially (or successively). An infant bilingual is unambiguously a simultaneous learner, but a child bilingual could be either a simultaneous or sequential learner. The terms for this contrast are Bilingual First Language Acquisition (BFLA) and early Second Language Acquisition (early SLA). When one language is learned first and then another one learned as a second language, they are called 'L1' and 'L2'. Both infant and child bilinguals are considered early bilinguals as opposed to someone learning a second language late, or after a critical age (yet to be determined).

It is not obvious what the limits are of 'early' in early SLA nor what the nature of second language learning is for the child learner. Early language learning is unlike other complex behaviours, such as figure skating or playing the piano, which seem like 'talents' and are normally distributed throughout the population. Children learning an L2 within an early sensitive period have a more universal expectation of success, as for other human endowments like walking or binocular vision (Hyltenstam & Abrahamsson 2000). Everyone with sufficient exposure and without a specific handicap – such as deafness – achieves native or near-native fluency. By contrast, late second language acquisition is more like a sport, or a talent.

21.2.3.1 The age factor

It is a matter of some debate whether second language learners have access to innate mechanisms (the LAD or Universal Grammar, UG) specialized for language learning, or whether they must use more general learning principles which are less efficient for language tasks. Early accounts (e.g. Lenneberg 1967) proposed that the cut-off between early second language learning (with UG) and late learning (with general learning principles) was puberty. However, studies of different language domains show no clear cut-off age but rather a gradual decline in ability for language tasks starting as early as age 7. Indeed, for some tasks, such as phonological discrimination in the laboratory, or processing the new language in the presence of noise, not every person who learned a second language before age 7 falls in the same range as monolingual learners (Caramazza *et al.* 1973, Hyltenstam & Abrahamsson 2000). Still, in the real world, within four or five years of starting the second language, the 'early sequential bilingual' is indistinguishable from the native speaker. For many people in many parts of the world, the L2 becomes their primary language.

For syntax the age of 9 or 10 seems a promising candidate for the language divide between early and late language learning. Hahne (2001), using ERP measures, found strong differences in syntactic (but not semantic) processing between bilinguals whose age of acquisition of the second language was younger or older than 10. Also, before age 9, learners of a second language were more likely to adopt a preference for L2 syntactic structures than were older learners, whose preferences did not shift away from the L1 (Jamshidiha & Marefat 2006). For phonology, Caramazza *et al.*'s (1973) findings indicate that the divide comes earlier particularly in perception, whereas there is no age limit for learning vocabulary or the pragmatics of discourse in two languages, and the older learner is perhaps better than the younger learner in those domains.

In sum, 'childhood bilingual' would be the general term for one who learned two languages natively before age 9, with the caution that the boundary between early and late is porous. Some rare individuals under 9 will not achieve native fluency (Ioup 1989), and some individuals older than 9 will (DeKeyser & Larson-Hall 2005). Even sequentially, the young child learns two languages in the implicit manner characteristic of first language acquisition. Given rich enough language interactions in two languages, children can learn them both without explicit, formal instruction.

21.2.3.2 Learning order

Also at stake in the difference between learning a language early or late is whether the second language is learned 'from scratch', independently from the first language, or whether it is filtered through the first language structures. In a University of Miami study of lexical learning by eighteen bilingual-learning infants (Pearson & Fernandez 1994), most children were observed to be learning new words in both languages and seemed to be learning both languages 'from the ground up'. One child, however, learned no words in her second language that she did not already know in her first language. So despite having begun both languages at birth, she seemed to be filtering the second language through the first, like a second-language learner. Other reports also indicate that transitory accents have been noted in preschoolers (Fantini 1985, Leopold 1939) and what looks like grammatical transfer (Dopke 1998), or other influence from one language to the other (Paradis & Genesee 1996), all indicating some degree of second-language learning.

21.2.4 Relationships between the two languages of a bilingual

Individuals can be balanced in their oral skills, but have a dominant language for reading and writing (or vice versa). Whether they are balanced or not, they can have their skills, like vocabulary, 'distributed' between the languages (Oller & Pearson 2002). For example, a scientist may know technical vocabulary learned in the L2 in that language only and not in the L1. Knowledge of household or sports terms may be more accessible in L1, and relatively fewer terms equally accessible in both.

In general, it is easier to learn a majority language than a minority language. That is, it takes more exposure to a minority language for the same degree of acquisition (Pearson *et al.* 1997, Vihman *et al.* 2006). When an elective/elite bilingual learns a second (minority) language, we expect the second language to be ADDED to the first. To learn French, the majority-language English speaker does not have to forget English first. French is added to English, in 'additive' bilingualism (Lambert 1977). When an immigrant learns a second language, especially a child under 10, it is often at the expense of the first language, resulting in 'subtractive' bilingualism, unless efforts are made to help the child continue growing the first language as well as the second.

The extreme case of subtractive bilingualism has been called 'serial monolingualism', where one language replaces the other, and the individual ends up not being bilingual at all. Serial monolingualism is observed in foreign adoptees who leave their country at an early age and subsequently lose all contact with their native language. For example, Pallier *et al.* (2003) showed that in word recognition tests and neuro-imaging data, French adults who had been adopted from Korea between ages 3 and 7 showed no greater response to Korean than to another unknown language. More usually, the first language skills persist. In a study of processing, Kohnert and colleagues (1999, 2002) documented the time course of the switch in language dominance among bilinguals who did not learn their L2 until the start of school. Among these children, their dominance shifted, and the L2 at different times (for different skills and subskills) became the stronger language. Still, both languages advanced during the time they examined (age 6 to adult), but the L1 at a slower rate than the L2. The researchers did not observe that the L1 actually regressed.

Another distinction between types of bilinguals derives from observations of how individuals use their languages, and how much interaction is envisioned between the two languages. Cummins' (1979) description of 'independent' versus 'interdependent' development echoes the earlier distinction from Weinreich (1953) between 'coordinate' versus 'compound' bilinguals. A coordinate bilingual was envisioned as having two independent systems that develop in parallel, but with minimal connection or overlap between them. Wierzbicka (2005) characterizes it as having 'two sets of mental furniture', a suite for each language. A compound bilingual, by contrast, would have only one set of mental furniture, with two sets of labels for the different pieces. The languages are pictured as interdependent.

21.3   Bilingual behaviours

Being bilingual also entails a certain amount of mental machinery involved, for example, in labelling elements as to which language they are part of and in coordinating the two languages. Psycholinguistic evidence indicates that both languages of a bilingual are always activated (Francis 2005), so there are elements of both conscious and subconscious choice in which language gets processed and which language gets suppressed in any situation.

21.3.1   Monolingual versus bilingual mode of speaking

Grosjean (1989) protests that a bilingual 'is not two monolinguals in one person', but in fact, some bilinguals operate in what he calls a 'monolingual mode' (Grosjean 2001). That is, they switch between being a monolingual speaker of one language with one person (or in one situation) to being a monolingual speaker of the other language with another person. Other people do not feel their languages are so separate from each other and they use both languages together in a 'bilingual mode', or 'rich language stew' (Gupta 2006) when the situation allows. Most bilingual people, regardless of whether they learned their languages together or separately, report that they can operate in either a monolingual or bilingual mode, depending on whom they are speaking with and what the situation requires.

21.3.2   Codeswitching (and code-mixing)

A phenomenon unique to the bilingual mode is 'code switching', where two languages are used within the same utterance or turn. Bilinguals' seamless switching between languages (here called codes) can happen either between sentences or within sentences at permissible points in the grammatical structure. The latter is often called 'code-mixing'. Some bilinguals have negative attitudes about code-switching and resist the impulse to mix, but many others profess to prefer it. In many bilingual parts of the world, for example in India, Singapore or south Florida, mixed language contexts are the standard, and people report it would feel unnatural to restrict conversations to one language (Gupta 2006). There is also a growing bilingual literature from writers who flow lyrically back and forth between languages, writing for others with knowledge of both languages (See de Courtivron 2003, or the Nuyorican Poetry Cafe 2007).

Code-mixing used to be thought of as a failure of bilingual behaviour. In fact, some of it is due to filling in words one does not know or cannot recall in one language, but code-mixing turns out to be a skilled behaviour that people master only after they have considerable skill in both languages. The principal constraint involves having the utterance respect the grammar of both languages at once. This is readily accomplished by adding an invariant tag, or a quotation, which has no syntactic links with the previous material. For example, "He said he'd be late, n'est-ce pas?" ('[isn't that] right'). A second kind of switch happens within sentences but at clause boundaries, as in the example from Poplack (1980), "Sometimes I begin a sentence in Spanish, y termino en espanol" ('and I finish [it] in Spanish'). A word or a phrase from one language can also be embedded within a constituent in the grammar of the other language where it takes the word order and morphosyntax of what is called the 'matrix language' frame (Myers-Scotton 2001). Generally, only a small percentage of switches involve insertions of one word into the grammar of the other language. Allen (2007a) gives examples from the highly inflected Inuktitut language, where the inserted English material ('mushy') follows the word order of the matrix sentence and takes its word endings: *mushy-u-nngi-tu-rulu-alu-runa*. ([mushy]-be-NEG-one.which-little-EMPH-this.one 'This little one isn't mushy.') Proper names and words with similar pronunciation are often 'triggers', as in this example from Clyne (2003): "Holland was too *smal voor ons. Het was te benauwd...* ('too narrow for us. It was too oppressive'). The shared pronunciation of *smal/small* appears to condition the switch from one language to the other.

Clyne (1980) noted that there is a micro-pause at the juncture where a switch takes place, and indeed in psycholinguistic experiments that force switching, the switch has been shown to have a measurable time cost. It takes longer to switch from a non-dominant language to the dominant language than vice versa (on average 143 milliseconds versus 85 ms). This may be counterintuitive, but Meuter (2005) argues that this asymmetry indicates the speaker is working harder (subconsciously) to suppress a dominant language than a non-dominant language, and thus it takes longer to release the suppression.

21.3.3   Code-switching in children

Children's mixed utterances have been examined to see whether there is a period of development during which their code-mixing is ungrammatical, or non-adultlike. While there are clearly some errors – just as adult speech contains performance errors that do not reflect the speaker's competence – only a small percentage of children's code-switches do not fit into the categories for adults. In Allen's (2007a) Inuktitut data, for example, all but 5 per cent of the code-switching, even at the earliest ages, fit the structure of both languages.

A certain amount of mixing is expected as children gradually master their target system. Sometimes, mixing is part of the child's target. When the people in the child's environment switch between languages freely, the child does, too. Lanza (1997) has shown that child rates of code-switching follow closely on parental code-switching rates, and also reflect the kinds of responses parents make to a child's switched utterances.

21.3.4   Non-converging dialogue

Another manifestation of the bilingual mode is 'non-converging dialogue'. In these asymmetrical conversations, bilingual and monolingual modes are mixed, so that people speak to each other in different languages. It is common for parents to use a minority language and their child to respond in the majority language. Or, when parents who speak different languages to their child address each other in the child's presence, they may choose to have non-converging conversations in which everyone is using a bilingual mode receptively to understand either language, but each person uses a different monolingual mode expressively.

21.4   Research areas

Research in child bilingualism spans the gamut of child language topics, but is concentrated on issues unique to bilinguals. Since a true experimental design is impossible – families cannot be randomly assigned to raise children bilingually or not – most of the research is either quasi-experimental, using already constituted groups that are as similar as possible, or involves short-term manipulations. One very strong paradigm uses two monolingual control groups for the bilingual group, one for each language (viz. Caramazza *et al.* 1973).

Interest is particularly great in the relationship between a bilingual's two languages, including how they are represented in the bilingual brain, and whether the representation will be different depending on when the languages were learned relative to each other, early versus late. Other lines of research seek to determine how bilingual learning might differ from first-language learning in monolinguals, for example, whether it is slower or less complete than FLA. Finally, many investigations explore the implications of two languages for educational and social policies.

21.4.1   One-language-or-two in development
21.4.1.1   Single representations versus dual (separate) representations

Historically, there has been great emphasis on trying to determine how bilingual children develop their two languages: Do they start with one 'unitary' system, with elements of both languages and gradually differentiate their single system into two systems? Or, do they have two languages from the outset, building both 'from the ground up'. Early observers like Leopold (1939) proposed the former, that children start with a single, fused system which later differentiated into two. Volterra and Taeschner (1978) took that idea further and proposed that the language separation took place first in the lexicon and then later in the grammar. From the perspective of phonology, Schnitzer and Krazinski (1994, 1996) suggest that the locus of differentiation is even more specific, that children first differentiate vowels, in the second year of life, and subsequently their consonants.

Much of the evidence for the unitary theory came from observations of children using the same elements and processes in both languages, or mixing elements of one language in the other. However, as more recent formulations argue (Paradis & Genesee 1996), children do not randomly use elements of both languages together regardless of the context, as they would if they had completely fused systems. Even two year olds with unbalanced proficiency use the language called for in the situation statistically more often than the other language (Genesee *et al.* 1996). Still, the existence of two separate systems does not mean that there is no influence of one language on the other.

Hulk and Muller (2000) argue that bilinguals develop like monolinguals of each language. Bilinguals do not take structures from their stronger language and use them in the other, but one language may still influence the acquisition of the other. They argue that when there is overlap at the surface level between structures in an individual's two languages, exposure to the structure in one language is taken as evidence for the structure in the other. The child will persist in that interpretation until more specific evidence from the second language permits the child to move from a more inclusive single (universal) analysis to two language-specific analyses. In their view, cross-language influence is limited to certain parts of the grammar and is more constrained than transfer.

21.4.1.2   Psycholinguistic and neurological evidence for the dual system hypothesis

Tools of analysis from psycholinguistic experiments and neuro-imaging provide further evidence against the unitary period in bilingual children's development. Around six months, when monolingual infants move from being universal listeners, (that is, they are equally sensitive to potential contrasts in any language), to becoming more responsive to their ambient language than to others (Werker & Tees 1984, 1992), bilingual infants give signs of recognizing the sounds of their two languages and also distinguishing between them (Sebastián-Gallés & Bosch 2005).

Brain-imaging techniques also offer new (but somewhat contradictory) evidence about whether the bilinguals' two languages appear to be fused or distinct. In the 1800s, aphasia studies had already suggested that bilinguals' two languages could be stored in different locations in the brain. When bilinguals suffer a stroke or other trauma to the brain, in most cases both languages are affected, but often enough it happens that one language is impaired and the other spared. When a number of bilinguals with aphasia were found to have damage not in the typical left or language hemisphere, but in the right hemisphere, it gave rise to the hypothesis that bilinguals might expand their language capacity by recruiting space for language in the right hemisphere (Albert & Obler 1978). Further, the well-known plasticity of children's brains, which allows a damaged language centre to relocate a first language to the right hemisphere (Caplan 1980), also fuelled speculation that in the right conditions, healthy (bilingual) brains could recruit the right hemisphere for language.

The bilingual aphasia evidence is ambiguous (Solin 1989), but the proposal seems to have a kernel of truth. New, non-invasive imaging techniques like functional magnetic resonance imaging (fMRI), positron emission tomography (PET) scans, and event-related potentials (ERPs), provide data from healthy individuals in the act of producing or understanding language stimuli. Experiments that map the activity of the brain while people are speaking or listening to one or both languages show activation for the two languages within the same or different spaces. Kim et al. (1997) suggested that the organization of two languages in the brain is a function of when they are learned relative to each other. They showed that when highly fluent child bilinguals were processing speech, the two languages activated the same areas of the brain, but when the subjects were late bilinguals, some areas activated did not overlap. In other studies (e.g. Perani et al. 1998), the key variable appears to be proficiency and not age of acquisition (although clearly the two are related). When the second language is more recent and less fluent, it might take up more space, whereas two highly practised languages would be handled efficiently in one area within one hemisphere. This pattern seems analogous to the pattern of development observed more generally for less practised behaviours to involve a larger area of weaker connections. As the behaviours become more practised, they become more 'focal', with stronger responses from fewer neurons (Eliot 1999).

Using infrared spectoscropy, Shalinsky et al. (2006) compared monolinguals with bilinguals when they were speaking in only one language (monolingual mode) and also when they were switching between languages (bilingual mode). In monolingual mode, the activity seen in the left hemisphere was the same as for monolinguals. However, when the bilinguals did a task that made them switch back and forth between their languages, there was activation in the analogous areas of the right hemisphere as well, in areas distinct from the first language.

Thus the neurological evidence seems to suggest that the bilingual brain does recruit more cortical areas for language than the monolingual brain, and to some extent or for some period of time, it may represent the two languages somewhat separately in different locations in the brain.

21.4.2   How is early bilingual learning different from late SLA?

Some people suggest that children are not better second-language learners than adults, but they learn in more helpful contexts and are less inhibited than adults. Evidence from diverse domains contradicts that view. In regression studies that include psychosocial variables along with age of arrival or length of residence, motivations and attitudes contribute very little if anything to the prediction of skill in the second language (DeKeyser & Larson-Hall 2005). Furthermore, learning a second language early results in different patterns at the processing level than if the individuals had learned the language later. In general, early bilinguals appear to have similar patterns to first-language learners for each of their languages. However, the phenomena are multifaceted, and so even for the early bilingual, some features may be similar to patterns observed in monolinguals of each language while others show a bi-directional influence of the languages on each other. Still, such influence is generally more subtle in early bilinguals than for late bilinguals, who are more likely to use the same processing patterns and biases in the second language that they learned for the first.

21.4.2.1   Evidence from syntax

Cross-language influence of this type is illustrated by work in syntax by Dussias (2001) in a series of experiments with ambiguous relative clauses. In a sentence like 'He shot the servant of the actress who was on the balcony', the final relative clause could be attached to the higher noun phrase (*servant*) or the lower noun phrase (*actress*). Both options are possible, but English speakers have been shown to prefer low attachment (Frazier 1987), whereas Spanish L1 speakers favour high attachment (Cuetos & Mitchell 1988). In Dussias' work, late bilinguals showed the preference from their first language regardless of whether the sentence was in English or Spanish. By contrast, early bilinguals showed an intermediate pattern, that is, less low attachment bias for English stimuli and more low attachment bias in Spanish than the respective monolinguals.

21.4.2.2   Evidence from phonology

Zampini and Green (2001) replicate and extend early work by Caramazza *et al.* (1973) which showed early bilinguals' segmental *productions* to be close to the respective monolinguals' (although their perception patterns were more mixed). Voice onset time (VOT), the interval between the release of air from the mouth and beginning the vibration of the vocal folds, has been identified as a sufficient cue to distinguish voiced from voiceless stops. In English, the VOT for the voiced stops are considered to be 'short-lag', that is, in the vicinity of 20 ms, whereas the voiceless counterpart is 'long-lag', generally greater than 35 ms. Spanish also has a voiced/voiceless stop contrast, but VOT production values measured for Spanish monolinguals are shifted downward. Thus, the Spanish voiceless stop (/p/) is short-lag (like the English voiced /b/), and the Spanish voiced /b/ is still shorter, that is, prevoiced with VOT -30 ms or less. Zampini and Green showed that the productive VOT values of early bilinguals (but not late second-language learners) matched those of monolinguals in the respective languages.

However, for these same subjects, even the production pattern was different from monolinguals when one looked at another parameter that distinguishes the voiced/voiceless contrast for Spanish speakers, the length of the voiceless closure interval (VCI). The VCI refers to how long the speaker keeps the closure before the release burst (i.e. the interval *before* the VOT interval). For English speakers, the Voiceless Closure Interval is the same for /b/ and /p/, but in Spanish, this interval is much shorter for /b/ than /p/ (10 ms versus 70 ms on average). Like the English monolinguals, early bilinguals showed no difference in closure time in English, and like Spanish monolinguals, they showed a large (50 millisecond) difference in Spanish. However, unlike the monolinguals, their closure value for Spanish /b/ was as high as the monolingual values for English /b/. In order to create the contrast in Spanish, the bilinguals' voiceless closure interval for Spanish /p/ was that much higher again than their /b/, making it higher than the Spanish monolinguals' /p/. Thus, the representations in each language seem distinct, but they also show influence of one language pattern on the other. As in the sentence-parsing example, the early bilinguals were both the same as and different from the respective monolinguals.

21.4.2.3   Evidence from semantics

Unlike phonology and syntax, semantic processing is thought in general to be less tied to the requirement of early acquisition of the L2. In electrophysiological studies by Weber-Fox and Neville (1996), measures from event-related potentials (ERPs) showed differences between early and late groups with respect to closed-class words (i.e. function words), but open-class words (nouns and verbs) and semantic anomalies were less sensitive to whether the participants were early or late learners. Illes *et al.* (1999) also found that some tasks, especially those that tapped semantic skills such as deciding whether a word was abstract or concrete, showed only a small and inconsistent effect of age of acquisition.

One of the main issues addressed in this area of research has been how different groups of bilinguals represent and access the words from their two languages in semantic memory, especially whether the words are represented in one merged storage area for both languages, or a separate storage area for each language. Current models of semantic memory propose more than one component (e.g. Kroll & de Groot 1997), so it is possible for word representations to be partially shared and partially separate. For example, there is considerable cross-language intrusion in memory tasks involving mixed-language sets (Francis 2005). In fact, memory for which language an utterance is spoken in is very poor. Kintsch (1970) showed that when recognizing items from a previous list, subjects were twice as likely to misclassify the language than to fail to recognize an item.

Data from priming experiments permit inferences about the relative association by form and meaning of words in a bilingual's two languages. In priming, a stimulus is used to sensitize the subject to a later presentation of the same or similar stimulus. Work by Sánchez-Casas and García-Alba (2005) contrasted four classes of words: identical words, cognates (which share both form and meaning, like *tower/torre*), translation equivalents that share the same meaning but do not sound similar (e.g. *book* versus *libro*) and false cognates, words of the same shape but with different meanings, like *librarie* in French to mean 'bookstore', not 'library'. At most timing intervals, cognate priming was almost as effective as priming with the exact same word, whereas non-cognate translation equivalents showed only a modest cross-language effect unless the priming interval was very long; false cognates showed a negative effect, unless the priming interval was very short (Sánchez-Casas & García-Alba 2005). Sánchez-Casas and García-Alba interpret these results as support for Kroll and de Groot's (1997) hypothesis that a word's form and concept are represented separately. The result with false cognates shows that the representation of the word form is activated in the early stages of word recognition, whereas the non-cognate translation equivalents suggest that conceptual representation is accessed later. Cognates, which have both form and concept associations, are effective for priming at all phases, and as effective as if they were repetitions of the original word. The magnitude of the priming effect for cognates is the same as for different forms of the same word, for example *door/doors* within languages and closer than within-language synonyms (which also share meaning but not form).

So there is considerable evidence in different domains of language that the outcomes of early bilingual learning – for BFLA and also for early SLA – are qualitatively different from later learning. However, little work has been done to delimit the differences between BFLA and early SLA.

21.4.3   How is bilingualism different from monolingualism?

Another common thread in the research literature on bilingual children concerns the relative advantage or disadvantage of bilinguals vis-à-vis monolingual children in language or cognitive development. As chronicled in a review by Hakuta (1986), comparisons of bilingual and monolingual children in the first half of the twentieth century reflected the anti-immigration attitudes of the times. Bilinguals were typically immigrants, and immigrants did poorly in school, so by a logical fallacy, bilingualism was seen as the cause of children doing poorly in school. When confounding factors like poverty and educational background were controlled for, and when children were tested in a language they could understand, most comparisons were no longer unfavourable for bilinguals (see also Oller & Eilers 2002).

21.4.3.1   Bilingual developmental milestones

Given the great variability in typical language acquisition milestones, it is very difficult to find statistical differences between matched bilingual and monolingual groups on any measures of language functioning. (School performance is a separate issue that we will address in Section 21.4.3.4.) Many early language milestones are similar, regardless of which language children are learning, or how many languages they are learning. Mature babbling typically appears at around 6 months of age, first words around 12–14 months, and first two-word combinations around 18–25 months (Fenson *et al.* 1994).

A similar timetable is observed for bilinguals, although often a child will be roughly comparable to a monolingual in only one of the two languages, not both. In fact, the bilingual groups that have been examined are squarely in the middle of what norms we have. (For babbling, see Oller *et al.* 1997; for first words, Pearson & Fernandez 1994; and Petitto *et al.* 2001; for early syntax, see reviews in de Houwer 1995, and Genesee *et al.* 2004.) Based on their own work and that of a large Bilingual First Language Acquisition research project in Hamburg Germany (Meisel 1994), Genesee *et al.* (2004: 73) conclude that bilinguals follow the same course and rate as monolinguals in each language in many aspects of their development, 'from the sound system to grammar'.

21.4.3.2   Meta-linguistic comparisons

In other language domains, bilinguals appear not just to equal monolinguals, but to exceed them. For example, bilinguals have been shown to excel at 'meta-linguistic awareness', a skill associated with learning to read and write. It also helps children learn a third language (Bild & Swain 1989). One illustration of precocious meta-linguistic awareness – that children can manipulate words independently of the sentences they occur in – is their ability to switch names for things without switching the object being named. In a study by Cummins (1978), while both monolinguals and bilinguals were able to agree, for example, to call the moon 'the sun', bilinguals were better at realizing that the night sky would still be dark, even with a moon that was now called 'sun'.

Similarly, at the emergent reading stage, work by Bialystok (1991) showed that bilinguals were more than a year in advance of the mono-linguals in recognizing that print does not change what it says depending on what it is labelling. In a pre-reading stage, children can usually say that a card under a toy rabbit says *rabbit*, but the harder test is to know what is on the card when it is moved under a bird. In Bialystok's study, only 18 per cent of the bilinguals at this stage of emergent reading erroneously said "bird", whereas 62 per cent of the monolinguals gave that answer. The 4-year-old bilinguals were ahead of the 5-year-old monolinguals on this task.

The bilingual advantage in reading was shown in a language and literacy study of 960 English–Spanish bilingual and English monolingual children in kindergarten, second and fifth grade in south Florida (Oller & Eilers 2002). Half of the bilinguals were in 'one-way' English-only schools, learn-ing Spanish at home, while the other half were in 'two-way' dual language programmes, where they learned to read in two languages from the very beginning. By second grade, differences in reading skill between the groups had emerged, favouring the group with instruction in two lan-guages, and the advantage was maintained at fifth grade. The most striking observation was that learning to read in Spanish as well as in English had clear benefits in terms of the children's reading scores not just in Spanish, but in English as well.

21.4.3.3   The effect of bilingualism on cognition

Research on the cognitive abilities of bilinguals conducted by Peal and Lambert (1962) is often credited with turning the tide toward more positive views of childhood bilingualism. These authors showed that bilingual elementary school children were more divergent thinkers, better problem solvers and ahead in content in school than matched monolinguals.

Bialystok (1999) proposes an Analysis and Control model to explain bilinguals' advantage in some tasks but not in others. According to this model, bilinguals and monolinguals perform equally well in analysis tasks, which demand explicit abstract representations, such as recogniz-ing syntactic errors in speech. By contrast, bilinguals do better in 'control' tasks, those which require them to focus on just one or two aspects of a task while *suppressing* attention to its other aspects. To be successful, the participant must ignore conflicting or extraneous information.

Bialystok (1999) used the dimension change card sort task to show bilin-guals' superior selective attention. She asked subjects to sort a set of cards twice, once according to the colour of the figures on the card, and a second time sorting according to the shape of the figures. Bilingual and monolin-gual children did the first sorting equally well. However, on the second sort, bilingual children responded more accurately and more quickly. They were better able to put the old response aside and pick up the new one.

21.4.3.4 Areas of slower development

In the two areas of grammar that are most sensitive to the amount of language exposure, vocabulary and morphosyntax, one may see a slower pace of learning in bilinguals compared to monolinguals. However, this difference need not translate into an academic deficit. We examine in this section how bilinguals' slower pace of learning in these domains relates to other academic skills differently than for monolinguals.

Bilingual children are by no means poor word learners. Their total lexicons – counting both languages – are considerably larger than those of monolinguals for reception and generally equivalent for production (Pearson *et al.* 1993). However, in the early stages of vocabulary development bilingual children may know fewer words in each language (perhaps as much as 30 or 50 per cent less). Gathercole (2002) suggests that there is a threshold mechanism. Learning is directly related to exposure up to a 'critical mass'. Once the critical mass is achieved, exposure differences will have less effect.

During the time when their single-language vocabularies are smaller, the close association often observed in monolinguals between vocabulary size and cognitive and academic measures is not observed in bilinguals. Oller *et al.* (2007) have demonstrated what they call a 'profile effect'. Bilingual and monolingual children took a battery of separately scaled tests covering oral language skills including receptive and productive vocabulary and literacy skills. Means for the monolingual groups in the separate tests were around the standardized mean of 100 across the board. That is, vocabulary patterned with the other skills. The bilingual group means for most tests were also around the standardized mean of 100, except in vocabulary, where the decrement ranged from 10 to 26 points. Thus, despite their lower scores in vocabulary, their scores in the other skills tested were not depressed. The extra time needed for them to reach a threshold, or 'catch up', in vocabulary did not appear to affect their language and literacy skills overall.

A similar dissociation has been shown between morphosyntactic accuracy and other language skills. That is, when words do not follow a general rule but have irregular forms like many plural forms in English (e.g. *sheep/sheep*), it takes longer to amass enough exposures to the forms to learn the irregulars. In a study of several hundred stories retold by monolingual and bilingual school children, discourse skills correlated closely with morphosyntax scores for the monolinguals, but not for the bilinguals (Pearson 2002). In monolingual children, the failure to have developed key areas of morphosyntax is often taken to be a sign of a processing problem indicative of a language delay more generally. In a bilingual child, by contrast, it is usually just an indication that the child had not yet had enough time and opportunity for exposure to the items equivalent to monolinguals.

21.5 Practical implications of bilingualism

21.5.1 Education for children with two languages
21.5.1.1 Immersion schooling
Communities (and families) that wish to support children's growth in a minority language can follow Fishman's (2001) advice to set aside times and functions for the minority language. Schooling in the medium of two languages supports families' efforts to keep up the minority language without harm to the majority language (Oller & Eilers 2002). Wong-Fillmore (1991) showed that families whose children went to English-only preschools were five times more likely to drop the minority language in the home than families of children who went to minority language, or bilingual preschools. Among the Inuits of Canada, Allen (2007a) also documents the diminished use and loss of proficiency in the minority language among schoolchildren instructed in an L2 with higher prestige, English or French. Within the first year of schooling in L2, Inuktitut proficiency declined significantly relative to children who were schooled in Inuktitut. Within two years, the gap widened, especially in the language for academic proficiency (as opposed to conversational proficiency).

In contrast, Allen (2007a) did not find the loss of L1 when two high prestige languages were involved. For example, French-speaking children schooled in English did not lose their French. Canadian immersion programmes have been in operation for decades, teaching English-speaking children French without loss to their English (Swain & Lapkin 1982). Likewise, in Northern Wales, making the minority language Welsh the language of instruction in public schools (since 1993) has led to the first upturn in the use of Welsh for more than a century. This has been accomplished without detriment to the children's English (Gathercole 2006).

21.5.1.2 Dual immersion schooling
However, strong arguments are made for children's need to learn the language of power on an equal footing with monolingual speakers in their country. One successful 'compromise' model used in the US is called dual immersion, or two-way schooling, where school subjects are taught in both the majority and minority languages equally. Children begin their academics in a language they know well, but do not delay learning in the majority language as well. Carefully controlled comparisons between children in two-way schools versus English-only schools in Miami showed that by fifth grade English scores for children in the two school types had only one standard score point difference, whereas the Spanish scores were ten standardized points better on average for children in the two-way schools (Pearson 2007).

Children in the two-way school could study the minority language without loss to the majority language. Furthermore, shared language provides a clear mechanism for helping the children identify with individuals in other ethnic groups. Learning a second language can play a crucial role in breaking down prejudice and fostering positive attitudes toward members of other groups as demonstrated by Wright and Tropp (2005). However, the small number of two-way programmes in the US, around 300 according to a database maintained by the Center for Applied Linguistics (Howard & Christian 2007), means that US policy makers have not heard or have not listened to the research evidence.

21.5.2   Language impairment and bilingualism

In a comprehensive treatment of the topic of language impairment and bilingualism, Genesee *et al.* (2004) demonstrate that most bilingual children with language impairment in one language show equivalent disorders in both languages – but different languages present different areas of vulnerability, so the actual symptoms of the disorders will be different in each language. With bilingual children whom one suspects of having a language impairment, Genesee *et al.* (2004) caution, only in rare cases will dropping one language, especially a first language, solve the language problem. Often it will cut children off from their most effective sources of help. By contrast, many cases show that children with language impairment can use two languages at a level that would be expected if they had learned just one. Bilingualism does not appear to cause or aggravate the language impairment.

However, it is important to distinguish between failure to use a feature of the morphology correctly (like lexical and grammatical gender agreement) because of faulty processing that prevents children with the same input conditions from learning like typically developing children and the absence of that morphology because of diminished input. Since bilingual children with SLI show both effects – a processing problem and diminished input – their morphology will show more errors than monolingual children with SLI (Baker & de Jong 2007). There is evidence for several constructions (Gathercole 2002) that bilinguals reach a critical mass and 'catch up' with monolinguals on points of morphosyntactic development. However, there is no evidence that processing problems associated with SLI will be eliminated if only one language is being learned.

21.6   Conclusion

The ability to learn two languages is within the human endowment, but not every child in a bilingual setting becomes bilingual. In a survey of 18,000 households in Flanders, de Houwer (2007) found approximately 12 per cent reported that two or more languages were spoken in the home. Of that number 75 per cent reported that their children were bilingual.

While it is clearly possible for children to become bilingual, it is not guaranteed. De Houwer's surveys confirm that parent attitudes are the best predictors of whether the parent will provide circumstances with adequate input in a minority language for their children to learn it (Pearson 2008). Early dual language learning, parents and schools have found, cannot be coerced; but with encouragement and continual reinforcement, children around the world can flourish in two languages.

Suggestions for further reading

Applied Psycholinguistics (2007), volume 28 (3). [The issue is devoted to the LAB (Language Acquisition and Bilingualism) symposium held in Toronto, May 2006.]

De Courtivron, I. (2003). *Lives in Translation*. New York: Palgrave Macmillan.

Genesee, F., Paradis, J., & Crago, M. (2004). *Dual Language Development and Disorders*. Baltimore: Paul Brookes.

Kroll, J., & de Groot, A. M. B. (Eds.). (2005). *Handbook of Bilingualism: Psycholinguistic Approaches*. Oxford: Oxford University Press.

Oller, D. K., & Eilers, R. E. (Eds.) (2002). *Language and Literacy in Bilingual Children*. Clevedon: Multilingual Matters.

Pearson, B. Z. (2008). *Raising a Bilingual Child: A Step-by-Step Guide for Parents*. New York: Random House.

22

Sign language acquisition studies

Diane Lillo-Martin

22.1   Introduction

In this chapter,[1] I overview aspects of sign language acquisition studies conducted over the past twenty years, and speculate on the future of such studies. I have organized the research into five themes, according to some of the goals of these works. These themes are as follows.

(1)   *Exploring the parallels between sign and spoken language acquisition.* In this category I include a variety of studies which show that sign language acquisition takes a similar path as spoken language acquisition, under comparable input conditions (i.e. children whose parents sign to them fluently from birth). Such studies serve to drive home the point that sign languages are fully natural languages and by implication, are deserving of all the rights associated with full natural languages.

(2)   *Explaining the differences between sign and spoken language acquisition.* In this category are studies which note potential differences in the path of acquisition of sign and spoken languages, and attempt to account for them, often by appealing to the modality. In some cases the differences are quite straightforwardly due to the modality (e.g. although sign phonology and spoken phonology have abstract principles in common, they are deeply rooted in modality differences); in others, a good argument has been made that ties the difference to a particular aspect of the modality.

[1] This chapter is a revised version of 'Sign language acquisition studies: Past, present and future' (Lillo-Martin 2008), published in the online proceedings of the conference on Theoretical Issues in Sign Language Research 9, held in Florianópolis, Brazil in December 2006. I sincerely thank Ronice Müller de Quadros and the organizing committee of TISLR 9 for inviting me to give the presentation on which this chapter is based. Preparation of this presentation and chapter was supported in part by a grant from the National Institutes of Health (NIDCD #00183).

(3)   A. *Using sign language acquisition data to inform us about sign language grammar.*
      B. *Using sign language grammar to inform us about sign language acquisition.*
      These two categories are grouped together to emphasize the importance of a strong, reciprocal relationship between studies of grammar and studies of acquisition. Studies in this category show how acquisition studies can bear on theoretical questions in grammatical analysis, and how grammatical developments can lead to new questions or reanalysis in acquisition studies. Such relationships between acquisition and grammar are not unique to sign language studies, of course, but sign language researchers can and do profitably participate in these kinds of works.

(4)   *Using sign language acquisition data to inform us about theories of language acquisition.* Again, sign language research is not alone in pursuing the goal of developing and testing explicit theories of how language acquisition proceeds, but it has much to contribute to such goals. It is particularly important to include sign languages in the database of language acquisition facts which theories strive to explain, since any such theory would have as its goal providing an explanation for the ability of *any* child to learn the natural language he or she is exposed to.

(5)   *Using sign language acquisition data to tell us about the nature of language.* Sign languages and deaf communities allow us to understand in more detail the nature of language since, due to experiments of nature, they sometimes reveal what happens to language in extreme circumstances. Information about what emerges is of great significance to theories of language.

Of course, many studies fall into more than one of the categories above, and others may not have been specifically directed at any of these topics. However, I think it can be useful to take this type of view and examine the broader impacts of studies, whatever their original goals were. The overview provided here is not meant to be exhaustive, but selects examples of studies falling into each theme, to give the reader an idea of directions and possibilities. Additional research in all of these areas is eagerly anticipated. Before discussing these five themes I provide a brief background.

22.2   Background

Any study of the acquisition of sign languages must begin with information regarding the participants and their language-learning situation. Unlike the vast majority of children, deaf children typically do not receive (accessible) linguistic input from birth. Only about 5 per cent of deaf children are born to deaf, signing parents (Mitchell & Karchmer 2004). These children are the focus of much research on sign language acquisition, since their input conditions are relatively comparable to that for children learning a spoken language. Most of the studies described here have been conducted with children in this condition, unless otherwise specified (primarily in theme 5). Other deaf children can be studied to gain a better understanding of the effects of delayed or imperfect input on the course of language acquisition (see Goldin-Meadow Ch. 9 for some discussion of the 'homesigning' sometimes produced by deaf children with no sign language model).

The sign languages under investigation here are natural languages, distinct from the spoken languages of the surrounding hearing communities. Most of the examples discussed here come from American Sign Language (ASL), and there are some examples from other sign languages including Brazilian Sign Language (LSB), and Sign Language of the Netherlands (SLN). It will be useful for the reader to understand that the sub-lexical (phonological) structure of individual signs is typically described in terms of handshape, location, and movement. In the research literature, signs are glossed using upper-case words from a spoken language with approximately the same meaning, with additional notational devices to indicate relevant modifications such as agreement and reduplication. Non-manual markers (facial expressions and body position) are usually noted on a line above the glosses which indicates their extent.

22.3   Five themes

22.3.1   Exploring the parallels between sign and spoken language acquisition

In this category I include research which aims to show that a particular sign language 'is a language' and is acquired on a par with spoken languages (see Lillo-Martin 1999, Newport & Meier 1985 for reviews of some of this research).

One clear example comes from the work of Laura Ann Petitto. Her body of research makes the strong claim that sign language is acquired in exactly the same way as oral language. For example, in one of her own overviews she claims, 'Deaf children exposed to signed languages from birth acquire these languages on an identical maturational time course as hearing children acquire spoken languages' (Petitto 2000: 43). Milestones claimed by Petitto to be 'identical' in signing and speaking children include babbling (7–12 months of age); the first-word stage (11–14 months); and the first two-word stage (16–22 months). Furthermore, Petitto says, 'social and conversational patterns of language use … as well as the types of things that they "talk" about … have demonstrated unequivocally that their language acquisition follows the identical path seen in age-matched hearing children acquiring spoken language' (Petitto 2000: 44).

Similar reports that the general path of language acquisition is similar for signed and spoken languages can be found in studies of sign languages other than ASL; for example, Italian Sign Language (Caselli & Volterra 1990), Brazilian Sign Language (Quadros 1997), and Sign Language of the Netherlands (Van den Bogaerde 2000), among others.

Consider the case of babbling. Research on the babbling of hearing children shows that vocal babbling (repetitive, syllabic sounds such as 'baba') emerges around 6 to 8 months of age, and continues (with certain changes) until it disappears as words come in (see also Vihman *et al.* Ch. 10). Petitto and Marentette (1991) similarly observed that deaf children exposed to sign language produced 'manual babbles' during this same period. They found manual babble activities occurring as 32–71 per cent of the gestures produced by two deaf children studied at 10, 12 and 14 months of age. Petitto and Marentette argued that manual babbling is like vocal babbling in satisfying three conditions. First, the babbles employed phonetic units restricted to those used in signing; second, they showed syllabic organization; and third, they were used non-communicatively. Petitto (2000: 45) concludes, 'the discovery of babbling in another modality confirmed the hypothesis that babbling represents a distinct and critical stage in the ontogeny of human language.'

The similarities in babbling between children learning a sign language and children learning a spoken language were emphasized and expanded on in studies by Meier and Willerman (1995) and Cheek *et al.* (2001), although they propose that babbling in both modalities is a consequence of motor development rather than an expression specifically of the linguistic faculty. Like Petitto and Marentette (1991), Meier and Willerman and Cheek *et al.* observed manual babbling in children exposed to sign language: they observed five deaf children at approximately 7, 10 and 13 months and reported manual babbling in between 25 and 93 per cent of all gestures produced. However, unlike Petitto and Marantette, who reported that manual babbling was much less frequent in the three hearing subjects they studied (about 20 per cent of gestures), Meier and Willerman and Cheek *et al.* report that the five hearing children not exposed to sign language whom they studied produce manual babbles much like those of deaf children, at rates of 44–100 per cent of all gestures.

Both of these studies find strong similarities between children developing sign language and children developing spoken language. Both also connect their findings to theoretical explanations which stress similarities in the development of sign and spoken languages, although their theories are different. Both are thus good examples of parallels between sign and spoken language acquisition.

Why is it important to demonstrate that deaf children with native signing input acquire sign languages along an 'identical' – or even parallel – time course as that of children learning spoken languages? For Petitto, the implication of this finding is that the human propensity for language is not modality dependent. Rather, the mechanisms that make language development possible apply equally well to a visual–gestural language as to an auditory–vocal language. As we seek to understand how language acquisition is possible, our theories might need to be changed to accommodate such modality independence.

Such conclusions about the nature of the language-acquisition mechanisms would not be warranted if sign languages were considered anything less than full, natural human languages with the same biological foundations as well as similar social environments. Nowadays, well-informed linguists and psychologists do not question the status of sign languages. However, there are still many people who are not well informed on this subject and oftentimes they are in positions which allow them to make decisions regarding the welfare of (potential) sign language users. For this reason, the point cannot be stressed too much.

22.3.2   Explaining the differences between sign and spoken language acquisition

This category of research focuses on where sign language and oral language acquisition might be different, and attempts to explain this as, for example, effects of the modality. Such modality effects may include iconicity and motor/articulatory development, among others.

An example of research considering the role of modality in explaining differences between sign language and spoken language development looks at the appearance of first signs versus spoken words. Numerous authors have claimed that first signs appear before first words by as much as six months, and the current enthusiasm for 'baby signing' in the hearing population is based on this idea. Meier and Newport (1990), in a thorough review of the literature documenting acquisition milestones for sign versus speech, came to several important general conclusions about the similarities and differences. First, the 'advantage' for signs seems to be about 1.5 to 2.5 months (roughly age 8.5 months for first signs versus age 10–11 months for first words), and this difference is seen only with the earliest context-bound signs, not purely symbolic ones. Second, they argued that the sign advantage exists only for first words, not for first word combinations (early syntax). Finally, Meier and Newport offered a possible explanation for the sign advantage in terms of 'peripheral' mechanisms – that is, the mechanisms used in the production and/or perception of signs versus words. They provided reasons to think that it takes longer for speaking children to develop sufficient articulatory control to produce utterances which can be recognized as words than for signing children to develop comparable control. Thus, the difference boils down to a *disadvantage* for spoken language at the earliest stages of lexical development.

Another body of research which examines effects of modality on sign language acquisition concerns early sign phonology. Researchers have studied which components of signs children are more or less accurate with, and found that in many cases children's development can be explained by appealing to the development of motor and perceptual mechanisms. Both of these explanations emphasize the role that modality plays in sign language acquisition. It may well be that modality plays an especially important role in explaining patterns of phonological development.

For example, several researchers find more errors on handshape than on location in early signs. Young children's first signs tend to use a handshape with all fingers extended, whether spread or lax (), or with the fingers all in a fist (), or with just the index finger extended (). These handshapes will often be substituted for others in target signs which use more complex handshapes. However, the location of signs is much more frequently produced correctly. A possible explanation offered for this pattern is that fine motor control is needed for handshape, but this develops later than the gross motor control which is needed for location (Cheek *et al.* 2001, Conlin *et al.* 2000, Marentette & Mayberry 2000). On the flip side of the coin, researchers suggest that it may be easier for children to perceive differences in location as compared with different handshapes, also contributing to the earlier accuracy with the former.

Researchers have also noticed that children's earliest signing often involves movement repetition (Meier 2006). This can be directly related to repeated movements in motoric development such as the stereotypes of repeated kicking or arm waving. Meier (2006) also observes that children sometimes produce certain two-handed signs with incorrect movement. In these signs, the target form has one hand acting on the other as a base. However, children may erroneously use identical movements on both hands. Meier proposes that such errors may be explainable by reference to a phenomenon known as 'sympathy', whereby children have difficulty inhibiting the action of one hand when the other is active.

Meier (2006) argues that studying articulatory factors in the development of sign phonology is important for at least two reasons. First, knowing which effects come from articulation helps identify those which require other explanations. Second, he suggests that articulatory factors may promote particular kinds of linguistic organization – especially for children – which might lead us to think that these effects may reflect not only different levels of performance with grammar (for signing and speaking children), but also different competences.

Identifying whether children's developing ability to produce signs reflects performance or competence differences is difficult, but there are some cases for which an articulatory/perceptual explanation is probably unwarranted. For example, Conlin *et al.* (2000) and Marentette and Mayberry (2000) suggest that some location errors are not consistent with a motoric explanation, but rather indicate that the child has misrepresented the target location of certain signs. This suggestion reinforces Meier's comment that understanding articulatory factors helps to identify those aspects of the development of signs which require alternative explanations.

These examples have emphasized the modality dependence of the proposed explanations of phonological development. However, it should be pointed out that articulatory factors may well explain some aspects of early phonological development in spoken languages as well (e.g. MacNeilage & Davis 1990). 'Modality' effects are present in both modalities, then, and in this sense attending to modality is not only a way of explaining how sign language development and spoken language development are different, but again how they are alike.

22.3.3 The reciprocal relationship between sign language grammar and acquisition

22.3.3.1 Using sign language acquisition data to inform us about sign language grammar

When competing grammatical models make different acquisition predictions, developmental data can be used to test the models. This is a principle of spoken language research as well as sign language research, although it has only been applied in sign language research relatively recently. Here I will discuss two examples, the first one only briefly.

Conlin *et al.* (2000: 52) state, 'Studies of early sign development … may help us decide between competing models of the adult language.' For example, they suggest that children's early signs may help in the determination of canonical signs. The usefulness of looking at child signing for this purpose is already clear. Researchers have identified certain handshapes as phonologically unmarked (for example, only these handshapes may appear as the base hand of certain two-handed signs). It has long been recognized that the earliest occurring handshapes come from the set of unmarked ones in the adult language (Battison 1978). Conlin *et al.* also hope that analyses of children's signing can help in the evaluation of models of adult grammar, in particular when certain models are better able to capture the generalizations about children's productions. Karnopp (2002) takes such an approach in her investigation of the development of phonology in Brazilian Sign Language. She adopts the Dependency model of van der Hulst (1993) and finds that it makes strong predictions about sign phonology acquisition which were borne out in the data she analysed from one deaf signing child. For example, the Dependency model identifies the finger selection aspect of handshape as a 'head', and the finger configuration aspect (e.g. whether the fingers are open or bent) as a 'dependent', and therefore predicts that finger configuration will be acquired only after finger selection. Karnopp concludes that the sign language acquisition data she analysed provide strong support for the theoretical model used.

A second example comes from the area of syntax. Lillo-Martin and Quadros (2006, in press) investigated the acquisition of topic, focus and wh-questions in American Sign Language (ASL) and Brazilian Sign Language (LSB). They argued that the child-language data helps to reveal the correct analyses of these structures. We will start with a few examples.

In both ASL and LSB, certain signs can appear in a sentence twice, once in their usual position and again at the end of the sentence, to indicate emphasis on that sign. These constructions are often called 'doubling'. Some examples are given in (1) (examples in this section are grammatical in both ASL and LSB; they are reproduced from Lillo-Martin & Quadros in press).

(1)   a. JOHN CAN READ CAN
          'John really CAN read.'
      b. MARY FINISH GO SPAIN FINISH
          'Mary ALREADY went to Spain.'
      c. I LOSE BOOK LOSE
          'I did LOSE the book indeed.'

Also in both of these languages, the same category of signs which can occur in doubling constructions can occur in the sentence-final position only. These sentences can be referred to as 'final constructions'. Examples are given in (2).

(2)   a. JOHN READ CAN
      b. MARY GO SPAIN FINISH
      c. I BOOK LOSE

According to one type of grammatical analysis, doubling and final constructions are related. Both are used for emphatic focus, and according to these theories, their derivations are related (Nunes & Quadros 2006, 2007, Petronio 1993, Wilbur, 1997).

However, there is another kind of focus, known as new information focus (for short, 'I-focus'). Unlike the emphatic focus, this places the focused material in the sentence-initial position (Lillo-Martin & Quadros in press, Neidle 2002). Such new information focus is used, for example, in the context of answering a question, as in example (3). The basic word order (SVO for both ASL and LSB) is also permitted in such contexts.

(3)   S1: WHAT YOU READ?
           'What did you read?'
                  I-focus
           ⎯⎯⎯⎯⎯⎯
      S2: BOOK STOKOE I READ
           or   I READ BOOK STOKOE
           'I read *Stokoe's book*.'

Table 22.1. Summary of results – Lillo-Martin
and Quadros (2005)

Child	Age of acquisition of each structure		
	I-focus	Doubling	Final
Aby	1;9 ***	2;1	2;0
Sal	1;7 ***	1;9	1;9
Ana	1;6 **	2;0	2;1
Leo	1;10 ***	2;1	2;2

** $p<0.005$
*** $p<0.001$

According to the proposals of Lillo-Martin and Quadros, I-focus is derived syntactically through a completely different mechanism from that of emphatic focus. They predicted that if their analyses are correct, children would acquire doubling and final constructions together, since these are both instances of emphatic focus, but these might be acquired independently from I-focus, since it is derived differently. Lillo-Martin and Quadros (2005) tested their prediction by looking at the longitudinal spontaneous production data from two deaf children acquiring ASL as a native language (Aby, Sal), and two deaf children acquiring LSB as a native language (Ana, Leo). All four children have deaf, signing parents. They were videotaped regularly starting before the age of 2. Their utterances were examined to determine when they started productively using I-focus, doubling and final constructions. The results of this study are summarized in Table 22.1.

It is clear that the children did acquire doubling and final constructions together, but these two constructions were acquired later than I-focus (highly significant by Binomial Exact Probability). These results can be taken to support theoretical analyses which relate doubling and final constructions in ASL and LSB over analyses which give them distinct derivations.

The two examples presented have shown areas in which data from sign language acquisition can bear on theoretical questions of grammatical analyses. For both sign and spoken languages, there are many cases in which different theoretical proposals do not obviously make different predictions for acquisition, so acquisition data may not bear on such issues. However, other cases lead to expectations of ordering, such that phenomena that are related in the adult grammar can be expected to be acquired together; or phenomena that are separated are expected to be acquired separately. In some cases, specific ordering predictions can be made, such as when a particular construction has others as prerequisites (for discussion of examples, see Snyder & Lillo-Martin in press). In these cases, language acquisition data can provide important support – or disconfirmation – of theoretical proposals.

22.3.3.2   Using sign language grammar to inform us about sign language acquisition

Category 3A looks at ways in which acquisition studies can inform studies of grammar. The present category of studies goes in the opposite direction, using new developments in grammar to inform acquisition studies. These two categories are closely related, since both show the close relationship between acquisition studies and linguistic theory, and in fact there is often a spiral effect such that both fields benefit from and influence each other in the same domain.

An example of this category comes from studies of children's development of word order. Coerts and Mills (1994) undertook a study of two deaf children's development of the subject – object – verb word order in the Sign Language of the Netherlands (SLN), between the ages of about one-and-a-half years to two-and-a-half years. They found that children showed a great deal of variability in their ordering of subjects and verbs. This variability in the acquisition of word order was puzzling and left without a full explanation. Then, Bos (1995) identified SLN as having a process known as Subject Pronoun Copy (SPC) (cf. Padden 1988). According to SPC, the subject of a sentence (glossed INDEX) can be repeated as a pronoun in the sentence-final position, as shown in (4a). However, it is also possible for the sentence-initial subject to be unexpressed (this is a general process found in SLN as well as in other sign languages). When the sentence-initial subject is left unexpressed, but the sentence-final subject pronoun is present, the surface order is verb – subject, as in (4) (examples from Coerts 2000).

(4)   a. INDEX$_{beppie}$ FILM INDEX$_{beppie}$
          'Beppie is filming'.
      b. CRY INDEX$_{dolls}$
          'The dolls are crying.'

Coerts (2000) then undertook to reanalyse the child data previously studied by Coerts and Mills (1994). First, it was clear that the children knew that SLN permits null subjects, as they used them appropriately and frequently. She then employed a fairly strict criterion for acquisition of the SPC process: the child must use a sentence-final subject pronoun in a sentence with an overt subject to show that they had acquired SPC. Once the children showed they had acquired SPC, at around two years, any later instances of verb – subject order in which the post-verbal subject is a pronoun were considered instances of SPC.

Using this reanalysis, Coerts found that the majority of the previously 'unexplained' word order examples were in fact explainable, and children's acquisition of word order was more in line with expectations. Coerts concludes:

knowledge of the adult language steers the choice of analysis procedures used for acquisition data … an analysis procedure that takes subject

pronoun copy into account results in a much clearer picture with respect
to the acquisition of subject and verb position.   (Coerts 2000: 107)

A project by Chen Pichler (2001a, 2001b) resulted in similar findings for
ASL, and her study goes beyond consideration of SPC alone to include
other instances of word order changes allowed in the adult grammar.
Although there had been early claims that children strictly followed the
adult basic SVO word order, Schick (2002) found no evidence for this
strategy in two year olds, concluding instead that children's word order
was 'random'. Chen Pichler used a similar approach to Coerts' and determined when children's use of verb–subject order could be considered cases
of SPC, and when their use of object–verb order could be considered as
following from adult-like word-order changing operations (for example,
object shift).

Chen Pichler established clear criteria for counting utterances as legal
order changes. For example, post-verbal subjects must be pronouns to be
considered SPC; preverbal objects occurring with verbs marked for aspect,
spatial location or handling classifier were considered instances of object
shift. Using these criteria, Chen Pichler found that children's word order use
demonstrates regularity in following grammatical options much earlier
than previously thought. Thus, taking into consideration such developments in the syntactic analyses leads to more reliable acquisition studies.

Both of the examples provided illustrate the importance of considering
the target adult grammar when studying language development. The goal of
studying language acquisition is to understand how children become adult-
like in their knowledge of language. When children differ from adults, an
explanation for this difference must be sought. But sometimes researchers
examining child development overlook developments in the study of the
adult grammar. The description of the language children are exposed to,
and will ultimately be users of, changes as researchers gather more data and
form hypotheses which point in new directions for further study.

22.3.4 Using sign language acquisition data to inform us about theories of language acquisition

In the previous section, we considered theories of adult grammar and their
relationship to studies of language acquisition. Here, we turn to theories of
the process of acquisition. Alternative theories of how language develops can
be tested and refined using real-time acquisition data from sign languages
just as they are tested using data from spoken languages. These theories are
general theories about language acquisition, not particular to sign languages
(and in general, not developed on the basis of sign language data).

As an example, consider the Verb Island Hypothesis of Tomasello (1992,
see also Tomasello Ch. 5). According to this model of language development, children go through an early period in which verbs are individual

'islands' of organization. It predicts that certain patterns (such as word order or inflections) will be found with individual verbs, although there will not be evidence that a whole class of verbs behaves in the same way. This early period of verb islands would begin when children are starting to use two-word combinations, but generalizations would be apparent some months later (say, around the age of two years for most children).

In support of this proposal, Morgan and Woll (2002: 275) conclude: 'we found no evidence for the child's exploitation of an abstract set of verb frames before 3;2. The child appeared to build argument structure afresh with each new verb and these verbs were uniquely tied to their communicative function.' Only later, they argue, do children build rules which hold over multiple verbs.

Schick (2002) also examined the verb island hypothesis in her study of early sign combinations. She found only limited evidence in support of the hypothesis, in that some of the children she studied showed consistent ordering patterns with some verbs. However, she found that in many cases, word order was quite varied even for individual verbs. This would appear to show neither verb islands, where individual verbs behave alike, nor evidence of word order rules which apply across the board to all different verbs.

In this context, we can return to the findings of Coerts (2000) and Chen Pichler (2001), reported in section 22.3.3.2. These authors reported systematic use of word order by young signing children when grammatical alternations allowed by the adult grammar are also considered. According to their results, children's signing is neither random nor organized into verb-specific islands. Rather, the rules which characterize the adult grammar are also found in this domain of children's language. Whether the data analysed by Morgan and Woll (BSL) and by Schick (ASL) are amenable to the same conclusion remains to be seen.

Another example can be raised from Reilly's study of the development of non-manual marking (as summarized in Reilly 2006). Reilly and colleagues have been interested in children's development of the use of linguistic non-manual markings versus often very similar affective and communicative facial expressions. Reilly sees this project as, in part, a test of the degree to which language is an innately specified independent cognitive function, because it assesses the separability of language from other cognitive functions. She suggests that an approach to language acquisition in which language is seen as a general cognitive system would predict that children would readily recruit their prelinguistic affective and communicative abilities in the service of linguistic functions, and thus acquire non-manual markings together with their co-occurring manual components. On the other hand, 'children would approach each linguistic structure and its morphology de novo' in a more modular approach (Reilly 2006: 268).

This question is clearly addressed with data from the development of non-manual marking of negation. The negative non-manual marker used in adult

ASL (indicated with 'neg' on the line above the sign glosses) is essentially like the negative headshake used communicatively by very young children, whether exposed to sign language or not. Negation can be expressed in adult ASL by a negative sign co-occurring with this negative headshake, or even by the negative headshake alone, as in the examples in (5) (examples from Reilly 2006; the notation 't' indicates a topic non-manual marker).

(5)   <u>   t   </u>   <u> neg </u>
    a. BOOK READ ME CAN'T
       I can't read the book.'
                           <u> neg </u>
    b. ME EAT ICE-CREAM
       'I don't eat ice cream.'

Reilly and her colleagues found that deaf children acquiring sign languages, like hearing, non-signing children, produce communicative negative headshakes by about 12 months of age. The first negative signs, NO and DON'T-WANT, emerge at 18–20 months, followed by other negative signs up to age 3;6. For seven of the eight negative signs investigated, Reilly found that the manual sign first appears without the required co-occurring headshake. Several months later, the negative headshake is used together with the negative signs. This separation occurred despite the fact that the negative headshake was used prelinguistically by these children to mean essentially the same thing. Reilly concludes that children treat the negative headshake as it is used in ASL as a linguistic element which must be analysed independently. This would not be expected under the theory of language as a more general cognitive system, but only by the modular approach.

The two theories under discussion in this section – the verb island hypothesis and the modularity of language with respect to other cognitive systems – can be further tested using data from sign language acquisition, as can other theories of language development. In some cases, sign languages provide a new form of data, unavailable using the study of spoken languages alone. The study of the non-manual marking of negation is one such case. In other cases, sign language research provides needed breadth and diversity of languages brought to bear on a theoretical question.

22.3.5 Using sign language acquisition data to tell us about the nature of language

The study of sign languages and deaf communities can provide information about language development under extreme circumstances which are not found elsewhere. This is a unique contribution to our understanding of the nature of language and the mechanisms which make language acquisition possible. Researchers studying such circumstances have a very special role to play in advancing scientific knowledge.

Examples of such contributions come from the study of recently developed sign languages, late first-language learners of sign languages, learners with degraded input, learners of invented sign systems, homesigners, etc. These studies tell us about the ranges of possible languages, the path and properties of language emergence, 'resilient' properties of language which appear in the absence of evidence, critical period effects in language acquisition, how the learner modifies the input she or he receives, etc. The range of outcomes from such studies is so broad and important that there is no way to give it justice here. However, I will give one example to whet the reader's appetite; for a fuller meal please see the original works in this area.

Late first-language learners are virtually unheard of in spoken language communities, but not so in signers. Since about 95 per cent of deaf children have hearing parents (Mitchell & Karchmer 2004), it is not surprising that the vast majority are not exposed to sign language from birth. Sometimes, parents decide to educate their children orally (without sign language); some of these children are later exposed to a sign language after having learned only a portion of spoken language (often, not enough to communicate effectively). In other cases, children experience late exposure to sign language simply because the resources for exposing the child earlier were not available to the family. For various reasons, children may be exposed to sign language only after the age of two years, or five years, or twelve years, etc. It is not well understood exactly how such delayed linguistic exposure affects language development, but it is clear that there are some effects.

Morford and Mayberry (2000) provide an overview of some of the research investigating effects of delayed input on (first) language acquisition and processing. Most of this research has been conducted with adults whose exposure to sign language began at different times. By studying adults, researchers investigate the outcome of the language-development process, after years of experience have made the use of sign language a well-practised, familiar skill.

Overall, studies with adults whose age of first exposure to ASL was between approximately 4 and 16 years, as compared to native signers (those with exposure from birth), have consistently reported differences in both production and comprehension tests. Furthermore, studies looking at language processing have also found differences for different age-of-exposure groups. The degree of an effect is not uniform across different studies. For example, Newport (1990) found that later learners (those with exposure after age 12) scored lower than 'early' learners (those with exposure between 4 and 6), who in turn scored lower than native signers, on tests of ASL morphology production and comprehension. However, the three groups were not different on a test of basic word order. Similarly, Emmorey et al. (1995) found that late learners were different from native signers in a study of online processing of verb agreement, but not in aspect marking.

Mayberry, Lock and Kazmi (2002) extended such findings by comparing late first-language learners of ASL with late *second*-language learners of ASL: late-deafened adults whose exposure to sign language began in the same period as the late first-language learners (9–13). Their study asked participants to judge the grammaticality of complex sentences. The effects of late exposure were strongest for late first-language learners; late second-language learners performed close to natives.

These results reinforce the idea that early exposure to language is crucial for its normal acquisition. But what factor(s) will be most affected by delayed input when other factors are relatively spared? Newport (1990) hypothesizes that young children have the ability to detect patterns of the 'correct grain size' for the development of complex morphology, while the greater cognitive capabilities of older children or adults actually interfere with this type of analysis, thus leading to the differences in performance on syntactic versus morphological tests she observed.

An alternative proposal is put forth by Morford and Mayberry (2000), who emphasize the differences in phonological processing skills for native or early learners versus late learners, and suggest that what is missing for late learners is what is learned by those with native exposure in the first year of life. In particular, a great deal of phonological development takes place during this period, and studies show infants' sensitivities to phonological information from a very early age. What Morford and Mayberry propose is that 'the true advantage of early exposure to language is the development of the phonological system prior to the development of the lexical–semantic and morpho-syntactic systems' (p. 124). Problems in phonological processing can have 'cascading' effects on other levels of language processing, showing up in the various areas of effects of language delay.

The study of late learners has much to contribute to theories of language and language development. The effects of delayed input should not be random or general, but rather should fall along fault lines which the grammar makes available. Theories of why children are better language learners than adults are must make reference to crucial aspects of the language-learning mechanism. Such theories have little data to go on outside of the realm of late first-language acquisition in deaf children, since second-language learning appears to have different constraints and consequences in some ways.

22.4   Research which cuts across themes

Many areas of sign language acquisition research touch on more than one of the themes discussed above. One area of research which touches on all of the themes is the acquisition of verb agreement, which has been a subject of attention for well over twenty years.

In ASL and other sign languages, subject and object person-agreement is expressed on a class of verbs (such as HELP and ASK) by modifying the initial and final locations of the verb. Agreement with source and goal location in another class of verbs (such as MOVE and GO) takes a similar form, but the endpoints represent location arguments rather than person. A third class of verbs (including LIKE and EAT) takes no agreement marking at all.

Meier (1982) examined the acquisition of verb agreement in ASL in comparison to the acquisition of verbal morphology in spoken languages. He argued that sign language agreement is acquired in a similar fashion as is complex, unstressed verb agreement in some spoken languages. On the other hand, Morgan, Barriere and Woll (2006), in their study of the acquisition of verb agreement in British Sign Language (BSL), argue that 'spatial' aspects of verb agreement in sign language make it unlike that in spoken languages. The form of agreement is not an affix, but a modification of the root, which Morgan *et al.* argue involves a high degree of simultaneity, making segmentation difficult for the young child. Both of these research groups found that children make errors of omission and commission in marking verbs for agreement, until at least the age of three years.

On the other hand, Quadros and Lillo-Martin (2007) found that verb agreement errors were extremely rare, for two children acquiring ASL and two children acquiring LSB. They attributed the differential error rate to a different theoretical view of contexts for obligatory use of verb morphology. They argue that the acquisition data support an approach which identifies verbs needing agreement in particular sentential contexts rather than lexically marking certain verbs as always requiring agreement, a view which is confirmed in studies with adult signers.

Verb agreement has also been studied in late learners, as it seems to be an area of special problems. Adult late learners have been shown to err on using verbal morphology (Newport 1990), and they also have processing difficulties in this domain (Emmorey *et al.* 1995). Studies of verb agreement in late learners provide some evidence that there are specifically grammatical differences between early and later learners as well as proposed processing differences. Berk (2003) studied two children whose exposure to ASL began at the age of six. She found that the later learners were particularly affected in their production of person-marking agreement on ASL verbs. They made numerous errors of both omission and commission, continuing without a decrease in error rate over four years of observation. Other verbal morphology, indicating location agreement, was not affected, as the late learners appropriately used such marking, although the form of location agreement is very similar to that of person agreement. A specifically grammatical deficit would seem to be implicated in order to explain such a difference.

22.5   The future of sign language acquisition research

What does the future of sign language acquisition research look like? Our hope is that future research on sign languages will continue to enhance connections with the questions asked of spoken language acquisition. Theories of language, and of language acquisition, need to accommodate sign language data, so sign language research that informs and benefits from studies of spoken languages is desirable. Even more studies of an enhanced range of populations is encouraged – for example, cross-sign language comparisons, studies of the effects of differences in input quality and timing, etc. Such studies have much to offer, both scientifically and practically.

Suggestions for further reading

Chamberlain, C., Morford, J. P., & Mayberry, R. I. (Eds.). (2000). *Language Acquisition by Eye*. Mahwah, NJ: Lawrence Erlbaum Associates.

Lillo-Martin, D. (1999). Modality effects and modularity in language acquisition: The acquisition of American Sign Language. In W. C. Ritchie & T. K. Bhatia (Eds.), *Handbook of Language Acquisition* (pp. 531–567). San Diego, CA: Academic Press.

Morgan, G., & Woll, B. (Eds.). (2002). *Directions in Sign Language Acquisition*. Amsterdam: John Benjamins.

Newport, E. L., & Meier, R. P. (1985). The acquisition of American Sign Language. In D. I. Slobin (Ed.), *The Crosslinguistic Study of Language Acquisition: Vol. 1*. (pp. 881–938). Hillsdale, NJ: Lawrence Erlbaum Associates.

Schick, B., Marschark, M., & Spencer, P. E. (Eds.). (2006). *Advances in the Sign Language Development of Deaf Children*. Oxford: Oxford University Press.

23

Children with specific language impairment

J. Bruce Tomblin

23.1 Introduction

During the past twenty years there has been an increasing amount of literature concerning one form of developmental language disorder that has come to be known as specific language impairment (SLI). Within this chapter, I will be focusing on the conceptual and empirical issues concerned with who these children are in relation to other children with or without language impairment and what is known about the course and aetiology of SLI. In the following chapter, Leonard (Ch. 24) will survey what we know about the particular language features of SLI and the explanations offered for these features.

23.2 Conceptualizing SLI

Much of the research concerning child language development has focused on mechanisms and characteristics that generalize across children. In such research, individual differences in language development are acknowledged, but often set aside. In contrast, these individual differences in language development are the central focus of those who study developmental language disorders. Consequently, developmental language disorders may be viewed as a particular region in a multidimensional space of individual differences among children with regard to language development and use. Conceptualizing SLI as a domain within a broader region of individual differences in language development helps highlight key issues that surrounded its development as a type of developmental language disorder and the manner in which it compares with individual differences of typically developing children. The current conceptualization of SLI can be traced back to the middle of the twentieth century where the term developmental aphasia or dysphasia was used to refer to language comprehension and/or production deficits in the context of a child who was not mentally retarded, mentally ill or deaf (Myklebust 1952). These children were described as having poor language development without concomitant intellectual disability or hearing impairment. By the early 1980s the term aphasia in reference to developmental language disorders began to give way to SLI (Fey & Leonard 1983). SLI was preferred over developmental aphasia largely due to the neurogenic implication of the term aphasia which refers to an acquired language disorder associated with brain lesions. The list of concomitant conditions that excluded children from being SLI also expanded. Leonard (1998) listed normal hearing, normal nonverbal IQ (performance IQ > 85), absence of recent otitis media, absence of seizure disorder, cerebral palsy, brain lesions, normal oral structure and function and normal reciprocal social interactions or restriction of activities. It is noteworthy that all these exclusionary conditions are diagnosed on the basis of behaviours other than language. As a result, SLI has come to be the only developmental disorder that is diagnosed on the basis of language itself. This feature of SLI means that it provides and in fact necessitates explicit consideration of when and why we say a child has language impairment.

23.2.1 Standards for language impairment

Although there were descriptions of children with language impairment for more than a century, much of this literature provided few explicit guidelines as to what would determine this. This is likely to be due to the absence of well-developed theory regarding language development and well-developed methods of measurement (For example, see Myklebust 1971). By the 1970s new language measures were being introduced and these provided guidelines for clinical interpretation (for example: Lee & Canter 1971, Rizzo & Stephens 1981). These guidelines defined language impairment as a discrepancy between a child's level of language achievement and the skills expected to be seen in a child of that chronological age – where these expectations were based on test norms. Referencing language achievement to chronological age was soon challenged by those who argued that the relevant benchmark for language development was not chronological age, but rather the child's cognitive development (Miller et al. 1978, Stark & Tallal 1981) and cognitive development was typically operationally defined as nonverbal IQ. This notion that achievement expectations should be based on some general cognitive or general intellectual benchmark was also being espoused in the fields of learning disabilities and dyslexia and came to be known as cognitive referencing. Thus, by the 1990s, SLI came to be viewed as language achievement that was to some degree poorer than would be expected on the basis of nonverbal IQ. This 'cognitive discrepancy' did not replace the chronological age criterion however, but rather was added to it. Thus, children with SLI needed to have language skills that were both below chronological age and nonverbal IQ expectations.

During the 1990s, several individuals voiced concerns about the value of cognitive referencing (Dale & Cole 1991, Lahey 1990). Concerns were raised that this standard excluded children with poor language skills and poor nonverbal intelligence from eligibility for services based on the assumption that their language skills could not be advanced beyond their nonverbal (cognitive) levels. Cole and Dale (Cole *et al.* 1990) demonstrated that in fact this assumption was not valid and further that discrepancy-based diagnoses were not stable over time. Thus, in 1997, my colleagues and I (Tomblin *et al.* 1996) presented a standard for language impairment that returned to the age-based reference. After surveying practising speech-language clinicians, we established that language achievement below the 10th percentile in two areas of language constituted language impairment. This criterion for the determination of language impairment was quite similar to one suggested by Paul (2001). Soon thereafter, we implemented this standard for the determination of the prevalence of SLI in kindergarten children (Tomblin *et al.* 1997). In this case, however, we continued to retain the requirement of a nonverbal discrepancy, by requiring children with SLI to have nonverbal IQs above 85. Thus, children with SLI were likely to have language skills below the 10th percentile and nonverbal intellectual skills above the 16th percentile. Subsequently, several studies have compared the language profiles of these children with SLI who had nonverbal IQs above 85 with those children who met the criteria for language impairment but who had nonverbal IQs between 70 and 85 termed non-specific language impaired (NLI) for lack of a better term (Ellis Weismer *et al.* 2000, Tomblin & Zhang 1999). In these studies the NLI group had generally lower language skills and slower processing than the SLI group. In many ways these two groups presented very similar profiles and also similar patterns of language change over time. Rice *et al.* (2005) did find some differences between these two groups concerning patterns of use of overgeneralization of regular past tense forms to irregular. Currently, common practice has retained some vestige of a nonverbal discrepancy at least in the form of fully normal (> 85) nonverbal IQ, however, Tager-Flusberg and Cooper (1999) noted that the inclusion of this practice bears reconsideration.

23.2.2　SLI and excluded conditions

As noted above, in addition to the presence of language impairment, SLI also requires the absence of excluded conditions. Common to these exclusionary conditions are factors that are known to influence language development and often result in language impairment. One could reasonably conclude that SLI represents individual differences in language that result in particularly poor levels of language for which we have no current explanation. A stronger claim would be that the application of these exclusionary conditions suggests that SLI is intended to refer to poor language achievement resulting from causes internal and possibly unique to the language systems, hence the term 'specific'. (See, for instance, Clahsen 1989, Friederici 2006, Gopnik 1997, Rice & Wexler 1996a, van der Lely & Stollwerck 1996.)

By creating a group of children with SLI that are distinguished from other children with language disorders within these excluded groups, we might infer that the language characteristics of children with SLI are also distinct from these other conditions. This hypothesis has only recently been put to empirical test with respect to several different populations. Children with Down syndrome (DS) usually are mentally retarded and have often been described as having particular difficulty with morpho-syntax (Chapman 1997), which is also often a characteristic weakness in children with SLI (see Leonard Ch. 24). Eadie and colleagues examined the use of grammatical morphology, particularly tense use, in mean-length-utterance-matched children with SLI and DS (Eadie *et al.* 2002). These authors reported no statistical differences in the use of grammatical mor-phology between the SLI and DS participants. More recently Laws and Bishop directly compared children with SLI with those DS after matching on nonverbal IQ with respect to lexical, sentence and narrative use (Laws & Bishop 2003) and pragmatics (Laws & Bishop 2004). Across these aspects of language, they found few differences between SLI and DS individuals in language and communication function. Williams syndrome (WS) repre-sents another group of individuals who often have intellectual disability. Pinker (1991) proposed that WS was a mirror image of SLI and thus these two conditions represented a double dissociation between rule learning and lexical learning systems where SLI represents a rule-learning deficit with preserved lexical abilities and the opposite for WS. This perspective was echoed by Clahsen and Almazan (2001) based upon their analysis of plural formation in the WS individuals. Laws and Bishop (2004) have directly compared children with SLI with children with WS and found that WS children were significantly better on measures of speech and grammar than the children with SLI, but both groups were poorer than the typically developing control group. In this study the children with SLI and WS were matched on nonverbal IQ, thus these data would support Rice *et al.*'s (2005) conclusion that children with SLI contrast with children with WS primarily with respect to the relationship between language and nonverbal cognitive skills. This contrast, however, becomes less interes-ting when we recall that children with SLI are selected in part because their language is poorer than their nonverbal skills whereas this is not so with WS (see Richardson & Thomas Ch. 26). Also, the extent to which language in WS exceeds general cognitive levels of development has been ques-tioned in recent reviews (Brock 2007, Donnai & Karmiloff-Smith 2000, Mervis & Becerra 2007). Therefore it is unlikely that a strong version of Pinker's double dissociation hypothesis that includes sparing of either rules or vocabulary across SLI and WS can hold. When one takes a broad view of the language features of SLI and those of children with DS or WS we find far greater similarities than differences. Where differences occur, they seem to be more in amount than kind. Whether these similarities also reflect shared causal factors remains an interesting and unanswered question.

The language features of children with SLI have also been contrasted with autism. For several decades there has been an ongoing interest in the relationship between SLI or earlier childhood aphasia and autism. Beginning with studies by Rutter and colleagues (Bartak *et al.* 1975, 1977) and extending through research more recently by Bishop and colleagues (Bishop & Norbury 2002) one common hypothesis has been that SLI and autism may be examples of a spectrum disorder involving communication. A portion of this hypothesis has been concerned with shared aetiology (see for instance, Folstein & Mankoski 2000), but this work has also considered the possible similarities and differences in language behaviours between SLI and autism. Any comparison between SLI and autism must recognize that the scope and variability of communication deficits within autism is much greater than in SLI. Common across this variability is always poor social use of language in autism whereas the features of phonology, grammar and semantics are highly variable ranging from complete mutism to, in some cases, relatively normal grammar and often spared phonology (Kjelgaard & Tager-Flusberg 2001, Sigman & Capps 1997, also see Luyster & Lord Ch. 25). Among those children with autism who are able to perform on standardized measures of language structure and content, and are thus higher functioning children with autism, the average language performance levels are similar albeit somewhat lower than those of children with SLI (Bartak *et al.* 1977, Tager-Flusberg 2004a). Currently there appears to be general agreement that SLI overlaps with autism with regard to core language features often found in SLI that involve impairments in grammar and semantics, but contrasts with autism with regard to the domain of pragmatics and social cognition (Bishop 2003). This overlap could be taken as support for the initial hypothesis that SLI is simply a milder variant of autism and thus resides on a continuum with it. An alternative hypothesis has surfaced in the past decade where the autism spectrum is viewed as having multiple components, one of which could be SLI. In this case the overlap of SLI and autism with respect to structure and meaning systems is not due to differences in severity but rather the joint occurrence of SLI with the social deficits that are more invariant in autism. In this regard, SLI is viewed as a common co-morbid condition with autism resulting in children with SLI and autism or children with autism without concomitant SLI. The manner in which these two accounts differ currently has more to do with alternative theories of shared versus unique aetiologies for SLI and autism because both assume that there is overlap in aspects of language characteristics.

One additional group of children with language impairment that is excluded from SLI is that of children with hearing impairment. The spoken language skills of children with hearing impairment are even more variable than those found in children with autism. Those children with congenital profound hearing loss often fail to acquire much functional spoken language and instead acquire their language and communication system via manual communication systems. Even those who do acquire the spoken language of their community usually have very limited skills unless they are provided with cochlear implants. The spoken language skills of children who have mild to moderate hearing loss (children who are hard of hearing; HH) are more likely to be comparable with those of SLI at least with regard to severity of the language deficit. Additionally, those theories that posit that SLI is caused by generalized central auditory processing deficits of acoustic stimuli (see, for instance, Tallal *et al.* 1993) support the prediction that the language profiles of children with SLI and HH may be similar. Bishop and her colleagues (Briscoe *et al.* 2001, Norbury *et al.* 2001) tested this prediction by comparing phonological memory, finite verb morphology and general spoken and written language abilities in children who were HH and children with SLI. With the exception of phonological memory measured by non-word repetition, the HH as a group was better than the age-matched children with SLI. These authors did note that there was considerable variability among the children with hearing loss and some were more similar to the SLI group with regard to language ability. Based upon very limited data, we can conclude that children with SLI do differ from children with HH in that the latter group approaches normal levels of spoken-language development.

This contrast of SLI with other forms of language impairment suggests that at least with regard to aspects of language other than pragmatics, children with SLI seem to be quite similar to children with certain forms of intellectual disability and autism and differ from the HH children largely because the latter group seems to have better language skills than children with SLI. Thus if we consider the multidimensional space containing individual differences in child language the predominant evidence suggests that children with SLI occupy a similar region as many other children with developmental disorders.

23.2.3   SLI and typically developing children

So far we have considered whether language comes apart in different ways for children with SLI than for other children with poor language ability. A more common question that has been asked over the years has been whether the features of SLI place them in a different space than younger children considered to have normal-language status (NL). Children with SLI have been hypothesized to contrast with NL children in one of two ways. One obvious way has been to consider these children as fundamentally different language learners and therefore it would be expected that features of their language are different from those of any NL children at any point in development. Additionally, the mechanisms by which language is acquired would be assumed to be different in some way. This hypothesis has been known as the deviance hypothesis. The alternative view has been one of delay which may be interpreted as a slowed learning trajectory that ultimately reaches full maturity or a slow trajectory that terminates at levels below full maturity (Leonard 1998). Key to the delay hypothesis is that the developmental trajectory of language for children with SLI follows the same course as that found in typically developing children. A somewhat weaker form of the delay hypothesis is one that permits variability in rates of development across language systems and therefore allows for relative strengths and weaknesses, but yet still constrains development of each system to follow the normal trajectory. Leonard (1998) referred to this as a profile difference. All of these forms of the delay hypothesis would be compatible with aetiologies for SLI that involve quantitative differences in underlying systems that contribute to individual differences in rates of language development. Constraints in rates of development arising from unique sources however could also conceivably produce a quantitative effect as well.

This issue of whether the language of children with SLI is delayed or deviant was a dominant topic of research during the 1970s and 1980s. Leonard (1987, 1998) has summarized this work and concluded that much of the research supports at least some form of the delay hypothesis and most particularly the profile difference model. The bulk of the language features of children with SLI are quite similar to younger typically developing children. However, as can be seen in the following chapter (Ch. 24 Leonard), there is considerable evidence that certain aspects of grammar are more challenging to children with SLI than other aspects of grammar or semantics. This greater vulnerability of particular aspects of grammar is very consistent with Leonard's view of a profile difference. Returning to our multidimensional space, we would then consider children with SLI in a region occupied by typically developing children of a younger age. This perspective however would not be shared by some accounts of SLI such as those of van der Laley and Battell (2003), Clahsen (e.g. 1999b) and Gopnik (1990). These researchers have interpreted this vulnerability in grammar as evidence for a specific defect in the grammatical system that is inherently deviant and thus, at least with regard to some aspects of grammar, they would place children with SLI in a different universe than typically developing children.

23.2.4   A developmental perspective on SLI

SLI represents a type of developmental disorder and therefore it has the potential to emerge at some point in development, change over time and converge on a state of maturity. We have established that much of the evidence concerning the nature of the language deficit in children with SLI is consistent with developmental processes that yield slower growth rates but qualitatively similar features as typically developing children.

23.2.4.1 Late talkers

It is generally believed that the developmental origins of SLI can be traced to very early periods of development. Studies of individual differences in basic perceptual skills during infancy have shown that these are predictive of later language status (Benasich & Tallal 2002, Newman *et al.* 2006). Given that the current diagnosis of SLI depends upon delays in expected patterns of language growth, children with potential SLI are rarely identified before 18 to 24 months of age at which time these children are referred to as late talkers. It is assumed that children with persisting SLI will emerge from this group of late talkers. The persistence of poor language (SLI) among late talkers has been found to be between 20 and 70 per cent (Rescorla, Dahlsgaard & Roberts 2000, La Paro *et al.* 2004, Paul 1993, Whitehurst & Fischel 1994). Because of the volatility in early language development, there has been a reluctance to diagnose SLI until the trajectory of language development in children becomes more stable. This developmental volatility appears to decline in four-year-old children (Bishop & Edmundson 1987). As a result Rescorla and Lee (2000) and Stothard *et al.* (1998) recommend reserving the diagnosis of SLI for children over 4 years.

23.2.4.2 SLI emergence

SLI thus emerges as persisting poor language achievement during the preschool years. If a child presents with SLI after 4 years of age there is considerable likelihood that this will persist. The extent to which normalization occurs during the school years has been the topic of several longitudinal studies of SLI during the school years and into adulthood (Aram & Nation 1980, Beitchman *et al.* 1996b, Conti-Ramsden & Botting 2004, Stark *et al.* 1984, Tomblin *et al.* 2003). In general, these studies show considerable persistence in SLI during the early school years. Some authors suggest that 81 to 89 per cent of these children continue to present a language problem throughout their school years (Silva 1987, Stark & Tallal 1988). Other authors have reported lower levels of persistence in the range of 54 to 56 per cent (Bishop & Edmundson 1987, Cole *et al.* 1995). My research group (Tomblin *et al.* 2003) has shown that it is possible that much of the apparent 'recovery' in these studies is likely to be due to the effect of regression to the mean that is inherent in methods that classify children on the basis of deviant performance on measures that contain measurement error and then subsequently reclassify the children with similar measures. Some of the children initially classified as having low language skills (i.e. SLI) are likely to be erroneously classified and thus when measured again they will appear to have resolved their impaired language when in fact their 'true' ability had not changed at all. Our analysis of the amount of change over a four year period of time suggested very little evidence of children changing their relative language standing across this time period. Recently this stable pattern of SLI, shown to exist during the early school years, has been extended into late adolescence and adulthood (Johnson *et al.* 1999, Rutter & Mawhood 1991, Stothard *et al.* 1998).

23.2.5 Summary of the construct of SLI

We can see that SLI is an evolving construct that defines a group of children who do poorly in language development although they do not present with the ordinary developmental or sensory disorders. There has been a considerable amount of work comparing these children with other atypical and typical language learners. These comparisons paint a picture of a pattern of language development that is surprisingly similar across all these groups. The principal way that children with SLI differ from other children has to do with the rate of development referenced to their chronological age. We also see that SLI emerges out of a period in development where there is considerable variability within and across children with regard to rates of acquisition. Predicting the long-term growth trajectory of language is difficult until children approach school age. At that time these language growth trajectories stabilize and SLI can be determined with greater confidence. Once children approach school age with SLI, they are very likely to persist in having poor language abilities throughout childhood and into adulthood. Thus the slow development does not appear to ultimately resolve into fully developed language abilities that are achieved at a later time point, but rather appear to represent persisting poor language skills into adulthood.

23.3 Aetiology of SLI

The general picture above suggests that the aetiological factors that create the individual differences in language represented by SLI are likely to overlap with the factors that create individual differences among both NL children and children with excluded conditions. Questions of causation for complex developmental systems such as language have to contend with the fact that causation is likely to be a pathway with multiple levels with multiple inputs. Figure 23.1 depicts this scheme. As can be seen in the figure, some of these levels are more proximal to the actual language behaviour of the child at any point in time whereas other levels are more likely to be distal. We can assume that the most proximal causal factors are those that can be subsumed by the notion of cognition that encompasses language representations and processes involved in the activation of these representations. This cognitive level of explanation has been the focus of

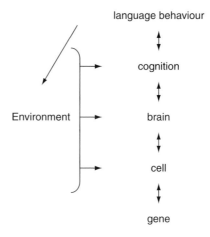

Figure 23.1 A model of the principal causal systems that contribute to individual differences. Note each level interacts with, as well as is acted on by, the adjoining levels and environmental influences can affect multiple levels.

considerable attention in research on SLI and is discussed in the next chapter (Ch. 24 by Leonard). Within the present chapter, we will focus on the more distal causal factors for SLI; namely genetics, neurological status and environmental factors.

23.3.1   Genetics of SLI

The observation that speech and language problems run in families and may be genetic can be found dating back to Ingram (1959); however, systematic studies are of more recent origin. Several studies have shown that speech and language problems are more common in families selected because a child (called a proband) had SLI in contrast with families with NL probands. Although family aggregation studies provide suggestive evidence that genes may play a role in a phenotype, twin studies provide a means of estimating whether there are genetic influences on a trait. If a dichotomous trait is genetically influenced we should find that monozygotic twins (MZ) more often have the same trait than do dyzygotic (DZ) twins. Concordance rates of SLI for MZ twins have run from 0.70 to 0.96 whereas they have ranged from 0.46 to 0.69 for DZ twins (Bishop *et al.* 1995, Lewis & Thompson 1992, Spinath *et al.* 2004, Tomblin & Buckwalter 1998). In each case the concordance for MZ was higher than for the DZ twins suggesting a genetic influence on SLI.

Heritability is an index that reflects the proportion of a quantitative trait variance that is attributable to genetic sources of variance. Quantitative measures of language within twinships containing children with SLI, have consistently shown moderate to strong levels of heritability (Fisher 2006). In addition to showing support for a genetic influence on language impairment, these studies have shown that phenotypes that are based on language status without regard to performance IQ yield higher heritability than those that employ a discrepancy criterion, and language heritability does not vary as a function of the performance IQ level of the sample. Heritability does appear to increase in groups that are sampled because of greater severity. Thus, the twin research supports a hypothesis that genetic factors play a role in the aetiology of SLI. It is important to note that this does not mean that SLI is genetically determined, nor should it be taken to mean that there are language genes that cause language disorder (Fisher 2006). Recall that these genetic effects are likely quite distant from the actual language behaviour and have many intervening processes that are highly interactive.

The evidence that SLI and by extension language in general may be genetically influenced has sparked interest in the identification of what these genes may be. Progress in this effort was advanced considerably by the discovery of a family (KE) where many of the members had specific speech and language impairment (Vargha-Khadem *et al.* 1995). Fisher *et al.* (1998) performed a genome-wide search using these family members and found the speech and language problem was linked to genetic markers on the long arm of chromosome 7 in the region of 7q31. The gene mutation accounting for the speech and language impairment in this family was then identified as *FOXP2* (Lai *et al.* 2001). *FOXP2* has been determined to be a regulatory gene that controls expression of other genes and the affected family members had a mutation that resulted in a protein product that could not perform the regulatory functions of the normal protein. Although these affected family members do present a profile of language impairment consistent with SLI, they also have substantial motor speech disorders characterized as apraxia. Thus, it is not clear that the impairment in these individuals can be described as SLI. At this time, however, there is no evidence that the particular mutation in *FOXP2* found in the KE family contributes to language impairment in the general population (Newbury *et al.* 2002, O'Brien *et al.* 2003, SLI Consortium 2004). It still remains possible that other mutations in *FOXP2* or in genes controlled by *FOXP2* are important to the aetiology of SLI.

Beyond the research concerning *FOXP2*, there have been additional studies using molecular genetic methods to identify genes influencing SLI during the last six years. A very small number of genome-wide scans have yielded potential regions of interest on chromosomes 2, 13, 16 and 19 (Bartlett *et al.* 2002, SLI Consortium 2004, The SLI Consortium 2002). The findings of the SLI Consortium and Newbury and colleagues are noteworthy in that they have been able to replicate linkage at chromosome 16 to non-word repetition. It is likely that several genes and various forms of genetic variation (single base pair substitutions, deletions and replications) will be contributing to individual differences in language development including that of SLI. By identifying these genes, it will become possible to form hypotheses concerning the pathways these genes act on and thus identify mechanisms important to language development and disorder.

23.3.2 Neurological findings and SLI

The aetiological pathway of genes to language behaviour has to involve the brain. If there are genes that predispose children to SLI then we might expect to find structural and/or functional differences in their brains. We will restrict ourselves to the question of whether there are structural differences associated with SLI as the functional differences may be an alternate manifestation of the language deficit rather than the cause.

Recall that the roots of the concept of SLI date back to the term childhood aphasia and this term suggested that these children had some type of brain lesion suggestive of minimal brain damage. With the development of magnetic resonance imaging (MRI), it has become possible to examine the structure of brains of individuals with SLI. There have now been several brain studies and as a part of these studies consideration has been given as to whether these individuals actually do have small focal lesions and so far there is no evidence of such type of brain abnormality associated with SLI (Trauner *et al.* 2000). Trauner and colleagues did, however, find a range of subtle non-language behavioural signs suggestive of abnormal neurological status. The search for anatomical bases of SLI has focused on whether there are differences in relative brain volumes across different brain regions. In particular, interest has focused on the cortical regions of Broca and Wernike (planum temporale) and their size in the left and right hemisphere. Within typical language learners, the planum is usually larger in the left than the right hemisphere. However, within individuals with SLI, several studies have shown that this relationship is often reduced or reversed and, as well, an absence of the expected larger Broca's area in the left hemisphere has been reported (Gauger *et al.* 1997, Herbert *et al.* 2005, Jernigan *et al.* 1991, Plante *et al.* 1991).

Most of the research concerning brain structure and SLI has concentrated on the study of brain regions that have long been associated with language functions. Such an approach assumes that there are language-specific brain regions and that language can be viewed as a special cognitive faculty. Under the alternate view that language arises from a widely distributed non-modular neural system, Herbert and colleagues (2003) have examined larger scale brain regions including subcortical structures. They report that children with SLI presented larger cortical volume that is due to greater amounts of white matter reflecting proportionately greater amounts of connectivity via myelinated fibre tracts. Although connectivity is generally considered important for neural networks, excessive connectivity could result in inefficient and noisy processing.

Overall, the studies of brain structure do provide consistent evidence of abnormal structural development that may serve as a basis for the language-learning difficulties associated with SLI. These abnormalities may point toward abnormalities in early formation of neural architecture and possibly also ongoing changes in activity-dependent neural connectivity. This latter dynamic process of neural development was suggested by

Locke (1994) who pointed out that differences in regional brain size may be the product of poor language learning rather than the cause of the learning difficulties. Disentangling this relationship is likely to be difficult.

23.3.3 The language environment and SLI

Nature and nurture have a long dialectical relationship in developmental science. In recent years, however, few will argue that these are in opposition, but rather nowadays nature and nurture have merged in such topics as epigenetics and behavioural embryology (Gottlieb 1997). Genes and brains only work in the context of environments. Furthermore, environments are shaped by the behaviour of individuals (Scarr & McCartney 1983), thus the direction of causality with regard to the child with SLI and the linguistic environment needs to be considered carefully.

There is a sizable literature that has shown a relationship between individual differences in the development of language and the communicative synchrony and reciprocity found in parent–child dyads. This quality of synchrony and reciprocity is reflected in the use of responses to child initiations, semantically contingent utterances and structural reformulations of prior child utterances sometimes called recasts. It stands to reason that one might expect this relationship to extend to children with SLI and indeed questions concerning the contribution of the linguistic environment to SLI were common a few decades ago. Most of this work was done in laboratory settings where adult–child dyads were observed and features of linguistic input examined. In much of this research (see Leonard 1998 for a summary), the language input to the child with SLI was found to be structurally less complex, and marked by discourse styles that were suggestive of poorer synchrony and reciprocity than was found with typically developing age mates. Leonard (1998) has pointed out that the fact that this pattern extended to other adults who were not parents (e.g. teachers), suggested that this language style was not unique to the parents and therefore this is not the principal cause of SLI, although he did acknowledge that this style, that may be elicited by the child, could compound an already existing language-learning problem.

What is particularly lacking are data concerning the quantity of input. Hart and Risley (1995) and Huttenlocher and colleagues (1991) have provided evidence that frequency of input may be an important contributor to individual differences among NL children. We have yet to learn whether such quantitative input differences in the home are associated with late talkers or children with SLI.

23.4 Academic and social outcomes of SLI

Earlier it was noted that SLI can be viewed as emergent during development. One aspect of this emergence concerns the extent to which aspects of early language status progresses into later reading and behaviour problems and what the possible bases of this emergent pattern may be. Two hypotheses have been prominent in this literature. One hypothesis is that the associations between spoken language and later outcomes are causal. Alternatively, the association of language and reading problems with behaviour problems may rest on a common underlying condition such as a neuromaturational delay that result in poor achievement in each domain.

Several investigators have examined the reading and psychosocial outcomes of children with LI in the early school years. Several studies reported poorer reading achievement and greater rates of reading disorder (RD) in children with language impairment (LI) (Aram *et al.* 1984, Bishop & Adams 1990, Catts 1993, Silva *et al.* 1987, Stark & Tallal 1988, Stark *et al.* 1984). In these studies, the prevalence of RD in children with SLI ranged from 25 per cent (Bishop & Adams 1990) to 90 per cent (Stark *et al.* 1984). The strong relationship between RD and LI has been shown to be attributable to the limitations these children have in both their ability to understand language and their phonological awareness (Catts *et al.* 1999, 2001). The phonological awareness deficits place them at risk for difficulties in learning decoding skills and the comprehension problems place them at risk for reading-comprehension problems.

Several studies have shown elevated rates of behaviour problems among children with LI (Beitchman *et al.* 1986b, 1987, 1989, 1990, 1996a, Benasich *et al.* 1993, Stevenson *et al.* 1985). The most common behavioural problem reported in these studies has been ADHD; however internalizing problems such as anxiety disorder are also reported. Some research has shown that these behaviour problems appear to vary with the setting in which the child is observed and in particular are reported by the children's teachers to a greater degree than their parents (Redmond & Rice 1998). This has been interpreted as evidence that these behaviour problems may arise more in the classroom situation than at home and are therefore reactions to classroom stress. Further support for this view arises from data showing that the excess of behaviour problems in children with RD and/or LI is found in those children with both conditions (Tomblin *et al.* 2000). Thus, these studies support the notion that LI in conjunction with RD results in the child facing excessive failure particularly with the classroom which in turn results in reactive behaviour problems. These conclusions however fail to explain why behaviour problems seem to be reported in preschool children with LI (Beitchman *et al.* 1986a). These findings could be used to argue for an underlying factor such as neurodevelopmental delay that contributes to all these conditions.

23.5 Conclusions

One way of viewing SLI is that it represents a region of individual differences in language development that represents impaired language development for which we have no well-supported explanation. The research to date has yet to offer a clear aetiologic candidate that serves as a singular and deterministic cause of SLI. It is possible and even likely that such a single deterministic aetiology cannot be found. I concluded earlier that these children with SLI are more likely inefficient language learners than qualitatively different learners. Therefore it is possible that the causes of SLI will encompass those mechanisms, whether genetic, neurological or environmental, that also contribute to individual differences in language development across groups of children, including the NL population. If so there are probably multiple factors that operate in a probabilistic interactive fashion. This type of aetiologic model has been termed a quantitative trait locus (QTL) by those studying genetics. Thus, the genetic contribution to SLI may simply consist of a combination of several gene variants such that each has a small deleterious effect on underlying systems for language. If so, these same gene variants may also be the basis for individual differences among NL children as well. Those who have been examining the influence of the linguistic environment on SLI appear to have approached the question of causation from this perspective, in that the type of parental input features they have examined are the same as those considered to be important for NL children. The research concerning structural brain differences have not been clearly motivated by a view of aetiologic continuity between SLI and NL. It remains quite possible, however, that the findings of differences in regional brain size and greater connectivity could be found to be associated with variation in language ability in other populations as well. The value of considering SLI as being continuous with NL is that SLI can both inform and be informed by research on the NL population in order to yield a comprehensive understanding of language development.

Suggestions for further reading

Bishop, D. V. M. (2006). What causes specific language impairment in children? *Current Directions in Psychological Science*, 15(5), 217–221.

Joanisse, M. F. (2004). Specific language impairments in children: phonology, semantics, and the English past tense. *Current Directions in Psychological Science*, 13(4), 156–160.

Montgomery, J. (2003) Working memory and comprehension in children with specific language impairment: What we know so far. *Journal of Communication Disorders*, 36, 221–231.

Schuele, C. M. (2004). The impact of developmental speech and language impairments on the acquisition of literacy skills. *Mental Retardation and Developmental Disabilities Research Reviews*, 10(3), 176–183.

Weismer S. E. (2006). Typical talkers, late talkers, and children with specific language impairment: A language endowment spectrum. In R. Paul (Ed.), *Language Disorders From a Developmental Perspective* (pp. 83–102). Hillsdale, NJ: Lawrence Erlbaum Associates.

24

Language symptoms and their possible sources in specific language impairment

Laurence B. Leonard

24.1 Introduction

In the previous chapter, Tomblin described a group of children exhibiting what has been termed a 'specific language impairment' (SLI). It was noted that the sources of these children's problems may be multifactorial, even in the many cases in which a genetic contribution seems likely. Although children with SLI are most often identified during the preschool years, the problems are often longstanding, adversely affecting not only the development of reading and other academic skills but social development as well. In Tomblin's chapter, factors that might contribute to an impairment in language were discussed. In the present chapter, the focus is on language itself, that is, the language symptoms that are associated with SLI.

There are good reasons to focus on the language characteristics of children with SLI. First, of course, these symptoms are frequently the means of identifying children with this disorder. As noted earlier, the weakest developmental area in children with SLI is language itself, and it is not uncommon for these children to be identified, at least initially, solely on the basis of their difficulties with language. Second, until or unless direct causal links can be found between non-linguistic factors and the children's language problems, language itself will be the direct focus of therapy. Therefore, it is important to have a firm grasp of the details of language that are more, and less, troublesome for these children. Third, a focus on the salient language symptoms of children with SLI can lead to possible explanations for SLI. These explanations, in the long run, may provide us with more effective methods of prevention or treatment.

Indeed, based on the accumulating data on the language symptoms of SLI, investigators have begun to advance proposals concerning the reasons for these special difficulties. In this chapter, we consider some of the accounts that have been offered to explain these salient language symptoms of children with SLI. We begin with a brief summary of the symptoms themselves.

24.2   Salient language symptoms in SLI

Children with SLI show a deficit in a range of language areas, such as vocabulary and phonology, but a more serious deficit in particular areas. During the preschool and kindergarten years, morphosyntax is an especially weak area, and, as these children gradually gain sufficient ability to participate in multi-utterance conversational turns, narrative skills, too, prove to be an area of extraordinary weakness. The details of the special difficulties differ according to the type of language being acquired. Here, we highlight the salient characteristics of SLI in some of the language types that have received significant investigative attention: (1) English; (2) German and Swedish; (3) Italian and Spanish; and (4) French. Although not discussed here, studies are also beginning to appear on such languages as Cantonese, Catalan, Dutch, Greek, Hebrew and Hungarian.

24.2.1   English

By far, the most studies of SLI have dealt with English-speaking children. Deficits observed in these children run a full range, from deficits in lexical skills (e.g. Gray 2004, McGregor et al. 2002) and argument structure (e.g. Grela 2003, Thordardottir & Ellis Weismer 2002) to problems with wh-questions and complement clauses (Owen & Leonard 2006, Schuele & Dykes 2005, van der Lely & Battel 2003), to difficulties with group negotiations and other conversational skills (e.g. Brinton et al. 1998, Liiva & Cleave 2005). Narrative skills (e.g. Dodwell & Bavin in press, Merritt & Liles 1987) and related skills such as inferencing (e.g. Ellis Weismer 1985, Norbury & Bishop 2002) also represent a weakness in these children.

   An especially well-documented problem in English-speaking children with SLI is a serious deficit in the use of grammatical morphemes that mark tense and agreement. These include the third-person singular -s and past tense -ed inflections and the copula and auxiliary forms of be. Children with SLI make less use of these morphemes than do younger typically developing children matched for mean length of utterance (MLU) or some other language measure (e.g. Cleave & Rice 1997, Leonard et al. 1997, Marshall & van der Lely 2006, Oetting & Horohov 1997). Problems in this area can continue into the early elementary school grades and beyond (Marchman et al. 1999, Norbury et al. 2001, Rice et al. 1998, van der Lely 1997). Composite measures of tense and agreement morpheme use exhibit good sensitivity and specificity in distinguishing children with SLI from their typically developing peers (Bedore & Leonard 1998, Rice 2003). Furthermore, measures of tense and agreement show promise as a method of identifying younger children at risk for SLI (Hadley & Short 2005).

Differences between children with SLI and typically developing comparison groups in the use of tense and agreement morphemes usually take the form of differences in degree of use. For example, whereas typically developing 3 year olds may use third-person singular -*s* in approximately 61 per cent of obligatory contexts in spontaneous speech, 5-year-old children with SLI may use this morpheme in 36 per cent of obligatory contexts (Rice & Wexler 1996b). With a few exceptions (see Owen & Goffman 2007), when children with SLI fail to use a tense and agreement morpheme in obligatory contexts, it appears as if they produce the non-finite form of the verb. Thus, in most instances, a verb form such as *run* in *Mummy run everyday* is not the child's failed attempt to articulate the final (-*s*) morpheme, but rather the child's selection of a form more akin to *run* in an adult utterance such as *We watch Mummy run everyday*.

24.2.2 German and Swedish

In German, verb inflections that mark tense and agreement are more frequent than in English. For example, in the present tense, third-person singular-*s* (e.g. *sings*) is the only overt inflection in English, whereas German possesses an inflection for each person and number combination (e.g. *singe* 'I sing', *singst* 'you sing', *singt* 'he/she sings'). As in English, differences between children with SLI and their younger MLU-matched compatriots are observed in these languages (e.g. Rice *et al.* 1997). Infinitives are often used in contexts requiring tense and agreement inflections and, in these languages, infinitives have overt inflections (e.g. German 'to sing' is *singen*, not the bare stem *sing*). However, bare stems have also been noted as substitutes on occasion.

Importantly, although German-speaking children with SLI have difficulties with tense and agreement inflections, their use of these inflections in obligatory contexts significantly exceeds the degree of use of tense and agreement inflections by English-speaking children with SLI. For example, whereas preschool-aged children with SLI acquiring English use third-person singular inflections in approximately 34 per cent of obligatory contexts (Leonard *et al.* 1997), the percentages for the corresponding inflections in German can range from 50 to 88 per cent (Rice *et al.* 1997, Roberts & Leonard 1997).

German is a 'verb-second' language; that is, the verb expressing agreement and/or tense must appear in second position in the sentence. Therefore, when utterances begin with a subject, as is common, the word order corresponds to that of English, as in the German utterance, *Jeanette fand die Kinder* 'Jeanette found the children'. However, when a constituent other than the subject appears in sentence-initial position, the verb that expresses tense and agreement appears next, not the subject, as seen in *gestern fand Jeanette die Kinder*. This utterance has the meaning of

'Yesterday Jeanette found the children' but is literally translated as 'Yesterday found Jeanette the children'.

German-speaking children with SLI sometimes fail to use the proper verb-second word order, often producing the lone verb in the sentence in final position. This sentence position is the typical position for non-finite lexical verbs, including infinitives, when an auxiliary also appears in the sentence, as in the German utterance *Chris kann Kaffee trinken* 'Chris can coffee drink' (= 'Chris can drink coffee') where *trinken* is the infinitive 'to drink'. However, children with SLI may also produce the infinitive form in sentence-final position even when no auxiliary appears in the utterance, as in *Chris Kaffee trinken* 'Chris coffee drink' (= 'Chris drink coffee'). Cases have also been observed in which a verb marked for tense and agreement appears in sentence-final position, as in *Chris Kaffee trinkt* 'Chris coffee drinks'.

Swedish is also a verb-second language, but differs from German in certain key respects. For example, verbs are inflected for tense but not agreement. In addition, infinitives do not appear in sentence-final position when an auxiliary such as 'can' is used in second position. Swedish-speaking children with SLI use tense inflections with higher percentages in obligatory contexts than do their English-speaking counterparts. For example, whereas English-speaking preschoolers with SLI use past tense inflections in approximately 50 per cent of obligatory contexts, Swedish-speaking preschoolers with SLI use past tense inflections in approximately 85 per cent of obligatory contexts (Leonard *et al.* 2005). When children fail to use a tense inflection in an obligatory context, infinitives are the usual substitute. Instead of *Karl dricker kaffe* 'Karl drinks coffee', for example, a child might produce *Karl dricka kaffe* 'Karl drink coffee'. The form *dricka* has the infinitive inflection -*a* in place of the present tense inflection -*er*. Although Swedish-speaking children with SLI produce sentences with word order errors (Hansson *et al.* 2000), they appear to do so with lower frequencies than in a language such as German. Rice *et al.* (1997) found that German-speaking children with SLI used tense-marked verb forms in the appropriate second position in 74 per cent of their utterances, whereas Leonard *et al.* (2005) observed that Swedish-speaking children with SLI used tense-marked verb forms in second position in 93 per cent of their utterances. Strikingly, the latter figure is based on non-subject-initial utterances that are the clearest test cases for the children's control of the verb-second pattern. Because subject-initial utterances reflect the canonical subject–verb–object word order of Swedish, they do not offer clear evidence that children grasp the verb-second rule of the language.

24.2.3 Italian and Spanish

In Romance languages such as Italian and Spanish, the subject of the sentence can be omitted when the referent is clear from the physical or discourse context. Thus, for example, in Italian, *dormono* '[they] sleep' would be a very natural response when asked "Tell me about the girls in this picture." For this reason, such languages are referred to as 'null-subject' languages. In these languages, verb inflections are abundant and bare stems are not permitted. Subject–verb–object is the basic word order, but the rich verb morphology permits considerable variation in the order in which words can be sequenced in a sentence.

Unlike the case for English and other Germanic languages, Italian- and Spanish-speaking children with SLI do not exhibit a serious difficulty in the use of verb inflections that mark tense and agreement (e.g. Bortolini *et al.* 1998). This is not to say that their verb inflection use is at age level. However, relative to younger MLU-matched children, few differences are found for many tense and agreement inflections (e.g. Bedore & Leonard 2001, 2005, Bortolini *et al.* 1997). In one sense this is rather paradoxical. In languages such as English, tense and agreement inflections are difficult for children with SLI. Because Italian and Spanish have an abundance of such inflections, one might expect even greater difficulties for children with SLI in these languages. Yet, instead of compounding the children's problems, the rich set of tense and agreement inflections in these languages appears to be relatively helpful, not only in comparison to English-speaking children with SLI but also in allowing them to narrow their disadvantage when compared to their typically developing compatriots.

The errors made by children with SLI in Italian and Spanish also differ from those seen in Germanic languages. Infinitives as substitutes are uncommon; instead, errors are usually productions of substitute inflections that differ from the appropriate inflections by a single feature, such as the use of a third person singular inflection in place of a third person plural inflection. These substitutes are not default forms, for they are not used unless they share features with the form that is obligated by the adult grammar. For example, first person singular inflections are sometimes produced in contexts requiring first person plural inflections, but they are not seen in contexts requiring third person plural inflections.

In contrast to the similarity between children with SLI and younger MLU controls in the use of verb inflections, Italian- and Spanish-speaking children with SLI show relative weaknesses in their use of function words. For Spanish, differences of this type have been documented for definite articles and direct object clitics (Bedore & Leonard 2001, 2005, Restrepo & Gutierrez-Clellan 2001). Direct object clitics are pronouns used when the referent is clear; they usually precede the verb marked for tense and agreement. For example, the utterance *La come* '(He/she) eats *it*' in Spanish has the clitic *la* that refers to a feminine singular direct object. For Italian, certain auxiliary verbs as well as definite articles and direct objects have emerged as problematic (Bortolini *et al.* 1997, Leonard & Bortolini 1998). An example of an auxiliary is *ha* as in the Italian utterance *Ha mangiato* '(He/she) *has* eaten'. This type of error is relevant because in most regions of Italy, the 'passato prossimo' (formed by combining the auxiliary with the past participle) is the most common way of referring to past events. Studies on Italian and Spanish that have employed only comparisons between children with SLI and their typically developing same-age peers have found, not surprisingly, differences favouring the typically developing children (Bortolini *et al.* 2002, 2006, Eng & O'Connor 2000, Jacobson & Schwartz 2002).

If there is a difference between these Romance languages in the way function words are used by children with SLI, it is that substitution errors as well as omissions are seen in Spanish, whereas omission errors predominate in Italian (e.g. Bedore & Leonard 2001, Bortolini *et al.* 2006). Prosodic differences between Spanish and Italian may be the basis for these differences, as Spanish weak syllables (including function words) differ from strong syllables to a smaller degree than in other languages (Delattre 1966), and thus may be less prone to weak syllable deletion.

24.2.4 French

Although French is a Romance language like Italian and Spanish, it differs from these other languages in important ways. First, it is not a null-subject language. Furthermore, although the distinctions among tense and agreement inflections are relatively preserved in the orthography, the pronunciation of these inflections results in a significant amount of homophony. For example, the inflected verb forms of 'speak' for first (*parle*), second (*parles*), and third person (*parle*) singular and third person plural (*parlent*) are pronounced alike. Subject nouns or pronouns (in this case, *je, tu, il/elle*, and *ils/elles*, respectively) are needed to properly identify the person and number of the verb.

To refer to past events, French makes use of the 'passé composé' which requires the auxiliary in combination with the past participle, as in the Italian passato prossimo. French-speaking children with SLI, like Italian-speaking children with SLI, seem to omit the auxiliary more often than younger typically developing children (Paradis & Crago 2001). However, the status of present tense inflections in the speech of French-speaking children with SLI is a source of disagreement. In contexts requiring these inflections, the children's choice of verb forms is quite accurate (Thordardottir & Namazi 2007). However, given the homophony involved in the present tense paradigm, coupled with the errors seen in the passé composé (created through the omission of auxiliaries), Paradis and Crago (2001) have argued that present tense forms produced by French-speaking children with SLI might constitute a type of default and do not reflect the tense properties that are reflected in the otherwise identical forms used in the adult grammar. We shall return to this issue in our discussion of one of the accounts of the tense and agreement morpheme difficulties in SLI.

Direct object clitics appear to be an area of special weakness for French-speaking children with SLI (Jakubowicz *et al.* 1998, Paradis 2007). As in Italian and Spanish, these forms typically precede the verb marked for tense and agreement in French (e.g. *le* in *Gina le voit* 'Gina sees him'). Clitics are often omitted by children with SLI. Interestingly, definite articles make use of the same phonetic forms as direct object clitics (e.g. *le* is the masculine singular form for 'the') and French-speaking children with SLI have very little difficulty with such articles (Jakubowicz *et al.* 1998).

24.3   Alternative accounts of SLI: the broader language deficit or areas of extraordinary difficulty?

Possible explanations for the language deficit in SLI have taken a wide range of forms. Many of these have proposed that the problem may not rest with language per se, but rather with children's ability to process and/or store information sufficiently well to learn language properly. Approaches of this type are concerned with the more general language problems of the children; particular details of language that are especially problematic for the children are usually not addressed. As will be seen, some accounts assume a subtle weakness in a wide range of cognitive operations, whereas others assume that one particular mechanism is awry. All of these accounts are discussed under the heading 'processing and memory accounts'.

Other types of accounts assume that children with SLI lack some essential linguistic principle or rule. These accounts pay close attention to particular details of language that tend to be especially weak in children with SLI. Thus, these accounts play an important role neglected by most processing and memory accounts – that of addressing pockets of great difficulty. At the same time, they suffer from the limitation of ignoring the broader deficit. These accounts will be discussed under the heading 'selective deficits in linguistic principles'. A goal of future research will be to find a theoretically coherent way of explaining both the mild-to-moderate broader deficit and the more serious deficit in select areas of language functioning.

The accounts discussed here are among the most prominent that have a focus on either the broader deficit or on selective areas of difficulty. Examples of other types of accounts include those of Leonard (1989), Tallal *et al.* (1996), Clahsen *et al.* (1997), van der Lely (1998) and Joanisse and Seidenberg (2003).

24.3.1   Processing and memory accounts

Processing can be viewed from several perspectives. Frequently, it is viewed from the perspective of time – the speed required to perform some task. It has also been viewed from the perspective of work space, that is, the amount of space available to perform the necessary computational operations, often referred to as processing 'capacity'. Of course, the two perspectives are related, given that the faster that information can be processed, the greater the amount of information that can be processed in any given unit of time. Nevertheless, the two types of perspectives are separable, especially when processing capacity is assessed through working memory. Working memory tasks are those that tap the child's ability to store small amounts of information for a brief time, while keeping the information available for mental manipulation. Although recent work recognizes the joint contributions that speed and working memory might make to a better understanding of SLI (Leonard *et al.* 2007), the prominent accounts focus primarily on one or the other. Following a brief review of each type of account, we will consider how the presumed speed or working memory limitations may impede language learning.

24.3.1.1   Generalized slowing

Studies of SLI have occasionally included measures of response time (RT) in an effort to detect subtle weaknesses even when accuracy is high. Investigators have typically reported slower RTs in children with SLI relative to same-age peers. Tasks on which children with SLI show relatively slow RTs are not limited to linguistic tasks such as picture naming or judging the grammatical accuracy of sentences; slow RTs have also been noted for non-linguistic tasks such as judging whether two abstract designs are identical. Kail (1994) proposed that this may be a generalized slowing, that is, slower processing speed across all tasks, including those of a non-linguistic nature. His evidence indicated that this was a proportional slowing. That is, Kail's analysis of data from a wide range of tasks revealed that, regardless of the task, children with SLI were approximately 33 per cent slower than their typically developing age-mates. If the slower RTs were due to a single inefficient operation (e.g. executing the response after a decision has been reached), the RTs for the SLI group should have differed from those of peers by a constant, absolute value (e.g. 100 milliseconds) rather than by a constant proportion. Since the initial work of Kail, other investigators have reported evidence consistent with generalized slowing, though with slightly smaller percentages of slowing relative to same-age peers (e.g. Miller *et al.* 2006) and some evidence that certain subdomains (e.g. picture naming) may show less slowing than others (Windsor *et al.* 2001).

24.3.1.2   Working memory

Evidence from tasks that emphasize working memory is rather clear in showing deficits in children with SLI (e.g. Gillam *et al.* 1998, Johnston 1994, Montgomery 2000). Tasks have included the recall of lists of words (e.g. Kail & Leonard 1986) as well as the recall of the last word in each of several sentences that must also be judged in terms of their truth value (e.g. Hoffman & Gillam 2004, Marton & Schwartz 2003). Verbal working memory deficits are most commonly reported, but evidence can also be found for deficits in visual working memory (e.g. Bavin *et al.* 2005, Hoffman & Gillam 2004).

24.3.1.3 Phonological working memory

An especially active area of research in SLI has been the area of phonological working memory. Most often, this ability has been gauged by children's performance on non-word repetition tasks, that is, tasks in which children must repeat non-words of varying lengths. Evidence showing significant weaknesses in children with SLI abound in the literature (Bishop *et al.* 2006, Conti-Ramsden 2003, Dollaghan & Campbell 1998, Ellis Weismer *et al.* 2000, Gathercole & Baddeley 1990). In a recent meta-analysis, Graf Estes *et al.* (2007b) provide evidence that this type of task consistently reveals differences between children with SLI and their typically developing peers.

24.3.1.4 Speed, working memory and the broader language deficit

One can see how deficits in speed and working memory can have a deleterious effect on the broader language deficit. For example, if children have limitations in phonological working memory, they may require more exposures to each new word before they can form an adequate phonological representation. This, in turn, could slow the pace of lexical acquisition. If verbs are among the lexical items that are acquired slowly, the children's development of argument structure could also be hampered. For example, if children have limited knowledge of the verb *draw*, they may not know that it can serve as both an intransitive verb with only the subject as an argument, as in *She's drawing*, and as a transitive verb with both the subject and direct object as arguments, as in *She's drawing a picture*. Similarly, knowledge of a verb such as *see* can affect complex sentence development, given that verbs of this type are used with complement clauses, as in *She sees that the dog is hungry*, as well as in simple sentences, as in *She sees the dog*.

Working memory limitations are also likely to affect sentence comprehension. For example, both Montgomery (1995) and Deevy and Leonard (2004) found that when sentences were lengthened simply by adding (non-contrastive) adjectives (e.g. *Who is the little gray bird chasing?*), the comprehension of the children with SLI showed a disproportionate decline relative to the same sentence structure without adjectives (*Who is the bird chasing?*). More sophisticated forms of sentence comprehension could also be hindered by working memory limitations. For example, sentences that can have multiple interpretations may be especially difficult because the children's working memory capacities may be inadequate to arrive at more than one interpretation of the sentence.

Limitations in speed of processing should also have broad effects on children's language comprehension. If children are processing the information in a sentence slowly, by the time some element of the sentence is interpreted, critical information that appears subsequently in the speech stream may be missed.

24.3.2 Selective deficits in linguistic principles

Although speed and working memory limitations may well contribute to the broader language deficit of children with SLI, there are, in addition, pockets of especially serious difficulties in SLI that do not lend themselves to a straightforward explanation by processing accounts. These areas of great difficulty have been the focus of several accounts that assume selective deficits in linguistic principles. We turn now to some of the prominent approaches of this type.

24.3.2.1 Extended optional infinitive (EOI) account

Rice, Wexler and their colleagues proposed that children with SLI treat tense as optional (e.g. Rice & Wexler 1996b, Rice *et al.* 1998). For example, in the children's grammars, both *Mummy likes coffee* and *Mummy like coffee* are acceptable. In languages such as English, German, Dutch and Swedish, typically developing children as well as children with SLI proceed through a developmental period of treating tense and agreement morphemes as optional in main clauses. However, for children with SLI, this period is significantly protracted, and may be attributable to a maturational principle not yet taking hold (Rice 2003). During this period of optionality, when children fail to express tense, they instead produce a non-finite form. For example, in the above example *Mummy like coffee*, the verb *like* would be assumed to be the infinitive form, which, in English is a bare stem.

There is considerable evidence that is consistent with the EOI account. For example, in presumably 'optional infinitive' languages that employ an overt inflection for infinitives (e.g. German, Swedish), children with SLI, do, in fact, often produce the overt infinitive form in contexts requiring a tense morpheme (Leonard *et al.* 2005, Rice *et al.* 1997).

Paradis and Crago (2001) reported that French, too, might show an optional period. However, in this case, instead of using infinitive forms to replace tense and agreement forms, children presumably select present tense forms and use them as default forms that lack tense. Given the homophony in the present tense paradigm of French, these default forms are not in any obvious way incorrect. Paradis and Crago base their argument in part on the fact that the auxiliaries required for the passé composé – the most frequent means of expressing past tense – are often omitted. However, comparable omission of auxiliaries is often seen by Italian-speaking children with SLI in using the passato prossimo, and these children are quite accurate in their use of present tense inflections. In Italian, there is no homophony in the present tense inflection paradigm (e.g. *parlo* '[I] speak', *parli* '[you] speak', *parla* '[he/she] speaks, *parlano* '[they] speak', each with a different pronunciation).

24.3.2.2 Agreement, tense omission model (ATOM)

According to the EOI account, children's failure to use a morpheme such as third person singular -*s* or auxiliary *is* can be attributed to a failure to express tense. That is, because these particular morphemes mark tense as well as agreement, if tense is not expressed, the entire morpheme is blocked. However, Wexler, Schütze and Rice (1998) suggested that agreement, too, might be optional in the grammars of children with SLI. The source of the failure to use *likes* in *Mummy like coffee* could be attributable to the lack of tense, but also to the lack of agreement. However, these investigators noted that children with SLI sometimes produce utterances such as *Yesterday him played*. In the general theoretical framework adopted by Wexler *et al.* nominative (subject) case is licensed by agreement in the verb, not tense. If agreement is missing, the child would adopt the default form for English, the accusative (object) case, as in *him*. Following this assumption, Wexler *et al.* proposed that utterances such as *Yesterday him played* reflected missing agreement, whereas those such as *Yesterday he play* reflected missing tense.

24.3.2.3   Extended unique checking constraint (EUCC)

Although the ATOM account expanded the range of tense and agreement difficulties of children with SLI that might be explained, there remained the problem of explaining why some languages do not appear to be 'optional infinitive' languages. Notable among these are languages that have rich verb inflection paradigms and allow for null subjects. These include Italian and Spanish, among others.

Wexler (1998, 2003) has provided a reformulation of the EOI and ATOM accounts that retains the original theoretical framework but attempts to explain why some languages and not others show this pattern of optional use. Instead of assuming that tense and agreement are optional, Wexler proposes that the grammars of children with SLI have a constraint that, in a language such as English, allows only one functional category to be projected. This constraint presumably reflects a maturational principle that is lacking in all children at the outset of development but is quickly grasped by typically developing children. Children with SLI, in contrast, are assumed to lack this maturational principle – and hence must operate with this constraint – for an extended period of time. According to Wexler, this constraint makes it difficult to generate an utterance such as *Yesterday he played* or *Mum runs everyday* because these utterances require the projection of both tense and agreement. As in the ATOM account, utterances such as *Yesterday him played* (or *Yesterday he play*) and *Mum run everyday* might result.

According to the EUCC framework, in null-subject languages with rich agreement morphology such as Italian and Spanish, the constraint does not apply to the agreement category, and therefore both tense and agreement can be projected. As discussed earlier, the data for Italian and Spanish are consistent with this assumption, as tense and agreement verb inflections are used by children with SLI in these languages to a degree that is comparable to that of MLU-matched control children.

Recall, though, that in Italian and Spanish, direct object clitics are quite problematic for children with SLI. Wexler (1998) assumes that clitics require two functional categories to be projected (one that ensures that the clitic receives accusative case, as is required for direct objects, and the other to allow the clitic to appear in front of the verb). Because the projection of two functional categories violates the constraint, clitics will often be absent from the children's utterances. It would seem that a similar line of reasoning might apply to explain the absence of direct object clitics from the speech of French-speaking children with SLI.

24.3.2.4   Linguistic principles and problems with tense and agreement morphology

A major contribution of the EOI, ATOM and EUCC accounts is that they deal explicitly with an area of special weakness in many children with SLI, the use of tense and agreement morphology. Furthermore, these accounts address the children's inconsistency, and the types of productions that occur when children fail to use the appropriate morpheme. The EUCC has an additional asset because it provides a means of explaining the less significant deficit in tense and agreement morphology in children with SLI acquiring Italian and Spanish.

Although the EOI, ATOM and EUCC accounts offer major advantages in precision, they leave certain facts unaccounted for. For example, these accounts do not provide a basis for expecting higher percentages of use by German- and Swedish-speaking children with SLI than by their English-speaking counterparts even though all of these languages can be regarded as optional infinitive languages (see Leonard & Deevy 2006).

24.3.3   Can processing accounts explain problems with tense and agreement morphology?

Although processing accounts tend to focus on the broader deficit and leave the explanation of pockets of special difficulties to accounts with a focus on linguistic principles, it seems possible that a processing approach might also be used to address problems of a more selective nature. In an attempt to evaluate the feasibility of considering difficulties with tense and agreement morphology as part of a processing limitation, Leonard and his colleagues proposed the 'morphological richness' account (Leonard 1998: 255–257, Leonard et al. 1987). According to this account, extraordinary difficulties with tense and agreement morphemes result from an interaction between a limited processing capacity and the properties of the particular system of grammar that must be learned. The typology of English is assumed to place significant processing demands on the learning of tense and agreement morphology. Inflections are sparse in English and bare stems are frequent. Faced with a limited processing capacity, then, children with SLI presumably devote their limited resources to the more prevalent structural information conveyed by word order. As a result, fewer resources remain for the learning of tense and agreement morphology, requiring more encounters with these morphemes before they can be learned. In contrast, children with SLI acquiring languages with a rich inflectional morphology such as Italian and Spanish are expected to devote their limited resources to this area of the grammar. Consequently, differences between these children and their typically developing peers will be smaller than in a language such as English.

However, given the processing capacity limitations assumed in this account, even if resources are directed toward tense and agreement morphology, problems could arise if the morphemes to be learned reflect a complex combination of grammatical dimensions. Following proposals of Pinker (1984), Leonard and his colleagues assumed that children first hypothesize dimensions (e.g. number, person, gender) one at a time and only hypothesize combinations of dimensions after the input contradicts the single-dimension solution. For example, *-s* does not appear in utterances such as *I run* or *They run* and therefore could not mark singular alone or third person alone, but rather the conjunction of third person and singular. The more dimensions children must consider simultaneously, the greater the demands on their limited processing capacity. These demands can result in incomplete processing, requiring more encounters with the inflection before it can become a stable part of the children's grammar.

As can be seen, then, a rich inflectional morphology offers children with SLI the advantage of allowing them to devote their limited resources to this aspect of language. However, if the inflections reflect a large number of dimensions, problems could be seen even in these languages. The data available thus far seem consistent with this general line of thinking. For example, children with SLI learning Italian and those learning Hebrew – both languages with a rich inflectional morphology – show significantly greater use of tense and agreement morphology than their English-speaking peers with SLI. However, Hebrew-speaking children with SLI have problems in select areas of inflectional morphology, specifically, those inflections that require the conjunction of four different dimensions, tense, person, number and gender (Dromi *et al.* 1999). Inflections involving combinations of only three of these dimensions are not problematic.

24.4   Conclusions

In the previous chapter, Tomblin examined many of the factors that might contribute to an impairment in language. In this chapter, we have examined many of the language symptoms of this impairment. We have seen that tense and agreement morphology is an area of difficulty that stands out in many children with SLI. However, the nature of this difficulty is shaped very much by the type of language being acquired. The proposals that have been offered to explain the language symptoms of SLI have ranged from those dealing principally with the broader deficit to those that examine selective deficits in tense and agreement morphology. Proposals of the first type emphasize limitations in processing and working memory; those of the second type emphasize deficits in linguistic principles. Both types of proposals have advantages but, taken singly, they fall well short of a complete account of the language difficulties seen in children with SLI. Future research should explore ways in which these two types of proposals might be merged in ways that are theoretically coherent. A greater understanding of this perplexing disorder might result from such efforts.

Suggestions for further reading

Bishop, D. V. M., & Leonard, L. (Eds.) (2000). *Speech and Language Impairments in Children*. Hove, East Sussex: Psychology Press.

Graf Estes, K., Evans, J., & Else-Quest, N. (2007b). Differences in the non-word repetition performance of children with and without specific language impairment: A meta-analysis. *Journal of Speech, Language, and Hearing Research*, 50, 177–195.

Leonard, L. (1998). *Children with Specific Language Impairment*. Cambridge, MA: MIT Press.

Rice, M., & Warren, S. (Eds.) (2004). *Developmental Language Disorders: From Phenotypes to Etiologies*. Mahwah, NJ: Lawrence Erlbaum Associates.

25

The language of children with autism

Rhiannon J. Luyster
Catherine Lord

25.1   Introduction

In its earliest clinical description (Kanner 1943), autism was characterized by marked social impairment and considerable heterogeneity in language. While eight of the eleven children with autism Kanner described eventually acquired language, the other three did not. Kanner noted that even those children who learned 'structurally sound' language did not use it in a communicative fashion, instead speaking in an undirected and repetitive manner. These observations of autism and the considerable variability in language skills, as well as the apparent divergence between language structure and language use within it, still ring remarkably true. In the years since Kanner's report, research has expanded what we know about linguistic development in this population, and as larger samples and more detailed measures are employed, our characterization of language continues to advance.

Autism is a developmental disorder with a strong genetic component (Freitag 2007, Gupta & State 2007). It is currently understood to be the most severe prototypic disorder on an 'autism spectrum', which also includes Asperger syndrome and Pervasive Developmental Disorder – Not Otherwise Specified (PDD-NOS), as well as several more rare disorders with some similar symptoms. These three most common diagnoses are the focus of this chapter and are considered together as autism spectrum disorder (ASD), an umbrella term now preferred by most autism researchers and families to the previous designation of Pervasive Developmental Disorders (World Health Organization 1992). ASD is characterized by three features: (1) impairments in social interaction; (2) impairments in communication (which includes speech); and (3) the presence of restricted

This work was supported by grants RO1MH066496 from the National Institute of Mental Health and HD 35482-01 from the National Institute of Child Health and Human Development to Catherine Lord.

and repetitive interests or behaviours (American Psychiatric Association 1994. Note: the terms autism and ASD will be used interchangeably throughout this chapter to refer to this broad group of individuals). ASD is about four times more common in males than in females; current estimates of the occurrence rate of the entire spectrum of disorders are one child per 150 children (Autism and Developmental Disabilities Monitoring Network 2007).

ASD is a lifelong disorder. There is no cure, although studies have indicated that the provision of early intervention can improve outcome for some children (Harris & Handleman 2000, Turner et al. 2006) and a small proportion of the least impaired children and adolescents may move out of the spectrum (Lord et al. 2006). Early studies of language outcome indicated that as many as half of all individuals with ASD remained non-verbal into adulthood, suggesting that the absence of language was a common feature of the disorder (Bailey et al. 1996, Lord & Rutter 1994). However, newer reports have suggested that only about 15 to 20 per cent of individuals with ASD fail to acquire at least communicative single words by late childhood or adolescence, and at least half obtain functional, complex expressive language (Eaves & Ho 2004, Turner et al. 2006). This change may be related to the increasing identification of individuals who are more mildly affected than those who were diagnosed two or three decades ago (Chakrabarti & Fombonne 2005, Yeargin-Allsopp et al. 2003).

Language impairment or delay is not required for an ASD diagnosis. However, a progression of language impairments are associated with ASD (Tager-Flusberg 2004b). The earliest language abnormality identified is usually a delay, but for many children, it gradually becomes apparent that the language the child comes to use is unusual (Chawarska et al. 2007). Figure 25.1 provides some typical early language profiles of children with ASD. As an example, a two-year-old boy with ASD may not yet be speaking, but by three years of age, he may have acquired functional language as well as some repetitive speech (reciting phrases from a favourite movie). As his language emerges, unusual intonation may become evident, and he may have difficulty appropriately using pronouns, such as *I* and *you*. Not surprisingly, the mastery of language in early childhood has been positively associated with a number of skills in later childhood and beyond. Children with relatively stronger language skills early in life have higher IQ scores, social skills, adaptive skills and school ability in adolescence (Eaves & Ho 2004, Lord, Risi & Pickles 2004). Language skills at age 2 are moderately correlated with later outcome, and language at age 3 is much more strongly related (Charman et al. 2005), such that a child who is still experiencing a language delay at age 3 has a reduced likelihood of becoming a fluent speaker. Interestingly, if one looks back at the early years of children with ASD who *have* acquired fluent language, a history of language delay makes relatively little difference in severity of social measures later in childhood (Eisenmajer et al. 1998) or eventual verbal IQ (Szatmari et al. 1995).

Case 1: Max

When Max was 16 months old, his parents were excited to notice that their son was learning new words. However, as the months went by, they started to get worried. Max seemed only to be using certain kinds of words. He was learning the names of his two favourite kinds of things: vehicles and shapes. Max had learned twelve words for different kinds of cars and trucks, and he knew almost fifteen different shapes. He learned a few words for some other things he really wanted, like "juice" and "cookie," but he never learned all the usual first words that his older sister had said, like "Mummy" or "hi" or "that". Occasionally, he would ask his parents for something he wanted (like juice), but mostly he talked when he was by himself. He would recite lists of shapes when he was sitting alone, and when he saw a truck on the street, he would say "truck" without ever looking at his parents or trying to get them to pay attention too.

Case 2: Amelia

Amelia's parents were surprised that she was using phrases by the time she was 20 months old, but the more they listened to her talk, the more it seemed like something wasn't quite right. Instead of putting words together on her own, Amelia just repeated things that she'd heard from the shows on television. While other people who heard Amelia talk were often impressed to hear such long phrases come from such a young child, her parents were more worried than pleased. Amelia would often say the same phrase over and over again in exactly the same way, and she didn't seem to understand what it meant. Her father also noticed that when he asked her a question, like "Do you want juice?", Amelia would just repeat the phrase "want juice?" instead of answering the question.

Figure 25.1 Early language development in children with ASD: two case studies

As just described, the acquisition of language varies widely across the autism spectrum. It is also of note that language abilities themselves are quite heterogeneous (Kjelgaard & Tager-Flusberg 2001). While the core structural features of language (i.e. phonology, syntax, grammar) have historically been assumed to be relatively intact, the ability to appropriately *use* language (i.e. pragmatics) has consistently shown impairments (Tager-Flusberg 2004b). The remainder of this chapter will summarize what is known about receptive and expressive language – in terms of structure and use – in children with ASD, starting with a description of prelinguistic development, followed by a presentation of research on early language mastery and change throughout childhood. Related research in augmentative communication and reading will be briefly addressed, and emerging bodies of research on language processing, the genetics of language and early intervention will be highlighted.

25.2   Early development

25.2.1   Prelinguistic development

It is important to begin our exploration even before speech emerges. The term 'social communication' refers to a set of nonverbal skills which are socially directed and intended to be communicative, including an extensive set of behaviours such as eye contact, facial expression, non-word vocalizations, gestures and shared affect. In typical development, these skills

The term 'Theory of Mind' (ToM) refers to an individual's ability to attribute mental states – such as desires, beliefs and intents – to other people. It is a set of skills which typically develops in the first several years of life and is understood to be a fundamental component of cognitive, social and language development. Many researchers have noted that children with ASD demonstrate ToM impairments and have suggested that ToM deficits are one possible explanation of the social and linguistic difficulties in ASD. For a discussion of how ToM impairments may be related to the language profile of children with ASD, see Baron-Cohen, 2000 and Walenski *et al.*, 2006.

Figure 25.2 Theory of Mind (ToM) in children with ASD

emerge in the first months of life and are believed to be important precursors to speech (Carpenter *et al.* 1998). They are also understood to be related to other socio-cognitive attainments often implicated in discussions of ASD, most importantly the mastery of a 'Theory of Mind' (see Figure 25.2 for a brief discussion).

A growing body of research has followed infants who are at risk for developing ASD (usually younger siblings of children on the spectrum because of their increased risk for ASD; Freitag 2007) from the first months of life. These reports have indicated that by 12 months of age, many children later diagnosed with ASD show impairments in eye contact, socially directed smiling and vocalization and interest/enjoyment in engaging with other people (Bryson *et al.* 2007, Chawarska *et al.* 2007, Zwaigenbaum *et al.* 2005). Other studies – which reviewed videotapes taken when the children were infants – revealed early differences in children's tendency to look at other people (Osterling *et al.* 2002) and their ability to respond when other people call their names (Baranek 1999, Werner *et al.* 2000). Overall, these results suggest an early difficulty in orienting to social stimuli (Dawson *et al.* 2002, 2005a).

Early abnormalities are evident in emerging language as well. Canonical babbling is not clearly impaired (Sheinkopf *et al.* 2000, Werner & Dawson 2005), but it may be less frequent (Iverson & Wozniak 2007). By their first birthday, children later diagnosed with ASD have consistently been shown to have receptive and expressive language impairments (Landa & Garrett-Mayer 2006, Mitchell *et al.* 2006, Zwaigenbaum *et al.* 2005) and to be delayed in early gesture use (Bryson *et al.* 2007, Zwaigenbaum *et al.* 2005). Moreover, whereas typically developing infants have a preference for speech sounds over non-speech sounds (e.g. synthesized analogues; Vouloumanos & Werker 2007), infants later diagnosed with ASD generally do not (Klin 1992, Kuhl *et al.* 2005). For children with autism, the degree of preference is negatively related to their concurrent expressive language development (Kuhl *et al.* 2005).

25.2.2   Assessment of language in young children with ASD

Researchers have questioned whether standard tests of language are valid for children diagnosed with ASD, particularly those who are very young or markedly impaired in either language or related nonverbal skills (Charman 2004, Risi *et al.* 2006). Partly, this is because children who are significantly language impaired may not be able to earn a meaningful score on some standardized tests, either because the norms do not extend to their age or because they cannot complete a sufficient number of tasks. In addition, individuals with ASD may be proficient at some things (i.e. identifying animals and reciting a script from a video) but experience profound deficits in others (i.e. answering questions or following directions). Consequently, their overall scores may be biased by a relative strength – such as single word vocabulary – or weakness, such as verb usage (Jarrold, Boucher & Russell 1997).

Tests which are designed to evaluate language in typically developing children are premised on the assumption that the child has certain other skills (such as the basic motivation to engage with the examiner). When these fundamental skills are impaired – as they are for children with ASD – results may not only reflect the child's language ability but also the child's ability to attend and engage in a social interaction. For this reason, many researchers have suggested that additional methods, like taking language samples and recruiting parent report, may be important complementary approaches (Charman 2004, Luyster *et al.* 2007b).

25.2.3   Trajectories of early language development

Studies have begun to explore the trajectories of language development in ASD during childhood. In general, the language skills of individuals with ASD improve over childhood (Ballaban-Gil *et al.* 1996, Lord *et al.* 2004a). However, a particularly striking path of development in ASD has been noted in a considerable minority of children who experience a *loss* of language, a developmental pattern which has not been observed in typically developing children. This 'regression' has been documented in about 25 per cent of children with ASD (Goldberg *et al.* 2003, Lord *et al.* 2004b). It is distinct from the losses observed in other developmental disorders (such as Rett syndrome) in that the language skills are usually re-acquired, and it is not accompanied by changes in motor or adaptive skill (e.g. using utensils, bladder control). Although this trajectory is unique to ASD, it is *not* unique to language. Language loss is accompanied by the loss of a number of related social communication skills, such as eye contact and social responsiveness (Goldberg *et al.* 2003, Lord *et al.* 2004b, Luyster *et al.* 2005). Regression has been associated with slightly poorer outcomes in some studies (Bernabei *et al.* 2007; Richler *et al.* 2006) but not others (Lord *et al.* 2004b, Werner *et al.* 2005).

25.3   Receptive language

Making a distinction between language understanding and production has been useful in identification efforts. *Receptive* language delay (as opposed to an *expressive* language delay) is important for distinguishing between ASD and other disorders (Bartak *et al.* 1977, Lord & Paul 1997). Furthermore, in typically developing children, receptive vocabulary is in advance of expressive usage: children understand more language than they can generate (Fenson *et al.* 1994). This is also generally understood to be the case in children with ASD.

However, some results have indicated that children with ASD show less of an advantage in receptive skills than do their typically developing peers (Charman *et al.* 2003). When language scores were compared to age expectations for adults with ASD, there was a greater deficit in receptive vocabulary than in expressive vocabulary (Howlin 2003). Similarly, children with ASD demonstrated a profile in which expressive language standard scores were higher than the receptive scores; the opposite profile was observed in a group of children with specific language impairment (Lloyd *et al.* 2006). Other studies have not confirmed this profile. Neither Jarrold and colleagues (1997) nor Kjelgaard and Tager-Flusberg (2001) found any relative advantage in expressive language versus receptive language in ASD.

Studies have also explored children's understanding of the structure of language. Swensen *et al.* (2007), using a preferential looking paradigm, found that the understanding of subject–verb–object (SVO) word order preceded the production of SVO structure in two- and three-year-old children with ASD. Similar reports of intact SVO understanding have been reported by other researchers (Kelley *et al.* 2006, Paul *et al.* 1988). While children with ASD and concurrent language impairment have difficulty using sentence context to decide which meaning of a homograph is most appropriate (e.g. *bank*, which could refer either to a financial institution or the side of a river), children with ASD and average language scores perform as well as their typically developing peers (Norbury 2005).

Of late, researchers have begun to look beyond such basic characterizations of the receptive abilities of young individuals with ASD to explore the complex underlying processes of early language understanding. Theories of typical language development have invoked word learning biases (see Clark Ch.16), suggesting that children have a tendency to interpret new words in certain ways (i.e. as referring to objects rather than actions, called the 'noun bias'). Young children with ASD appear to abide by some of these biases (i.e. the noun bias, Swensen *et al.* 2007) but not others (i.e. the shape bias, Tek *et al.* 2007).

Other researchers have investigated children's understanding of how language can be used in different ways, where the focus is the intended meaning within a social context. Examples of different kinds of language use include humour, sarcasm, irony and metaphor. Understanding these different non-literal uses of words has consistently been found to be impaired in children with ASD (Happé 1994, Wang *et al.* 2006).

25.4 Expressive language

The study of expressive language in ASD has addressed children's ability to produce structurally correct language and their ability to use language appropriately, (the latter is considered 'pragmatics', see section 25.4.2). Given the centrality of language for the development of children with ASD, one might suppose that the field had firmly established the characterization of expressive language. In fact, the degree of language integrity and impairment is still up for discussion, partly due to inconsistent findings across projects and partly due to heterogeneity within samples.

25.4.1 Structural aspects of expressive language

Phonological abilities of children with ASD appear to be intact. Some studies have indicated possible phonological and articulation abnormality lingering into adolescence (Shriberg *et al.* 2001), while other studies have confirmed delay but not chronic impairment (Bartak *et al.* 1975, Kjelgaard & Tager-Flusberg 2001). The prosody and intonation of speech is often unusual in individuals with ASD (see McCann & Peppe 2003 for a review, Paul *et al.* 2005). Some children speak in an almost mechanical manner, lacking the ups and downs of normal speech. Others have the opposite problem, using intonations which are exaggerated and 'sing-songy'. In addition to abnormalities of intonation, other aberrations of speech are often reported, such as inappropriate volume or speed.

The acquisition of vocabulary is an area of some uncertainty. The lexicons of children with ASD have been reported to be comprised similarly to those of typically developing children across different word categories (e.g. nouns, predicates) (Charman *et al.* 2003, Luyster *et al.* 2007a). On the other hand, impairments have been noted in the appropriate use of emotional terms (Hobson *et al.* 1989) and deictic terms (which mark the differential reference of language between speaker and listener, such as *this* or *that*) (Lord & Paul, 1997, Tager-Flusberg 1994). A particularly salient example of deictic impairments are pronoun errors (Le Couteur *et al.* 1989); at some point in development, a high proportion of children with ASD consistently reverse their pronouns, saying 'you' for 'I' (Lee *et al.* 1994).

The question of semantics and underlying conceptual organization has also yielded varied results. In some reports, children with ASD demonstrated lexical organization similar to typically developing children (meaning that they form conceptual categories in the same way, e.g. Tager-Flusberg 1985, Ungerer & Sigman 1987). Other studies reported deficits in connectedness and depth of lexical knowledge (Dunn *et al.* 1996, Minshew *et al.* 2002). A recent study revealed differential performance of ASD children across different *kinds* of words, suggesting that impairments may be related specifically to the conceptual understanding of animate things (Kelley *et al.* 2006).

In their mastery of syntax and grammar, children with ASD generally follow a normal, albeit delayed, developmental progression (Tager-Flusberg *et al.* 1990, Waterhouse & Fein 1982). Nevertheless, some studies have suggested that they may show important differences from typically developing children in their use of morphological and syntactic terms, either in the ability to use forms correctly (Volden & Lord 1991) or in the range of produced forms (Bartolucci *et al.* 1980, Fein *et al.* 1996). One recent study indicated that the inconsistency of results may be partly due to the particular skill in question: when given a variety of standardized and experimental tests, school-aged children with ASD performed as well as their typically developing peers on most morphology and syntax tasks but showed difficulties with verb argument structure (Kelley *et al.* 2006). Verb agreement has been shown elsewhere to be an area of difficulty for children with ASD who also have receptive vocabulary deficits (Roberts *et al.* 2004b).

25.4.2 Pragmatic aspects of expressive language

Perhaps the most noted language deficits of children with ASD are in the realm of pragmatics. In general, challenges in the appropriate social use of language are associated with ASD in particular, although some researchers have suggested that pragmatic impairment can also be present in children without ASD (Bishop & Norbury 2002). In the ASD population, pragmatic impairments have been observed in a variety of manifestations. A boy may repeat words or phrases that he has just heard (a behaviour called 'echo-lalia') or has heard in the past ('delayed echolalia'). This 'echoed' language is frequently used in an undirected repetitive fashion (though some researchers have discussed its communicative function, see Prizant & Duchan 1981). In addition, children may use stereotyped words or phrases – that is, they may say the same thing repeatedly, even if the word or phrase is used appropriately (e.g. a young child named James saying "Good job, Mr James!" every time he completes a task).

The term 'neologism' refers to the generation of a non-word (for instance, saying *bloosers* for 'bruises', or *plin* for floating pieces of paper or fabric; Volden & Lord 1991). The use of neologisms is somewhat rare; what may be more frequent is an idiosyncratic use of language, in which the child phrases things in an unusual manner (Bartak *et al.* 1975, Kanner 1943). An example of this is asking "When was it born?" (instead of "When was it made?") or referring to tears as "sad water". Interestingly, these abnormalities have been linked to concept formation, such that children's unusual use of words or phrases may indicate that they are not abiding by common concepts or accepted meanings of a word (see Volden & Lord 1991 for a discussion).

In typical development, children use language for a variety of reasons: ask a question, make a request, comment on an object or event or just chat.

Children with ASD tend to use language in a more limited manner. They are much more likely to speak in order to make a request than to share their interest in something with another person (Landry & Loveland 1989, Stone & Caro-Martinez 1990). Often, this renders individuals profoundly impaired in conversational ability. Individuals with ASD who are able to engage in reciprocal dialogue with another person generally find it difficult to move flexibly from topic to topic, often responding inappropriately to the cues of others (Tager-Flusberg & Anderson 1991, Volden 2004). A child with ASD who was particularly interested in bus schedules might be capable of maintaining a simple discussion about local public transportation but would have a difficult time following the conversation if the topic changed to the price of gasoline and its effect on public transportation.

Rigidity in language use is demonstrated in other ways as well. Some individuals engage in verbal rituals, in which either they feel a need to say something in a certain way or demand that their social partner provide a particular verbal response (Le Couteur *et al.* 1989). For instance, a child might recite a favourite scene from a television show and, if interrupted, start over again until he completes the entire script. Alternatively, a young girl might repeatedly ask her father "Does the elevator go up or down?" until her father answers, "The elevator goes down."

One very important aspect of language in typically developing children is its integration with other nonverbal communication skills, such as gaze, facial expression and gestures. This too is an area of difficulty for children with ASD, as discussed in section 25.2.1. As children with ASD age, deficits become clear in other, more complex nonverbal behaviours, such as using 'beat' gestures while speaking and nodding or shaking one's head to indicate engagement with one's conversational partner (Garcia-Perez *et al.* 2007).

25.5   Issues related to language development

As discussed above, a minority of children with ASD remain nonverbal into adolescence, and these children require assistance in order to communicate. Augmentative and alternative communication (AAC) systems have been developed to meet this need. A recent meta-analysis of AAC on speech production (for individuals with ASD as well as other developmental disabilities) reported that, overall, AAC programmes appear to be successful in increasing expressive language (Millar *et al.* 2006). Perhaps the best-known AAC system is the Picture Exchange Communication System (PECS), which requires the child to hand a picture to a recipient in order to make a request, and there is some emerging evidence that PECS may be particularly valuable in increasing communication use (Howlin *et al.* 2007, Yoder & Stone 2006).

Reading ability in children with ASD has not yet been extensively researched. Results suggest – as in other areas of language ability – considerable heterogeneity across individuals. For instance, a recent study of children with ASD between 6 and 15 years of age reported that nine children (about 22 per cent) were unable to read at all (Nation *et al.* 2006). For those children who do master some reading skills, studies have fairly consistently reported that decoding skills (that is, deciphering unfamiliar words) exceed comprehension skills (Minshew *et al.* 1994, Whitehouse & Harris 1984).

25.6   Emerging areas of research in language development

A particularly relevant approach for our knowledge of language and language processing in ASD is neuro-imaging. Results from these endeavours suggest that individuals with ASD may have atypical associations between language and brain structure and function, characterized by diminished left hemisphere lateralization (the left hemisphere is associated with language processing in typically developing individuals) and increased association with the right hemisphere (e.g. Bigler *et al.* 2007, Boddaert *et al.* 2003). These findings suggest the failure of the left hemisphere to 'specialize' in language the way that it does in typical development (Dick *et al.* 2007), resulting in a less integrated and efficient neural network; this observation is similar to others noted in electrophysiological studies addressing the ability of children with ASD to process faces (see Dawson *et al.* 2005b for a review).

A second emerging body of research has to do with exploring genetic differences. It has become increasingly clear that ASD has a strong genetic component, and investigators are currently exploring the ways in which the genetic profile of ASD may be related to the behavioural profile of ASD. Studies have explored whether associations of ASD with specific genetic regions are increased for children who have autism *and* language delay. Results have been somewhat inconsistent, but some promising linkages have been reported both with age of language acquisition (Alarcon *et al.* 2002, Schellenberg *et al.* 2006) and the pattern of developmental regression (Molloy *et al.* 2005, Schellenberg *et al.* 2006). Further research will be required in order to explore observed associations between language development and other confounding factors, such as IQ, age and autism severity (Hus *et al.* 2007). These associations make replication difficult and cloud the relationship between language itself and underlying genetic profiles.

Finally, with the growing numbers of children diagnosed with ASD and the increasing demands on families, schools, and communities to provide long-term support, considerable attention has been paid to providing high-quality intervention services. Because of the evidence that early language mastery is associated with positive outcomes, intervention programmes often primarily emphasize children's verbal development. The provision of intervention services varies widely, although speech and language therapy is most commonly sought (Thomas *et al.* 2007). Research has indicated that individuals with ASD who receive intensive intervention early in childhood have better language than their peers who did not receive such services (Harris & Handleman 2000, Turner *et al.* 2006). It remains unclear whether there are certain intervention approaches that work better than others (see Goldstein 2002 for a review). Moreover, while large effects of intervention were initially claimed (Lovaas 1987), recent reports have suggested that the influence is much more modest, though still meaningful (Eikeseth *et al.* 2007, Kasari *et al.* 2006).

25.7 Conclusions

There remain challenges ahead for the study of language in children with ASD. Despite having been widely studied, language in ASD does not yet have a generally accepted standardized measure. Currently, there are a range of tests (primarily normed on typically developing children) which are commonly used but which present a number of difficulties, as discussed above (see section 25.2.2). With the growing numbers of children with ASD and the increasing need for appropriate standardized measures, many researchers have begun to tailor tests for this population and then work to establish basic psychometric properties. Measuring language (especially expressive) in children with ASD can be particularly difficult because of the inconsistency of language use across situations. Ideally, it would be possible to find a reliable and meaningful set of behaviours which has concurrent validity and also provides unique information about language development. Formalizing these behaviours as part of an ASD-specific language assessment would support efforts to clarify a number of the observed discrepancies in the literature.

Furthermore, the varied observations of language and social impairment in ASD have led many diagnosticians to contemplate the ways in which language, nonverbal communication and social interaction are intertwined. We are now beginning to consider the notion that the building blocks of language are separable from communication but communication is not separable from social interaction, as evidenced by indications that behaviours such as social imitation and play load onto social *and* communication factors (Bishop 1998, Lecavalier *et al.* 2006) There is a movement in the field to restructure the formal diagnostic guidelines to reflect this new conception of ASD. Whereas there are currently three required domains of symptomatology outlined in the *Diagnostic and Statistical Manual of Mental Disorders – Fourth Edition* (DSM-IV; American Psychiatric Association 1994), the upcoming revision is anticipated to outline two core features, both of which have been established in the literature (Gotham *et al.* 2007, Lecavalier *et al.* 2006): social communication and repetitive behaviours. According to the updated criteria, these two features may have associated impairments in nonverbal IQ and language. The shift of language impairment from a required to a possible symptom is largely the result of the many observations discussed throughout this chapter: language impairment is not specific to or universal throughout ASD, so it is less useful as a defining feature. Nevertheless, along with nonverbal IQ, language characteristics are central to both the diagnostic process and treatment planning. As we continue to study the language skills of individuals with ASD, it will be important to include well-matched comparison samples in order to clarify whether there are certain abnormalities (e.g. verbal rituals) which *are* unique to ASD. These new discoveries can, in turn, inform the refinement of diagnostic frameworks and enrich our understanding of ASD itself.

Suggestions for further reading

Charman, T., & Stone, W. (Eds.). (2006). *Social and Communication Development in Autism Spectrum Disorders: Early Identification, Diagnosis, and Intervention.* New York: Guilford Press.

Paul, R. (2006). *Language Disorders from Infancy Through Adolescence: Assessment and Intervention* (3rd edn.). St. Louis, MO: Mosby.

Volkmar, F., Paul, R., Klin, A., & Cohen, D. (Eds.). (2005). *Handbook of Autism and Pervasive Developmental Disorders* (3rd edn. Vol. 1–3). New York: Wiley Press.

26

Language development in genetic disorders

Fiona M. Richardson
Michael S. C. Thomas

26.1 Introduction

The study of language in developmental disorders is an important endeavour for several reasons. First, it is essential to identify areas of relative strength and weakness in order to gain a profile of the disorder, so that we may best support and facilitate the development of language and communication skills in these individuals. Second, such research allows us the opportunity to gain an insight into questions about the process of normal language development. For example: to what extent do biological factors influence language development? Does language learning rely on general cognitive processes, or processes that are specific to language? In this chapter, we focus on the process of language development in two contrasting developmental disorders: (i) Williams syndrome and (ii) Down syndrome. This chapter will describe what has been learned about normal language development through the study of these disorders and discuss unresolved issues that still exist in this field.

Both Williams syndrome (WS) and Down syndrome (DS) are genetically defined disorders. WS is caused through the deletion of approximately 28 genes from one copy of chromosome 7.[1] The incidence of WS is rare, occurring in approximately 1 in 20,000 live births (Morris *et al.* 1998). DS is more common by comparison, affecting approximately 14 in 10,000 live births (Roberts *et al.* 2007) and is the result of three copies (referred to as 'trisomy') of chromosome 21 (Tassabehji 2003). In normal individuals, there are only two copies of chromosome 21 – one from each parent. Both disorders result in some degree of learning disability or learning

This research was supported by MRC Career Establishment Grant GO300188 and British Academy Grant SG-40400 awarded to Dr Michael Thomas.

[1] The length of missing DNA is well understood while the functional role of the relevant base pairs is a topic of active research.

difficulties, with IQ in WS typically falling between 51 and 70 (Donnai & Karmiloff-Smith 2000, Mervis & Becerra 2007), and in DS ranging from 35 to 70 (Chapman & Hesketh 2000). Both disorders are also accompanied by a series of clearly distinguishable physical characteristics. For example, individuals with WS and DS frequently suffer from co-occurring heart problems and growth deficiency; individuals with DS may also suffer from respiratory problems. A prominent feature of both disorders is that they are also typically accompanied by a distinctive facial appearance (Morris 2006, Roizen & Patterson 2003).

The profile of verbal and nonverbal skills differs between disorders. In WS, overall IQ measures mask areas of relative strength and weakness in mental abilities, such as language, problem-solving ability and visuo-spatial processing, resulting in an uneven *cognitive* profile. Language in WS is frequently hailed as being a particularly strong skill. Notably, individuals with WS tend to develop extensive vocabularies that exceed expectations when compared to typically developing children with the same mental age (Bellugi *et al.* 1988). Children with WS also have relatively good auditory rote memory processing, having a longer forward and backward digit span than normally developing individuals matched for both chronological age and mental age, as well as individuals with DS (Klein & Mervis 1999). By contrast, visuo-spatial skills in WS are particularly poor, for example as measured through the use of drawing and pattern construction tasks (Mervis *et al.* 2000, Udwin & Yule 1991, Wang & Bellugi 1994). WS is also characterized by a distinctive personality profile, which is described as hypersocial or 'over-friendly'. However, individuals with WS are also prone to suffering from anxiety, particularly when in unfamiliar surroundings, or faced with a new set of circumstances (Klein-Tasman & Mervis 2003).

In terms of the profile of strengths and weaknesses in DS, visuo-spatial and visuo-motor skills are considered to be relatively good compared to overall mental age (Klein & Mervis 1999). However, in DS spoken language can be problematic. In part this is due to differences in facial musculature and oral structure (such as a larger tongue and smaller palette) that can limit the speed and range of motion in mouth movements making articulation more difficult, and resulting in poor clarity of speech (Dodd & Thompson 2001, Miller & Leddy 1998). Moreover, cranial facial differences and narrow auditory canals, in conjunction with a slight deficiency of the immune system, results in a susceptibility to Otitis media – inflammation or infection of the middle ear. This can lead to fluctuations in clarity of hearing or even hearing loss, which occurs in approximately two thirds of children with DS (American Academy of Paediatrics 2004, Roberts *et al.* 2004a, Roizen 2002). These additional factors make it more difficult for individuals with DS to develop clear well-articulated spoken language. Nevertheless, children with DS are still capable of effective communication through the support of nonverbal methods, and are socially motivated, affectionate and engaging (Moore *et al.* 2002).

In the following section, we consider the similarities and differences in the process of early language development in WS and DS in comparison to normally developing children, indicating how the initial characteristics of these disorders shape language learning from the very beginning of the acquisition process.

26.2   Early communicative development

The initial development of communication skills begins in infancy, with the use of nonverbal elements, such as gestures and eye gaze. This communication takes place between the infant and caregiver (dyadic interactions), and subsequently between the infant, caregiver and object or toy (triadic interactions). It is these initial patterns of interaction that underpin the development of *conceptual knowledge* – learning how objects are used and in what context; and *vocabulary* – learning what objects are called. In this section, we take a look at these early stages of language development in WS and DS, where initial differences from normally developing infants may be clearly identified.

26.2.1   Early communicative development in WS
The strong desire for social interaction that characterizes individuals with WS is apparent in infancy through a keen interest in faces. However, this results in infants with WS preferring to look at the face of their caregiver, as opposed to engaging in gaze-following behaviour, which is typically seen in normally developing infants (Bellugi *et al.* 1992). This initial reluctance makes more complex interactions between the infant, caregiver and an object or toy problematic. This is because toddlers with WS have difficulty switching their attention from the caregiver to an object being referred to in communication (via pointing, looking and naming).

During the early stages of communication development, normally developing children use deictic gestures such as pointing, as well as eye gaze, to direct the attention of their caregiver to objects. This behaviour facilitates the child in learning the terms of reference for objects and events. Since shared attention to newly named objects is one of the main routes into the development of vocabulary knowledge (see Tomasello Ch. 5, Carpenter *et al.* 1998), difficulty in triadic interactions places toddlers with WS at a disadvantage in vocabulary development. Indeed, difficulty in triadic interactions is considered to be a major source of the delay in the development of vocabulary knowledge in WS (Laing *et al.* 2002, Mervis *et al.* 2003). Mervis and Bertrand (1997) found that in WS the use of pointing behaviour emerges after these children start to use verbal labels. This finding was confirmed by Laing *et al.* (2002), and could not be attributed to any *deficit* (difficulty in performance below normal level) in fine motor skills that could potentially impede the development of pointing behaviour. Thus the development of early nonverbal communication skills in WS deviates from that found in normal development.

However, the development of productive vocabulary in WS usually matches, or sometimes even extends beyond, mental-age expectations. In WS, growth in vocabulary is remarkably rapid, equalling or even extending beyond that of children with the same mental age. This rapid growth has been attributed to the high attentional value placed on verbal input and increased auditory memory for words found in WS, rather than the early use of *semantic* knowledge to support vocabulary growth (Mervis & Bertrand 1997, Singer-Harris *et al.* 1997). Indeed, there is preliminary evidence that compared to typically developing children, those with WS show a reduced comprehension vocabulary in comparison to their production vocabulary (Paterson 2000), implying that these children have a poorer understanding of word knowledge than their use of vocabulary suggests.

26.2.2   Early communicative development in DS

Like infants with WS, infants with DS also encounter difficulties that result in a delay in establishing early nonverbal communication skills. Specifically, infants with DS usually have difficulty in establishing mutual eye contact with the caregiver, which makes the development of patterns of interaction more challenging (Berger & Cunningham 1981, Jansow *et al.* 1988). Moreover, once this initial problem is resolved, infants with DS prefer to continue to focus on the eyes of their caregiver, rather than the facial features, as young infants typically do (Berger & Cunningham 1981). This can subsequently lead to further difficulties in establishing more complex nonverbal exchanges, such as in triadic interactions. There is also usually delay in the onset of babbling, which is in part attributed to the articulatory difficulties that can occur in conjunction with this disorder (Miller *et al.* 1992).

Young children with DS also differ in their use of nonverbal communicative gestures, producing more gestures than those seen in normal development (and more than observed in WS). It is postulated that this additional use of gesture may be a method of compensating for the delay in the onset of developing spoken language due to frequently occurring articulatory difficulties (Singer-Harris *et al.* 1997). Recent research has investigated the types of gesture used in DS in comparison to normally developing children. Children with DS produce deictic gestures (pointing, giving, showing) and iconic gestures (depicting the use of an object – such as gesturing the use of a spoon) more than normally developing children, and use a particularly large number of iconic gestures in their communication (Stefanini *et al.* 2007). The use of iconic gestures, in particular, implies that these children have conceptual knowledge and are extracting meaning from their environment, which is not necessarily evident through their language production.

However, not all children with DS suffer from such profound articulatory difficulties that spoken language becomes insurmountable. Although vocabulary development is delayed, with some children with DS taking over 3 years to produce their first words (Berglund *et al.* 2001), once this process begins the subsequent rate of development is comparable to that seen in normally developing children of the same mental age MA (Tager-Flusberg & Sullivan 1998). Upon reaching the two-word stage, the progress of productive language development in DS varies – as some children do not extend beyond this stage until 4 years of age, or even as late as 5 or 6 years (Fowler 1998). Moving beyond the two-word stage, the use of grammatical knowledge develops.

26.2.3 Summary

Overall, early communication development in WS and DS may be summarized in terms of two main characteristics. First, there is a delay in the onset of language development in both disorders. Second, when language development does get underway, there is an imbalance between productive vocabulary and actual word knowledge. In children with WS, the development of productive vocabulary is rapid and indeed exceeds expectations based on mental age, whereas the development of intelligible speech in DS is frequently hampered by articulatory difficulties. However, children with DS do demonstrate conceptual knowledge of their environment through the use of gesture, whereas the rapid development of productive vocabulary in WS is not necessarily met with a corresponding level of understanding.

26.3   Patterns of language development

The development of language is heavily dependent upon the extent of the learning difficulties of the individual. Although there are cases of children who show exceptional language proficiency despite low IQ (Cromer 1994), it is usually expected that language ability in a child with learning difficulties will not surpass that of their mental age (Miller *et al.* 1978). For example, children with DS with a low IQ (below 50) may never develop complex structured language (Miller 1988). Furthermore, in order to succeed in acquiring language, children must also be socially motivated with the desire to communicate, and have some ability to understand the thoughts and intentions of others. In conjunction, these factors are crucial to the level of overall proficiency attained.

In the following section, we consider different aspects of language development in WS and DS, and discuss how these children differ from the typically developing population.

26.3.1   Later language learning in WS

Although the main feature of language development in WS is delay (Brock 2007, Thomas *et al.* 2001, 2006), the eventual outcome is relatively successful in that in most cases children with WS become proficient users of language. However, this is not to say that language in these individuals is normal; indeed, there is disparity between different aspects of language that results in an *atypical* profile (differing from normal development). Moreover, there is also variability in terms of the relative strengths and weaknesses found in both linguistic and cognitive skills (Porter & Coltheart 2005). Children with WS usually develop an extensive vocabulary and complex syntax – though their vocabulary skills generally exceed their syntactic ability in terms of mental age (Karmiloff-Smith *et al.* 1997). This profile of language skills contrasts with that found in children with specific language impairment (SLI), who have a particular difficulty in processing grammatical constructions (see Leonard Ch. 24, Tomblin Ch. 23 for discussion). In typically developing children there is a relationship between the length of utterance and the complexity of grammatical structure – this relationship also holds in WS (Mervis *et al.* 1999).

Children with WS make more errors in morphology than in syntax, that is, in verb tense and agreement and personal pronouns (Karmiloff-Smith *et al.* 1997, Volterrra *et al.* 1996). Also, French-speaking children with WS find grammatical gender particularly difficult (Karmiloff-Smith *et al.* 1997). Whilst the cognitive profiles of children with WS have been studies across many different languages, current work reflects a similar profile to that found in English-speaking children with WS (Levy & Bechar 2003). Although syntactic complexity is higher than expected upon the basis of non-linguistic skills, such as visuo-spatial construction or reasoning, they are nevertheless lower than expectations based upon levels of receptive vocabulary ability or auditory short-term memory (Mervis *et al.* 1999). A close inspection of grammatical abilities was carried out by Mervis *et al.* using the Test of Receptive Grammar (TROG: Bishop 1983), which assesses the ability to understand different types of sentence constructions of varying levels of complexity. This study was carried out with a large sample of 77 individuals between the ages of 5 and 52 years. Only 18 per cent of the participants (22 per cent of the adults) passed the test block that assessed right branching relative clauses (e.g. *The girl chases the dog that is jumping*) and only 5 per cent (9 per cent of the adults) passed the block assessing centre-embedded relative clauses (e.g. *The duck the ball is on is yellow*).

In terms of the development of semantic knowledge, children with WS exhibit a relative strength in category concepts (e.g. the distinctions between animals, tools, clothing, furniture). This contrasts with problems understanding semantic relational concepts. For example, children with WS have difficulty in understanding sentences containing spatial terms of reference (such as: *The bottle is in the boat* – Phillips *et al.* 2004). Within category concepts, recent evidence has indicated differential naming problems across categories, such as animals being named better than foods (Temple *et al.* 2002, Thomas *et al.* 2006). On the basis of such evidence it has been argued that the *lexicon* is an area of specific anomalies in WS (Clahsen & Almazan 1998, Rossen *et al.* 1996, Temple *et al.* 2002). Fractionation such as this also appears in other areas of the WS language system (Thomas 2006). For example, in the area of pragmatics children with WS have relatively good social sensitivity (e.g. making dyadic eye contact, sensitivity to nonverbal cues) but exhibit problems in areas such as greeting behaviours, topic maintenance and answering questions (Semel & Rosner 2003).

Thomas and Karmiloff-Smith (2003) recently characterized two types of hypotheses regarding the developmental profile of WS: (i) a series of 'imbalance' hypotheses, which account for the profile shown in WS in terms of an imbalance in the integration of phonological and semantic processing, and (ii) a 'conservative hypothesis', which proposes that language development in WS is delayed but not fundamentally altered. In the latter case, any anomalies in the language profile of children with WS would be accounted for by non-linguistic characteristics of the disorder – such as a strong desire for social interaction and poor visuo-spatial skills (Brock 2007).

26.3.2 Later language learning in DS

There are limitations in the overall level of complexity of language attained in DS. Moreover, the production of intelligible speech can be particularly challenging. Phonological development is delayed, proceeding at a slower rate in terms of mental age expectations and is associated with more error-prone production (Bleile & Schwartz 1984, Roberts *et al.* 2005, Stoel-Gammon 1980). The development of vocabulary knowledge in DS is also slow, but there is some consistency with those patterns observed in normal development. For example, some children with DS experience a vocabulary spurt (Berglund *et al.* 2001, Klein & Mervis 1999); however, this tends to occur at a more advanced age than seen in typically developing children. On the other hand, the development of receptive vocabulary is more consistent with mental age expectations, and is greatly enhanced throughout adolescence and adulthood, through life experience (Chapman 2006, Miller 1999).

Grammatical development varies widely in DS, and can only be partially explained in terms of IQ differences. For individuals with DS whose language development does progress beyond the use of two-word utterances,

utterances tend to be shorter in comparison to normally developing children (as measured by mean length of utterance) and are of lower syntactic complexity (Mervis *et al.* 1999). Also, like children with SLI there are difficulties in grammatical morphology. Children with DS are also more imitative than normally developing children in their use of language (Tager-Flusberg & Sullivan 1998). However, the development of syntax in DS has a prolonged developmental span, with increases in syntactic complexity and utterance length being known to continue throughout adolescence and into early adulthood (Chapman *et al.* 2002).

In terms of pragmatics abilities, children with DS are socially motivated in their use of language, and display the same range of communicative interests and interactions as typically developing children. However, the strength of these pragmatic abilities seems to be closely tied to mental age (Fowler 1998). This may in part contribute to some of the inconsistencies reported in the literature concerning the range of pragmatic abilities reported in DS such as taking into account the needs of the listener during conversation (Roberts *et al.* 2007). However, overall it is clear that individuals with DS are capable of holding and maintaining conversations in a similar way to typically developing children.

26.3.3 Summary

In later language learning, disparities between the normally developing population and WS and DS become more obvious. This is not only due to the limitations placed on language ability by learning difficulties, but also in terms of the differential profile of strengths and weaknesses shown both within and across different aspects of language skill (phonology, grammar, semantics and pragmatics). Language in WS appears to be strong at surface level, and is characterized by its particular use in social engagement. However, in spite of the development of an extensive vocabulary and complex syntax, there are elements of grammar, receptive vocabulary and semantic knowledge that do not match this proficiency. By comparison, language development in DS appears to asymptote at a lower level of complexity and the development of spoken language can be hindered by articulatory difficulties. However, the receptive abilities of those with DS exceed those of productive language, and individuals with DS display sensitivity to the thoughts and intentions of others and enjoy social interaction through conversation.

26.4 What can WS and DS tell us about language development?

The differing profiles of linguistic and non-linguistic skills in WS and DS illustrate the ways in which the normal developmental process may be deflected. The comparison of language skills across syndromes is particularly informative in terms of establishing what skills are crucial to successful language acquisition. In general, the contrasting language skills of those with WS and DS indicate that general cognitive ability cannot be considered to be a reliable indicator of all aspects of language function in children with learning difficulties. Comparisons carried out both in early development (Tager-Flusberg & Sullivan 1998) and later childhood (Fowler 1998) suggest that pragmatics and semantics are more closely linked to overall mental age across different disorders, while phonology and syntax can dissociate. McDonald (1997) compared language acquisition across different disorder groups (including WS and DS) who exhibited varying degrees of success and concluded that good representations of speech sounds (phonology) are a critical requirement to the successful development of language. However, Morton (2004) argues that successful language acquisition is dependent upon multiple cognitive components, and that impairment in any one of these can potentially result in the system failing to develop normally. Therefore, under Morton's view, good phonological skills may be a necessary but not sufficient requirement for successful language acquisition.

Consideration of what components of language are critical to successful acquisition raises key questions about how these components emerge as a process of development and what happens when something goes wrong. In current developmental theory, there are two potential interpretations. The first takes as its starting point the functional organization of normal adult cognitive processes. The field of neuropsychology has identified case studies of healthy adults who exhibit specific deficits in particular aspects of language processing following brain damage. From these dissociations, the language system is inferred to be organized into specific processing components or 'modules'. As applied to developmental disorders, a specific difficulty or strength in a given aspect of language processing is viewed as reflecting the under-development or over-development of that specific component of the language system (Clahsen & Temple 2003).

This framework provides a comfortable fit between the results of standardized language tests and atypical functional structure. Assuming we have tests that give an indication of the integrity of individual modules (e.g. tests of vocabulary, tests of grammar, tests of phonological processing), scores in the normal range of performance on a given test can be interpreted as reflecting a normally developed component. By contrast scores above or below the normal range can be read as reflecting an (atypically) over- or under-developed component. This mapping of test results to modular structure in developmental disorders rests on one of two assumptions. Either the modular system identified in the adult is also present in the infant, so that language development can commence with an initially selective anomaly in one or more components; or the modular structure emerges through development in such a way that when things go wrong, some parts emerge with atypical functionality while the rest nevertheless manage to emerge displaying their normal functionality. Together, these alternatives constitute the assumption of 'residual normality' (Thomas & Karmiloff-Smith 2002). Formally, the assumption is that the rest of the system can develop normally irrespective of the selective difficulty in one processing component.

The second, contrasting explanatory framework argues that development must play some role in shaping the profile of any given developmental disorder. This approach, known as 'neuroconstructivism', is based on the premise that components of the adult cognitive system are a *product* of the process of development and not initially present in infancy (Mareschal *et al.* 2007). This view is strongly motivated by data from developmental cognitive neuroscience (Elman *et al.* 1996, Karmiloff-Smith 1998). It calls into question a key assumption made by the modular view, that performance within the normal range on a given test of cognitive ability is an indicator of normal functional structure. Instead, neuroconstructivism argues that performance within the normal range may be achieved through atypical means, and that the underlying mechanisms that give rise to the same level of performance may be fundamentally different. The debate between these two explanations of uneven linguistic profiles has at times become polarized. On the one hand, there are strong claims that for given developmental disorders, certain cognitive structures must have developed normally, given behaviour in the normal range (sometimes these are referred to as *intact* or *spared* systems). On the other hand, there are counter-claims that since the developmental processes we know about could not have produced such an uneven modular outcome, the relevant behaviour must be produced by structures that are qualitatively different and atypical.

At the neurological level, brain-imaging techniques have been applied to the study of brain development in developmental disorders such as WS and DS. These studies look at a range of aspects of brain development, such as exploring anatomical differences between brain structures. For example, they look for differences in overall size or in the volume of a specific brain structure (in terms of amount of grey or white matter), or differences in patterns of brain symmetry (between left and right hemispheres) or connectivity, known as 'structural' differences. In WS, structural techniques have identified regions of reduced grey matter volume in the intraparietal sulcus and the orbitofrontal cortex (Meyer-Lindenberg *et al.* 2006). Abnormalities in the folds of the cerebral cortex have also been identified (Gaser *et al.* 2006, Kippenhan *et al.* 2005, Van Essen *et al.* 2006). In children with DS, brain regions such as the hippocampus, prefrontal cortex and cerebellum have been found to have a low volume (Nadel 2003). Exactly how these differences in brain structure affect brain 'function' is as yet unclear, and raises further questions. To what extent can we expect normal brain function in a system with structural differences?

As the different constraints placed on the system in developmental disorders put these children at a disadvantage, it is likely that their cognitive systems will attempt to overcome the challenges they face through the process of 'compensation' (Thomas 2005a, 2005b). The process of compensation within the context of developmental disorders is frequently incomplete, as evidenced by children failing to deliver levels of performance within the range of normally developing children. This may be because the process of compensation has resulted in the atypical system utilizing a secondary, less efficient route to task success, or the system has a reduced capacity or less efficient processing resources (i.e. Bishop 1994). However, children are renowned for the adaptive capacity, which is generally attributed to a property known as 'plasticity' – the flexibility of the learning system to adapt and alter in order to incorporate new information from the environment. This property of the learning system is generally considered to decrease over age (Uylings 2006), and may offer only a short window of opportunity for optimal adaptive change (known as a 'sensitive period', M. Johnson 2005). In conjunction, these factors play an important role in shaping the language systems of children with developmental disorders (Fowler 1998).

Finally, we shift our focus to consider the role of the environment in shaping the course of developmental disorders. In terms of environmental influences, there are two main points for consideration. The first of these is the extent to which differences in the internal cognitive system result in differences in the way in which the environment is perceived. We know that the neurology of the cognitive system in children differs from that of normally developing children, which may in turn result in differences in which the external environment is perceived by children with developmental disorders. Autism is a particularly good example of this (Happé & Frith 1996). Thus, although the external environment may not have been altered in any explicit manner, it may be fundamentally different from that of a normally developing child. In addition, children with developmental disorders display different initial preferences as to what they find interesting in their external environment (such as a keen interest in faces in WS). This means that the way they manipulate their external environment in order to participate in exchanges they perceive as rewarding may result in a subtly altered role for the environment in shaping the course of development. The second environmental influence and one of the most important motivating factors for the study of developmental disorders, is how we might support and facilitate effective development through a process of intervention. The degree and type of intervention appropriate may depend upon a number of factors. These include the profile of the individual child and the level of intervention services that may be accessed. Interventional methods seek to manipulate the environment and in doing so attempt to influence the course of development for those with disorders in a positive way. Somewhat counterintuitively, it may often be useful to interfere and further bolster an area of relative strength (such as language in WS) so that this ability can be used strategically to aid areas of weakness (such as visuo-spatial skills: Semel & Rosner 2003). For example, a series of memorized verbal cues may be one way to improve picture drawing or tying of shoe laces.

In sum, development is a process of change – in developmental disorders it is vital that we understand what changes are occurring and when, in order to establish the similarities and differences in children with disorders and typically developing children. Exploring the nature of these transitions not only enhances our understanding of developmental disorders but also provides us with an insight into cognitive processes in general, in terms of the emergence of modularity and expertise, and the scale and flexibility of cognitive processes during learning. In exploring the mechanisms of development, understanding the impact of the environment is also crucial. In this respect, the environment should not be viewed as a static influence; the environment can be changed externally, and may also undergo internal changes as the child's ability to interpret the environment or gain knowledge from it alters over time.

26.5   Unanswered questions and future challenges

In this chapter, we have explored the profiles of language development in WS and DS. We did so first to gain an insight into the relative patterns of strengths and weaknesses that characterize these disorders, and second to understand how the course of typical language development may be altered. However, a range of unanswered questions remains, which pose challenges for future research. Specifically, how does the functional organization of the language system emerge, and to what extent is this constrained by the processing properties of our neurology? These key questions are important to modular theorists and neuroconstructivists alike.

Within the context of developmental disorders, we need to be able to answer questions such as: does deficiency in one component (say, phonology) affect the development of another (say, syntax)? And, what level of disruption is necessary to produce a developmental disorder? Moreover, understanding the processing capabilities of different neural substrates in both typical development and developmental disorders is an important step towards understanding what kinds of differences result in a disorder. In short, we need to understand the parameters that affect the course of development and the different paths that development may take when faced with adverse circumstances. In this respect methods such as brain-imaging and computational modelling of language development may help in characterizing typical and atypical developmental processes (Thomas & Karmiloff-Smith 2003).

Suggestions for further reading

The following reviews provide a useful summary of language and communication skills in DS and WS:

Mervis, C., & Becerra, A. (2007). Language and communication development in Williams syndrome, *Mental Retardation and Developmental Disabilities Research Reviews*, 13, 3–15.

Roberts, J., Price, J., & Malkin, C. (2007). Language and communication development in Down syndrome. *Mental Retardation and Developmental Disabilities Research Reviews*, 13, 26–35

For more information on cross-syndrome comparisons see the following useful chapters:

Bellugi, U., Bihrle, A., Neville, H., Jernigan, T., & Doherty, S. (1992). Language, cognition, and brain organization in a neurodevelopmental disorder. In M. R. Gunnar & C. A. Nelson (Eds.), *Developmental Behavioral Neuroscience* (pp. 201–232). Hillsdale, NJ: Lawrence Erlbaum Associates.

Tager-Flusberg, H., & Sullivan, K. (1998). Early language development in children with mental retardation. In J. A. Burack, R. M. Hodapp & E. Zigler (Eds.), *Handbook of Mental Retardation and Development* (pp. 208–239). Cambridge: Cambridge University Press.

For further reading into how the study of developmental disorders can provide an insight into the process of language development, see:

Thomas, M., & Karmiloff-Smith, A. (2005). Can developmental disorders reveal the component parts of the human language faculty? *Language Learning and Development*, 1, 65–92.

For further reading into the development of cognitive processes, see:

Mareschal, D., Johnson, M., Sirios, S., Spratling, M., & Thomas, M. (2007). *Neuroconstructivism: How the Brain Constructs Cognition*. Oxford: Oxford University Press.

References

Abbeduto, L., & Short-Myerson, K. (2002). Linguistic influences on social interaction. In H. Goldstein, L. Kaczmarek & K. English (Eds.), *Promoting Social Communication* (pp. 27–54). Baltimore: Paul H. Brookes.

Abbot-Smith, K., & Tomasello, M. (2006). Exemplar-learning and schematization in a usage-based account of syntactic acquisition. *The Linguistic Review*, 23, 275–290.

Abbot-Smith, K., Lieven, E., & Tomasello, M. (2001). What preschool children do and do not do with ungrammatical word orders. *Cognitive Development*, 16, 679–692.

(2004). Training 2;6-year-olds to produce the transitive construction: The role of frequency, semantic similarity and shared syntactic distribution. *Developmental Science*, 7, 48–55.

(in press). Graded representations in the acquisition of English and German transitive constructions. *Cognitive Development*.

Abercombrie, D. (1967). *Elements of General Phonetics*. Chicago: Aldine.

Abu-Akel, A., Bailey, A., & Thum, Y.-M. (2004). Describing the acquisition of determiners in English: A growth modeling approach. *Journal of Psycholinguistic Research*, 33, 407–424.

Acredolo, L. P., & Goodwyn, S. W. (1988). Symbolic gesturing in normal infants. *Child Development*, 59, 450–466.

Akhtar, N. (1999). Acquiring basic word order: Evidence for data-driven learning of syntactic structure. *Journal of Child Language*, 26, 339–356.

Akhtar, N., & Tomasello, M. (1996). Two-year-olds learn words for absent objects and actions. *British Journal of Developmental Psychology*, 14, 79–93.

(1997). Young children's productivity with word order and verb morphology. *Developmental Psychology*, 33, 952–965.

Aksu-Koç, A. (1998). The role of input vs. universal predispositions in the emergence of tense–aspect morphology: Evidence from Turkish. *First Language*, 18, 255–280.

Aksu-Koç, A., & Slobin, D.I. (1985). The acquisition of Turkish. In D.I. Slobin (Ed.), *The Crosslinguistic Study of Language Acquisition: Vol. 1. The Data* (pp. 839–878). Hillsdale, NJ: Lawrence Erlbaum Associates.

Aksu-Koç, A., & von Stutterheim, C. (1994). Temporal relations in narrative: Simultaneity. In R.A. Berman & D.I. Slobin (Eds.), *Relating Events in Narrative: A Crosslinguistic Developmental Study* (pp. 393–456). Hillsdale, NJ: Lawrence Erlbaum Associates.

Alarcon, M., Cantor, R.M., Liu, J., Gilliam, T.C., The Autism Genetic Resource Exchange Consortium, & Geschwind, D.H. (2002). Evidence for a language quantitative trait locus on chromosome 7q in multiplex families. *American Journal of Human Genetics*, 70, 60–71.

Albert, M., & Obler, L.K. (1978). *The Bilingual Brain: Neuropsychological and Neurolinguistc Aspects of Bilingualism*. New York: Academic Press.

Allen, G.D., & Hawkins, S. (1978). The development of phonological rhythm. In A. Bell & J.B. Hooper (Eds.), *Syllables and Segments* (pp. 173–185). Amsterdam: North Holland.

   (1980). Phonological rhythm: Definition and development. In G. Yeni-Komshian, J.S. Kavanagh & C.A. Ferguson (Eds.), *Child Phonology: Vol. 1.* (pp. 227–256). New York: Academic Press.

Allen, R., & Shatz, M. (1983). 'What says meow?' The role of context and linguistic experience in very young children's responses to *what*-questions. *Journal of Child Language*, 10, 14–23.

Allen, S.E.M. (2000). A discourse-pragmatic explanation for argument representation in child Inuktitut. *Linguistics*, 38, 483–521.

   (2007a). The future of Inuktitut in the face of majority languages: Bilingualism or language shift? *Applied Psycholinguistics*, 28, 515–536.

   (2007b). Interacting pragmatic influences on children's argument realization. In M. Bowerman & P. Brown (Eds.), *Crosslinguistic Perspectives on Argument Structure: Implications for Learnability* (pp. 191–210). New York: Lawrence Erlbaum Associates.

Allen, S.E.M., & Crago, M. (1996). Early passive acquisition in Inuktitut. *Journal of Child Language*, 23, 129–155.

Allen, S.E.M., & Schröder, H. (2003). Preferred Argument Structure in early Inuktitut spontaneous speech data. In J.W. Du Bois, L.E. Kumpf & W.J. Ashby (Eds.), *Preferred Argument Structure: Grammar as Architecture for Function* (pp. 301–338). Amsterdam: John Benjamins.

Allen, S.E.M., Özürek, A., Kita, S., *et al.* (2006). Language-specific and universal influences in children's syntactic packaging of manner and path: A comparison of English, Japanese and Turkish. *Cognition*, 102, 16–48.

Allen, S.E.M., Skarabela, B., & Hughes, M. (2008). Using corpora to examine discourse effects in syntax. In H. Behrens (Ed.), *Corpora in Language Acquisition Research* (pp. 99–137). Amsterdam: Benjamins.

Allopenna, P.D., Magnuson, J.S., & Tanenhaus, M.K. (1998). Tracking the time course of spoken word recognition using eye movements: Evidence for continuous mapping models. *Journal of Memory & Language*, 38, 419–439.

Altmann, G. (1998) Ambiguity in Sentence Processing. *Trends in Cognitive Sciences*, 2, 146–152.

   (2001). The language machine: Psycholinguistics in review. *British Journal of Psychology*, 92, 129–170.

Altmann, G., & Steedman, M. (1988). Interaction with context during human sentence processing. *Cognition*, 30, 191–238.

Ambridge, B., Rowland, C., Theakston, A., & Tomasello, M. (2006). Comparing different accounts of auxiliary inversion errors. *Journal of Child Language*, 33, 519–557.

Ameel, E., Malt, B. C., & Storms, G. (2008). Object naming and later lexical development: From baby bottle to beer bottle. *Journal of Memory & Language*, 58, 262–285.

American Academy of Pedriatrics (2004). Clinical practice guideline: Otis media with effusion. *Pedriatrics*, 113, 1412–1429.

American Psychiatric Association (1994). *Diagnostic and Statistical Manual of Mental Disorders* (4th edn). Washington, DC: Author.

Andersen, E. S. (1975). Cups and glasses: Learning that boundaries are vague. *Journal of Child Language*, 2, 79–103.

   (2000). Exploring register knowledge: The value of 'controlled improvisation'. In L. Menn & N. B. Ratner (Eds.), *Methods for Studying Language Production* (pp. 225–248). Mahwah, NJ: Lawrence Erlbaum Associates.

Andersen, E. S., Dunlea, A., & Kekelis, L. S. (1984). Blind children's language: Resolving some differences. *Journal of Child Language*, 11, 645–664.

Anderson, J. L., Morgan, J. L., & White, K. S. (2003). A statistical basis for speech sound discrimination. *Language and Speech*, 46, 155–182.

Andrews, A. (1985). *Studies in the Syntax of Relative and Comparative Clauses*. New York: Garland.

Aram, D. M., & Nation, J. (1980). Preschool language disorders and subsequent language and academic difficulties. *Journal of Communication Disorders*, 13, 159–170.

Aram, D. M., Ekelman, B. L., & Nation, J. E. (1984). Preschoolers with language disorders: Ten years later. *Journal of Speech and Hearing Research*, 22, 232.

Archibald, J. (Ed.) (1995). *The Acquisition of Non-linear Phonology*. Hillsdale, NJ: Lawrence Erlbaum Associates.

Ariel, M. (1990). *Accessing Noun-Phrase Antecedents*. London: Routledge.

Arnold J., Eisenband J., Brown-Schmidt S., & Trueswell, J. (2000). The rapid use of gender information: Evidence of the time course of pronoun resolution from eyetracking, *Cognition*, 76, B13–B26.

Arunachalam, S., Gould, D., Andersen, E., Byrd, D., & Narayanan, S. (2001, September). *Politeness and Frustration Language in Child–Machine Interactions*. Paper presented at the 7th European Conference on Speech Communication and Technology, Aalborg, Denmark.

Aslin, R. N., & Pisoni, D. B. (1980). Some developmental processes in speech perception. In G. H. Yeni-Komshian, J. F. Kavanagh & C. A. Ferguson (Eds.), *Child Phonology: Vol. 2. Perception* (pp. 67–96). New York: Academic Press.

Aslin, R. N., Pisoni, D. B., Hennessy, B. L., & Perey, A. J. (1981). Discrimination of voice onset time by human infants: New findings and implications for the effects of early experience. *Child Development*, 52, 1135–1145.

Aslin, R. N., Saffran, J. R., & Newport, E. L. (1998). Computation of conditional probability statistics by 8-month-old infants. *Psychological Science*, 9, 321–324.

Austin, J. L. (1975). *How to do Things with Words*. Cambridge, MA: Harvard University Press.

Autism and Developmental Disabilities Monitoring Network (2007). Prevalence of autism spectrum disorders – autism and developmental disabilities monitoring network, 14 sites, United States, 2002. *MMWR Surveillance Summaries*, 56, 12–28.

Bailey, A., Phillips, W., & Rutter, M. (1996). Autism: Towards an integration of clinical, genetic, neuropsychological, and neurobiological perspectives. *Journal of Child Psychology and Psychiatry*, 37, 89–126.

Bailey, T., & Plunkett, K. (2002). Phonological specificity in early words. *Cognitive Development*, 17, 1267–1284.

Baker, A., & de Jong, J. (2007, July). The Nature of Bilingual Specific Language Impairment (SLI). Keynote speech presented at the Child Language Seminar, University of Reading.

Baker, C. I., Olson, C. R., & Behrmann, M. (2004). Role of attention and perceptual grouping in visual statistical learning. *Psychological Science*, 15, 460–466.

Baker, C. L. (1979). Syntactic theory and the projection problem. *Linguistic Inquiry*, 10, 533–581.

Baker, M. (1988). *Incorporation: A Theory of Grammatical Function Changing*. Chicago: University of Chicago Press.

Baker, N. D., & Nelson, K. E. (1984). Recasting and related conversational techniques for triggering syntactic advances by young children. *First Language*, 5, 3–22.

Ballaban-Gil, K., Rapin, I., Tuchman, R., & Shinnar, S. (1996). Longitudinal examination of the behavioral, language, and social changes in a population of adolescents and young adults with autistic disorder. *Pediatric Neurology*, 15, 217–223.

Ballem, K. D., & Plunkett, K. (2005). Phonological specificity in children at 1;2. *Journal of Child Language*, 32, 159–173.

Bamberg, M. (1986). The acquisition of anaphoric relationships. *Linguistics*, 26, 227–284.

  (1987). *The Acquisition of Narratives: Learning to use Language*. Berlin: Mouton de Gruyter.

(in press). Sequencing events in time or sequencing events in storytelling? From cognition to discourse – with frogs paving the way. In J. Guo, S. Ervin-Tripp & N. Budwig (Eds.), *Festschrift for Dan Slobin*. Mahwah, NJ: Lawrence Erlbaum Associates.

Baranek, G. T. (1999). Autism during infancy: A retrospective video analysis of sensory–motor and social behaviors at 9–12 months of age. *Journal of Autism and Developmental Disorders*, 29, 213–224.

Barlow, J. A. (1997). A constraint-based account of syllable onsets: Evidence from developing systems. Unpublished doctoral dissertation, Indiana University, Bloomington.

(2001). The structure of /s/-sequences: Evidence from a disordered system. *Journal of Child Language*, 28, 291–324.

Baron-Cohen, S. (2000). Autism and 'Theory of Mind'. In J. Harley and A. Braithwaite (Eds.) *The Applied Psychologist*. Milton Keynes: Open University Press.

Bartak, L., Rutter, M., & Cox, A. (1975). A comparative study of infantile autism and specific developmental receptive language disorder: I. The children. *British Journal of Psychiatry*, 126, 127–145.

(1977). A comparative study of infantile autism and specific developmental receptive language disorders: III. Discriminant function analysis. *Journal of Autism & Childhood Schizophrenia*, 7(4), 383–396.

Bartlett, C. W., Flax, J. F., Logue, M. W., *et al.* (2002). A major susceptibility locus for specific language impairment is located on 13q21. *American Journal of Human Genetics*, 71, 45–55.

Bartolucci, G., Pierce, S. J., & Streiner, D. L. (1980). Cross-sectional studies of grammatical morphemes in autistic and mentally retarded children. *Journal of Autism and Developmental Disorders*, 10, 39–50.

Barton, M., & Tomasello, M. (1991). Joint attention and conversation in mother–infant–sibling triads. *Child Development*, 62, 517–529.

(1994). The rest of the family: The role of fathers and siblings in early language development. In C. Gallaway & B. Richards (Eds.), *Input and Interaction in Language Acquisition* (pp. 109–134). Cambridge: Cambridge University Press.

Bates, E. (1976). *Language and Context: The Acquisition of Pragmatics*. New York: Academic Press.

Bates, E., & Goodman, J. C. (1999). On the emergence of grammar from the lexicon. In B. MacWhinney (Ed.), *The Emergence of Language* (pp. 29–79). Mahwah, NJ: Lawrence Erlbaum Associates.

Bates, E., & MacWhinney, B. (1987). Competition, variation and language learning. In B. MacWhinney (Ed.), *Mechanisms of Language Acquisition* (pp. 157–194). Hillsdale, NJ: Lawrence Erlbaum Associates.

(1989). Functionalism and the competition model. In B. MacWhinney & E. Bates (Eds.), *The Crosslinguistic Study of Sentence Processing* (pp. 3–73). New York: Cambridge University Press.

Bates, E., Benigni, L., Bretherton, I., Camaioni, L., & Volterra, V. (1979). *The Emergence of Symbols: Cognition and Communication in Infancy*. New York: Academic Press.

Bates, E., McNew, S., MacWhinney, B., Devescovi, A., & Smith, S. (1982). Functional constraints on sentence comprehension: A crosslinguistic study. *Cognition*, 11, 245–299.

Bates, E., MacWhinney, B., Caselli, C., Devescovi, A., Natale, F., & Venza, V. (1984). A cross-linguistic study of the development of sentence interpretation strategies. *Child Development*, 55, 341–354.

Bates, E., Bretherton, I., & Snyder, L. S. (1988). *From First Words to Grammar: Individual Differences and Dissociable Mechanisms*. Cambridge: Cambridge University Press.

Battison, R. (1978). *Lexical Borrowing in American Sign Language*. Silver Spring: Linstok Press.

Bavin, E. L., (2000). Ellipsis in Warlpiri children's narratives: An analysis of Warlpiri frog stories. *Linguistics*, 38, 569–589.

(2004). Focusing on 'where': An analysis of Warlpiri frog stories. In S. Stromqvist & L. Verhoeven (Eds.), *Relating Events in Narrative: Typological and Contextual Perspectives* (pp. 17–35). Mahwah, NJ: Lawrence Erlbaum Associates.

Bavin, E. L., & Growcott, C. (1999). Infants of 24–30 months understand verb frames. In M. Perkins & S. Howard (Eds.), *New Directions in Language Development and Disorders* (pp. 169–177). New York: Kluwer.

Bavin, E. L., Wilson, P., Maruff, P., & Sleeman, F. (2005). Spatio-visual memory of children with specific language impairment: Evidence for generalized processing problems. *International Journal of Language and Communication Disorders*, 40, 319–332.

Bazzanella, C., & Calleri, D. (1991). Tense coherence and grounding in children's narrative. *Text*, 11, 175–187.

Bechtel, W., & Abrahamsen, A. (2002). *Connectionism and the Mind: Parallel Processing, Dynamics, and Evolution in Networks* (2nd edn.). Oxford: Blackwell.

Becker, J. (1982). Children's strategic use of requests to mark and manipulate social status. In S. Kuczaj (Ed.), *Language Development: Language, Thought, and Culture* (pp. 1–35). Hillsdale, NJ: Lawrence Erlbaum Associates.

(1984). Implications of ethology for the study of pragmatic development. In S. Kuczaj (Ed.), *Discourse Development* (pp. 1–17). New York: Springer-Verlag.

(1988). The success of parents' indirect techniques for teaching their preschoolers pragmatic skills. *First Language*, 8, 173–181.

(1990). Processes in the acquisition of pragmatic competence. In G. Conti-Ramsden & C. Snow (Eds.), *Children's Language: Vol. 7.* (pp. 7–24). Hillsdale, NJ: Lawrence Erlbaum Associates.

(1994a). Pragmatic socialization: Parental input to preschoolers. *Discourse Processes*, 17, 131–148.

(1994b). 'Sneak shoes', 'sworders', and 'nose beards': A case study of lexical innovation. *First Language*, 40, 95–121.

Becker, J., & Hall, M. (1989). Adult beliefs about pragmatic development. *Journal of Applied Developmental Psychology*, 10, 1–17.

Becker, J., Place, K., Tenzer, S., & Frueh, C. (1991). Teachers' impressions of children varying in pragmatic skills. *Journal of Applied Developmental Psychology*, 12, 397–412.

Becker, M. (2000). The development of the copula in child English: The lightness of be. Unpublished doctoral dissertation, University of California, Los Angeles.

Bedore, L., & Leonard, L. (1998). Specific language impairment and grammatical morphology: A discriminant function analysis. *Journal of Speech, Language, and Hearing Research*, 41, 1185–1192.

(2001). Grammatical morphology deficits in Spanish-speaking children with specific language impairment. *Journal of Speech, Language, and Hearing Research*, 44, 905–924.

(2005). Verb inflections and noun phrase morphology in the spontaneous speech of Spanish-speaking children with specific language impairment. *Applied Psycholinguistics*, 26, 195–225.

Behrens, H. (2002). Learning multiple regularities: Evidence from overgeneralization errors in the German plural. In A. H.-J. Do, L. Domínguez & A. Johansen (Eds.), *Proceedings of the 26th Annual Boston University Conference on Language Development* (pp. 72–83). Somerville, MA: Cascadilla Press.

(2003). Bedeutungserwerb, Grammatikalisierung und Polysemie: Zum Erwerb von 'gehen' im Deutschen, Niederländischen und Englischen. In S. Haberzettl & H. Wegener (Eds.), *Spracherwerb und Konzeptualisierung* (pp. 161–181). Frankfurt: Peter Lang.

Beilin, H., & Lust, B. (1975). Connectives: Logical, linguistic and psychological theory (pp. 186–216). A study in the development of logical and linguistic connectives: Linguistic data (pp. 217–284). A study of the development of logical and linguistic connectives: Cognitive data (pp. 285–337). In H. Beilin (Ed.), *Studies in the Cognitive Basis of Language Development*. New York: Academic Press.

Beitchman, J. H., Nair, R., Clegg, M., & Ferguson, B. (1986a). Prevalence of psychiatric disorders in children with speech and language disorders. *Journal of the American Academy of Child Psychiatry*, 25, 528–535.

Beitchman, J. H., Nair, R., Clegg, M., & Patel, P. G. (1986b). Prevalence of speech and language disorders in 5-year-old kindergarten children in the Ottawa-Carleton region. *Journal of Speech and Hearing Disorders*, 51, 98–110.

Beitchman, J. H., Tuckett, M., & Batth, S. (1987). Language delay and hyperactivity in preschoolers: Evidence for a distinct subgroup of hyperactives. *Canadian Journal of Psychiatry*, 32, 683–687.

Beitchman, J. H., Hood, J., Rochon, J., & Peterson, M. (1989). Empirical classification of speech/language impairment in children: II. Behavioral characteristics. *Journal of the American Academy of Child and Adolescent Psychiatry*, 28, 118–123.

Beitchman, J. H., Hood, J., & Inglis, A. (1990). Psychiatric risk in children with speech and language disorders. *Journal of Abnormal Child Psychology*, 18, 283–296.

Beitchman, J. H., Brownlie, E. B., & Wilson, B. (1996a). Linguistic impairment and psychiatric disorder: Pathways to outcome. In J. H. Beitchman, N. J. Cohen, M. M. Konstantareas & R. Tannock (Eds.), *Language, Learning, and Behavior Disorders: Developmental, Biological, and Clinical Perspectives* (pp. 493–514). New York: Cambridge University Press.

Beitchman, J. H., Wilson, B., Brownlie, E. B., Walters, H., & Lancee, W. (1996b). Long-term consistency in speech/language profiles: I. Developmental and academic outcomes. *Journal of the American Academy of Child & Adolescent Psychiatry*, 35, 804–814.

Bekken, K. (1989). Is there 'Motherese' in gesture? Unpublished doctoral dissertation, University of Chicago, Chicago.

Bellugi, U., Marks, S., Bihrle, A., & Sabo, H. (1988). Dissociation between language and cognitive functions in Williams syndrome. In D. V. M. Bishop & K. Mogford (Eds.), *Language Development in Exceptional Circumstances* (pp. 177–189). London: Churchill.

Bellugi, U., Bihrle, A., Neville, H., Jernigan, T., & Doherty, S. (1992). Language, cognition, and brain organization in a neurodevelopmental disorder. In M. R. Gunnar & C. A. Nelson (Eds.), *Developmental Behavioral Neuroscience* (pp. 201–32). Hillsdale, NJ: Lawrence Erlbaum Associates.

Benasich, A. A., & Tallal, P. (2002). Infant discrimination of rapid auditory cues predicts later language impairment. *Behavioural Brain Research*, 136, 31–49.

Benasich, A. A., Curtiss, S., & Tallal, P. (1993). Language, learning, and behavioral disturbances in childhood: A longitudinal perspective. *Journal of the American Academy of Child and Adolescent Psychiatry*, 32, 585–594.

Bennet-Kastor, T. (1983). Noun phrases and coherence in child narrative. *Journal of Child Language*, 10, 133–149.

Berger, J., & Cunningham, C. (1981). The development of eye contact between mothers and normal versus Down syndrome infants. *Developmental Psychology*, 17, 678–689.

Berglund, E., Eriksson, M., & Johansson, I. (2001). Parental reports of spoken language skills in children with Down syndrome. *Journal of Speech, Language and Hearing Research*, 44, 179–191.

Berk, S. (2003). Sensitive period effects on the acquisition of language: A study of language development. Unpublished doctoral dissertation, University of Connecticut, Storrs.

Berko, J. (1958). The child's learning of English morphology. *Word*, 14, 150–177.

Berman, R. A. (1986). A step-by-step model of language learning. In I. Levin (Ed.), *Stage and Structure: Re-Opening the* Debate (pp. 191–219). Norwood, NJ: Ablex.

(1988). On the ability to relate events in narratives. *Discourse Processes*, 11, 469–497.

(1990). Acquiring an (S)VO language: Subjectless sentences in children's Hebrew. *Linguistics*, 28, 1135–1166.

(1993). Marking verb transitivity in Hebrew-speaking children. *Journal of Child Language*, 20, 641–670.

(1995). Narrative competence and storytelling performance: How children tell stories in different contexts. *Journal of Narrative and Life History*, 5, 285–313.

(1996). Form and function in developing narrative abilities: The case of 'and'. In D. I. Slobin, J. Gerhardt, A. Kyratzis & J. Guo (Eds.), *Social Interaction, Social Context, and Language: Essays in Honor of Susan Ervin-Tripp* (pp. 243–268). Mahwah, NJ: Lawrence Erlbaum Associates.

(1998). Typological perspectives on connectivity. In N. Dittmar & Z. Penner (Eds.), *Issues in the Theory of Language Acquisition* (pp. 203–224). Bern: Peter Lang.

(2004a). Between emergence and mastery: The long developmental route of language acquisition. In R. A. Berman (Ed.), *Language Development across Childhood and Adolescence: Psycholinguistic and Crosslinguistic Perspectives. Trends in Language Acquisition Research (TILAR): Vol. 3.* (pp. 9–34). Amsterdam: John Benjamins.

Berman, R. (Ed.). (2004b). *Language Development across Childhood and Adolescence*. Philadelphia, PA: John Benjamins.

(2007). Developing linguistic knowledge and language use across adolescence. In E. Hoff & M. Shatz (Eds.), *Blackwell Handbook of Language Development* (pp. 347–367). Malden, MA: Blackwell.

Berman, R. A., & Dromi, E. (1984). On marking time without aspect in child language. *Papers and Reports on Child Language Development*, 23, 21–32.

Berman, R. A., & Katzenberger, I. (1998). Cognitive and linguistic factors in development of picture-series narration. *Studia Italiani i Linguistica Teorica e Applicata*, 27, 21–47.

Berman, R. A., & Neeman, Y. (1994). Development of linguistic forms: Hebrew. In R. A. Berman & D. I. Slobin (Eds.), *Relating Events in Narrative: A Crosslinguistic Developmental Study* (pp. 285–428). Hillsdale, NJ: Lawrence Erlbaum Associates.

Berman, R. A., & Nir-Sagiv, B. (2004). Linguistic indicators of inter-genre differentiation in later language development. *Journal of Child Language*, 31, 339–380.

(2007). Comparing narrative and expository text construction across adolescence: A developmental paradox. *Discourse Processes*, 43, 79–120.

(in press). Clause-packaging in narratives: A crosslinguistic developmental study. In J. Guo, E. Lieven, N. Budwig, S. Ervin-Tripp, K. Nakamura & S. Ozcaliskan (Eds.), *Crosslinguistic Approaches to the Psychology of Language: Research in the Tradition of Dan I. Slobin*. Mahwah, NJ: Lawrence Erlbaum Associates.

Berman, R. A., & Slobin, D. I. (Eds.). (1994). *Relating Events in Narrative: A Crosslinguistic Developmental Study*. Hillsdale, NJ: Lawrence Erlbaum Associates.

Bernabei, P., Cerquiglini, A., Cortesi, F., & D'Ardia, C. (2007). Regression versus no regression in the autistic disorder: Developmental trajectories. *Journal of Autism and Developmental Disorders*, 37, 580–588.

Bernal, S., Lidz, J., Millotte, S., & Christophe, A. (2007). Syntax constrains the acquisition of verb meaning. *Language Learning and Development*, 3, 325–341.

Bernhardt, B. H., & Stemberger, J. P. (1998). *Handbook of Phonological Development from the Perspective of Constraint-Based Nonlinear Phonology*. San Diego: Academic Press.

Bernstein, I. L., & Borson, S. (1986). Learned food aversion: A component of anorexia nervosa syndromes. *Psychological Review*, 93, 462–472.

Bertoncini, J., Bijeljac-Babic, R., Blumstein, S., & Mehler, J. (1987). Discrimination of very short CV syllables by neonates. *Journal of the Acoustical Society of America*, 82, 31–37.

Berwick, R., & Niyogi, P. (1996). Learning from triggers. *Linguistic Inquiry*, 27, 605–622.

Best, C. T. (1994). The emergence of native-language phonological influences in infants: A perceptual assimilation model. In J. C. Goodman & H. C. Nusbaum (Eds.), *The Development of Speech Perception: The Transition from Speech Sounds to Spoken Words* (pp. 167–224). Cambridge, MA: MIT Press.

Best, C. T., & McRoberts, G. W. (2003). Infant perception of nonnative contrasts that adults assimilate in different ways. *Language and Speech*, 46, 183–216.

Best, C. T., McRoberts, G. W., & Sithole, N. M. (1988). Examination of perceptual reorganization for nonnative speech contrasts: Zulu click discrimination by English-speaking adults and infants. *Journal of Experimental Psychology: Human Perception and Performance*, 14, 345–360.

Best, C. T., McRoberts, G. W., LaFleur, R., & Silver-Isenstadt, J. (1995). Divergent developmental patterns for infants' perception of two nonnative consonant contrasts. *Infant Behavior and Development*, 18, 339–350.

Bialystok, E. (1991). Letters, sounds, and symbols: Changes in children's understanding of written language. *Developmental Psychology*, 28, 654–664.

(1999). Cognitive complexity and attentional control. *Child Development*, 70, 636–644.

(2007). Language acquisition and bilingualism: Consequences for a multilingual society. *Applied Psycholinguistics*, 28, 393–397.

Bialystok, E., & Hakuta, K. (1999). Confounded age: Linguistic and cognitive factors in age differences for second language acquisition. In D. Birdsong

(Ed.), *Second Language Acquisition and the Critical Period Hypothesis* (pp. 161–181). Mahwah, NJ: Lawrence Erlbaum Associates.

Bickel, B., & Nichols, J. (2005), Inflectional synthesis of the verb. In M. Haspelmath, M. S. Dryer, D. Gil, & B. Comrie (Eds.), *World Atlas of Language Structures* (pp. 94–97). Oxford: Oxford University Press.

Bickel, B., Banjade, G., Gaenszle, M., *et al.* (2007). Free prefix ordering in Chintang. *Language*, 83, 8–43.

Bigler, E. D., Mortensen, S., Neeley, E. S., *et al.* (2007). Superior temporal gyrus, language function, and autism. *Developmental Neuropsychology*, 31, 217–238.

Bild, E., & Swain, M. (1989). Minority language students in a French programme: Their French proficiency. *Journal of Multilingual and Multicultural Development*, 10, 255–274.

Birdsong, D., & Molis, M. (2001). On the evidence for maturational constraints in second-language acquisition. *Journal of Memory and Language*, 44, 235–249.

Bishop, D. V. M. (1983). *The Test for Reception of Grammar*. Age and Cognitive Performance Research Centre, University of Manchester.

(1994). Grammatical errors in specific language impairment: Competence of performance limitations? *Applied Psycholinguistics*, 15, 507–550.

(1998). Development of the Children's Communication Checklist (CCC): A method for assessing qualitative aspects of communicative impairment in children. *Journal of Child Psychology and Psychiatry*, 39(6), 879–891.

(2003). Autism and Specific Language Impairment: Categorical Distinction or Continuum? In G. Bock & J. Goode (Eds.), *Autism: Neural Basis and Treatment Possibilities* (pp. 213–234). Chichester: John Wiley.

Bishop, D. V. M., & Adams, C. (1990). A prospective study of the relationship between specific language impairment, phonological disorders and reading retardation. *Journal of Child Psychology and Psychiatry and Allied Disciplines*, 31, 1027–1050.

Bishop, D. V. M., & Edmundson, A. (1987). Specific language impairment as a maturational lag: Evidence from longitudinal data on language and motor development. *Developmental Medicine and Child Neurology*, 29, 442–459.

Bishop, D. V. M., & Norbury, C. F. (2002). Exploring the borderlands of autistic disorder and specific language impairment: A study using standardized diagnostic instruments. *Journal of Child Psychology and Psychiatry*, 43, 917–929.

Bishop, D. V. M., North, T., & Donlan, C. (1995). Genetic basis of specific language impairment: Evidence from a twin study. *Developmental Medicine and Child Neurology*, 37, 56–71.

Bishop, D. V. M., Adams, C., & Norbury, C. F. (2006). Distinct influences on grammar and phonological short-term memory deficits: Evidence from six-year-old twins. *Genes, Brain and Behavior*, 5, 158–169.

Bittner, D. (2000). Sprachwandel durch Spracherwerb? Pluralerwerb. In A. Bittner, D. Bittner & K.-M. Köpcke (Eds.), *Angemessene Strukturen:*

Systemorganisation in Phonologie, Morphologie und Syntax (pp. 123–141). Hildesheim: Olms.

Bittner, D., Dressler, W.U., & Kilani-Schoch, M. (2003). Introduction. In D. Bittner, W.U. Dressler & M. Kilani-Schoch (Eds.), *The Development of Verb Inflection in First Language Acquisition: A Cross-Linguistic Perspective* (pp. vii–xxxvii). Berlin: Mouton de Gruyter.

Black, B., & Hazen, N. (1990). Social status and patterns of communication in acquainted and unacquainted preschool children. *Developmental Psychology*, 26, 379–387.

Black, B., & Logan, A. (1995). Links between communication patterns in mother–child, father–child, and child–peer interactions and children's social status. *Child Development*, 66, 255–271.

Bleile, K., & Schwartz, I. (1984). Three perspectives on the speech of children with Down syndrome. *Journal of Communication Disorders*, 17, 87–94.

Blenn, L., Seidl, A., & Höhle, B. (2003). Recognition of phrases in early language acquisition: The role of morphological markers. In B. Beachley, A. Brown & F. Conlin (Eds.), *BUCLD 27: Proceedings of the 27th Annual Conference on Language Development*. Sumerville: Cascadilla Press.

Blom, E. (2007). *From Root Infinitive to Finite Sentence: The Acquisition of Verbal Inflections and Auxiliaries*. Berlin: Mouton de Gruyter.

Bloom, L. (Ed.). (1970). *Language Development: Form and Function in Emerging Grammars*. Cambridge, MA: MIT Press.

Bloom, L. (1971). Why not pivot grammar? *Journal of Speech and Hearing Disorders*, 36, 40–50.

(1973). *One Word at a Time*. The Hague: Mouton.

(1992). *Language Development from Two to Three*. Cambridge: Cambridge University Press.

Bloom, L., Lahey, M., Hood, L., Lifter, K., & Fiess, K. (1980). Complex sentences: Acquisition of syntactic connectives and the semantic relations they encode. *Journal of Child Language*, 7, 235–261.

Bloom, L., Rispoli, M., Gartner, B., & Hafitz, J. (1989). Acquisition of complementation. *Journal of Child Language*, 16, 101–120.

Bloom, P. (1990a). Subjectless sentences in child language. *Linguistic Inquiry*, 21(4), 491–504.

(1990b). Syntactic distinctions in child language. *Journal of Child Language*, 17, 343–355.

(1997). Intentionality and word learning. *Trends in Cognitive Sciences*, 1, 9–12.

(2000). *How Children Learn the Meanings of Words*. Cambridge, MA: MIT Press.

Blum-Kulka, S. (1997). *Dinner Talk: Cultural Patterns of Sociability and Socialization in Family Discourse*. Mahwah, NJ: Lawrence Erlbaum Associates.

(2004). The role of peer interaction in later pragmatic development. In R.A. Berman (Ed.), *Language Development across Childhood and Adolescence* (pp. 191–210). Philadelphia, PA: John Benjamins.

(2005). 'I will tell you the <u>whole</u> story now': Sequencing the past, present, and future in children's conversational narratives. In D. D. Ravid, H. B.-Z. Shyldkrot & R. A. Berman (Eds.), *Perspectives on Language and Language Development* (pp. 275–288). Dordrecht: Kluwer.

Blum-Kulka, S., & Snow, C. (Eds.) (2002). *Talking to Adults: The Contribution of Multi-party Discourse to Language Acquisition*. Mahwah, NJ: Lawrence Erlbaum Associates.

Blum-Kulka, S., & Snow, C. (2004). Introduction: The potential of peer talk. *Discourse Studies*, 6, 291–306.

Bock, J. K. (1986). Syntactic persistence in language production. *Cognitive Psychology*, 18, 355–387.

Bod, R., Hay. J., & Jannedy, S. (2003). Introduction. In R. Bod, J. Hay & S. Jannedy (Eds.), *Probabilistic Linguistics* (pp. 1–10). Cambridge, MA: MIT Press.

Boddaert, N., Belin, P., Chabane, N., Poline, J., *et al.* (2003). Perception of complex sounds: Abnormal pattern of cortical activation in autism. *American Journal of Psychiatry*, 160, 2057–2060.

Boersma, P., & Weenink, D. (2005). Praat: Doing phonetics by computer (Version 4.4.07) [Computer Software].

Bohannon, N., & Stanowicz, L. (1988). The issue of negative evidence: Adult responses to children's language errors. *Developmental Psychology*, 24, 684–689.

Boland, J. E. (2005). Visual arguments. *Cognition*, 95, 237–274.

Boland, J. E., & Cutler, A. (1996). Interaction with autonomy: Multiple output models and the inadequacy of the Great Divide. *Cognition*, 58, 309–320.

Boneva, B., Quinn, A., Kraut, R., Kiesler, S., & Shklovski, I. (2006). Teenage communication in the instant messaging era. In R. Kraut, M. Brynn & S. Kiesler (Eds.), *Computers, Phones, and the Internet* (pp. 201–218). New York: Oxford University Press.

Booij, G. (2005). *The Grammar of Words*. Oxford: Oxford University Press.

Bookheimer, S. (2002). Functional MRI of language: New approaches to understanding the cortical organization of semantic processing. *Annual Review of Neuroscience*, 25, 151–188.

Bornkessel, I., & Schlesewsky, M. (2006). The extended argument dependency model: A neurocognitive approach to sentence comprehension across languages. *Psychological Review*, 113, 787–821.

Bornstein, M. H., Haynes, O. M., Painter, K. M., & Genevro, J. L. (2000). Child language with mother and with stranger at home and in the laboratory: A methodological study. *Journal of Child Language*, 27, 407–420.

Bornstein, M. H., Painter, K., & Park, J. (2002). Naturalistic language sampling in typically developing children. *Journal of Child Language*, 29, 687–699.

Bortfeld, H., Rathbun, K., Morgan, J., & Golinkoff, R. (2005). Mommy and me. *Psychological Science*, 16, 298–304.

Bortolini, U., Caselli, M. C., & Leonard, L. (1997). Grammatical deficits in Italian-speaking children with specific language impairment. *Journal of Speech, Language, and Hearing Research*, 40, 809–820.

Bortolini, U., Leonard, L., & Caselli, M. C. (1998). Specific language impairment in Italian and English: Evaluating alternative accounts of grammatical deficits. *Language and Cognitive Processes*, 13, 1–20.

Bortolini, U., Caselli, M. C., Deevy, P., & Leonard, L. (2002). Specific language impairment in Italian: First steps in the search of a clinical marker. *International Journal of Language and Communication Disorders*, 37, 77–93.

Bortolini, U., Arfé, B., Caselli, M. C., Degasperi, L., Deevy, P., & Leonard, L. (2006). Clinical markers for specific language impairment in Italian: The contribution of clitics and nonword repetition. *International Journal of Language and Communication Disorders*, 41, 695–712.

Bos, H. (1995). Pronoun copy in Sign Language of the Netherlands. In H. Bos & T. Schermer (Eds.), *Sign Language Research 1994: Proceedings of the 4th European Congress on Sign Language Research* (pp. 121–147). Hamburg: Signum.

Bosch, L., & Sebastián-Gallés, N. (2001). Evidence of early language discrimination abilities in infants from bilingual environments. *Infancy*, 2(1), 29–49.

(2003). Simultaneous bilingualism and the perception of a language-specific vowel contrast in the first year of life. *Language and Speech*, 46, 217–243.

Bowerman, M. (1974). Learning the structure of causative verbs: A study in the relationship of cognitive, semantic, and syntactic development. *Papers and Reports on Child Language Development*, 8, 142–178.

(1979). The acquisition of complex sentences. In P. Fletcher & M. Garman (Eds.), *Language Acquisition: Studies in First Language Development* (pp. 285–305). Cambridge: Cambridge University Press.

(1982a). Evaluating competing linguistic models with language acquisition data: Implications of developmental errors with causative verbs. *Quaderni di Semantica*, 3, 5–66.

(1982b). Reorganizational processes in lexical and syntactic development. In E. Wanner & L. R. Gleitman (Eds.), *Language Acquisition: The State of the Art*. Cambridge: Cambridge University Press.

(1985). What shapes children's grammar? In D. I. Slobin (Ed.), *The Crosslinguistic Study of Language Acquisition: Vol. 2. Theoretical Issues* (pp. 1257–1319). Hillsdale, NJ: Lawrence Erlbaum Associates.

(1988). The 'no negative evidence' problem. How do children avoid constructing an overgeneral grammar? In J. A. Hawkins (Ed.), *Explaining Language Universals* (pp. 73–101). Oxford: Basil Blackwell.

(1990). Mapping thematic roles onto syntactic functions: Are children helped by innate linking rules? *Linguistics*, 28, 1253–1289.

(1994). From universal to language-specific in early grammatical development. *Philosophical Transactions of the Royal Society of London*, 346, 37–45.

(1996). Learning how to structure space for language: A cross-linguistic perspective. In P. Bloom, M. Peterson, L. Nadel & M. Garret (Eds.), *Language and Space* (pp. 385–436). Cambridge, MA: MIT Press.

(2005). Why can't you 'open' a nut or 'break' a cooked noodle? Learning covert action categories in action word meanings. In L. Gershkoff-Stowe & D. Rakison (Eds.), *Building Object Categories in Developmental Time* (pp. 209–243). Mahwah, NJ: Lawrence Erlbaum Associates.

Bowerman, M., & Brown, P. (2007). Introduction. In M. Bowerman & P. Brown (Eds.), *Crosslinguistic Perspectives on Argument Structure: Implications for Learnability* (pp. 1–26). New York: Lawrence Erlbaum Associates.

Bowerman, M., & Choi, S. (2003). Space under construction: Language specific spatial categorization in first language acquisition. In D. Gentner & S. Goldin-Meadow (Eds.), *Language in Mind: Advances in the Study of Language and Cognition* (pp. 387–427). Cambridge, MA: MIT Press.

Bowerman, M., & Croft, W. (2007). The acquisition of the English causative alternation. In M. Bowerman & P. Brown (Eds.), *Crosslinguistic Perspectives on Argument Structure: Implications for Learnability* (pp. 279–307). New York: Lawrence Erlbaum Associates.

Bowerman, M., & Levinson, S. C. (Eds.). (2001). *Language Acquisition and Conceptual Development*. Cambridge: Cambridge University Press.

Bowerman, M., de León, L., & Choi, S. (1995). Verbs, particles, and spatial semantics: Learning to talk about spatial actions in typologically different languages. In E. V. Clark (Ed.), *The Proceedings of the 27th Annual Child Language Research Forum* (pp. 101–110). Stanford, CA: CSLI.

Braine, M. D. S. (1963). The ontogeny of English phrase structure: The first phase. *Language*, 39, 1–13.

(1994). Is nativism sufficient? *Journal of Child Language*, 21, 9–31.

Braine, M. D. S., & Brooks, P. (1995). Verb argument structure and the problem of avoiding an overgeneral grammar. In M. Tomasello & W. Merriman (Eds.), *Beyond Names of Things: Young Children's Acquisition of Verbs* (pp. 353–376). Hillsdale, NJ: Lawrence Erlbaum Associates.

Brandt, S., Diessel, H., & Tomasello, M. (2008). The acquisition of German relative clauses: A case study. *Journal of Child Language*, 35, 325–348.

Brandt, S., Lieven, E., & Tomasello, M. (submitted). The development of sentential-complement constructions in German.

Bregman, E. O. (1934). An attempt to modify the emotional attitudes of infants by the conditioned response technique. *Journal of Genetic Psychology*, 45, 169–198.

Bresnan, J. (2001). *Lexical-Functional Syntax*. Oxford: Blackwell.

Brinton, B., & Fujiki, M. (1995). Conversational intervention with children with specific language impairment. In M. Fey, J. Windsor & S. Warren (Eds.), *Language Intervention: Preschool through the Elementary Years: Vol. 5. Communication and Language Intervention Series* (pp. 183–212). Baltimore: Paul H. Brookes.

Brinton, B., Fujiki, M., & McKee, L. (1998). The negotiation skills of children with specific language impairment. *Journal of Speech, Language, and Hearing Research*, 41, 927–940.

Briscoe, J., Bishop, D. V. M., & Norbury, C. F. (2001). Phonological processing, language, and literacy: A comparison of children with mild-to-moderate sensorineural hearing loss and those with specific language impairment. *Journal of Child Psychology and Psychiatry and Allied Disciplines*, 42, 329–340.

Broaders, S., Cook, S. W., Mitchell, Z., & Goldin-Meadow, S. (2007). Making children gesture brings out implicit knowledge and leads to learning. *Journal of Experimental Psychology: General*, 136(4), 539–550.

Brock, J. (2007). Language abilities in Williams syndrome: A critical review. *Development and Psychopathology*, 19, 97–127.

Brodmann, K. (1909). *Vergleichende Lokalisationslehre der Großhirnrinde in ihren Prinzipien dargestellt auf Grund des Zellenbaues*. Leipzig: Barth JA.

Brooks, P., & Tomasello, M. (1999a). How young children constrain their argument structure constructions. *Language*, 75, 720–738.

(1999b). Young children learn to produce passives with nonce verbs. *Developmental Psychology*, 35, 29–44.

Brooks, P., Tomasello, M., Lewis, L., & Dodson, K. (1999). Children's overgeneralization of fixed transitivity verbs: The entrenchment hypothesis. *Child Development*, 70, 1325–1337.

Browman, C. P., & Goldstein, L. (1986). Towards an articulatory phonology. *Phonology Yearbook*, 3, 219–252.

Brown, P. (1998a). Children's first verbs in Tzeltal: Evidence for an early verb category. *Linguistics*, 36, 713–753.

(1998b). Conversational structure and language acquisition: The role of repetition in Tzeltal adult and child speech. *Journal of Linguistic Anthropology*, 8, 197–221.

(1998c). Early Tzeltal verbs: Argument structure and argument realization. In E. V. Clark (Ed.), *Proceedings of the 29th Annual Child Language Research Forum* (pp. 129–140). Stanford, CA: Center for Studies in Language and Information (CSLI).

Brown, R. (1957). Linguistic determinism and the part of speech. *Journal of Abnormal and Social Psychology*, 55, 1–5.

(1973). *A First Language: The Early Stages*. Cambridge, MA: Harvard University Press.

Brown, R., & Hanlon, C. (1970). Derivational complexity and order of acquisition in child speech. In J. R. Hayes (Ed.), *Cognition and the Development of Language* (pp. 11–54). New York: John Wiley.

Bruner, J. (1983). *Child's Talk: Learning to Use Language*. New York: Norton.

(1986). *Actual Minds, Possible Worlds*. Cambridge, MA: Harvard University Press.

Bryant, J. B. (1999). Perspectives on pragmatic socialization. In A. Greenhill (Ed.), *Proceedings of the 23rd Annual Boston University Conference on Language Development: Vol. 1.* (pp. 132–137). Somerville, MA: Cascadilla Press.

Bryson, S., Zwaigenbaum, L., Brian, J., *et al.* (2007). A prospective case series of high-risk infants who developed autism. *Journal of Autism and Developmental Disorders*, 37, 12–24.

Bull, D., Eilers, R. E., & Oller, D. K. (1984). Infants' discrimination of intensity variation in multisyllabic stimuli. *Journal of the Acoustical Society of America*, 76, 13–17.

Burnham, D., & Dodd, D. (1999). Familiarity and novelty preferences in infants' auditory–visual speech perception: Problems, factors, and a solution. In C. Rovee-Collier, L. Lipsitt & H. Hayne (Eds.), *Advances in Infancy Research: Vol. 12.* (pp. 170–187). Stamford: Ablex.

Burns, T., Werker, J. F., & McVie, K. (2003). Development of phonetic categories in infants raised in bilingual and monolingual environments. In B. Beachley, A. Brown & F. Colin (Eds.), *Proceedings of the 27th Annual Boston University Conference on Language Development.* Somerville, MA: Cascadilla Press.

Butcher, C., & Goldin-Meadow, S. (2000). Gesture and the transition from one- to two-word speech: When hand and mouth come together. In D. McNeill (Ed.), *Language and Gesture* (pp. 235–25). New York: Cambridge University Press.

Butterworth, G., & Grover, L. (1988). The origins of referential communication in human infancy. In L. Weiskrantz (Ed.), *Thought without Language* (pp. 5–24). Oxford: Clarendon.

Bybee, J. (1985). *Morphology: A Study of the Relation between Meaning and Form.* Amsterdam: John Benjamins.

  (1995). Regular morphology and the lexicon. *Language and Cognitive Processes*, 10, 425–455.

  (1998). The emergent lexicon. *Proceedings of the Chicago Linguistics Society*.

Bybee, J., & Noonan, M. (Eds.). (2001). *Complex Sentences in Grammar and Discourse: Essays in Honor of Sandra A. Thompson.* Amsterdam: John Benjamins.

Cairns, H. S., McDaniel, D., & Hsu, J. (1993). A reply to 'Children are in control'. *Cognition*, 48, 193–194.

Callanan, M. A. (1985). How parents label objects for young children: The role of input in the acquisition of category hierarchies. *Child Development*, 56, 508–523.

Calvert, S. (2002). Identity construction on the internet. In S. Calvert, A. Jordan & R. Cocking (Eds.), *Children in the Digital Age: Influences of Electronic Media on Development* (pp. 57–70). Westport, CT: Praeger.

Cameron-Faulkner, T., Lieven, E., & Tomasello, M. (2003). A construction based analysis of child directed speech. *Cognitive Science*, 27, 843–873.

Campbell, A. L., & Tomasello, M. (2001). The acquisition of English dative constructions. *Applied Psycholinguistics*, 22, 253–267.

Campos, J. J., Anderson, D. I., Barbu-Roth, M. A., Hubbard, E. M., Hertenstein, M. J., & Witherington, D. (2000). Travel broadens the mind. *Infancy*, 1, 149–219.

Capirci, O., Montanari, S., & Volterra, V. (1998). Gestures, signs, and words in early language development. In J. M. Iverson & S. Goldin-Meadow (Eds.), *The Nature and Functions of Gesture in Children's Communications* (pp. 45–60). San Francisco: Jossey-Bass.

Caplan, D. (1980). *Biological Studies of Mental Processes.* Cambridge, MA: MIT Press.

Caramazza, A., Yeni-Komshian, G., Zurif, E., & Carbone, E. (1973). The acquisition of a new phonological contrast: The case of stop consonants in French–English bilinguals. *The Journal of the Acoustical Society of America,* 54, 421–428.

Carnie, A. (2006). *Syntax: A Generative Introduction* (2nd edn.). Malden, Oxford: Blackwell.

Carpenter, M., Nagell, K., & Tomasello, M. (1998). Social cognition, joint attention, and communicative competencies from 9 to 15 months of age. *Monographs of the Society of Research in Child Development,* 63, Serial No. 255.

Carter, A., & Gerken, L. (2004). Do children's omissions leave traces? *Journal of Child Language,* 31, 561–586.

Cartwright, T. A., & Brent, M. R. (1997). Syntactic categorization in early language acquisition: Formalizing the role of distributional analysis. *Cognition,* 63, 121–170.

Caselli, M. C., & Volterra, V. (1990). From communication to language in hearing and deaf children. In V. Volterra & C. J. Erting (Eds.), *From Gesture to Language in Hearing and Deaf Children* (pp. 263–277). Berlin: Springer Verlag.

Casenhiser, D., & Goldberg, A. (2005). Fast mapping between a phrasal form and meaning. *Developmental Science,* 8, 500–508.

Cassell, J., Huffaker, D., Tversky, D., & Ferriman, K. (2006). The language of online leadership: Gender and youth engagement on the internet. *Developmental Psychology,* 42, 436–449.

Catts, H. W. (1993). The relationship between speech–language impairments and reading disabilities. *Journal of Speech & Hearing Research,* 36, 948–958.

Catts, H., Fey, M., Zhang, X., & Tomblin, J. B. (1999). Language bases of reading and reading disabilities: Evidence from a longitudinal investigation. *Journal of the Scientific Study of Reading,* 3, 331–361.

Catts, H., Fey, M., Zhang, X., & Tomblin, J. B. (2001). Estimating the risk of future reading difficulties in kindergarten children: A research-based model and its clinical implementation. *Language Speech and Hearing Services in Schools,* 32, 38–50.

Cazden, C. B. (1968). The acquisition of verb and noun inflection. *Child Development,* 39, 433–448.

Chakrabarti, S., & Fombonne, E. (2005). Pervasive developmental disorders in preschool children: Confirmation of high prevalence. *American Journal of Psychiatry,* 162, 1133–1141.

Chambers, C., Tanenhaus, M. & Magnuson, J. (2004). Actions and Affordances in Syntactic Ambiguity Resolution. *Journal of Experimental Psychology: Learning, Memory, and Cognition*, 30, 687–696.

Chambers, K. E., Onishi, K. H., & Fisher, C. (2003). Infants learn phonotactic regularities from brief auditory experiences. *Cognition*, 87, B69–B77.

Chan, A., Lieven, E., & Tomasello, M. (in press). Children's understanding of the agent–patient relations in the transitive construction: Cross-linguistic comparisons between Cantonese, German, and English. *Cognitive Linguistics*.

Chao, Y. R. (1968/1976). *A Grammar of Spoken Chinese*. Berkeley, CA: University of California Press.

Chapman, R. (1997). Language development in children and adolescents with Down Syndrome. *Mental Retardation and Developmental Disabilities*, 3, 307–312.

  (2006). Language learning in Down syndrome: The speech and language profile compared to adolescents with cognitive impairment of unknown origin. *Down Syndrome Research and Practice*, 10, 61–66.

Chapman, R., & Hesketh, L. (2000). Behavioral phenotype of individuals with Down syndrome. *Mental Retardation and Developmental Disabilities Research Reviews*, 6, 84–95.

Chapman, R., Hesketh, L., & Kistler, D. (2002). Predicting longitudinal change in language production and comprehension in individuals with Down syndrome. *Journal of Speech, Language and Hearing Research*, 45, 902–915.

Charette, M. (1991). *Conditions on Phonological Government*. Cambridge: Cambridge University Press.

Charman, T. (2004). Matching preschool children with autism spectrum disorders and comparison children for language ability: Methodological challenges. *Journal of Autism and Developmental Disorders*, 34, 59–64.

Charman, T., Drew, A., Baird, C., & Baird, G. (2003). Measuring early language development in pre-school children with autism spectrum disorder using the MacArthur Communicative Development Inventory (Infant Form). *Journal of Child Language*, 30, 213–236.

Charman, T., Taylor, E., Drew, A., Cockerill, H., Brown, J., & Baird, G. (2005). Outcome at 7 years of children diagnosed with autism at age 2: Predictive validity of assessments conducted at 2 and 3 years of age and pattern of symptom change over time. *Journal of Child Psychology & Psychiatry*, 46, 500–513.

Chawarska, K., Klin, A., Paul, R., & Volkmar, F. (2007). Autism spectrum disorder in the second year: Stability and change in syndrome expression. *Journal of Child Psychology and Psychiatry*, 48, 128–138.

Cheek, A., Cormier, K., Repp, A., & Meier, R. P. (2001). Prelinguistic gesture predicts mastery and error in the production of first signs. *Language*, 77(2), 292–323.

Chen, L. & Kent, R. (2005). Consonant–vowel co-occurrence patterns in Mandarin-learning infants. *Journal of Child Language*, 32, 507–534.

Chen Pichler, D. (2001a). Evidence for early word order acquisition in a variable word order language. In A. H.-J. Do, L. Dominguez & A. Johansen (Eds.), *Proceedings of the 25th Boston University Conference on Language Development*. Sommerville, MA: Cascadilla Press.

(2001b). Word order variability and acquisition in American Sign Language. Unpublished doctoral dissertation, University of Connecticut, Storrs.

Cheour, M., Alho, K., Sainio, K., *et al.* (1997). The mismatch negativity to changes in speech sounds at the age of three months. *Developmental Neuropsychology*, 13, 167–174.

Cheour, M., Alho, K., Ceponiene, K., *et al.* (1998a). Maturation of mismatch negativity in infants. *International Journal of Psychophysiology*, 29, 217–226.

Cheour, M., Ceponiene, R., Lehtokoski, A., (1998b). Development of language-specific phoneme representations in the infant brain. *Nature Neuroscience*, 1, 351–353.

Cheour, M., Ceponiene, R., Leppanen, P., *et al.* (2002). The auditory sensory memory trace decays rapidly in newborns. *Scandinavian Journal of Psychology*, 43, 33–39.

Cheour-Luhtanen, M., Alho, K., Kujala, T., *et al.* (1995). Mismatch negativity indicates vowel discrimination in newborns. *Hearing Research*, 82, 53–58.

Cheour-Luhtanen, M., Alho, K., Sainio, K., *et al.* (1996). The ontogenetically earliest discriminative response of the human brain. *Psychophysiology*, 33, 478–481.

Chien Y. C., & Lust, B. (1983). Topic-comment structure and grammatical subject in first language acquisition of Mandarin Chinese: A study of equi-constructions. *Papers and Reports on Child Language Development*, 22, 74–82.

(1985). The concepts of topic and subject in first language acquisition of Mandarin Chinese. *Child Development*, 6, 1359–1375.

Childers, J., & Tomasello, M. (2001). The role of pronouns in young children's acquisition of the English transitive construction. *Developmental Psychology*, 37, 730–748.

Chin, S. B., & Dinnsen, D. A. (1992). Consonant clusters in disordered speech: Constraints and correspondence patterns. *Journal of Child Language*, 19, 259–285.

Choi, S., & Bowerman, M. (1991). Learning to express motion events in English and Korean: The influence of language-specific lexicalization patterns. *Cognition*, 41, 83–121.

Choi, S., & Gopnik, A. (1995). Early acquisition of verbs in Korean: A cross-linguistic study. *Journal of Child Language*, 22, 497–529.

Choi, S., McDonough, L., Bowerman, M., & Mandler, J. M. (1999). Early sensitivity to language-specific spatial categories in English and Korean. *Cognitive Development*, 14, 241–268.

Choi, Y., & Mazuka, R. (2003). Young children's use of prosody in sentence parsing. *Journal of Psycholinguistic Research*. 32, 197–217.

Chomsky, C. (1969). *The Acquisition of Syntax in Children from 5 to 10*. Cambridge, MA: MIT Press.

Chomsky, N. (1957). *Syntactic Structures*. The Hague: Mouton.

  (1965). *Aspects of the Theory of Syntax*. Cambridge, MA: MIT Press.

  (1970). Remarks on nominalization. In R. Jacobs & P. Rosenbaum (Eds.), *Readings in English Transformational Grammar* (pp. 184–221). Waltham, MA: Gin & Co.

  (1980). Rules and representations. *Behavioral and Brain Sciences*, 3, 1–61.

  (1981). *Lectures on Government and Binding*. Dordrecht: Foris.

  (1988). *Language and Problems of Knowledge: The Managua Lectures*. Cambridge, MA: MIT Press.

  (1995). *The Minimalist Program*. Cambridge, MA: MIT Press.

  (2006). *Language and Mind* (3rd edn). Cambridge: Cambridge University Press.

Chomsky, N., & Halle, M. (1968). *The Sound Pattern of English*. New York: HarperRow.

Christiansen, M. H., & Monaghan, P. (2006). Discovering verbs through multiple-cue integration. In K. Hirsh-Pasek & R. M. Golinkoff (Eds.), *Action Meets Word: How Children Learn Verbs* (pp. 88–107). Oxford: Oxford University Press.

Christiansen, M. H., Allen, J., & Seidenberg, M. S. (1998). Learning to segment speech using multiple cues: A connectionist model. *Language and Cognitive Processes*, 13, 221–268.

Chun, M. M., & Jiang, Y. (1999). Top-down attentional guidance based on implicit learning of visual covariation. *Psychological Science*, 10, 360–365.

Church, R. B., & Goldin-Meadow, S. (1986). The mismatch between gesture and speech as an index of transitional knowledge. *Cognition*, 23, 43–71.

Clahsen, H. (1984). Der Erwerb von Kasusmarkierungen in der deutschen Kindersprache. *Linguistische Berichte*, 89, 1–31.

  (1989). The grammatical characterization of developmental dysphasia. *Linguistics*, 27, 897–920.

  (1999a). Lexical entries and rules of language: A multidisciplinary study of German inflection. *Behavioral and Brain Sciences*, 22, 991–1060.

  (1999b). Linguistic perspectives on specific language impairment. In W. C. Ritchie (Ed.), *Handbook of Child Language Acquisition* (pp. 675–704). San Diego, CA: Academic Press, Inc.

  (2008). Behavioral methods for investigating morphological and syntactic processing in children. In I. Sekerina, E. Fernández & H. Clahsen, (Eds.), *Developmental Psycholinguistics: On-line Methods in Children's Language Processing* (pp. 1–27). Benjamins: Amsterdam.

Clahsen, H., & Almazan, M. (1998). Syntax and morphology in Williams Syndrome. *Cognition*, 68, 167–198.

  (2001). Compounding and inflection in language impairment: Evidence from Williams syndrome (and SLI). *Lingua*, 111, 729–757.

Clahsen, H., & Penke, M. (1992). The acquisition of agreement morphology and its syntactic consequences: New evidence on German child language from the Simone corpus. In J. M. Meisel (Ed.), *The Acquisition of Verb Placement: Functional Categories and V2 Phenomena in Language Acquisition* (pp. 181–223). Dordrecht: Kluwer.

Clahsen, H., & Temple, C. (2003). Words and rules in Williams syndrome. In Y. Levy & J. Schaeffer (Eds.), *Towards a Definition of Specific Language Impairment in Children* (pp. 323–352). Hillsdale, NJ: Lawrence Erlbaum Associates.

Clahsen, H., Bartke, S., & Göllner, S. (1997). Formal features in impaired grammars: A comparison of English and German SLI children. *Journal of Neurolinguistics*, 10, 151–171.

Clancy, P. M. (1985). The acquisition of Japanese. In D. I. Slobin (Ed.), *The Crosslinguistic Study of Language Acquisition: Vol. 1. The Data* (pp. 373–524). Hillsdale, NJ: Lawrence Erlbaum Associates.

  (1996). Referential strategies and the co-construction of argument structure in Korean acquisition. In B. Fox (Ed.), *Studies in Anaphora* (pp. 33–68). Amsterdam: John Benjamins.

  (1997). Discourse motivations for referential choice in Korean acquisition. In H.-M. Sohn & J. Haig (Eds.), *Japanese/Korean Linguistics: Vol. 6.* (pp. 639–659). Stanford, CA: CSLI.

  (2003). The lexicon in interaction: Developmental origins of preferred argument structure in Korean. In J. W. Du Bois, L. E. Kumpf & W. J. Ashby (Eds.), *Preferred Argument Structure: Grammar as Architecture for function* (pp. 81–108). Amsterdam: John Benjamins.

Clark, E. V. (1973). Nonlinguistic strategies and the acquisition of word meanings. *Cognition*, 2, 161–182.

  (1985). The acquisition of Romance with special reference to French. In D. I. Slobin (Ed.), *The Cross-linguistic Study of Language Acquisition* (pp. 687–782). Hillsdale, NJ: Lawrence Erlbaum Associates.

  (1987). The principle of contrast: A constraint on language acquisition. In B. MacWhinney (Ed.), *Mechanisms of language acquisition* (pp. 1–33). Hillsdale, NJ: Lawrence Erlbaum Associates.

  (1997). Conceptual perspective and lexical choice in acquisition. *Cognition*, 64, 1–37.

  (2002). Making use of pragmatic inferences in the acquisition of meaning. In D. Beaver, S. Kaufmann, B. Z. Clark & L. Casillas (Eds.), *The Construction of Meaning* (pp. 45–58). Stanford, CA: CSLI.

  (2003). *First Language Acquisition*. (2nd ed.). Cambridge: Cambridge University Press.

  (2007). Young children's uptake of new words in conversation. *Language in Society*, 36, 157–182.

  (2009). *The Lexicon in Acquisition*. (2nd edn). Cambridge: Cambridge University Press.

  (in press). Learning a language the way it is: Conventionality and semantic domains. In B. Malt & P. Wolff (Eds.), *Words and the World*. Oxford: Oxford University Press.

Clark, E. V., & Grossman, J. B. (1998). Pragmatic directions and children's word learning. *Journal of Child Language*, 25, 1–18.

Clark, E. V., & Kelly, B. F. (Eds.). (2006). *Constructions in Acquisition*. Stanford, CA: CSLI.

Clark, E. V., & Wong, A. D.-W. (2002). Pragmatic directions about language use: Words and word meanings. *Language in Society*, 31, 181–212.

Clark, H. H. (1996). *Using Language*. Cambridge: Cambridge University Press.

Cleave, P., & Rice, M. (1997). An examination of the morpheme BE in children with specific language impairment: The role of contractibility and form class. *Journal of Speech, Language, and Hearing Research*, 40, 480–492.

Clements, G. N. (1990). The role of the sonority cycle in core syllabification. In J. Kingston & M. E. Beckman (Eds.), *Papers in Laboratory Phonology I* (pp. 283–333). Cambridge: Cambridge University Press.

Clements, G. N., & Keyser, S. J. (1983). *CV Phonology : A Generative Theory of the Syllable*. Cambridge, MA: MIT Press.

Clyne, M. (2003). *Dynamics of Language Contact*. New York: Cambridge University Press.

 (1980). Triggering and language processing. *Canadian Journal of Psychology*, 34, 400–406.

Cochran, B. P., McDonald, J. L., & Parault, S. J. (1999). Too smart for their own good: The disadvantage of a superior processing capacity for adult language learners. *Journal of Memory and Language*, 41, 30–58.

Coerts, J. (2000). Early sign combinations in the acquisition of Sign Language of the Netherlands: Evidence for language-specific features. In C. Chamberlain, J. P. Morford & R. I. Mayberry (Eds.), *Language Acquisition by Eye* (pp. 9–109). Mahwah, NJ: Lawrence Erlbaum Associates.

Coerts, J., & Mills, A. E. (1994). Early sign combinations of deaf children in Sign Language of the Netherlands. In I. Ahlgren, B. Bergman & M. Brennan (Eds.), *Perspectives on Sign Language Usage: Papers from the Fifth International Symposium on Sign Language Research: Vol. 2.* (pp. 319–331). Durham: ISLA.

Cohen Sherman, J. (1983). The acquisition of control in complement sentences: The role of structural and lexical factors. Unpublished doctoral dissertation, Cornell University, New York.

Cohen Sherman, J., & Lust, B. (1986). Syntactic and lexical constraints on the acquisition of control in complement sentences. In B. Lust (Ed.), *Studies in the Acquisition of Anaphora: Vol. 1. Defining the Constraints* (pp. 279–310). Dordrecht: Reidel.

 (1993). Children are in control. *Cognition*, 46, 1–51.

Cole, K. N., Dale, P. S., & Mills, P. E. (1990). Defining language delay in young children by cognitive referencing: Are we saying more than we know? *Applied Psycholinguistics*, 11, 291–302.

Cole, K. N., Schwartz, I., Notari, A., Dale, P., & Mills, P. E. (1995). Examination of the stability of two methods of defining specific language impairment. *Applied Psycholinguistics*, 16, 103–123.

Comeau, L., Genesee, F., & Mendelson, M. (2007). Bilingual children's repairs of breakdowns in communication. *Journal of Child Language*, 34, 159–174.

Comrie, B., & Kuteva, T. (2005). Relativization strategies. In M. Haspelmath, M. S. Dryer & B. Comrie (Eds.), *The World Atlas of Language Structures* (pp. 494–501). Oxford: Oxford University Press.

Conlin, K. E., Mirus, G. R., Mauk, C., & Meier, R. P. (2000). The acquisition of first signs: Place, handshape, and movement. In C. Chamberlain, J. P. Morford & R. I. Mayberry (Eds.), *Language Acquisition by Eye* (pp. 51–69). Mahwah, NJ: Lawrence Erlbaum Associates.

Connelly, M. (1984). Basotho children's acquisition of noun class morphology. Unpublished doctoral dissertation, University of Essex.

Conti-Ramsden, G. (2003). Processing and linguistic markers in young children with specific language impairment. *Journal of Speech, Language, and Hearing Research*, 46, 1029–1037.

Conti-Ramsden, G., & Botting, N. (2004). Social difficulties and victimization in children with SLI at 11 years of age. *Journal of Speech, Language and Hearing Research*, 47, 145–161.

Conway, C. M., & Christiansen, M. H. (2005). Modality-constrained statistical learning of tactile, visual, and auditory sequences. *Journal of Experimental Psychology: Learning, Memory, and Cognition*, 31, 24–39.

Conwell, E., & Demuth, K. (2007). Early syntactic productivity: Evidence from dative shift. *Cognition*, 103, 163–179.

Cook, M., & Mineka, S. (1990). Selective associations in the observational conditioning of fear in rhesus monkeys. *Journal of Experimental Psychology: Animal Behavior Processes*, 16, 372–389.

Cook, S. W., Mitchell, Z., & Goldin-Meadow, S. (2008). Gesturing makes learning last. *Cognition*, 106, 1047–1058.

Cooper, D. C., & Anderson-Inman, L. (1998). Language and socialization. In M. A. Nippold (Ed.), *Later Language Development: Ages Nine Through Nineteen* (pp. 225–245). Boston: College-Hill.

Cooper, R. P., & Aslin, R. (1990). Preference for infant-directed speech in the first month after birth. *Child Development*, 61, 1584–1595.

Courchesne, E. (1990). Chronology of postnatal human brain development: Event-related potential, positron emission tomography, myelinogenesis, and synaptogenesis studies. In J. W. Rohrbaugh, R. Parasuraman & R. J. Johnson (Eds.), *Event-Related Brain Potentials: Basic Issues and Applications* (pp. 210–241). New York: Oxford University Press.

Courtney, E. (1998). Child acquisition of Quechua morphosyntax. Unpublished doctoral dissertation, University of Arizona.

(2006). Adult and child production of Quechua relative clauses. *First Language*, 26, 317–338.

Craig, H., & Washington, J. (1993). Access behaviors of children with specific language impairment. *Journal of Speech and Hearing Research*, 36, 322–337.

Crain, S., & McKee, C. (1985). Acquisition of structural restrictions on anaphors. *Proceedings of the Sixteenth Annual Meeting of the North Eastern Linguistics Society (NELS)* (pp. 94–110). Montreal: McGill University.

Crain, S., & Nakayama, M. (1987). Structure dependence in grammar formation. *Language*, 63, 522–543.

Crain, S., & Pietroski, P. (2001). Nature, Nurture and Universal Grammar. *Linguistics and Philosophy*, 24, 138–185.

Crain, S. & Steedman, M. (1985). On not being led up the garden path: The use of context by the psychological parser. In D. R. Dowty, L. Karttunen & A. Zwicky (Eds.) *Natural Language Parsing*, (pp. 320–358). Cambridge: Cambridge University Press.

Crain, S., & Thornton, R. (1998). *Investigations in Universal Grammar: A Guide to Experiments on the Acquisition of Syntax and Semantics*. Cambridge MA: MIT Press.

Crain, S., McKee, C., & Emiliani, M. (1990). Visiting relatives in Italy. In L. Frazier & J. deVilliers (Eds.), *Language Processing and Language Acquisition* (pp. 335–356). Dordrecht: Kluwer.

Crain, S., Ni, W., & Conway, L. (1994). Learning, parsing, and modularity. In C. Clifton, L. Frazier & K. Rayner (Eds.), *Perspectives on Sentence Processing* (pp. 443–467). Hillsdale, NJ: Lawrence Erlbaum Associates.

Crain, S., Thornton, R., Boster, C., Conway, L., Lillo-Martin, D., & Woodams, E. (1996). Quantification without qualification. *Language Acquisition*, 5 (2), 83–153.

Crain, S., Gardner, A., Gualmini, A., & Rabin, B. (2002). Children's command of negation. In Y. Otsu (Ed.), *Proceedings of the Third Tokyo Conference on Psycholinguistics* (pp. 71–95). Tokyo: Hituzi.

Creel, S. C., Newport, E. L., & Aslin, R. N. (2004). Distant melodies: Statistical learning of nonadjacent dependencies in tone sequences. *Journal of Experimental Psychology: Learning, Memory, & Cognition*, 30, 1119–1130.

Cromer, R. (1994). A case study of dissociations between language and cognition. In H. Tager-Flusberg (Ed.), *Constraints on Language Acquisition: Studies of Atypical Children* (pp. 141–53). Hillsdale, NJ: Lawrence Erlbaum Associates.

Crystal, D. (2004). *The Language Revolution*. Cambridge: Polity Press.

Cuetos, F., & Mitchell, D. C. (1988). Cross-linguistic influence in parsing: Restrictions on the use of the Late Closure strategy in Spanish. *Cognition*, 30, 73–105.

Cummins, J. (1978). Bilingualism and the development of metalinguistic awareness. *Journal of Cross-Cultural Psychology*, 9, 131–149.

(1979). Cognitive/academic language proficiency, linguistic interdependence, the optimum age question and some other matters. *Working Papers on Bilingualism*, 19, 121–129.

Curtin, S., Mintz, T. H., & Byrd, D. (2001). Coarticulatory cues enhance infants' recognition of syllable sequences in speech. In A. H. J. Do, L. Dominguez & A. Johansen (Eds.), *Proceedings of the 25th Annual Boston*

University Conference on Language Development (pp. 190–201). Somerville, MA: Cascadilla Press.

Curtin, S., Mintz, T. H., & Christiansen, M. H. (2005). Stress changes the representational landscape: Evidence from word segmentation. *Cognition*, 96, 233–262.

Curtin, S., Fennell, C. T., Escudero, P., & Werker, J. F. (submitted). Weighting of acoustic cues explains patterns of word–object associative learning.

Cutler, A., & Carter, D. M. (1987). The predominance of strong initial syllables in the English vocabulary. *Computer Speech and Language*, 2, 133–142.

Cutler, A., & Foss, D. J. (1977). On the role of sentence stress in sentence processing. *Language and Speech*, 20, 1–10.

Cutler, A., & Swinney, D. A. (1987). Prosody and the development of comprehension. *Journal of Child Language*, 14, 145–167.

Cutler, A., Mehler, J., Norris, D. G., & Segui, J. (1986). The syllable's differing role in the segmentation of French and English. *Journal of Memory and Language*, 25, 385–400.

Dahl, Ö. (1990). Standard average European as an exotic language. In J. Bechert, G. Bernini & C. Buridant (Eds.), *Towards a Typology of European Languages* (pp. 3–8). Berlin: Mouton de Gruyter.

Dale, P. S., & Cole, K. N. (1991). What's normal? Specific language impairment in an individual differences perspective. *Language, Speech, and Hearing Services in Schools*, 22, 80–83.

Dauer, R. M. (1983). Stress-timing and syllable-timing reanalyzed. *Journal of Phonetics*, 11, 51–62.

Davidson, R., & Snow, C. (1996). Five-year-olds' interactions with fathers versus mothers. *First Language*, 16, 223–242.

Davis, B. L., & MacNeilage, P. F. (1995). The articulatory basis of babbling. *Journal of Speech and Hearing Research*, 38, 1199–1211.

Dawson, G., Carver, L., Meltzoff, A., Panagiotides, H., McPartland, J., & Webb, S. J. (2002). Neural correlates of face recognition and object recognition in young children with autism spectrum disorder, developmental delay and typical development. *Child Development*, 73, 700–717.

Dawson, G., Webb, S. J., & McPartland, J. (2005a). Understanding the nature of face processing impairment in autism: Insights from behavioral and electrophysiological studies. *Developmental Neuropsychology*, 27, 403–424.

Dawson, G., Webb, S., Wijsman, E., *et al.* (2005b). Neurocognitive and electrophysiological evidence of altered face processing in parents of children with autism: Implications for a model of abnormal development of social brain circuitry in autism. *Development and Psychopathology*, 17, 679.

De Courtivron, I. (2003). *Lives in Translation*. New York: Palgrave Macmillan.

De Houwer, A. (1995). Bilingual language acquisition. In P. Fletcher & B. MacWhinney (Eds.), *The Handbook of Child Language* (pp. 219–250). Oxford: Blackwell.

(2007). Parental language input patterns and children's bilingual use. *Applied Psycholinguistics*, 28, 411–424.

de León, L. (1998). The emergent participant: Interactive patterns in the socialization of Tzotzil (Mayan) infants. *Journal of Linguistic Anthropology*, 8, 131–161.

(in press). Between frogs and black winged-monkeys: Orality, evidentials, and authorship in Tzotzil (Mayan) children's narratives. In J. Guo, E. Lieven, N. Budwig, S. Ervin-Tripp, K. Nakamura & S. Ozcaliskan (Eds.), *Crosslinguistic Approaches to the Psychology of Language: Research in the Tradition of Dan I. Slobin*. Mahwah, NJ: Lawrence Erlbaum Associates.

DeCasper, A. J., & Fifer, W. P. (1980). Of human bonding: Newborns prefer their mothers' voices. *Science*, 208, 1174–1176.

DeCasper, A. J., & Spence, M. J. (1986). Prenatal maternal speech influences newborns' perception of speech sounds. *Infant Behavior and Development*, 9, 133–150.

Deen, K. (2002). The omission of inflectional prefixes in the acquisition of Nairobi Swahili. Unpublished doctoral dissertation, University of California, Los Angeles.

(2004). Object agreement and specificity in Nairobi Swahili. In A. Brugos, L. Micciulla & C. E. Smith (Eds.), *The Proceedings to the 28th Boston University Conference on Language Development* (pp. 129–140). Somerville, MA: Cascadilla Press.

(2005). *The Acquisition of Swahili*. Amsterdam: John Benjamins.

Deevy, P., & Leonard, L. (2004). The comprehension of wh-questions in children with specific language impairment. *Journal of Speech, Language and Hearing Research*, 47, 802–815.

Dehaene-Lambertz, G. (2000). Cerebral specialization for speech and non-speech stimuli in infants. *Journal of Cognitive Neuroscience*, 12, 449–460.

Dehaene-Lambertz, G., & Baillet, S. (1998). A phonological representation in the infant brain. *NeuroReport*, 9, 1885–1888.

Dehaene-Lambertz, G., & Dehaene, S. (1994). Speed and cerebral correlates of syllable discrimination in infants. *Nature*, 370, 292–295.

Dehaene-Lambertz, G., & Gliga, T. (2004). Common neural basis for phoneme processing in infants and adults. *Journal of Cognitive Neuroscience*, 16, 1375–1387.

Dehaene-Lambertz, G., & Peña, M. (2001). Electrophysiological evidence for automatic phonetic processing in neonates. *NeuroReport*, 12, 3155–3158.

Dehaene-Lambertz, G., Dehaene, S., & Hertz-Pannier, L. (2002). Functional neuroimaging of speech perception in infants. *Science*, 298, 2013–2015.

DeHart, G. (1999). Conflict and averted conflict in preschoolers' interactions with siblings and friends. In W. A. Collins & B. Laursen (Eds.), *Relationships in Developmental Contexts: The Minnesota Symposia on Child Psychology: Vol. 30.* (pp. 281–303). Mahwah, NJ: Lawrence Erlbaum Associates.

DeKeyser, R., & Larson-Hall, J. (2005). What does the critical period really mean? In J. Kroll & A. M. B. de Groot (Eds.), *Handbook of Bilingualism: Psycholinguistic Approaches* (pp. 88–108). Oxford: Oxford University Press.

Delattre, P. (1966). A comparison of syllable length conditioning among languages. *International Review of Applied Linguistics in Language Teaching*, 4, 183–198.

Demuth, K.. (1989). Maturation and the acquisition of the Sesotho passive. *Language*, 65, 56–80.

(1992). The acquisition of Sesotho. In D. I. Slobin (Ed.), *The Crosslinguistic Study of Language Acquisition: Vol. 3.* (pp. 557–638). Hillsdale, NJ: Lawrence Erlbaum Associates.

(1993). Issues in the acquisition of the Sesotho tonal system. *Journal of Child Language*, 20, 275–301.

(1994). On the 'underspecification' of functional categories in early grammars. In B. Lust, M. Suñer & J. Whitman (Eds.), *Syntactic Theory and First Language Acquisition: Cross-Linguistic Perspectives*, (pp. 119–134). Hillsdale, NJ: Lawrence Erlbaum Associates.

(1995a). Markedness and the development of prosodic structure. In J. Beckman (Ed.), *Proceedings of the North East Linguistic Society: Vol. 25.* (pp. 13–25). Amherst, MA: GLSA, University of Massachusetts.

(1995b). Questions, relatives and minimal projection. *Language Acquisition*, 4, 49–71.

(1998). Argument structure and the acquisition of Sesotho applicatives. *Linguistics*, 36, 781–806.

(2001). Prosodic constraints on morphological development. In J. Weissenborn & B. Höhle (Eds.), *Approaches to Bootstrapping: Phonological, Syntactic and Neurophysiological Aspects of Early Language Acquisition* (pp. 3–21). Amsterdam: John Benjamins.

(2007). Acquisition at the prosody-morphology interface. In Alyona Belikova, Luisa Meroni & Mari Umeda, (Eds.), *Proceedings of the 2nd Conference on Generative Approaches to Language Acquisition North America (GALANA)* (pp. 84–91). Somerville, MA: Cascadilla Proceedings Project.

Demuth, K., & Ellis, D. (in press). Revisiting the acquisition of Sesotho noun class prefixes. In J.-S. Guo, E. Lieven, S. Ervin-Tripp, N. Budwig, S. Ozcaliskan & K. Nakamura. (Eds.), *Crosslinguistic Approaches to the Psychology of Language: Festschrift for Dan Slobin*. Mahwah, NJ: Lawrence Erlbaum Associates.

Demuth, K., & Fee, J. E. (1995). Minimal prosodic words in early phonological development. Unpublished manuscript.

Demuth, K., & Johnson, M. (2003). Truncation to subminimal words in early French. *Canadian Journal of Linguistics*, 48, 211–241.

Demuth, K., & Kehoe, M. (2006). The acquisition of word-final clusters in French. *Journal of Catalan Linguistics*, 5, 59–81.

Demuth, K., & Kline, M. (2006). The distribution of passives in spoken Sesotho. *Southern African Linguistics and Applied Language Studies*, 24, 377–388.

Demuth, K., & McCullough, E. (in press-a). The acquisition of clusters in French. *Journal of Child Language*.

(in press-b). The prosodic (re)organization of children's early English articles. *Journal of Child Language*.

Demuth, K., & Tremblay, A. (in press). Prosodically conditioned variability in children's production of French determiners. *Journal of Child Language*.

Demuth, K., Culbertson, J., & Alter, J. (2006). Word-minimality, epenthesis, and coda licensing in the acquisition of English. *Language and Speech*, 49, 137–174.

Demuth, K., Machobane, M., & Moloi, F. (2000). Learning word order constraints under conditions of object ellipsis. *Linguistics*, 38, 1–24.

(2003). Rules and construction effects in learning the argument structure of verbs. *Journal of Child Language*, 30, 797–821.

Demuth, K., Machobane, M., Moloi, F., & Odato, C. (2005). Learning animacy hierarchy effects in Sesotho double object applicatives. *Language*, 81, 421–447.

DePaolis, R. A. (2006). The influence of production on the perception of speech. In D. Bamman, T. Magnitskaia & C. Zaller (Eds.), *Proceedings of the 30th Boston University Conference on Language Development*. Somerville, MA: Cascadilla Press.

de Villiers, J. (1995). Empty categories and complex sentences: The case of wh-questions. In P. Fletcher & B. MacWhinney (Eds.), *The Handbook of Child Language Acquisition* (pp. 508–540). Oxford: Blackwell.

de Villiers, J., & de Villiers, P. A. (1973a). A cross sectional study of the acquisition of grammatical morphemes in child speech. *Journal of Psycholinguistic Research*, 2, 267–278.

(1973b). Development of the use of word order in comprehension. *Journal of Psycholinguistic Research*, 2, 331–341.

de Villiers, J., Flusberg, H. T., & Hakuta, K. (1977). Deciding among theories of the development of coordination in child speech. *Papers and Reports on Child Language Development*, 13, 118–125.

Dick, F., Saygin, A. P., Galati, G., *et al.* (2007). What is involved and what is necessary for complex linguistic and nonlinguistic auditory processing: Evidence from functional magnetic resonance imaging and lesion data. *Journal of Cognitive Neuroscience*, 19, 799–816.

Diessel, H. (2004). *The Acquisition of Complex Sentences*. New York: Cambridge University Press.

Diessel, H., & Tomasello, M. (2000). The development of relative clauses in spontaneous child speech. *Cognitive Linguistics*, 11, 131–151.

(2001). The acquisition of finite complement clauses in English: A usage based approach to the development of grammatical constructions. *Cognitive Linguistics*, 12, 97–141.

(2005). A new look at the acquisition of relative clauses. *Language*, 81, 882–906.

Dimroth, C., Gretsch, P., Jordens, P., Perdue, C., & Starren, M. (2003). How to express finiteness in Germanic languages: A stage-model for first and second language acquisition. In C. Dimroth & M. Starren (Eds.), *Linguistic Structure and the Dynamics of Acquisition* (pp. 65–94). Amsterdam: John Benjamins.

Dittmar, M., Abbot-Smith, K., Lieven, E., & Tomasello, M. (2008). Comprehension of case marking and word order cues by German children. *Child Development*, 79, 1152–1167.

Dodd, B., & Thompson, L. (2001). Speech disorder in children with Down's syndrome. *Journal of Intellectual Disability Research*, 45, 308–316.

Dodge, K., Schlundt, D., Schocken, I., & Delugach, J. (1983). Social competence and children's sociometric status: The role of peer group entry strategies. *Monographs of the Society for Research in Child Development*, 5, Serial No. 213.

Dodwell, K., & Bavin, E. L. (in press). Children with specific language impairment: An investigation of their narratives and memory. *International Journal of Language and Communication Disorders*.

Dollaghan, C., & Campbell, T. (1998). Nonword repetition and child language impairment. *Journal of Speech, Language, and Hearing Research*, 41, 1136–1146.

Donnai, D., & Karmiloff-Smith, A. (2000). Williams syndrome: From genotype through to cognitive phenotype. *American Journal of Medical Genetics*, 97, 164–171.

Dopke, S. (1998). Competing language structures: The acquisition of verb placement by bilingual German–English children. *Journal of Child Language*, 25, 555–584.

dos Santos, C. (2007). Développement phonologique en français langue maternelle: Une étude de cas. Unpublished doctoral dissertation, Université Lumière Lyon 2, Lyon.

Dougherty, T. M., & Haith, M. M. (2002). Infants' use of constraints to speed information processing and to anticipate events. *Infancy*, 3, 457–473.

Dromi, E., Leonard, L., Adam, G., & Zadunaisky-Ehrlich, S. (1999). Verb agreement morphology in Hebrew-speaking children with specific language impairment. *Journal of Speech, Language, and Hearing Research*, 42, 1414–1431.

Drozd, K., & van Loosbroek, E. (1999). Weak quantification, plausible dissent, and the development of children's pragmatic competence. *Proceedings of the 23rd Annual Boston University Conference on Language Development*. Somerville, MA: Cascadilla Press.

Du Bois, J. W. (1987). The discourse basis of ergativity. *Language*, 63, 805–855.

Du Bois, J. W., Kumpf, L. E., & Ashby, W. J. (Eds.). (2003). *Preferred Argument Structure: Grammar as Architecture for Function*. Amsterdam: Benjamins.

Dunn, M., Gomes, H., & Sebastian, M. (1996). Prototypicality of responses of autistic, language disordered, and normal children in a word fluency task. *Child Neuropsychology*, 2, 99–108.

Durieux, G., & Gillis, S. (2001). Predicting grammatical classes from phonological cues: An empirical test. In J. Weissenborn & B. Höhle (Eds.), *Approaches to Bootstrapping: Phonological, Lexical, Syntactic and Neurophysiological Aspects of Early Language Acquisition: Vol. 1.* (pp. 189–229). Amsterdam: Benjamins.

Dussias, P. (2001). *Sentence parsing in fluent Spanish–English bilinguals.* In J. Nicol (Ed.), *One Mind, Two Languages* (pp. 159–176). Oxford: Blackwell.

Dye, C. (2005). Identifying auxiliaries in first language acquisition: Evidence from a new child French corpus. Unpublished doctoral dissertation, Cornell University, New York.

Eadie, P. A., Fey, M. E., Douglas, J. M., & Parsons, C. L. (2002). Profiles of grammatical morphology and sentence imitation in children with specific language impairment and Down syndrome. *Journal of Speech Language and Hearing Research*, 45, 720–732.

Eaves, L., & Ho, H. (2004). The very early identification of autism: Outcome to age 4 1/2 – 5. *Journal of Autism and Developmental Disorders*, 34(4), 367–378.

Ebeling, K. S., & Gelman, S. A. (1994). Children's use of context in interpreting 'big' and 'little'. *Child Development*, 65, 1178–1192.

Echols, C. H., Crowhurst, M. J., & Childers, J. B. (1997). The perception of rhythmic units in speech by infants and adults. *Journal of Memory and Language*, 36, 202–225.

Edelman, G. (1987). *Neural Darwinism: The Theory of Neuronal Group Selection.* New York: Basic Books.

Edwards, J., Beckman, M. E., & Munson, B. R. (2004). The interaction between vocabulary size and phonotactic probability effects on children's production accuracy and fluency in nonword repetition. *Journal of Speech, Language, and Hearing Research*, 47, 421–436.

Eikeseth, S., Smith, T., Jahr, E., & Eldevik, S. (2007). Outcome for children with autism who began intensive behavioral treatment between ages 4 and 7: A comparison controlled study. *Behavior Modification*, 31(3), 264–278.

Eilers, R. E., Bull, D. H., Oller, D. K., & Lewis, D. C. (1984). The discrimination of vowel duration by infants. *Journal of the Acoustical Society of America*, 75, 1213–1218.

Eimas, P. D., Siqueland, E. R., Jusczyk, P., & Vigorito, J. (1971). Speech perception in infants. *Science*, 171, 303–306.

Eisenberg, A. (1985). Learning to describe past experiences in conversation. *Discourse Processes*, 8, 177–204.

Eisenberg S. L., & Cairns, H. S. (1994). The development of infinitives from three to five. *Journal of Child Language*, 21, 713–734.

Eisenmajer, R., Prior, M., Leekam, S., *et al.* (1998). Delayed language onset as a predictor of clinical symptoms in pervasive developmental disorders. *Journal of Autism and Developmental Disorders*, 28, 527–533.

Ejiri, K., & Masataka, N. (2001). Co-occurrence of preverbal vocal behavior and motor action in early infancy. *Developmental Science*, 4, 40–48.

Elbers, L., & Ton, J. (1985). Play pen monologues: The interplay of words and babble in the first words period. *Journal of Child Language*, 12, 551–565.

Elbers, L., & Wijnen, F. (1992). Effort, production skill, and language learning. In C. A. Ferguson, L. Menn & C. Stoel-Gammon (Eds.), *Phonological Development: Models, Research, Implications* (pp. 337–368). Timonium, MD: York Press.

Eliot, L. (1999). *What's Going On in There? How the Brain and Mind Develop in the First Five Years of Life*. New York: Bantam Books.

Ellis Weismer, S. (1985). Constructive comprehension abilities exhibited by language-disordered children. *Journal of Speech and Hearing Research*, 28, 175–184.

Ellis Weismer, S., & Hesketh, L. J. (1993). The influence of prosodic and gestural cues on novel word acquisition by children with specific language impairment. *Journal of Speech and Hearing Research*, 36, 1013–1025.

Ellis Weismer, S., Tomblin J. B., Zhang, X., Buckwalter, P., Chynoweth, J., & Jones, M. (2000). Nonword repetition performance in school-age children with and without language impairment. *Journal of Speech, Language, and Hearing Research*, 43, 865–878.

Elman, J. (1993). Learning and development in neural networks: The importance of starting small. *Cognition*, 48, 71–99.

  (2001). Connectionism and language acquisition. In M. Tomasello & E. Bates (Eds.), *Language Development: The Essential Readings* (pp. 295–306). Oxford: Blackwell.

Elman, J., Bates, E. A., Johnson, M. H., Karmiloff-Smith, A., Parisi, D. & Plunkett, K. (1996). *Rethinking Innateness: A Connectionist Perspective on Development*. Cambridge, MA: MIT Press.

Elman, J., Hare, M. & McRae, K. (2005). Cues, Constraints, and Competition in Sentence Processing. In M. Tomasello & D. I. Slobin (Eds.) *Beyond nature–nurture: Essays in honor of Elizabeth Bates* (pp. 111–138). Mahwah, NJ: Lawrence Erlbaum Associates.

Ely, R., & Gleason, J. (1995). Socialization across contexts. In P. Fletcher & B. MacWhinney (Eds.), *The Handbook of Child Language* (pp. 251–276). Cambridge, MA: Blackwell.

Ely, R., Gleason, J., MacGibbon, A., & Zaretsky, E. (2001). Attention to language: Lessons learned at the dinner table. *Social Development*, 10, 355–373.

Emmorey, K., Bellugi, U., Friederici, A., & Horn, P. (1995). Effects of age of acquisition on grammatical sensitivity: Evidence from on-line and off-line tasks. *Applied Psycholinguistics*, 16, 1–23.

Endress, A. D., Scholl, B. J., & Mehler, J. (2005). The role of salience in the extraction of algebraic rules. *Journal of Experimental Psychology: General*, 134, 406–419.

Eng, N., & O'Connor, B. (2000). Acquisition of definite article + noun agreement of Spanish–English bilingual children with specific language impairment. *Communication Disorders Quarterly*, 21, 114–124.

Ervin-Tripp, S. (1977). Wait for me, roller skate! In S. Ervin-Tripp & C. Mitchell-Kernan (Eds.), *Child Discourse* (pp. 165–188). New York: Academic Press.

(1979). Children's verbal turn-taking. In E. Ochs & B. Schieffelin (Eds.), *Developmental Pragmatics* (pp. 391–413). New York: Academic Press.

Ervin-Tripp, S., Strage, A., Lampert, M., & Bell, N. (1987). Understanding requests. *Linguistics*, 25, 107–143.

Eschenlohr, S. (1997). Zur kategorialen Determiniertheit von Wortformen im Deutschen. In E. Löbel & G. Rauh (Eds.), *Lexikalische Kategorien und Merkmale* (pp. 27–43). Tübingen: Niemeyer.

Estigarribia, B., & Clark, E. V. (2007). Getting and maintaining attention in talk to young children. *Journal of Child Language*, 34, 799–814.

Evans, J. L., Alibali, M. W., & McNeil, N. M. (2001). Divergence of embodied knowledge and verbal expression: Evidence from gesture and speech in children with Specific Language Impairment. *Language and Cognitive Processes*, 16, 309–331.

Eyer, J. A., Leonard, L. B., Bedore, L. M., McGregor, K. K., Anderson, B., & Viescas, R. (2002). Fast mapping of verbs by children with specific language impairment. *Clinical Linguistics & Phonetics*, 16, 59–77.

Fantini, A. (1985). *Language Acquisition of a Bilingual Child: A Sociolinguistic Perspective (to Age Ten)*. Clevedon: Multilingual Matters.

Farrar, J. (1992). Negative evidence and grammatical morpheme acquisition. *Developmental Psychology*, 28, 90–98.

Fee, J. E. (1995). Segments and syllables in early language acquisition. In J. Archibald (Ed.), *Phonological Acquisition and Phonological Theory* (pp. 43–61). Hillsdale, NJ: Lawrence Erlbaum Associates.

Fein, D., Dunn, M., Allen, D., *et al.* (1996). Language and neuropsychological findings. In I. Rapin (Ed.), *Preschool Children with Inadequate Communication* (pp. 123–154). London: MacKeith Press.

Fennell, C. T. (2004). Infant attention to phonetic detail in word forms: Knowledge and familiarity effects. Unpublished doctoral dissertation, The University of British Columbia, Vancouver.

Fennell, C. T., & Werker, J. F. (2003). Early word learners' ability to access phonetic detail in well-known words. *Language and Speech*, 46, 245–264.

Fenson, L., Dale, P., Reznick, J., Bates, E., Thal, D., & Pethick, S. (1994). Variability in Early Communicative Development. *Monographs of the Society for Research in Child Development*, 59 Serial No. 242.

Fenson, L., Marchman, V., Thal, D, Dale, P., Reznick, J. S., & Bates, E. (2007). *MacArthur–Bates Communicative Development Inventories: Users' Guide and Manual* (2nd edn). Baltimore: Paul Brookes.

Ferguson, C. A., & Farwell, C. B. (1975). Words and sounds in early language acquisition. *Language*, 51, 419–439. Reprinted with Appendix in W. S.-Y. Wang (Ed.) (1997). *The Lexicon in Phonological Change* (pp. 7–68). The Hague: Mouton.

Fernald, A. (1985). Four-month-old infants prefer to listen to Motherese. *Infant Behavior and Development*, 8, 181–195.

(1992). Maternal vocalisations to infants as biologically relevant signals: An evolutionary perspective. In J. H. Barkow, L. Cosmides & J. Tooby (Eds.), *The Adapted Mind: Evolutionary Psychology and the Generation of Culture* (pp. 391–428). Oxford: Oxford University Press.

Fernald, A., & Kuhl, P. K. (1987). Acoustic determinants of infant preference for Motherese speech. *Infant Behavior and Development*, 10, 279–293.

Fernald, A., Taeschner, T., Dunn, J., Papousek, M., Boysson-Bardies, B. D., & Fuko, I. (1989). A cross-language study of prosodic modifications in mothers' and fathers' speech to preverbal infants. *Journal of Child Language*, 16, 477–501.

Fernald, A., Pinto, J., Swingley, D., Weinberg, A., & McRoberts, G. (1998). Rapid gains in speed of verbal processing by infants in the 2nd year. *Psychological Science*, 9, 228–231.

Fernald, A., Swingley, D., & Pinto, J. P. (2001). When half a word is enough: Infants can recognize spoken words using partial phonetic information. *Child Development*, 72, 1003–1015.

Fernald, A., Perfors, A. & Marchman, V. (2006). Picking up speed in understanding: Speech processing efficiency and vocabulary growth across the 2nd year. *Developmental Psychology*, 42, 98–116.

Fernald, A., Zangl, R., Portillo, A. L., & Marchman, V. A. (2008). Looking while listening: Using eye movements to monitor spoken language comprehension by infants and young children. In I. Sekerina, E. Fernández & H. Clahsen, (Eds.), *Developmental Psycholinguistics: On-line Methods in Children's Language Processing* (pp. 97–135). Amsterdam: Benjamins.

Fernandes, K., Marcus, G., Di Nubila, J., & Vouloumanos, A. (2006). From semantics to syntax and back again: Argument structure in the third year of life. *Cognition*, 100, B10–B20.

Fey, M. E., & Leonard, L. (1983). Pragmatic skills of children with specific language impairment. In T. Gallagher & C. Prutting (Eds.), *Pragmatic Assessment and Intervention Issues in Language* (pp. 65–82). San Diego, CA: College Hill Press.

Fikkert, P. (1994). *On the Acquisition of Prosodic Structure*. Amsterdam: Holland Institute of Generative Linguistics.

Fillmore, C., Kay, P., & O'Connor, M. C. (1988). Regularity and idiomaticity in grammatical constructions: The case of let alone. *Language*, 64, 501–538.

Firth, J. R. (1948). Sounds and prosodies. *Transactions of the Philological Society*, 1948, 127–152.

Fiser, J., & Aslin, R. N. (2001). Unsupervised statistical learning of higher-order spatial structures from visual scenes. *Psychological Science*, 12, 499–504.

(2005). Encoding multielement scenes: Statistical learning of visual feature hierarchies. *Journal of Experimental Psychology: General*, 134, 521–537.

Fisher, C. (1996). Structural limits on verb mapping: The role of analogy in children's interpretation of sentences. *Cognitive Psychology*, 31, 41–81.

(2002a). The role of abstract syntactic knowledge in language acquisition: A reply to Tomasello (2000). *Cognition*, 82, 259–278.

(2002b). Structural limits on verb mapping: The role of abstract structure in 2.5-year-olds' interpretations of novel verbs. *Developmental Science*, 5, 55–64.

Fisher, C., Hall, D. G., Rakowitz, S., & Gleitman, L. (1994). When it is better to receive than to give: Syntactic and conceptual constraints on vocabulary growth. *Lingua*, 92, 333–375.

Fisher, C., Klingler, S. L., & Song, H. (2006). What does syntax say about space? 2-year-olds use sentence structure to learn new prepositions. *Cognition*, 101, B19–B29.

Fisher, S. E. (2006). Tangled webs: Tracing the connections between genes and cognition. *Cognition*, 101, 270–297.

Fisher, S. E., Vargha-Khadem, F., Watkins, K. E., Monaco, A. P., & Pembrey, M. E. (1998). Localisation of a gene implicated in a severe speech and language disorder. *Nature Genetics*, 18, 168–170.

Fishman, J. (2001). *Can Threatened Languages Be Saved: Reversing Language Shift, Revisited*. Clevedon: Multilingual Matters.

Fitch, W. T., & Hauser, M. D. (2004). Computational constraints on syntactic processing in a nonhuman primate. *Science*, 303, 377–380.

Fivush, R., Gray, J., & Fromhoff, F. (1987). Two-year olds talk about the past. *Cognitive Development*, 2, 393–409.

Flynn, S., & Lust, B. (1981). Acquisition of relative clauses: Developmental changes in their heads. In W. Harbert & J. Herchensohn (Eds.), *Cornell Working Papers in Linguistics: Vol. 1*. (pp. 33–45). Ithaca, NY: Department of Modern Languages and Linguistics, Cornell University.

Fodor, J. D. (1998a). Unambiguous triggers. *Linguistic Inquiry*, 29, 1–36.
(1998b). Parsing to learn. *Journal of Psycholinguistic Research*, 27, 339–374.

Fodor, J. D., & Crowther, C. (2002). Understanding stimulus poverty arguments. *Linguistic Review*, 19, 105–146.

Foley, C. (1996). Knowledge of the syntax of operators in the initial state: The acquisition of relative clauses in French and English. Unpublished doctoral dissertation, Cornell University, Ithaca, NY.

Foley, C., Núñez del Prado, Z., Barbier, I., & Lust, B. (2003). Knowledge of variable binding in VP ellipsis: Language acquisition research and theory converge. *Syntax*, 6, 52–83.

Foley, W. A., & van Valin, R. D. (1984). *Functional Syntax and Universal Grammar*. Cambridge: Cambridge University Press.

Folstein, S. E., & Mankoski, R. E. (2000). Chromosome 7q: Where autism meets language disorder? *American Journal of Human Genetics*, 67, 278–281.

Fowler, A. (1998). Language in mental retardation: Associations with dissociations from general cognition. In J. A. Burack, R. M. Hodapp & E. Zigler (Eds.), *Handbook of Mental Retardation and Development* (pp. 290–333). Cambridge: Cambridge University Press.

Fragman, C., Goodluck, H., & Heggie, L. (2007). Child and adult construal of relative clauses: Knowledge of grammar and differential effects of syntactic context. *Journal of Child Language*, 34, 345–380.

Francis, W. S. (2005). Bilingual semantic and conceptual representation. In J. Kroll & A. M. B. de Groot (Eds.), *Handbook of Bilingualism: Psycholinguistic Approaches* (pp. 251–267). Oxford: Oxford University Press.

Frank, R. (1998). Structural complexity and the time course of grammatical development. *Cognition*, 66, 249–301.

Frazier, L. (1987). Sentence processing: A tutorial review. In M. Coltheart (Ed.), *Attention and Performance XII* (pp. 559–586). Hillsdale, NJ: Lawrence Erlbaum Associates.

Frazier, L. & Clifton, C. Jr. (1996). *Construal*. Cambridge, MA: MIT Press.

Frazier, L. & Fodor, J. D. (1978). The sausage machine: A new two-stage parsing model. *Cognition*, 6, 291–325.

Freitag, C. M. (2007). The genetics of autistic disorders and its clinical relevance: A review of the literature. *Molecular Psychiatry*, 12, 2–22.

French, L. A., & Nelson, K. (1985). *Children's Acquisition of Relational Terms: Some Ifs, Ors, and Buts*. New York: Springer-Verlag.

Freudenthal, D., Pine, J. M., & Gobet, F. (2006). Modelling the developmental patterning of finiteness marking in English, Dutch, German and Spanish using MOSAIC. *Cognitive Science*, 30, 277–310.

Friederici, A. D. (2002). Towards a neural basis of auditory sentence processing. *Trends in Cognitive Sciences*, 6, 78–84.

(2005). Neurophysiological markers of early language acquisition: from syllables to sentences. *Trends in Cognitive Sciences*, 9(10), 481–488.

(2006). The neural basis of language development and its impairment. *Neuron*, 52, 941–952.

Friederici, A. D., & Wessels, J. M. I. (1993) Phonotactic knowledge of word boundaries and its use in infant speech perception. *Perception and Psychophysics*, 54, 287–295.

Friederici, A. D., Friedrich, M., & Weber, C. (2002). Neural manifestation of cognitive and precognitive mismatch detection in early infancy. *NeuroReport*, 13, 1251–1254.

Friederici, A. D., Gunter, T. C., Hahne, A., & Mauth, K. (2004). The relative timing of syntactic and semantic processes in sentence comprehension. *NeuroReport*, 15, 165–169.

Friederici, A. D., Friedrich, M., & Christophe, A. (2007) Brain responses in 4-month-old infants are already language specific. *Current Biology*, 17, 1208–1211.

Friedrich, M. (2007, August). Maturation of semantic integration mechanisms and behavioural language development. Paper presented at the British Psychological Society, Developmental Section, University of Plymouth, Plymouth.

(2008). Neurophysiological correlates of picture-word priming in one-year-olds. In A. D. Friederici & G. Thierry (Eds.), *Early Language Development: Bridging Brain and Behaviour. Series: Trends in Language Acquisition Research* (pp. 137–160). Amsterdam: John Benjamins.

Friedrich, M., & Friederici, A. D. (2004). N400-like semantic incongruity effect in 19-month-olds: Processing known words in picture contexts. *Journal of Cognitive Neuroscience*, 16, 1465–1477.

Friedrich, M., & Friederici, A. D. (2005a). Phonotactic knowledge and lexical–semantic processing in one-year-olds: Brain responses to words and nonsense words in picture contexts. *Journal of Cognitive Neuroscience*, 17, 1785–1802.

(2005b). Lexical priming and semantic integration reflected in the ERP of 14-month-olds. *NeuroReport*, 16, 653–656.

Gair, J., Lust, B., Sumangala, L., & Rodrigo, M. (1998). Acquisition of null subjects and control in some Sinhala adverbial clauses. In J. Gair (Ed.), *Studies in South Asian Linguistics: Sinhala and Other South Asian* Languages (pp. 271–285). Oxford: Oxford University Press.

Gamez, P. B., Shimpi, P. M., & Huttenlocher, J. (2005). Emerging syntactic representations as evident through priming. Poster presented at the 2005 SRCD Biennial Meeting, Atlanta, GA.

Garcia, J., & Koelling, R. A. (1966). Relation of cue to consequence in avoidance learning. *Psychonomic Science*, 4, 123–124.

Garcia-Perez, R., Lee, A., & Hobson, P. (2007). On intersubjective engagement in autism: A controlled study of nonverbal aspects of conversation. *Journal of Autism and Developmental Disorders*, 37, 1310–1322.

Garvey, C. (1975). Requests and responses in children's speech. *Journal of Child Language*, 2, 41–63.

(1984). *Children's Talk*. Cambridge, MA: Harvard University Press.

(1990). *Play* (2nd edn.). Cambridge, MA: Harvard University Press.

Gaser, C., Luders, E., Thompson, P., *et al.* (2006). Increased local gyrification mapped in Williams syndrome. *Neuroimage*, 33, 46–54.

Gathercole, S., & Baddeley, A. (1990). Phonological memory deficits in language disordered children: Is there a causal connection? *Journal of Memory and Language*, 29, 336–360.

Gathercole, V. (2002). Monolingual and bilingual acquisition: Learning different treatments of *that*-trace phenomena in English and Spanish. In D. K. Oller & R. E. Eilers (Eds.), *Language and Literacy in Bilingual Children* (pp. 220–254). Clevedon: Multilingual Matters.

(2006). *Language Transmission in Bilingual Families in Wales*. Bangor, Wales: Welsh Language Board.

Gauger, L. M., Lombardino, L. J., & Leonard, C. M. (1997). Brain morphology in children with specific language impairment. *Journal of Speech Language and Hearing Research*, 40, 1272–1284.

Gelman, S. A., & Markman, E. M. (1985). Implicit contrast in adjectives vs. nouns: Implications for word-learning in preschoolers. *Journal of Child Language*, 12, 125–143.

Gelman, S. A., & Taylor, J. (1984). How two-year-old children interpret proper and common names for unfamiliar objects. *Child Development*, 55, 1535–1540.

Gelman, S. A., Coley, J. D., Rosengren, K. S., Hartman, E., & Pappas, A. (1998). Beyond labeling: The role of maternal input in the acquisition of richly structured categories. *Monographs of the Society for Research in Child Development*, 63, Serial No. 253.

Genesee, F., Boivin, I., & Nicoladis, E. (1996). Talking with strangers: A study of bilingual children's communicative competence. *Applied Psycholinguistics*, 17, 427–442.

Genesee, F., Paradis, J., & Crago, M. (2004). *Dual Language Development and Disorders: A Handbook on Bilingualism and Second Language Acquisition*. Baltimore: Paul H. Brooks.

Gentner, D. (1982). Why nouns are learned before verbs: Linguistic relativity versus natural partitioning. In S. Kuczaj (Ed.), *Language Development: Vol. 2. Language, Thought, and Culture* (pp. 301–334). Hillsdale, NJ: Lawrence Erlbaum Associates.

(2003). Why we are so smart. In D. Gentner & S. Goldin-Meadow (Eds.), *Language in Mind: Advances in the Study of Language and Cognition* (pp. 195–235). Cambridge, MA: MIT Press.

Gentner, D., & Markman, A. (1997). Structure mapping in analogy and similarity. *American Psychologist*, 52, 45–56.

Gerken, L. A. (1991). The metrical basis of children's subjectless sentences. *Journal of Memory and Languages*, 30, 431–451.

(1994). A metrical template account of children's weak syllable omissions from multisyllabic words. *Journal of Child Language*, 21, 565–584.

(1996). Prosodic structure in young children's language production. *Language*, 72, 683–712.

(2004). Nine-month-olds extract structural principles required for natural language. *Cognition*, 93, B89–B96.

Gerken, L. A., & McIntosh, B. (1993). The interplay of function morphemes and prosody in early language. *Developmental Psychology*, 29, 448–457.

Gerken, L. A., Landau, B., & Remez, R. E. (1990). Function morphemes in young children's speech perception and production. *Developmental Psychology*, 26, 204–216.

Gertner, B., Rice, M., & Hadley, P. (1994). Influence of communicative competence on peer preferences in a preschool classroom. *Journal of Speech and Hearing Research*, 37, 913–923.

Gertner, Y., Fisher, C., & Eisengart, J. (2006). Learning words and rules: Abstract knowledge of word order in early sentence comprehension. *Psychological Science*, 17, 684–691.

Gervain, J., Nespor, M., Mazuka, R., Horie, R., & Mehler, J. (2008). Bootstrapping word order in prelexical infants: A Japanese–Italian cross-linguistic study. *Cognitive Psychology*, 57, 56–74.

Geurts, B. (2003). Quantifying kids. *Language Acquisition*, 11, 197–218.

Gibson, E., & Wexler, K. (1994.) Triggers. *Linguistic Inquiry*, 25, 407–454.

Gierut, J. A. (1999). Syllable onsets: Clusters and adjuncts in acquisition. *Journal of Speech, Language, and Hearing Research*, 42, 708–726.

Gil, D. (2000). Syntactic categories, cross-linguistic variation and universal grammar. In P. M. Vogel & B. Comrie (Eds.), *Approaches to the Typology of Word Classes* (pp. 173–216). Berlin: Mouton de Gruyter.

Gillam, R., Cowan, N., & Marler, J. (1998). Information processing by school-age children with specific language impairment: Evidence from a modality effect paradigm. *Journal of Speech, Language, and Hearing Research*, 41, 913–926.

Gillette, J., Gleitman, L., Gleitman, H., & Lederer, A. (1999). Human simulations of vocabulary learning. *Cognition*, 73, 135–176.

Gleason, J. B. (1975). Fathers and other strangers: Men's speech to young children. In D. Dato (Ed.), *Developmental Psycholinguistics: Theory and Applications. Georgetown University Roundtable on Language and Linguistics* (pp. 289–297). Washington, DC: Georgetown University Press.

Gleason, J. B., Perlmann, R., & Greif, E. (1984). What's the magic word: Learning language through politeness routines. *Discourse Processes*, 7, 493–502.

Gleitman, L. R. (1990). The structural sources of verb meanings. *Language Acquisition*, 1, 3–55.

Gleitman, L. R., & Wanner, E. (1982). Language acquisition: The state of the art. In E. Wanner & L. R. Gleitman (Eds.), *Language Acquisition: The State of the Art* (pp. 3–48). New York: Cambridge University Press.

Gleitman, L. R., Gleitman, H., Landau, B., & Wanner, E. (1988). Where learning begins: Initial representations for language learning. In F. J. Newmeyer (Ed.), *Linguistics: The Cambridge Survey: Vol. 3. Language: Psychological and Biological Aspects* (pp. 150–193). Cambridge: Cambridge University Press.

Gleitman, L. R., Cassidy, K., Nappa, R., Papafragou, A., & Trueswell, J. (2005). Hard words. *Language Learning and Development*, 1, 23–64.

Gnanadesikan, A. (2004). Markedness and faithfulness constraints in child phonology. In R. Kager, J. Pater & W. Zonneveld (Eds.), *Constraints in Phonological Acquisition*. Cambridge: Cambridge University Press.

Goad, H., & Brannen, K. (2003). Phonetic evidence for phonological structure in syllabification. In J. van de Weijer, V. J. van Heuven & H. van der Hulst (Eds.), *The Phonological Spectrum: Vol. 2. Suprasegmental Structure* (pp. 3–30). Amsterdam: John Benjamins.

Goad, H., & Buckley, M. (2006). Prosodic structure in child French: Evidence for the Foot. *Catalan Journal of Linguistics*, 5, 109–142.

Goad, H., & Rose, Y. (2004). Input elaboration, head faithfulness and evidence for representation in the acquisition of left-edge clusters in West Germanic. In R. Kager, J. Pater & W. Zonneveld (Eds.), *Constraints in Phonological Acquisition* (pp. 109–157). Cambridge: Cambridge University Press.

Goldberg, A. (1995). *Constructions: A Construction Grammar Approach to Argument Structure*. Chicago: University of Chicago Press.

(1999). The emergence of the semantics of argument structure constructions. In B. MacWhinney (Ed.), *The Emergence of Language* (pp. 197–212). Mahwah, NJ: Lawrence Erlbaum Associates.

(2006). *Constructions at Work: The Nature of Generalization in Language.* Oxford: Oxford University Press.

Goldberg, A., Casenhiser, D., & Sethuraman, N. (2004). Learning argument structure generalizations. *Cognitive Linguistics*, 15, 289–316.

(2005). The role of prediction in construction-learning. *Journal of Child Language*, 32, 407–426.

Goldberg, W., Osann, K., Filipek, P., *et al.* (2003). Language and other regression: Assessment and timing. *Journal of Autism and Developmental Disorders*, 33, 607–616.

Goldin-Meadow, S. (2003a). *Hearing Gesture: How our Hands Help us Think.* Cambridge, MA: Harvard University Press.

(2003b). *The Resilience of Language: What Gesture Creation in Deaf Children can tell us about how all Children Learn Language.* New York: Psychology Press.

(2005). What language creation in the manual modality tells us about the foundations of language. *Linguistic Review*, 22, 199–225.

Goldin-Meadow, S., & Butcher, C. (2003). Pointing toward two-word speech in young children. In S. Kita (Ed.), *Pointing: Where Language, Culture, and Cognition Meet* (pp. 85–107). Hillbaum, NJ: Lawrence Erlbaum Associates.

Goldin-Meadow, S., & Morford, M. (1985). Gesture in early child language: Studies of deaf and hearing children. *Merrill-Palmer Quarterly*, 31, 145–176.

Goldin-Meadow, S., & Saltzman, J. (2000). The cultural bounds of maternal accommodation: How Chinese and American mothers communicate with deaf and hearing children. *Psychological Science*, 11, 311–318.

Goldin-Meadow, S., & Singer, M. A. (2003). From children's hands to adults' ears: Gesture's role in teaching and learning. *Developmental Psychology*, 39, 509–520.

Goldin-Meadow, S., & Wagner, S. M. (2005). How our hands help us learn. *Trends in Cognitive Science*, 9, 234–241.

Goldin-Meadow, S., Goodrich, W., Sauer, E., & Iverson, J. (2007). Young children use their hands to tell their mothers what to say. *Developmental Science*, 10, 778–785.

Goldstein, H. (2002). Communication intervention for children with autism: A review of treatment efficacy. *Journal of Autism and Developmental Disorders*, 32(5), 373–396.

Golinkoff, R. M., Hirsh-Pasek, K., Cauley, K. M., & Gordon, L. (1987). The eyes have it – lexical and syntactic comprehension in a new paradigm. *Journal of Child Language*, 14, 23–45.

Gombert, J. E. (1992). *Metalinguistic Development.* London: Harvester Wheatsheaf.

Gómez, R. L. (2002) Variability and detection of invariant structure. *Psychological Science*, 13, 431–436.

Gómez, R. L., & Gerken, L. (1999). Artificial grammar learning by one-year-olds leads to specific and abstract knowledge. *Cognition*, 70, 109–135.

Gómez, R. L., & Lakusta, L. (2004). A first step in form-based category abstraction by 12-month-old infants. *Developmental Science*, 7, 567–580.

Goodluck, H. (1978). *Linguistic principles in children's grammar of complement interpretation*. PhD dissertation, University of Massachusetts, Amherst, MA. Published by the Graduate Linguistic Student Association, Department of Linguistics.

  (1981). Children's grammar of complement-subject interpretation. In S. Tavakolian (Ed.), *Language Acquisition and Linguistic Theory* (pp. 139–166). Cambridge, MA: MIT Press.

Goodluck, H., & Tavakolian, S. (1982). Competence and processing in children's grammar of relative clauses. *Cognition*, 11, 1–27.

Goodman, J. C., McDonough, L., & Brown, N. B. (1998). The role of semantic context and memory in the acquisition of novel nouns. *Child Development*, 69, 1330–1344.

Goodwyn, S. W., & Acredolo, L. P. (1993). Symbolic gesture versus word: Is there a modality advantage for onset of symbol use? *Child Development*, 64, 688–701.

  (1998). Encouraging symbolic gestures: A new perspective on the relationship between gesture and speech. In J. M. Iverson & S. Goldin-Meadow (Eds.), *The Nature and Functions of Gesture in Children's Communication* (pp. 61–73). San Francisco: Jossey-Bass.

Goodwyn, S., Acredolo, L., & Brown, C. A. (2000). Impact of symbolic gesturing on early language development. *Journal of Nonverbal Behavior*, 24, 81–104.

Gopnik, M. (1990). Feature-blind grammar and dysphasia. *Nature*, 344, 715.

  (1997). Language deficits and genetic factors. *Trends in Cognitive Sciences*, 1, 5–9.

Gordon, D., & Ervin-Tripp, S. (1984). The structure of children's requests. In R. Schiefelbusch & J. Pickar (Eds.), *The Acquisition of Communicative Competence: Vol. 8. Language Intervention Series* (pp. 295–321). Baltimore: University Park Press.

Gordon, P. (2003). The origin of argument structure in infant event representations. In A. Brugos, L. Micciulla & C. Smith (Eds.), *Proceedings of the 28th Annual Boston University Conference on Language Development* (pp. 189–198). Somerville, MA: Cascadilla Press.

Gordon, P., & Chafetz, J. (1990). Verb-based versus class-based accounts of actionality effects in children's comprehension of passives. *Cognition*, 36, 227–254.

Goro, T. (2004). The emergence of Universal Grammar in the emergence of language: The acquisition of Japanese logical connectives and positive polarity. Unpublished manuscript, University of Maryland at College Park.

Goro, T., & Akiba, S. (2004). The acquisition of disjunction and positive polarity in Japanese. In *Proceedings of the 23rd West Coast Conference on Formal Linguistics* (pp. 251–264). Somerville, MA: Cascadilla Press.

Goro, T., Minai, U., & Crain, S. (2005). Two disjunctions for the price of *only* one. In A. Brugos, M. R. Clark-Cotton & S. Ha (Eds.), In *Proceedings of the 29th Boston University Child Language Development Conference* (pp. 228–239). Somerville, MA: Cascadilla Press.

Gotham, K., Risi, S., Pickles, A., & Lord, C. (2007). The Autism Diagnostic Observation Schedule (ADOS): Revised algorithms for improved diagnostic validity. *Journal of Autism and Developmental Disorders, 37*, 613–627.

Gottlieb, G. (1997). *Synthesizing Nature–nurture: Prenatal Roots of Instinctive Behavior*. Mahwah, NJ: Lawrence Erlbaum Associates.

Graf Estes, K., Evans, J. L., Alibali, M. W., & Saffran, J. R. (2007a). Can infants map meaning to newly segmented words? Statistical segmentation and word learning. *Psychological Science, 18*, 254–260.

Graf Estes, K., Evans, J., & Else-Quest, N. (2007b). Differences in the nonword repetition performance of children with and without specific language impairment: A meta-analysis. *Journal of Speech, Language, and Hearing Research, 50*, 177–195.

Grassman, S., & Tomasello, M. (2007). Two-year-olds use primary sentence accent to learn new words. *Journal of Child Language, 34*, 677–687.

Gray, S. (2004). Word learning by preschoolers with specific language impairment: Predictors and poor learners. *Journal of Speech, Language, and Hearing Research, 47*, 1117–1132.

Greenfield, P. (1997). You can't take it with you: Why ability assessments don't cross cultures. *American Psychologist, 52*, 1115–1124.

Greenfield, P., & Savage-Rumbaugh, E. S. (1990). Grammatical combinations in *Pan paniscus*: Processes of learning and invention in the evolution and development of language. In S. T. Parker & K. R. Gibson (Eds.), *'Language' and intelligence in monkeys and apes: Comparative developmental perspectives* (pp. 540–578). New York: Cambridge University Press.

Greenfield, P., & Smith, J. (1976). *The Structure of Communication in Early Language Development*. New York: Academic Press.

Greenfield, P., & Subrahmanyam, K. (2003). Online discourse in a teen chatroom: New codes and new modes of coherence in a visual medium. *Applied Developmental Psychology, 24*, 713–738.

Greenfield, P., Gross, E., Subrahmanyam, K., Suzuki, L., & Tynes, B. (2006). Teens on the internet: Interpersonal connection, identity, and information. In R. Kraut, M. Brynn & S. Kiesler (Eds.), *Computers, Phones, and the Internet* (pp. 185–200). New York: Oxford University Press.

Greenwood, A. (1998). Accommodating friends: Niceness, meanness, and discourse norms. In S. Hoyle & C. Adger (Eds.), *Kids Talk: Strategic Language use in Later Childhood* (pp. 68–81). New York: Oxford University Press.

Greenwood, C., Walker, D., & Utley, C. (2002). Relationships between social-communicative skills and life achievements. In H. Goldstein, L. Kaczmarek, & K. English (Eds.), *Promoting Social Communication: Children with Developmental Disabilities from Birth to Adolescence* (pp. 345–370). Baltimore: Paul H. Brookes.

Grela, B. (2003). The omission of subject arguments in children with specific language impairment. *Clinical Linguistics and Phonetics, 17*, 153–169.

Grice, H. P. (1989). *Studies in the Way of Words*. Cambridge, MA: Harvard University Press.

Grieser, D., & Kuhl, P. K. (1988). Maternal speech to infants in a tonal language: Support for universal prosodic features in motherese. *Developmental Psychology*, 24, 14–20.

Griffin, R., Hemphill, L., Camp, L., & Wolf, D. (2004). Oral discourse in the preschool years and later literacy skills. *First Language*, 24, 123–147.

Grinstead, J. (2000). Case, inflection and subject licensing in child Catalan and Spanish. *Journal of Child Language*, 27, 119–155.

Gropen, J., Pinker, S., Hollander, M., Goldberg, R., & Wilson, R. (1989). The learnability and acquisition of the dative alternation in English. *Language*, 65, 203–257.

Grosjean, F. (1989). Neurolinguists, beware! The bilingual is not two mono-linguals in one person. *Brain and Language*, 36, 3–15.

(2001). The bilingual's language modes. In J. Nicol (Ed.), *One Mind, Two Languages: Bilingual Language Processing* (pp. 1–22). Oxford: Blackwell.

Gualmini, A. (2004). *The Ups and Downs of Child Language: Outstanding Dissertations in Linguistics Series*. New York: Routledge.

Gualmini, A., Meroni, L., & Crain, S. (2003). An asymmetric universal in child language. In M. Weisgerber (Ed.), *Proceedings of Sinn und Bedeutung VII – Arbeitspapiere des Fachbereichs Sprachwissenschaft 'Konstanz Linguistics Working Papers': Vol. 114*. (pp. 136–148). Konstanz, Germany.

Guasti, M. T. (1993/1994). Verb syntax in Italian child grammar: finite and non-finite verbs. *Language Acquisition*, 3, 1–40.

(2002). *Language Acquisition: The Growth of Grammar*. Boston, MA: MIT Press.

Guasti, M. T., & Shlonsky, U. (1995). The acquisition of French relative clauses reconsidered. *Language Acquisistion*, 4, 257–276.

Guerriero, S., Cooper, A., Oshima-Takane, Y., & Kuriyama, Y. (2001). A discourse–pragmatic explanation for argument realization and omission in English and Japanese children's speech. In A. Do, L. Dominguez & A. Johansen (Eds.). *Proceedings of the 25th Annual Boston University Conference on Language Development* (pp. 319–330). Somerville, MA: Cascadilla Press.

Guerriero, S., Oshima-Takane, Y., & Kuriyama, Y. (2006). The development of referential choice in English and Japanese: A discourse–pragmatic perspective. *Journal of Child Language*, 33, 823–857.

Guidetti, M. (2005). Yes or no? How young French children combine gestures and speech to agree and refuse. *Journal of Child Language*, 32, 911–924.

Gupta, A. (2006). *Bilingual and Multilingual Children: Another Perspective. Ask-A-Linguist FAQ*. Retrieved June 10, 2006, from www.linguistlist.org/.

Gupta, A. R., & State, M. W. (2007). Recent Advances in the Genetics of Autism. *Biological Psychiatry*, 61, 429–437.

Hadley, P., & Short, H. (2005). The onset of tense marking in children at risk for specific language impairment. *Journal of Speech, Language, and Hearing Research*, 48, 1344–1362.

Haegeman, L. (1991). *Introduction to Government and Binding Theory*. Oxford: Blackwell.

Hahne, A. (2001). What's different in second-language processing? Evidence from event-related potentials. *Journal of Psycholinguistic Research*, 30, 251–266.

Haiman, J., & Thompson, S. A. (Eds.). (1988). *Clause Combining in Grammar and Discourse*. Amsterdam: John Benjamins.

Hakuta, K. (1986). *The Mirror of Language*. New York: Basic Books.

(1988). A wordly look at language acquisition. Review of Dan Isaac Slobin (Ed.) The crosslinguistic study of language acquisition, Volumes 1 & 2. *Contemporary Psychology*, 33, 576–578.

Hall, D. G. (2000). Preschoolers' use of form class cues in word learning. *Developmental Psychology*, 36, 449–462.

Hallé, P. A., & de Boysson-Bardies, B. (1994). Emergence of an early lexicon. *Infant Behavior and Development*, 17, 119–129.

(1996). The format of representation of recognized words in infants' early receptive lexicon. *Infant Behavior and Development*, 19, 463–481.

Hallé, P. A., Durand, C., & de Boysson–Bardies, B. (2008). Do 11–month-old French infants process articles? *Language and Speech*, 51, 23–44.

Halliday, M. A. K., & Hasan, R. (1976). *Cohesion in English*. London: Longman.

Hamann, C., & Plunkett, K. (1998). Subjectless sentences in child Danish. *Cognition*, 69, 35–72.

Hamburger, H. (1980). A deletion ahead of its time. *Cognition*, 8, 389–416.

Hamburger, H., & Crain, S. (1982). Relative acquisition. In S. A. Kuczaj (Ed.), *Language Development: Syntax and Semantics*. Hillsdale, NJ: Lawrence Erlbaum Associates.

Hamilton, A., Plunkett, K., & Schafer, G. (2001). Infant vocabulary development assessed with a British CDI. *Journal of Child Language*, 27, 689–705.

Hansson, K., Nettelbladt, U., & Leonard, L. (2000). Specific language impairment in Swedish: The status of verb morphology and word order. *Journal of Speech, Language, and Hearing Research*, 43, 848–864.

Happé, F. (1994). An advanced test of theory of mind: Understanding of story characters' thoughts and feelings by able autistic, mentally handicapped, and normal children and adults. *Journal of Autism and Developmental Disorders*, 24, 129–154.

Happé, F., & Frith, U. (1996). The neuropsychology of Autism. *Brain*, 119, 1377–1400.

Harris, S. L., & Handleman, J. S. (2000). Age and IQ at intake as predictors of placement for young children with autism: A four- to six-year follow up. *Journal of Autism and Developmental Disorders*, 30, 137–142.

Harris, T., & Wexler, K. (1996). The optional-infinitive stage in child English: Evidence from negation. In H. Clahsen (Ed.), *Generative Perspectives on Language Acquisition: Empirical Findings, Theoretical Considerations and Crosslinguistic Comparisons* (pp. 1–42). Philadelphia, PA: John Benjamins.

Harrison, P. A. (2000). Acquiring the phonology of lexical tone in infancy. *Lingua*, 110, 581–616.

Hart, B., & Risley, T. (1995). *Meaning Differences in the Everyday Experiences of Young American Children*. Baltimore, MD: Paul Brooks.

Haspelmath, M. (2001). The European linguistic area: Standard average European. In M. Haspelmath, E. Konig, W. Osterreicher & W. Raible (Eds.), *Language Typology and Language Universals: An International Handbook* (pp. 1492–1510). Berlin: Mouton de Gruyter.

Haspelmath, M., Dryer, M. S., & Comrie, B. (Eds.). (2005). *The World Atlas of Language Structures*. Oxford: Oxford University Press.

Hauser, M. D., Weiss, D., & Marcus, G. (2002). Rule learning by cotton-top tamarins. *Cognition*, 86, B15–B22.

Hayes, J. R., & Clark, H. H. (1970). Experiments on the segmentation of an artificial speech analogue. In J. Hayes (Ed.), *Cognition and the Development of Language* (pp. 221–234). New York: John Wiley.

He, C., Hotson, L., & Trainor, L. J. (2007). Mismatch responses to pitch changes in early infancy. *Journal of Cognitive Neuroscience*, 19, 878–892.

Heath, S. (1998). Working through language. In S. Hoyle & C. Adger (Eds.), *Kids Talk: Strategic Language use in Later Childhood* (pp. 217–240). New York: Oxford University Press.

Heibeck, T. H., & Markman, E. M. (1987). Word learning in children: An examination of fast mapping. *Child Development*, 58, 1021–1034.

Herbert, M. R., Ziegler, D. A., Makris, N., *et al.* (2003). Larger brain and white matter volumes in children with developmental language disorder. *Developmental Science*, 6, F11–F22.

Herbert, M. R., Ziegler, D. A., Deutsch, C. K., *et al.* (2005). Brain asymmetries in autism and developmental language disorder: A nested whole-brain analysis. *Brain*, 128, 213–226.

Herot, C. (2002). Socialization of affect during mealtime interactions. In S. Blum-Kulka & C. Snow (Eds.), *Talking to Adults: The Contribution of Multi-Party Discourse to Language Acquisition* (pp. 155–179). Mahwah, NJ: Lawrence Erlbaum Associates.

Hickmann, M. (1980). Creating referents in discourse: A developmental analysis of linguistic cohesion. In J. Kreiman & E. Ojeda (Eds.), *Papers from the Parasession on Pronouns and Anaphora* (pp. 192–203). Chicago: Chicago Linguistic Society.

(1982). The development of narrative skills: Pragmatic and metapragmatic aspects of discourse cohesion. Unpublished doctoral dissertation, University of Chicago, Chicago.

(1987). The pragmatics of reference in child language: Some issues in developmental theory. In M. Hickmann (Ed.), *Social and Functional Approaches to Language and Thought* (pp. 165–184). Orlando: Academic Press.

(1995). Discourse organization and the development of reference to person, space, and time. In P. Fletcher & B. MacWhinney (Eds.), *Handbook of Child Language* (pp. 194–218). Oxford: Basil Blackwell.

(2003). *Children's Discourse: Person, Time, and Space across Languages*. Cambridge: Cambridge University Press.

(2004). Coherence, cohesion, and context: Some comparative perspectives in narrative development. In S. Strömqvist & L. Verhoeven (Eds.), *Relating Events in Narrative: Typological and Contextual Perspectives* (pp. 281–306). Mahwah, NJ: Lawrence Erlbaum Associates.

Hickmann, M., & Liang, J. (1990). Clause-structure variation in Chinese narrative discourse: A developmental analysis. *Linguistics*, 28, 1167–2000.

Hickmann, M., Kail, M., & Roland, F. (1995). Cohesive anaphoric relations in French children's narratives as a function of mutual knowledge. *First Language*, 15, 177–300.

Hickmann, M., Hendriks, H., Roland, F., & Liang, J. (1996). The marking of new information in children's narratives: A comparison of English, French, German, and Mandarin Chinese. *Journal of Child Language*, 23, 591–619.

Hickok, G., & Poeppel, D. (2007). The cortical organization of speech processing. *Nature Reviews Neuroscience*, 8, 393–402.

Hirsh-Pasek, K., & Golinkoff, R. M. (1996). *The Origins of Grammar: Evidence from Early Language Comprehension*. Cambridge, MA: MIT Press.

Hirsh-Pasek, K., & Golinkoff, R. M. (Eds.). (2006). *Action meets Words: How Children Learn Verbs*. New York: Oxford University Press.

Hobson, R. P., Ouston, J., & Lee, A. (1989). Naming emotion in faces and voices: Abilities and disabilities in autism and mental retardation. *British Journal of Developmental Psychology*, 7, 237–250.

Hoff-Ginsberg, E. (1991). Mother–child conversation in different social classes and communicative settings. *Child Development*, 62, 782–796.

(1998). The relation of birth order and socioeconomic status to children's language experience and language development. *Applied Psycholinguistics*, 19, 603–629.

Hoff-Ginsberg, E., & Krueger, W. (1991). Older siblings as conversational partners. *Merrill-Palmer Quarterly*, 37, 465–482.

Hoffman, L., & Gillam, R. (2004). Verbal and spatial information processing constraints in children with specific language impairment. *Journal of Speech, Language, and Hearing Research*, 47, 114–125.

Höhle, B. (2002). *Der Einstieg in die Grammatik: Die Rolle der Phonologie–Syntax–Schnittstelle für Sprachverarbeitung und Spracherwerb*. Habilitationsschrift, Berlin: Freie Universität.

Höhle, B., & Weissenborn, J. (2000). The origins of syntactic knowledge: Recognition of determiners in one year old German children. In S. C. Howell, S. A. Fish & T. Keith-Lucas (Eds.), *BUCLD 24: Proceedings of the 24th Annual Boston University Conference on Language Development: Vol. 2* (pp. 418–429). Somerville: Cascadilla Press.

Höhle, B., & Weissenborn, J. (2003). German-learning infants' ability to detect unstressed closed-class elements in continuous speech. *Developmental Science*, 6, 122–127.

Höhle, B., Schmitz, M., Santelmann, L. M., & Weissenborn, J. (2006). The recognition of discontinuous verbal dependencies by German

19-month-olds: Evidence for lexical and structural influences on children's early processing capacities. *Language Learning and Development*, 2, 277–300.

Höhle, B., Bijeljac-Babic, R., Nazzi, T., Herold, B., & Weissenborn, J. (submitted). The emergence of language specific prosodic preferences during the first half year of life: Evidence from German and French infants.

Höhle, B., Weissenborn, J., Kiefer, D., Schulz, A., & Schmitz, M. (2004). Functional elements in infants' speech processing: The role of determiners in the syntactic categorization of lexical elements. *Infancy*, 5, 341–353.

Hollich, G. J., Hirsh-Pasek, K., & Golinkoff, R. M. (2000). Breaking the language barrier: An emergentist coalition model for the origins of word learning. *Monographs of the Society for Research in Child Development*, 65, Serial No. 262.

Homae, F., Watanabe, H., Nakano, T., Asakawa, K., & Taga, G. (2006). The right hemisphere of sleeping infant perceives sentential prosody. *Neuroscience Research*, 54, 276–280.

Horn, L. R. (1996). Presupposition and implicature. In S. Lappin (Ed.), *Handbook of Contemporary Semantic Theory* (pp. 299–319). Oxford: Blackwell.

Hornstein, N., & Lightfoot, D. (1981). Introduction. In N. Hornstein, & D. Lightfoot (Eds.), *Explanation in Linguistics: The Logical Problem in Language Acquisition* (pp. 9–31). London: Longman.

Houston, D. M., & Jusczyk, P. W. (2000). The role of talker-specific information in word segmentation by infants. *Journal of Experimental Psychology: Human Perception and Performance*, 26, 1570–1582.

(2003). Infants' long-term memory for the sound patterns of words and voices. *Journal of Experimental Psychology: Human Perception and Performance*, 29, 1143–1154.

Houston, D. M., Juscyzk, P. W., Kuijpers, C., Coolen, R., & Cutler, A. (2000). Cross-language word segmentation by 9-month-olds. *Psychonomics Bulletin Review*, 7, 504–509.

Houston-Price, C., & Nakai, S. (2004). Distinguishing novelty and familiarity effects in infant preference procedures. *Infant and Child Development*, 13, 341–348.

Howard, E., & Christian, D. (no date). Two-way immersion 101: Designing and implementing a two-way immersion education program at the elementary level. Retrieved June 20, 2007, from www.cal.org/crede/pubs/edpractice/EPR9.htm/.

Howlin, P. (2003). Outcome in high-functioning adults with autism with and without early language delays: Implications for the differentiation between autism and Asperger syndrome. *Journal of Autism and Developmental Disorders*, 33, 3–13.

Howlin, P., Gordon, R. K., Pasco, G., Wade, A., & Charman, T. (2007). The effectiveness of Picture Exchange Communication System (PECS) training for teachers of children with autism: A pragmatic, group randomised controlled trial. *Journal of Child Psychology & Psychiatry*, 48, 473–481.

Hoyle, S., & Adger, C. (Eds.). (1998). *Kids Talk: Strategic Language Use in Later Childhood*. New York: Oxford University Press.

Hsieh, L., Leonard, L. B., & Swanson, L. (1999). Some differences between English plural noun inflections and third singular verb inflections in the input: The contributions of frequency, sentence position, and duration. *Journal of Child Language*, 26, 531–543.

Hsu, J., Cairns, H. S., & Fiengo, R. W. (1985). The development of grammars underlying children's interpretation of complex sentences. *Cognition*, 20, 25–48.

Huang, Y. & Snedeker, J. (2006). On-line Interpretation of Scalar Quantifiers: Insight into the Semantics–Pragmatics Interface. *Proceedings of the Twenty-eighth Annual Conference of the Cognitive Science Society, Vancouver, BC*. (pp. 351–356). New York: Taylor & Francis.

Hudson, J. A. (1993). Reminiscing with mothers and others: Autobiographical memory in young 2-year-olds. *Journal of Narrative and Life History*, 3, 1–31.

Hudson Kam, C. L., & Newport, E. L. (2005). Regularizing unpredictable variation: The roles of adult and child learners in language formation and change. *Language Learning and Development*, 1, 151–195.

Hulk, A., & Muller, N. (2000). Bilingual first language acquisition at the interface between syntax and pragmatics. *Bilingualism: Language and Cognition*, 3(3), 227–244.

Hulst, H. van der (1993). Units in the analysis of signs. *Phonology*, 10, 209–242.

Hunt, K. W. (1965). *Grammatical Structures Written at Three Grade Levels (Research Report No.3)*. Champaign, IL: National Council of Teachers of English.

Hunter, M. A., & Ames, E. W. (1988). A multifactor model of infant preferences for novel and familiar stimuli. In L. Lipsitt & C. Rovee-Collier (Eds.), *Advances in Infancy Research: Vol. 5* (pp. 69–95). Norwood, NJ: Ablex.

Hus, V., Pickles, A., Cook, E. H., Risi, S., & Lord, C. (2007). Using the Autism Diagnostic Interview – revised to increase phenotypic homogeneity in genetic studies of autism. *Biological Psychiatry*, 61, 438–448.

Huttenlocher, J., & Smiley, P. (1987). Early word meanings: The case of nouns. *Cognitive Psychology*, 19, 63–89.

Huttenlocher, J., Haight, W., Bryk, A., Seltzer, M., & Lyons, T. (1991). Early vocabulary growth: Relation to language input and gender. *Developmental Psychology*, 27, 236–248.

Huttenlocher, J., Vasilyeva, M., & Shimpi, P. (2004). Syntactic priming in young children. *Journal of Memory and Language*, 50, 182–195.

Hyams, N. (1989a). The Domain Problem in Language Acquisition. Invited lecture at Syracuse University.

  (1989b). The null subject parameter in language acquisition. In O. Jaeggli & K. J. Safir (Eds.), *The Null Subject Parameter* (pp. 215–238). Dordrecht: Kluwer.

Hyams, N., & Wexler, K. (1993). On the grammatical basis of null subjects. *Linguistic Inquiry*, 24, 421–459.

Hyltenstam, K., & Abrahamsson, N. (2000). Who can become native-like in a second language? All, some, or none? *Studia Linguistica*, 54, 150–166.

Hymes, D. (1967). Models of the interaction of language and social setting. *Journal of Social Issues*, 23, 8–28.

Ihns, M., & Leonard, L. (1988). Syntactic categories in early child language: Some additional data. *Journal of Child Language*, 15, 673–678.

Illes, J., Francis, W., Desmond, J., *et al.* (1999). Convergent cortical representation in semantic processing in bilinguals. *Brain and Language*, 70, 347–363.

Imai, M., & Gentner, D. (1997). A cross-linguistic study of early word meaning: Universal ontology and linguistic influence. *Cognition*, 62, 169–200.

Ingram, T. T. S. (1959). Specific developmental disorders of speech in childhood. *Brain*, 82, 450–454.

Inhelder, B., & Piaget, J. (1964). *The Early Growth of Logic in the Child*. London: Routledge & Kegan Paul.

Ioup, G. (1989). Immigrant children who have failed to acquire native English. In S. Gass, C. Madden, D. Preston & L. Selinker (Eds.), *Variation in Second Language Acquisition: Vol. 2. Psycholinguistic Issues* (pp. 160–175). Clevedon: Multilingual Matters.

Iverson, J. M. (1999). How to get to the cafeteria: Gesture and speech in blind and sighted children's spatial descriptions. *Developmental Psychology*, 35, 1132–1142.

Iverson, J. M., & Fagan, M. K. (2004). Infant vocal–motor coordination: Precursor to the gesture–speech system? *Child Development*, 75, 1053–1066.

Iverson, J. M., & Goldin-Meadow, S. (1998). Why people gesture as they speak. *Nature*, 396, 228.

  (2005). Gesture paves the way for language development. *Psychological Science*, 16, 367–371.

Iverson, J. M., & Thelen, E. (1999). Hand, mouth, and brain: The dynamic emergence of speech and gsture. *Journal of Consciousness Studies*, 6, 19–40.

Iverson, J. M., & Wozniak, R. H. (2007). Variation in vocal–motor development in infant siblings of children with autism. *Journal of Autism and Developmental Disorders*, 37, 158–170.

Iverson, J. M., Capirci, O., & Caselli, M. S. (1994). From communication to language in two modalities. *Cognitive Development*, 9, 23–43.

Iverson, J. M., Capirci, O., Longobardi, E., & Caselli, M. C. (1999). Gesturing in mother–child interaction. *Cognitive Development*, 14, 57–75.

Iverson, J. M., Longobardi, E., & Caselli, M. C. (2003a). Relationship between gestures and words in children with Down's syndrome and typically developing children in the early stages of communicative development. *International Journal of Language and Communication Disorders*, 38, 179–197.

Iverson, P., Kuhl, P. K., Akahane-Yamada, R., *et al.* (2003b). A perceptual interference account of acquisition difficulties for non-native phonemes. *Cognition*, 87, B47–B57.

Iverson, J. M., Hall, A. J., Nickel, L., & Wozniak, R. H. (2007). The relationship between reduplicated babble onset and laterality biases in infant rhythmic arm movements. *Brain and Language*, 101, 198–207.

Iverson, J. M., Capirci, O., Volterra, V., & Goldin-Meadow, S. (2008). Learning to talk in a gesture-rich world: Early communication in Italian vs. American children. *First Language*, 28, 164–181.

Jacobson, P., & Schwartz, R. (2002). Morphology in incipient bilingual Spanish-speaking preschool children with specific language impairment. *Applied Psycholinguistics*, 23, 23–41.

Jaeger, J. J. (1997). How to say 'Grandma': The problem of developing phonological representations. *First Language*, 17, 1–29.

Jakobson, R. (1941). *Kindersprache, aphasie und allgemeine lautgesetze.* Uppsala: Almqvist & Wiksells boktryckeri a.-b.

  (1968). *Child Language, Aphasia, and Phonological Universals* (A. R. Keiler, Trans.). The Hague: Mouton (original work published 1941).

Jakubowicz, C., Nash, L., Rigaut, C., & Gérard, C. (1998). Determiners and clitic pronouns in French-speaking children with SLI. *Language Acquisition*, 7, 113–160.

Jamshidiha, H., & Marefat, H. (2006). L1 Persian attrition. *Linguistics Journal*, 1, 17–46.

Jancovic, M. A., Devoe, S., & Wiener, M. (1975). Age-related changes in hand and arm movements as nonverbal communication: Some conceptualizations and an empirical exploration. *Child Development*, 46, 922–928.

Janda, A. (1978). The linguistic analysis of the honey bee's dance language. Unpublished doctoral dissertation, City University of New York, Graduate Center.

Jansow, W., Crown, C., Feldstein, S., Taylor, L., Beebe, B., & Jaffe, J. (1988). Coordinated interpersonal timing of Down-syndrome and non-delayed infants with their mothers: Evidence for a buffered mechanism of social interaction. *Biological Bulletin*, 174, 355–360.

Jarrold, C., Boucher, J., & Russell, J. (1997). Language profiles in children with autism: Theoretical and methodological implications. *Autism*, 1 (1), 57–76.

Jernigan, T. L., Hesselink, J. R., Sowell, E., & Tallal, P. A. (1991). Cerebral structure on magnetic-resonance-imaging in language-impaired and learning-impaired children. *Archives of Neurology*, 48, 539–545.

Jisa, H. (1985). French preschoolers' use of *et pis* ('and then'). *First Language*, 5, 169–184.

  (1987). Sentence connnectors in French children's monologue performance. *Journal of Pragmatics*, 11, 607–621.

Joanisse, M., & Seidenberg, M. (2003). Phonology and syntax in specific language impairment: Evidence from a connectionist model. *Brain and Language*, 86, 40–56.

Johnson, C. J., Beitchman, J., Young, A., *et al.* (1999). Fourteen-year follow-up of children with and without speech/language impairments: Speech/language stability and outcomes. *Journal of Speech–Language–Hearing Research*, 42, 744–760.

Johnson, E. K. (2005) English-learning infants' representations of word forms with iambic stress. *Infancy*, 7, 99–109.

Johnson, E. K., & Jusczyk, P. W. (2001). Word segmentation by 8-month-olds: When speech cues count more than statistics. *Journal of Memory and Language*, 44, 548–567.

Johnson, J. S., & Newport, E. L. (1989). Critical period effects in second language learning: The influence of maturational state on the acquisition of English as a second language. *Cognitive Psychology*, 21, 60–99.

Johnson, M. (2005). Sensitive periods in functional brain development: Problems and prospects. *Developmental Psychobiology*, 46, 287–292.

Johnston, J. R. (1985). Cognitive prerequisites: The evidence from children learning English. In D. I. Slobin (Ed.), *The Crosslinguistic Study of Language Acquisition: Vol. 2. Theoretical Issues* (pp. 961–1004). Hillsdale, NJ: Lawrence Erlbaum Associates.

(1994). Cognitive abilities of children with language impairment. In R. Watkins & M. Rice (Ed.), *Language Impairments in Children* (pp. 107–121). Baltimore, MD: Paul H. Brookes.

Johnston, J. R., & Slobin, D. I. (1979). The development of locative expressions in English, Italian, Serbo-Croatian and Turkish. *Journal of Child Language*, 6, 529–545.

Jonas, D. (1995). On the acquisition of verb syntax in child Faroese. *MIT Working Papers in Linguistics*, 26, 265–280.

Jongstra, W. (2003). Variation in reduction strategies of Dutch word-initial consonant clusters. Unpublished doctoral dissertation, University of Toronto.

Jusczyk, P. W. (1997). *The Discovery of Spoken Language.* Cambridge, MA: MIT Press.

Jusczyk, P. W., & Aslin, R. N. (1995). Infants' detection of the sound patterns of words in fluent speech. *Cognitive Psychology*, 29, 1–23.

Jusczyk, P. W., & Hohne, E. A. (1997). Infants' memory for spoken words. *Science*, 277, 1984–1986.

Jusczyk, P. W., & Luce, P. A. (1994). Infants' sensitivity to phonotactic patterns in the native language. *Journal of Memory and Language*, 33, 630–645.

Jusczyk, P. W., & Thompson, E. J. (1978). Perception of a phonetic contrast in multisyllabic utterances by 2-month-old infants. *Perception and Psychophysics*, 23, 105–109.

Jusczyk, P. W., Cutler, A., & Redanz, N. (1993a). Infants' preference for the predominant stress patterns of English words. *Child Development*, 64, 675–687.

Jusczyk, P. W., Friederici, A. D., Wessels, J., Svenkerud, V. Y., & Jusczyk, A. M. (1993b). Infants' sensitivity to the sound patterns of native language words. *Journal of Memory and Language*, 32, 402–420.

Jusczyk, P. W., Luce, P. A., & Charles-Luce, J. (1994). Infants' sensitivity to phonotactic patterns in the native language. *Journal of Memory and Language*, 33, 630–645.

Jusczyk, P. W., Goodman, M., & Bauman, A. (1999a). 9-month-olds' attention to sound similarities in syllables. *Journal of Memory and Language*, 40, 62–82.

Jusyczk, P. W., Hohne, E. A., & Bauman, A. (1999b). Infants' sensitivity to allophonic cues for word segmentation. *Perception and Psychophysics*, 62, 1465–1476.

Jusczyk, P. W., Houston, D. M., & Newsome, M. (1999c). The beginnings of word segmentation in English-learning infants. *Cognitive Psychology*, 39, 159–207.

Kabak, B., & Vogel, I. (2001). The phonological word and stress assignment in Turkish. *Phonology*, 18, 315–360.

Kail, M., & Hickmann, M. (1992). French children's ability to introduce referents in narratives as a function of mutual knowledge, *First Language*, 12, 73–94.

Kail, M., & Sanchez y Lopez, I. (1997). Referent introductions in Spanish children's narratives as a function of contextual constraints. *First Language*, 17, 103–130.

Kail, R. (1994). A method of studying the generalized slowing hypothesis in children with specific language impairment. *Journal of Speech and Hearing Research*, 37, 418–421.

Kail, R., & Leonard, L. (1986). Word-finding abilities in language-impaired children. *ASHA Monographs*, 25.

Kajikawa, S., Fais, L., Werker, J., & Amano, S. (2006). Cross-language sensitivity to phonotactic patterns in infants. *The Journal of the Acoustical Society of America*, 120, 2278–2284.

Kako, E. (1999). Elements of syntax in the systems of three language-trained animals. *Animal Learning and Behavior*, 27, 1–14.

Kamide, Y., Altmann, G. T. M., & Haywood, S. L. (2003). The timecourse of prediction in incremental sentence processing: Evidence from anticipatory eye movements. *Journal of Memory and Language*, 49, 133–156.

Kanner, L. (1943). Autistic disturbances of affective contact. *Nervous Child*, 2, 217–250.

Karmiloff-Smith, A. (1979). *A Functional Approach to Child Language: A Study of Determiners and Reference*. Cambridge: Cambridge University Press.

   (1980). Psychological processes underlying pronominalization and non-pronominalization in children's connected discourse. In J. Kreiman & A. E. Ojeda (Eds.), *Papers from the Parasession on Pronouns and Anaphora* (pp. 231–250). Chicago: Chicago Linguistic Society.

   (1981). The grammatical marking of thematic structure in the development of language production. In W. Dutch (Ed.), *The Child's Construction of Language* (pp. 121–147). New York: Academic Press.

   (1983). Language acquisition as a problem solving process. *Papers and Reports from the Stanford Child Language Forum*, 22, 1–23.

(1987). Function and process in comparing language and cognition. In M. Hickmann (Ed.), *Social and Functional Approaches to Language and Thought* (pp. 185–202). Orlando, FL: Academic Press.

(1992). *Beyond Modularity: A Developmental Perspective on Cognitive Science*. Cambridge, MA: Bradford.

(1998). Development itself is the key to understanding developmental disorders. *Trends in Cognitive Sciences*, 2, 389–398.

Karmiloff-Smith, A., Grant, J., Berthoud, I., Davies, M., Howlin, P., & Udwin, O. (1997). Language and Williams syndrome: How intact is 'intact'? *Child Development*, 68, 246–262.

Karnopp, L. B. (2002). Phonology acquisition in Brazilian Sign Language. In G. Morgan & B. Woll (Eds.), *Directions in Sign Language Acquisition* (pp. 29–53). Amsterdam: John Benjamins.

Karzon, R. G. (1985). Discrimination of polysyllabic sequences by one-to-four-month-old infants. *Journal of Experimental Child Psychology*, 39, 326–342.

Kasari, C., Freeman, S., & Paparella, T. (2006). Joint attention and symbolic play in young children with autism: a randomized controlled intervention study. *Journal of Child Psychology and Psychiatry*, 47, 611–620.

Kaschak, M. P., Loney, R. A., & Borregine, K. L. (2006). Recent experience affects the strength of structural priming. *Cognition*, 99, B73–B82.

Katz, J. J. (1978). Effability and translation. In F. Guenthner & M. Guenthner-Reutter (Eds.), *Meaning and Translation: Philosophical and Linguistic Approaches* (pp. 191–234). London: Duckworth.

(1981). *Language and other Abstract Objects*. Totowa, NJ: Rowman & Littlefield.

Katz, N., Baker, E., & Macnamara, J. (1974) What's in a name? A study of how children learn common and proper names. *Child Development*, 45, 469–473.

Katzenberger, I. (1994). Cognitive, linguistic, and developmental factors in the narration of picture series. Unpublished doctoral dissertation (in Hebrew), Tel Aviv University.

Kedar, Y., Casasola, M., & Lust, B. (2006). Getting there faster: 18- and 24-month-old infants' use of function words to determine reference. *Child Development*, 77, 325–338.

Kegl, J., Senghas, A., & Coppola, M. (1999). Creation through contact: Sign language emergence and sign language change in Nicaragua. In M. DeGraff (Ed.), *Language Creation and Language Change: Creolization, Diachrony, and Development* (pp. 179–237). Cambridge, MA: MIT Press.

Kehoe, M., & Stoel-Gammon, C. (2001). Development of syllable structure in English-speaking children with particular reference to rhymes. *Journal of Child Language*, 28, 393–432.

Kehoe, M., Hilaire-Debove, G., Demuth, K., & Lléo, C. (2008). The structure of branching onsets and rising diphthongs: Evidence from the acquisition of French and Spanish. *Language Acquisition*, 15, 5–57.

Kelley, E., Paul, J.J., Fein, D., & Naigles, L.R. (2006). Residual language deficits in optimal outcome children with a history of autism. *Journal of Autism and Developmental Disorders*, 36, 807–828.

Kelly, M. (1996) The role of phonology in grammatical category assignment. In J. Morgan & K. Demuth (Eds.), *From Signal to Syntax. Bootstrapping from Speech to Grammar in Early Acquisition* (pp. 249–262). Hillsdale, NJ: Lawrence Erlbaum Associates.

Kelly, S.D. (2001). Broadening the units of analysis in communication: Speech and nonverbal behaviours in pragmatic comprehension. *Journal of Child Language*, 28, 325–349.

Kemp, C., Perfors, A., & Tennenbaum, J.B. (2007). Learning overhypotheses with hierarchical Bayesian models. *Developmental Science*, 10, 307–321.

Kempe, V., & MacWhinney, B. (1998). The acquisition of case marking by adult learners of Russian and German. *Studies in Second Language Acquisition*, 20, 543–587.

Kemple, K., Speranza, H., & Hazen, N. (1992). Cohesive discourse and peer acceptance: Longitudinal relationships in the preschool years. *Merill-Palmer Quarterly*, 38, 364–381.

Kendon, A. (1980). Gesticulation and speech: Two aspects of the process of utterance. In M.R. Key (Ed.), *Relationship of Verbal and Nonverbal Communication* (pp. 207–228). The Hague: Mouton.

Kernan, K.T. (1977). Semantic and expressive elaboration in children's narratives. In S.M. Ervin-Tripp & C. Mitchell-Kernan (Eds.), *Child Discourse* (pp. 91–102). New York: Academic Press.

Kidd, E.J. (2003). An investigation of children's sentence processing: A developmental perspective. Unpublished Doctoral Dissertation, La Trobe University.

Kidd, E.J., & Bavin, E.L. (2002). English-speaking children's comprehension of relative clauses: Evidence for general-cognitive and language-specific constraints on development. *Journal of Psycholinguistic Research*, 31, 599–617.

Kim, K.H., Relkin, N.R., Lee, K.M., & Hirsch, J. (1997). Distinct cortical areas associated with native and second languages. *Nature*, 388, 171–174.

Kintsch, W. (1970). Recognition memory in bilingual subjects. *Journal of Verbal Learning and Verbal Behavior*, 9, 405–409.

Kiparsky, P., & Menn, L. (1977). On the acquisition of phonology. In J. Macnamara (Ed.), *Language Learning and Thought* (pp. 47–78). New York: Academic Press.

Kippenhan, J., Olsen, R., Mervis, C., et al. (2005). Genetic contributions to human gyrification: Sulcal morphology in Williams syndrome. *Journal of Neuroscience*, 25, 7840–7846.

Kirk, C. (2008). Substitution errors in the production of word-initial and word-final consonant cluster. *Journal of Speech, Language, and Hearing Research*, 51, 35–48.

Kirk, C., & Demuth, K. (2005). Asymmetries in the acquisition of word-initial and word-final consonant clusters. *Journal of Child Language*, 32, 709–734.

(2006). Accounting for variability in 2-year-olds' production of coda consonants. *Language Learning and Development*, 2, 97–118.

Kirkham, N. Z., Slemmer, J. A., & Johnson, S. P. (2002). Visual statistical learning in infancy: Evidence for a domain general learning mechanism. *Cognition*, 83, B35–B42.

Kjelgaard, M. M., & Speer, S. R. (1999). Prosodic facilitation and interference in the resolution of temporary syntactic closure ambiguity. *Journal of Memory and Language* 40, 153–194.

Kjelgaard, M. M., & Tager-Flusberg, H. (2001). An investigation of language impairment in autism: Implications for genetic subgroups. *Language and Cognitive Processes*, 16, 287–308.

Klein, B., & Mervis, C. (1999). Cognitive strengths and weaknesses of 9- and 10-year-old children with Williams syndrome. *Developmental Neuropsychology*, 16, 177–196.

Klein-Tasman, B., & Mervis, C. (2003). Distinctive personality characteristics of 8-, 9-, and 10-year-old children with Williams syndrome. *Developmental Neuropsychology*, 23, 271–292.

Klin, A. (1992). Listening preferences in regard to speech in four children with developmental disabilities. *Journal of Child Psychology and Psychiatry*, 33, 763–769.

Kluender, K. R., Lotto, A. J., Holt, L. L., & Bloedel, S. L. (1998). Role of experience for language-specific functional mappings of vowel sounds. *Journal of the Acoustical Society of America*, 104, 3568–3582.

Knowlton, B. J., & Squire, L. R. (1993). The learning of categories: Parallel brain systems for item memory and category knowledge. *Science*, 262, 1747–1749.

Kohnert, K., & Bates, E. (2002). Balancing bilinguals II: Lexical comprehension and cognitive processing in children learning Spanish and English. *Journal of Speech, Language, and Hearing Research*, 45, 347–359.

Kohnert, K., Bates, E., & Hernandez, A. (1999). Balancing bilinguals: Lexical–semantic production and cognitive processing in children learning Spanish and English. *Journal of Speech, Language, and Hearing Research*, 42, 1400–1413.

Kooijman, V., Hagoort, P., & Cutler, A. (2005). Electrophysiological evidence for prelinguistic infants' word recognition in continuous speech. *Cognitive Brain Research*, 24, 109–116.

Köpcke, K.-M. (1998). The acquisition of plural marking in English and German revisited: Schemata vs. rules. *Journal of Child Language*, 25, 293–319.

Krämer, I. (1993). The licensing of subjects in early child language. *Papers on Case and Agreement II: MIT Working Papers in Linguistics*, 19, 197–212.

Kroll, J., & de Groot, A. M. B. (1997). Lexical and conceptual memory in the bilingual: Mapping form to meaning in two languages. In A. M. B. de Groot & J. Kroll (Eds.), *Tutorials in Bilingualism: Psycholinguistic Perspectives* (pp. 169–199). Mahwah, NJ: Lawrence Erlbaum Associates.

Kuhl, P. K. (1993). Innate predispositions and the effects of experience in speech perception: The native language magnet theory. In B. de Boysson-Bardies, S. de Schonen, P. Jusczyk, P. McNeilage & J. Morton (Eds.), *Developmental Neurocognition: Speech and Face Processing in the First Year of Life* (pp. 259–274). Dordrecht: Kluwer Academic Publisher.

(2004). Early language acquisition: cracking the speech code. *Nature Reviews Neuroscience*, 5, 831–843.

Kuhl, P. K., & Coffey-Corina, S. (2001, November). Language and the developing brain: Changes in ERPs as a function of linguistic experience. Paper presented at the meeting of the Cognitive Neuroscience Society, New York.

Kuhl, P. K., Coffey-Corina, S., Padden, D., & Dawson, G. (2005). Links between social and linguistic processing of speech in preschool children with autism: Behavioral and electrophysiological measures. *Developmental Science*, 8, F1–F12.

Kuhl, P. K., Stevens, E., Hiyashi, A., Deguchi, T., Kiritani, S., & Iverson, P. (2006). Infants show a facilitation effect for native language perception between 6 and 12 months. *Developmental Science*, 9, F1–F9.

Kuhl, P. K., Williams, K. A., Lacerda, F., Stevens, K. N., and Lindblom, B. (1992). Linguistic experience alters phonetic perception in infants by 6 months of age. *Science*, 225, 606–608.

Kujala, T., & Näätänen, R. (2001). The mismatch negativity in evaluating central auditory dysfunction in dyslexia. *Neuroscience and Behavioral Review*, 25, 535–543.

Kunene, E. (1979). The acquisition of SiSwati as a first language: A morphological study with special reference to noun prefixes, noun classes and some agreement markers. Unpublished doctoral dissertation, University of California, Los Angeles.

Kupersmitt, J. (2006). Temporality in texts: A crosslinguistic developmental study of form–function relations in narrative and expository discourse. Unpublished doctoral dissertation, Bar Ilan University, Israel.

Kushnerenko, E., Čeponiene, R., Balan, P., Fellman, V., & Näätänen, R. (2002). Maturation of the auditory change detection response in infants: A longitudinal ERP study. *NeuroReport*, 13, 1843–1848.

Kutas, M., & Federmeier, K. D. (2000). Electrophysiology reveals semantic memory use in language comprehension. *Trends in Cognitive Sciences*, 4, 463–470.

Kutas, M., & Van Petten, C. K. (1994). Psycholinguistics electrified: Event-related brain potential investigations. In M. A. Gernsbacher (Ed.), *Handbook of Psycholinguistics* (pp. 83–143). San Diego: Academic Press.

La Paro, K. M., Justice, L., Skibbe, L. E., & Pianta, R. C. (2004). Relations among maternal, child, and demographic factors and the persistence of preschool language impairment. *American Journal of Speech-Language Pathology*, 13, 291–303.

Labelle, M. (1990). Predication Wh-movement and the development of relative clauses. *Language Acquisition*, 1, 95–119.

Labov, W. (1972). The transformation of experience in narrative syntax. In W. Labov (Ed.), *Language in the Inner City* (pp. 355–396). Philadelphia: University of Pennsylvania Press.

Labov, W., & Waletzky, J. (1967). Narrative analysis: Oral versions of personal experience. In J. Helm (Ed.), *Essays on the Verbal and Visual Arts* (pp. 12–44). Seattle, WA: University of Washington Press.

Ladefoged, P. (1993). *A Course in Phonetics* (3rd edn). Fort Worth: Harcourt Brace Jovanovich College Publishers.

  (2006). *A Course in Phonetics* (5th edn). London: Thomson.

Lahey, M. (1990). Who shall be called language disordered? Some reflections and one perspective. *Journal of Speech and Hearing Disorders*, 55, 612–620.

Lai, C. S., Fisher, S., Hurst, J. A., Vargha-Khadem, F., & Monaco, A. (2001). A forkhead-domain gene is mutated in a severe speech and language disorder. *Nature*, 413, 519–523.

Laing, E., Butterworth, G., Ansari, D., *et al.* (2002). Atypical development of language and social communication in toddlers with Williams syndrome. *Developmental Science*, 5, 233–246.

Lambert, W. E. (1977). The effects of bilingualism on the individual: Cognitive and sociocultural consequences. In P. Hornby (Ed.), *Bilingualism. Psychological, Social, and Educational Implications* (pp. 15–28). New York: Academic Press.

Landa, R., & Garrett-Mayer, E. (2006). Development in infants with autism spectrum disorders: A prospective study. *Journal of Child Psychology & Psychiatry*, 47, 629–638.

Landau, B., & Gleitman, L. R. (1985). *Language and Experience: Evidence from the Blind Child*. Cambridge, MA: Harvard University Press.

Landau, B., Smith, L. B., & Jones, S. S. (1988). The importance of shape in early lexical learning. *Cognitive Development*, 3, 299–321.

Landry, S. H., & Loveland, K. A. (1989). The effect of social context on the functional communication skills of autistic children. *Journal of Autism and Developmental Disorders*, 19, 283–299.

Langacker, R. W. (1987). *Foundations of Cognitive Grammar: Vol. 1*. Stanford, CA: Stanford University Press.

  (2000). A dynamic usage-based model. In M. Barlow & S. Kemmer (Eds.), *Usage-Based Models of Language* (pp. 1–63). Stanford: CSLI.

Lanza, E. (1997). Language contact in bilingual two-year-olds and code-switching: Language encounters of a different kind? *International Journal of Bilingualism*, 1, 135–162.

Lasky, R. E., Syrdal-Lasky, A., & Klein, R. E. (1975). VOT discrimination by four- to six-and-a-half-month-old infants from Spanish environments. *Journal of Experimental Child Psychology*, 20, 215–225.

Laubitz, Z. (1987). Conjunction in children's discourse. *Papers and Reports on Child Language Development*, 26, 64–71.

Laws, G., & Bishop, D. V. (2003). A comparison of language abilities in adolescents with Down syndrome and children with specific language impairment. *Journal of Speech, Language and Hearing Research*, 46, 1324–1339.

Laws, G., & Bishop, D. (2004). Pragmatic language impairment and social deficits in Williams syndrome: A comparison with Down's syndrome and specific language impairment. *International Journal of Language and Communication Disorders*, 39, 45–64.

Leaper, C., Anderson, K. J., & Sanders, P. (1998). Moderators of gender effects on parents' talk to their children: A meta-analysis. *Developmental Psychology*, 34, 3–27.

Le Couteur, A., Rutter, M., & Lord, C. (1989). Autism Diagnostic Interview: A standardized investigator-based instrument. *Journal of Autism and Developmental Disorders*, 19, 363–387.

Lebeaux, D. (1990). The grammatical nature of the acquisition sequence: Adjoin-alpha and the formation of relative clauses. In L. Frazier & J. deVilliers (Eds.), *Language Processing and Language Acquisition* (pp. 13–82). Dordrecht: Kluwer.

Lecanuet, J.-P., Granier-Deferre, C., & Busnel, M. C. (1995). Human fetal auditory perception. In J.-P. Lecanuet & W. P. Fifer (Eds.), *Fetal Development: A Psychobiological Perspective* (pp. 239–262). Hillsdale, NJ: Lawrence Erlbaum Associates.

Lecavalier, L., Aman, M. G., Scahill, L., *et al.* (2006). Validity of the Autism Diagnostic Interview – Revised. *American Journal on Mental Retardation*, 111, 199–215.

Lee, A., Hobson, R. P., & Chiat, S. (1994). I, you, me, and autism: An experimental study. *Journal of Autism and Developmental Disorders*, 24(2), 155–176.

Lee, J., & Naigles, L. (2005). Input to verb learning in Mandarin Chinese: A role for syntactic bootstrapping. *Developmental Psychology*, 41, 529–540.

   (2008). Mandarin learners use syntactic bootstrapping in verb acquisition. *Cognition*, 106, 1028–1037.

Lee, K.-Y. (1991). On the first language acquisition of relative clauses in Korean: The universal structure of COMP. Unpublished doctoral dissertation, Cornell University, New York.

Lee, K.-Y., Lust, B., & Whitman, J. (1991). On functional categories in Korean: A study of the first language acquisition of Korean relative clauses. In E. -J. Baek (Ed.), *Papers from the Seventh International Conference on Korean Linguistics* (pp. 312–333). International Circle of Korean Linguists and Osaka University of Economics and Law.

Lee, L., & Canter, S. (1971). Developmental sentence scoring: A clinical procedure for estimating syntactic development in children's spontaneous speech. *Journal of Speech and Hearing Disorders*, 36, 315–340.

Lee, T. (1991). Linearity as a scope principle for Chinese: The evidence from first language acquisition. In D. Napoli & J. Kegl (Eds.), *Bridges Between*

Psychology and Linguistics (pp. 183–206). Hillsdale, NJ: Lawrence Erlbaum Associates.

(1997). Scope and distributivity in child Mandarin. *Proceedings of the 28th Annual Boston University Conference on Language Development* (pp. 183–206). Somerville, MA: Cascadilla Press.

Legate, J.A., & Yang, C.D. (2002). Empirical re-assessment of stimulus poverty arguments. *Linguistic Review*, 19, 151–163.

Lenneberg, E. (1967). *Biological Foundations of Language*. New York: Wiley.

Leonard, L. (1987). Is specific language impairment a useful construct? In S. Rosenberg (Ed.), *Advances in Applied Psycholinguistics: Vol. 1. Disorders of First-Language Development; Vol. 2. Reading, Writing, and Language Learning* (pp. 1–39). New York: Cambridge University Press.

(1989). Language learnability and specific language impairment in children. *Applied Psycholinguistics*, 10, 179–202.

(1998). *Children with Specific Language Impairment*. Cambridge, MA: The MIT Press.

Leonard, L., & Bortolini, U. (1998). Grammatical morphology and the role of weak syllables in the speech of Italian-speaking children with specific language impairment. *Journal of Speech, Language, and Hearing Research*, 41, 1363–1374.

Leonard, L., Wilcox, J., Fulmer, K., & Davis, A. (1978). Understanding indirect requests: An investigation of children's comprehension of pragmatic meanings. *Journal of Speech and Hearing Research*, 21, 528–537.

Leonard, L., Sabbadini, L., Leonard, J., & Volterra, V. (1987). Specific language impairment in children: A cross-linguistic study. *Brain and Language*, 32, 233–252.

Leonard, L., Eyer, J., Bedore, L., & Grela, B. (1997). Three accounts of the grammatical morpheme difficulties of English-speaking children with specific language impairment. *Journal of Speech, Language, and Hearing Research*, 40, 741–753.

Leonard, L., Hansson, K., Nettelbladt, U., & Deevy, P. (2005). Specific language impairment in children: A comparison of English and Swedish. *Language Acquisition*, 12, 219–246.

Leonard, L., & Deevy, P. (2006). Cognitive and linguistic issues in the study of children with specific language impairment. In M. Traxler & M.A. Gernsbacher (Eds.), *Handbook of Psycholinguistics* (2nd edn, pp. 1143–1171). London: Academic Press.

Leonard, L., Ellis Weismer, S., Miller, C., Francis, D., Tomblin, J.B., & Kail, R.V. (2007). Speed of processing, working memory, and language impairment in children. *Journal of Speech, Language, and Hearing Research*, 50, 408–428.

Leopold, W. (1939–1949). *Speech Development of a Bilingual Child: A Linguist's Record: Vols. 1–4*. Evanston, IL: Northwestern University Press.

Leppänen, P.H.T., Richardson, U., & Lyytinen, H. (1997). Brain ERPs to changes of speech segment durations in six-month-olds. *International Journal of Psychophysiology* 25, 55.

Leppänen, P. H. T, Pihko, E., Eklund, K. M. & Lyytinen, H. (1999). Cortical responses of infants with and without a genetic risk for dyslexia: II. Group effects. *NeuroReport*, 10, 969–973.

Leung, E., & Rheingold, H. (1981). Development of pointing as a social gesture *Developmental Psychology*, 17, 215–20.

Levelt, C. C., Schiller, N. O., & Levelt, W. J. (2000). The acquisition of syllable types. *Language Acquisition*, 8, 237–264.

Levin, B. (1993). *English Verb Classes and Alternations*. Chicago: University of Chicago Press.

Levinson, S. C. (2003). Language and mind: Let's get the issues straight! In D. Gentner & S. Goldin-Meadow (Eds.), *Language in Mind* (pp. 25–46). Cambridge, MA: MIT Press.

Levy, E., & Nelson, K. (1994). Words in discourse: A dialectical approach to the acquisition of meaning and use. *Journal of Child Language*, 21, 367–389.

Levy, Y., & Bechar, T. (2003). Cognitive, lexical and morpho-syntactic profiles of Israeli children with Williams syndrome. *Cortex*, 39, 255–271.

Lewis, B. A., & Thompson, L. A. (1992). A study of developmental speech and language disorders in twins. *Journal of Speech and Hearing Research*, 35, 1086–1094.

Lewis, C. (1997). Fathers and preschoolers. In M. Lamb (Ed.), *The Role of Fathers in Child Development* (pp. 121–142). New York: Wiley.

Li, C. N., & Thompson S. A. (1981). *Mandarin Chinese: A Functional Reference Grammar*. Berkeley, CA: University of California Press.

Li, P., & Shirai, Y. (2000). *The Acquisition of Lexical and Grammatical Aspect*. New York: Mouton de Gruyter.

Lidz, J., Gleitman, H., & Gleitman, L. (2003a). Understanding how input matters: Verb learning and the footprint of universal grammar. *Cognition*, 87, 151–178.

Lidz, J., Waxman, S., & Freedman, J. (2003b). What infants know about syntax but couldn't have learned: Experimental evidence for syntactic structure at 18 months. *Cognition*, 89, B65–B73.

Liebel, K., Behne, T., Carpenter, M. & Tomasello, M. (in press). Infants use shared experience to interpret pointing gestures. *Developmental Science*.

Lieven, E. V. M. (1994). Crosslinguistic and crosscultural aspects of language addressed to children. In C. Gallaway & B. J. Richards (Eds.), *Input and Interaction In Language Acquisition* (pp. 56–73). New York: Cambridge University Press.

  (1997). Variation in a crosslinguistic context. In D. I. Slobin (Ed.), *The Crosslinguistic Study of Language Acquisition: Vol. 5.* (pp. 199–263). Hillsdale, NJ: Lawrence Erlbaum Associates.

Lieven, E. V. M., & Tomasello, M. (2008). Children's first language acquisition from a usage-based perspective. In N. Ellis (Ed.), *Handbook of Cognitive Linguistics and Second Language Acquisition* (pp. 168–196). New York and London: Routledge.

Lieven, E. V. M., Pine, J. M., & Barnes, H. D. (1992). Individual differences in early vocabulary development: Redefining the referential–expressive distinction, *Journal of Child Language*, 19, 287–310.

Lieven, E. V. M., Pine, J. M., & Baldwin, G. (1997). Lexically-based learning and early grammatical development. *Journal of Child Language*, 24, 187–220.

Lieven, E. V. M., Behrens, H., Speares, J., & Tomasello, M. (2003). Early syntactic creativity: A usage based approach. *Journal of Child Language*, 30, 333–370.

Lightfoot, D. (1989). The child's trigger experience: Degree-0 learnability. *Behavioral and Brain Sciences*, 12, 321–334.

Liiva, A., & Cleave, P. (2005). Roles of initiation and responsiveness in access and participation for children with specific language impairment. *Journal of Speech, Language, and Hearing Research*, 48, 868–883.

Lillo-Martin, D. (1999). Modality effects and modularity in language acquisition: The acquisition of American Sign Language. In W. C. Ritchie & T. K. Bhatia (Eds.), *Handbook of Child Language Acquisition* (pp. 531–567). San Diego, CA: Academic Press.

Lillo-Martin, Diane (2008). Sign language acquisition studies: Past, present and future. In R. M. d. Quadros (Ed.), *Sign Languages: Spinning and unraveling the past, present and future. TISLR9, forty-five papers and three posters from the 9th Theoretical Issues in Sign Language Research Conference, Florianópolis, Brazil, December 2006* (pp. 244–263). Petrópolis, Brazil: Editora Arara Azul. www.editora-arara-azul.com.br/EstudosSurdos.php.

Lillo-Martin, D. & Quadros, R. M. D(2005). The acquisition of focus constructions in Amercian Sign Language and Língua de Sinais Brasileira. In A. Burgos, M. R. Clark-Cotton, & S. Ha (Eds.), *Proceedings of the 29th Boston Unverisity Conference on Language Development* (pp. 365–375). Somerville, MA: Cascadilla Press.

(2006). The position of early wh-elements in American Sign Language and Brazilian Sign Language. In K. Ud Deen, J. Nomura, B. Schulz & B. D. Schwartz (Eds.), *The Proceedings of the Inaugural Conference on Generative Approaches to Language Acquisition – North America, Honolulu, HI* (pp. 195–203). Cambridge, MA: MITWPL.

(in press). Focus constructions in American Sign Language and Língua de Sinais Brasileira. In J. Quer (Ed.), *Signs of the Time: Selected Papers from TISLR 2004* (pp 163–178). Hamburg: Signum Verlag.

Limber, J. (1973). The genesis of complex sentences. In T. Moore (Ed.), *Cognitive Development and the Acquisition of Language*. New York: Academic Press.

Lindner, K. (2003). The development of sentence interpretation strategies in monolingual German-learning children with and without specific language impairment. *Linguistics*, 41, 213–254.

Ling, R., & Yttri, B. (2006). Control, emancipation, and status: The mobile telephone in teens' parental and peer relationships. In R. Kraut, M. Brynn & S. Kiesler (Eds.), *Computers, Phones, and the Internet* (pp. 219–234). New York: Oxford University Press.

Lisker, L., & Abramson, A. S. (1967). Some effects of context on voice onset time in English stops. *Language and Speech*, 10, 1–28.

Lizskowski, U., Carpenter, M., Striano, T., & Tomasello, M. (2006). 12- and 18-month-olds point to provide information for others. *Journal of Cognition and Development*, 7, 173–187.

Lizskowski, U., Carpenter, M., & Tomasello, M. (2007). Pointing out new news, old news, and absent referents at 12 months of age. *Developmental Science*, 10, F1–F7.

Lleó, C. (1996). To spread or not to spread: different styles in the acquisition of Spanish phonology. In B. H. Bernhardt, J. G. Ingram & D. Ingram (Eds.), *Proceedings of the UBC International Conference on Phonological Acquisition* (pp. 215–228). Somerville, MA: Cascadilla Press.

   (2001). The interface of phonology and morphology: The emergence of the article in the early acquisition of Spanish and German. In J. Weissenborn & B. Höhle (Eds.), *Approaches to Bootstrapping: Phonological, Syntactic and Neurophysiological Aspects of Early Language Acquisition* (pp. 23–44). Amsterdam: John Benjamins.

   (2003). Prosodic licensing of codas. *Probus*, 15, 257–281.

   (2006). The acquisition of prosodic word structures in Spanish by monolingual and Spanish–German bilingual children. *Language and Speech*, 49, 207–231.

Lleó, C. & Demuth, K. (1999). Prosodic constraints on the emergence of grammatical morphemes: Crosslinguistic evidence from Germanic and Romance languages. In A. Greenhill, H. Littlefield & C. Tano (Eds.), *Proceedings of the 23rd Annual Boston University Conference on Language Development* (pp. 407–418). Somerville, MA: Cascadilla Press.

Lleó, C., & Prinz, M. (1996). Consonant clusters in child phonology and the directionality of syllable structure assignment. *Journal of Child Language*, 23, 31–56.

   (1997). Syllable structure parameters and the acquisition of affricates. In S. J. Hannahs & M. Young-Scholten (Eds.), *Focus on Phonological Acquisition*. Amsterdam: John Benjamins.

Lloyd, H., Paintin, K., & Botting, N. (2006). Performance of children with different types of communication impairment on the Clinical Evaluation of Language Fundamentals (CELF). *Child Language Teaching and Therapy*, 22, 47–67.

Lloyd, P. (1992). The role of clarification requests in children's communication of route directions by telephone. *Discourse Processes*, 15, 357–374.

Lloyd, P., Mann, S., & Peers, I. (1998). The growth of speaker and listener skills from five to eleven years. *First Language*, 18, 81–103.

Loban, W. (1976) *Language development: Kindergarten through Grade Twelve. Research Report No. 18.* Urbana, IL: National Council of Teachers of English.

Locke, J. L. (1983). *Phonological Acquisition and Change*. New York: Academic Press.

   (1994). Gradual emergence of developmental language disorders. *Journal of Speech & Hearing Research*, 37, 608–616.

Lord, C., & Paul, R. (1997). Language and communication in autism. In D. Cohen & F. Volkmar (Eds.), *Handbook of Autism and Pervasive Developmental Disorders* (pp. 460–483). New York: Wiley Press.

Lord, C., & Rutter, M. (1994). Autism and pervasive developmental disorders. In E. Taylor (Ed.), *Child and Adolescent Psychiatry: Modern approaches: Vol. 3.* (pp. 569–593). Oxford: Blackwell.

Lord, C., Risi, S., & Pickles, A. (2004a). Trajectory of language development in Autistic Spectrum Disorders. In M. Rice & S. Warren (Eds.), *Developmental Language Disorders: From Phenotypes to Etiologies* (pp. 7–29). Mahwah, NJ: Lawrence Erlbaum Associates.

Lord, C., Shulman, C., & DiLavore, P. (2004b). Regression and Word Loss in Autism Spectrum Disorder. *Journal of Child Psychology and Psychiatry*, 45, 936–955.

Lord, C., Risi, S., DiLavore, P., Shulman, C., Thurm, A., & Pickles, A. (2006). Autism from two to nine. *Archives of General Psychiatry*, 63(6), 694–701.

Lovaas, O. I. (1987). Behavioral treatment and normal educational and intellectual functioning in young autistic children. *Journal of Consulting and Clinical Psychology*, 55, 3–9.

Lucy, J. A. (1992). *Language Diversity and Thought*. Cambridge: Cambridge University Press.

Lust, B. (1977). Conjunction reduction in child language. *Journal of Child Language* 4, 257–297.

  (1981). On coordinating studies of coordination: Problems of method and theory in first language acquisition – a reply to Ardery. *Journal of Child Language*, 8, 457–470.

  (1994). Functional projection of CP and phrase structure parameterization: An argument for strong continuity. In B. Lust, M. Suñer & J. Whitman (Eds.), *Syntactic Theory and First Language Acquisition: Crosslinguistic Perspectives: Vol. 1. Heads Projections and Learnability* (pp. 85–118). Mahwah, NJ: Lawrence Erlbaum Associates.

  (2006). *Child Language: Acquisition and Growth*. Cambridge: Cambridge University Press.

Lust, B., & Chien, Y. C. (1984). The structure of coordination in first language acquisition of Mandarin Chinese: Evidence for a universal. *Cognition* 17, 49–83.

Lust, B., & Mervis, C. A. (1980). Coordination in the natural speech of young children. *Journal of Child Language*, 7, 279–304.

Lust, B., & Wakayama, T. K. (1979). The structure of coordination in young children's acquisition of Japanese. In F. R. Eckman & A. J. Hastings (Eds.), *Studies in First and Second Language Acquisition* (pp. 134–152). Rawley MA: Newbury House.

  (1981). Word order in Japanese first language acquisition. In P. Dale & D. Ingram (Eds.), *Child Language: An International Perspective* (pp. 73–90). Baltimore, MD: University Park Press.

Lust, B., Wakayama, T., Snyder, W., & Bergman, M. (1980). A study of natural speech of young Japanese children. Paper presented at Fifth Annual Boston University Conference on Child Language, Boston, MA.

Lust, B., Wakayama T., Snyder W., Mazuka, R., & Oshima, S. (1985). Configurational factors in Japanese anaphora: Evidence from acquisition. Paper presented at Linguistic Society of America, Seattle, WA.

Lust, B., Solan, L., Flynn, S., Cross, C., & Schuetz, E. (1986). Distinguishing bound and free anaphora. In B. Lust (Ed.), *Studies in the Acquisition of Anaphora: Vol. 1. Defining the Constraints* (pp. 245–77). Dordrecht: Reidel.

Lust, B,. Eisele, J., & Mazuka, R. (1992). The binding theory module: Evidence from first language acquisition for Principle C. *Language*, 68, 333–358.

Lust, B., Hermon, G., & Kornfilt, J. (Eds.). (1994). *Syntactic Theory and First Language Acquisition: Cross-Linguistic Perspectives: Vol. 2. Binding Dependencies and Learnability.* Mahwah, NJ: Lawrence Erlbaum Associates.

Lust, B., Bhatia, T., Gair J., Sharma, V. & Khare J. (1995). Children's acquisition of Hindi anaphora in 'jab' clauses: A parameter-setting paradox. In V. Gambhir (Ed.), *The Teaching and Acquisition of South Asian languages* (pp. 172–189). Philadelphia, PA: University of Pennsylvania Press.

Lust, B., Chien, Y. C., Flynn, S., & Krawiec, B. (in press). First language acquisition of coordination: The mud puddle study and beyond. In W. D. Lewis, S. Karimi, H. Harley & S. Farrar (Eds.), *Time and Again* (pp. 151–175). Amsterdam: John Benjamins.

Luyster, R., Richler, J., Risi, S., *et al.* (2005). Early regression in social communication in Autistic Spectrum Disorders: A CPEA study. *Developmental Neuropsychology*, 27, 311–336.

Luyster, R., Lopez, K., & Lord, C. (2007a). Characterizing communicative development in children referred for autism spectrum disorder using the MacArthur–Bates Communicative Development Inventory (CDI). *Journal of Child Language*, 34, 623–654.

Luyster, R., Qiu, S., Lopez, K., & Lord, C. (2007b). Predicting outcomes of children referred for autism using the MacArthur–Bates Communicative Development Inventory (CDI). *Journal of Speech, Language & Hearing Research*, 50, 667–681.

MacDonald, M. C., Pearlmutter, N. J., & Seidenberg, M. S. (1994). The lexical nature of syntactic ambiguity resolution. *Psychological Review*, 1001, 676–703.

Macken, M. A. (1978). Permitted complexity in phonological development: One child's acquisition of Spanish consonants. *Lingua*, 44, 219–253.

  (1979). Developmental reorganization of phonology: A hierarchy of basic units of acquisition. *Lingua*, 49, 11–49.

  (1980). Aspects of the acquisition of stop systems. In G. Yeni-Komshian, J. F. Kavanagh, & C. A. Ferguson (Eds.), *Child Phonology, I: Production.* New York: Academic Press.

Macken, M. A., & Ferguson, C. A. (1983). Cognitive aspects of phonological development: Model, evidence, and issues. In K. E. Nelson (Ed.), *Children's language: Vol. 4.* (pp. 256–282). Hillsdale, NJ: Lawrence Erlbaum Associates.

Macnamara, J. (1977). From sign to language. In J. Macnamara (Ed.), *Language Learning and Thought*. New York: Academic Press.

MacNeilage, P. F., & Davis, B. L. (1990). Acquisition of speech production: Frames, then content. In M. Jeannerod (Ed.), *Attention and Performance: Vol. 11. Motor Representation and Control* (pp. 453–476). Hillsdale, NJ: Lawrence Erlbaum Associates.

MacWhinney, B. (Ed.) (1999). *The Emergence of Language*. Mahwah, NJ: Lawrence Erlbaum Associates.

MacWhinney, B. (2000). *The CHILDES project: Tools for analyzing talk* (3rd edn.). Mahwah, NJ: Lawrence Erlbaum Associates.

(2004a). A multiple process solution to the logical problem of language acquisition. *Journal of Child Language*, 31, 883–914.

(2004b). New directions in the competition model. In D. I. Slobin & M. Tomasello (Eds.), *Beyond Nature–Nurture: Essays in Honor of Elizabeth Bates* (pp. 81–110). Mahwah, NJ: Lawrence Erlbaum Associates.

(2005). A unified model of language acquisition. In A. M. B. de Groot & J. F. Kroll (Eds.), *Handbook of Bilingualism: Psycholinguistic Approaches* (pp. 49–67). Oxford: Oxford University Press.

MacWhinney, B., & Bates, E. (1989). *The Cross-Linguistic Study of Sentence Processing*. New York: Cambridge University Press.

Maddieson, I. (2005). Consonant Inventories. In M. Haspelmath, M. S. Dryer, D. Gill & B. Comrie (Eds.), *The World Atlas of Language Structures* (pp. 10–14). Oxford: Oxford University Press.

Männel, C., & Friederici, A. D. (submitted). Pauses and intonational phrasing: ERP studies in 5-month-old German infants and adults. *Journal of Cognitive Neuroscience*.

Magnuson, J. S., Tanenhaus, M. K., Aslin, R. N., & Dahan, D. (2003). The time-course of spoken word learning and recognition: studies with artificial lexicons. *Journal of Experimental Psychology: General*, 132, 202–227.

Malone, M. J., & Guy, R. (1982). A comparison of mothers' and fathers' speech to their three-year-old sons. *Journal of Psycholinguistic Research*, 11, 599–608.

Mandel, D. R., Jusczyk, P. W., & Pisoni, D. B. (1995). Infants' recognition of the sound patterns of their own names. *Psychological Science*, 6, 315–318.

Mandel-Emer, D. (1997). Names as early lexical candidates: Helpful in language processing? Unpublished doctoral dissertation, State University of New York, Buffalo.

Mannle, S., & Tomasello, M. (1987). Fathers, siblings, and the bridge hypothesis. In K. E. Nelson & A. van Kleeck (Eds.), *Children's Language: Vol. 6.* (pp. 23–41). Hillsdale, NJ: Lawrence Erlbaum Associates.

Mannle, S., Barton, M., & Tomasello, M. (1991). Two-year-olds' conversations with their mothers and preschool-aged siblings. *First Language*, 12, 57–71.

Maratsos, M. (1974). How preschool children understand missing complement subjects. *Child Development*, 45, 700–706.

Maratsos, M., & Chalkley, M. A. (1980). The internal language of children's
syntax: The ontogenesis and representation of syntactic categories. In
K. Nelson (Ed.), *Children's Language: Vol. 2*. (pp. 127–214). New York:
Gardner Press.

Maratsos, M., Fox, D., Becker, J., & Chalkley, M. A. (1985). Semantic restrictions on children's passives. *Cognition*, 19, 167–191.

Marchman, V., Wulfeck, B., & Ellis Weismer, S. (1999). Morphological productivity in children with normal language and SLI: A study of the
English past tense. *Journal of Speech, Language, and Hearing Research*, 42,
206–219.

Marcus, G. F. (2000). Children's overregularization and its implications for
cognition. In P. Broeder & J. Murre (Eds.), *Models of Language Acquisition*
(pp. 154–176). Oxford: Oxford University Press.

    (2003). *The Algebraic Mind: Integrating Connectionism and Cognitive Science*.
Cambridge, MA: MIT Press.

Marcus, G. F., & Fisher, S. E. (2003). FOXP2 in focus: What can genes tell us
about speech and language? *TRENDS in Cognitive Sciences*, 7, 257–262.

Marcus, G. F., Pinker, S., Ullman, M., Hollander, M., Rosen, T. J., & Xu, F.
(1992). Overregularization in language acquisition. *Monographs of the
Society for Research in Child Development*, 57 (4, Serial No. 228).

Marcus, G. F., Vijayan, S., Rao, S. B., & Vishton, P. M. (1999). Rule learning by
seven-month-old infants. *Science* 283: 77–80.

Marean, G. C., Werner, L. A., & Kuhl, P. K. (1992). Vowel categorization by
very young infants. *American Psychological Association*, 28, 396–405.

Marentette, P. F., & Mayberry, R. I. (2000). Principles for an emerging
phonological system: A case study of early ASL acquisition. In C.
Chamberlain, J. P. Morford & R. I. Mayberry (Eds.), *Language Acquisition
by Eye* (pp. 71–90). Mahwah, NJ: Lawrence Erlbaum Associates.

Mareschal, D., Johnson, M., Sirios, S., Spratling, M., & Thomas, M. (2007).
Neuroconstructivism: How The Brain Constructs Cognition. Oxford: Oxford
University Press.

Markman, E. M. (1989). *Categorization and Naming in Children: Problems of
Induction*. Cambridge, MA: MIT/Bradford Books.

    (1991). The whole-object, taxonomic, and mutual exclusivity assump-
tions as initial constraints on word meaning. In S. Gelman & J. Byrnes
(Eds.), *Perspectives on Language and Thought: Interrelations in Development*
(pp. 72–106). Cambridge: Cambridge University Press.

Marshall, C., & van der Lely, H. (2006). A challenge to current models
of past tense inflection: The impact of phonotactics. *Cognition*, 100,
302–320.

Marslen-Wilson, W. D., & Welsh, A. (1978). Processing interactions and
lexical access during word recognition in continuous speech.
Cognitive Psychology, 10, 29–63

Marton, K., & Schwartz, R. (2003). Working memory capacity and language processes in children with specific language impairment. *Journal of Speech, Language, and Hearing Research*, 46, 1138–1153.

Martynova, O., Kirjavainen, J., & Cheour, M. (2003). Mismatch negativity and late discriminative negativity in sleeping human newborns. *Neuroscience Letters*, 340, 75–78.

Matthei, E. H. (1989). Crossing boundaries: More evidence for phonological constraints on early multi-word utterances. *Journal of Child Language*, 16, 41–54.

Matthews, D., Lieven, E. V., Theakston, A., & Tomasello, M. (2005). The role of frequency in the order of English word order. *Cognitive Development*, 20, 121–136.

(2006). The effect of perceptual availability and prior discourse on young children's use of referring expressions. *Applied Psycholinguistics*, 27, 403–422.

Matthiessen, M. I. M. (2002). Combining clauses into clause complexes: A multi-faceted view. In J. Bybee & M. Noonan (Eds.), *Complex Sentences in Grammar and Discourse: Essays in Honor of Sandra A. Thompson* (pp. 235–319). Amsterdam: John Benjamins.

Mattock, K., & Burnham, D. (2006) Chinese and English infants' tone perception: Evidence for perceptual reorganization. *Infancy*, 10, 241–265.

Mattys, S. L., & Jusczyk, P. W. (2001a). Do infants segment words or continuous recurring patterns? *Journal of Experimental Psychology: Human Perception and Performance*, 27, 644–655.

(2001b) Phonotactic cues for segmentation of fluent speech by infants. *Cognition*, 78, 91–121.

Mattys, S. L., Jusczyk, P. W., Luce, P. A., & Morgan, J. L. (1999). Phonotactic and prosodic effects on word segmentation in infants. *Cognitive Psychology*, 38, 465–494.

Mayberry, R. I. (1992). The cognitive development of deaf children: Recent insights. In S. Segalowitz & I. Rapin (Eds.), *Handbook of Neuropsychology: Vol. 7.* (pp. 51–68). Amsterdam: Elsevier.

Mayberry, R. I., Lock, E., & Kazmi, H. (2002). Linguistic ability and early language exposure. *Nature*, 417(6884), 38.

Maye, J., & Weiss, D. (2003). Statistical cues facilitate infants' discrimination of difficult phonetic contrasts. *Proceedings of the 27th Annual Boston University Conference on Language Development* (pp. 508–518). Somerville, MA: Cascadilla Press.

Maye, J., Weiss, D., & Aslin, R. N. (2008). Statistical phonetic learning in infants: Facilitation and feature generalization. *Developmental Science*, 11, 122–134.

Maye, J., Werker, J. F., & Gerken, L. (2002). Infant sensitivity to distributional information can affect phonetic discrimination. *Cognition*, 82, B101–B111.

Mayer, M. (1969). *Frog, Where Are You?* New York: Dial.

Mazuka, R. (1996). Can a grammatical parameter be set before the first word? Prosodic contributions to an early setting of a grammatical parameter. In J. L. Morgan & K. Demuth (Eds.), *Signal to Syntax: Bootstrapping from Speech to Grammar in Early Acquisition* (pp. 313–330). Hillsdale, NJ: Lawrence Erlbaum Associates.

(1998). *The Development of Language Processing Strategies: A Cross-linguistic Study between Japanese and English.* Hillsdale, NJ: Lawrence Erlbaum Associates.

Mazuka, R., Lust, B., Wakayama, T., & Snyder, W. (1986). Distinguishing effects of parameters in early syntax acquisition: A cross-linguistic study of Japanese and English. *Papers and Reports on Child Language Development*, 25, 73–82.

Mazuka, R., Lust, B., Wakayama, T., & Snyder, W. (1995). 'Null subject grammar' and phrase structure in early syntax acquisition: A cross-linguistic study of Japanese and English. In C. Jakubowicz. (Ed.), *Recherches Linguistiques de Vincennes*, 24, 55–81.

Mazurkewich, I., & White, L. (1984). The acquisition of the dative alternations: Unlearning overgeneralizations. *Cognition*, 16, 261–283.

McCann, J., & Peppe, S. (2003). Prosody in autism spectrum disorders: A critical review. *International Journal of Language & Communication Disorders*, 38, 325–350.

McCarthy, J. J., & Prince, A. (1994). The emergence of the unmarked: Optimality in prosodic morphology. *Proceedings of the North East Linguistics Society: Vol. 24.* (pp. 333–379).

McClelland, J. L., McNaughton, B. L., & O'Reilly, R. C. (1995). Why there are complementary learning systems in the hippocampus and neocortex. *Psychological Review*, 102, 419–517.

McClure, K., Pine, J., & Lieven, E. (2006). Investigating the abstractness of children's early knowledge of argument structure. *Journal of Child Language*, 33, 693–720.

McCune, L. (1992). First words: A dynamic systems view. In C. A. Ferguson, L. Menn, & C. Stoel-Gammon (Eds.), *Phonological Development: Models, Research, Implications* (pp. 312–336). Timonium, MD: York Press.

McCune, L., & Vihman, M. M. (2001). Early phonetic and lexical development. *Journal of Speech, Language and Hearing Research*, 44, 670–684.

McCutchen, D., &. Perfetti, C. (1982). Coherence and connectedness in the development of discourse production, *Text*, 2, 113–139.

McDonald, J. L. (1986). The development of sentence comprehension strategies in English and Dutch. *Journal of Experimental Child Psychology*, 41, 317–35.

(1997). Language acquisition: The acquisition of linguistic structure in normal and special populations. *Annual Review of Psychology*, 48, 215–41.

McDonald, J. L., & MacWhinney, B. (1989). Maximum likelihood models for sentence processing. In B. MacWhinney & E. Bates (Eds.), *The Crosslinguistic Study of Sentence Processing* (pp. 397–421). Cambridge: Cambridge University Press.

McGann, W., & Schwartz, A. (1988). Main character in children's narratives. *Linguistics*, 26, 423–445.

McGregor, K., Newman, R., Reilly, R., & Capone, N. (2002). Semantic representation and naming in children with specific language impairment. *Journal of Speech, Language, and Hearing Research*, 45, 998–1014.

McKee, C. (1996). On-line methods. In D. McDaniel, C. McKee, & H. S. Cairns (Eds.), *Methods for assessing children's syntax* (pp. 189–212). Cambridge, MA: MIT Press.

McMurray, B., & Aslin, R. N. (2005). Infants are sensitive to within-category variation in speech perception. *Cognition*, 95, B15–B26.

McNeill, D. (1992). *Hand in Mind*. Chicago: University of Chicago Press.

McTear, M. (1988). *Children's Conversation*. Oxford: Blackwell.

Mehler, J., & Christophe, A. (1995). Maturation and learning of language in the first year of life. In M. S. Gazzaniga (Ed.), *The Cognitive Neurosciences: A Handbook for the Field* (pp. 943–954). Cambridge, MA: MIT Press.

Mehler J., Jusczyk, P., Lambertz, G., Halsted, N., Bertoncini, J., & Amiel-Tison, C. (1988). A precursor of language acquisition in young infants. *Cognition*, 29, 143–178.

Meier, R. P. (1982). Icons, analogues, and morphemes: The acquisition of verb agreement in ASL. Unpublished PhD dissertation, University of California, San Diego.

(2006). The form of early signs: Explaining signing children's articulatory development. In B. Schick, M. Marschark & P. E. Spencer (Eds.), *Advances in the Sign Language Development of Deaf Children* (pp. 202–230). Oxford: Oxford University Press.

Meier, R. P., & Newport, E. L. (1990). Out of the hands of babes: On a possible sign advantage in language acquisition. *Language*, 66, 1–23.

Meier, R. P., & Willerman, R. (1995). Prelinguistic gesture in deaf and hearing infants. In K. Emmorey & J. Reilly (Eds.), *Language, Gesture, and Space* (pp. 391–410). Hillsdale, NJ: Lawrence Erlbaum Associates.

Meisel, J. (1994). *Bilingual First Language Acquisition: French and German Grammatical Development*. Amsterdam: John Benjamins.

Menn, L. (1971). Phonotactic rules in beginning speech. *Lingua*, 26, 225–251.

(1983). Development of articulatory, phonetic, and phonological capabilities. In B. Butterworth (Ed.), *Language Production: Vol. 2.* (pp. 3–49). London: Academic Press.

(2006). Saving the baby: Making sure that old data survive new theories. In R. Kager, J. Pater & W. Zonneveld (Eds.), *Constraints in Phonological Acquisition* (pp. 54–72). Cambridge: Cambridge University Press.

Menn, L., & Matthei, E. H. (1992). The 'two-lexicon' account of child phonology: Looking back, looking ahead. In C. A. Ferguson, L. Menn & C. Stoel-Gammon (Eds.), *Phonological Development: Models, Research, Implications* (pp. 211–247). Timonium, MD: York Press.

Meroni, L., Gualmini, A., & Crain, S. (2006). Everybody knows. In V. van Geenhoven (Ed.). *Acquisition meets Semantics* (pp. 89–114). Dordrecht: Kluwer.

Merritt, D., & Liles, B. (1987). Story grammar ability in children with and without language disorders: Story generation, story retelling, and story comprehension. *Journal of Speech and Hearing Research*, 30, 539–552.

Mervis, C., & Becerra, A. M. (2007). Language and communicative development in Williams syndrome. *Mental Retardation and Developmental Disabilities Research Reviews*, 13, 3–15.

Mervis, C. & Bertrand, J. (1997). Developmental relations between cognition and language: Evidence from Williams syndrome. In L. B. Adamson & M. A. Romski (Eds.), *Research on Communication and Language Disorders: Contributions to Theories of Language Development* (pp. 75–106). New York: Brookes.

Mervis, C., Morris, C., Bertrand, J., & Robinson, B. (1999). Williams syndrome: Findings from an integrated program of research. In H. Tager-Flusberg (Ed.), *Neurodevelopmental Disorders* (pp. 65–110). Cambridge, MA: MIT Press.

Mervis, C., Robinson, B., Bertrand, J., Morris, C., Klein-Tasman, B., & Armstrong, S. (2000). The Williams syndrome cognitive profile. *Brain and Cognition*, 44, 604–628.

Mervis, C., Morris, C., Klein-Tasman, B., *et al.* (2003). Attentional characteristics of infants and toddlers with Williams syndrome during triadic interactions. *Developmental Neuropsychology*, 23, 243–268.

Meuter, R. (2005). Language selection in bilinguals: Mechanisms and processes. In J. Kroll & A. M. B. de Groot (Eds.), *Handbook of Bilingualism: Psycholinguistic Approaches* (pp. 349–370). Oxford: Oxford University Press.

Meyer, M., Alter, K., Friederici, A. D., Lohmann, G., & von Cramon, D. Y. (2002). FMRI reveals brain regions mediating slow prosodic modulations in spoken sentences. *Human Brain Mapping*, 17, 73–88.

Meyer, M., Steinhauer, K., Alter, K., Friederici, A. D., & von Cramon, D. Y. (2004). Brain activity varies with modulation of dynamic pitch variance in sentence melody. *Brain and Language*, 89, 277–289.

Meyer-Lindenberg, A., Mervis, C., & Berman, K. (2006). Neural mechanisms in Williams syndrome: A unique window to genetic influences on cognition and behavior. *Nature Reviews Neuroscience*, 7, 380–393.

Millar, D. C., Light, J. C., & Schlosser, R. W. (2006). The impact of augmentative and alternative communication intervention on the speech production of individuals with developmental disabilities: A research review. *Journal of Speech, Language, and Hearing Research*, 49, 248–264.

Miller, C., Leonard, L., Kail, R., Zhang, X., Tomblin, J. B., & Francis, D. (2006). Response time in fourteen-year-olds with language impairment. *Journal of Speech, Language, and Hearing Research*, 49, 713–728.

Miller, J. F. (1988). The developmental asynchrony of language development in children with Down syndrome. In L. Nadel (Ed.), *The Psychobiology of Down Syndrome* (pp. 167–198). Cambridge, MA: MIT Press.

(1999). Profiles of language development in children with Down Syndrome. In J. F. Miller, M. Leddy & L. A. Leavitt (Eds.), *Improving the Communication of People with Down Syndrome* (pp. 11–39). Baltimore, MD: Brookes Publishing.

Miller, J. F., Chapman, R., & Bedrosian, J. (1978) Defining developmentally disabled subjects for research: The relationship between etiology, cognitive development, and language and communicative performance. *New Zealand Speech Therapists Journal*, 33, 2–19.

Miller, J. F., & Leddy, M. (1998). Down Syndrome: The impact of speech production on language development. In R. Paul (Ed.), *Exploring the Speech and Language Connection* (pp. 11–39). Baltimore, MD: Brookes Publishing.

Miller, J. F., Sedley, A., Miolo, G., Murray-Branch, J., & Rosin, M. (1992). Longitudinal investigation of vocabulary acquisition in children with Down Syndrome. *Symposium on Research in Child Language Disorders*. Madison, WI.

Miller J. L. & Eimas P. D. (1996). Internal structure of voicing categories in early infancy. *Perception and Psychophysics*, 58(8), 1157–1167.

Miller, P. J., & Sperry, L. L. (1988). Early talk about the past: Origins of conversational stories of personal experience. *Journal of Child Language*, 15, 293–315.

Mills, A. (1985) The acquisition of German. In D. I. Slobin (Ed.), *The Crosslinguistic Study of Language Acquisition, Vol. 1: The Data* (pp. 141–254). Hillsdale, NJ: Lawrence Erlbaum Associates.

Mills, D. L., Coffey-Corina, S., & Neville, H. J. (1997). Language comprehension and cerebral specialization from 13 to 20 months. *Developmental Neuropsychology*, 13, 397–445.

Minshew, N. J., Goldstein, G., Taylor, H. G., & Siegel, D. J. (1994). Academic achievement in high functioning autistic individuals. *Journal of Clinical and Experimental Neuropsychology*, 16, 261–270.

Minshew, N. J., Meyer, J., & Goldstein, G. (2002). Abstract reasoning in autism: A disassociation between concept formation and concept identification. *Neuropsychology*, 16, 327–334.

Mintz, T. H. (2002). Category induction from distributional cues in an artificial language. *Memory and Cognition*, 30, 678–686.

(2003). Frequent frames as a cue for grammatical categories in child directed speech. *Cognition*, 90, 91–117.

(2006). Finding the verbs: Distributional cues to categories available to young learners. In K. Hirsh-Pasek & R. M. Golinkoff (Eds.), *Action meets Words: How Children Learn Verbs* (pp. 31–63). New York: Oxford University Press.

Mitchell, R. E., & Karchmer, M. A. (2004). Chasing the mythical ten percent: Parental hearing status of deaf and hard of hearing students in the United States. *Sign Language Studies*, 4, 138–163.

Mitchell, S., Brian, J., Zwaigenbaum, L., et al. (2006). Early language and communication development of infants later diagnosed with autism spectrum disorder. *Journal of Developmental and Behavioral Pediatrics*, 27, S69.

Molloy, C., Keddache, M., & Martin, L. J. (2005). Evidence for linkage on 21q and 7q in a subset of autism characterized by developmental regression. *Molecular Psychiatry*, 10, 741–746.

Montanari, S., Yildirim, S., Andersen, E., & Narayanan, S. (2004). Reference marking in children's computer-directed speech. Available at www.isca-speech.org/archive/interspeech_2004/i04_1841.html/.

Montgomery, J. (1995). Sentence comprehension in children with specific language impairment: The role of phonological working memory. *Journal of Speech, Language, and Hearing Research*, 38, 187–199.

  (2000). Relation of working memory to off-line and real-time sentence processing in children with specific language impairment. *Applied Psycholinguistics*, 21, 117–148.

Moore, D., Oates, J., Hobson, R. & Goodwin, J. (2002). Cognitive and social factors in the development of infants with Down Syndrome. *Down Syndrome Research and Practice*, 8, 43–52.

Morford, J. P., & Mayberry, R. I. (2000). A reexamination of 'early exposure' and its implications for language acquisition by eye. In C. Chamberlain, J. P. Morford & R. I. Mayberry (Eds.), *Language Acquisition by Eye* (pp. 111–127). Mahwah, NJ: Lawrence Erlbaum Associates.

Morford, M., & Goldin-Meadow, S. (1992). Comprehension and production of gesture in combination with speech in one-word speakers. *Journal of Child Language*, 19, 559–580.

Morgan, G., & Woll, B. (2002). The development of complex sentences in British Sign Language. In G. Morgan & B. Woll (Eds.), *Directions in Sign Language Acquisition* (pp. 255–275). Amsterdam: John Benjamins.

Morgan, G., Barriere, I., & Woll, B. (2006). The influence of typology and modality on the acquisition of verb agreement morphology in British Sign Language. *First Language*, 26, 19–43.

Morgan, J. L., Meier, R. P., & Newport, E. L. (1989). Facilitating the acquisition of syntax with cross-sentential cues to phrase structure. *Journal of Memory and Language*, 28, 360–374.

Morgan, J. L., & Saffran, J. R. (1995) Emerging integration of sequential and suprasegmental information in preverbal speech segmentation. *Child Development*, 66, 911–936.

Morr, M. L., Shafer, V. L., Kreuzer, J. A. & Kurtzberg, D. (2002). Maturation of mismatch negativity in typically developing infants and preschool children. *Ear and Hearing*, 23, 118–136.

Morris, C. A. (2006). The dysmorphology, genetics, and natural history of Williams–Beuren syndrome. In C. A. Morris, H. W. Lenhoff & P. P. Wang (Eds.), *Williams–Beuren Syndrome: Research, Evaluation, and Treatment* (pp. 3–17). Baltimore, MD: Johns Hopkins University Press.

Morris, C. A., Demsey, S., Leonard, C., Dilts, C., & Blackburn, B. (1998). Natural history of Williams syndrome: Physical characteristics. *Journal of Pediatrics*, B, 318–326.

Morton, J. (2004). *Developmental Disorders: A Causal Modelling Approach*. Oxford: Blackwell.

Mowrer, D. E., & Burger, S. (1991). A comparative analysis of phonological acquisition of consonants in the speech of 21 2–6-year-old Xhosa- and English-speaking children. *Clinical Linguistics and Phonetics*, 3, 139–164.

Mueller, J. H., Pavur, E. J., & Yadrick, R. M. (1974). Verbal-discrimination learning as a function of encoding variability. *Bulletin of the Psychonomic Society*, 4, 41–43.

Murasugi K. (2000). An antisymmetry analysis of Japanese relative clauses. In A. Alexiadou, P. Law, A. Meinunger & C. Wilder (Eds.), *The Syntax of Relative Clauses* (pp. 231–263). Groningen: John Benjamins.

Murphy, C. M., & Messer, D. J. (1977). Mothers, infants and pointing: A study of gesture. In H. R. Schaffer (Ed.), *Studies in Mother–Infant Interaction* (pp. 325–354). New York: Academic Press.

Musolino, J. (1998). Universal Grammar and the acquisition of semantic knowledge. Unpublished doctoral dissertation, University of Maryland, College Park.

Myers-Scotton, C. (2001). The matrix language frame model: Developments and responses. In R. Jacobson (Ed.), *Codeswitching Worldwide II* (pp. 23–58). Berlin: Mouton de Gruyter.

Myklebust, H. (1952). Aphasia in children. *Journal of Exceptional Child*, 19, 9–14.

(1971). Childhood aphasia: An evolving concept. In L. E. Travis (Ed.), *Handbook of Speech Pathology and Audiology* (pp. 1181–1202). New York: Appleton-Century Crofts.

Näätänen, R., Tervaniemi, M., Sussman, E., Paavilainen, P., & Winkler, I. (2001). 'Primitive intelligence' in the auditory cortex, *Trends in Neurosciences*, 24, 283–288.

Nadel, L. (2003). Down's syndrome: A genetic disorder in biobehavioral perspective. *Genes, Brain and Behavior*, 2, 156–166.

Naigles, L. R. (1990). Children use syntax to learn verb meanings. *Journal of Child Language*, 17, 357–374.

(1996). The use of multiple frames in verb learning via syntactic bootstrapping. *Cognition*, 58, 221–251.

(2002). Form is easy, meaning is hard: Resolving a paradox in early child language. *Cognition*, 86, 157–199.

Naigles, L. R., & Hoff-Ginsberg, E. (1995). Input to verb learning: Evidence for the plausibility of syntactic bootstrapping. *Developmental Psychology*, 31, 827–837.

(1998). Why are some verbs learned before other verbs? Effects of input frequency and structure on children's early verb use. *Journal of Child Language*, 25, 95–120.

Naigles, L. R., & Kako, E. (1993). First contact in verb acquisition: Defining a role for syntax. *Child Development*, 64, 1665–1687.

Naigles, L. R., & Lehrer, N. (2002). Language-general and language-specific influences on children's acquisition of argument structure: A comparison of French and English. *Journal of Child Language*, 29, 545–566.

Naigles, L. R., & Swensen, L. (2007). Syntactic supports for word learning. In E. Hoff & M. Shatz (Eds.), *Blackwell Handbook of Language Development* (pp. 212–231). Malden, MA: Blackwell.

Naigles, L. R., Fowler, A., & Helm, A. (1992). Developmental changes in the construction of verb meanings. *Cognitive Development*, 7, 403–427.

Naigles, L. R., Gleitman, H., & Gleitman, L. R. (1993). Acquiring the components of verb meaning from syntactic evidence. In E. Dromi (Ed.), *Language and Cognition: A Developmental Perspective* (pp. 104–140). Norwood, NJ: Ablex.

Nakamura, K. (2001). The acquisition of polite language by Japanese children. In K. E. Nelson, A. Aksu-Koch, & C. Johnson (Eds.), *Children's Language: Vol. 10* (pp. 93–112). Mahwah, NJ: Lawrence Erlbaum Associates.

Namy, L. L., & Waxman, S. R. (1998). Words and gestures: Infants' interpretations of different forms of symbolic reference, *Child Development*, 69, 295–308.

Namy, L. L., Acredolo, L., & Goodwyn, S. (2000). Verbal labels and gestural routines in parental communication with young children. *Journal of Nonverbal Behavior*, 24, 63–80.

Narasimhan, B., Budwig, N., & Murty, L. (2005). Argument realization in Hindi caregiver–child discourse. *Journal of Pragmatics*, 37, 461–495.

Nation K., Marshall C., & Altmann G. (2003). Investigating individual differences in children's real-time sentence comprehension using language-mediated eye movements. *Journal of Experimental Child Psychology*, 86, 314–329.

Nation, K., Clarke, P., Wright, B., & Williams, C. (2006). Patterns of reading ability in children with Autism Spectrum Disorder. *Journal of Autism and Developmental Disorders*, 36, 911–919.

Nazzi, T. (2005). Use of phonetic specificity during the acquisition of new words: Differences between consonants and vowels. *Cognition*, 98(1), 13–30.

Nazzi, T., & Ramus, F. (2003) Perception and acquisition of linguistic rhythm by infants. *Speech Communication*, 41, 233–243.

Nazzi, T., Bertoncini, J., & Mehler, J. (1998) Language discrimination by newborns: Toward an understanding of the role of rhythm. *Journal of Experimental Psychology: Human Perception and Performance*, 24, 756–766.

Nazzi, T., Jusczyk, P. W., & Johnson, E. K. (2000) Language discrimination by English-learning 5-month-olds: Effects of rhythm and familiarity. *Journal of Memory and Language*, 43, 1–19.

Nazzi, T., Iakimova, G., Bertoncini, J., Frédonie, S., & Alcantara, C. (2006). Early segmentation of fluent speech by infants acquiring French: Emerging evidence for crosslinguistic differences. *Journal of Memory and Language*, 54, 283–299.

Neidle, C. (2002). ASL focus and question constructions. *Linguistic Variation Yearbook*, 2, 71–98.

Nelson, K. (Ed.). (1986). *Event Knowledge: Structure and Function in Development.* Hillsdale, NJ: Lawrence Erlbaum Associates.

Nelson, K. (1996). *Language in Cognitive Development.* New York: Cambridge University Press.

Nespor, M. (1990). On the rhythm parameter in phonology. In I. M. Roca (Ed.), *Logical Issues in Language Acquisition* (pp. 157–176). Dordrecht: Foris.

Nespor, M., & Vogel, I. (1986). *Prosodic Phonology.* Dordrecht: Foris.

Newbury, D. F., Bonora, E., Lamb, J. A., *et al.* (2002). FOXP2 is not a major susceptibility gene for autism or specific language impairment. *American Journal of Human Genetics*, 70, 1318–1327.

Newman, R., Ratner, N. B., Jusczyk, A. M., Jusczyk, P. W., & Dow, K. A. (2006). Infants' early ability to segment the conversational speech signal predicts later language development: A retrospective analysis. *Developmental Psychology*, 42, 643–655.

Newport, E. L. (1988). Constraints on learning and their role in language acquisition: Studies of the acquisition of American Sign Language. *Language Sciences*, 10, 147–172.

   (1990). Maturational constraints on language learning. *Cognitive Science*, 14, 11–28.

Newport, E. L., & Aslin, R. N. (2000). Innately constrained learning: Blending old and new approaches to language acquisition. In S. Howell, S. Fish & T. Keith-Lucas (Eds.), *Proceedings of the 24th Boston University Conference on Language Development* (pp. 1–21). Somerville, MA: Cascadilla Press.

   (2004). Learning at a distance I: Statistical learning of non-adjacent dependencies. *Cognitive Psychology*, 48, 127–162.

Newport, E. L., & Meier, R. P. (1985). The acquisition of American Sign Language. In D. I. Slobin (Ed.), *The Cross-Linguistic Study of Language Acquisition: Vol.1. The Data* (pp. 881–938). Hillsdale, NJ: Lawrence Erlbaum Associates.

Newport, E. L., Weiss, D. J., Wonnacott, E., & Aslin, R. N. (2004). *Statistical Learning in Speech: Syllables or Segments?* Paper presented at the 29th Annual Boston University Conference on Language Development.

Newsome, M., & Jusczyk P. (1995). Do infants use stress as a cue in segmenting fluent speech? In D. MacLaughlin & S. McEwen (Eds.), *19th Annual Boston University Conference on Language Development: Vol. 2.* Somerville, MA: Cascadilla Press.

Ngonyani, D. (1996). The morphosyntax of applicatives. Unpublished doctoral dissertation, UCLA.

Nicolopoulou, A. (1997). Children and narratives: Toward an interpretive and sociocultural approach. In M. Bamberg (Ed.), *Narrative Development: Six Approaches* (pp. 179–215). Mahwah, NJ: Lawrence Erlbaum Associates.

Nicolopoulou, A., & Richner, E. (2004). 'When your powers combine, I am Captain Planet': The developmental significance of individual- and group-authored stories by preschoolers. *Discourse Studies*, 6, 347–371.

Ninio, A. (1988). The roots of narrative: Discussing recent events with very young children. *Language Sciences I*, 10, 32–52.

(2005). Testing the role of semantic similarity in syntactic development. *Journal of Child Language*, 32, 35–61.

Ninio, A., & Snow, C. (1996). *Pragmatic Development*. Boulder, CO: Westview Press.

(1999). The development of pragmatics: Learning to use language appropriately. In W. Ritchie & T. Bhatia (Eds.), *Handbook of Child Language Acquisition* (pp. 347–383). San Diego, CA: Academic Press.

Nippold, M. (1998). *Later Language Development: The School-age and Adolescent Years* (2nd edn). Austin, TX: Pro-Ed.

Norbury, C. F. (2005). Barking up the wrong tree? Lexcial ambiguity resolution in children with language impairments and autistic spectrum disorders. *Journal of Experimental Child Psychology*, 90, 142–171.

Norbury, C. F., & Bishop, D. V. M. (2002). Inferential processing and story recall in children with communication problems: A comparison of specific language impairment, pragmatic language impairment, and high-functioning autism. *International Journal of Language and Communication Disorders*, 37, 227–251.

Norbury, C. F., Bishop, D. V. M., & Briscoe, J. (2001). Production of English finite verb morphology: A comparison of SLI and mild-moderate hearing impairment. *Journal of Speech Language and Hearing Research*, 44, 165–178.

Nunes, J., & Quadros, R. M. d. (2006). Duplication of wh-elements in Brazilian Sign Language. In C. Ussery & L. Bateman (Eds.), *Proceedings of the Thirty-Fifty Annual Meeting of the North East Linguistic Society, Vol. II* (pp. 463–478). Charleston, SC: Booksurge.

(in press). Phonetic realization of multiple copies in Brazilian Sign Language. In J. Quer (Ed.), *Signs of the Time: Selected Papers from TISLR 2004*. Hamburg: Signum Verlag.

Núñez del Prado, Z., Foley, C., Proman, R., & Lust, B. (1993). The significance of CP to the pro-drop parameter: An experimental study comparing Spanish and English. In E. Clark (Ed.), *The Proceedings of the 25th Annual Child Language Research Forum* (pp. 146–57). Stanford: Center for the Study of Language and Information.

Nuyorican Poetry. Available at www.nuyorican.org/AboutUs/AboutUs.html

O'Brien, E. K., Zhang, X. Y., Nishimura, C., Tomblin, J. B., & Murray, J. C. (2003). Association of specific language impairment (SLI) to the region of 7q31. *American Journal of Human Genetics*, 72, 1536–1543.

O'Grady, W. (Ed.). (1997). Passives. *Syntactic Development* (pp. 192–214). Chicago: University of Chicago Press.

O'Grady, W. (2005). *Syntactic Carpentry: An Emergentist Approach to Syntax*. Mahwah, NJ: Lawrence Erlbaum Associates.

O'Leary, C., & Crain, S. (1994). Negative polarity (a positive result) and positive polarity (a negative result). Paper presented at the 18th Annual Boston University Conference on Language Development.

O'Neill, D. (1996). Two-year-old children's sensitivity to a parent's knowledge state when making requests. *Child Development*, 67, 659–677.

O'Neill, D., Pearce, M., & Pick, J. (2004). Preschool children's narratives and performance on the Peabody Individualized Achievement Test-Revised: Evidence of a relation between early narrative and later mathematical ability. *First Language*, 24, 149–183.

Oberecker, R., & Friederici, A. D. (2006). Syntactic ERP components in 24-month-olds' sentence comprehension. *NeuroReport*, 17, 1017–1021.

Oberecker, R., Friedrich, M. & Friederici, A. D. (2005). Neural correlates of syntactic processing in two-year-olds. *Journal of Cognitive Neuroscience*, 17, 1667–1678.

Ochs, E., & Schieffelin, B. (1984). Language acquisition and socialization: Three developmental stories and their implications. In R. Shweder & R. LeVine (Eds.), *Culture Theory: Mind, Self, and Emotion* (pp. 276–320). Cambridge: Cambridge University Press [Reprinted in *Language, Culture, and Society: A Book of Readings*. B. Blount (Ed.) (pp. 470–512). Long Groue, IL: Waveland Press.]

Oehrle, R. T. (1976). The grammatical status of the English dative alternation. Unpublished doctoral dissertation, Massachusetts Institute of Technology.

Oetting, J., & Horohov, J. (1997). Past tense marking by children with and without specific language impairment. *Journal of Speech, Language, and Hearing Research*, 40, 62–74.

Ohala, D. K. (1996). Cluster reduction and constraints in acquisition. Unpublished doctoral dissertation, University of Arizona.

(1999). The influence of sonority on children's cluster reductions. *Journal of Communication Disorders*, 32, 397–422.

Oller, D. K. (1980). The emergence of the sounds of speech in infancy. In G. Yeni-Komshian, J. F. Kavanagh & C. A. Ferguson (Eds.), *Child Phonology, Vol. I: Production*. New York: Academic Press.

Oller, D. K., & Eilers, R. E. (2002). *Language and Literacy in Bilingual Children*. Clevedon: Multilingual Matters.

Oller, D. K., & Pearson, B. Z. (2002). Assessing the effects of bilingualism: A background. In D. K. Oller & R. E. Eilers (Eds.), *Language and Literacy in Bilingual Children* (pp. 3–21). Clevedon: Multilingual Matters.

Oller, D. K., Wieman, L. A., Doyle, W. J., & Ross, C. (1976). Infant babbling and speech. *Journal of Child Language*, 3, 1–11.

Oller, D. K., Eilers, R. E., Urbano, R., & Cobo-Lewis, A. B. (1997). Development of precursors to speech in infants exposed to two languages. *Journal of Child Language*, 27, 407–425.

Oller, D. K., Pearson, B. Z., & Cobo-Lewis, A. B. (2007). Profile effects in early bilingual language and literacy. *Applied Psycholinguistics*, 28 (2), 191–230.

Onishi, K. H., Chambers, K. E., & Fisher, C. (2002) Learning phonotactic constraints from brief auditory experience. *Cognition*, 83, B13–B23.

Oshima, S. & Lust, B. (1997). Remarks on anaphora in Japanese adverbial clauses. *Cornell Working Papers in Linguistics*, 15, 88–100.

Osterling, J., Dawson, G., & Munson, J. (2002). Early recognition of 1-year-old infants with autism spectrum disorder versus mental retardation. *Development and Psychopathology*, 14, 239–251.

Ota, M., (1999). Phonological theory and the acquisition of prosodic structure: Evidence from child Japanese. Unpublished doctoral dissertation, University of Georgetown.

(2006). Input frequency and word truncation in child Japanese: Structural and lexical effects. *Language and Speech*, 49, 261–295.

Otake, T., Hatano, G., Cutler, A., & Mehler, J. (1993). Mora or syllable? Speech segmentation in Japanese. *Journal of Memory and Language*, 32, 258–278.

Owen, A., & Goffman, L. (2007). Acoustic correlates of inflectional morphology in the speech of children with specific language impairment and their typically developing peers. *Clinical Linguistics and Phonetics*, 21, 501–522.

Owen, A., & Leonard, L. (2006). The production of finite and nonfinite complement clauses by children with specific language impairment and their typically developing peers. *Journal of Speech, Language, and Hearing Research*, 49, 548–571.

Ozcaliskan, S., & Goldin-Meadow, S. (2005a). Gesture is at the cutting edge of early language development, *Cognition*, 96, B01–113.

(2005b). Do parents lead their children by the hand? *Journal of Child Language*, 32, 481–505.

(2008). When gesture–speech combinations do and do not index linguistic change, *Language and Cognitive Processes*.

Ozcaliskan, S., Levine, S., & Goldin-Meadow, S. (2008). Gesturing with an injured brain: How gesture helps children with early brain injury learn linguistic constructions, under review.

Ozeki H., & Shirai Y. (2005). Semantic bias in the acquisition of relative clauses in Japanese. *Proceedings of 29th Boston University Conference on Language Development* (pp. 459–470). Somerville, MA: Cascadilla Press.

Packard, J. (1987). The first language acquisition of prenominal modification with *de* in Mandarin. *Journal of Chinese Linguistics*, 16, 31–54.

Padden, C. A. (1988). *Interaction of Morphology and Syntax in American Sign Language*. New York: Garland.

Pak, R., Sprott, R., & Escalera, E. (1996). Little words, big deal: The development of discourse and syntax. In D. I. Slobin, J. Gerhrdt, A. Kyratzis & J. Guo (Eds.), *Social Interaction, Context, and Language: Essays in Honor of Susan Ervin-Tripp* (pp. 287–308). Mahwah, NJ: Lawrence Erlbaum Associates.

Pallier, C., Dehaene, S., Poline, J. B., *et al.* (2003). Brain imaging of language plasticity in adopted adults: Can a second language replace the first? *Cerebral Cortex*, 13, 155–161.

Pan, B., & Snow, C. (1999). The development of conversational and discourse skills. In M. Barrett (Ed.), *The Development of Language* (pp. 229–249). Hove, East Sussex: Psychology Press.

Pannekamp, A., Toepel, U., Alter, K., Hahne, A., & Friederici, A. D. (2005). Prosody-driven sentence processing: An event-related brain potential study. *Journal of Cognitive Neuroscience*, 17, 407–421.

Pannekamp, A., Weber, C., & Friederici, A. D. (2006). Prosodic processing at sentence level in infants. *NeuroReport*, 17, 675–678.

Papafragou, A., & Tantalou, N. (2004). The computation of implicatures by young children. *First Language*, 12, 71–82.

Papafragou, A., Cassidy, K., & Gleitman, L. (2007). When we think about *thinking*: The acquisition of belief verbs. *Cognition*, 105, 125–165.

Papousek, M., Papousek, H., & Symmes, D. (1991), The meanings of melodies in motherese in tone and stress languages. *Infant Behavior and Development*, 14, 415–440.

Paradis, J. (2007). Bilingual children with specific language impairment: Theoretical and applied issues. *Applied Psycholinguistics*, 28, 551–564.

Paradis, J., & Crago, M., (2001). The morphosyntax of specific language impairment in French: An extended optional default account. *Language Acquisition*, 9, 269–300.

Paradis, J., & Genesee, F. (1996). Syntactic acquisition in bilingual children: Autonomous or interdependent? *Studies in Second Language Acquisition*, 18, 1–25.

Parker, J., & Gottman, J. (1989). Social and emotional development in a relational context. In T. Berndt & G. Ladd (Eds.), *Peer Relationships in Child Development* (pp. 95–131). New York: Wiley.

Pater, J. (1997). Minimal violation and phonological development. *Language Acquisition*, 6, 201–253.

Pater, J., & Barlow, J. A. (2003). Constraint conflict in cluster reduction. *Journal of Child Language*, 30, 487–526.

Pater, J., Stager, C. L., & Werker, J. F. (2004). The lexical acquisition of phonological contrasts. *Language*, 80, 361–379.

Paterson, K. B., Liversedge, S. P., Rowland, C., & Filik, R. (2003). Children's comprehension of sentences with focus particles. *Cognition*, 89, 263–294.

Paterson, S. (2000). The development of language and number understanding in Williams syndrome and Down's syndrome: Evidence from the infant and mature phenotypes. Unpublished doctoral thesis. University College London.

Paul, R. (1993). Outcomes of early expressive language delay. *Journal of Communication Disorders*, 15, 7–14.

  (2001). *Language Disorders from Infancy through Adolescence*. St Louis: Mosby.

Paul, R., Fischer, M. L., & Cohen, D. J. (1988). Brief report: Sentence comprehension strategies in children with autism and specific language disorders. *Journal of Autism and Developmental Disorders*, 18, 669–679.

Paul, R., Augustyn, A., Klin, A., & Volkmar, F.R. (2005). Perception and production of prosody by speakers with Autism Spectrum Disorders. *Journal of Autism and Developmental Disorders*, 35, 205–220.

Peal, E., & Lambert, W. (1962). The relation of bilingualism to intelligence. *Psychological Monographs*, 76, 1–23.

Pearson, B.Z. (2002). Narrative competence in bilingual school children in Miami. In D.K. Oller & R.E. Eilers (Eds.), *Language and Literacy in Bilingual Children* (pp. 135–174). Clevedon: Multilingual Matters.

(2007). Social factors in childhood bilingualism in the United States. *Applied Psycholinguistics*, 28, 399–410.

(2008). *Raising a Bilingual Child: A Step-by-Step Guide for Parents*. New York: Random House.

Pearson, B.Z., & Fernandez, S.C. (1994). Patterns of interaction in the lexical development in two languages of bilingual infants. *Language Learning*, 44, 617–653.

Pearson, B.Z., Fernandez, S.C., & Oller, D.K. (1993). Lexical development in bilingual infants and toddlers: Comparison to monolingual norms. *Language Learning*, 43, 93–120.

Pearson, B.Z., Fernandez, S.C., Lewedag, V., & Oller, D.K. (1997). Input factors in lexical learning of bilingual infants (ages 10 to 30 months). *Applied Psycholinguistics*, 18, 41–58.

Pegg J.E., & Werker J.F. (1997). Adult and infant perception of two English phones. *Journal of the Acoustical Society of America*, 102, 3742–3753.

Pelphrey, K.A., & Reznick, J.S. (2003). Working memory in infancy. In R. Kail (Ed.), *Advances in Child Development and Behavior: Vol. 31* (pp. 173–227). San Diego: Elsevier.

Pelzer, L., & Höhle, B. (2006) Processing of morphological markers as a cue to syntactic phrases by 10-month-old German-learning infants. In A. Belletti, E. Bennati, C. Chesi, E. DiDomenico & I. Ferrari (Eds.), *Language Acquisition and Development* (pp 427–439). Cambridge: Cambridge Scholars Press.

Peña, M., Maki, A., Kovacic, D., *et al.* (2003). Sounds and silence: An optical topography study of language recognition at birth. *Proceedings of the National Academy of Sciences*, 100, 11702–11705.

Peperkamp, S. (2003). Introduction. *Language and Speech*, 46, 87–113.

Peperkamp, S., le Calvez, R., Nadal, J., & Dupoux, E. (2006). The acquisition of allophonic rules: Statistical learning with linguistic constraints. *Cognition*, 101, B31–B41.

Perani, D., Paulesu, E., Sebastián-Gallés, N., *et al.* (1998). The bilingual brain: Proficiency and age of acquisition of the second language. *Brain*, 121, 1841–1852.

Perry, M., Church, R.B., & Goldin-Meadow, S. (1988). Transitional knowledge in the acquisition of concepts. *Cognitive Development*, 3, 359–400.

Peters, A.M. (1985). Language segmentation: Operating principles for the perception and analysis of language. In D.I. Slobin (Ed.), *The*

Crosslinguistic Study of Language Acquisition: Vol. 2. Theoretical Issues (pp. 1029–1067). Hillsdale, NJ: Lawrence Erlbaum Associates.

(1997). Language typology, prosody, and the acquisition of grammatical morphemes. In D.I. Slobin (Ed.), *The Crosslinguistic Study of Language Acquisition: Vol. 5. Expanding the Contexts* (pp. 135–197). Mahwah, NJ: Lawrence Erlbaum Associates.

Peterson, C., & Dodsworth, D. (1991). A longitudinal analysis of young children's cohesion and noun specification in narratives. *Journal of Child Language*, 18, 397–416.

Peterson, C., & McCabe, A. (1983). *Developmental Psycholinguistics: Three Ways of Looking at a Child's Narrative*. New York: Plenum.

(1988). The connective 'and' as discourse glue. *First Language*, 8, 9–28.

(1991). Linking connective use to connective macrostructure. In A. McCabe & C. Peterson, *Developing Narrative Structure* (pp. 29–54). Hillsdale, NJ: Lawrence Erlbaum Associates.

Petitto, L.A. (2000). The acquisition of natural signed languages: Lessons in the nature of human language and its biological foundations. In C. Chamberlain, J.P. Morford & R.I. Mayberry (Eds.), *Language Acquisition by Eye* (pp. 41–50). Mahwah, NJ: Lawrence Erlbaum Associates.

Petitto, L.A., & Marentette, P.F. (1991). Babbling in the Manual Mode: Evidence for the Ontogeny of Language. *Science*, 251, 1493–1496.

Petitto, L.A., Katerelos, M., Levy, B., Gauna, K., Tétrault, K., & Ferraro, V. (2001). Bilingual signed and spoken language acquisition from birth: Implications for the mechanisms underlying early bilingual language acquisition. *Journal of Child Language*, 28, 453–496.

Petronio, K. (1993). Clause structure in American Sign Language. Unpublished PhD dissertation, University of Washington.

Philip, W. (1995). Event quantification in the acquisition of universal quantification. Unpublished doctoral dissertation, University of Massachusetts, Amherst.

Philips, S. (1993). *The Invisible Culture: Communication in the Classroom and Community on the Warm Springs Indian Reservation* (Rev. edn). Prospect Heights, IL: Waveland Press.

Phillips, C. (1995). Syntax at age 2: Cross-linguistic differences. *MIT Working Papers in Linguistics*, 26, 325–382.

Phillips, C., Jarrold, C., Baddeley, A., Grant, J., & Karmiloff-Smith, A. (2004). Comprehension of spatial language terms in Williams syndrome: Evidence for an interaction between domains of strength and weakness. *Cortex*, 40, 85–110.

Piaget, J. (1952). *The Origins of Intelligence in Children*. (M. Cook, Trans.) New York: Norton.

(1974). *The Language and Thought of the Child*. (M. Gabain, Trans.) New York: New American Library (Original work published 1926).

Picton, T. W., Bentin, S., Berg, P., *et al.* (2000). Guidelines for using human event-related potentials to study cognition: Recording standards and publication criteria. *Psychophysiology*, 37, 127–152.

Pierce, A. (1989). On the emergence of syntax: a cross-linguistic study. Unpublished doctoral dissertation, MIT.

Pierrehumbert, J. (2003). Phonetic diversity, statistical learning, and acquisition of phonology. *Language and Speech*, 46, 115–154.

Pihko, E., Leppänen, P. H. T., Eklund, K. M., Cheour, M., Guttorm, T. K., & Lyytinen, H. (1999). Cortical responses of infants with and without a genetic risk for dyslexia: I. Age effects. *NeuroReport*, 10, 901–905.

Pike, K. L. (1945). *The Intonation of American English*. Ann Arbor: University of Michigan Press.

Pine, J. M., & Lieven, E. V. M. (1997). Slot and frame patterns and the development of the determiner category. *Applied Psycholinguistics*, 18, 123–138.

Pine, J. M., & Martindale, H. (1996). Syntactic categories in the speech of young children: The case of the determiner. *Journal of Child Language*, 23, 369–395.

Pine, K. J., Lufkin, N., & Messer, D. (2004). More gestures than answers: Children learning about balance. *Developmental Psychology*, 40, 1059–1067.

Pinker, S. (1984). *Language Learnability and Language Development*. Cambridge, MA: Harvard University Press.

   (1989). *Learnability and Cognition: The Acquisition of Verb-Argument Structure.* Cambridge, MA: Harvard University Press.

   (1990). Language Acquisition. In D. N. Osherson & H. Lasnik (Eds.), *An Invitation to Cognitive Science: Vol. 1.* (pp. 107–133). Cambridge, MA: MIT Press.

   (1991). Rules of language. *Science*, 253, 530–535.

   (1994). *The Language Instinct*. New York: HarperCollins.

   (1997). *How the Mind Works*. New York: W. W. Norton.

   (1999). *Words and Rules: The Ingredients of Language*. New York: HarperCollins.

Pinker, S., & Bloom, P. (1990). Natural language and natural selection. *Behavioral and Brain Sciences*, 13, 707–784.

Pinker, S., & Prince, A. (1991). Regular and irregular morphology and the psychological status of rules of grammar. *BLS*, 17, 230–251.

Pinker, S., Lebeaux, D., & Frost, L. (1987). Productivity and constraints in the acquisition of the passive. *Cognition*, 26, 195–267.

Pisoni, D. B., & Lively, S. E. (1995). Variability and invariance in speech perception: A new look at some old problems in perceptual learning. In W. Strange (Ed.), *Speech Perception and Linguistic Experience* (pp. 433–459). Timonium, MD: York Press.

Pizzuto, E., & Caselli, M. C. (1992). The acquisition of Italian morphology: Implications for models of language development. *Journal of Child Language*, 19, 491–558.

Place, K., & Becker, J. (1991). The influence of pragmatic competence on the likeability of grade-school children. *Discourse Processes*, 14, 227–241.

Plante, E., Swisher, L., Vance, R., & Rapcsak, S. (1991). MRI findings in boys with specific language impairment. *Brain and Language*, 41, 52–66.

Platzack, C. (1992). Functional categories and early Swedish. In J. Meisel (Ed.), *The Acquisition of Verb Placement: Functional Categories and V2 Phenomena in Language Acquisition*. Dordrecht: Kluwer.

Poeppel, D., & Wexler, K. (1993). The full competence hypothesis of clause structure in early German. *Language*, 69, 1–33.

Polka, L., & Bohn, O. S. (1996). A cross-language comparison of vowel perception in English-learning and German-learning infants. *Journal of the Acoustical Society of America*, 100, 577–592.

(2003). Asymmetries in vowel perception. *Speech Communication*, 41, 221–231.

Polka, L., & Sundara, M. (2003) Word segmentation in monolingual and bilingual infant learners of English and French. *Proceedings of the 15th International Congress of Phonetic Sciences*. Barcelona, Spain.

Polka, L., & Werker, J. F. (1994). Developmental changes in perception of nonnative vowel contrasts. *Journal of Experimental Psychology: Human Perception and Performance*, 20, 421–435.

Polka, L., Colantonio, C., & Sundara, M. (2001). A cross-language comparison of /d/-/th/ perception: Evidence for a new developmental pattern. *Journal of the Acoustical Society of America*, 109, 2190–2201.

Polka, L., Sundara, M., & Blue, S. (2002). The role of language experience in word segmentation: A comparison of English, French, and bilingual infants. Paper presented at the 143rd meeting of the Acoustical Society of America: Special session in memory of Peter Jusczyk, June, Pittsburgh, PA.

Pollock, J.-Y. (1989). Verb movement, UG and the structure of IP. *Linguistic Inquiry*, 20, 365–424.

Poplack, S. (1980). Sometimes I'll start a sentence in Spanish y termino en español: Toward a typology of code-switching. *Linguistics*, 18, 581–618.

Porter, M., & Coltheart, M. (2005). Cognitive heterogeneity in Williams syndrome. *Developmental Neuropsychology*, 27, 275–306.

Priestly, T. M. S. (1977). One idiosyncratic strategy in the acquisition of phonology. *Journal of Child Language*, 4, 45–66.

Prieto, P. (2006). The relevance of metrical information in early prosodic word acquisition: A comparison of Catalan and Spanish. *Language and Speech*, 49, 231–259.

Prince, A., & Smolensky, P. (2004). *Optimality Theory: Constraint Interaction in Generative Grammar*. Malden, MA: Blackwell.

Prizant, B. M., & Duchan, J. F. (1981). The functions of immediate echolalia in autistic children. *Journal of Speech & Hearing Disorders*, 46, 241–249.

Pullum, G. K., & Scholz, B. C. (2002). Empirical assessment of stimulus poverty arguments. *The Linguistic Review*, 19, 9–50.

Pye, C., & Quixtan Poz, P. (1988). Precocious passives (and antipassives) in Quiche Mayan. *Papers and Reports on Child Language Development*, 27, 71–80.

Pye, C., Pfeiler, B., de León, L., Brown, P., & Mateo, P. (2007), Roots or Edges? Explaining variation in children's early verb forms across five Mayan languages. In B. Pfeiler (Ed.), *Learning Indigenous Languages: Child Language Acquisition In Mesoamerica* (pp. 15–46), New York: Mouton de Gruyter.

Pynte, J., & Prieur, B, (1996). Prosodic breaks and attachment decisions in sentence parsing. *Language and Cognitive Processes*, 11, 165–192.

Quadros, R. M. d. (1997). *Educação de Surdos: A Aquisição da Linguagem*. Porto Alegre: Editora Artes Médicas.

Quadros, R. M. d., & Lillo-Martin, D. (2007). Gesture and the acquisition of verb agreement in sign languages. In H. Caunt-Nulton, S. Kulatilake & I.-H. Woo (Eds.), *Proceedings of the 31st Boston University Conference on Language Development: Vol. 2* (pp. 520–531). Somerville, MA: Cascadilla Press.

Quine, W. V. O. (1964). *Word and Object*. Boston: MIT Press.

Radford, A. (1986). Small children's small clauses. *Research Papers in Linguistics: Vol. 1* (pp. 1–44). University College of North Wales, Bangor.
  (1990). *Syntactic Theory and the Acquisition of English Syntax*. Oxford: Basil Blackwell.

Ramus, F. (2002). Language discrimination by newborns: Teasing apart phonotactic, rhythmic, and intonation cues. *Annual Review of Language Acquisition*, 2, 85–115.

Ramus, F., Nespor, M., & Mehler, J. (1999). Correlates of linguistic rhythm in the speech signal. *Cognition*, 73, 265–292.

Ramus, F., Hauser, M. D., Miller, C., Morris, D., & Mehler, J. (2000). Language discrimination by human newborns and by cotton-top tamarin monkeys. *Science*, 288, 349–351.

Ramus, F., Dupoux, E., & Mehler, J. (2003). The psychological reality of rhythm classes: Perceptual studies. *Proceedings of the 15th ICPhS*, Barcelona, Spain.

Ratner, N. B., & Pye, C. (1984). Higher pitch in BT is not universal: Acoustic evidence from Quiche Mayan. *Journal of Child Language*, 11, 515–522.

Ravid, D., & Berman, R. A. (2006). Information density in the development of spoken and written narratives in English and Hebrew. *Discourse Processes*, 41, 117–149.

Reber, A. S. (1967). Implicit learning of artificial grammars. *Journal of Verbal Learning and Verbal Behavior*, 6, 855–863.

Reber, A. S., & Lewis, S. (1977). Implicit learning: An analysis of the form and structure of a body of tacit knowledge. *Cognition*, 5, 333–361.

Reddy, V. (1999). Prelinguistic communication. In M. Barrett (Ed.), *The Development of Language* (pp. 25–50). Hove, East Sussex: Psychology Press.

Redington, M., Chater, N., & Finch, S. (1998). Distributional information: A powerful cue for acquiring syntactic categories. *Cognitive Science: A Multidisciplinary Journal*, 22, 425–469.

Redmond, S., & Rice, M. L. (1998). The socioemotional behaviors of children with SLI: Social adaptation or social deviance. *Journal of Speech, Language, and Hearing Research*, 41, 688–689.

Reeder, K., & Shapiro, J. (1996). A portrait of the literate apprentice. In K. Reeder, J. Shapiro, R. Watson & H. Goelman (Eds.), *Literate Apprenticeships: The Emergence of Language and Literacy in the Preschool Years* (pp. 119–133). Norwood, NJ: Ablex.

   (1997). Children's attributions of pragmatic intentions and early literacy. *Language Awareness*, 6, 17–31.

Reeder, K., Shapiro, J., Watson, R., & Goelman, H. (Eds.). (1996). *Literate Apprenticeships: The Emergence of Language and Literacy in the Preschool Years*. Norwood, NJ: Ablex.

Regier, T., & Gahl, S. (2004). Learning the unlearnable: The role of missing evidence. *Cognition*, 93, 147–155.

Reilly, J. S. (1992). How to tell a good story: The intersection of language and affect in children's narratives. *Journal of Narrative and Life History*, 2, 355–377.

   (2006). How faces come to serve grammar: The development of nonmanual morphology in American Sign Language. In B. Schick, M. Marschark & P. E. Spencer (Eds.), *Advances in the Sign Language Development of Deaf Children* (pp. 262–290). Oxford: Oxford University Press.

Rescorla, L., & Lee, E. C. (2000). Language impairments in young children. In T. L. Layton & L. Watson (Eds.), *Handbook of Early Language Impairment in Children: Nature* (pp. 1–38). New York: Delmar.

Rescorla, L., Dahlsgaard, K., & Roberts, J. (2000). Late-talking toddlers: MLU and IPSyn outcomes at 3;0 and 4;0. *Journal of Child Language*, 27, 643–664.

Restrepo, M. A., & Gutierrez-Clellan, V. (2001). Article use in Spanish-speaking children with SLI. *Journal of Child Language*, 28, 433–452.

Rice, M. (1993). Social consequences of specific language impairment. In H. Grimm & H. Skowronek (Eds.), *Language Acquisition Problems and Reading Disorders: Aspects of Diagnosis and Intervention* (pp. 111–128). New York: Walter de Gruyter.

   (2003). A unified model of specific and general language delay: Grammatical tense as a clinical marker of unexpected variation. In Y. Levy & J. Schaeffer (Eds.), *Language Competence Across Populations: Toward a Definition of SLI* (pp. 63–94). Mahwah, NJ: Lawrence Erlbaum Associates.

Rice, M., & Wexler, K. (1996a). Phenotypes of SLI: Extended optional infinitives. In M. Rice (Ed.), *Toward a Genetics of Language*. Mahwah, NJ: Lawrence Erlbaum Associates.

   (1996b). Toward tense as a clinical marker of specific language impairment in English-speaking children. *Journal of Speech, Language, and Hearing Research*, 39, 1239–1257.

Rice, M., Noll, K. R., & Grimm, H. (1997). An extended optional infinitive stage in German-speaking children with specific language impairment. *Language Acquisition*, 6, 255–295.

Rice, M., Wexler, K., & Hershberger, S. (1998). Tense over time: The longitudinal course of tense acquisition in children with specific language impairment. *Journal of Speech, Language, and Hearing Research*, 41, 1412–1431.

Rice, M., Warren, S. F., & Betz, S. K. (2005). Language symptoms of developmental language disorders: An overview of autism, Down syndrome, fragile X, specific language impairment, and Williams syndrome. *Applied Psycholinguistics*, 26, 7–27.

Richards, B. J. (1994), Child-directed speech and influences on language acquisition: Methodology and interpretation. In C. Gallaway & B. J. Richards (Eds.), *Input and Interaction in Language Acquisition* (pp. 74–106). Cambridge: Cambridge University Press.

Richler, J., Luyster, R., Risi, S., *et al.* (2006). Is there a regressive 'phenotype' of autism spectrum disorder associated with the measles–mumps–rubella vaccine? A CPEA study. *Journal of Autism & Developmental Disorders*, 36, 299–316.

Risi, S., Lord, C., Gotham, K., *et al.* (2006). Combining information from multiple sources in the diagnosis of autism spectrum disorders. *Journal of the American Academy of Child & Adolescent Psychiatry*, 45, 1094.

Rispoli, M. (1987). The acquisition of transitive and intransitive action verb categories in Japanese. *First Language*, 7, 183–200.

(1995). Missing arguments and the acquisition of predicate meanings. In M. Tomasello & W. E. Merriman (Eds.), *Beyond Names for Things: Young Children's Acquisition of Verbs* (pp. 331–352). Hillsdale, NJ: Lawrence Erlbaum Associates.

Rivera-Gaxiola, M., Silva-Pereyra, J., Garcia-Sierra, A., Klarman, L., & Kuhl, P. K. (2003). Event-related potentials to native and non-native speech contrasts in 7 and 11 month old American infants. Paper presented at the 10th annual meeting of the Cognitive Neuroscience Society, New York, April.

Rivera-Gaxiola, M., Silva-Pereyra, J., & Kuhl, P. K. (2005). Brain potentials to native and non-native speech contrasts in 7-and 11-month-old American infants. *Developmental Science*, 8, 162–172.

Rizzi, L. (1994). Some notes on linguistic theory and language development: The case of root infinitives. *Language Acquisition*, 3, 371–393.

Rizzo, J., & Stephens, M. (1981). Performance of children with normal and impaired oral language production on a set of auditory comprehension tests. *Journal of Speech and Hearing Disorders*, 46, 150–159.

Roach, P. (1982). On the distinction between 'stress-timed' and 'syllable-timed' languages. In D. Crystal (Ed.), *Linguistic Controversies* (pp. 73–79). London: Edward Arnold.

Roark, B., & Demuth, K. (2000). Prosodic constraints and the learner's environment: A corpus study. In S. C. Howell, S. A. Fish & T. Keith-Lucas (Eds.), *Proceedings of the 24th Annual Boston University Conference on Language Development* (pp. 597–608). Somerville, MA: Cascadilla Press.

Roberts, J., Hunter, L., Gravel, J., *et al.* (2004a). Otis media, hearing loss, and language learning: Controversies and current research. *Developmental and Behavioral Paediatrics*, 25, 1–13.

Roberts, J., Rice, M., & Tager-Flusberg, H. (2004b). Tense marking in children with autism. *Applied Psycholinguistics*, 25, 429–448.

Roberts, J., Long, S., Malkin, C., *et al.* (2005). A comparison of phonological skills of boys with Fragile X syndrome and Down syndrome. *Journal of Speech, Language and Hearing Research*, 48, 980–995.

Roberts, J., Price, J., & Malkin, C. (2007). Language and communication development in Down syndrome. *Mental Retardation and Developmental Disabilities Research Reviews*, 13, 26–35.

Roberts, S. S., & Leonard, L. (1997). Grammatical deficits in German and English: A cross-linguistic study of children with specific language impairment. *First Language*, 17, 131–150.

Rochat, P. (1998). Self-perception and action in infancy. *Experimental Brain Research*, 123, 102–109.

Rogers, D. (1978). Information about word-meaning in the speech of parents to young children. In R. N. Campbell & P. T. Smith (Eds.), *Recent Advances in the Psychology of Language* (pp. 187–198). London: Plenum.

Rohde, D. L. T., & Plaut, D. C. (1999). Language acquisition in the absence of explicit negative evidence: How important is starting small? *Cognition*, 72, 67–109.

Roizen, N. (2002). Down syndrome. In M. Batshaw (Ed.), *Children with Disabilities*, (5th edn., pp. 361–76). Baltimore, MD: Johns Hopkins University Press.

Roizen, N., & Patterson, D. (2003). Down syndrome. *Lancet*, 361, 1281–1289.

Rondal, J. (1980). Fathers' and mothers' speech in early language development. *Journal of Child Language*, 7, 353–369.

Rose, Y. (2000). Headedness and prosodic licensing in the L1 acquisition of phonology. Unpublished doctoral dissertation, McGill University.

Rose, Y., MacWhinney, B., Byrne, R., *et al.* (2006). Introducing Phon: A software solution for the study of phonological acquisition. In D. Bamman, T. Magnitskaia & C. Zaller (Eds.), *Proceedings of the 30th Annual Boston University Conference on Language Development* (pp. 489–500). Somerville, MA: Cascadilla Press.

Rosenbaum P. (1967). *The Grammar of English Predicate Complement Constructions*. Cambridge MA: MIT Press.

Rossen, M., Klima, E. S., Bellugi, U., Birhle, A., & Jones, W. (1996). Interaction between language and cognition: Evidence from Williams syndrome. In J. H. Beitchman, N. J. Cohen, M. M. Konstantareas & R. Tannock (Eds.), *Language, Learning and Behavior Disorders: Developmental, Biological, and Clinical Perspectives* (pp. 367–392). New York: Cambridge University Press.

Rowe, M. L., Ozcaliskan, S., & Goldin-Meadow, S. (2008). Learning words by hand: Gesture's role in predicting vocabulary growth. *First Language*, 28, 182–199.

Rowland, C., & Pine, J. M. (2000). Subject-auxiliary inversion errors and wh-question acquisition: 'What children do know?' *Journal of Child Language*, 27, 157–181.

Rubino, R., & Pine, J. M. (1998). Subject agreement in Brazilian Portuguese: What low error rates hide. *Journal of Child Language*, 25, 35–59.

Russell, B. (1948). *Human Knowledge: Its Scope and Limits*. London: Allen and Unwin.

Rutter, M., & Mawhood, L. (1991). The long-term psychosocial sequelae of specific developmental disorders of speech and language. In M. C. P. Rutter & P. Casaer (Eds.), *Biological Risk Factors For Psychosocial Disorders* (pp. 233–259). Cambridge: Cambridge University Press.

Sachs, J. (1983). Talking about the there and then: The emergence of displaced reference in parent–child discourse. *Children's Language: Vol. 4* (pp. 1–48). New York: Gardner Press.

Saffran, J. R. (2002). Constraints on statistical language learning. *Journal of Memory and Language*, 47, 172–196.

  (2003). Statistical language learning: Mechanisms and constraints. *Current Directions in Psychological Science*, 12, 110–114.

Saffran, J. R., & Griepontrog, G. J. (2001). Absolute pitch in infant auditory learning: Evidence for developmental reorganization. *Developmental Psychology*, 37, 74–85.

Saffran, J. R., & Thiessen, E. D. (2003). Pattern induction by infant language learners. *Developmental Psychology*, 39, 484–494.

Saffran, J. R., Aslin, R. N., & Newport, E. L. (1996a). Statistical learning by 8-month-old infants. *Science*, 274, 1926–1928.

Saffran, J. R., Newport, E. L., & Aslin, R. N. (1996b). Word segmentation: The role of distributional cues. *Journal of Memory and Language*, 35, 606–621.

Saffran, J. R., Newport, E. L., Aslin, R. N., Tunick, R. A., & Barrueco, S. (1997). Incidental language learning: Listening (and learning) out of the corner of your ear. *Psychological Science*, 8, 101–105.

Saffran, J. R., Reeck, K., Niebuhr, A., & Wilson, D. (2005). Changing the tune: The structure of the input affects infants' use of absolute and relative pitch. *Developmental Science*, 8, 1–7.

Saffran, J. R., Werker, J. F., & Werner, L. (2006). The infant's auditory world: Hearing, speech, and the beginnings of language. In D. Kuhn & R. Siegler (Eds.), *Handbook of Child Psychology: Vol. 2. Cognition, Perception, and Language* (6th edn, pp. 58–108). New York: John Wiley.

Sag, I., & Wasow, T. (1999). *Syntactic Theory: A Formal Introduction*. Stanford: CSLI.

Samter, W. (2003). Friendship interaction skills across the life span. In J. Greene & P. Burleson (Eds.), *Handbook of Communication and Social Interaction Skills* (pp. 637–684). Mahwah, NJ: Lawrence Erlbaum Associates.

Samuelson, L. K. (2002). Statistical regularities in vocabulary guide language acquisition in connectionist models and 15–20-month-olds. *Developmental Psychology*, 38, 1016–1037.

Sánchez-Casas, R., & García-Alba, J. E. (2005). The representation of cognate and non-cognate words in bilingual memory: Can cognate status be characterized as a special kind of morphological relation? In J. Kroll & A. M. B. de Groot (Eds.), *Handbook of Bilingualism: Psycholinguistic Approaches* (pp. 226–250). Oxford: Oxford University Press.

Sandbank, A. (2004). Writing narrative texts: A developmental and cross-linguistic study, Unpublished doctoral dissertation, Tel Aviv University.

Sandler, W. & Lillo-Martin, D. (2006). *Sign Language and Linguistic Universals*. Cambridge: Cambridge University Press.

Sano, T. (1995). Roots in language acquisition: A comparative study of Japanese and European languages. Unpublished doctoral dissertation, UCLA.

Sano, T., & Hyams, N. (1994). Agreement, finiteness, and development of null arguments. In Gonzalez, M. (Ed.), *The Proceedings to NELS 24* (pp. 543–558). Amherst, MA: GLSA Publications.

Santelmann, L., & Jusczyk, P. W. (1998) Sensitivity to discontinuous dependencies in language learners: evidence for limitations in processing space. *Cognition*, 69, 105–134.

Sasse, H.-J. (1993). Syntaktische Phänomene in den Sprachen der Welt I: Syntaktische Kategorien und Relationen [Syntactic phenomena in the world's languages I: categories and relations]. In J. Jakobs (Ed.), *Syntax* (pp. 646–686). New York: Mouton de Gruyter.

Savage, C., Lieven, E., Theakston, A., & Tomasello, M. (2003). Testing the abstractness of children's linguistic representations: Lexical and structural priming of syntactic constructions in young children. *Developmental Science*, 6, 557–567.

Savage, C., Lieven, E., Theakston, A., & Tomasello, M. (2006). Structural priming as implicit learning in language acquisition. *Language, Learning and Development*, 2, 27–49.

Savage-Rumbaugh, E. S., Murphy, J., Sevcik, R. A., Brakke, K. E., Williams, S. L., & Rumbaugh, D. M. (1993). *Language Comprehension in Ape and Child*. Monographs of the Society for Research in Child Development, 58, Nos. 3–4.

Scarr, S., & McCartney, K. (1983). How people make their own environments: A theory of genotype greater than environment effects. *Child Development*, 54, 424–435.

Schafer, A. J. (1997). Prosodic parsing: The role of prosody in sentence comprehension. Unpublished doctoral dissertation, Amherst, MA: University of Massachusetts.

Schafer, G., & Punkett, K. (1998). Rapid word learning by fifteen-month-olds under tightly controlled conditions. *Child Development*, 69, 309–320.

Schellenberg, G. D., Dawson, G., Sung, Y. J., *et al.* (2006). Evidence for multiple loci from a genome scan of autism kindreds. *Molecular Psychiatry*, 11, 1049–1060.

Schick, B. S. (2002). The expression of grammatical relations by deaf toddlers learning ASL. In G. Morgan & B. Woll (Eds.), *Directions in Sign Language Acquisition* (pp. 143–158). Amsterdam: John Benjamins.

Schieffelin, B. (1985). The acquisition of Kaluli. In D. I. Slobin (Ed.), *The Crosslinguistic Study of Language Acquisition: Vol. 1. The Data* (pp. 525–594). Hillsdale, NJ: Lawrence Erlbaum Associates.

Schieffelin, B., & Ochs, E. (Eds.). (1986). *Language Socialization across Cultures.* New York: Cambridge University Press.

Schieffelin, B., & Ochs, E. (1996). The microgenesis of competence: Methodology in language socialization. In D. Slobin, J. Gerhardt, A. Kyratzis & J. Guo (Eds.), *Social Interaction, Social Ccontext, and Language: Essays in Honor of Susan Ervin-Tripp* (pp. 251–263). Mahwah, NJ: Lawrence Erlbaum Associates.

Schnitzer, M., & Krasinski, E. (1994). The development of segmental phonological production in a bilingual child. *Journal of Child Language*, 21, 585–622.

(1996). The development of segmental phonological production in a bilingual child: A contrasting second case. *Journal of Child Language*, 23, 547–571.

Schuele, C. M., & Dykes, J. (2005). Complex syntax acquisition: A longitudinal case study of a child with specific language impairment. *Clinical Linguistics and Phonetics*, 19, 295–318.

Schulz, L. E., & Gopnik, A. (2004). Causal learning across domains. *Developmental Psychology*, 40, 162–176.

Scobbie, J., Gibbon, F., Hardcastle, W., & Fletcher, P. (2000). Covert contrast as a stage in the acquisition of phonetics and phonology. In M. Broe & J. Pierrehumbert (Eds.), *Papers in Laboratory Phonology: Vol 5. Acquisition and the Lexicon* (pp. 194–207). Cambridge: Cambridge University Press.

Scott, C. (1984). Adverbial connectivity in conversations of children aged 6–12. *Journal of Child Language*, 11, 423–452.

(1988). Spoken and written syntax. In M. A. Nippold (Ed.), *Later Language Development: Ages 9 through 19* (pp. 45–95). San Diego, CA: College Hill Press.

Scott, C., & Windsor, J. (2000). General language performance measures in spoken and written narrative and expository discourse of school-age children with language learning disabilities. *Journal of Speech, Language, and Hearing Research*, 43, 324–339.

Sebastián, E., & Slobin, D. I. (1994). Development of linguistic forms: Spanish. In R. A. Berman & D. I. Slobin (Eds.), *Relating Events in Narrative: A Crosslinguistic Developmental Study* (pp. 239–284). Hillsdale, NJ: Lawrence Erlbaum Associates.

Sebastián-Gallés, N., & Bosch, L. (2005). Phonology and bilingualism. In J. Kroll & A. M. B. de Groot (Eds.), *Handbook of Bilingualism: Psycholinguistic Approaches* (pp. 68–87). Oxford: Oxford University Press.

Sedivy, J., Demuth, K., Chunyo, G., & Freeman, S. (2000). Incremental referentiality-based language processing in young children: Evidence from eye movement monitoring. In S. C. Howell, S. A. Fish & T. Keith-Lucas, (Eds.) *Proceedings of the 24th Annual Boston University Conference on Language Development* (pp. 684–695). Somerville, MA: Cascadilla Press.

Seidl, A. (2007). Infants' use and weighting of prosodic cues in clause segmentation. *Journal of Memory and Language*, 57, 24–48.

Sekerina, I., & Brooks, P. (2007). Eye movements during spoken word recognition in Russian children, *Journal of Experimental Child Psychology*, 98, 20–45.

Sekerina, I., Stromswold, K., & Hestvik, A. (2004). How do adults and children process referentially ambiguous pronouns? *Journal of Child Language*, 31, 123–152.

Sekerina, I., Fernandéz, E. M., & Clahsen, H. (2008). *Developmental Psycholinguistics. On-Line methods in Children's Language Processing.* Amsterdam: John Benjamins.

Selkirk, E. O. (1984). *Phonology and Syntax: The Relation between Sound and Structure.* Cambridge, MA: MIT Press.

  (1996). The prosodic structure of function words. In J. L. Morgan & K. Demuth (Eds.), *Signal to Syntax: Bootstrapping from Speech to Grammar in Early Acquisition* (pp. 187–213). Mahwah, NJ: Lawrence Erlbaum Associates.

Semel, E., & Rosner, S. (2003). *Understanding Williams Syndrome.* Malwah, NJ: Lawrence Erlbaum Associates.

Senghas, A. (2003). Intergenerational influence and ontogenetic development in the emergence of spatial grammar in Nicaraguan Sign Language. *Cognitive Development*, 18, 511–531.

Senghas, A., & Coppola, M. (2001). Children creating language: How Nicaraguan Sign Language acquired a spatial grammar. *Psychological Science*, 12, 323–328.

Senghas, A., Kita, S., & Özyürek, A. (2004). Children creating core properties of language: Evidence from an emerging sign language in Nicaragua. *Science*, 305, 1779–1782.

Serratrice, L. (2005). The role of discourse pragmatics in the acquisition of subjects in Italian. *Applied Psycholinguistics*, 26, 437–462.

Seuss, Dr (1965). *Fox in Socks.* New York: Beginner Books.

Shady, M. (1996). Infants' sensitivity to function morphemes. Unpublished doctoral dissertation, The State University of New York, Buffalo.

Shafer, V. L., Shucard, D. W., Shucard, J. L., & Gerken L. A. (1998). An electrophysiological study of infants' sensitivity to the sound patterns of English speech. *Journal of Speech, Language, and Hearing Research*, 41, 874–886.

Shalinsky, M., Kovelman, I., Berens, M., & Petitto, L. A. (2006, Oct.). Near-infrared spectroscopy: Shedding light on the neural signature of bilingualism. Poster presented at the Society for Neuroscience Annual Meeting, Atlanta, GA.

Shapiro, L. R., & Hudson, J. A. (1991). Tell me a make-believe story: Coherence and cohesion in young children's picture elicited narratives. *Developmental Psychology*, 27, 960–974.

Shatz, M. (1978). Children's comprehension of their mothers' question directives. *Journal of Child Language*, 5, 39–46.

   (1982). On mechanisms of language acquisition: Can features of the communicative environment account for development? In E. Wanner & L. R. Gleitman (Eds.), *Language Acquisition: The State of the Art* (pp. 102–127). New York: Cambridge University Press.

Shatz, M., & Gelman, R. (1973). The development of communication skills: Modifications in the speech of young children as a function of listener. *Monographs of the Society for Research in Child Development*, 38, Serial No. 152.

Sheinkopf, S., Mundy, P., Oller, D. K., & Steffens, M. (2000). Vocal atypicalities of preverbal autistic children. *Journal of Autism and Developmental Disorders*, 30(4), 345–354.

Shi, R., & Lepage, M. (in press). The effect of functional morphemes on word segmentation in preverbal infants. *Developmental Science*.

Shi, R., Morgan, J., & Allopenna, P. (1998). Phonological and acoustic bases for earliest grammatical category assignment: A crosslinguistic perspective. *Journal of Child Language*, 25, 169–201.

Shi, R., Werker, J. F., & Morgan, J. (1999). Newborn infants' sensitivity to perceptual cues to lexical and grammatical words. *Cognition*, 72, B11–B21.

Shi, R., Cutler, A., Werker, J., & Cruickshank, M. (2006a). Frequency and form as determinants of functor sensitivity in English-acquiring infants. *Journal of the Acoustical Society of America*, 119, EL61–EL67.

Shi, R., Marquis, A., & Gauthier, B. (2006b). Segmentation and representation of function words in preverbal French-learning infants. In D. Bamman, T. Magnitskaia & C. Zaller (Eds.), *BUCLD 30: Proceedings of the 30th Annual Boston University Conference on Language Development: Vol. 2*. Somerville: Cascadilla Press.

Shi, R., Werker, J. F., & Cutler, A. (2006c) Recognition and representation of function words in English-learning infants. *Infancy*, 10, 187–198.

Shimpi, P., Gámez, P., Huttenlocher, J., & Vasilyeva, M. (2007). Syntactic priming in 3- and 4-year-old children: Evidence for abstract representations of transitive and dative forms. *Developmental Psychology*, 43, 1334–1346.

Shirai, Y., Slobin, D. I., & Weist, R. E. (1998). Introduction: The acquisition of tense-aspect morphology. *First Language*, 18(54), 245–254.

Shriberg, L., Paul, R., McSweeny, J., Klin, A., Cohen, D. J., & Volkmar, F. (2001). Speech and prosody characteristics of adolescents and adults with high-functioning autism and Asperger syndrome. *Journal of Speech, Language & Hearing Research*, 44, 1097–1115.

Sigman, M., & Capps, L. (1997). *Children with Autism*. Cambridge, MA: Harvard University Press.

Silliman, E., & Wilkinson, L. (1991). *Communicating for Learning: Classroom Observation and Collaboration*. Gaithersburg, MD: Aspen.

Silva, P. A. (1987). Epidemiology, longitudinal course and some associated factors: An update. In W. Yule & M. Rutter (Eds.), *Language Development and Disorders* (pp. 1–15). Oxford: Blackwell Scientific Publications Ltd.

Silva, P. A., Williams, S., & McGee, R. (1987). A longitudinal study of children with developmental language delay at age three: Later intelligence, reading and behaviour problems. *Developmental Medicine and Child Neurology*, 29, 630–640.

Silva-Pereyra, J., Rivera-Gaxiola, M., & Kuhl, P. K. (2005). An event-related brain potential study of sentence comprehension in preschoolers: Semantic and morphosyntactic processing. *Cognitive Brain Research*, 23, 247–258.

Singer-Harris, N., Bellugi, U., Bates, E., Jones, W., & Rossen, M. (1997). Contrasting profiles of language development in children with Williams and Down syndromes. *Developmental Neuropsychology*, 13, 345–370.

Singh, L. (2008). Effects of high and low variability on infant word recognition. *Cognition*, 106, 833–870.

Singh, L., Morgan, J., & White, K. (2004). Preference and processing: The role of speech affect in early speech spoken word recognition. *Journal of Memory and Language*, 51, 173–189.

Skarabela, B. (2006). The role of social cognition in early syntax: The case of joint attention in argument realization in child Inuktitut. Unpublished doctoral dissertation, Boston University, Boston, MA.

SLI Consortium. (2002). A genomewide scan identifies two novel loci involved in specific language impairment. *American Journal of Human Genetics*, 70, 384–398.

  (2004). Highly significant linkage to the SLI1 locus in an expanded sample of individuals affected by specific language impairment. *American Journal of Human Genetics*, 74, 1225–1238.

Slobin, D. I. (1973). Cognitive prerequisites for the development of grammar. In C. A. Ferguson & D. I. Slobin (Eds.), *Studies of Child Language Development* (pp. 175–208). New York: Holt, Rinehart and Winston.

  (1982). Universal and particular in the acquisition of language. In E. Wanner & L. R. Gleitman, (Eds.). *Language Acquisition: The State of the Art* (pp. 128–170). Cambridge: Cambridge University Press.

  (1985a). *The Crosslinguistic Study of Language Acquisition: Vol. 1. The Data.* Hillsdale, NJ: Lawrence Erlbaum Associates.

  (1985b). *The Crosslinguistic Study of Language Acquisition: Vol. 2. Theoretical Issues.* Hillsdale, NJ: Lawrence Erlbaum Associates.

  (1985c). Crosslinguistic evidence for the language-making capacity. In D. I. Slobin (Ed.), *The Crosslinguistic Study of Language Acquisition: Vol. 2. Theoretical Issues* (pp. 1157–1249). Hillsdale, NJ: Lawrence Erlbaum Associates.

Slobin, D. I. (1988). The development of clause-chaining in Turkish child language. In S. Koç (Ed.), *Studies on Turkish linguistics* (pp. 27–54). Ankara: Middle East Technical University.

Slobin, D. I. (Ed.). (1992). *The Crosslinguistic Study of Language Acquisition: Vol. 3.* Hillsdale, NJ: Lawrence Erlbaum Associates.

Slobin, D. I. (1996). From 'thought and language' to 'thinking for speaking'. In J. J. Gumperz & S. C. Levinson (Eds.), *Rethinking Linguistic Relativity* (pp. 70–96). Cambridge: Cambridge University Press.

Slobin, D. I. (Ed.). (1997a). *The Crosslinguistic Study of Language Acquisition: Vol. 4.* Mahwah, NJ: Lawrence Erlbaum Associates.

(Ed.). (1997b). *The Crosslinguistic Study of Language Acquisition: Vol. 5. Expanding the Contexts.* Mahwah, NJ: Lawrence Erlbaum Associates.

Slobin, D. I. (1997c). The origins of grammaticizable notions: Beyond the individual mind. In D. I. Slobin (Ed.), *The Crosslinguistic Study of Language Acquisition: Vol. 5. Expanding the Contexts* (pp. 265–323). Mahwah, NJ: Lawrence Erlbaum Associates.

(1997d). The universal, the typological, and the particular in acquisition. In D. I. Slobin (Ed.), *The Crosslinguistic Study of Language Acquisition: Vol. 5. Expanding the Contexts* (pp. 1–39). Mahwah, NJ: Lawrence Erlbaum Associates.

(2001). Form-function relations: How do children find out what they are? In M. Bowerman & S. C. Levinson (Ed.), *Language Acquisition and Conceptual Development* (pp. 406–449). Cambridge: Cambridge University Press.

(2004). The many ways to search for a frog: Linguistic typology and the expression of motion events. In S. Strömqvist & L. Verhoeven (Eds.), *Relating Events in Narrative: Typological and Contextual Perspectives* (pp. 219–257). Mahwah, NJ: Lawrence Erlbaum Associates.

Smith, L. B. (1999). Children's noun learning: How general learning processes make specialized learning mechanisms. In B. MacWhinney, (Ed.) *The Emergence of Language* (pp. 277–303). Mahwah, NJ: Lawrence Erlbaum Associates.

(2005). Emerging idea about categories. In L. Gershkoff-Stowe & D. H. Rakison (Eds.), *Building Object Categories in Developmental Time* (pp. 159–173). Mahwah, NJ: Lawrence Erlbaum Associates.

Smith, L. B., Jones, S. S., Landau, B., Gershkoff-Stowe, L., & Samuelson, L. K. (2002). Object learning provides on-the-job training for attention. *Psychological Science*, 13, 13–19.

Smith, N. V. (1973). *The Acquisition of Phonology: A Case Study.* Cambridge: Cambridge University Press.

Smoczyńska, M. (1985). The acquisition of Polish. In D. I. Slobin (Ed.), *The Crosslinguistic Study of Language Acquisition: Vol. 1. The Data* (pp. 595–686). Hillsdale, NJ: Lawrence Erlbaum Associates.

Smolensky, P. (1996). On the comprehension/production dilemma in child language. *Linguistic Inquiry*, 27, 720–731.

Snedeker, J., & Gleitman, L. (2004). Why is it hard to label our concepts? In D. G. Hall & S. R. Waxman (Eds.), *Weaving a Lexicon* (pp. 603–636). Cambridge, MA: MIT Press.

Snedeker, J., & Thothathiri, M. (2008). What Lurks Beneath: Syntactic Priming During Language Comprehension in Preschoolers (and Adults). In I. Sekerina, E. Fernández & H. Clahsen (Eds.), *Developmental Psycholinguistics: On-Line Methods in Children's Language Processing* (pp. 137–167), Amsterdam: Benjamins.

Snedeker, J., & Trueswell, J. C. (2003). Using Prosody to Avoid Ambiguity: Effects of Speaker Awareness and Referential Context, *Journal of Memory and Language*, 48, 103–130.

(2004). The developing constraints on parsing decisions: The role of lexical-biases and referential scenes in child and adult sentence processing. *Cognitive Psychology*, 49, 238–299.

Snedeker, J., & Yuan, S. (2008). The role of prosodic and lexical constraints in parsing in young children (and adults). *Journal of Memory and Language*, 58, 574–608.

Snow, C. (1994). What is so hard about learning to read? A pragmatic analysis. In J. Duchan, L. Hewitt & R. Sonnenmeier (Eds.), *Pragmatics: From Theory to Practice* (pp. 164–184). Englewood Cliffs, NJ: Prentice-Hall.

Snow, C., & Blum-Kulka, S. (2002). From home to school: School-age children talking with adults. In S. Blum-Kulka & C. Snow (Eds.), *Talking to Adults: The Contribution of Multi-party Discourse to Language Acquisition* (pp. 327–341). Mahwah, NJ: Lawrence Erlbaum Associates.

Snow, C., & Ferguson, C. A. (1977). *Talking to Children: Language Input and Acquisition*. New York: Cambridge University Press.

Snow, C., Perlmann, R., Gleason, J. B., & Hooshyar, N. (1990). Developmental perspectives on politeness: Sources of children's knowledge. *Journal of Pragmatics*, 14, 289–305.

Snow, C., Porche, M., Tabors, P., & Harris, S. R. (2007). *Is Literacy Enough?* Baltimore: Paul H. Brookes.

Snyder, W., & Lillo-Martin, D. (in press). Language acquisition and the principles and parameters framework. In P. Hogan (Ed.), *Cambridge Encyclopedia of the Language Sciences*. Cambridge: Cambridge University Press.

Snyder, W., & Stromswold, K. (1997). The structure and acquisition of English dative constructions. *Linguistic Inquiry*, 28, 281–317.

Sobel, D. M., & Kirkham, N. Z. (2007). Bayes nets and babies: Infants' developing statistical reasoning and their representation of causal knowledge. *Developmental Science*, 10, 298–306.

Sobel, D. M., Tenenbaum, J. B., & Gopnik, A. (2004). Children's causal inferences from indirect evidence: Backwards blocking and Bayesian reasoning in preschoolers. *Cognitive Science*, 28, 303–333.

Soderstrom, M., White, K. S., Conwell, E., & Morgan, J. L. (2007). Receptive grammatical knowledge of familiar content words and inflection in 16-month-olds. *Infancy*, 12, 1–29.

Solin, D. (1989). The systematic misrepresentation of bilingual crossed-aphasia data and its consequences. *Brain and Language*, 36, 92–116.

Somashekar, S. (1999). Developmental trends in the acquisition of relative clauses: Cross-linguistic experimental study of Tulu. Unpublished doctoral dissertation, Cornell University, New York.

Song, H., & Fisher, C. (2004). *Syntactic priming in 3-year-old children*. Paper presented at the 29th Annual Boston University Conference on Language Development, Boston, MA.

  (2005). Who's 'she'? Discourse prominence influences preschoolers' comprehension of pronouns. *Journal of Memory and Language*, 52, 29–57.

Song, J. Y., & Demuth, K. (in press). Compensatory vowel lengthening for omitted coda consonants: A phonetic investigation of children's early prosodic representations. *Language and Speech*.

Song, J. Y., Sundara, M. & Demuth, K. (in submission). Effects of phonology on children's production of English 3rd person singular -*s*.

Spelke, E. S. (1979). Perceiving bimodally specified events in infancy. *Developmental Psychology*. 15, 626–636.

Spelke, E. S., & Kinzler, K. D. (2007). Core knowledge. *Developmental Science*, 10, 89–96.

Spelke, E. S., & Newport, E. (1998). Nativism, empiricism, and the development of knowledge. In W. Damon & R. Lerner (Eds.), *Handbook of Child Psychology: Vol. 1. Theoretical Models of Human Development* (5th edn, pp. 275–340). New York: John Wiley.

Spinath, F. M., Price, T. S., Dale, P. S., & Plomin, R. (2004). The genetic and environmental origins of language disability and ability. *Child Development*, 75, 445–454.

Squire, L. R., & Kandel, E. R. (1999). *Memory: From Mind to Molecules*. New York: Henry Holt.

Stadler, M. A. (1992). Statistical structure and implicit serial learning. *Journal of Experimental Psychology: Learning, Memory, and Cognition*, 18, 318–327.

  (1995). Role of attention in implicit learning. *Journal of Experimental Psychology: Learning, Memory, and Cognition*, 21, 674–685.

Stager, C. L., & Werker, J. F. (1997). Infants listen for more phonetic detail in speech perception than in word learning tasks. *Nature*, 388, 381–382.

Stark, R., & Tallal, P. (1981). Selection of children with specific language deficits. *Journal of Speech and Hearing Disorders*, 46, 114–122.

  (1988). *Language, Speech, and Reading Disorders in Children*. Boston: Little, Brown and Co.

Stark, R., Bernstein, L., Condino, R., Bender, M., Tallal, P., & Catts, H. (1984). Four-year follow-up study of language impaired children. *Annals of Dyslexia*, 34, 49–68.

Stefanini, S., Caselli, M., & Volterra, V. (2007). Spoken and gestural production in a naming task by young children with Down syndrome. *Brain and Language*, 101, 208–221.

Steinhauer, K., Alter, K., & Friederici, A. D. (1999). Brain potentials indicate immediate use of prosodic cues in natural speech processing. *Nature Neuroscience*, 2, 191–196.

Stemberger, J. P., & Bernhardt, B. H. (1997). Phonological constraints and morphological development. In E. Hughes, M. Hughes & A. Greenhill (Eds.), *Proceedings of the 21st Annual Boston University Conference on Language Development* (pp. 602–614). Somerville, MA: Cascadilla Press.

Sternberg S. (1998). Discovering mental processing stages: The method of additive factors. In D. Scarborough and S. Sternberg (Eds.) *An invitation to cognitive science: methods, models, and conceptual issue* (pp. 703–863). Cambridge, MA: MIT Press.

Stevenson, J., Richman, N., & Graham, P. (1985). Behaviour problems and language abilities at three years and behavioural deviance at eight years. *Journal of Child Psychology and Psychiatry and Allied Disciplines*, 26, 215–230.

Stites, J., Demuth, K., & Kirk, C. (2004). Markedness versus frequency effects in coda acquisition. In A. Brugos, L. Micciulla & C. E. Smith (Eds.), *Proceedings of the 28th Annual Boston University Conference on Language Development* (pp. 565–576). Somerville, MA: Cascadilla Press.

Stoel-Gammon, C. (1980). Phonological analysis of four Down's syndrome children. *Applied Psycholinguistics*, 1, 31–48.

Stoel-Gammon, C., & Buder, E. (2002). American and Swedish children's acquisition of vowel duration: Effects of vowel identity and final stop voicing. *Journal of the Acoustical Society of America*, 111, 1854–1864.

Stoll, S. (2001). The acquisition of Russian aspect. Unpublished doctoral dissertation, University of California, Berkeley.

(2005). Beginning and end in the acquisition of the Russian perfective aspect. *Journal of Child Language*, 32, 805–825.

Stoll, S., & Gries, S. T. (in press). How to measure development? An association strength approach. *Journal of Child Language*.

Stoll, S., Abbot-Smith, K., & Lieven, E. (in press). Lexically restricted utterances in Russian, German and English. *Cognitive Science*.

Stone, W., & Caro-Martinez, L. M. (1990). Naturalistic observations of spontaneous communication in autistic children. *Journal of Autism and Developmental Disorders*, 20(4), 437–453.

Storkel, H. L. (2001). Learning new words. *Journal of Speech, Language, and Hearing Research*, 44, 1321–1337.

(2004). The emerging lexicon of children with phonological delays: Phonotactic constraints and probability in acquisition. *Journal of Speech, Language, and Hearing Research*, 47, 1194–1212.

Stothard, S. E., Snowling, M. J., Bishop, D. V. M., Chipchase, B. B., & Kaplan, C. A. (1998). Language-impaired preschoolers: A follow-up into adolescence. *Journal of Speech Language and Hearing Research*, 41, 407–418.

Streeter, L. A. (1976). Language perception in 2-month-old infants shows effects of both innate mechanisms and experience. *Nature*, 259, 39–41.

Strömqvist, S., & Verhoeven, L. (Eds.). (2004). *Relating Events in Narrative: Vol. 2. Typological and Contextual Perspectives*. Mahwah, NJ: Lawrence Erlbaum Associates.

Strömqvist, S., Ragnarsdóttir, H., Toivainen, K., *et al.* (1995). The inter-Nordic study of language acquisition. *Nordic Journal of Linguistics*, 18, 3–29.

Sudhalter, V., & Braine, M. (1985). How does comprehension of passives develop? A comparison of actional and experiential verbs. *Journal of Child Language*, 12, 455–470.

Suzman, S. (1991). Language acquisition in Zulu. Unpublished doctoral dissertation, University of Witwatersrand, Johannesburg.

Swain, I. U., Zelazo, P. R., & Clifton, R. K. (1993). Newborn infants' memory for speech sounds retained over 24 hours. *Developmental Psychology*, 29, 312–323.

Swain, M., & Lapkin, S. (1982). *Evaluating Bilingual Education: A Canadian Case Study*. Clevedon: Multilingual Matters.

Swensen, L. D., Kelley, E., Fein, D., & Naigles, L. R. (2007). Processes of language acquisition in children with autism: Evidence from preferential looking. *Child Development*, 78, 542–557.

Swift, M. D., & Allen, S. E. (2002). Contexts of verbal inflection dropping in Inuktitut child speech. In B. Skarabela, S. Fish & A. H.-J. Do (Eds.), *Proceedings from the 26th Annual Boston Conference on Language Development* (pp. 689–700). Somerville, MA: Cascadilla Press.

Swingley, D. (2003). Phonetic detail in the developing lexicon. *Language and Speech*, 46, 265–294.

   (2005). Statistical clustering and the contents of the infant vocabulary. *Cognitive Psychology*, 50, 86–132.

Swingley, D., & Aslin, R. N. (2000). Spoken word recognition and lexical representation in very young children. *Cognition*, 76, 147–166.

   (2002). Lexical neighborhoods and the word-form representations of 14-month-olds. *Psychological Science*, 13, 480–484.

Swingley, D. & Fernald, A. (2002). Recognition of words referring to present and absent objects by 24-month-olds. *Journal of Memory and Language*, 46, 39–56.

Swingley, D., Pinto, J. P., & Fernald, A. (1999). Continuous processing in word recognition at 24 months. *Cognition*, 71, 73–108.

Swoboda, P. J., Morse, P. A., & Leavitt, L. A. (1976). Continuous vowel discrimination in normal and at risk infants. *Child Development*, 47, 459–465.

Szabolcsi, A. (2002). Hungarian disjunctions and positive polarity. In I. Kenesei & P. Siptar (Eds.), *Approaches to Hungarian 8* (pp. 217–241). Budapest: Akademiai Kiado.

Szatmari, P., Archer, L., Fisman, S., Streiner, D. L., & Wilson, F. J. (1995). Asperger's syndrome and autism: Differences in behavior, cognition, and adaptive functioning. *Journal of the American Academy of Child & Adolescent Psychiatry*, 34, 1662–1670.

Tager-Flusberg, H. (1985). Basic level and superordinate level categorization by autistic, mentally retarded and normal children. *Journal of Experimental Child Psychology*, 40, 450–469.

(1994). Dissociations in form and function in the acquisition of language by autistic children. In H. Tager-Flusberg (Ed.), *Constraints on Language Acquisition: Studies of Atypical Children* (pp. 175–194). Hillsdale, NJ: Lawrence Erlbaum Associates.

(2004a). Do autism and specific language impairment represent overlapping language disorders? In M. Rice & S. Warren (Eds.), *Developmental Language Disorders: From Phenotypes to Etiologies* (pp. 31–52). Mahwah, NJ: Lawrence Erlbaum Associates.

(2004b). Strategies for conducting research on language in autism. *Journal of Autism and Developmental Disorders*, 34, 75–80.

Tager-Flusberg, H., & Anderson, M. (1991). The development of contingent discourse ability in autistic children. *Journal of Child Psychology and Psychiatry*, 32, 1123–1134.

Tager-Flusberg, H., & Cooper, J. (1999). Present and future possibilities for defining a phenotype for specific language impairment. *Journal of Speech, Language and Hearing Research*, 42, 1275–1278.

Tager-Flusberg, H., & Sullivan, K. (1998). Early language development in children with mental retardation. In J. A. Burack, R. M. Hodapp & E. Zigler (Eds.), *Handbook of Mental Retardation and Development* (pp. 208–239). New York: Cambridge University Press.

Tager-Flusberg, H., Calkins, S., Nolin, T., Baumberger, T., Anderson, M., & Chadwick-Dias, A. (1990). A longitudinal study of language acquisition in autistic and Down syndrome children. *Journal of Autism & Developmental Disorders*, 20, 1–21.

Tallal, P., Miller, S., & Fitch, R. H. (1993). Neurobiological basis of speech: A case for the preeminence of temporal processing. *Annals of the New York Academy of Sciences*, 682, 27–47.

Tallal, P., Miller, S., Bedi, G., *et al.* (1996). Language comprehension in language-learning children improved with acoustically modified speech. *Science*, 271, 81–84.

Talmy, L. (1985). Lexicalization patterns: Semantic structures in lexical forms. In T. E. Shopen (Ed.), *Language Typology and Syntactic Description: Vol. 3. Grammatical Categories and the Lexicon* (pp. 57–149). Cambridge: Cambridge University Press.

Tanenhaus, M., Spivey-Knowlton, M., Eberhard, K., & Sedivy, J. (1995). Integration of visual and linguistic information in spoken language comprehension. *Science*, 268, 1632–1634.

Taraban, R., & McClelland, J. (1988). Constituent attachment and thematic role assignment in sentence processing: Influences of content-based expectations. *Journal of Memory and Language*, 27, 1–36

Tardif, T. (1996). Nouns are not always learned before verbs: Evidence from Mandarin speakers' early vocabularies. *Developmental Psychology*, 32, 492–504.

Tardif, T., Gelman, S. A., & Xu, F. (1999). Putting the 'noun bias' in context: A comparison of English and Mandarin. *Child Development*, 70, 620–35.

Tassabehji, M. (2003). Williams–Beuren syndrome: A challenge for genotype–phenotype correlations. *Human Molecular Genetics*, 15, 229–237.

Tavakolian, S. (1978). The conjoined-clause analysis of relative clauses and other structure. In H. Goodluck & L. Solan (Eds.), *Papers in the Structure and Development of Child Language* (pp. 37–83). Amherst: University of Massachusetts, Linguistics Department, GLSA Publications.

   (1981). The conjoined-clause analysis of relative clauses. In S. Tavakolian (Ed.), *Language Acquisition and Linguistic Theory* (pp. 167–187). Cambridge MA: MIT Press.

Taylor, J. R. (2003). *Linguistic Categorization* (3rd edn). Oxford: Oxford University Press.

Taylor, M., & Gelman, S. A. (1988) Adjectives and nouns: Children's strategies for learning new words. *Child Development*, 59, 411–419.

Tek, S., Jaffery, G., Swensen, L., Fein, D., & Naigles, L. (2007). *The Shape Bias: Investigations of Word Learning in Children with Autism*. Paper presented at the International Meeting for Autism Research, Seattle, WA.

Temple, C., Almazan, M., & Sherwood, S. (2002). Lexical skills in Williams syndrome: A cognitive neuropsychological analysis. *Journal of Neurolinguistics*, 15, 463–495.

Terrace, H. S. (1987). *Nim: A Chimpanzee who Learned Sign Language*. New York: Columbia University Press.

Thal, D., Tobias, S., & Morrison, D. (1991). Language and gesture in late talkers: A one year followup. *Journal of Speech and Hearing Research*, 34, 604–612.

Theakston, A. L. (2004). The role of entrenchment in children's and adults' performance on grammaticality judgment tasks. *Cognitive Development*, 19, 15–34.

Theakston, A. L., Lieven, E. V. M., Pine, J. M., & Rowland, C. F. (2002). Going, going, gone: The acquisition of the verb 'go'. *Journal of Child Language*, 29, 783–811.

Thelen, E. (1981). Rhythmical behavior in infancy. *Developmental Psychology*, 17, 237–257.

(1991). Motor aspects of emergent speech: A dynamic approach. In N. A. Krasnegor, D. M. Rumbaugh, R. L. Schiefelbusch & M. Studdert-Kennedy (Eds.), *Biological and Behavioral Determinants of Language Development* (pp. 339–362). Hillsdale, NJ: Lawrence Erlbaum Associates.

Thelen, E., & Smith, L. B. (1994). *A Dynamic Systems Approach to the Development of Cognition and Action.* Cambridge, MA: MIT Press.

Thierry, G., Vihman, M., & Roberts, M. (2003). Familiar words capture the attention of 11-month-olds in less than 250 msec. *Neuroreport,* 14, 2307–2310.

Thiessen, E. D. (2007). The effect of distributional information on children's use of phonemic contrasts. *Journal of Memory and Language,* 56, 16–34.

Thiessen, E. D., & Saffran, J. R. (2003). When cues collide: Use of stress and statistical cues to word boundaries by 7- to 9-month-old infants. *Developmental Psychology,* 39, 706–716.

(2007). Learning to learn: Infants' acquisition of stress-based strategies for word segmentation. *Language Learning and Development,* 3, 73–100.

Thiessen, E. D., Hill, E. A., & Saffran, J. R. (2005). Infant-directed speech facilitates word segmentation. *Infancy,* 7, 53–71.

Thomas, E. M., & Gathercole, V. C. (2007). Children's productive command of grammatical gender and mutation in Welsh: An alternative to rule-based learning. *First Language,* 27, 251–278.

Thomas, K., Morrissey, J., & McLaurin, C. (2007). Use of autism-related services by families and children. *Journal of Autism and Developmental Disorders,* 37(5), 818–830.

Thomas, M. (2005a). *Constraints on language development: Insights from developmental disorders.* In P. Fletcher & J. F. Miller (Eds.), *Language Disorders and Developmental Theory* (pp. 11–34). Philadelphia: John Benjamins.

(2005b). Characterising compensation. *Cortex,* 41(3), 434–442.

(2006). Williams syndrome: fractionation all the way down? *Cortex,* 42, 1053–1057.

Thomas, M., & Karmiloff-Smith, A. (2002). Residual normality: Friend or foe? *Behavioral and Brain Sciences,* 25, 772–780.

(2003). Modelling language acquisition in atypical phenotypes. *Psychological Review,* 110, 647–682.

Thomas, M., Grant, J., Gsödl, M., *et al.* (2001). Past tense formation in Williams syndrome. *Language and Cognitive Processes,* 16, 143–176.

Thomas, M., Dockrell, J., Messer, D., Parmigiani, C., Ansari, D., & Karmiloff-Smith, A. (2006). Speeded naming, frequency and the development of the lexicon in Williams syndrome. *Language and Cognitive Processes,* 21, 721–759.

Thomson, J. R., & Chapman, R. S. (1977). Who is 'Daddy' revisited: The status of two-year-olds' over-extended words in use and comprehension. *Journal of Child Language,* 4, 359–375.

Thordardottir, E. T., & Ellis Weismer, S. (2002). Verb argument structure weakness in specific language impairment in relation to age and utterance length. *Clinical Linguistics and Phonetics*, 16, 233–250.

Thordardottir, E. T., & Namazzi, M. (2007). Specific language impairment in French-speaking children: Beyond grammatical morphology. *Journal of Speech, Language, and Hearing Research*, 50, 698–715.

Thothathiri, M., & Snedeker, J. (2008). Syntactic priming during language comprehension in three- and four-year-old children. *Journal of Memory and Language*.

Tincoff, R., Santelmann, L. M., & Jusczyk, P. W. (2000). Auxiliary verb learning and 18-month-olds' acquisition of morphological relationships. In S. C. Howell, S. A. Fish & T. Keith-Lucas (Eds.) (pp. 726–737). *Proceedings of the 24th Annual Boston University Conference on Language Development: Vol. 2*. Somerville, MA: Cascadilla Press.

Tincoff, R., Hauser, M., Tsao, F., Spaepen, G., Ramus, F., & Mehler, J. (2005). The role of speech rhythm in language discrimination: Further tests with a nonhuman primate. *Developmental Science*, 8, 26–35.

To Kit Sum, C. (2006). Use of reference in Cantonese narratives: A developmental study. Unpublished doctoral dissertation, Hong Kong University, Hong Kong.

Tomasello, M. (1987). Learning to use prepositions: A case study. *Journal of Child Language*, 14, 79–98.

(1988). The role of joint attentional process in early language development. *Language Sciences*, 10, 69–88.

(1992). *First Verbs: A Case Study of Early Grammatical Development*. Cambridge: Cambridge University Press.

(1995). Joint attention as social cognition. In C. Moore & P. J. Dunham (Eds.), *Joint Attention: Its Origins and Role in Development* (pp. 103–130). Hillsdale, NJ: Lawrence Erlbaum Associates.

(2000a). Do young children have adult syntactic competence? *Cognition*, 74, 209–253.

(2000b). First steps toward a usage-based theory of language acquisition. *Cognitive Linguistics*, 11(1–2), 61–82.

(2000c). The item-based nature of children's early syntactic development. *Trends in Cognitive Sciences*, 4, 156–163.

(2000d). The social-pragmatic theory of word learning. *Pragmatics*, 10, 401–414.

(2001). Perceiving intentions and learning words in the second year of life. In M. Bowerman & S. Levinson (Eds.), *Language Acquisition and Conceptual Development* (pp. 132–158). Cambridge: Cambridge University Press.

(2003). *Constructing a Language: A Usage-Based Theory of Language Acquisition*. Cambridge, MA: Harvard University Press.

(2004). Syntax or semantics? Response to Lidz *et al*. *Cognition*, 93, 139–140.

(2008). *Origins of Human Communication*. MIT Press.

Tomasello, M., & Abbot-Smith, K. (2002). A tale of two theories: Response to Fisher. *Cognition*, 83, 207–214.

Tomasello, M., & Brooks, P. (1998). Young children's earliest transitive and intransitive constructions. *Cognitive Linguistics*, 9, 379–395.

Tomasello, M., & Mannle, S. (1985). Pragmatics of sibling speech to one-year-olds. *Child Development*, 56, 911–917.

Tomasello, M., & Stahl, D. (2004). Sampling children's spontaneous speech: How much is enough? *Journal of Child Language*, 31, 101–121.

Tomasello, M., Conti-Ramsden, G., & Ewert, B. (1990). Young children's conversations with their mothers and fathers: Differences in breakdown and repair. *Journal of Child Language*, 17, 115–130.

Tomasello, M., Carpenter, M., & Lizskowski, U. (2007). A new look at infant pointing. *Child Development*, 78, 705–722.

Tomblin, J. B., & Buckwalter, P. (1998). The heritability of poor language achievement among twins. *Journal of Speech and Hearing Research*, 41, 188–199.

Tomblin, J. B., & Zhang, X. (1999). Are children with SLI a unique group of language learners? In H. Tager-Flusberg (Ed.), *Neurodevelopmental Disorders: Contributions to a New Framework from the Cognitive Neurosciences* (pp. 361–382). Cambridge, MA: MIT Press.

Tomblin, J. B., Records, N. L., & Zhang, X. (1996). A system for the diagnosis of specific language impairment in kindergarten children. *Journal of Speech & Hearing Research*, 39, 1284–1294.

Tomblin, J. B., Records, N. L., Buckwalter, P., Zhang, X., Smith, E., & O'Brien, M. (1997). Prevalence of specific language impairment in kindergarten children. *Journal of Speech Language Hearing Research*, 40, 1245–1260.

Tomblin, J. B., Zhang, X., & Buckwalter, P. (2000). The association of reading disability, behavioral disorders, and language impairment among second-grade children. *Journal of Child Psychology & Psychiatry & Allied Disciplines*, 41, 473–482.

Tomblin, J. B., Zhang, X., Buckwalter, P., & O'Brien, M. (2003). The stability of primary language impairment: Four years after diagnosis. *Journal of Speech–Language–Hearing Research*, 46, 1283–1296.

Toro, J. M., Sinnett, S. & Soto-Faraco, S. (2005). Speech segmentation by statistical learning depends on attention. *Cognition*, 67, B25–B34.

Toro, J. M., & Trobalon, J. B. (2005). Statistical computations over a speech stream in a rodent. *Perception and Psychophysics*, 67, 867–875.

Torrens, V. (1995). The acquisition of the functional category inflection in Spanish and Catalan. *MIT Working Papers in Linguistics*, 26, 451–472.

Traill, A. (1985). *Phonetic and Phonological Studies of !Xóõ Bushman*. Hamburg: Helmut Buske Verlag.

Trainor, L. J., McFadden, M., Hodgson, L., *et al.* (2003). Changes in auditory cortex and the development of mismatch negativity between 2 and 6 months of age. *International Journal of Psychophysiology*, 51, 5–15.

Trask, R. (1993). *A Dictionary of Grammatical Terms in Linguistics.* New York: Routledge.

Trauner, D., Wulfeck, B., Tallal, P., & Hesselink, J. (2000). Neurological and MRI profiles of children with developmental language impairment. *Developmental Medicine and Child Neurology*, 42, 470–475.

Traxler, M. (2002). Plausibility and subcategorization preference in children's processing of temporarily ambiguous sentences: Evidence from self-paced reading. *Quarterly Journal of Experimental Psychology A: Human Experimental Psychology*, 55A, 75–96.

Trehub, S. E. (1976). The discrimination of foreign speech contrasts by infants and adults. *Child Development*, 47, 466–472.

Treiman, R., Clifton, C., Meyer, A. & Wurn, A. (2003). Language comprehension and production. In A. Healy, & R. Proctor (Eds.), *Handbook of Psychology: Vol. 4. Experimental Psychology*, (pp. 527–547). Hoboken, NJ: John Wiley.

Tremblay, A., & Demuth, K. (2007). Prosodic licensing of determiners in children's early French. In A. Belikova, L. Meroni & M. Umeda (Eds.), *Proceedings of the 2nd Conference on Generative Approaches to Language Acquisition North America (GALANA)* (pp. 84–91). Somerville, MA: Cascadilla Proceedings Project.

Trueswell, J. C. & Gleitman, L. R. (2004). Children's eye movements during listening: evidence for a constraint-based theory of parsing and word learning. In J. M. Henderson & F. Ferreira (Eds.). *Interface of Vision, Language, and Action.* (pp. 319–346). New York: Psychology Press.

Trueswell, J. C., Tanenhaus, M. K. & Kello, C. (1993). Verb-specific constraints in sentence processing: Separating effects of lexical preference from garden paths. *Journal of Experimental Psychology: Learning, Memory and Cognition*, 19, 528–553.

Trueswell, J. C., Sekerina, I., Hill, N. M., & Logrip, M. L, (1999). The kindergarten-path effect: Studying on-line sentence processing in young children. *Cognition*, 73, 89–134.

Turner, L., Stone, W. L., Pozdol, S., & Coonrod, E. E. (2006). Follow-up of children with autism spectrum disorders from age 2 to age 9. *Autism*, 10, 243–265.

Udwin, O., & Yule, W. (1991). A cognitive and behavioral phenotype in Williams syndrome. *Journal of Clinical and Experimental Neuropsychology*, 13, 232–244.

Ungerer, J., & Sigman, M. (1987). Categorization skills and receptive language development in autistic children. *Journal of Autism and Developmental Disorders*, 17(1), 3–16.

Uylings, H. (2006). Development of the human cortex and the concept of 'critical' or 'sensitive' periods. *Language Learning*, 56, 59–91.

Valian, V. (1986). Syntactic categories in the speech of young children. *Developmental Psychology*, 22, 562–579.

(1990). Null subjects: A problem for parameter setting models of language acquisition. *Cognition*, 35, 105–122.

(1991). Syntactic subjects in the early speech of American and Italian children. *Cognition*, 40, 21–81.

(1999). Rethinking learning: Comments on 'Rethinking innateness'. *Journal of Child Language*, 26, 248–253.

Valian, V., & Coulson, S. (1988) Anchor points in language learning: The role of marker frequency. *Journal of Memory and Language*, 27, 71–86.

Valian, V., Solt, S., & Stewart, J. (in press). Abstract categories or limited-scope formulae? The case of children's determiners. *Journal of Child Language*.

Vallabha, G. K., McClelland, J. L., Pons, F., Werker, J. F., & Amano, S. (2007). Unsupervised learning of vowel categories from infant-directed speech. *Proceedings of the National Academy of Sciences*, 104, 13273–13278.

Van den Bogaerde, B. (2000). Input and Interaction in Deaf Families. *Sign Language and Linguistics*, 3, 143–151.

van der Lely, H. K. (1997). Language and cognitive development in a grammatical SLI boy: Modularity and innateness. *Journal of Neurolinguistics*, 10, 75–107.

(1998). SLI in children: Movement, economy, and deficits in the computational–syntactic system. *Language Acquisition*, 7, 161–192.

van der Lely, H. K., & Battell, J. (2003). Wh-movement in children with grammatical SLI: A test of the RDDR hypothesis. *Language*, 79, 153–181.

van der Lely, H. K., & Stollwerck, L. (1996). A grammatical specific language impairment in children: An autosomal dominant inheritance? *Brain Language*, 52, 484–504.

van Dijk, M. (2004). Child language cuts capers: Variability and ambiguity in early child development. Unpublished doctoral dissertation, Rijksuniversiteit Groningen, The Netherlands.

van Dijk, T. (1980). *Macrostructures: An Interdisciplinary Study of Global Structures in Discourse, Interaction, and Cognition*. Hillsdale, NJ: Lawrence Erlbaum Associates.

Van Essen, D., Dierker, D., Snyder, A., Raichle, M., Reiss, A., & Korenberg, J. (2006). Symmetry of cortical folding abnormalities in Williams syndrome revealed by surface-based analyses. *Journal of Neuroscience*, 26, 5470–5483.

van Geert, P. (1994). *Dynamic Systems of Development: Change between Complexity and Chaos*. New York: Harvester Wheatsheaf.

Van Valin, R. D. (1992). An overview of ergative phenomena and their implications for language acquisition. In D. I. Slobin (Ed.), *The*

Crosslinguistic Study of Language Acquisition: Vol. 3 (pp. 15–37). Hillsdale, NJ: Lawrence Erlbaum Associates.

Vargha-Khadem, F., Watkins, K., Alcock, K., Fletcher, P., & Passingham, R. (1995). Praxic and nonverbal cognitive deficits in a large family with a genetically transmitted speech and language disorder. *Proceedings of the National Academy of Sciences*, 92, 930–933.

Vasilyeva, M., Huttenlocher, J., & Waterfall, H. (2006). Effects of language intervention on syntactic skill levels of preschoolers. *Developmental Psychology*, 42, 164–174.

Viau, J. (2006). *Give = CAUSE + HAVE / GO*: Evidence for early semantic decomposition of dative verbs in English child corpora. In D. Bamman, T. Magnitskaia & C. Zaller (Eds.), *Proceedings of the 30th Annual Boston University Conference on Language Development* (pp. 665–670). Somerville, MA: Cascadilla Press.

Vigário, M., Freitas, M. J., & Frota, S. (2006). Grammar and frequency effects in the acquisition of prosodic words in European Portuguese. *Language and Speech*, 49, 175–203.

Vihman, M. M. (1993). Variable paths to early word production. *Journal of Phonetics*, 21, 61–82.

(1996). *Phonological Development: The Origins of Language in the Child.* Cambridge: Blackwell.

Vihman, M. M., & Croft, W. (2007). Phonological development: Toward a 'radical' templatic phonology. *Linguistics*, 45, 683–725.

Vihman, M. M., & Kunnari, S. (2006). The sources of phonological knowledge: A cross-linguistic perspective. *Recherches Linguistiques de Vincennes*, 35, 133–164.

Vihman, M. M., & McCune, L. (1994). When is a word a word? *Journal of Child Language*, 21, 517–542.

Vihman, M. M., & Miller, R. (1988). Words and babble at the threshold of language acquisition. In M. D. Smith & J. L. Locke (Eds.), *The Emergent Lexicon: The Child's Development of a Linguistic Vocabulary* (pp. 151–183). New York: Academic Press.

Vihman, M. M., Macken, M. A., Miller, R., Simmons, H., & Miller, J. (1985). From babbling to speech: A reassessment of the continuity issue. *Language*, 61, 395–443.

Vihman, M. M., & Velleman, S. L. (1989). Phonological reorganization. *Language and Speech*, 32, 149–170.

Vihman, M. M., Velleman, S. L., & McCune, L. (1994). How abstract is child phonology? Toward an integration of linguistic and psychological approaches. In M. Yavas (Ed.), *First and Second Language Phonology* (pp. 9–44). San Diego: Singular Publishing Group.

Vihman, M. M., Nakai, S., DePaolis, R. A., & Hallé, P. (2004). The role of accentual pattern in early lexical representation. *Journal of Memory and Language*, 50, 336–353.

Vihman, M. M., Lum, J., Thierry, G., Nakai, S., & Keren-Portnoy, T. (2006). The onset of word form recognition in one language and in two. In P. McCardle & E. Hoff (Eds.), *Childhood Bilingualism: Research on Infancy through School Age* (pp. 30–44). Clevedon: Multilingual Matters.

Volden, J. (2004). Conversational repair in speakers with autism spectrum disorder. *International Journal of Language & Communication Disorders*, 39, 171–189.

Volden, J., & Lord, C. (1991). Neologisms and idiosyncratic language in autistic speakers. *Journal of Autism & Developmental Disorders*, 21(2), 109–130.

Volterra, V., & Taeschner, T. (1978). The acquisition and development of language by bilingual children. *Journal of Child Language*, 5, 311–326.

Volterra, V., Capirci, O., Pezzini, G., Sabbadini, L., & Vicari, S. (1996). Linguistic abilities in Italian children with Williams syndrome. *Cortex*, 32, 663–677.

von Frisch, K. (1967). *The Dance Language and Orientation of Bees*. Cambridge, MA: Harvard University Press.

Vouloumanos, A., & Werker, J. F. (2007). Listening to language at birth: Evidence for a bias for speech in neonates. *Developmental Science*, 10, 159–164.

Walenski, M., Tager-Flusberg, H., and Ullman, M. T. (2006). Language in Autism. In S. O. Moldin and J. L. R. Rubenstein (Eds.) *Understanding Autism: From Basic Neuroscience to Treatment* (pp. 175–203). Boca Raton, FL: Taylor and Francis Books.

Wang, A. T., Lee, S. S., Sigman, M., & Dapretto, M. (2006). Neural basis of irony comprehension in children with autism: The role of prosody and context. *Brain: A Journal of Neurology*, 129, 932–943.

Wang, P., & Bellugi, U. (1994). Evidence from two genetic syndromes for a dissociation between verbal and visual-spatial short-term memory. *Journal of Clinical and Experimental Neuropsychology*, 16, 317–322.

Wang, X.-L., Mylander, C., & Goldin-Meadow, S. (1993). Language and environment: A cross-cultural study of the gestural communication systems of Chinese and American deaf children. *Belgian Journal of Linguistics*, 8, 167–185.

Warren, A., & Tate, C. (1992). Egocentrism in children's telephone conversations. In R. Diaz & L. Berk (Eds.), *Private Speech: From Social Interaction to Self-regulation* (pp. 245–264). Hillsdale, NJ: Lawrence Erlbaum Associates.

Waterhouse, L., & Fein, D. (1982). Language skills in developmentally disabled children. *Brain and Language*, 15, 307–333.

Waterson, N. (1971). Child phonology: A prosodic view. *Journal of Linguistics*, 7, 179–211.

(1987). *Prosodic Phonology: The Theory and its Application to Language Acquisition and Speech Processing*. Tübingen: Gunter Narr Verlag.

Watkins, K. E., Dronkers, N. F., & Vargha-Khadem, F. (2002). Behavioural analysis of an inherited speech and language disorder: Comparison with acquired aphasia. *Brain*, 125, 452–464.

Waxman, S., & Booth, A. (2001). Seeing pink elephants: Fourteen-month-olds' interpretations of novel nouns and adjectives. *Cognitive Psychology*, 43, 217–242.

(2003). The origins and evolution of links between word learning and conceptual organization: New evidence from 11-month-olds. *Developmental Science*, 6, 128–135.

Weber, C., Hahne, A., Friedrich, M., & Friederici, A. D. (2004). Discrimination of word stress in early infant perception: Electrophysiological evidence. *Cognitive Brain Research*, 18, 149–161.

Weber-Fox, C., & Neville, H. (1996). Maturational constraints on functional specializations for language processing: ERP and behavioral evidence in bilingual speakers. *Journal of Cognitive Neuroscience*, 8, 231–256.

Weinreich, U. (1953). *Languages in Contact: Finding and Problems*. New York: Linguistic Circle of New York.

Weissenborn, J. (1992). Null subjects in early grammars: Implications for parameter-setting theories. In J. Weissenborn, H. Goodluck & T. Roeper (Eds.), *Theoretical Issues in Language Acquisition* (pp. 269–299). Hillsdale NJ: Lawrence Erlbaum Associates.

Weizman, Z. O., & Snow, C. E. (2001). Lexical input as related to children's vocabulary acquisition: Effects of sophisticated exposure and support for meaning. *Developmental Psychology*, 37, 265–279.

Welsh, M., Pennington, B., & Groisser, D. (1991). A normative–developmental study of executive function: A window on prefrontal function in children. *Developmental Neuropsychology*. 7, 131–149.

Werker, J. F. (1989). Becoming a native listener: A developmental perspective on human speech perception. *American Scientist*, 77, 54–59.

(1995). Exploring developmental changes in cross-language speech perception. In L. R. Gleitman & M. Liberman (Eds.), *Language: An Invitation to Cognitive Science: Vol. 1* (2nd edn, pp. 87–106). Cambridge, MA: MIT Press.

Werker, J. F., & Curtin, S. (2005). PRIMIR: A developmental framework of infant speech processing. *Language Learning and Development*, 1, 197–234.

Werker, J. F., & Fennell, C. T. (2004). From listening to sounds to listening to words: Early steps in word learning. In G. Hall & S. Waxman (Eds.), *Weaving a Lexicon* (pp. 79–109). Cambridge, MA: MIT Press.

Werker, J. F., & Lalonde, C. E. (1988). Cross-language speech perception: Initial capabilities and developmental change. *Developmental Psychology*, 24, 672–683.

Werker, J. F., & McLeod, P. J. (1989). Infant preference for both male and female infant-directed talk: A developmental study of attentional and affective responsiveness. *Canadian Journal of Psychology*, 43, 230–246.

Werker, J. F., & Tees, R. C. (1984). Cross-language speech perception: Evidence for perceptual reorganization during the first year of life. *Infant Behavior and Development*, 7, 49–63.

  (1992). The organization and reorganization of human speech perception. *Annual Review of Neuroscience*, 15, 377–402.

Werker, J. F., & Yeung, H. H. (2005). Infant speech perception bootstraps word learning. *Trends in Cognitive Sciences*, 9, 519–527.

Werker, J. F., Cohen, L. B., Lloyd, V. L., Casasola, M., & Stager, C. L. (1998). Acquisition of word-object associations by 14-month-old infants. *Developmental Psychology*, 34, 1289–1309.

Werker, J. F., Corcoran, K., Fennell, C. T., & Stager, C. L. (2002). Infants' ability to learn phonetically similar words: Effects of age and vocabulary size. *Infancy*, 3, 1–30.

Werker, J. F., Pons, F., Dietrich, C., Kajikawa, S., Fais, L., & Amano, S. (2007). Infant-directed speech supports phonetic category learning in English and Japanese. *Cognition*, 103, 147–162.

Werner, E., & Dawson, G. (2005). Validation of the phenomenon of autistic regression using home videotapes. *Archives of General Psychiatry*, 62, 889–895.

Werner, E., Dawson, G., Osterling, J., & Dinno, N. (2000). Brief report: Recognition of autism spectrum disorder before one year of age: a retrospective study based on home videotapes. *Journal of Autism & Developmental Disorders*, 30, 157–162.

Werner, E., Dawson, G., Munson, J., & Osterling, J. (2005). Variation in early developmental course in autism and its relation with behavioral outcomes at 3–4 years of age. *Journal of Autism and Developmental Disorders*, 35, 337–350.

West, W. C., & Holcomb, P. J. (2002). Event-related potentials during discourse-level semantic integration of complex pictures. *Cognitive Brain Research*, 13, 363–375.

Westermann, G., & Miranda, E. R. (2004). A new model of sensorimotor coupling in the development of speech. *Brain and Language*, 89, 393–400.

Weverink, M. (1989). The subject in relation to inflection in child language. Unpublished master thesis, University of Utrecht, Netherlands.

Wexler, K. (1994). Optional infinitives, head movement, and economy of derivation. In D. Lightfoot & N. Hornstein (Eds.), *Verb Movement* (pp. 305–350). Cambridge: Cambridge University Press.

  (1998). Very early parameter setting and the unique checking constraint. *Lingua*, 106, 23–79.

  (2003). Lenneberg's dream: Learning, normal language development, and specific language impairment: In Y. Levy & J. Schaeffer (Eds.), *Language Competence across Populations: Toward a Definition of Specific Language Impairment* (pp. 11–61). Mahwah, NJ: Lawrence Erlbaum Associates.

Wexler, K., & Culicover, P. (1980.) *Formal Principles of Language Acquisition.* Cambridge, MA: MIT Press.

Wexler, K., Schütze, C., & Rice, M. (1998). Subject case in children with SLI and unaffected controls: Evidence for the Arg/Tns omission model. *Language Acquisition,* 7, 317–344.

White, L. (1987). Children's overgeneralization of the dative alternation. In K. Nelson & A. Van Kleeck (Eds.), *Children's Language: Vol. 6.* (pp. 261–287). Hillsdale, NJ: Lawrence Erlbaum Associates.

Whitehouse, D., & Harris, J.C. (1984). Hyperlexia in infantile autism. *Journal of Autism and Developmental Disorders,* 14, 281–289.

Whitehurst, G.J., & Fischel, J.E. (1994). Practitioner review: Early developmental language delay: What, if anything, should the clinician do about it? *Journal of Child Psychology and Psychiatry and Allied Disciplines,* 35, 613–648.

Wierzbicka, A. (2005). Universal human concepts as a tool for exploring bilingual lives. *International Journal of Bilingualism,* 9, 7–26.

Wigglesworth, G. (1990). Children's narrative acquisition: A study of some aspects of reference and anaphora. *First Language,* 10, 105–125.

(1997). Children's individual approaches to the organization of narrative. *Journal of Child Language,* 24, 279–330.

Wijnen, F. (1997). Temporal reference and eventivity in root infinitives. *MIT Occasional Papers in Linguistics,* 12, 1–25.

Wijnen, F., Kempen, M., & Gillis, S. (2001). Root infinitives in early Dutch child language: An effect of input? *Journal of Child Language,* 28, 629–660.

Wilbur, R.B. (1997). A prosodic/pragmatic explanation for word order variation in ASL with typological implications. In M. Vespoor, K.D. Lee & E. Sweetser (Eds.), *Lexical and Syntactical Constructions and the Constructions of Meaning* (pp. 89–104). Amsterdam: John Benjamins.

Wilcoxon, H.C., Dragoin, W.B., & Kral, P.A. (1971). Illness-induced aversions in rat and quail: Relative salience of visual and gustatory cues. *Science,* 171, 826–828.

Windsor, J., Milbrath, R., Carney, E., & Rakowski, S. (2001). General slowing in language impairment: Methodological considerations in testing the hypothesis. *Journal of Speech, Language, and Hearing Research,* 44, 446–461.

Winskel, H. (2004). The acquisition of temporal reference cross-linguistically using two acting-out comprehension tasks. *Journal of Psycholinguistic Research,* 33, 333–355.

Wittek, A. (2007). What adverbs have to do with learning the meaning of verbs. In M. Bowerman & P. Brown (Eds.), *Crosslinguistic Perspectives on Argument Structure: Implications for Learnability* (pp. 309–329). New York: Lawrence Erlbaum Associates.

Wittek, A., & Tomasello, M. (2005). German-speaking children's productivity with syntactic constructions and case morphology: Local cues help locally. *First Language*, 25, 103–125.

Wittgenstein, L. (1953). *Philosophical Investigations*. New York: Macmillan.

Wong-Fillmore, L. (1991). When learning a second language means losing a first. *Early Childhood Research Quarterly*, 6, 323–346.

Wood, B., & Gardner, R. (1980). How children 'get their way': Directives in communication. *Communication Education*, 29, 264–272.

Wood, N., & Cowan, N. (1995). The cocktail party phenomenon revisited. *Journal of Experimental Psychology: Learning, Memory, and Cognition*, 21, 255–260.

Woodward, A. L., & Guajardo, J. J. (2002). Infants' understanding of the point gesture as an object-directed action. *Cognitive Development*, 17, 1061–1084.

Woodward, A. L., Markman, E., & Fitzsimmons, C. M. (1994). Rapid word learning in 13- and 18-month-olds. *Developmental Psychology*, 30, 553–566.

World Health Organization. (1992). *The ICD 10 Classification of Mental and Behavioral Disorders: Clinical Descriptions and Diagnostic Guidelines*. Geneva, Switzerland: World Health Organization.

Wright, S., & Tropp, L. (2005). Investigating the impact of bilingual instruction on children's intergroup attitudes. *Group Processes and Intergroup Relations*, 8, 309–328.

Xu, F., & Tenenbaum, J. B. (2007). Sensitivity to sampling in Bayesian word learning. *Developmental Science*, 10, 288–297.

Yang, C. D. (2002). *Knowledge and Learning in Natural Language*. Oxford: Oxford University Press.

(2004). Universal grammar, statistics, or both? *Trends in Cognitive Science*, 8, 451–456.

Yavas, M. S. (1994). *First and Second Language Phonology*. San Diego: Singular Publishing Group.

Yeargin-Allsopp, M., Rice, C., Karapurkar, T., Doernberg, N., Boyle, C., & Murphy, C. (2003). Prevalence of Autism in a US Metropolitan Area. *Journal of the American Medical Association*, 289, 49–55.

Yoder, P., & Stone, W. (2006). A randomized comparison of the effect of two prelinguistic communication interventions on the acquisition of spoken communication in preschoolers with ASD. *Journal of Speech, Language, and Hearing Research*, 49, 698–711.

Younger, B. A., & Fearing, D. D. (1998). Detecting correlations among form attributes: An object-examining test with infants. *Infant Behavior and Development*, 21, 289–297.

Yu, C., & Smith, L. B. (2007). Rapid word learning under uncertainty via cross-situational statistics. *Psychological Science*, 18, 414–420.

Yule, G. (1997). *Referential Communication Tasks*. Mahwah, NJ: Lawrence Erlbaum Associates.

Zampini, M. L., & Green, K. P. (2001). The voicing contrast in English and Spanish: The relationship between perception and production. In J. Nicol (Ed.), *One Mind, Two Languages* (pp. 23–48). Oxford: Blackwell.

Zamuner, T. S. (2006). Sensitivity to word-final phonotactics in 9- to 16-month-old infants. *Infancy*, 10, 77–95.

Zamuner, T. S., Gerken, L., & Hammond, M. (2004). Phonotactic probabilities in young children's speech production. *Journal of Child Language*, 31, 515–536.

Zangl, R., & Fernald, A. (2007). Increasing flexibility in children's online processing of grammatical and nonce determiners in fluent speech. *Language Learning and Development*, 3, 199–231.

Zwaigenbaum, L., Bryson, S., Rogers, T., Roberts, W., Brian, J., & Szatmari, P. (2005). Behavioral manifestations of autism in the first year of life. *International Journal of Developmental Neuroscience*, 23, 143–152.

Index

in Down syndrome 155, 462
gestural input received 153–154
iconic gestures 146–147, 462
integration with speech: one-word period
  147–148
and language learning difficulties 154–156
and other cognitive domains 150–151
pointing 70–72, 146, 461, 462
and specific language impairment 155–156
as stepping stone to first words 145–147
and two-word combinations 149–150
versatility of gesture 158–159
Gleason, J. B. *et al.* 348
Gleitman, L. R. 139
Gnanadesikan, A. 188
Goad, H. 190, 191, 192
Goldberg, A. 220
Goldin-Meadow, S. 149, 150, 152, 154
Gómez, R. L. 64
Goodluck, H. 252
Goodwyn, S. W. 146
Gopnik, A. 38
Gordon, P. 220
Goro, T. 303, 306, 307
government-and-binding theory: absolute
  universals 21
Graf Estes, K. *et al.* 441
grammatical aspect 97
grammatical categories 199–215
  Competition model 93, 213
  compositional or holistic forms? 203
  derivational morphology and compounding
    210
  dual route vs. single route processing 211–212
  generalization and schema formation
    206–207
  grammaticizable notions 201–202
  inflectional morphology: acquisition 205–210
  linguistic relativity 213–214
  morpheme-order studies 205–206
  operating principles 212–213
  paradigm building 207–210
  productivity criteria 203–205
  theories 211–214
grammatical morphemes 133–138, 193–195, 200
grammaticizable notions 201–202
Green, K. P. 390
Greenfield, P. 100
Grice, H. P. 284
Gropen, J. *et al.* 230
Grosjean, F. 384
Gualmini, A. *et al.* 309, 311
Guasti, M. T. 253, 264

Hakuta, K. 392
Hamburger, H. 253
Harris, T. 268
Hart, B. 429
Hawkins, S. 186
Hazen, N. 353
headturn preference paradigm 110, 127
Hebrew
  narrative contexts 364, 366, 367–369, 370,
    371, 372–373
  specific language impairment 445
Herbert, M. R. *et al.* 428
Hickmann, M. *et al.* 358, 361, 362, 363
Hindi 110, 232, 235, 250

Hoff-Ginsberg, E. 351
Höhle, B. *et al.* 133, 135–136, 137, 141
Hohne, E. A. 117
holophrases 73–75, 76
home languages 381
homesigning 157–158
Horn, L. R. 316
Hsu, J. *et al.* 242
Hudson, J. A. 361
Hulk, A. 387
Hungarian 21, 93, 434
Hunter, M. A. 127
Huttenlocher, J. *et al.* 225, 429
Hyams, N. 263, 267
hypothesis-testing 25

identificationals 78
Illes, J. *et al.* 390
illocutionary acts 340, 345
imperatives 78
implicatures 296–298
Indo-European languages 89
Indonesian 95, 101
inflection 30, 64, 65, 66, 96, 127, 199, 200, 202,
    211, 255, 256, 259–280,292, 363, 410,
    434–438, 442–445
inflectional morphology 202, 205–210, 259
  generalization and schema formation
    206–207
  morpheme-order studies 205–206
  paradigm building 207–210
  see also morphology acquisition
Ingram, T. T. S. 426
Inhelder, B. 312
initial state 16, 17, 31
innateness 15–33
  acquisition and learnability mechanisms
    25–27
  animals and language 27–30
  arguments against nativism 23–25
  empirical evidence 27–33
  genetic involvement 30
  language/cognition dissociation 30
  and language variation 91
  linguistic evidence 20–21; (indirect negative
    evidence 20, 21; negative evidence 20, 21;
    positive evidence 20)
  linguistic universals 18–19
  logical arguments for innateness 20–23
  nativism–empiricism debate 15–18
  poverty-of-the-stimulus: case filter 20, 21–23
  sensitive period 30, 48
  syntactic categories 31–32
  word order 2, 17–18, 19, 32–33
intention-reading 69, 70, 74, 86
interactionism 16
intermodal preferential looking paradigm (IPL)
  99, 325
intonation in autism 453
intonational phrase boundaries (IPh) 62
intonational phrases 184
intransitives 78
Inuktitut
  argument structure 232, 233, 234
  bilingualism 385, 386, 395
  productivity 205
IPh (intonational phrase boundaries) 62
IPL *see* intermodal preferential looking paradigm